VRML
Bringing Virtual Reality to the Internet

**DISK
DO NOT
DESENSITIZE**

LIMITED WARRANTY AND DISCLAIMER OF LIABILITY

ACADEMIC PRESS, INC. ("AP") AND ANYONE ELSE WHO HAS BEEN INVOLVED IN THE CREATION OR PRODUCTION OF THE ACCOMPANYING CODE ("THE PRODUCT") CANNOT AND DO NOT WARRANT THE PERFORMANCE OR RESULTS THAT MAY BE OBTAINED BY USING THE PRODUCT. THE PRODUCT IS SOLD "AS IS" WITHOUT WARRANTY OF ANY KIND (EXCEPT AS HEREAFTER DESCRIBED), EITHER EXPRESSED OR IMPLIED, INCLUDING, BUT NOT LIMITED TO, ANY WARRANTY OF PERFORMANCE OR ANY IMPLIED WARRANTY OF MERCHANTABILITY OR FITNESS FOR ANY PARTICULAR PURPOSE. AP WARRANTS ONLY THAT THE MAGNETIC CD-ROM(S) ON WHICH THE CODE IS RECORDED IS FREE FROM DEFECTS IN MATERIAL AND FAULTY WORKMANSHIP UNDER THE NORMAL USE AND SERVICE FOR A PERIOD OF NINETY (90) DAYS FROM THE DATE THE PRODUCT IS DELIVERED. THE PURCHASER'S SOLE AND EXCLUSIVE REMEDY IN THE EVENT OF A DEFECT IS EXPRESSLY LIMITED TO EITHER REPLACEMENT OF THE CD-ROM(S) OR REFUND OF THE PURCHASE PRICE, AT AP'S SOLE DISCRETION.

IN NO EVENT, WHETHER AS A RESULT OF BREACH OF CONTRACT, WARRANTY OR TORT (INCLUDING NEGLIGENCE) WILL AP OR ANYONE WHO HAS BEEN INVOLVED IN THE CREATION OR PRODUCTION OF THE PRODUCT BE LIABLE TO PURCHASER FOR ANY DAMAGES, INCLUDING ANY LOST PROFITS, LOST SAVINGS OR OTHER INCIDENTAL OR CONSEQUENTIAL DAMAGES ARISING OUT OF THE USE OR INABILITY TO USE THE PRODUCT OR ANY MODIFICATIONS THEREOF, OR DUE TO THE CONTENTS OF THE CODE, EVEN IF AP HAS BEEN ADVISED OF THE POSSIBILITY OF SUCH DAMAGES, OR ANY CLAIM BY ANY OTHER PARTY.

Any request for replacement of a defective CD-ROM must be postage prepaid and must be accompanied by the original defective CD-ROM, your mailing address and telephone number, and proof of date of purchase and purchase price. Send such requests, stating the nature of the problem, to Academic Press Customer Service, 6277 Sea Harbor Drive, Orlando, FL 32887, 1-800-321-5068. APP shall have no obligation to refund the purchase price or to replace a CD-ROM based on the claims of defects in the nature or operation of the Product.

Some states do not allow limitation on how long an implied warranty lasts, nor exclusions or limitations of incidental or consequential damage, so the above limitations and exclusions may not apply to you. This Warranty gives you specific legal rights, and you may also have other rights which may vary from jurisdiction to jurisdiction.

THE RE-EXPORT OF UNITED STATES ORIGIN SOFTWARE IS SUBJECT TO THE UNITED STATES LAWS UNDER THE EXPORT ADMINISTRATION ACT OF 1969 AS AMENDED. ANY FURTHER SALE OF THE PRODUCT SHALL BE IN COMPLIANCE WITH THE UNITED STATES DEPARTMENT OF COMMERCE ADMINISTRATION REGULATIONS. COMPLIANCE WITH SUCH REGULATIONS IS YOUR RESPONSIBILITY AND NOT THE RESPONSIBILITY OF AP.

VRML

Bringing Virtual Reality to the Internet

John Vacca
Houston, TX

AP PROFESSIONAL

Boston San Diego New York
London Sydney Tokyo Toronto

This book is printed on acid-free paper

Copyright © 1996 by Academic Press, Inc.
All rights reserved.
No parts of this publication may be reproduced or
transmitted in any form or by any means, electronic
or mechanical, including photocopy, recording, or
any information storage and retrieval system, without
permission in writing from the publisher.

All brand names and product names mentioned
in this book are trademarks or registered trademarks
of their respective companies.

AP PROFESSIONAL
1300 Boylston Street, Chestnut Hill, MA 02167
World Wide Web Site at http://www.apnet.com

An imprint of ACADEMIC PRESS, INC.
A Division of HARCOURT BRACE & COMPANY

United Kingdom Edition published by
ACADEMIC PRESS LIMITED
24-28 Oval Road, London NW1 7DX

Library of Congress Cataloging-in-Publication Data
Vacca, John R.
    VRML, bringing virtual reality to the Internet / John Vacca
        p. cm.
    Includes bibliographical references and index.
    ISBN 0-12-709910-7 -- ISBN 0-12-709911-5 (CD-ROM)
      1. Computer graphics 2. Three-dimensional display systems.
   3. Virtual reality. 4. VRML (Document markup language) 5. Internet
(Computer network) I. Title.
T385.V322 1996
006--dc20   96-3546
                                                                                                     CIP

Printed in the United States of America
96 97 98 99 IP 9 8 7 6 5 4 3 2 1

For my mother, Antonia Vacca;

whose remarkable life has inspired mine.

Contents

Acknowledgments **xxi**
Preface **xxiii**
Introduction **xxv**ii

Part I Identifying the Future 1

**1   Bringing 3-D Environments to the Web:
     The VRML Connection 3**
Why All the Excitement about VRML? 4
Current 3-D Environments on the Web 5
The Good, the Bad, and the Ugly 7
Build It and They Will Come 10
Ease of Build 13
Ease of Access 14
The Practical Value of 3-D Environments on the Web 16
Available Tools for Browsing and Building VRML Worlds 18
What Are the 3-D Tools For? 25
This Calls for Introductions 25
What a Difference a 3-D Web Tool Makes 26
The Future Promise for 3-D Environments on the Web 29
From Here 30

2 The Emerging VRML Standard 31

The VRML Standard 32
   Implications of the VRML Standard 32
   VRML Browser Standards 33
VRML Development Stage 35
Availability in the Commercial World 38
   VRML Viewers 39
   Extensions to HTML Browsers 39
   VRML Authoring Tools 39
VRML's Planned Use by Vertical Industries 40
Planned Applications for VRML's Use 40
   Engineering Applications 41
   Research, Including Medical Research 41
   Commercial Applications and Marketing 42
   Virtual Museums and Art Galleries 42
Implications of VRML in the Client-Server Environment 44
Implications of VRML in Client-Server Applications
   Development Environments 45
Business and Technology Advantages of VRML 45
Requirements for Business Benefits of VRML 47
   Standardization 48
   Development of Content 48
   The Installed Base 49
The Future 49
From Here 49

3 Virtual Reality Modeling Language Visions 51

Vision One: The U. S. Holocaust Museum (USHM) 52
Vision Two: The U. S. Library of Congress 53
Vision Three: Earth 53
Vision Four: The World Wide Marketplace 55
Vision Five: The Agora and the Senate 56
From Here 57

4 OpenGL: The Open Graphics Standard 59

Features/Application Portability 60
Architecture 61

Integration **62**
Governance **64**
OpenGL News **64**
OpenGL Licensing Program **64**
From Here **65**

5   Open Inventor Object-Oriented 3-D Toolkit and VRML   67

Object-Oriented File Format **67**
Scene Graphs **68**
   Node Contents **69**
   Coordinates and Normals **73**
   Bindings **74**
   Primitive Shapes **76**
   Groups **77**
   Textures **80**
   Texture Coordinates **81**
   Transformations **81**
   Cameras **82**
   Lights **84**
   Info **84**
VRML Extensions to Open Inventor **85**
Other Open Inventor Nodes **86**
   Text2, Text3, Font **86**
   NURBS **87**
   Nodekits **87**
   Draggers **87**
   Array, MultipleCopy **88**
   Blinker, Rotor, Shuttle, Pendulum **88**
   ClipPlane **88**
   DrawStyle **88**
   Environment **88**
   LightModel **89**
   ResetTransform, Units, AntiSquish, RotationXYZ **89**
   TextureCoordinateEnvironment, TextureCoordinatePlane **90**
   Coordinate4, ProfileCoordinate2, ProfileCoordinate3 **90**
   Binary Format **90**
Field Syntax **91**
   Field Classes **91**
Naming **92**

Instancing 92
Extensibility 93
Header 94
Comments 95
Whitespace 95
File Contents 95
File Extension 95
Coordinate Space Conventions 96
Is That Everything? 96
Looking Ahead 96
From Here 96

6 CAVEview: Netscape and Mosaic-Based Virtual Reality 99

The Cave 100
The Cave Simulator 101
Motivation 102
CAVEview Features 103
  CAVEview as a Presentation Tool 104
  CAVE Movement and Viewpoint 104
Stereo, Tracking, and the Flying Mouse 105
Audio 105
Scripts 106
Implementation and Development 106
CAVEview Data File 107
Web Browsers' File Transfer 107
Dynamic Link 107
Field Test: VROOM, SIGGRAPH '94 108
Summary 108
From Here 109

7 Surrogate Travel on the Internet 111

Inline Graphics Surrogate Travel 113
External Graphics Surrogate Travel 114
Future Directions 115
From Here 116

8 Real Virtual Reality on the Internet 117

Immersive Technologies **118**
Emerging Technologies **118**
The Diaspar Virtual Reality Network—the Next Generation **121**
For the Future **122**
   Toward Low Cost Home Virtual Reality **123**
   The Lunar Teleoperations Model 1 {LTM1} **123**
   Information about Virtual Networks **124**
   Getting Started **125**
From Here **126**

9 MOO-Based Collaborative Hypermedia System for WWW 127

Hypermedia Models **128**
Storyspace **130**
MOO **131**
   Hypertext in the MOO **132**
   Creation of the Hypertext MOO **132**
   Creating a WWW Site Server from the MOO **133**
   Dynamic Delivery of HTML Texts **134**
   Extensions to HTML **134**
   Adding State to WWW **135**
   Forms-Based Authoring Tools **136**
   Security Issues **136**
Applications **137**
WAXweb **138**
Future Work **139**
Summary **140**
From Here **140**

10 Cyberspace 141

Sushi Lunch **141**
   The Wheels Start Rolling **142**
   The Hard Part **143**
   Future **144**
Visualization and VRML **145**
Cyberspace **147**

Metrics in Cyberspace 147
Implementation of Cyberspace Protocol 148
Cyberspace Web Site Servers 149
Cyberspace and the World Wide Web 150
Labyrinth 151
Data Abstraction Protocols 152
Summary 152
From Here 153

PART II Implementing the Future 155

11 VRML Architecture Group (VAG) 157

Beyond VRML 157
   Priorities 158
Changes to VRML Document 159
Nodes 161
   Animation 161
   Materials 162
   Perspective and Orthographic Cameras 163
   Rendering 164
   Navigation 165
   Lights 166
Geometry 167
   Cylinder 167
   Sphere 168
The Tower of VRML 169
   Goal 169
   Physics 170
   Behavior 171
   Distributed Objects 171
   MOO/MUD/Shared Space 171
   Java Shell 172
   ACE (Avatar Control Environment) 172
   Protocol Conservation 172
   Network Issues 172
The Role of Sound in VRML 173

History **174**
Starting Point for the VRML X.X Audio Extentions **175**
Areas for Further Development **178**
VRML's Associated Behavior **179**
Existing Systems **180**
Language Extension Mechanisms **181**
Prototyping New Nodes **182**
VAG's Proposed Extension Mechanism **182**
Messages **185**
A Convention for Multimethods **186**
Time-Critical Behaviors **187**
Primitives **188**
API Considerations **189**
Sample Behavior Extensions **191**
Collision Detection **192**
URNs and VRML **193**
VRML VAG Proposal **196**
Fix Trouble Spots and Correct Minor Oversights **196**
Add Useful Open Inventor Constructs **197**
Support for Simple Reality **198**
Add API and Behavior Hooks **198**
Add Location-Independent Name Support **198**
From Here **198**

12 Open Inventor **199**

IRIS Inventor Overview **200**
An Open Inventor Sampler: Hello Cone **201**
Variation 1: Using Engines to Make the Cone Spin **202**
Variation 2: Adding a Trackball Manipulator **202**
Variation 3: Adding the Examiner Viewer **203**
Naming Scenes **203**
Coordinate Systems **203**
Building a Scene Graph **204**
Nodes and Groups **204**
Paths **209**
Fields **209**
Node Mechanisms **210**
Cameras **211**
Lights **212**

Shapes, Properties, and Binding **212**
    Shapes **212**
    Properties **213**
    Bindings **215**
    Normals **215**
    Transformations **216**
Text **216**
Textures **217**
Nodekits **219**
From Here **220**

13 Virtual Reality Modeling Language (VRML) **221**

VRML Overview **222**
History **223**
Requirements **224**
VRML Language Specification **225**
    Language Basics **225**
    Node Characteristics **226**
    Coordinate System **228**
    Fields **229**
    Nodes **232**
    Issues for Low-End Rendering Systems **237**
    New Nodes for VRML **248**
    Pros **251**
    Pros **253**
    Prototyping **256**
    Extensibility **259**
    URNs **261**
Browser Considerations **262**
From Here **262**

14 The OpenGL Graphics System **263**

Three Views of OpenGL **263**
OpenGL Operation **265**
    Floating-Point Computation **267**
    GL State **267**
    GL Command Syntax **268**
    Basic GL Operation **271**
    GL Errors **272**

      Begin/End Paradigm **273**
      Vertex Specification **280**
      Coordinate Transformations **283**
      Current Raster Position **284**
      Colors and Coloring **285**
   Rasterization **294**
      Invariance **295**
      Points **297**
      Line Segments **298**
      Polygons **301**
      Pixel Rectangles **303**
      Texturing **311**
   Per Fragment Operations and the Frame Buffer **317**
      Per Fragment Operations **318**
      Whole Frame Buffer Operations **326**
      Drawing, Reading, and Copying Pixels **331**
   Special Functions **337**
      Evaluators **337**
      Selection **340**
      Feedback **342**
      Display Lists **345**
      Flush and Finish **347**
      Hints **348**
   State and State Requests **348**
   Invariance **355**
      Repeatability **355**
      Multipass Algorithms **355**
      Invariance Rules **356**
   From Here **358**

PART III   Results and Future Directions **359**

15   Proposed VRML Systems **361**

   Adding Behavior to VRML **361**
      GMD's Goals **362**
      Subclassing **363**
      Events **363**

   Behavior **364**
   Distributed Behavior **364**
  MultiUser Representation of Virtual Worlds to Support VRML **364**
   Multiuser Representation **369**
   Sharing and Distributed Interactions **373**
   Further Extensions **380**
  Distributed Interactive Virtual Environment {DIVE} **381**
  Behavior Representation **382**
   Principal Features of BEF **383**
   VRML Extension Process **385**
   Separable Aspects of this Proposal **386**
   User Interaction **387**
   Kinematics and Motion **388**
  High-Performance Rendering Capabilities of High-End VR Systems **388**
   Characteristics of a 3-D Environment **390**
   The i3-D System **392**
   Application Examples **395**
  MPh 1a—{Metaphysical Modeling Language} **399**
  Interacting with Intelligent Objects with Simple Behaviors **400**
  VR Data Structures **401**
  Virtual Society Project **402**
  Other Proposed VRML Systems **403**
  From Here **404**

16   VRML Concepts **405**

  Platform Independent VR **406**
  Universal Resource Locators (URLS) **408**
  Multipurpose Internet Mail Extensions {MIME} **409**
  VRML Issues **409**
   Indoor Scenes **410**
   Outdoor Scenes **411**
   Actions and Scripts **413**
   Achieving Realism **413**
  Virtual Presence Teleconferencing **414**
  Where Next? **415**
  From Here **416**

17 The OpenGL Graphics Interface Design 417

Overview of OpenGL **420**
Design Considerations **421**
 Performance **422**
 Orthogonality **422**
 Completeness **423**
 Interoperability **423**
 Extensibility **424**
 Acceptance **424**
Design Features **424**
 Based on IRIS GL **424**
 Low-Level API **425**
 Fine-Grained Control **426**
 Modal API **429**
 Frame Buffer **431**
 Not Programmable **432**
 Geometry and Images **434**
 Immediate Mode and Display Lists **435**
 Depth Buffer **437**
 Rendering Only **438**
 API Not Protocol **440**
Example: Three Kinds of Text **440**
Summary **443**
From Here **444**

18 Virtual Behavior Engines 445

Overview of BE **445**
Objects and Classes **446**
Naming **447**
BEings **447**
Assembly **447**
Time and Concurrency **448**
Programming the Behavior Engine **449**
Comparison to Other Simulation Technology **449**
Example Applications **452**
 Repositories of Parameterized Objects, Behaviors, and Documents **454**
Behavior Engine Products **455**

BE Designer 456
  BE Player 456
 Virtual Reality Behavior System (VRBS) 456
  The VRBS System Structure 458
  The WWWScript Node 459
  VRBS Behavior Protocol Goals and Style 461
  VRBS Protocol Messages 464
  Opcode Classes and Opcodes 466
  World Identifiers 468
  Events 469
  Handshaking 469
  Interpreter and Behavior Startup Sequence 471
  Changing Other Worlds 473
 Perl: The Standard VRML Behavior Language 474
  Functional Requirements 475
  Perl Behavior System (PBS) 476
  PBS/VRBS-Browser Interaction 477
  Perl-VRBS User Bindings 478
  PBS Internals 479
  Behavior Language Restraints 480
  Sanitizing Perl 484
 From Here 485

19 Other VR Research 487

 Commercial: VRML Making VISA More Competitive in the Financial Services Market 487
 Military: DIVE Technology 489
  Technical Approach 490
  Physiological and Psychological Requirements 493
  Unencumbered Virtual Reality Technology 497
  Proposed Solution 498
 Government: NASA Virtual Reality Projects 499
  Ames Research Center (ARC) 499
  Goddard Space Flight Center (GSFC) 506
  Johnson Space Center (JSC) 508
  Marshall Space Flight Center (MSFC) 512
 Medical: VR Technology and Project ARCANA 514
  ARCANA 1 Project Description 514
  The Cognitive Demands and the Interpretive Model 516

Evaluation of the Cognitive Performance **518**
Automatic Scoring of Events **519**
Biomedical Data Acquisition and Analysis **520**
Hardware and Software **522**
Limitations and Constraints of Present-Time VR Technology **525**
Comment **526**
From Here **528**

20 Summary, Conclusions, and Recommendations **529**
Performance and Price **530**
Software and Hardware **531**
Artificial Intelligence and Virtual Reality **532**
Market Drivers **534**

Index **535**

Acknowledgments

There are many people whose efforts on this book have contributed to its successful completion. I owe each a debt of gratitude and want to take this opportunity to offer my sincere thanks.

A very special thanks to my editor Jenifer Niles, whose initial interest and support made this book possible. And editorial assistant Jacquelyn Young, who provided staunch support and encouragement when it was most needed. Thanks to my production manager Karen Pratt and my production editor Peter Sullivan, whose fine work has been invaluable. Thanks also to my marketing manager Kira Glass and marketing coordinator Josh Mills, whose efforts on this book have been greatly appreciated.

Thanks to my technical editor and good friend, Dennis Pleticha, whose expertise in Internet and network technology were indispensable. In addition to his work as technical editor, Dennis contributed technical support and time, without which the work would have been much less enjoyable.

Thanks to my wife, Bee Vacca, for her love, her help, and her understanding of my long work hours.

I wish to thank the organizations and individuals who granted me permission to use the research material and information necessary for the completion of this book (cited in the CD-ROM), and the software and demonstrations which are in the CD-ROM.

As always, thanks to my agent, Margot Malley, for guidance and encouragement over and above the business of being an agent.

Preface

The Problems of Goggles and Gloves

Unless you've been stranded on a desert island the past few months, you know that Virtual Reality (VR) is all the rage these days. In fact, it seems to be the media's current darling. Every week brings news of something new in virtual reality—accessories for home video game systems, arcade machines, and even virtual reality theme parks. This may portend a future in which there is still a Disney and we still pay $30, but there is no land. If so, one presumes that Michael Eisner is already working on it. Using virtual reality, we can explore distant places easily, enter dangerous environments safely, and experience past, future, and fictional worlds from the comfort of our homes and offices. Unfortunately there is a dirty little secret to virtual reality: Those goggles and gloves we see so often don't work. Don't believe it? Read on.

Virtual reality gloves are called the light pens of the 1990s. Research done at Lord Corporation in the late 1980s indicates that these are crippled by the lack of force feedback. In real life force feedback is what happens when you push or pull or grab something: You meet resistance. Force feedback is crucial for delicate or precise work with our hands; without it, we are clumsy and awkward at best. Further, due to the way our muscles work, pushing or pulling an object with mass is easier than simply holding one's arm out in space, which most of us can do for about five minutes. Without resistance, this is about how long the average person can effectively use a virtual reality glove—five minutes.

Goggles show more long-term promise than gloves but are still difficult to use today. Try the best goggles made, using the best software available, on the fastest hardware in the world, and they still exhibit disconcerting flaws. One such flaw, lag, occurs when the goggles can't keep up with the user's head movements and display images that are out of date. Other technical problems exist, but the social problems may be even more severe: Can you picture yourself wearing virtual reality goggles for a significant portion of your day at home or in the office? Can you imagine your family members or coworkers doing so? Until the technical problems of goggles are solved and until they become far less intrusive and obvious, they will remain curiosities at best.

Despite these problems, some in our industry have suggested that goggles and gloves are essential to the virtual reality experience. Not coincidentally these people often turn out to have goggles and gloves for sale. If this is true, we're in trouble, because they don't work, at least not today.

Fortunately there's good news: Goggles and gloves aren't required for virtual reality. It turns out that monitors and televisions are perfectly adequate display devices, and mice and joysticks are perfectly adequate input devices. In other words, we can experience virtual reality with the hardware we have today. Companies are producing software that allows people to enter virtual environments, using their existing Microsoft Windows and Apple Macintosh personal computers, with no special peripherals. The virtual environment is displayed on a computer monitor, and the user walks or flies through environments by simply moving the mouse.

The environments users create, and the uses they find for the software, prove that virtual reality is not defined by what we wear on our heads or on our hands. For example, Steve Milligan, a North Carolina architect, sought permission from the National Trust for Historic Preservation to use VR software to construct a model of Frank Lloyd Wright's Pope-Leighy house. The National Trust not only granted this permission but also, after viewing the completed work, commissioned a run-time version of the model so that disabled persons unable to physically enter the house could explore it by using a standard desktop computer.

Although virtual reality gloves may not work, other input devices arriving in the marketplace work far better at far lower cost. For example, joysticks with six degrees of freedom—able to move and rotate along and around all three axes—are now available for approximately $100 and less. Mice with similar capabilities are also available at comparable prices. As such devices become popular, we can expect that many 3-D software manufacturers will support them. These input devices will enhance the virtual reality experience and make it easier to navigate and build in a 3-D world. The concept of experiencing 3-D environments on the Web is not new. A standard approach for defining such 3-D environments, called VRML (Virtual Reality Modeling Language), has been embraced by a number of companies, most notably Silicon Graphics.

However, this raises a question: What is virtual reality? To be specific, virtual reality is the suspension of disbelief in an unreal environment. This may sound intimidating, but it really isn't. Using this definition, great literature, great theater, and other art forms qualify, as well they should. If you have lost yourself staring into a painting or forgotten you were in a cinema in the midst of a film, you have suspended your disbelief of an environment that doesn't exist—at least not right in front of you.

This raises another question: If we already have art forms that can place us in virtual environments, why should we use computers for the same task? The answer is simple: navigation. Although literature, theater, and other art forms may place us in virtual environments, they usually do not allow us to take control, moving when and where we wish. Ideally we should be free to navigate through virtual environments as we see fit. This dramatically increases our ability to suspend disbelief and imagine ourselves within the environment. Further, free navigation within a virtual environment results in a unique and wholly personalized experience every time it is entered. Contrast this with many multimedia titles, which provide the same experience for every user, every time.

Now we know what virtual reality is and why computers can help it. But why should we use virtual reality? The answer is simple, and it has to do with imagination, the most powerful tool our species has. With the computers we have today, we can enhance our imagination, traveling through distant, unreachable, or imaginary worlds on our desktops. We can more easily and more vividly imagine what it must have been like to live as an Athenian in ancient Greece if we have the ability to immerse ourselves in a simulation of that environment. When virtual reality software is available on every desktop and every television — when it is no longer perceived as something fantastic but rather as a tool for learning, working, and entertaining ourselves — we will have enhanced the imagination of every person who uses it.

What do the next few years hold for virtual reality? Instead of focusing on the next new peripheral that will finally push virtual reality over the top, we look to basic performance improvements that will enhance the virtual reality experience from the bottom up. Over the next year or so, we will see numerous introductions of graphics adapters with 3-D acceleration at prices only slightly above those of their unaccelerated counterparts. These accelerators will offer up to 100,000 polygons per second, all texture-mapped, Gouraud-shaded, antialiased and z-buffered. In other words, they will make great-looking 3-D environments. At the same time, a new generation of machines, based on the Pentium Chip and the PowerPC, will provide increased computing power to make the worlds more interesting, with more interactivity. Improving the graphics and interactivity of virtual environments will make them richer, which will make them more compelling. More compelling environments will lead to better work, learning, and entertainment.

Whenever humans have explored a new frontier, we have learned more about ourselves and our world. We have learned about the composition of the earth by visiting the moon, and we have found treatments for new diseases in ancient rain forests. What will we find when any one of us can explore Pompeii before Vesuvius, the bottom of the Cayman Trench, or the surface of Mars? We are about to find out in this book.

Introduction

No one really knows how many people are really on the Internet. Recent estimates have put the number at 30 million Netizens in America. One forecast even predicted a worldwide Internet population of 300 million by the year 2000. A new study, however, took much of the hype out of cyberspace. An industry survey put the number of people in the United States with direct access to the Internet at 6.9 million. In addition, 5 million use commercial on-line services exclusively. While not as explosive as some had predicted, growth has continued to remain robust. The industry survey envisions 7 million new users by the end of 1996. Nevertheless, much in the survey is not surprising.

Internet users, for instance, prove to be 3-to-2 male—mostly young and relatively well-to-do. Still, demographic measurements will be critical to commercial users who fuel the Internet's undeniable but hard to quantify surge.

Web Sites for Virtualnauts

More Web statistics than you can handle? After all, the World Wide Web (WWW) is jazzy but confusing. But not so confusing that the good life can't be had by all.

For example, imagine a wine shop (http://www.virtwalvin.com) where the salesperson is a chatty virtual reality (VR) interactive expert who delivers strong opinions but always amiably and without a trace of condescension. Or, virtual snippets from the latest alternative rock tracks. Expert advice on gardening, bicycling and movie reviews from a self-proclaimed typical teenager. That's the WWW today.

The WWW teems with information, opinions and advice on just about every topic you can think of — and most of it is free to anyone who pays $20 or so a month for an Internet account. Think of it now as a VR multinational library and coffee-house all rolled into one. A novice virtualnaut can drown in the sheer volume of VR stuff out there on the Web—the inner sanctum of the Internet that graduates from plain text to 3-D graphics, virtual reality, and photos (and is careening into sound and video).

The Flatness of the Internet

Today's WWW promises to be realized with a new technology called Virtual Reality Modeling Language (VRML). VRML is literally the glue that allows a range of technologies, including multimedia-equipped personal computers, high-speed communications and others to bring networked virtual reality to the end-user. The key to VRML's potential success lies, however in the explosive growth of the Internet—that phenomenon of cyberspace has an almost palpable reality for users. Many people talk of going to an Internet site, or a particular Internet address, and say: I've been there. This is a testament to the power of human imagination. The Internet today is largely a text-based, or at best a two-dimensional graphical (the Web) environment. VRML promises to take this strongly imaginative experience of cyberspace and enhance it significantly through multimedia technology.

The Origin of VRML

The abbreviation VRML sounds somewhat like the abbreviation for another Internet standard: HTML or Hyper-Text Markup Language. HTML is a standard that allows the creation of hypertext documents on the Worldwide Web that contain links to other documents, either on the same computer, or across the globe.

While VRML utilizes Web technology, it really has no relation directly to HTML. It is not 3-D HTML as its name might suggest. In fact, VRML was developed by technologists in the field of graphics and 3-D rendering who foresaw the potential benefit of bringing three-dimensionality to the Worldwide Web.

In particular, engineers at Silicon Graphics—the same company that developed the technology that allowed the stunning morph effects in the film *Terminator 2: Judgment Day*—had a major part in its initial specification. Their Open Inventor 3-D technology was chosen by an independent standards group as the underpinning for VRML. A portion of this technology with enhancements to support networking, form the basis for VRML as we know it today.

How VRML Works

VRML is not in fact a programming language in the strictest sense. At least, it is not what programmers refer to as a compiled language. This is where a software program can issue instructions directly to the computer without the need of an intermediary program called an interpreter.

VRML code consists of descriptions of 3-D scenes, and the expected behavior of those scenes based on actions of the user. The code is (like HTML) actually written in plain text or ASCII format. It commonly consists of hundreds, or even thousands of polygons (the basic building block of a three-dimensional scene on a computer).

When the user encounters a VRML-based site, the VRML viewer or browser receives instructions from the server on the other end. The server sends VRML code, commonly called a homespace or world to the viewer, which then interprets the instructions and displays the initial scene elements.

Each world is a self-contained environment that is loaded locally for navigation. These files range in size from 100 kilobytes to several megabytes. So, bandwidth directly affects download/access time. Once the world is loaded, the user's experience is dictated by CPU performance. Higher performance processors handle more MIPS, allowing faster and smoother navigation through the world.

Given the relatively low performance and limited bandwidth of today's installed base of personal computers, developers will begin to build VRML sites so as to minimize the back-and-forth communication between the viewer and the server-based VRML programming code. One way to do this is to utilize the power and storage capacity of the PC itself to store certain VRML elements such as commonly-used texture maps and audio files in a local reference file.

As the user moves through the environment, the client viewer and the server are in intermittent contact—exchanging requests and instructions as the user clicks on links to other worlds, audio displays, streaming video, and complex behaviors. VRML worlds will become true multimedia experiences on the World Wide Web.

Who Should Read this Book?

This book is primarily for non-programmers interested in learning how to use VRML to create virtual reality environments and 3-D graphics on the Internet. This will include graphics designers and programmers, marketing professionals, advertising professionals, publishers, software developers and game developers.

What's So Special About this Book?

This book thoroughly explains how to use VRML for creating 3-D graphics and virtual reality applications for the Internet. No previous experience with VRML is required and all of the latest standards are covered.

The key features of this book include, but are not limited to the following:

- Contains extensive coverage of OpenGL Graphics Standards, fundamentals and libraries.
- Provides numerous VRML applications as examples as well as VRML browsers.
- Includes tutorial on graphic techniques from polygon edges to rasterization.
- Contains the latest VRML standards developed by the VRML Architecture Group (VAG).
- Provides instructions for installing and configuring specific 3-D viewers or browsers that are required to view VRML files.

- Includes the latest VRML applications in the areas of: architecture, art, astronomy, telemedicine, biomedical sciences, chemistry, sports, animation, military, space, commercial, computer science, and engineering.
- Features a CD-ROM that includes over 20 VRML browsers and the applications that they support (authoring tools, modeling, viewers, etc.); and, examples that show how to create your own applications.

Organization of this Book

This book presents instant Internet gratification for all those would-be 3-D graphics Web cruisers who are tantalized by all the hoopla of VRML, but haven't got a clue as to how to view any of the interactive virtual reality environments. You'll begin by exploring the future of the last great multimedia virtual information mall to come to the WWW—VR 3-D graphics. You'll continue your exploration of VRML by learning to implement the language in order to create any type of 3-D applications, advertisements or Web pages that are needed by corporate decision makers, business owners, and technical professionals.

Many people feel daunted about cruising the net, in part because of all the techie terms in cyberspace. This book will make you feel at ease in using the 3-D viewers and browsers to view the VRML applications. The final part of this book concludes by linking you—the interactive virtualnaut to resources around the world with effective and easy to use VRML browsers that allow the display of text, video, graphics, and sound on a local computer screen. In other words, the book concludes with a description of what the future of Virtual Reality on the Net holds for you.

Part I: Identifying the Future

In this part of the book, a discussion about why there's so much excitement about VRML is presented. You'll discover the development of a whole new breed of web browsers to accommodate this new medium. You'll next explore the reasons why real virtual reality on the Internet does not exist yet. In addition, you'll find out why the concept of bringing 3-D environments to the Web is not new.

Next, you'll examine why Silicon Graphics' Open Inventor Object-oriented 3-D toolkit is proposed as the basis for VRML. Also, you'll examine why CAVEview is an interactive tool for exploring virtual reality applications over the Internet—via Web browsers. In addition, you'll learn why now—after existing for 17 years, surrogate travel in it's graphical form looms large on the VR horizon by allowing users to interact with information in a virtual intuitive manner.

Finally, Part I reaches its climax with a discussion of real virtual reality on the Internet. It will also describe the development of the networked collaborative hypermedia system intended to support groups of writers and scholars in writing and publishing hypertext fiction and criticism in a virtual reality environment. Part I concludes with an historical account about stumbling into Cyberspace with an idea that didn't get away—VRML!

Part II: Implementing the Future

Part II begins by outlining a direction for VRML based upon trends and directions found in the rapidly forming 3-D graphics and networking markets. Next, it discusses the development and implementation of Open Inventor as an object-oriented 3-D toolkit offering a comprehensive solution to interactive graphics programming problems. Also, Part II discusses the success of the VRML process that was committed to being open and flexible; and, responsive to the needs of a growing Web community. It concludes with a description of the Open GL graphics system: what it is, how it acts, and what is required to implement it.

Part III: Results and Future Directions

Part III begins the visionary quest of visiting the numerous proposed VRML research projects and systems. It describes the preliminary ideas for extending the World Wide Web to incorporate virtual reality (VR)—the primary focus of this book. Next, you'll learn how various considerations have governed the selection and presentation of graphical operators in OpenGL. The theme contains a detailed discussion of OpenGL's procedural interfaces which allows a graphics programmer to describe rendering tasks, whether simple or complex, easily and efficiently. You'll even learn about VRML behavior engine technology which allows simulations, as well as documentation through which a reader accesses and links them with an embedded component distributed on the Net.

In addition, Part III also looks at the numerous VRML applications that have been developed for viewing and interacting on the Internet. As you near conclusion, you'll be guided through the development of ongoing realistic VR Projects within the commercial, military, government, and medical community that will eventually be imported to the Internet as possible VRML applications. Finally, how far can high performance VRML go? In what directions will it develop? How fast will it evolve? These questions and more are answered in this part of the book by examining the various pieces of the puzzle and looking at application trends and future possibilities.

What's on the CD-ROM?

The CD-ROM of this book should be thought of as a treasure trove of tools and software that you can use to build your 3-D graphics and Virtual reality applications for the Internet. Here's a quick and dirty overview of what is contained in the CD-ROM:

Neat VRML Sites Dozens of sites that have lists of sites and accompanying URLs.

The VRML Repository A resource for information relating to VRML and acocmpanying URLs.

The OpenGL Graphics System Utility Library A set of routines designed to complement the OpenGL graphics system is included here by providing support for mipmapping, matrix manipulation, polygon tessellation, quodrics, NURBS, and error handling.

OpenGL Graphics with the Xwindow System A description of GLX and the OpenGL extension to the X Window System is provided here.

GLX Extension for OpenGL Protocol Specification A description is provided here of the network protocol for GLX as it is encapsulated within the X protocol bytestream.

News Groups and Mailing Lists Dozens of discussion groups, news groups and mailing lists are provided for your enjoyment.

Software/Browsers Dozens of browsers are provided for viewing VRML files.

VRML Applications Dozens of VRML applications that have been developed for viewing and interacting on the Internet are provided, as well as various VR applications that are in the process of being designed for implementation on the net.

Tools/Software Last but not least, the CD-ROM also includes a comprehensive interactive array of shareware and demo versions of some of the most popular 3-D and VRML Web Browsers, Authoring Tools, Viewers, 3-D modeling tools, and other VRML products.

A Word from the Author

Most information on the WWW is already free—as is much software. Experienced, virtualnauts, not used to paying for things they download, may be reluctant to pay as they go. As spectacular as Web technology is, it still has a considerable way to go to become attractive to the millions of consumers who are used to the amenities of mall and catalog culture.

In time, though, everything from home appliances to automobiles could be linked to a virtual reality environment on the Web. As it so grows, so will VR applications such as telemedicine, in which rural doctors will share virtual diagnostic tools like MRIs with specialists around the world. Or a car might plug into a holographic VR network in which engineers at a manufacturing plant could comment on the car's condition in a holodeck type setting. Perhaps home refrigerators will report their inventory to grocery store computers that they are running low in food stapes and require home delivery—billed to the customer's account. The customer could then select new items by viewing them in a virtual grocery store. Nevertheless, all of this VR commerce will begin in earnest on the Web when the computer becomes as easy to use as a telephone or a microwave oven.

If you're looking to use the Web in this way now, it would be worth your while to phone a help-line consultant to learn how to use the 3-D software and seek help often to figure out how to negotiate virtualspace. The computer is evolving into an information appliance. But that day won't truly arrive until computers get easier to use and conveyor—telephone and cable companies—hook up homes with high-speed data lines that end those annoying delays when virtualnauts try to download their favorite VRML application from a Web site.

Remember, the Web is out there! Have fun!

>John R. Vacca
>2318 Gemini Avenue
>Houston, Texas 77058
>(713) 480-1688 (voice)
>(713) 486-8346 (fax)
>74044.164@compuserve.com (internet)
>jvacca@hti.net (Internet)
>URL—http://www.commerce.com/ctw (Web Page)

PART I

Identifying the Future

Bringing 3-D Environments to the Web: The VRML Connection

An android entity named the "The Face" is leading me around the ancient Martian city of Cydonia. "Have you visited the 'Fortress yet?" she wants to know, and when I ask her what she's talking about, she just says, "Follow me." We walk and walk across the Martian desert until finally, after meeting up with a giant Terrain being named Richard and an overgrown ancient Egyptian cat named Ray, we arrive.

The 3-D view of the Fortress goes on and on. It is awesome, its linear battlements built so as to afford the occupants with an uninterrupted view out across the desert. I see alien Martian armies, pennants flying, sallying forth from the massive Fortress squatting on the rust-hued Martian desert, off on some ancient, inexplicable military campaign.

"So what do you think?" The Face wants to know. "I can show you some more ancient ruins, if you want." I spend the next four hours following The Face around, and I'm not the only one. By the end of the day, there's a whole parade of Martians following The Face's every lead. "Where did The Face go?" my new friend the Red King asks the minute The Face disappears. "Still here" comes The Face's message. "Sorry, but I had to go to the kitchen to get my diet drink."

A Ray Bradbury *Martian Chronicles* surrealistic dream? Not quite. As it turns out, The Face was actually a colleague of mine from her home in London.

Suddenly, 3-D environments like the scenario just described are popping up all over the Web. We're seeing lots of workstation vendors, animation vendors, and virtual reality (VR) software vendors coming to market—with all kinds of 3-D Web browsers, Builders, and authoring tools. At SIGGRAPH '95, VRML (Virtual Reality Modeling Language) and related products were all the rage. So, what's going on? What does it all mean?

Why All the Excitement about VRML?

VRML is to 3-D what HTML (Hypertext Markup Language) is to 2-D. VRML is the whole point. Without a standard 3-D graphics interchange format, the whole 3-D WWW is pointless.

Whereas HTML specifies how two-dimensional documents are represented, VRML is a format that describes how three-dimensional environments can be explored and created on the World Wide Web (WWW). Since 2-D is really just a subset of 3-D, any two-dimensional object can be easily represented in a three-dimensional environment. In Mark Pesce's book *VRML: Browsing and Building in Cyberspace,* Tim Berners-Lee, the father of the Web, reasons that VRML is the future of the Web because it is more natural for us to be immersed in a three-dimensional space than to click our way through hyperlinked pages.

VRML is exciting to the computer graphics community because it represents a clear first step toward truly widespread use of 3-D graphics. By agreeing on a standard mechanism for sharing 3-D graphics over the WWW, 3-D graphics can move outside of niche application areas and into everyday use. This is exciting because there are compelling reasons to believe that 3-D graphics can enable better ways to communicate, learn, and conduct business.

What's going on here is that one good idea leads to another. Very few people saw the Web coming. Even fewer saw 3-D on the Web looming over the horizon. Now that 3-D and the Web are irrevocably wed, people are raving about the brave new world. SIGGRAPH, the premier show for interactive media technologies and solutions, has been true to its image. What better environment than the free-spirited

SIGGRAPH to help disseminate the notion of the Web as a carrier of interactive media technologies? And of course serious businesses have become interested in making some extra money with the concept!

What all this means is that everybody is exploring new possibilities. It is too early for a sure voice to be heard over the Web's cacophony. The experiments of today will pave the future for real applications of 3-D environments on the Web. By the end of 1997, with the large percentage of personal computers (the client of choice for Web exploration) equipped with on-board 3-D acceleration and increased line bandwidth, 3-D will be the natural choice for navigating the Web and visualizing distributed information. The inherent topology of the Web, with all of its interconnections, is certainly not two-dimensional, and better visualization tools are required. By providing an extra dimension, 3-D seems to fill the gap.

Current 3-D Environments on the Web

An increasing number of 3-D environments are available. Each environment is different. There are sites displaying objects of all kinds: hand tools, mathematical entities, buildings, molecules, and even conference floor plans.

For example, Dimension's X's Liquid Reality with HotJava, shown in Figure 1.1, provides the Web's first interactive 3-D experience—where you can interact with objects in the environment in realtime. Intervista has World View, as shown in Figure 1.2, and TGS and SGI have Web Space (see Figure 1.3). These last three all act as external helper applications to a regular Web browser, although they all have plans to go In Plane with Netscape Navigator to be viewed from within the regular browser window. They also provide *static* 3-D spaces; you can wander through the spaces but can't interact with anything in the spaces.

On the other hand, what is currently available are not 3-D worlds but more like 3-D islands—some with links to other islands. Most of the 3-D environments available are simply 3-D models translated to VRML. They are really just preliminary demo environments put out by R&D organizations. Very few models exist that take advantage of key VRML features: level of detail and the ability to include other nodes from across the Web, etc.

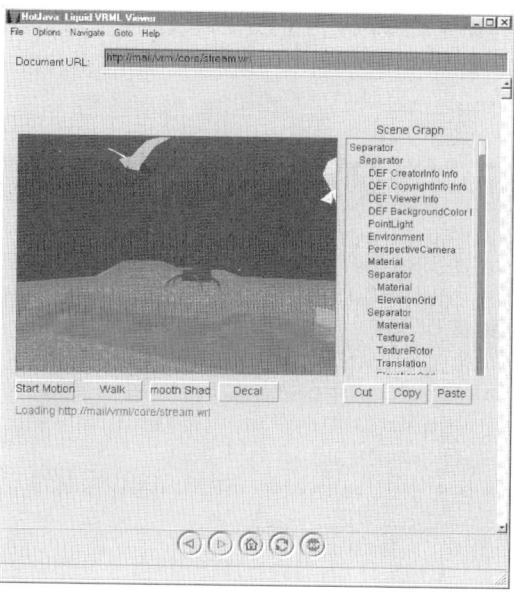

Figure 1.1 Dimension's X's Liquid Reality with Hot Java

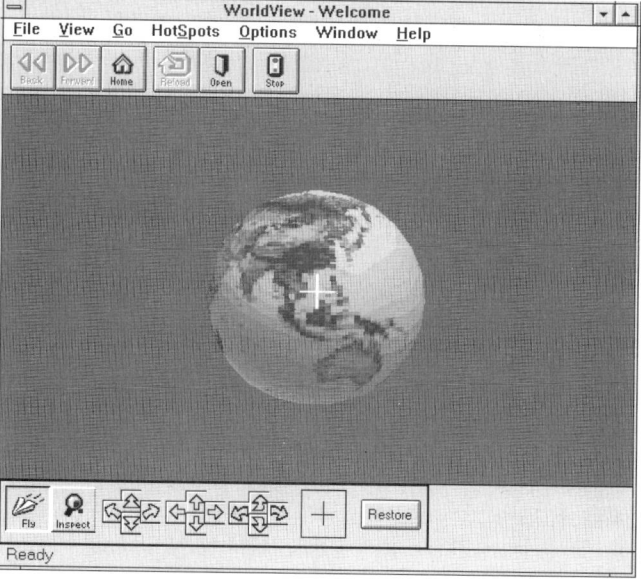

Figure 1.2 Intervista's World View

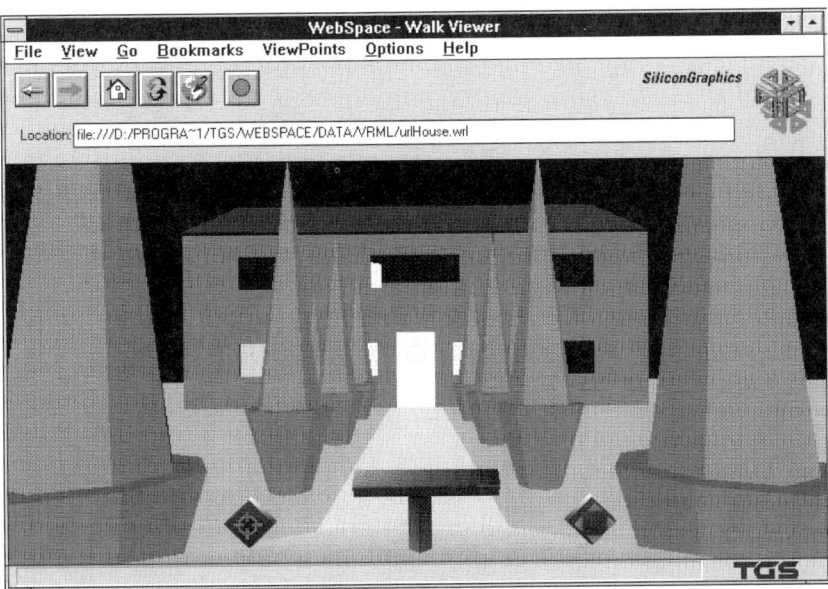

Figure 1.3 Web Space

The Good, the Bad, and the Ugly

The current crop of 3-D environments on the Web cover the entire gamut—the good, the bad, and the ugly. The same sins committed when creating traditional Web pages are also well represented in 3-D. The key aspects of the Web are *content* and *form*. The very nature of the Web makes it impossible to separate both. The ideal 3-D environment offers a well-thought structure, easy navigation, and above all useful content. Today's 3-D environments are largely exploratory in nature and more a vehicle for learning the new medium than a carrier of content.

The ones this author has viewed have not been very interesting. This is a result of several factors: First, the viewers are pretty slow, even on something as high-end as an SGI Indigo Extreme. Second, the ones viewed so far have not been compressed and have to run on several megabytes (MB)—which is a long download time, even on a fast connection. Finally, VRML as a language is still in its infancy, and static scenes with a few hyperlinks cannot be all that interesting.

People are still learning how to take full advantage of VRML. Simply converting existing 3-D models into VRML via file translators does not usually yield good results. VRML is designed for use on low-end machines over low-bandwidth networks. Polygon count and file sizes are important concerns.

Two unique features of VRML that help manage these concerns are the LOD (level of detail) node and the inline node, as shown in Figures 1.4 and 1.5, respectively. The LOD node allows the author to specify multiple representations of objects at varying complexities. The version of the object that is displayed is chosen automatically, based on the distance between the object and the user's eyepoint. This is a time-honored trick used for years in real-time visual simulation applications. Effective use of the LOD node greatly improves graphics performance by helping to limit the total number of polygons displayed at any one time.

The inline node points to other VRML files and can be used to break up large VRML files into smaller pieces. As a VRML file is being read into the user's machine, the browser interprets the file and builds the appropriate geometry. When the browser encounters an inline node in the VRML file, it begins fetching this new piece. In the meantime, the

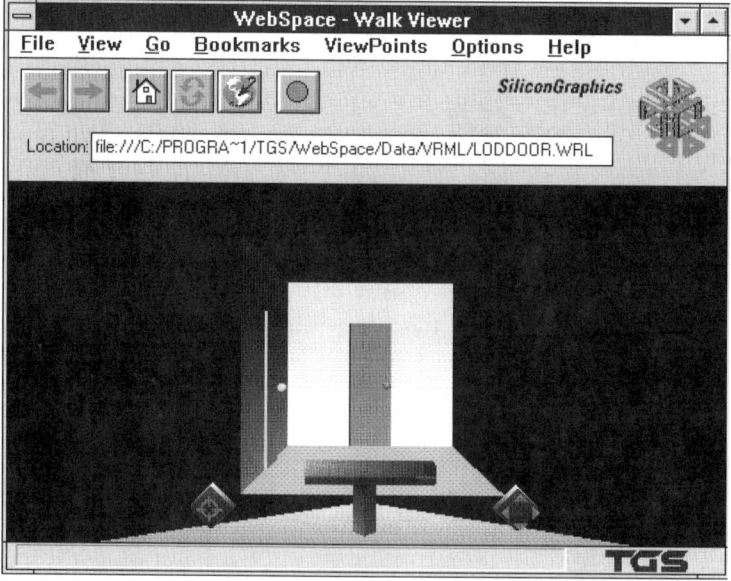

Figure 1.4 LOD (Level of Detail) Node

Chapter 1 Bringing 3-D Environments to the Web: The VRML Connection

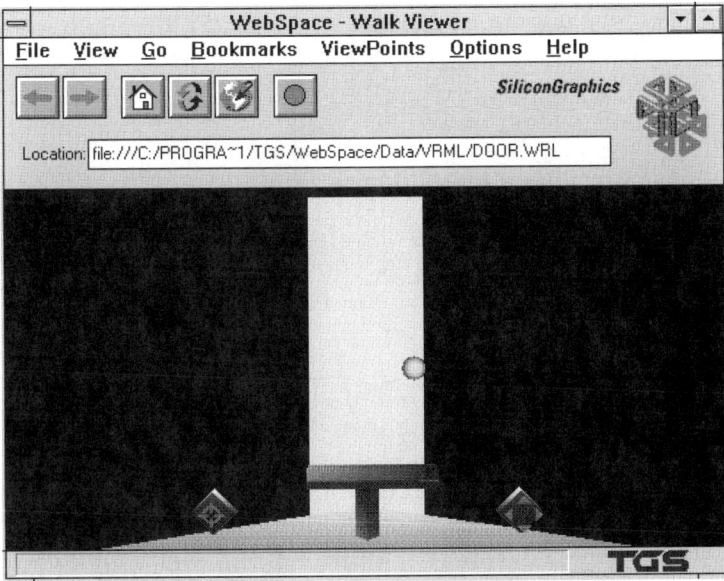

Figure 1.5 Inline Node

user can begin navigating through the scene even while it is being constructed. This is especially useful if the user has a low-bandwidth network connection.

When inlines are wrapped inside LODs, a double advantage occurs. If the user happens to navigate away from the location of an inlined part of the scene and never activates the LOD that contains this inline, the browser will not even attempt to load that part of the scene across the network. This is especially efficient, since it reduces both network traffic and polygon count.

Until recently, it's been difficult for VRML authors to take advantage of these features of VRML because to do so would require carefully editing the VRML text files to add these nodes at the appropriate place in the scene. This requires intimate knowledge of the VRML file format. However, interactive VRML authoring applications are now appearing that greatly simplify this task. With the use of these tools, we will begin to see more and better-performing VRML sites than are available today.

Build It and They Will Come

Builders of 3-D environments range from universities to businesses to individuals just passing through who are interested in exploring the new medium. Recently there has been a proliferation of sites of architectural nature—where buildings and, sometimes, the main components of a town are represented. Another trend is to offer conference attendees a glimpse of an exhibition floor plan, complete with booth and vendor information. The ability to walk through a conference before even getting there is the perfect planning tool to optimize one's time.

It's still early for VRML, but more and more 3-D sites are going up every day. Just as the number of HTML Web pages grew exponentially over the last couple years, so will the number of VRML sites increase.

Most of the VRML work being done right now is coming from academic and research institutions. These include architecture (UCLA); chemistry (Imperial College, Technical University of Darmstadt, Virginia Tech, Oxford); computer science (University of Illinois); national labs (NCSA, SDSC); and, math departments (University of Minnesota), as shown in Figures 1.6, 1.7, 1.8, 1.9, and 1.10, respectively.

Figure 1.6 Architecture

Chapter 1 Bringing 3-D Environments to the Web: The VRML Connection 11

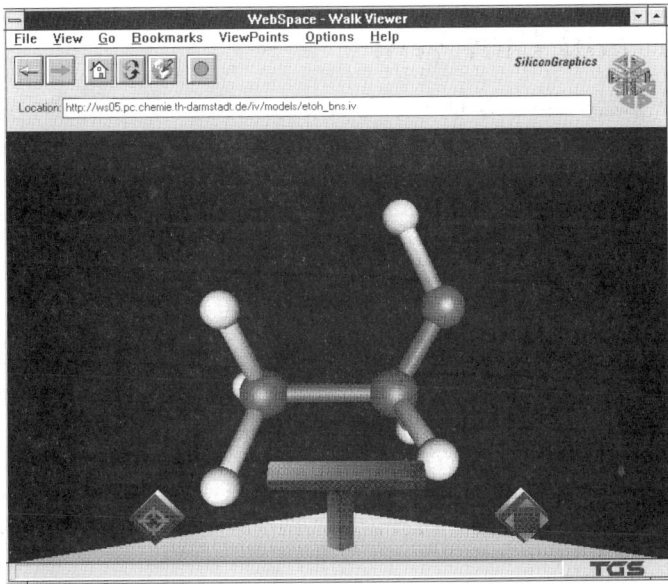

Figure 1.7 Chemistry

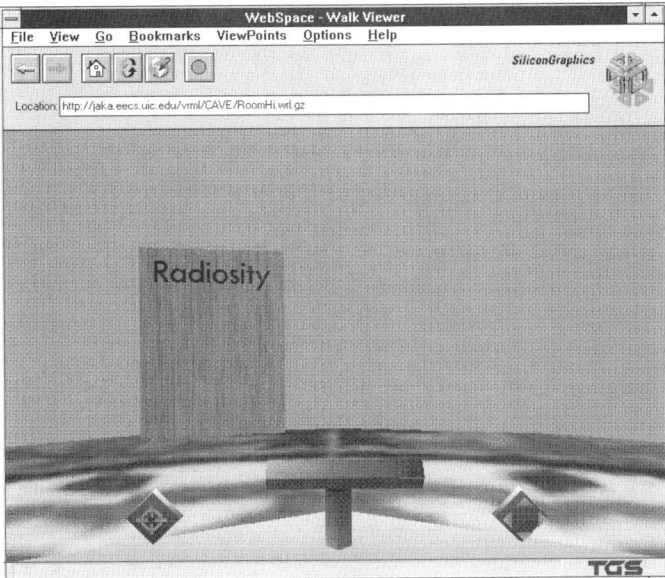

Figure 1.8 Computer Science

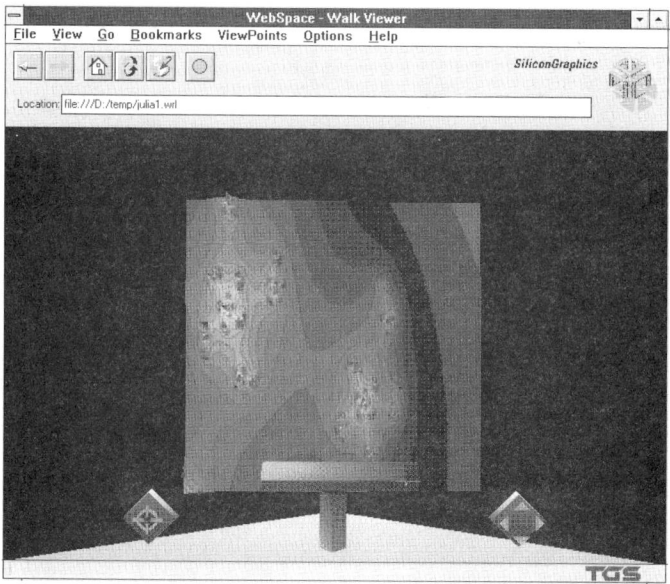

Figure 1.9 National Labs

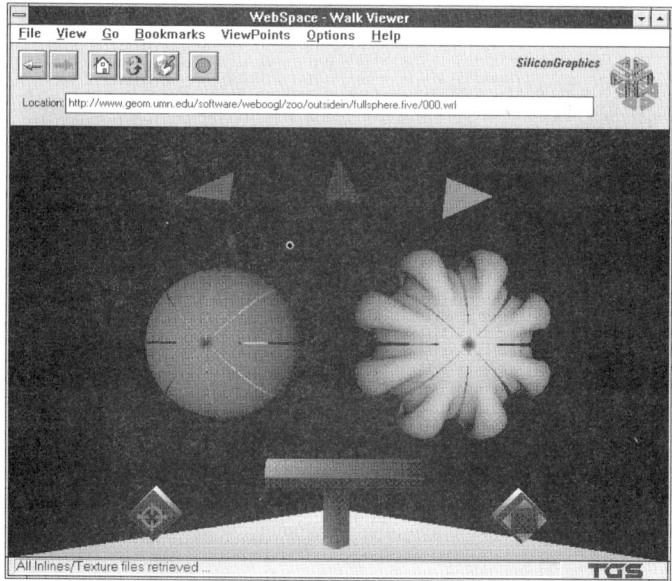

Figure 1.10 Math Departments

Of course, software and hardware developers that are somehow involved with VRML also tend to have VRML models on their Web sites (Silicon Graphics, Lightscape, Paragraph, Radiance, 3-D/Eye). Among the more interesting sites are those created as virtual representations of real-world exhibitions like that done for the Interactive Media Festival and, of course, the SIGGRAPH kiosks. The most notable commercial site is the British Telecom Laboratories home space called Portal (as shown in Figure 1.11), which uses VRML as an interface to public information about BT Labs, facilities and projects.

Ease of Build

Most tools for building 3-D environments on the Web are existing applications modified to save files in the VRML format. As such, the difficulty in building these environments has little to do with the Web itself. Perhaps the main challenge is not of graphical nature but rather how to attach Web-specific information (URLs) to existing or newly created 3-D models. A limitation of today's 3-D environments

Figure 1.11 Portal

on the Web is their artificial nature. Some models lack floors or ceilings; some even lack walls—certainly not what Web warriors might expect.

There are two basic steps to building 3-D environments for use on the Web: building the geometry and adding links. Building 3-D models is not rocket science, but it can be tedious. Good modeling tools are widely available as far as file translators to convert geometry to the VRML format. Structuring the geometry into inlines and LODs as described earlier can be difficult or easy, depending on your access to interactive VRML authoring tools. The same is true for enriching VRML sites by adding links to other Web-based content.

Nevertheless, every day it is becoming easier to build 3-D Web sites, because industry is embracing the VRML standard. All of the 3-D modeling packages are now exporting VRML files. All of the vendors of 3-D models are now offering VRML versions of their wares. Soon 3-D objects will become a commodity product. This is inevitable. With VRML products becoming more and more accessible, it makes it that much easier for you or me to create a 3-D Web site. Nonetheless, the authoring software still has a long way to go before it is trivial to build a 3-D Web site.

Ease of Access

Interacting with 3-D information on the Web can be a frustrating experience. On the one hand, the inherent limitations in bandwidth and computing power on the client side restrict the complexity and richness of 3-D environments to mere sketchy models. On the other hand, the very fact that humans are used to living in a 3-D environment makes the Web a sterile place. All interaction cues we all depend on to live in our 3-D world merely disappear when surfing the Web. Current research has concentrated almost exclusively on file formats and rendering performance at the expense of better user interaction models. Lack of proper user interaction support is the second biggest impediment to make 3-D on the Web reach widespread use; lack of interacting and compelling content is the first. Let's be honest: Going through walls and flying upside down can be appealing to certain types of users, and even so, the novelty wears off pretty quickly. The next generation of 3-D environments will offer easily affordable immersive VR on the Web with head-gear and gloves, provide intelligent content and intelligent access, take care of detecting collisions, and direct users to interesting places.

Nevertheless, viewing 3-D environments on the Web today requires a VRML-compatible browser or viewing application. Currently quite a few are available on various platforms (see http://sdsc.edu/SDSC/Partners/vrml/software/browsers.html), as shown in the example in Figure 1.12. How good the experience of browsing 3-D sites is depends on a number of factors. Obviously the more graphics horsepower you have in your computer and the faster connection you have to the Internet, the smoother the experience will be. But other factors come into play as well.

A good VRML authoring package, as shown in Figure 1.13, helps an author take full advantage of the power of VRML to perform well in low-end situations. Making extensive use of LODs and inlines will help tremendously. Structuring the geometric data as efficiently as possible and compressing the VRML files using standard compression routines, such as gzip, will also help. Adding a list of camera views to the scene will also do much to help the user navigate by providing a guided tour to preferred viewpoints.

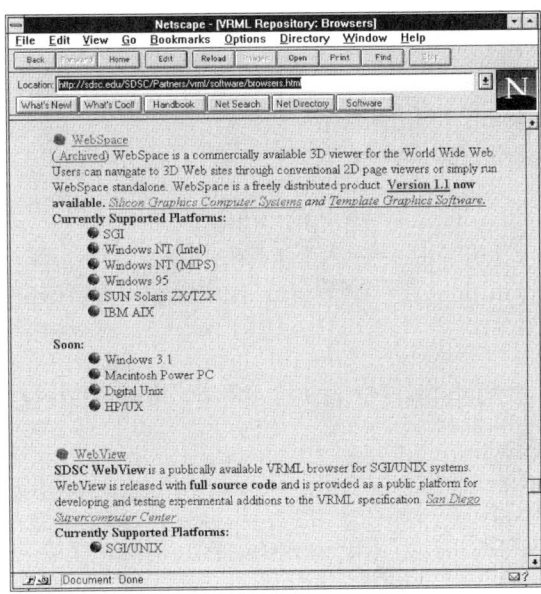

Figure 1.12 San Diego Super Computing (SDSC)

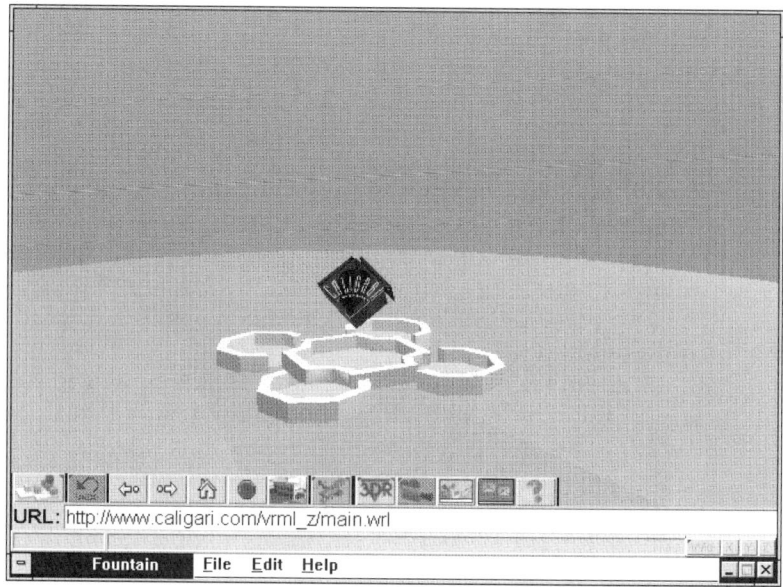

Figure 1.13 VRML Authoring Package

Browsers are getting pretty stable now but are by no means perfect yet. It's best to have a standalone browser. Viewers like WebSpace from Silicon Graphics have to rely on HTML browsers to get them the data, and errors do occur during the transmission. Nevertheless, VRML browser WebSpace Navigator V1.1 (as shown in Figure 1.14) includes several options in the interface to allow the user to make tradeoffs between frame rate and image quality. Of course, the best navigation paradigms are those that leverage what people already know. Games like DOOM have been used as inspiration.

The Practical Value of 3-D Environments on the Web

Seen as the next interaction metaphor—whether on the desktop or in distributed fashion—3-D promises to expand our ability to interact with the surrounding digital world. The very nature of the World Wide Web, where information acquires a multidimensional character, fosters

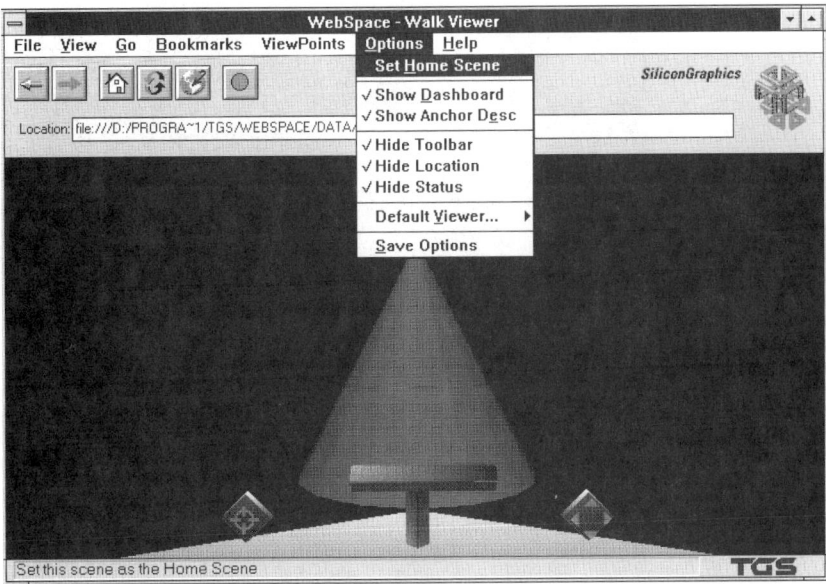

Figure 1.14 VRML Browser Web Space Navigator

the use of 3-D graphics as a natural interface. Existing HTML-based pages cannot adequately convey the Web's topology-cyberspace that knows no boundaries.

Today three major areas of practical uses for 3-D environments on the Web exist: flying through 3-D worlds, visualizing information, and inspecting 3-D models. The first category refers to the application of VRML for entertainment and advertising. Enriching a Web site with 3-D can further differentiate a site and help attract traffic. Silicon Graphics recently sponsored a VRML-based game called the Rift (as shown in Figure 1.15) as part of a contest to win one of its new Impact computers. Some practical applications of flying through 3-D worlds include selecting seating in auditoriums and previewing travel accommodations.

Visualizing information refers to the many scientific and technical uses of VRML, which are among the most popular applications today. Several examples of this are in the fields of chemistry, biology, mathematics, astronomy, and environmental sciences. Other practical examples of this type of 3-D interactive environments include electronic merchandising (virtual mall for shopping), cyberbanking (virtual

Figure 1.15 Rift

teller), and virtual government (a government that has staffing online to interact with citizens 24 hours a day), as shown in Figures 1.16, 1.17, and 1.18, respectively.

Inspecting 3-D models will be a common use in product catalogs and design databases. Assembly, repair, and maintenance manuals can all be delivered online with illustrations in true 3-D. Expect to see consumer goods in the near future ship without physical manuals but instead with Web addresses attached to their undersides. Silicon Graphics created a VRML demo of such an application, in this case an assembly manual for a computer workstation desk. You can see it on http://webspace.sgi.com/Repository/SGI-Depot.

Available Tools for Browsing and Building VRML Worlds

Most tools today fall in one of the following categories: VRML browsers, VRML authoring packages or 3-D creation tools. Since the whole market is still very young, the tools vary not only by features

Figure 1.16 Virtual Shopping Mall

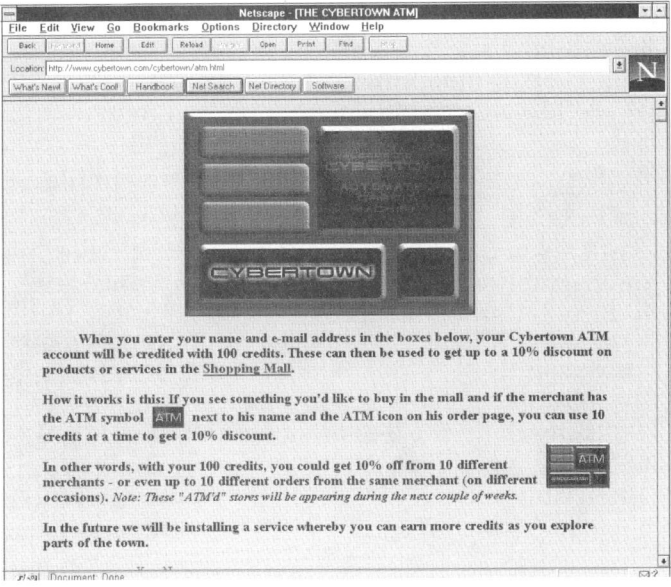

Figure 1.17 Virtual Teller

20 VRML: Bringing Virtual Reality to the Internet

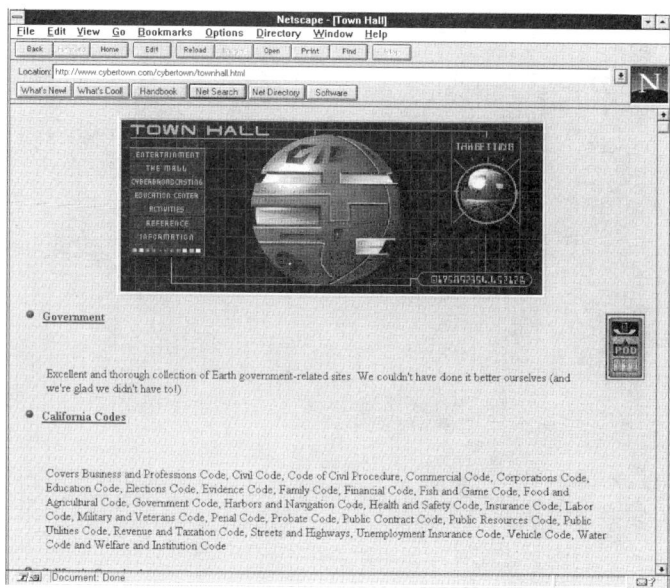

Figure 1.18 Virtual Government

but also by navigation paradigms and object manipulation methods. In addition, the tools differ considerably in terms of ease of learning, ease of use, reliability, price, and system requirements.

Although VRML is new, 3-D creation tools have been around for a long time. Also, whereas many CAD packages allow for 3-D design, the preferred tools for game designers and multimedia producers have been modeling and animation packages, such as Softimage, 3-D Studio, Strata Studio, and Caligari trueSpace, as shown in Figures 1.19, 1.20, 1.21, and 1.22. Although VRML does not support animation, it is very likely that it will do so in the future. So it is a good idea to purchase a 3-D creation tool from a vendor that will be able to add functionality as VRML evolves into a language for describing interactive multiparticipant environments.

Although some 3-D creation tools already allow models to be saved in VRML, others require you to purchase or download separate translation utilities that convert from the vendor's internal format to VRML. Direct VRML output is preferable to converters, since something always gets lost during a translation. It is a good idea to make sure that the tool you are considering not only writes VRML files but also

Chapter 1 Bringing 3-D Environments to the Web: The VRML Connection   21

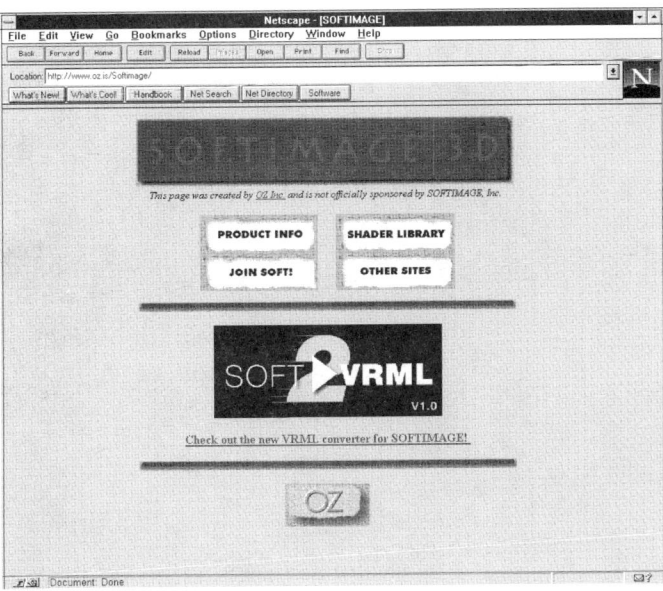

Figure 1.19 Softimage

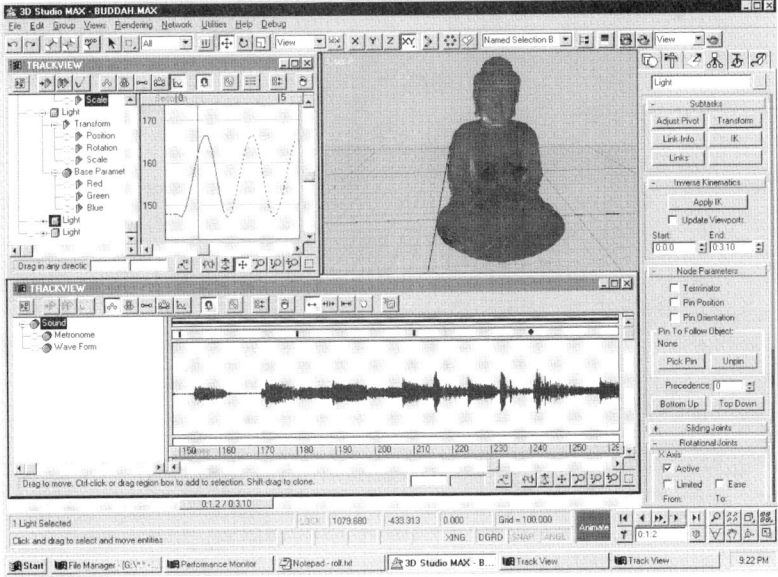

Figure 1.20 3-D Studio

22   VRML: Bringing Virtual Reality to the Internet

Figure 1.21 Strata Studio

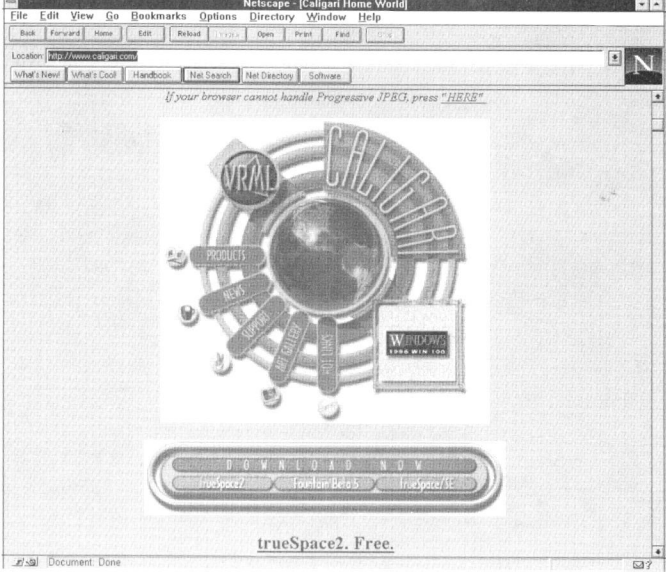

Figure 1.22 Caligari trueSpace

can import them. In addition, you should be aware of what elements get lost when you save a scene in VRML rather than in the vendor's format; otherwise, you find yourself with completely washed-out scenes because your tool supports light attenuation, but VRML doesn't. Since there are various levels of VRML support, you should also check to what extent VRML is supported. For example, most modeling packages cannot write out VRML primitives.

Although most 3-D creation tools are developed by established vendors, many VRML browsers are written by companies that were started after the first VRML spec was drafted in late 1994. Most of these companies have a networking rather than 3-D graphics background, but they were able to beat larger competitors to the market because they recognized the importance of VRML early on.

Some browsers (WebSpace) rely on HTML browsers to fetch VRML scenes, but others (WorldView and worldSpace) have built-in networking support and need to communicate with HTML browsers only when they encounter an HTML document. Although most VRML browsers rely on DDE to communicate with HTML browsers, WebF/X integrates seamlessly with HTML browsers, such as QMosaic. Caligari's worldSpace is the only VRML browser that also includes 3-D creation tools and VRML authoring.

Many other specialized VRML browsers are available in the industry. In the fourth quarter of 1995, IBM and Worlds Inc. began distributing a free VRML+ browser that supports multiuser virtual environment for IBM OS/2 Warp, Apple Power Macintosh, and Microsoft Windows 95 and NT platforms (see Sidebar: "VRML+ Lets Groups Communicate, Share Experiences in Virtual Worlds"). The VRML+ browser is for viewing the 3-D environments and also allows users on the Web to interact and communicate with one another in real time through the Internet.

Virtus Walk through, Web-Space author, Home Space Builder, and Caligari worldSpace are the most popular authoring tools. Although all of them allow you to add hyperlinks, only WebSpace Author and Caligari worldSpace support inlining and levels of detail. WebSpace Author runs on SGI machines and includes some sophisticated polygon reduction technology. However, unlike Caligari, worldSpace does not include any 3-D creation tools. Caligari worldSpace runs on Windows 3.1 and Windows 95 and is freely downloadable for noncommercial use.

VRML+ Lets Groups Communicate, Share Experiences in Virtual Worlds

Click on the Internet and begin an exciting journey with other people through a virtual environment. Travel around the world with other cybersurfers from who, like you, can be seen as real-life avatars, or visual embodiments of people. Chat with your cyberpals as you tour an art gallery of renowned paintings. Conduct business by talking to sales representatives about their products and services. Buy and sell products that can be demonstrated and seen in full-motion 3-D form.

Fantasy? A page from a C. S. Lewis novel? No, all of these virtual collaborations are possible now. At SIGGRAPH '95 IBM and Worlds Inc. demonstrated Virtual Reality Modeling Language+ (VRML+)—a jointly proposed extension to the emerging Internet standard: Virtual Modeling Language (VRML). The two companies are offering VRML+ to the computer industry as a first step toward an enhanced VRML and are making the protocols freely available.

In the fourth quarter of 1995, IBM and Worlds Inc. began distributing a free VRML+ browser that supports multiuser virtual environments for IBM OS/2 Warp, Apple Power Macintosh, and Microsoft Windows 95 and NT platforms. Servers will be available for RISC System/6000 (RS/6000) Silicon Graphics Inc. Challenge and Indigo, Linux, Sun Solaris, and Windows NT platforms.

The ability to turn the Web into a universe of friendly and fascinating cyberworlds offers a huge realm of potential for leading consumer product and service organizations. VISA is one of the companies working with Worlds Inc. to create 3-D applications for its member banks and their customers.

- **Virtual branch office:** For private conferences and cyberchats, users will be welcome to arrange meetings in virtual conference rooms, living rooms, or even pool side.
- **IBM digital library:** Cybersurfers can tour the wonders of an art museum through IBM's newest multimedia technology, which allows owners of information content to maximize their assets and make them available through networks around the world.

> - **New-product gallery:** Cybersurfers can virtually test-drive hot IBM products, technologies, and services.
>
> Additional details on the VRML+ protocols may be found on the World Wide Web at http://www.worlds.net/vrml/protocols.

What Are the 3-D Tools For?

The current crop of 3-D Web tools are mostly of experimental nature or adaptations of existing applications. The trend for content creation is to take existing 3-D applications and change them so as to also save models in the VRML format. For 3-D browsing, the easiest approach is to rely on a traditional Web browser (Netscape being the all-time favorite) as a front-end and to develop a compatible helper application.

The 3-D Web browsers let any Web user experience a 3-D Web site. The 3-D Web builders let any Web site creator add 3-D functionality to its Web site. World builders, such as Virtus Walk through Pro 2.5, enable users to build 3-D environments, and 3-D browsers enable people to view 3-D sites on the Web.

This Calls for Introductions

Who's introducing these 3-D Web tools? Macintosh users can count on a number of tools for content creation and 3-D browsing. For content creation, Strata Inc., a well-known provider of 3-D graphics rendering and animation tools, has taken the lead and adapted Studio Pro to save models and URLs as VRML files. Strata's approach to attaching URL information to 3-D models makes it very easy to deploy existing content on the Web. It also allows designers to use a well-known tool, without having to deal with the subtleties of the VRML format. For browsing VRML files on the Macintosh, users can rely on applications that use QuickDraw 3-D (the 3-D graphics API recently introduced by Apple Computer) to display 3-D models across the Power Macintosh family. The freeware Whurlwind application is one example. Whurlwind not only reads VRML files but also understands models created in 3-DMF—the native file format built in QuickDraw 3-D.

Integrated Data Systems (IDS) has released its new VRML browser, which will work on Windows 95 and Windows NT. Its partner in this venture, Portable Graphics, will also port this to various UNIX platforms. Later it will be available for OS/2 and the Mac. IDS is also starting an authoring package called VRealm Builder, which will allow developers to easily create 3-D worlds. This will be available the second quarter of 1996.

What a Difference a 3-D Web Tool Makes

Since products differ so widely, you need to evaluate which features are essential and which ones would be merely nice to have. For example, if you already have certain 3-D models in-house that you want to use, you need to make sure that your VRML authoring tool can import those objects. In particular, you should make sure that your tool imports VRML objects, or else you will not be able to take advantage of all the objects that you can grab off of various VRML sites on the Web.

Even if you heavily rely on prebuilt models, chances are that you will want to create a few objects of your own or merely modify some of the ones that you found on the Web. If you already have a modeling tool and your artist knows how to use it, you probably don't need to purchase another. However, you should keep in mind that many traditional 3-D modelers were built with photorealistic output in mind and may be overly complicated or lack features essential for interactive 3-D graphics.

Although most modelers still force you to work in wireframe mode, the latest breed of tools allows you to manipulate texture-mapped objects in realtime. Before spending a lot of money on a high-end tool, you should evaluate whether traditional modeling features, such as lathing and extrusions, are sufficient, or whether you will need advanced functions, such as organic deformations and 3-D Booleans. Deformations can add sizzle to your environment, but they also bump up file size and place a heavy burden on your visitors' computers that need to render your environments in realtime.

Although it is always a good idea to keep the average configuration of your target audience in mind, you also need to check which authoring tools run on your platform and how much memory they require. If you have an SGI, you have access to some of the best modeling tools in the industry. However, you will pay a high price for your software, and the selection of VRML authoring tools will be much more limited than on the PC. Pricing for Macintoshes is more in line with those for the PC, but software selections is much more limited. Most VRML browsers don't even work on the Mac yet.

Your best selection of tools will be on the PC, and the stiff competition will continue to keep prices both for software and hardware lower than on any other platform. However, some tools may require you to purchase more RAM, or you may have to deal with incompatibilities and crashes. Since most of your users will explore your VRML worlds with Windows browsers, you should have a very good reason if you choose not to use the PC as your primary development platform.

Rather than settling on one VRML tool, you may consider purchasing several and using each of them for the tasks for which they are best suited. In this case you need to make sure, though, that the best tools interoperate well and that there are no unexpected surprises when transferring scenes from one tool to the next.

If you have existing 2-D assets, you should make sure that your VRML tool can leverage these assets. If you want to use 2-D illustrations, you should make sure that you can import at least PostScript files. You can convert most image maps to JPEG format, but it is a good idea to check out what bitmap formats are supported by both your VRML authoring and browsing tools. Compatibility problems are minimized, of course, if you choose an integrated tool that can do it all. However, unless you want to optimize your VRML site for a particular browser, you still need to check on how your scenes look in the most common browsers.

Since VRML is hot, you will encounter many packages that claim to do VRML authoring. However, please keep in mind that VRML is an ASCII format and that any text editor can technically claim to be a VRML authoring tool. However, unless you enjoy working directly with a straight ASCII file, you should make sure that you can create levels of detail and inline objects without having to do any editing by hand. If modeling is not your strongest suit, you should select a tool that includes polygon reduction, so that you don't have to model levels of detail separately.

Although you need strong 3-D creation tools to generate the objects and spaces you want, the material-editing capabilities will determine how those objects and spaces will look. To keep maximum flexibility, you should look for tools that let you assign material attributes not only for entire objects but also on a perface basis. For example, you might want to use one texture map for someone's pants and another for his belt. Since texture maps increase the amount of data that has to be transferred, you should look for advanced paint tools, such as vertex painting. Vertex painting allows you to create multicolor gradients across surfaces and often eliminates the need for texture maps.

When evaluating VRML tools, you should pay close attention to options for reducing file size. By stripping out normals, ASCII formatting, and default values, a good VRML tool can reduce file sizes by as much as 50 percent. Files can be reduced even further by collapsing hierarchies, reducing precision, using VRML primitives and saving only one instance of an object that appears in various places. If you use gzip after having trimmed the VRML file to the bone, you may end up with files that are only 5 percent of their original sizes. This will dramatically speed up loading times for your users, and it will allow you to serve more users without adding disk space or bandwidth.

However, if you don't recommend a specific VRML tool for browsing, you will have to be careful about what tricks you employ to reduce file size. For example, many browsers do not accept zipped VRML files. If you do not have a tool that includes VRML browsing, you need to be prepared for a lot of testing and switching between your browser and your authoring application to make sure the links work. The navigation is more comfortable and all the objects look right. You may also have to switch to a separate browser to see whether inlines load as intended and whether objects that contain levels of detail are displayed properly.

When recommending browsers to visitors of your site, you should check how each of them performs on a similar system. The differences in speed can be quite dramatic. Some browsers are already set up to take advantage of a new breed of 3-D acceleration chips. Other factors to consider are ease of use and stability. Many of the newer browsers have not been tested adequately, so it is safer to recommend a browser that has been thoroughly debugged. Ease of use is to a certain extent a matter of taste. Some people prefer to use extensive navigation controls, whereas others feel more at home just using the mouse and keyboard shortcuts. A good browser gives you lots of choices for navigating around.

If you do decide to recommend a VRML tool for browsing, you should check with the developer of the tool to see whether you can make it available for downloading from your site. Many developers will be honored that you chose their tool and will allow you to distribute it free of charge. If the tool you distribute also includes authoring capabilities, you may find that your visitors will want to add to your VRML site or make improvements. In this case you should let them know ahead of time what your policy is regarding VRML scenes uploaded to your server.

The Future Promise for 3-D Environments on the Web

This technology is truly going to change our way of life. Imagine logging on in Chicago and playing basketball in 3-D on the Web with your friend in Tokyo. Imagine flying through a virtual store, trying out virtual products, and purchasing those you want to buy. Imagine accessing a database in 3-D whereby you can actually grab a 3-D data entity in front of you and inspect it. Imagine traveling to Antarctica on the Web. All of these things will ultimately be possible.

The Web today reminds me of Christopher Columbus. When Columbus was sailing west in his quest for a round earth, he reached a point where he was hopelessly lost. Legend has it that he gathered all the sailors and exclaimed: "We've arrived at uncharted waters much sooner than I had anticipated. Rejoice!" This is the current situation with the Web. Several explorers are experimenting with different paradigms, looking for brand new opportunities. Whether it be in education or entertainment, the future promise for 3-D environments on the Web relies on bringing users a level of experience otherwise impossible.

Most people involved with VRML agree that there are three major areas of functionality that remain to be incorporated into VRML: interaction with objects in the scene (to pick them up, change their color, or bounce off of them), behavioral dynamics (objects that function according to certain rules—like machines that move or birds that flock), and support for multiuser shared worlds (where you can meet and converse with others in a virtual world).

At SIGGRAPH '95, Silicon Graphics demonstrated a 3-D environment called the Dragonfly demo. Users at four workstations participated in a shared networked world. Each user was represented in the world as a fully three-dimensional avatar that could move freely through the space and interact with objects in the world. An image of each user was captured from a video camera and texture mapped onto the face of his or her respective avatar. The world featured simple physics that provided collision detection and mock gravity. Via open microphones, users could speak to one another at any time. Audio cues were used extensively whenever objects collided or interacted. Ambient sounds of crickets chirping pervaded the scene. A spider could be seen meandering about, flying creatures passed by in the air, and floating lilypads grew flowers over time. Users could turn lights on and off by pressing buttons placed on pedestals in the scene.

One of the objects of the demo was to build a dragonfly. The various pieces of the dragonfly lay on the floor inertly. When a wing was attached to the body of the dragonfly, it automatically began to flap. When the dragonfly was completely assembled, it flew away.

The Dragonfly demonstration exhibited a rich, interactive, shared virtual world that hopefully sparked the imagination of SIGGRAPH attendees. Although this application may have been somewhat frivolous, the technology behind it has countless important applications: online commerce, distance learning, and entertainment, to name a few. Unlike monolithic military simulations, the Dragonfly demo prototypes a lighter-weight, more flexible simulation whereby users could inhabit the shared world and bring intelligent objects into it. This is like the beginnings of a true cyberspace as depicted in numerous science fiction books and movies of late.

From Here

VRML is literally the glue that allows a range of technologies—including multimedia-equipped personal computers, high-speed communications, and others—to bring networked virtual reality to the end user. The next chapter identifies the key standard to VRML's potential success in the explosive phenomenon known as the Internet.

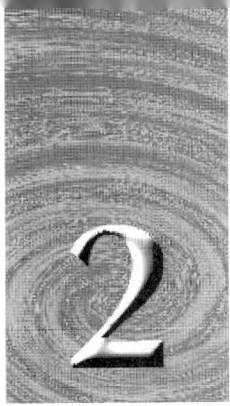

The Emerging VRML Standard

In his groundbreaking 1985 science fiction novel *Neuromancer*, author William Gibson defined what he called *cyberspace*, a future world in which humans would interface directly with computers and networks in a digital reality that seemed as real, or perhaps more real, than our physical world.

Gibson's vision was more fiction than science. But he did foresee that advances in computer and communications technology would, perhaps sooner than anyone thought at the time, yield a rich, highly interactive, networked environment that for all intents and purposes is Gibson's cyberspace.

Today that environment promises to be realized in part with Virtual Reality Modeling language, or VRML. As discussed in Chapter 1, VRML is a next-generation programming standard that allows personal computer users to visit and move through three-dimensional environments over the Internet, with much of the graphical sophistication of interactive video games or CD-ROM software. In VRML you can manipulate objects in 3-D space—rotate them, zoom in on detail, fly around them. For example, instead of just looking at a blueprint of a building an architect has finished, he or she could take you inside to look around. Or, instead of clicking on text and pictures to take you to different places on the Net, you could walk through doors, up stairways, or fly through windows.

A whole new breed of Web browsers has been developed to accommodate this new medium. We're seeing lots of workstation vendors, animation vendors, and VR software vendors coming to market—with all kinds of VRML Web browsers, builders and authoring tools.

The VRML Standard

The official organization developing VRML technology is, first, the whole community. The official organization tasked with leading the next version of the standard is the VRML Architecture Group (VAG). The group is made up of 10 technologists in the 3-D computer graphics industry (from Virtus Corp.; Silicon Graphics; Intervista Software; Sun Microsystems; IBM; Worlds, Inc.; Integrated Data Systems; Visible Decisions; and Strata; Caligari). VAG currently has plans to publish the next standard as soon as possible.

VAG—see http://vrml.wired.com/VAG/—also controls the VRML specification documents, as shown in Figure 2.1. A set of mailing lists on the Internet is used to generate discussion on what should go into the standard, with anybody free to submit proposals to the VAG.

Implications of the VRML Standard

VRML enables the communication and sharing of 3-D objects and worlds. That alone is very powerful—allowing chemists, for example, to publish 3-D models that they can use to communicate some aspect of molecular structure that they're studying.

The VRML standard is evolving to include more complex notions, such as objects that change over time. This will allow even more compelling applications to be created.

For example, the VRML spec is available for V1.0. This is a subset of SGI's Open Inventor with three extensions: level of detail control, winlin, and www.anchor. It also acts as a hyperlink to other VRML scenes. V1.1 specs are in the works. They're being debated. There will be minor corrections and clarifications. Requests are being sent to Bernie Roehl at the University of Waterloo; he then posts them to a Web page.

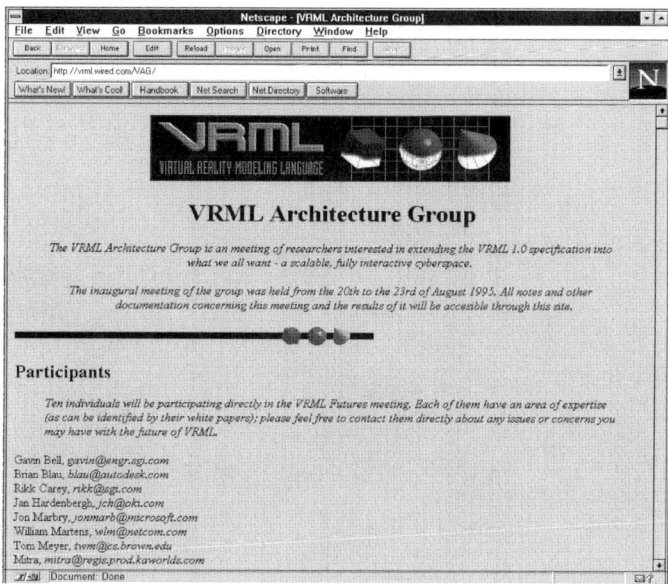

Figure 2.1 VRML Architecture Group (VAG)

V2.0 specs, on the other hand, are being debated now. Religious wars are occurring. The debate is on what types of behavior to include and whether the focus should be on client/server or peer/peer connections.

VRML Browser Standards

Browsers should implement every VRML feature, but some don't. Since VRML V1.0 is a little open, the browsers implement different effects (lighting models). Some browsers extend the standard. Among VRML browsers are the following:

- Webspace from SGI and Template Graphics (UNIX and Win/NT browser based on Open Inventor), as shown in Figure 2.2;
- Webfx from Paper Inc. (PC browser not based on Open Inventor), as shown in Figure 2.3;
- Worldview from Intervista (PC browser not based on Open Inventor), as shown in Figure 2.4.

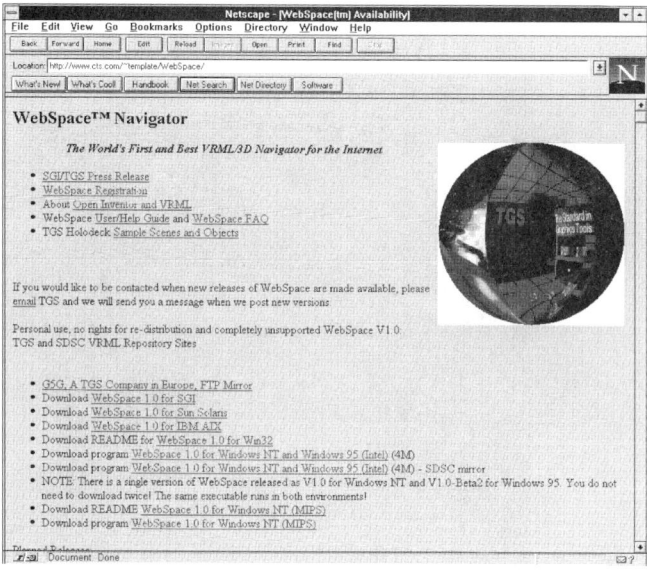

Figure 2.2 Webspace

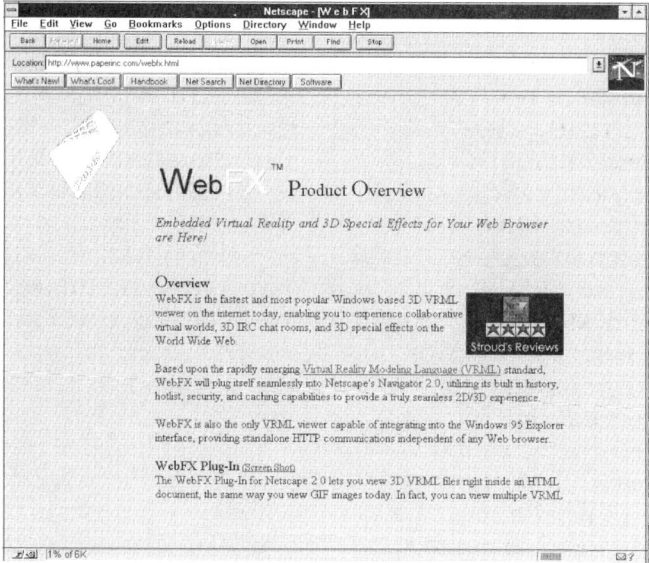

Figure 2.3 Webfx

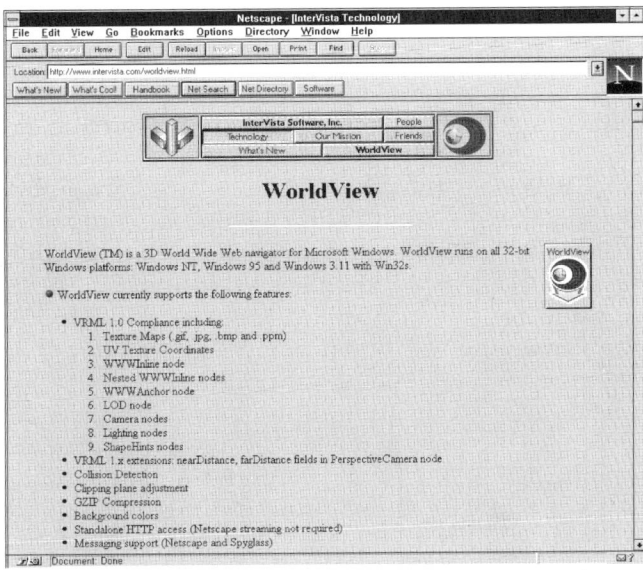

Figure 2.4 Worldview

VRML Development Stage

The VRML technology is immature, and current implementations are crude at best. An emerging standard for emerging technology, VRML currently does little more than whet the appetite for the inevitable evolution of this still crude discipline. Specifically, VRML V1.0 defines objects, textures, lights, and cameras but lacks important features of interactive 3-D, such as object behaviors and cause-and-effect relationships.

Many factors will push the evolution of this technology along. Intel and Motorola, for example, love compute-intensive technologies because applications based on those technologies help pull the new, more powerful computers into the market. Another group is backing the concept of cable modems—which allow you to experience the Internet through your cable line. Cable modem vendors are going to back VRML applications because Internet applications that are sexy and need a lot of bandwidth are what ultimately create their market. Microsoft is pushing 3-D in a big way. Thus there are a lot of companies with substantial power that will push this technology into the market.

At the same time, the amazing things that you will be able to do with this technology will cause consumers to pull it into the market.

VRML is for the time being an evolving organism. The VRML Architecture Group has proposed extensions and clarifications leading to a V1.1 specification. The challenges VAG faces are several. On one hand, it is clear that the current specification is somewhat a compromise and that changes are inevitable. On the other hand, there is strong pressure for managing changes in a way that minimizes the impact on existing commercial ventures. This latter point is very important, since widespread adoption of VRML as a standard for 3-D graphics on the Web will not happen until developers can stop chasing a moving target.

Existing and potential VRML developers face another type of challenge: the parser itself. The VRML syntax and the required integration with 3-D graphics libraries alien to VRML create problems of their own. Most current browsers rely on a publicly available parser (QVlib) that, although a good starting point, does have shortcomings. The fact that VRML is a subset of SGI's Open Inventor file format and that QVlib itself had its roots in Open Inventor leads to files that cannot be rendered correctly. A VRML validation suite or perhaps a reference implementation are sorely missed.

The VRML community, as demonstrated during the SIGGRAPH '95 conference, is also bracing itself for the unavoidable schism that VRML V2.0 will bring. VRML V2.0 will specify support for behaviors, a topic for which multiple and often conflicting solutions exist. Someone once said that instead of standing on each other's shoulders and move forward, 3-D graphics professionals always stand on other people's toes. Perhaps the best contribution the VRML Architecture Group ought to make is to focus at getting the core functionality right and to make extensibility through plug-ins an integral component of its architecture.

The notion of extensibility through plug-ins is being implemented by Apple Computer as part of its 3-D graphics program. QuickDraw 3-D, Apple's 3-D graphics API (application program interface), empowers developers and end users, allowing them to extend that product's core behavior in a well-defined manner, as shown in Figure 2.5. This means that as time goes by, with the natural evolution of 3-D and related technologies, the API (a specific library where an executable application program can be created) can be kept current and fulfill the needs of an ever-growing number of users.

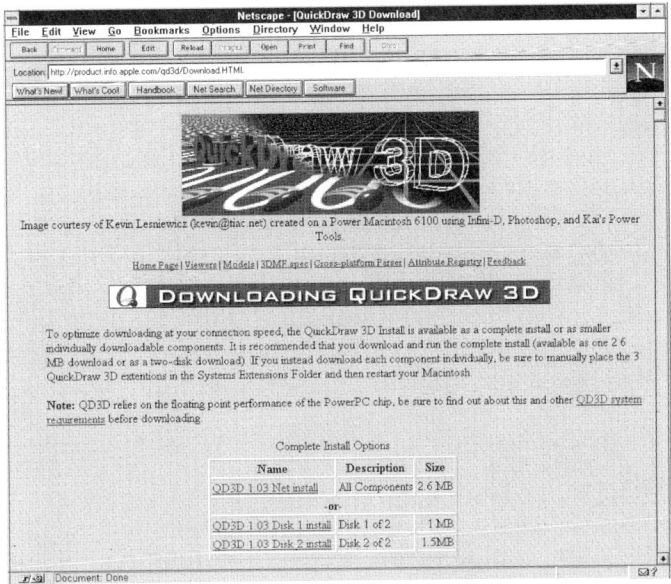

Figure 2.5 QuickDraw 3-D

QuickDraw 3-D is, naturally, the preferred way to render 3-D scenes on Power Macintosh systems. It will soon become available on other systems, offering a cross-platform solution to those wanting to experience 3-D graphics on the Web. An integral part of QuickDraw 3-D is its 3-DMF file format. Not unlike VRML, 3-DMF also has support for Web attributes and an integral custom attribute architecture that supports plug-ins at the operating system level. Some see 3-DMF and VRML as competitors. That might be true at a very low level. But let's not miss the forest for the trees. In the big scheme of things, users want the freedom to pick and choose whatever format serves their needs. The market is big enough to support multiple formats, and users will dictate their segmentation. For example, VRML, as a committee-driven effort, is a compromise (and a very good one indeed); it addresses most customers' needs but not all. Enter 3-DMF. Its close integration at the operating system level offers users the ability to take 3-D information well beyond the Web domain and into the existing corporate infrastructure.

Currently VRML V1.x is in common use by most VRML browsers. It basically defines the geometry, textures, and basic lights. But it's not interactive. You can load a world and fly through it, but the objects themselves do not respond to user input. The VRML Architecture Group is defining VRML V2.0, which will include some interactivity—most likely to be provided by the introduction of Java-based behaviors. Karl Jacob and the technogurus at Dimension in San Francisco (www.dimensionx.com) have created some great examples of VRML worlds with Java-charged behaviors attached to models. It's likely that the VAG will look to include a good deal of what Dimension X has done with this Liquid Reality into the spec for VRML V2.0. Other companies, such as MultiGen, Sense8, and Superscape, have many years experience building behaviors into real-time models. Their contributions are sure to be valued as well.

Availability in the Commercial World

Let's try to distinguish between commercially available and commercially viable. This is a central for any Web-based business today. Right now we're creating a billion-dollar industry by spending a billion dollars creating it. But the people really making a profit today are companies selling modems (until Intel puts 10 MBps cable modem access on the mother board), companies selling Internet access (until AT&T and the Baby Bells launch their services defensively), people creating Web pages on a fee-for-service basis (not really scalable), and magazines and books telling us all about it (always a good bet).

As with many technologies, the market for VRML is being driven largely by its potential for commercial applications. Major corporations are attracted to the ideas of building 3-D worlds for their customers to visit, perhaps creating a truly memorable experience that causes them to return over and over again. One of the limits of today's HTML-based Web sites is that, regardless of how beautiful their 2-D graphics are, the customer still experiences a flat, text-oriented world that can seem disappointing when compared with television or, for that matter, the real world. As a result, the customer may not be compelled to pay a return visit to learn more about the company or its products. Corporate developers currently have their choice of three major types of product: VRML viewers, related products that provide VRML extensions to existing HTML browsers, and VRML authoring tools.

VRML Viewers

Similar to HTML browsers, these are standalone software packages, written for PCs running Microsoft Windows, the Macintosh, or other PCs or workstations, that allow the PC user to visit and navigate VRML worlds. They typically feature controls for moving forward and backward, the ability to remember or record camera positions (3-D bookmarks that allow the user to return to a particular location later on), and handle such essential things as preventing the user from walking into or through a wall.

Extensions to HTML Browsers

Many firms are developing products that provide these capabilities as enhancements or plug-ins to existing Web browsers, such as Netscape Navigator or Spyglass Mosaic. These products allow users to access VRML worlds with their current browser technologies.

VRML Authoring Tools

Many of the same firms developing VRML viewers are also developing home space development tools. These tools allow developers to design and build the 3-D worlds in VRML format and to incorporate Internet-standard audio files, video files, and behavior engines that allow user interaction with and animation of 3-D objects in a world.

Thus many firms are bringing viewers and development tools to market, and some of the products are already shipping. As with any new technology, however, corporate developers and end users are taking a cautious approach. They know from experience that the second, or even third, version of a standard or product is often the one that contains the most satisfying combination of functionality, performance, and an attractive price.

A new medium must do one of two things to last. It must either lead the user to an economic transaction (in which case the value of the medium is as an advertising vehicle) or provide the user with an experience he or she is willing to pay for. VRML is unique in that it can do both. We're speaking of interactive advertising. It's expected that we'll see such applications deployed by advertisers within three months to start with and on a more regular basis within a year. As the VRML spec improves and Internet/Web and 3-D accelerator penetration into the home increases, we'll see a rapid increase in the demand for better, more compelling interactive advertisements delivered over the Web, using VRML. Look for critical mass in 1997.

VRML's Planned Use by Vertical Industries

Vertical industries, such as the construction industry, are already using VRML to explore exact representations of architectural drawings and models prior to the start of building. The real estate industry is planning to capitalize on VRML worlds, showing houses on the Internet to potential long-distance clientele. The museum industry is quite far along in offering 3-D worlds of various well-known pieces of art. The games industry is already a huge VRML market, and online 3-D chat worlds are becoming more popular.

Chemists are using VRML to visualize molecules before they're chemically synthesized. Travel companies are using VRML as a navigational aid in advertisements. Game publishers are using VRML to promote their 3-D games on the Web (Sega's Vectorman). Manufacturers will use VRML as an aid in training workers about production processes. Designers and architects will use VRML to help clients visualize their buildings before they're built. Advertisers will use VRML to sell real estate, cars, electronics, games, and even groceries.

Planned Applications for VRML's Use

The very fact that VRML can use existing technology is one of its major attractions to Internet technologists. It means that sites developed now will be, in the very near future, visitable by a large number of PC users.

Potential applications of VRML, if the market grows as expected, are both varied and remarkable. The following represent a few examples of VRML applications that might be built, given the state of the technology today.

Engineering Applications

Engineering today is a field that is largely dependent on graphical tools for visualizing and even building models for various products, as shown in Figure 2.6. The ability for engineers to use VRML to work on such 3-D models, across a network in a collaborative way, holds strong appeal for companies trying to increase productivity and cut costs.

Research, Including Medical Research

Medical researchers might use VRML to share not only their ideas, in text or chart form, but also their 3-D models of molecules or genes, across vast distances, as shown in Figure 2.7. This could not only speed up research but also spur ideas for new research.

Figure 2.6 Engineering

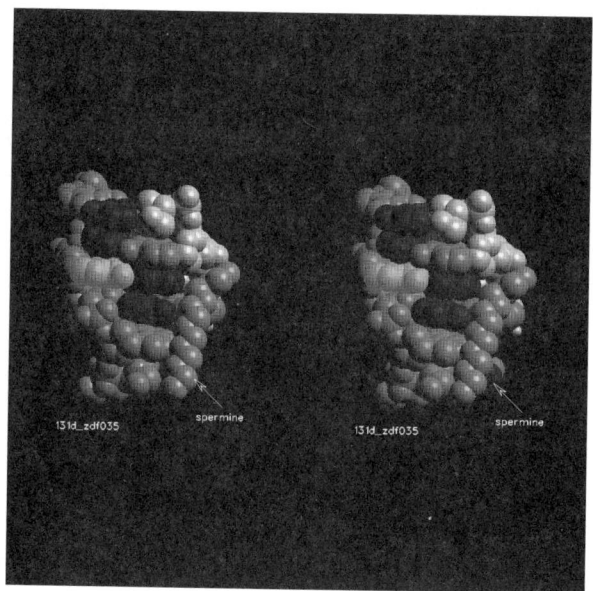

Figure 2.7 Medical Researchers

Commercial Applications and Marketing

The World Wide Web holds great appeal to firms wishing to establish direct links to customers, in particular via electronic advertising on their home pages. VRML holds the potential to enhance the customer/product experience dramatically. For example, customers could visit virtual malls and virtual shops, pick up, and look at the products they are thinking about purchasing, as shown in Figure 2.8. Or, vacationers could visit a resort in advance and walk through the hotel's facilities, including the guest's room itself, while checking out amenities, reviewing a schedule of local events, and pondering the streaming video view out the window.

Virtual Museums and Art Galleries

It would be possible to build a virtual museum in which users could browse around and look at works of art from various angles, as shown in Figure 2.9. Although this certainly could not match the richness

Chapter 2 The Emerging VRML Standard   43

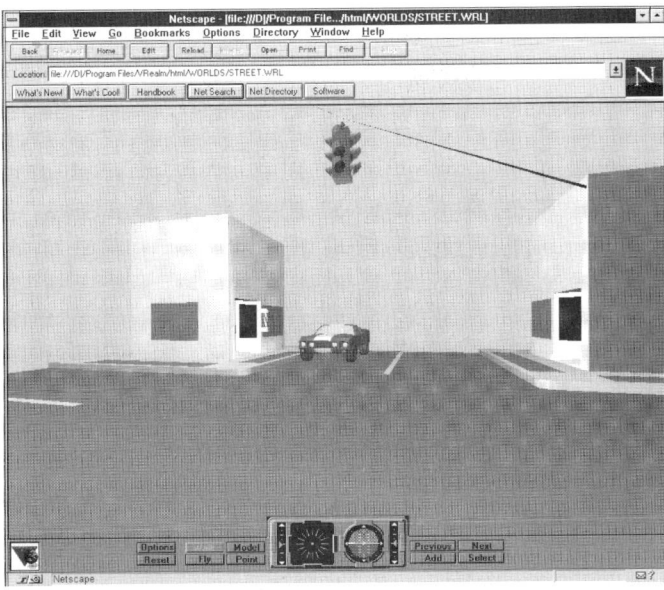

Figure 2.8 Commercial Application

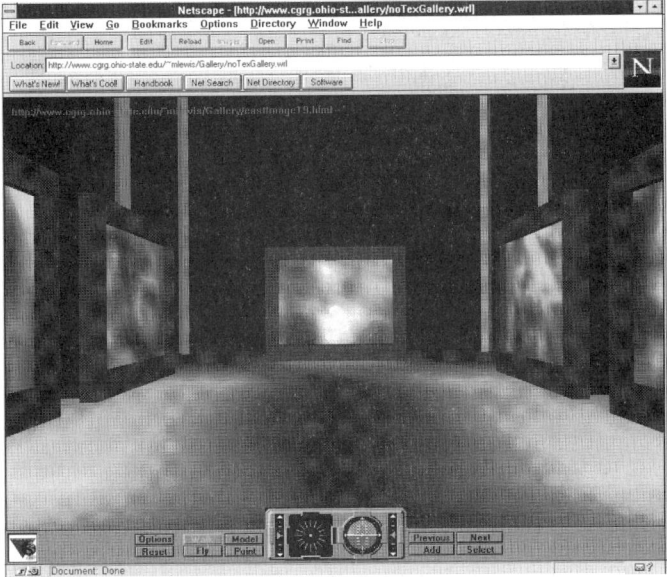

Figure 2.9 Virtual Museum

of a live experience, the ability to combine 3-D images of art with text and explanatory information could make VRML-based museums a significant source of art education and enrichment.

Implications of VRML in the Client-Server Environment

In the client-server environment, VRML will allow the development of a 3-D standard for the exchange of 3-D information over the Internet and among various systems. This creates a very powerful medium for interchange of information.

VRML brings interactive 3-D to client-server environments. If you can think of ways in which having interactive 3-D objects or 3-D environments be components of your particular client-server application and can add value, you probably should start to study up on virtual reality as a technology. The biggest impact may be in the area of graphical user interfaces in that an intuitive 3-D interface can make a lot of sense for many companies.

Corporations worldwide are discovering the strategic advantages of using internal Web sites for disseminating information company-wide. Not only the thorny issues of groupware computing get alleviated, but also internal Web sites open the door to finally tracking the Holy Grail: concurrent engineering. In the context of concurrent engineering, the need to unambiguously share product information across divisions makes 3-D a definite win. First of all, the added dimension of 3-D graphics increases the level of understanding among those accessing information. Then, the existence of a common database, composed of a well-defined format to represent 3-D information, makes it possible to move information from the conceptual-design phase down to manufacturing, without losses. Transferring data from one application to another is akin to moving sand from one place to another: When you move something, you always drop some sand and pick up some dirt.

VRML as it stands today lacks the richness necessary to represent the different data types and, even more important, the relationship among all data components. Until that happens, VRML will be confined to representing the graphics portion of a product's data. Perhaps that is not a bad idea, since graphics and VRML go hand in hand. Ideally,

VRML will prove versatile enough to play along with other richer file formats. In that scenario VRML would be the carrier of graphical information, whereas, perhaps, the intelligence behind a model would be carried by another file format.

Implications of VRML in Client-Server Applications Development Environments

VRML has no special implications for client-server applications development environments. You may use the server to download a VRML environment, but after that the role of the server (and even the Internet) is minimal. You can view the VRML environment off line without losing anything. However, the server will become more important as VRML environments become more functional. Right now, many companies rely on servers in their non-VRML environments to enable multiuser communication, to convey positioning, to update environments, and to show changes to them (either since your last visit or while you are there). The server will also play this role in VRML+ spaces. However, over time you will start to see VRML specifically, and virtual reality in general, integrated into client-server development software. This will allow the physical and logical components of the network—software and data—to be accessible and maintainable through intuitive, interactive 3-D interfaces.

Business and Technology Advantages of VRML

Despite its rapid evolution to date, the computer is still deficient in one very important area. Specifically, we as humans live in a 3-D world, yet the computer represents us with 2-D text and images. What the concept of VRML brings to the worlds of business and technology is, both literally and figuratively, a new dimension. Not only does it finally bring 3-D to the computer, but it also delivers *interactive* 3-D to us. VRML delivers 3-D to us quickly and efficiently across a wire, whether that be a local area network or the World Wide Web. Exactly what this technology gives us is difficult to say, just as it was difficult to predict useful applications of the computer when it was first conceptualized and commercialized. Suffice it to say that over time, more and more people will come to understand the power of interactive virtual reality. Its applications will become more and more prevalent, materializing in ways we probably cannot predict at this time.

VRML will allow us to go places that we currently cannot go and to see things that we currently cannot see, either because of physical, logistical, or financial constraints or because the places and things do not exist in our physical world. You cannot go inside of your computer, because you are too big. You cannot visit the Playboy Mansion, because access is restricted. You cannot test drive a new car design, because building a prototype is too expensive. You cannot walk through a database and examine data connections, because no such place exists. You cannot travel to the moon or perhaps even to the Bahamas, because it is too expensive. You cannot pick up hazardous materials, because it is not safe. Virtual reality lets us do all the things that we currently cannot do. The applications are limited only by the imagination.

VRML allows information to be represented in a three dimensional format, which is better matched to the delivery of certain types of information and allows the user to interact with the information presented. This has dramatic technological implications. VRML will allow technology currently available only to users of high-powered workstations (with expensive software) to be available to consumers and individuals in corporations with common PCs via the Internet. The business implications are that corporations can use VRML software to allow engineering designs to be reviewed by a larger number of individuals within a corporation in various locations. This will result in improved marketing and product review. Additionally, consumers will be allowed to better review products and to receive better service information.

For the industry as a whole, VRML as an emerging standard presents an opportunity to move away from proprietary tool-centered formats toward a more neutral geometry format. This presents new business challenges. VRML is, in a unique way, a new medium. Throughout the history of communication, economic value, in any medium, is shared between the content author or copyright holder and the publisher/distributor. We must build into the VRML specification a way to identify the original author and copyright holder of the model and perhaps the path that model took to get to the ultimate viewer.

Technologically VRML's primary advantage today is its independence and its flexibility. Since VRML is not sponsored by any single authoring tool or platform, the specification is independent and able to improve as quickly as the architecting parties can agree. Of course, it's a rare case in this industry that a committee-created specification ever reaches the status of *de facto* standard. This is usually because the committee members (VAG), with their built-in biases, can rarely agree on a neutral and advanced standard quickly enough to make it relevant to the market. It's like herding cats. But in this case there is significant leadership from neutral parties (Pesce and Parisi and others) who have shown an ability to help bring closure to issues quickly and then promote the result with religious fervor.

But VRML's polygonal format comes with the same challenge of any polygonal format. That is that its resolution is relatively fixed. Ideally, a user should be able to dialin the desired resolution (based on bandwidth and local processor and 3-D accelerator capability). This will require some nontrivial extensions to today's VRML specification.

Another challenge today is that many of the early viewers have been optimized to ship sooner and render later. Only a few have taken the opportunity to take advantage of some of the powerful and quick real-time rendering tools available. This will change and Moore's Law (and 36 new PC 3-D accelerator cards on the market by August of '96) will bless us with ever-increasing desktop 3-D power.

Requirements for Business Benefits of VRML

One wonderful aspect of VRML is that it surpasses language barriers. Content that is not culturally biased makes a site more attractive to a general audience. When we use spaces to communicate, we appeal to fairly fundamental cause-and-effect relationships. For example, other cultures may not understand American humor or moral debates; however, visitors from China may enter a Notre Dame world and instinctively know that this is a sacred space and behave accordingly. Without having to read the literature, visitors leave with a sense of what Notre Dame is all about. In this way businesses can apply international symbols and signs to conduct business over the Internet.

Commercial acceptance of VRML depends on a large number of factors. Certainly a commitment on the part of software companies to build tools and viewers is critical, and this has already been demonstrated with the flood of products in recent months. There are perhaps three critical success factors for VRML and VRML-based products: standardization, content development, and the installed base of PCs and modems.

Standardization

One problem that VRML users encounter today is incompatibility between their browser software and the many 3-D worlds they visit. Some browsers view only worlds built using that company's tools. Others view a broad number of worlds but are limited in the number of advanced features, behaviors, or site enhancements they can interpret or process. Advancement of the VRML standard itself, and adherence to that standard by software companies, is essential if VRML technology is to become widely deployed and used.

VRML standardization to increase compatibility among worlds and browser technologies is essential to improve user experiences, encouraging them to continue their exploration of the 3-D Web. As is the case with the current Netscape extensions (the site optimized for Netscape Navigator V1.1), many firms intend to market VRML viewers that are optimized for sites developed using their tools or to sell tools that build sites that look best when accessed with their viewer. These added features will be among the differentiating factors in initial product choice and will ultimately help guide future standard specifications.

Development of Content

Another market driver is the widespread development of worlds and home spaces with meaningful content. It won't do anyone a lot of good to pour hundreds of thousands of VRML viewers into the market if there is nowhere for users to go or nowhere that they *want* to go. Developers need to start building worlds now and to get familiar enough with VRML that they can imagine capabilities that go beyond the current technology, thus providing valuable feedback to the industry. However, developers also need to pay attention to such issues as polygon count, file size, network bandwidth and others so that end users don't have to wait forever to download a world or even more than half a second for a movement they have initiated to display on the screen.

The Installed Base

Finally, and perhaps most critical, is the current state of the Internet and the installed base of personal computers. As it stands today, VRML will work with a good deal of the existing PCs, which in the home market are largely 486 machines with 14.4 KBps modems and probably multimedia capabilities and will run over a 14.4 KBps Internet connection.

Critically the vast majority of PCs being sold today are more powerful and have higher-speed modems. This, combined with improvements in the Internet itself, mean that just about the time that VRML is ready for prime time (that is, a large number of worlds are built), the installed base of technology should have changed, making and using VRML quite satisfying for the end user.

The Future

Clearly VRML has great promise as a technology to help carry the Internet into the future. The ability to use three-dimensional virtual-reality types of interfaces in a networked environment holds the potential for developing new applications that allow multiple users to experience rich environments, in some cases simultaneously, connected over vast distances.

In order for this technology to become a reality, highly functional, standards-based tools need to be on the market, together with a large number of VRML-based sites developed that nonetheless recognize the reality of today's Internet and PC technology. Within the next year, it may become obvious whether the market is meeting its critical success factors and VRML really is destined to become the wave of the future.

From Here

Whether VRML is destined to become the wave of the future is really in the eye of the visionaries. The next chapter takes a look at some very large and complicated VRML projects that are currently under way for release in the near future.

Virtual Reality Modeling Language Visions

Real virtual reality (VR) on the Internet does not exist! This may come as a shock to those cyberjunkies who don't know what time it is—sometimes letting weeks go by—as they ride through those interactive games, checking out different points of view.[1]

The absence of and limited use of VR hardware while working those virtual scenarios is very high. Much of that use is just to move a head-mounted or hand-held tracker to verify that the program is receiving and handling the position information correctly; that does not immerse a "nettime junkie" into the real virtual environment.

Don't hold that thought, though! All hope is not lost for all those cyberpunks who enter the World Wide Web (WWW). Mark Pesce, coordinator for the Virtual Reality Markup Language (VRML), the Labyrinth research group (in Laguna Beach, CA), and others have been working on the development of a VR interface through Mosaic to the WWW for several months. During this period they have been inspired by what will be possible through VRML when their work is complete.

The hardware and software requirements to be able to use these applications via VRML are Apple Macintosh Power PC and UNIX

---

[1] Vacca, John. "The Outer Limits: Virtual Reality on the Internet," *Internet World* (March 1995), p. 42.

systems. A bandwidth of at least 10 MB (megabytes) per second for a LAN or the equivalent of 10,000 kilobytes, with a normal 9600 baud rate modem, is required. No special ISDN infrastructure or T1 lines are required. Physical access to VRML requires no special headset device or computer graphics.

VRML design is being approached from various points of view. Despite differing needs, goals are quite often congruent, and we must strive to develop a technology that meets the needs of the vast majority of its users without sacrificing elegance or intelligence. Mark Pesce has formulated several visions in the hope of meeting the needs for VRML now and into the future.

Vision One: The U. S. Holocaust Museum (USHM)

The USHM project (due for release in late 1996) is a joint development between Husky Labs (Washington, D.C.) and the Labyrinth Group to produce a WWW site that has both documentary and spatial exhibits.[2] The USHM is a unique museum; the architecture of the space plays an important role in the story being told. Parts of the museum look like villages in Eastern Europe, a concentration camp, an oven. Visitors to the museum are overwhelmed by the gestalt that is created. That a space is so evocative is one of the strengths of the museum; without it, the museum loses some of its impact on the imagination and the soul.

When completed, the museum will be accessible, as a space, from anywhere on the Internet, to any WWW client that is VRML-capable. It will be possible to tour the museum, just as is done in real space, with many links from the virtual space of the museum into Web pages that describe in greater detail the content of the museum's exhibits.

This project requires technology that has already been developed and demonstrated at WWW '94. The VRML language (the specification for which is given at the VRML Forum WWW site) is capable, with very few extensions, of handling the expression of the entire space, with extensive linkages to WWW pages to be viewed from Netscape, Mosaic, or another Web/MIME reviewer.

---

[2] "Web-Posium," *Internet World* (October 1994), p. 27.

Vision Two: The U. S. Library of Congress

Pesce's initial inspiration for the creation of Labyrinth and VRML was to develop a way to model the complexity and richness of the Web in such a manner that it is intrinsically navigable, without any instruction required on anyone's part.[3] He used, as an example, the U.S. Library of Congress GOPHER site (due for completion in early 1997). It is rich, it is deep, but it is difficult to navigate or browse, especially if one is unacquainted with the site or doesn't know precisely what one is looking for.

Pesce asserts that it is possible to model the Web in three dimensions so that it is intrinsically navigable, such that the form of an object within a particular space is derived from the content of that object. It is possible, then, to build a library, or data repository, that looks only coincidentally like a library in the real world. In fact, users are better served if this virtual library looks like its content. If Pesce succeeds in this, it should be possible for anyone, of any age, to browse the collected content of the world's greatest library or as much of it as is placed on line, without having to be taught hermetic classification systems, searching methodologies, and the like.

At the very least, it is possible to take the GOPHER site marvel.loc.gov and wrap a VRML interface around it. In so doing, the library is made accessible to people who would otherwise be intimidated by a GOPHER interface, and the space can be organized so as to facilitate browsing and examination of the resources at the site. This, again, requires very little technology that VRML does not already have.

Vision Three: Earth

One of the most inspirational parts of the Web are the pages at the Michigan State University where the current weather maps/movies are kept and maintained, as shown in Figure 3.1. This is a collaborational effort of many people at many university sites across the

---

[3] Vacca, John. *Op. cit.*, p. 46.

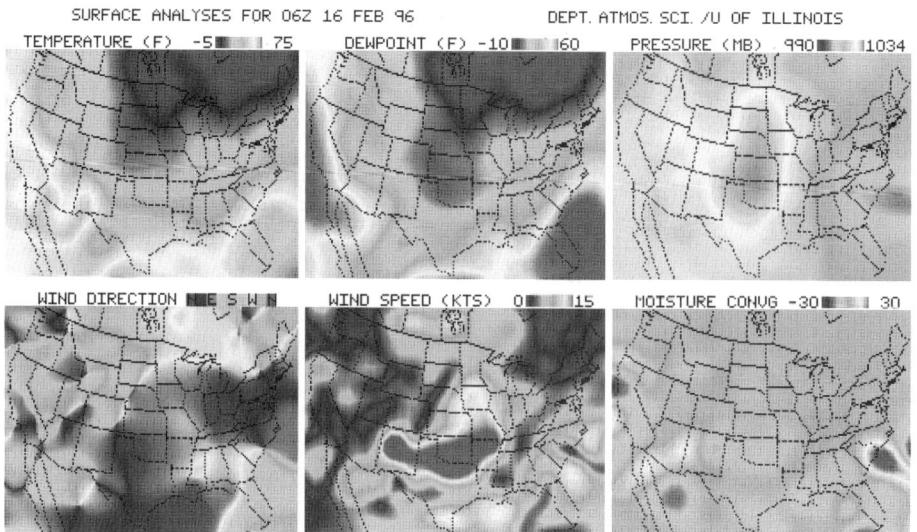

Figure 3.1 Michigan State University Current Weather Maps/Movies

country, and is a truly brilliant example of what is already possible with the Web.

Extending this into the virtual world, Pesce would like to be able to create a real, live earth on his desktop (not unlike the version described by Neal Stephenson in *Snow Crash*—a book full of good ideas), which would take the satellite data, massage it just slightly, and wrap it onto a sphere that represented the planet.[4] This is certainly possible right now and would be an extremely effective demonstration of the combined capabilities of VR and the World Wide Web.

Further, one can imagine that this earth simulation (due for completion in late 1997) can become one of the interfaces for NASA's EOS project, the Mission to Planet Earth, which has already begun and will result in exabytes (10^{15} bytes) of cartographic and other ecological mappings of the planet. VRML is used to create a rich, dense, yet easy-to-use interface to what will be the single largest data collection task ever undertaken by humanity.

---

[4] *Ibid.*

VR/cyberspace represents an effective, necessary technology for planetary management. In an age when we must always be conscious of our effect on the surrounding environment, we need powerful tools to visualize it and to track our effect on it.

Technically this project is only a little more advanced than those that have been described already. It would be useful for VRML to incorporate the concept of a data stream (something in the works for the WWW libraries) so that real-time data flows could be incorporated into the planetary simulation.

Vision Four: The World Wide Marketplace

Many commercial organizations are excited by the possibility of being able to offer goods and services through Internet-based channels. In fact, it should be possible to create a space with a very wide array of goods, both physical and more ephemeral, without advertising (or with it, if desired), so that the marketplace can exist for trade. Moreover, this market need not be (should not be) monolithic—no single Macy's or HSC or what have you—but more like a bazaar, with a dense, organic ecology of businesses that work together (and are colocated) in order to support one another.[5]

It might look like a suburban shopping mall, although that will not have a great appeal for everyone. It might look more like Marrekesh than Minneapolis. It does need to be flexible, though, so that there is a wide availability of goods/services and so that organizations can come and go quickly as a market need arises, is satisfied, and disappears. Although cooperation is necessary, any monolithic entity that attempts to own the entire retail space would end only in stifling the diversity of the market. It has to be possible to create a concatenated space that can draw from sources (Web sites) all across the Internet and yet can create a continuous, regular perception of space. Finally, it all has to be integrated seamlessly with other Web-based markets.

This project (due for completion in early 1998) is somewhat more complicated than the others outlined. It requires an overall protocol architecture to support a distributed description of a virtual space.

---

[5] *Ibid.*

Vision Five: The Agora and the Senate

This project (due for completion in late 1998) will be one of the great benefits of communications technology in that it can create and nurture communities that exist outside of demographic bounds.[6] However, demographic communities need to be brought together as well, for the purposes of self-governance. VRML is instrumental in the implementation of these systems of self-governance.

Democracy is founded on the conceptualization of informed consent. This means that you, as a citizen, have a right and a responsibility to exercise your franchise based on the best possible information. Although the history of politics is the history of disputes about which information is true, right, or moral, underlying all of it is an understanding that information, in whatever form, from whomever it comes, is necessary for informed consent and that informed consent is necessary for democracy.

In the United States, our founding fathers did not give us a direct democracy at the national level, because no communications infrastructure of the eighteenth century could support such a proposition. However, in New England and in several of the other colonies, towns governed themselves directly, and rather anarchically, through a system of town meetings, in which all the citizenry could play a role. This itself was modeled after systems that had evolved in England and before that in Athens and Rome, whereby all of the citizens of the state were free to participate in the debate on the issues of the day. To them, government was a place as much as a process; the area around the Senate in Rome contained the library, a public area for discussion and debate, the baths (where more discussion, debate, and dealmaking went on), and an amphitheater for speeches.

If we attempt to augment our own mechanisms of self-governance, we will need to look at this model and adapt its most functional aspects to our own methodologies and create a Senate of our own. This is done with what is available now and with what is being developed, although VRML will have to move toward complete interactivity before it is possible to stage a "street debate" complete with an attentive (or heckling) audience. Already it is possible to peruse the budget of the United States, and the town of San Carlos, California just announced its own WWW site. VRML is used to put an attractive interface on these

---

[6] *Ibid*, p. 47.

gold mines of useful data; that alone is worth doing. But further, the Web and VRML are used to create a place where democracy can happen. That is a noble goal, one worth working toward.

Pesce has shared his visions with you; these projects are possible immediately in the future, not in some distant, barely imagined cyberpunk evocation. Together we can sculpt the tools that will define these worlds, define their behaviors, and allow us all to share in one another's creations.

From Here

In order to develop Pesce's vision, tools must exist to develop 3-D graphics. The next chapter briefly examines OpenGL: the high performance tool for the 3-D graphics applications.

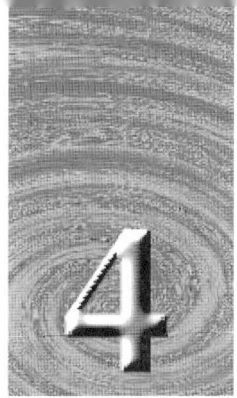

OpenGL: The Open Graphics Standard

The concept of bringing 3-D environments to the Web is not new. However, before these enviroments can be brought over by VRML they have to be developed. This is where OpenGL comes into play.

OpenGL™, the high-performance tool from Silicon Graphics Computer Systems, is the premier environment for developing 2-D and 3-D graphics applications. The OpenGL application programming interface (API) is a vendor-neutral, multiplatform industry standard. Licensees of OpenGL support the API on a range of computers: from PCs to workstations to all types of computers. Porting OpenGL applications among conforming OpenGL implementations is simple and easy.

Leading PC, workstation, and supercomputer vendors, including 3-Dlabs, AccelGraphics, AT&T, Cirrus Logic, Cray Research, Daikin, Digital Equipment, Evans & Sutherland, Harris Computer, Hitachi, IBM, Intel, Intergraph, Japan Radio Company, MediaVision, Microsoft, NEC, NeTpowerm, Samsung, Sony, and Silicon Graphics, are committed to OpenGL as a strategic open standard for high-performance 2-D and 3-D graphics. Third-party solutions for Apple, Hewlett-Packard, and Sun® products are available from several companies, including Portable Graphics and Template Graphics Software.

OpenGL is the direct descendant of IRIS Graphics Library™ (IRIS GL™), invented in 1982. More than 1500 3-D applications are currently written with IRIS GL. OpenGL inherits that legacy of experience in applications development. It preserves all critical rendering functionality from IRIS GL. The OpenGL applications are, and will be, ported from IRIS GL, and new applications will be written directly with OpenGL.

Features/Application Portability

OpenGL provides a wide range of graphics abilities, from rendering a simple geometric point, line, or filled polygon to the most sophisticated lighted and texture-mapped NURBS curved surface, as shown in Figure 4.1. The 250 routines of OpenGL give software developers access to the following capabilities:

- geometric and raster primitives,
- RGBA or color index mode,
- display list or immediate mode,
- viewing and modeling transformations,
- lighting and shading,
- hidden surface removal (depth buffer),
- alpha blending (translucency),
- anti-aliasing,
- texture mapping,
- atmospheric effects (fog, smoke, haze),
- feedback and selection,
- stencil planes, and
- accumulation buffer.[1]

These functions are provided on every conforming OpenGL implementation to make applications (written with OpenGL) easily portable among platforms. All licensed OpenGL implementations are required to pass conformance tests and come from a single specification and language-binding document.

---

[1] Silicon Graphics Computer Systems, Corporate Office, 2011 N. Shoreline Boulevard, Mountain View, CA 94043.

Figure 4.1 Texture Maps and Shadows

Architecture

The OpenGL state machine is a good model for representing graphics problems. Figure 4.2[2] provides a high-level block diagram of how OpenGL processes data. Commands enter from the left and proceed through what can be thought of as a processing pipeline. Some commands specify geometric objects to be drawn, and others control how the objects are handled. All elements of the OpenGL state—even the contents of the texture memory and the frame buffer—can be obtained by an OpenGL application.

If you want to draw a 3-D model consisting of lighted, smooth shaded polygons, for example, turn on the lighting state and set your values for the material properties. Turn on the smooth shading. Set your viewing transformation. For each polygon, declare a current surface normal to define its orientation. Now that you've established the current state, issue the vertices that comprise each polygon. The

---

[2] *Ibid.*

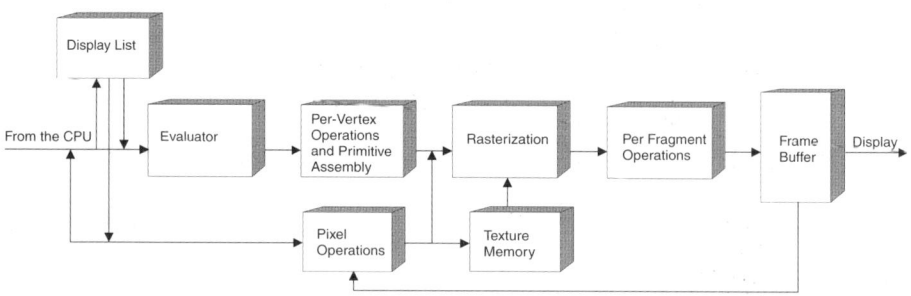

Figure 4.2 OpenGL Diagram

OpenGL state machine will process and render those polygons into the frame buffer.

In subsequent renderings you can further enhance your model. Turn on the depth buffer and remove hidden surfaces, or even add fog or apply a texture map to your model.

Integration

The model for interpreting OpenGL commands is the client-server process, as shown in Figure 4.3.[3] A client application issues commands, which are interpreted and processed by an OpenGL server. The server and client may operate on different machines; thus OpenGL is network transparent. If it is not going over a network, the client-server communication can be replaced by local rendering, which may be faster.

OpenGL is hardware, window, and operating system independent, as shown in Figure 4.4.[4] On one implementation OpenGL may run

---

[3] *Ibid.*
[4] *I bid.*

Chapter 4 OpenGL: The Open Graphics Standard

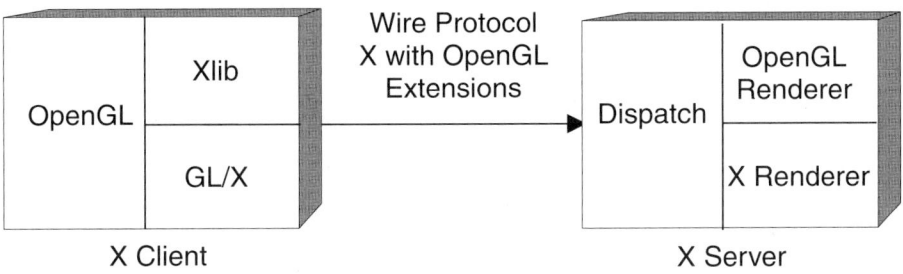

Figure 4.3 Integration

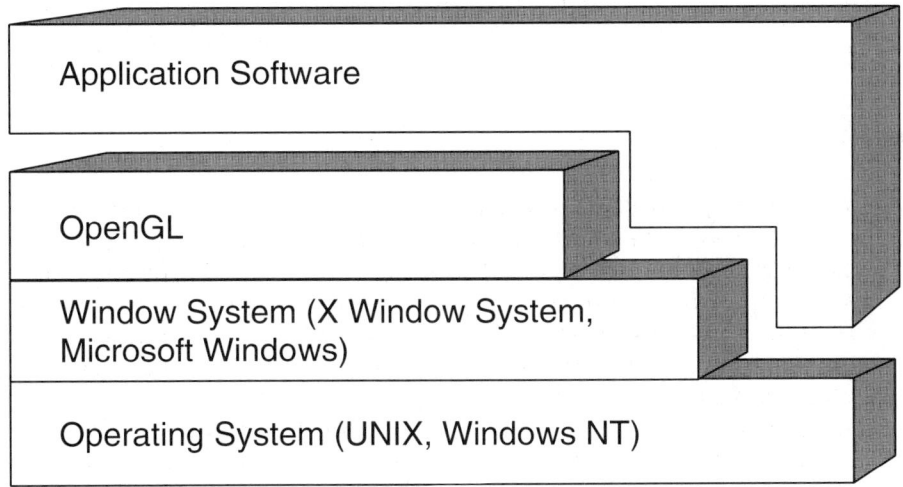

Figure 4.4 Extensibility of OpenGL

with the X Window System™ and UNIX®. On another implementation OpenGL may run with Microsoft Windows™, MS DOS®, Microsoft Windows NT™, and IBM® OS/2™. OpenGL is or will soon be compatible with other APIs, such as Xlib, OSF/Motif™, IRIS Open Inventor™, Image Vision™, and IRIS Performer™. OpenGL is callable from C, C++, FORTRAN, and Ada.

Governance

OpenGL is defined and released by the seven-member OpenGL Architecture Review Board (ARB): Digital Equipment, Evans & Sutherland, IBM, Intel, Intergraph, Microsoft, and Silicon Graphics. Every member of the ARB has a single vote to determine the future of OpenGL. The OpenGL ARB oversees the administration of the OpenGL Specification and Conformance Test Suite.

OpenGL News

Information about OpenGL is readily available online. You can get source code examples, documentation, and news about product availability. Just follow the Internet news group comp.graphics.opengl, or browse the OpenGL home page on the World Wide Web (http://www.sgi.com/tech /openGL/opengl.html).

OpenGL Licensing Program

OpenGL can be licensed at three levels. Only system vendors, peripherals suppliers, or software companies providing an OpenGL development or run-time environment are required to license OpenGL. End users or software developers writing code based on the OpenGL API use OpenGL free of licensing requirements. The ARB-approved OpenGL specification and source code are available.

From Here

Chapter 5 continues this theme of OpenGL with a brief but detailed overview of Open Inventor: the object-oriented 3-D graphics programming tool, a virtual must in the VRML environment. A further discussion of Open Inventor can be found in Chapter 12.

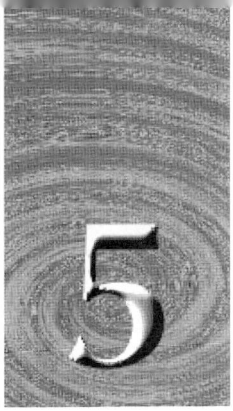

Open Inventor Object-Oriented 3-D Toolkit and VRML

Open Inventor has taken many programmer years to design and implement and is a fairly large, very general system. VRML must be much smaller to become a success; otherwise, implementations will either be incompatible or will take too long to produce. Therefore only the most commonly used subset of Open Inventor is proposed here as the basis for VRML.

The Open Inventor group at Silicon Graphics has committed to separating the ASCII file-reading code from the rest of the Open Inventor library, repackaging it, and putting it in the public domain as the start of a VRML toolkit to make implementing VRML easier. The file reader will be C++ code that produces a hierarchical structure of C++ classes. A VRML implementor would need to define appropriate render methods for these classes to implement rendering—a pick method to implement picking, etc.—or, alternatively, traverse these classes and create a completely different internal representation for the scene.

Object-Oriented File Format

At the highest level of abstraction, the Open Inventor file format is just a way for objects to read and write themselves. Theoretically the objects can contain anything—3-D geometry, MIDI data, JPEG images, anything. Open Inventor defines a set of objects useful for doing 3-D graphics. These objects are called *nodes*.

Scene Graphs

Nodes are arranged in hierarchical structures called *scene graphs*, as shown in Figure 5.1. Scene graphs are more than just a collection of nodes; a scene graph defines an ordering for the nodes. The Open Inventor scene graph has a notion of state: Nodes earlier in the scene can affect nodes that appear later in the scene. For example, a Rotation or Material node will affect the nodes after it in the scene. A mechanism is defined to limit the effects of properties (Separator nodes), allowing parts of a scene graph to be functionally isolated from other parts.

This notion of order in the scene graph may be the most controversial feature of Open Inventor. Most other systems attempt to attach properties to objects, with the properties affecting only that one object. In fact, an early prototype of Open Inventor was written that way. However, treating properties differently from geometry resulted in several problems. First, if a shape has several properties associated with it, you must still define an order in which the properties are applied. Second, some objects, such as lights and cameras, act as both

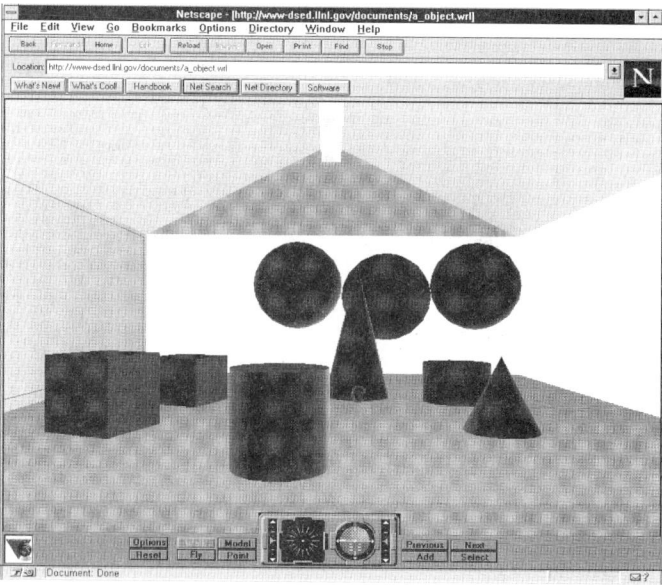

Figure 5.1 Scene Graphs

shapes (things that have a position in the world) and properties (things that affect the way other things look). Getting rid of the distinction between shapes and properties simplified both the implementation and the use of the library.

Node Contents

A node can be characterized by what kind of object it is. A node might be a cube, a sphere, a texture map, a transformation, etc. Further, parameters distinguish this node from other nodes of the same type. For example, each Sphere node might have a different radius, and different texture maps nodes will certainly contain different images to use as the texture maps, as shown in Figure 5.2. These parameters are called fields. A node can have zero or more *fields*.

Being able to name nodes and to refer to them elsewhere is very powerful. It allows a scene's author to give hints to applications using the scene about what is in the scene and creates possibilities for very powerful scripting extensions. Nodes do not have to be named, but if they are named, they have only one name.

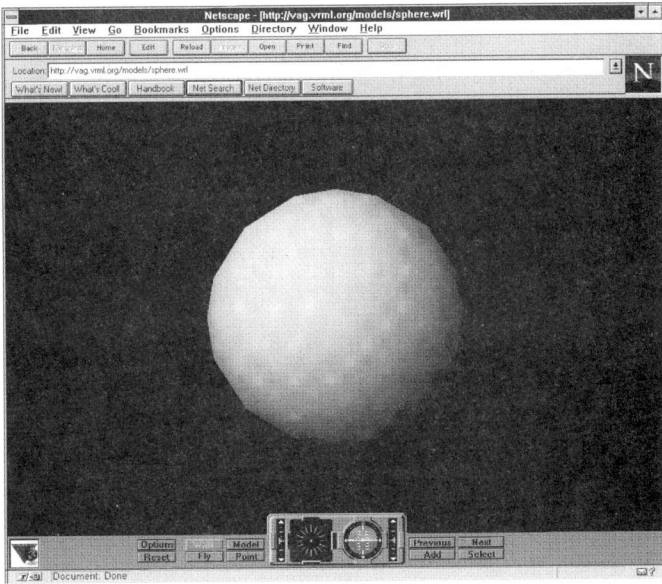

Figure 5.2 Sphere Node

Object hierarchy is implemented by allowing nodes to contain other nodes. Parent nodes traverse their children in order during rendering. Nodes that may have children are referred to as *group nodes*. Group nodes can have zero or more children.

The syntax chosen to represent these pieces of information is straightforward:

```
DEF objectname objecttype { fields children }
```

Only the objecttype and braces are required. Nodes may or may not have a name, fields, and children. The following sections describe the types of objects that should be the basis of VRML and describe details of this basic syntax.

IndexedFaceSet

Open Inventor has eight ways of specifying a polygonal shape or surface (FaceSet, IndexedFaceSet, QuadMesh, TriangleStripSet, IndexedTriangleStripSet, NurbsSurface, IndexedNurbsSurface, and Text3). To ease the implementation burden, it is proposed that only IndexedFaceSet be part of VRML, as shown in Figure 5.3. IndexedFaceSets can be used to represent any of the other polygonal shape types, are fairly space-efficient, and are the most common type of geometry. IndexedFaceSet supports overall, per face, and per vertex materials and normals. IndexedFaceSet will automatically generate normals if the user doesn't specify them. Faces with fewer than three vertices will be ignored. Here is a simple example of two Open Inventor V2.0 ASCII IndexedFaceSets, showing some of its more advanced features (per vertex coloring, for example), as shown in Figures 5.4 and 5.5.

Each of the faces of an IndexedFaceSet is assumed to be convex by default. A ShapeHints node (see following) can be used to change this assumption to allow concave faces. However, all faces must be simple (they must not self-intersect).

If not enough normals are specified to satisfy the current normal binding, normals will be automatically generated, based on the IndexedFaceSet's geometry. If explicit texture coordinates are not specified using a TextureCoordinate2 node, default texture coordinates will be automatically generated. A simple planar projection along one of the primary axes is used, mapping the width of the texture image onto the longest dimension of the IndexedFaceSet's bounding box, with the

Chapter 5 Open Inventor Object-Oriented 3-D Toolkit and VRML

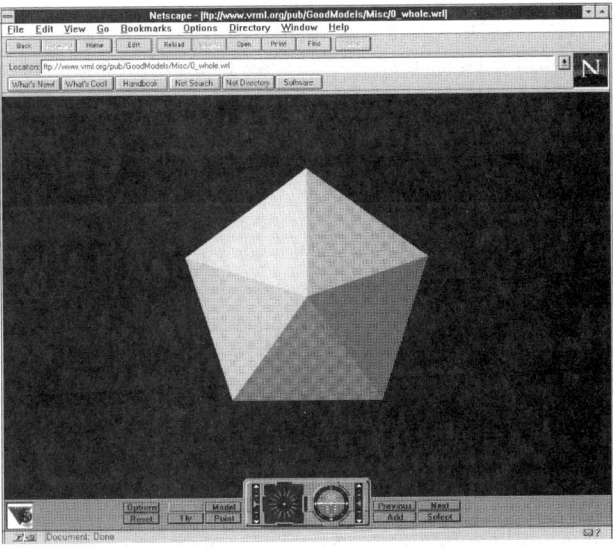

Figure 5.3 IndexedFaceSets

```
#Inventor V2.0 ascii
# Two IndexedFaceSets each describing a cube.
# Normals are per polygon. The first has OVERALL material binding, and
# appears all one color.
# The second has colors indexed per vertex. This allows the colors
# to be defined in any order and then randomly accessed for each vertex.

Separator {
  Coordinate3 {
     point [ -1  1  1,   -1 -1  1,   1 -1  1,   1  1  1,
             -1  1 -1,   -1 -1 -1,   1 -1 -1,   1  1 -1 ]
  }
  Material { diffuseColor [ 1 0 0,  0 1 0,  0 0 1,  1 1 0 ] }# indices 0,1,2,3
  Normal {
    vector [ 0.0  0.0  1.0,   1.0  0.0  0.0,   # front and right faces
             0.0  0.0 -1.0,  -1.0  0.0  0.0,   # back and left faces
             0.0  1.0  0.0,   0.0 -1.0  0.0 ]  # top and bottom faces
  }
  NormalBinding { value PER_FACE_INDEXED }
  MaterialBinding { value OVERALL }
  IndexedFaceSet {
    coordIndex [ 0,  1,  2,  3, -1,    3,  2,  6,  7, -1,  # front and right faces
                 7,  6,  5,  4, -1,    4,  5,  1,  0, -1,  # back and left faces
                 0,  3,  7,  4, -1,    1,  5,  6,  2, -1 ] # top and bottom faces
    normalIndex [ 0,  1,  2,  3,  4,  5, ]     # Apply normals to faces, in order
  }
}
```

Figure 5.4 IndexedFaceSet describing a cube; normals are per polygon. This one has OVERALL material binding and appears all one color.

```
Translation { translation 3 0 0 }
MaterialBinding { value PER_VERTEX_INDEXED }
IndexedFaceSet {
  coordIndex [ 0, 1, 2, 3, -1, 3, 2, 6, 7, -1,   # front and right faces
               7, 6, 5, 4, -1, 4, 5, 1, 0, -1,   # back and left faces
               0, 3, 7, 4, -1, 1, 5, 6, 2, -1 ] # top and bottom faces
  materialIndex [ 0, 0, 1, 1, -1,        # red/green front
                  2, 2, 3, 3, -1,        # blue/yellow right
                  0, 0, 1, 1, -1,        # red/green back
                  2, 2, 3, 3, -1,        # blue/yellow left
                  0, 0, 0, 0, -1,        # red top
                  2, 2, 2, 2, -1 ]       # blue bottom
  }
}
```

Figure 5.5 Here colors are indexed per vertex. This allows the colors to be defined in any order and then randomly accessed for each vertex.

height of the texture image going in the direction of the next-longest dimension of its bounding box.

ShapeHints

The ShapeHints node gives extra information about the shapes in the scene that a renderer can use to optimize rendering, as shown in Figure 5.6. It has a faceType field that can be either CONVEX (meaning that all of the polygons in all shapes to follow are convex) or UNKNOWN_FACE_TYPE (meaning that the polygons may be either concave or convex). Its vertexOrdering field lets a renderer know whether faces are defined CLOCKWISE, COUNTERCLOCKWISE, or have an UNKNOWN_ORDERING. Its shapeType field defines whether the shape is SOLID (the faces completely enclose a volume of space) or an UNKNOWN_SHAPE_TYPE. Open Inventor uses these hints to turn off or on backface removal, two-sided lighting, and the tesselation of concave polygons.

ShapeHints also has a creaseAngle field used during normal generation. It is a hint to the normal generator about where sharp creases between polygons should be created. If two faces sharing an edge have a dihedral angle less than the creaseAngle, the normals will be smoothed across the edge; otherwise, the edge will appear as a sharp crease.

```
VERTEX ORDERING ENUMS
        UNKNOWN_ORDERING         Ordering of vertices is unknown
        CLOCKWISE                Face vertices are ordered clockwise
                                    (from the outside)
        COUNTERCLOCKWISE         Face vertices are ordered counterclockwise
                                    (from the outside)
SHAPE TYPE ENUMS
        UNKNOWN_SHAPE_TYPE       Nothing is known about the shape
        SOLID                    The shape encloses a volume

FACE TYPE ENUMS
        UNKNOWN_FACE_TYPE        Nothing is known about faces
        CONVEX                   All faces are convex

FILE FORMAT/DEFAULTS
    ShapeHints {
        vertexOrdering           UNKNOWN_ORDERING
        shapeType                UNKNOWN_SHAPE_TYPE
        faceType                 CONVEX
        creaseAngle              0.5
    }
```

Figure 5.6 ShapeHints

Coordinates and Normals

Coordinate3 and Normal nodes are considered properties, like materials or textures, as shown in Figure 5.7. Specifying coordinates and normals separately from the shape makes it much easier to extend the format to support other representations for coordinates and normals.

If a binary format for VRML is developed, it will be worthwhile to specify low-bandwidth alternatives to the standard Open Inventor Coordinate3 and Normal nodes, which store each coordinate or normal as three floating-point numbers. Lighting is usually good enough even with byte-sized normals. A ByteNormal with normal XYZ vectors with components from (127 to 127 would save a significant amount of network bandwidth. Similarly, a ShortCoordinate3 that specified vertices in the range of (32767 to 32767 (the model would need an appropriate scale to make it reasonably sized, of course) could also save significant network bandwidth. Note that in the ASCII file format, new nodes aren't necessary; you can just limit the precision of the ASCII numbers in your scene to a few digits of accuracy. For example, instead of specifying a normal as [.7071067811865 .7071067811865 0], specify it as [.707 .707 0] to save bandwidth.

```
Coordinate3 {
    point [ -1  1  1,   -1 -1  1,   1 -1  1,   1  1  1,
            -1  1 -1,   -1 -1 -1,   1 -1 -1,   1  1 -1 ]
}
Material { diffuseColor [ 1 0 0,   0 1 0,   0 0 1,   1 1 0 ] }# indices 0,1,2,3
Normal {
  vector [ 0.0  0.0  1.0,    1.0  0.0  0.0,   # front and right faces
           0.0  0.0 -1.0,   -1.0  0.0  0.0,   # back and left faces
           0.0  1.0  0.0,    0.0 -1.0  0.0 ]  # top and bottom faces
}
NormalBinding { value PER_FACE_INDEX }
MaterialBinding { value OVERALL }
IndexedFaceSet {
    coordIndex [ 0,  1,  2,  3, -1,   3,  2,  6,  7, -1,  # front and right faces
                 7,  6,  5,  4, -1,   4,  5,  1,  0, -1,  # back and left faces
                 0,  3,  7,  4, -1,   1,  5,  6,  2, -1 ] # top and bottom faces
    normalIndex [ 0,  1,  2,  3,  4,  5, ]     # Apply normals to faces, in order
}
```

Figure 5.7 Coordinated and Normal ModesIndexedFaceSets

Bindings

Binding nodes (MaterialBinding and NormalBinding) specify how to apply properties to primitives. Open Inventor has eight ways of binding materials or normals to primitives. The _INDEXED bindings use the index fields in IndexedFaceSet (coordIndex, normalIndex) to index into the list of current materials or normals, as shown in the sidebar.

Specifying how materials or normals are applied to shapes allows the same set of materials (or, much less common, normals) to be used for several different shapes. For example, a program may use only a limited palette of materials that it applies to either the vertices or the faces of IndexedFaceSets. The same Material {} node may be used by all of the IndexedFaceSets, with MaterialBinding nodes switching between PER_VERTEX_INDEXED and PER_FACE_INDEXED materials.

Open Inventor has a TextureCoordinateBinding node with DEFAULT, PER_VERTEX, and PER_VERTEX_INDEXED values. Because binding texture coordinates PER_VERTEX is very rare (PER_VERTEX_INDEXED is infinitely more common), the node should not be part of VRML.

Bindings

- DEFAULT — Each shape chooses a reasonable binding. The primitive shapes and IndexedFaceSet all choose OVERALL as their default material binding; the DEFAULT normal binding for IndexedFaceSet is PER_VERTEX_INDEXED (the primitive shapes generate their own normals and ignore the normal binding).
- OVERALL — One material or normal used for the entire object.
- PER_PART, PER_PART_INDEXED — One material or normal for each part of the shape. For IndexedFaceSet, these are the same as PER_FACE and PER_FACE_INDEXED. Primitive shapes treat PER_PART_INDEXED the same as PER_PART.
- PER_FACE, PER_FACE_INDEXED — One material or normal for each face of the shape. Since primitive shapes do not have faces, they interpret these bindings the same as OVERALL.
- PER_VERTEX, PER_VERTEX_INDEXED — One material or normal for each vertex of the shape. Since primitive shapes do not have explicit vertices, they interpret these bindings the same as OVERALL.[1]

IndexedLineSet

IndexedLineSet is just like IndexedFaceSet, only open line segments are drawn instead of polygons. For example, Figure 5.8 shows this as two line segments: The first is a closed triangle (note that the first index is repeated to close the loop), and the second is a zig-zag of four connected line segments.

Unlike IndexedFaceSet, an IndexedLineSet will be drawn with lighting turned off if normals are not specified. Lines with fewer than two vertices are ignored.

---

[1] Gavin Bell, *Inventor and VRML*, Silicon Graphics, 1996.

```
FILE FORMAT/DEFAULTS
   IndexedLineSet {
       coordIndex              0
       materialIndex          -1
       normalIndex            -1
       textureCoordIndex      -1
   }
```

Figure 5.8 IndexedLineSet

PointSet

Points are drawn using the PointSet primitive, as shown in Figure 5.9. Its startIndex and numPoints fields are used to specify which points from the current coordinate node should be drawn. By default, startIndex is zero and numPoints is (1, meaning draw all of them. PointSet uses the current coordinates in order, starting at the index specified by the startIndex field. The number of points in the set is specified by the numPoints field. A value of (1 for this field indicates that all remaining values in the current coordinates are to be used as points.

Like IndexedLineSet, if normals are not specified, the points will be drawn unlighted. *Note:* An IndexedPointSet primitive isn't terribly useful, because coordinates used for a PointSet aren't typically shared (unlike polygons and lines, where several polygons or line segments may meet at a vertex).

Primitive Shapes

The Open Inventor Cube, Sphere, Cylinder, and Nit: yes cubes aren't really cubes if they have different widths, heights, and depths, as shown in Figure 5.10. But a nonuniform scale can also make a sphere not a sphere.

```
FILE FORMAT/DEFAULTS
   PointSet {
       startIndex      0
       numPoints      -1
   }
```

Figure 5.9 PointSet

Chapter 5 Open Inventor Object-Oriented 3-D Toolkit and VRML

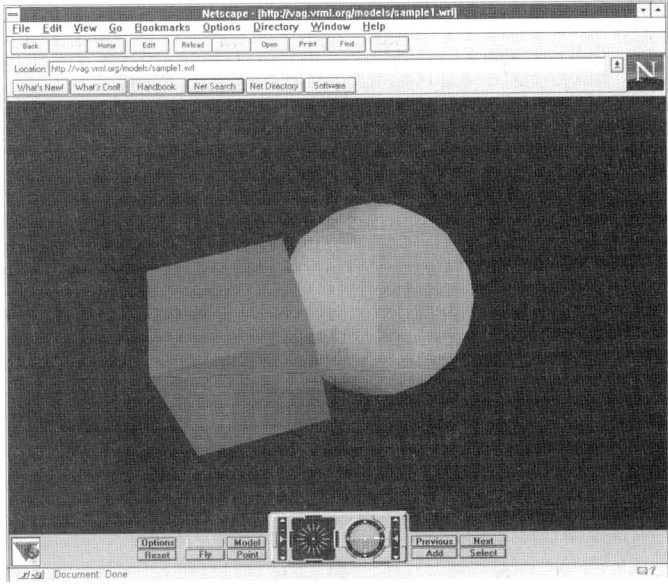

Figure 5.10 Primitive Shapes

Open Inventor has a Complexity node with a 0.0 to 1.0 value that can be used to control the quality of these shapes. The complexity control should be left to the browser, which could control the complexity to get good interactive performance.

Groups

Group nodes (Separator, Group, TransformSeparator, Switch, and LevelOfDetail) are used to create the scene hierarchy, as shown in Figure 5.11. Separator is most commonly used; it separates the effects of its children (material changes, translates/rotates/scales, etc.) from the rest of the scene.

```
FILE FORMAT/DEFAULTS
     Group {
     }
```

Figure 5.11 Groups

Open Inventor's Separator node has several fields to control its caching (whether it should build a display list when rendering) and culling (whether it should draw its children, based on whether or not it is in the view volume) behavior. It is proposed that VRML require only the renderCulling field, since the caching fields is specific to APIs like GL, which have a notion of display lists (and the default, Open Inventor's AUTO caching, works very well).

Another group that is very useful is TransformSeparator, which separates the effects of transformations inside it from the rest of the scene but allows other properties to leak out. This node wasn't implemented to improve performance over Separator. On a well-implemented system, Separator should do a lazy push/pop of attributes—saving/restoring only attributes that matter. Nevertheless, the node was implemented to allow transformations to transform lights and cameras without affecting the objects that the camera is viewing or the lights are illuminating.

The Switch node traverses none, one, or all of its children, based on its whichChild field. It is most useful in programs (for example, a scene may contain two representations of a world, with a named Switch used to switch between them), but it can be very useful for commenting out part of the scene.

LevelOfDetail

LevelOfDetail is a special group that traverses one of its children, based on approximately how much screen area its children occupy. It approximates the screen area by taking the 3-D bounding box of its children, projecting it onto the 2-D screen, and then taking the area of the 2-D bounding box that contains that projected 3-D bounding box. The different levels of detail are stored as the LevelOfDetail node's children. The first child should be the most detailed version of the object, with subsequent children being less detailed versions of the object. For example, here is a very simple LevelOfDetail node that display a sphere as the most detailed object. When its bounding box is larger than 10,000 pixels (about 100 by 100), a cube as the middle level of detail (when the object is between 10,000 and 100 pixels big) displays nothing (an Info node) when it is smaller than 100 pixels:

```
LevelOfDetail {
    screenArea [ 10000, 100 ]
    Sphere { } # Highest level of detail
    Cube   { } # Next level of detail
    Info   { } # Lowest level of detail
}[2]
```

Will implementing this be too difficult? It wouldn't be too bad if it were a much simpler node that just chose a child based on how far away it is from the eye (called DistanceSwitch, perhaps). Distance-Switch could switch, based on the distance of the center of its children's bounding box from the eye (but then that forces implementors to be able to figure out bounding boxes for objects); or it could just switch, based on the distance of point (0,0,0) in object space from the eye (this assumes that objects are modeled around (0,0,0) and translated into position).

Thus the Open Inventor LevelOfDetail node (Open Inventor's primitive shapes—*Cube/Sphere/Cone/Cylinder) pay attention to the current complexity value, stored in the Complexity node (a lower complexity value causes LevelOfDetail to choose simpler levels of detail). Therefore it is okay for VRML to leave complexity as a global value controlled by the browser.

Materials

Open Inventor's Material node supports a simple model for how light reflects off the surface of an object. Materials are intended to be easily implementable, not to capture a truly accurate physical description of the surface. The parameters are ambient, diffuse, specular and emissive colors, a shininess parameter (specular exponent for the geeks reading this), and how transparent or opaque the material is. The ambient, diffuse, specular, and emissive colors are specified as RGB triples in the range 0.0 to 1.0.

Open Inventor has two other material nodes: BaseColor is equivalent to a Material except that it sets only the diffuseColor for subsequent shapes. PackedColor is a compact form of BaseColor, with diffuse colors and transparency specified as 32-bit unsigned long values. The red, green, blue, and alpha components are specified with eight bits of precision. Thus BaseColor doesn't add enough function-

---

[2] *Ibid.*

ality to justify its inclusion in VRML. However, PackedColor does use significantly less bandwidth than Material and should be included.

Textures

The Texture2 node specifies a 2-D array of colors (possibly with transparency) to be mapped onto 3-D objects, as shown in Figure 5.12. It allows the image either to be specified in an external file or to be stored in an SFImage field directly in the Open Inventor file. It also specifies how the colors should interact with the material of the object (whether they should combine with or replace the object's material) and whether the texture should repeat (see Texture Coordinates, following).

Open Inventor's Texture2 node has a model field that controls how the texture image and the object's lighted color are combined. BLEND is used with greyscale and greyscale+alpha images. It uses the intensity of the texture image to control how much of the object's color is used and how much of a constant blending color. Specified in the Texture2 Issue: for VRML, the filename field should take a URL. The same image formats as HTML should be supported. The SFImage field is an uncompressed, eight bits per component format; should it be eliminated from VRML as too much of a bandwidth hog?

```
WRAP ENUM
    REPEAT      Repeats texture outside 0-1 texture coordinate range
    CLAMP       Clamps texture coordinates to lie within 0-1 range
}

FILE FORMAT/DEFAULTS
    Texture2 {
        filename    ""
        image       0 0 0
        wrapS       REPEAT
        wrapT       REPEAT
    }
```

Figure 5.12 Texture2 Node

Texture Coordinates

Open Inventor's primitive shapes define how the texture image is mapped onto their geometry. A TextureCoordinate2 node is used to specify how the texture is mapped onto the IndexedFaceSet primitive. The texture image is mapped into the (0,0) to (1,1) space of texture coordinates. TextureCoordinate2 allows each vertex of the IndexedFaceSet to be given a different texture coordinate, allowing arbitrary mappings. Texture coordinates outside the range (0,0) to (1,1) will either cause the texture image to repeat itself or will be clamped, causing the border pixel in the texture image to be reused, depending on the fields of the Texture2 node.

The Texture2Transform node can be used to modify a shape's texture coordinates. A Texture2Transform is a 2-D version of the Transform node that transforms texture coordinates instead of vertex coordinates. It has fields that specify a 2-D translation, 2-D rotation, 2-D scale, and a 2-D center about which the transformations will be applied. Texture coordinates are either specified explicitly in a TextureCoordinate2 node or are implicitly generated by shapes. The cumulative texture transformation is applied to the texture coordinates, and the transformed texture coordinates are used to find the appropriate texel in the texture image. Note that like regular transformations, Texture2Transform nodes have a cumulative effect.

Texture2Transforms allow the default mapping of textures onto primitive shapes to be changed, as shown in Figure 5.13. For example, you might build a house out of Cube primitives (if you didn't really care about performance!) and change the Texture2Transform so that a wallpaper texture was repeated across the walls instead of the default mapping of the texture being repeated once across the faces of the cube.

Transformations

Open Inventor defines 12 transformation nodes. The following should be part of VRML. Translation has a single field that specifies an XYZ translation for subsequent objects. Note that all transformations are relative.

```
FILE FORMAT/DEFAULTS
    Texture2Transform {
        translation    0 0
        rotation       0
        scaleFactor    1 1
        center         0 0
    }
```

Figure 5.13 Texture2 Transforms

For example:

```
Translation {  translation   1  0  0     }
Translation {  translation   3  5  2  1  }

Cube {      }
```

will result in the cube's having a total translation of (4.5,2,1).[3]

Scale has a single field that specifies a relative scale. The scale will be nonuniform in the X, Y, or Z directions if all of the components of scaleFactor are not the same.

Rotation has a single field that specifies an axis to rotate about and an angle (in radians) specifying how much right-hand rotation about that axis to apply. It would have been more convenient if the angle were specified in degrees instead of radians.

MatrixTransform has a single field containing an arbitrary 4-by-4 rotation matrix. It is to be combined with previous transformations and applied to subsequent objects.

The Transform node combines several common transformation tasks into one convenient node. It has fields specifying a translation, rotation, and scaleFactor, along with scaleOrientation and center fields for specifying what coordinate axes the scale should be applied along and about which point the scale and rotation should occur.

Cameras

Open Inventor defines two types of cameras PerspectiveCamera and OrthographicCamera. PerspectiveCamera has position and orientation fields that specify the camera's location and orientation relative to world space (the space objects are in after all transformations have been applied), as shown in Figure 5.14. PerspectiveCamera also has a heightAngle that specifies how wide or narrow the field of view

---

[3] *Ibid.*

```
FILE FORMAT/DEFAULTS
    PerspectiveCamera {
        position            0 0 1
        orientation         0 0 1 0
        image               0 0 0
        focalDistance       5
        heightAngle         0.785398
    }
```

Figure 5.14 PerspectiveCamera

should be. Changing the heightAngle is like using a zoom lens to zoom in and out. The focalDistance field is a hint to browsers about where the person behind the camera is looking. Browsers can use this information to do correct stereo rendering (basing the stereo eye separation on the focalDistance), to adjust how quickly the viewer should move through the scene, and to do fancy depth-of-field blur effects.

ViewportMapping, nearDistance, farDistance, or aspectRatio fields should not be part of VRML. ViewportMapping is almost always left at its default value of ADJUST_CAMERA. The near and far clipping planes distances are best calculated by the VRML browser and adjusted automatically. And we should assume that the aspectRatio will match the window. Authors who want their scenes to look squished can insert nonuniform scales.

OrthographicCamera is exactly like PerspectiveCamera. Only instead of a heightAngle field to control the field of view, it has a height field that specifies how tall the viewing volume is in world-space coordinates, as shown in Figure 5.15.

This spec doesn't define any way of specifying a recommended viewing paradigm—walk-through versus fly-through versus looking at a single object. Most common paradigms will be a single object (you just want to move around the object and look at it from all sides)—an immersive room or environment (you want to walk or fly or crawl or

```
FILE FORMAT/DEFAULTS
    OrthographicCamera {
        position            0 0 1
        orientation         0 0 1 0
        focalDistance       5
        height              2
    }
```

Figure 5.15 OrthographicCamera

hop around it exploring). Smart browsers should be able to distinguish between these two cases pretty easily (using position of camera versus rest of scene, plus viewer size (focalDistance) versus rest of scene).

Lights

Open Inventor defines three basic kinds of lights. All lights have an intensity, color, and an on field that can be used to turn them on or off. DirectionalLight has a direction field that specifies what direction the light is traveling. A PointLight has a position in space and radiates light uniformly in all directions from that point. A SpotLight has both a location and a direction, plus fields to control the width and focus of its beam. Note that light positions and directions *are* transformed by the current transformation, allowing lights to be attached to objects.

Info

Storing arbitrary information in a file is handy for recording who created an object, copyright information, etc. The Info node contains a single field, called string, that contains an arbitrary ASCII string that can be used for this.

For example:

```
Info {
    string "Created by Thad Beier.
Slightly ill-behaved model: has some clockwise polygons.
Public domain.
"
}[4]
```

Note that newlines are are allowed in string fields, allowing one Info node to contain several lines of information. Should conventions for the information inside Info nodes be established to allow browsers to interpret that information? For example, the convention for author information could be a line of the form: Author: author_name.

---

[4] *Ibid.*

VRML Extensions to Open Inventor

For the first release of VRML, two new nodes are proposed: WWWInline and WWWAnchor.

WWWInline would look like this:

```
WWWInline {
    name "http://www.sgi.com/FreeStuff/CoolScene.vrml"
    bboxCenter 0 0 4
    bboxSize 10.5 4.5 8
}[5]
```

The name field is an SFString containing the URL for the file. A smart implementation can delay the retrieval of the file until it is rendered instead of reading it right away. Combined with LevelOfDetail, this provides an automatic mechanism for delayed loading of complicated scenes.

The bboxCenter and bboxSize fields allow an author to specify the bounding box for this WWWInline. Specifying a bounding box this way allows a browser to decide whether the WWWInline can be seen from the current camera location without reading the WWWInline's contents. If a bounding box is not specified, the contents of the WWWInline do have to be read to determine the WWWInline's bounding box.

WWWAnchor looks very much like WWWInline, except that it is a group node and can have children.

```
WWWAnchor {
    name "http://www.sgi.com/FreeStuff/CoolScene.vrml"
    Separator {
       Material { diffuseColor 0 0 .8 }
       Cube { }
    }
}
```

WWWAnchor is a strange node. It must somehow communicate with the browser and cause the browser to load the scene specified in its name field when a child of the WWWAnchor is picked, replacing the current scene that the WWWAnchor is part of. Specifying how that

---

5 *Ibid.*

happens is up to the browser and implementor of WWWAnchor, as is implementing the picking code.

So what happens when you nest WWWAnchors (you have WWWAnchors as children of WWWAnchors)? *Suggestion:* The lowest WWWAnchor wins.

WWWAnchor also has a map field that adds the object-space point on the object the user picked to the URL in the name field. This is like the image-map feature of HTML and allows scripts to do different things, based on exactly what part of an object is picked.

For example, given this WWWAnchor:

```
WWWAnchor   {
    name "http://www.foo.com/cgi-bin/pickMapper"
    map POINT
    Cube    {  }
}
```

Picking on the top of the Cube might produce the URL http://www.foo.com/cgi-bin/pickMapper?.211,1.0,-.56.

Other Open Inventor Nodes

Several other Open Inventor nodes are not common enough or will be too difficult to implement to include in VRML. The following are the most interesting, along with my reasons for not including them in this chapter.

Text2, Text3, Font

Text2 is two-dimensional screen-aligned text. Adding a 2-D primitive whose size is not in 3-D object coordinates but window coordinates turns up a lot of annoying implementation issues. As 3-D text is pretty complicated to implement implementing the full Open Inventor functionality would necessitate adding four more nodes to specify the font, coordinates for the 3-D extrusion bevel on the text, and specification whether the extrusion is a curve or a set of line segments (Font, ProfileCoordinate2, LinearProfile, and NurbsProfile). Also, allowing different fonts to be specified opens up a whole can of worms on what font names are allowed, where fonts are defined, what format fonts are in, etc.

NURBS

NURBS curves and surfaces are also complicated, especially if trimming of NURBS surfaces is supported (Open Inventor supports that). VRML can be very successful without them.

Nodekits

Open Inventor's nodekits impose a structure on the scene graph, making it easier for applications to manipulate the scene. For example, figuring out where to insert a material node to affect a picked object is not trivial for an arbitrary scene. If you use nodekits, it is trivial. Each ShapeKit has an associated AppearanceKit, and you just tell the AppearanceKit what you want the material to be. Nodekits should not be part of VRML only because they add yet another thing to be implemented, and the design must be kept as minimal as possible.

Draggers

Draggers are incredibly powerful interactive objects that respond to user interaction by moving themselves. For example, a RotateSpherical dragger will rotate itself when the mouse is clicked and dragged over it. Draggers become powerful when their fields (which change as they move) are wired to other parts of the scene, using field-to-field connections. Because behaviors, engines, and field-to-field connections should not be part of VRML, draggers should not be, either.

Array, MultipleCopy

An Array node copies its children several times, each translated differently. A MultipleCopy node is similar, except that arbitrary transformation matrices are specified. They aren't used very much (although they are useful for things like regular grids).

Blinker, Rotor, Shuttle, Pendulum

Blinker, a subclass of the Switch node, changes which child is drawn over time. Rotor is a rotation that changes over time. Shuttle is a translation that changes between two locations over time, and Pendulum changes between two rotations over time. The notion of animating objects that change over time should wait for VRML V2.0 and should include full-fledged engines and behaviors.

ClipPlane

ClipPlane specifies an arbitrary clipping plane that can be used to clip out parts of the scene. Useful for specific CAD applications, ClipPlane is not very useful generally (and not typically saved as part of a scene).

DrawStyle

This functionality allows parts of the scene to be drawn as LINES or POINTS but can be left to the browser. Authors can use PointSet or IndexedLineSet if they want lines or points in their scene.

Environment

The Environment node specifies global illumination settings, such as fog and the ambient light intensity of the scene. Those are pretty advanced features that VRML can do without, at least for now.

LightModel

Open Inventor supports either a BASE_COLOR lighting model, which is basically no lighting at all, or the default PHONG lighting model, which is a simple lighting approximation. The BASE_COLOR lighting model is useful mainly for scenes that have already had their lighting precomputed, such as a scene for which a radiosity solution has been calculated. These kinds of scenes are not common enough to justify the addition of the LightModel node to VRML.

ResetTransform, Units, AntiSquish, RotationXYZ

ResetTransform can be painful to implement correctly and is almost never specified in scene files. The same is true for AntiSquish. Also, Units shouldn't be used, because strange things happen when you nest them.

For example:

```
Separator {
    Units { units FEET }
    DEF FootCube Cube { }
    Separator {
        Units { units METERS }
        DEF MeterCube Cube { }
    }
}
```

Applications that try to be smart about rearranging the object hierarchy will have trouble figuring out exactly what effect the second Units node will have, since its effect will change if it is moved out from under the first Units node. The rules are much simpler if a simple Scale node is used instead.

RotationXYZ allows rotation about one of the primary axes. The generality of Rotation is preferred here, which allows rotation about an arbitrary axis. However, it might make sense to replace Rotation with RotationXYZ, since the general Transform node can also be used to rotate about an arbitrary axis.

TextureCoordinateEnvironment, TextureCoordinatePlane

These specify a fairly simple mapping of object geometry to texture coordinates. The TextureCoordinatePlane should be part of VRML. However, it will add a fair amount of complexity to a VRML implementation's code for handling texture coordinates.

Coordinate4, ProfileCoordinate2, ProfileCoordinate3

Coordinate4 specifies homogeneous coordinates (X, Y, Z, and W), which are not very common. ProfileCoordinate2 and ProfileCoordinate3 specify coordinates for the bevels on 3-D text and the trim curves of NURBS objects. Since 3-D text or NURBS should not be part of VRML V1.0, they aren't necessary, either.

Binary Format

To make implementation of VRML easier, a binary format should not initially be part of VRML. Experience with Open Inventor has shown that using a standard compression utility (such as compress, pack, or gzip) to compress ASCII Open Inventor files results in files that are just as small as Open Inventor's binary format (compressing the binary format typically has very little effect). If a new protocol for transmitting VRML scenes is designed, servers and browsers could automatically compress and decompress ASCII VRML files to save network bandwidth. Actually, this is orthogonal to VRML. HTML files could also be stored and sent compressed to save network bandwith. Parsing time is greatly improved with a binary format. However, for VRML browsers the network transmission time will be much greater than the ASCII parsing time.

Field Syntax

Each node has zero or more fields that store the data for the node. Each of the fields is written as the field's name, followed by the data in the field.

For example, a Sphere has a single radius field that contains a single floating-point value and is written as Sphere { radius 1.0 }. Each node defines reasonable default values for its fields, which are used if the field does not appear as part of the node's definition.

Some fields can contain multiple values. The syntax for a multiple-valued field is a superset of the syntax for single-valued fields. The values are all enclosed in brackets ([]) and are separated by commas. The final value may optionally be followed by an extra comma. If a multiple-valued field has only one value, the brackets and commas may be omitted, resulting in the same syntax as single-valued fields. A multiple-valued field may also contain zero values, in which case just a set of empty brackets appears.

Field Classes

Single-valued fields have type names that begin with SF. Multiple-valued fields have type names that begin with MF. Open Inventor defines 42 types of fields.

VRML should consist of the subset used by the nodes defined by VRML, which are:

* SFFloat
* MFVec3f
* SFVec3f
* MFColor
* SFColor
* SFRotation
* SFMatrix
* SFEnum
* SFBitMask
* MFString
* SFString
* SFImage

Some of the types for fields are tied to the C programming language (Float; Open Inventor also has Long and Short). It will be misleading on some machines. An Open Inventor SFFloat is a 32-bit floating-point number, even though floats are larger or smaller on different machines.

Naming

A node may be given a name by prepending its definition with the reserved token DEF, followed by whitespace, the name of the node, and whitespace to separate the name from the type of the node. For example, to give the name SquareHead to a Cube, use the following: DEF SquareHead Cube {}. Names must not start with a digit (0–9), and must not contain ASCII control characters, whitespace, or the following characters: +,\,',",{}.

Note: The + character is illegal for compatibility with Open Inventor programs in which the characters after the + are used to disambiguate multiple nodes with the same name. For example, a user of an Open Inventor program may give two nodes the name Joe; when written, these might appear as Joe+0 and Joe+1. The other characters are illegal, to make parsing easier and to leave room for future format extensions.

Instancing

A node may be the child of more than one group. This is called *instancing* (using the same instance of a node multiple times, or aliasing or multiple references by other systems). It is accomplished by using the USE keyword.

The DEF keyword both defines a named node and creates a single instance of it. The USE keyword indicates that the most recently defined instance should be used again. If several nodes were given the same name, the last DEF encountered during parsing wins. DEF/USE is limited to a single file. There is no mechanism for using USE on nodes which is used DEF in other files.

For example, rendering this scene will result in three spheres being drawn. Both of the spheres are named Joe; the second (smaller) sphere is drawn twice:

```
Separator {
    DEF Joe Sphere { }
    Translation { translation 2 0 0 }
    DEF Joe Sphere { radius .2 }
    Translation { translation 2 0 0 }
    USE Joe
}
```

Extensibility

Open Inventor's file format has two mechanisms to support easy extensibility: self-declaring nodes and alternative representations for nodes. Objects that are not built in write out a description of themselves first. This allows them to be read in and ignored by applications that don't understand them.

This description is written just after the opening brace for the node and consists of the keyword fields, followed by a list of the types and names of fields used by that node. To save space, fields with default values that won't be written also will not have their descriptions written.

For example, if Cube was not built into the core library, it would be written like this:

```
Cube {
    fields [ SFFloat width, SFFloat height, SFFloat depth ]
    width 10 height 4 depth 3
}
```

By describing the types and names of the Cube's fields, a parser can correctly read the new node. Field-to-field connections and engines (which should not be part of VRML V1.0) require that the parser know the names and types of fields in unknown nodes. It isn't good enough just to search for matching curly-braces outside of strings and store unknown node contents as an unparsed string.

The other feature that allows easy extensibility is the ability to supply an alternative representation for objects. This is done by adding a special field, named alternateRep of type SFNode, to your new nodes. For example, to implement a new kind of Material that supported indexOfRefraction, a regular Material would be needed as an alternative representation for applications that do not understand RefracMaterial.

The file format would look like:

```
RefracMaterial {
    fields [ SFNode alternateRep, MFFloat indexOfRefraction,
        MFColor diffuseColor ]
    indexOfRefraction 0.2
    diffuseColor 0.9 0.0 0.2
    alternateRep Material { diffuseColor 0.9 0.0 0.2 }
}
```

Open Inventor uses DSOs (dynamic shared objects; DLLs, or dynamic link libraries, on the Windows NT port of Open Inventor) to support run-time loading of the code for a new node. A RefracMaterial.so is needed, with an implementation (written in C++) of the new RefracMaterial. At this point existing Open Inventor applications will then work, thus recognizing the new node, and *not* use the alternateRep. However, it is beyond the scope of VRML to try to define a method for the dynamic loading of platform-independent code across the network. That issue is completely independent of VRML.

Header

For easy identification of VRML files, every VRML file must begin with the characters:

```
#VRML V1.0 ascii
```

Any characters after these on the same line are ignored. The line is terminated by either the ASCII newline or carriage-return characters.

It would be a little more convenient if VRML shared the same identifying header as Open Inventor (Open Inventor V2.0 ASCII). However, in the long run there will be many fewer problems if it is easy to distinguish VRML files from Open Inventor files. It would be trivial to write a translator for VRML to Open Inventor and only moderately difficult to write one for Open Inventor to VRML that tesselated any primitives that were not part of VRML (NURBS) into IndexedFaceSets.

Comments

The "#" character begins a comment. All characters until the next newline or carriage return are ignored. The only exception to this is within string fields, where the # character will be part of the string.

Comments and whitespace may not be preserved. In particular, a VRML document server may strip comments and extraneous whitespace from a VRML file before transmitting it. Info nodes should be used for persistent information, such as copyrights or author information.

Whitespace

Blanks, tabs, newlines, and carriage returns are whitespace characters wherever they appear outside of string fields. One or more whitespace characters separate the syntactical entities in VRML files, where necessary.

File Contents

After the required header, a VRML file contains exactly one VRML node. That node may in turn contain any number of other nodes.

Open Inventor allows a series of root nodes to be parsed from a single file. This causes problems for filters that operate on Open Inventor files. (Instancing between the nodes in the different roots tends to get broken as each root is worked on independently.) It doesn't really add any functionality.

File Extension

The standard file extension for VRML files is .vrml. It seems safe to assume that there is no issue with a four-character suffix, since the standard suffix for HTML documents is .html.

Coordinate Space Conventions

Open Inventor's default unit is the meter. Open Inventor uses a right-handed coordinate system. If you are looking at your computer monitor, the default Open Inventor coordinate axes are +X toward the right, +Y toward the top, and +Z coming out of the screen toward you.

The consensus on the mailing list was +X right, +Y into the screen, and +Z up. Is it worth having VRML be incompatible with Open Inventor? It is also easy for a translator to add a Rotation node.

Is That Everything?

Not quite! Let's define a list of terms and features *here* in order to place the remainder of this chapter and the ones that follow in perspective.

Looking Ahead

Open Inventor's field-to-field connections, global fields, and engine objects (which should not be part of VRML V1.0) provide the infrastructure for creating objects with behaviors. Open Inventor is missing a good set of engines for doing simple keyframed animated behaviors of objects. It is also missing some simple interactive nodes, such as buttons (like the WWWAnchor node, only more general). The Open Inventor team at Silicon Graphics will be designing and implementing these kinds of nodes and engines in the near future.

From Here

If this wasn't enough, a further detailed discussion of Open Inventor will be coming up in Chapter 12. Chapter 16 will give a brief overview of an interactive tool for exploring VR applications over the Internet via Mosiac and Netscape.

Terminology and Features

- Platform independence—This is an ASCII file format that has already proved to be easily transportable to other platforms.
- True 3-D information (not prerendered texture maps a la DOOM)—All of the primitives are true 3-D objects.
- PHIGS-ish lighting and view model—Material, the lights, and PerspectiveCamera give a simple but powerful way of specifying views and lights.
- Unrecognized data types are ignored (to leave open future development)—Extensibility has been designed in.
- Hierarchical data structure—Groups create the hierarchy, with Separators providing appropriate encapsulation so subparts do not affect their parents.
- Lightweight design—You'll have to judge, but it should be kept minimal.
- Convex and concave objects allowed—IndexedFaceSets allow arbitrary geometry.
- Fill-in-the-details support (pictures in a museum)—LevelOfDetail combined with a lazy-load WWWInline node give this functionality.
- The file format is public domain—The Open Inventor file format is usable by anybody, and Silicon Graphics will be releasing a public domain parser for it to make it easier to write applications that understand the file format.
- Level of detail support—LevelOfDetail supports this directly.
- Geometric primitives—{Cube, Sphere, Cylinder} (Anybody want to argue hard for others?).
- Object-oriented—Most people would agree that Open Inventor is object-oriented, and that this is reflected in its file format.
- Texture mapping—Texture2 and TextureCoordinate2 provide a general method for doing simple texture mapping.
- Engines—This is the one feature that it would be a mistake to add to VRML V1.0. This can safely wait for a later version of VRML.

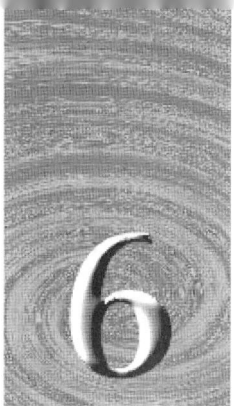

CAVEview: Netscape and Mosaic-Based Virtual Reality

CAVEview (Cave Automatic Virtual Environmentview) is an interactive tool for exploring virtual reality applications over the Internet via Web browsers: Netscape and Mosaic. Mosaic and Netscape (henceforth known as "Web browsers" in this chapter) currently use external viewers to present hypertext documents with images, text, sounds, and animation. With CAVEview, virtual reality applications are inserted into hypertext documents. CAVEview operates like other external viewers by bringing data files over the network. However, the transferred data is an application object file. The object file fully describes the environment, allowing the user to explore the scene for an unlimited amount of time.

Accessing application program files lets the user have control over the story. This is in sharp contrast to being able to upload and view animations in which the exploration of the scene is restricted to a fixed interval of a prerecorded sequence. To attain a variation of that sequence, the animator would have to add more frames, increasing the size of the data file that must be transferred. CAVEview adds stereo realism, interactivity, and sound to viewing 3-D objects in Web browsers, without the cost of large animation files.

Web browsers give access to hypertext documents on the Internet, most of which contain primarily text and inline images. However, some documents contain high-resolution images, audio clips, animations, and video sequences. The Web browsers present these items by invoking an external viewer, such as xv, ghostview, or mpeg. Web browsers serve as an interface to a viewer by locating, retrieving, and storing the data and calling the viewer with the appropriate arguments. Viewers have specific control functionality that allows the user to modify or change viewing parameters of an image, animation, or sound. The user may be able to change color, size or crop an image, replay an animation at different speeds, or view the animation backward.

Recently the Web browsers added forms support, which allows the user to input parameters and to receive back information reflecting those choices. A user may request an image of the U. S. weather system, designed to his or her own specifications. CAVEview expands this kind of user-driven data and information-gathering system to three-dimensional computer graphics and virtual reality by presenting interactive CAVE applications within the Web browsers' HTML documents.

The CAVE

The CAVE (Cave Automatic Virtual Environment) is a virtual reality environment designed and implemented at the Electronic Visualization Laboratory at the University of Illinois at Chicago. The CAVE, shown in Figure 6.1, is a surround screen, surround sound, projection-based virtual reality environment system. The actual environment is a 10×10×10 foot cube, where images are rear-projected in stereo on two or three walls, and down-projected onto the floor. The viewer explores a virtual world by moving around inside the cube and grabbing objects with the wand, the CAVE input device. In the CAVE high-resolution stereoscopic images are generated by a multiprocessor Silicon Graphics workstation or multiple workstations and are rear-projected onto several walls and from there projected onto the floor. Several people can be in the CAVE simultaneously, all wearing stereo glasses. One person is tracked, and as he or she moves in the

Chapter 6 CAVEview: Netscape and Mosaic-Based Virtual Reality

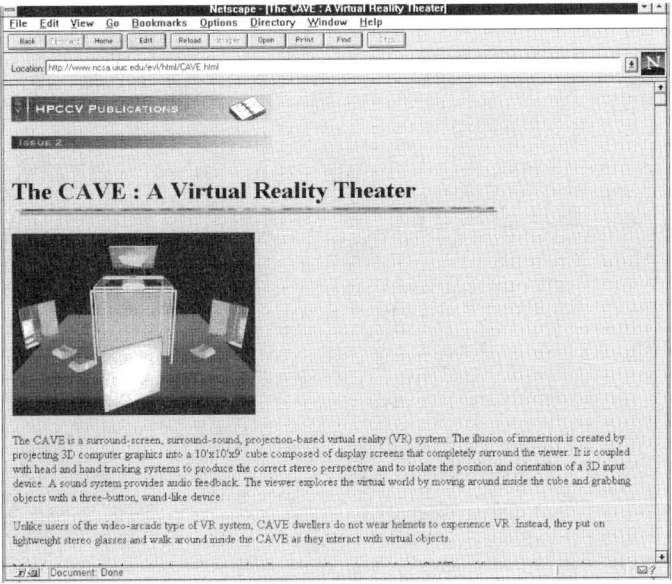

Figure 6.1 The CAVE

CAVE, the correct perspective and stereo projections of the environment are updated to match the person's viewpoint. The rest of the participants are passive viewers, as though watching a 3-D movie.

The CAVE Simulator

To aid in the development of CAVE applications, the CAVE simulator, shown in Figure 6.2, has been developed. The CAVE simulator emulates the CAVE by providing control of navigation, viewpoint, and wand input. Recently the CAVE has grown in popularity. Many research scientists, application programmers, and artists have begun using the CAVE and the CAVE simulator. As interest in the CAVE grew, there was a need for a presentation tool for CAVE applications. This tool needed to be geared toward the novice user, the individual who has little or no experience with the CAVE environment. This chapter presents an application called CAVEview, which serves as a

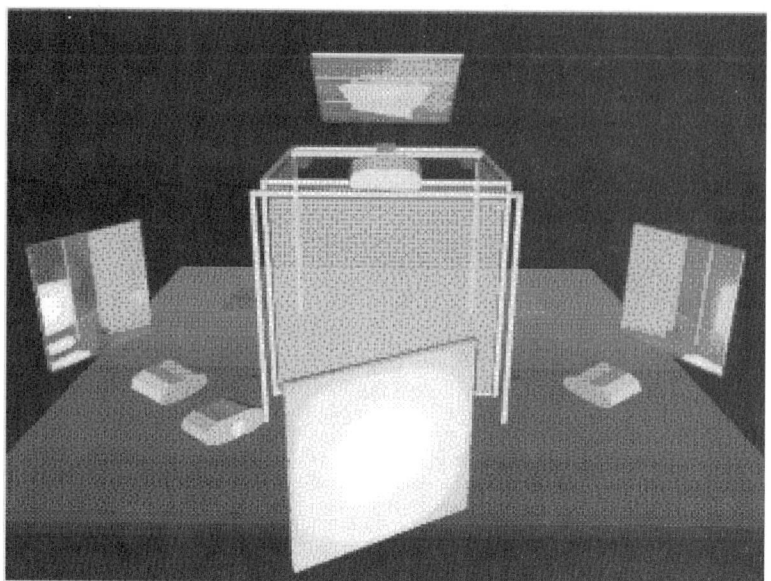

Figure 6.2 The CAVE simulator

viewing environment for CAVE programs on the World Wide Web using Web browsers.

Motivation

Animation, the Web browsers' traditional method for visualizing three-dimensional data, has many drawbacks. The amount of time it takes to download an animation is proportional to the size and number of frames contained in the animation. An animation typically gives some information or tells a story. Unfortunately the story remains the same each time the animation is played. An animator can create a new story by creating other animations or by adding more frames to change or lengthen the animation. But both of these alternatives increase download time. No matter how many changes the animator makes to the animation, the user is still left with no control over the plot.

In order to overcome these drawbacks, CAVEview needed to be interactive and to have a reasonable download time. It had to be versatile enough to allow many types of applications to be ported to CAVEview. A solution was to develop CAVEview as an interface to the CAVE simulator. By using the CAVE simulator, existing CAVE applications could easily be converted to CAVEview and consequently the Web browsers' environment. CAVE application developers would have little or no changes in their code to view their applications in the CAVEview environment.

CAVEview Features

CAVEview achieves interactivity by executing the application locally on the Mosaic user's machine. Instead of a large image file, an application object file and required resource files are transferred. Download time is decreased, since animation files are typically larger than application object files. Since the application is executed locally, the graphics are created in real time as the user selects a path through the data. Similarly, the user can interactively change the size of the graphics window, as shown in Figure 6.3, and explore the scene

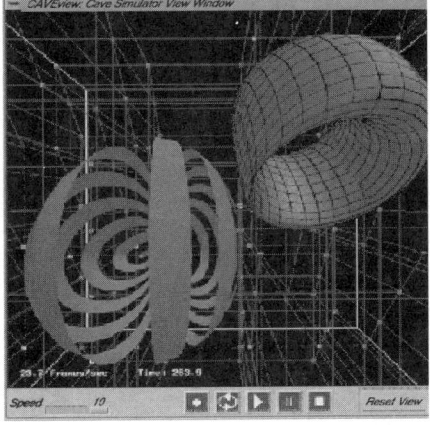

Figure 6.3 The Graphics Window

without time limitation or extra loading time. CAVEview allows each user to explore and collect information on the scene he or she is viewing at his or her own pace.

CAVEview as a Presentation Tool

The CAVE simulator was designed as a development tool whereby input commands are given to the CAVE simulator through the keyboard. CAVEview is designed as a presentation and viewing tool. Consequently there had to be a user interface that would allow the CAVE novice to quickly and easily move about the data and the CAVE space. The CAVEview interface allows users to interact with objects in 3-D as they might in the actual CAVE. CAVEview has all the functionality of the CAVE simulator environment, with the additional enhancement of script record and playback features. Use of the Logitech tracking system and stereo glasses provides the option of stereo viewing and enhanced object manipulation.

CAVE Movement and Viewpoint

CAVEview has three areas for user input: the control panel, the graphics window, and the scripts panel. The control panel, shown in Figure 6.4, consists of Motif widgets that control navigation, perspective,

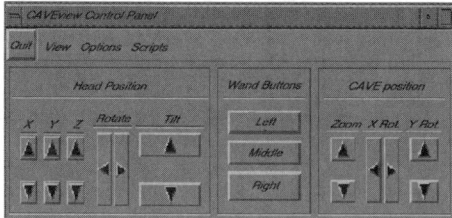

Figure 6.4 The Control Panel

wand input, and available visual cues for the CAVE. CAVEview maintains CAVE simulator features, such as an outline of the CAVE structure, a virtual CAVE person, and a wand. There are widgets for moving the virtual CAVE person around the CAVE space and tilt controls for the virtual person's head and wand. There are three viewing modes: wall, perspective, and outside view. Head tilt controls are used in the perspective and outside view modes, and wand orientation controls are available in all view modes.

Stereo, Tracking, and the Flying Mouse

The mouse, tracking, and stereo viewing are features that add realism to the simulated CAVE experience. The operation of the wand buttons changes, depending on the application. Typical operations for these buttons are fly-through capabilities, data manipulations, and menu selections. The Web browser's documentation that accompanies each CAVEview application should describe the operation for each of the buttons.

In order to make user interaction with the applications more natural, tracking and three-dimensional input capabilities were added. Use of these features requires a magnetic tracking device and a three dimensional mouse, such as the Logitech 3-D mouse. When the user is equipped with a head-tracking system, CAVEview calculates the scene in viewer-centered perspective. In other words, the computer generates the image-based on the user's distance from the screen, interoccular distance, and head orientation. The three-dimensional mouse presents the wand in the CAVE. The user has direct control of each of the size degrees of freedom. In the CAVE the wand can be moved up and down, left and right, forward and backward, as well as azimuth, elevation, and roll, the three orientation controls. It is very difficult to represent these six degrees of freedom with a two-dimensional input device, such as the traditional mouse. These 3-D input features create a physical relationship between the way the user moves and what he or she sees.

Audio

The CAVE currently uses a sound Web site server called VSS to create sounds for the virtual reality applications. Most of the CAVE applications use this server to play sounds created by frequency modulation, additive synthesis, digital sampling, and MIDI (musical instrument digital interface). Likewise, the sound server is run while using CAVEview. Consequently CAVEview users experience the same audio feedback as they would in the CAVE.

Scripts

Scripts, the record and playback feature available in CAVEview offer an animationlike experience without a frame-by-frame playback. Prerecorded scripts provide a suggested path for user exploration and playback. Both the user and the application developer can record a script or multiple scripts through the Scripts Control Panel. The script file contains the widget, keyboard, and mouse presses that specify a path or data manipulation. The script file is then saved in the user-specified directory or packaged within the application object file. Scripts designed by the developer are automatically loaded when the application is started in CAVEview. Users can insert their own scripts to be loaded upon startup, by changing a resource file.

Implementation and Development

The file that is downloaded when a Web browser user selects a CAVEview application for viewing has a .cave extension. This file is an archive of several files, with contents varying from application to application. Generally a .cave file would contain the application object and data files, along with the CAVEview script and data files.

CAVEview Data File

This data file contains application-specific information that is required by CAVEview. All CAVE applications share a similar structure. Drawing and calculation routines are separate functions. In addition, the GL graphics initialization and regular initialization must be in separate functions. CAVEview obtains names for these functions by accessing a file with the extension .cv_data. The application designer can also set certain visual cues to be automatically turned on or off upon application startup. This information resides in a file with the extension .cv. The application object and data files, the CAVEview script, and data files are all archived together into one file with the .cave extension. The .cave is the file Mosaic downloads when a user selects a link to a CAVEview application.

Web Browsers' File Transfer

When Web browsers download an image, animation, or HTML document across the network, they attempt to put the information in the datacache. However, for large animation and image files, the Web browser writes the files temporarily to /usr/tmp. Like the Web browsers, CAVEview also writes files to /usr/tmp. However, CAVEview creates a temporary directory, /usr/tmp/CAVEviewXXXX, where XXXX is the process ID number. The application object, data files, CAVEview script, and data files are extracted from the .cave file into this temporary directory. CAVEview then accesses files from this directory during execution. When the CAVEview application exits, this temporary directory is removed.

Dynamic Link

External viewers work independently of the data or image presented. Unfortunately the CAVE simulator library must be compiled with each CAVE application. In order for CAVEview to operate like other external viewers, CAVEview was designed to dynamically link the CAVE application shared object file to CAVEview using rld, the SGI runtime linker. Using rld allows any application in the .cave format to be accessed by CAVEview.

Field Test: VROOM, SIGGRAPH '94

The virtual reality exhibit VROOM at SIGGRAPH '94 provided a unique opportunity to showcase VROOM applications in the Web browsers and to test CAVEview on a broad spectrum of users. More than 20 CAVE applications were featured in CAVEview, including Interactive Molecular Modeling, A Walk Through the Chesapeake Bay, A 3-D Model of the Heart, Parallel Real Time Radiocity, and Getting Physical in 4D. Seven SGI Indigo 2 Extremes and three IndigoElans were used to run the Mosaic based documentation. Workstations were linked via a local area network that allowed access to VROOM documentation only. This documentation included CAVEview simulations, animations, and text. Each of the media described the projects and served as a supplement to the CAVE experience. Unlike the VROOM CAVE experience, where there is one navigator and many passive viewers, CAVEview allows the user direct control over navigation, wand input, and length of interaction. Moreover, CAVEview allowed the user to view any number of the VROOM applications. Overall, the CAVEview user interface proved quite intuitive and did not require additional instructions or assistance other than those provided in the documents.

Summary

CAVEview was designed to take Web browsers into the realm of interactive three-dimensional computer graphics. As shown at VROOM SIGGRAPH '94, CAVEview has been successful in meeting this goal. However, there are serious security problems with its implementation, and it may not be realistic for widespread use on the Web. The security problem lies within the dynamic linking procedure, which in effect runs the CAVE application locally. Any process a user runs on a workstation, has the same rights and privileges as the user. Any process running in a CAVEview application has access to the file system of the machine that it is running on. As the number of Web browsers users grows, there will be a greater need for a system such as CAVEview. Future interactive 3-D graphical systems for Netscape and Mosaic should be cross-platform, standardized, easy to use, and have a minimal security risk.

From Here

Surrogate travel on the Internet is here to stay. Chapter 7 briefly discusses surrogate travel in a virtual intuitive manner, as a natural interface with computers.

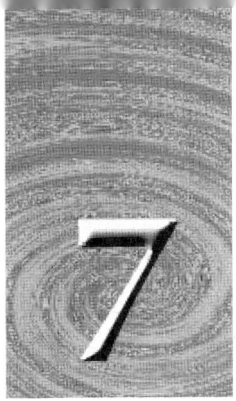

Surrogate Travel on the Internet

Mosaic—the first Internet killer application—and now Netscape have brought the Internet into the popular culture. Users can begin to use simple point-and-click interfaces rather than a myriad of arcane commands and protocols. As another step toward a more natural interface, it's recommended here that a first-person point of view (POV) model be used that allows a user to interact with information in a virtual intuitive manner.

Surrogate travel has been around in a graphical form for more than 17 years. The concept of first-person POV has been used to convey a sense of place to a user interacting with a computer. The nature of the interaction has varied quite a bit, depending on the context of the application. In the late 1970s the Aspen movie map work at the Architecture Machine Lab (now known as the Media Lab) at MIT pioneered the concept of real-time surrogate travel with photo-realistic images. The movie map work was extended to the use of these environments as front ends to information. More recently Apple Computer is in the process of commercializing the concept of first-person POV interfaces with QuickTime Virtual Reality (VR). Travel through an abstract space, such as a hierarchical file system, has been demonstrated with Silicon Graphics' FSN (Full Service Network).

Examples of first-person POV interfaces come from many domains. Games, such as 7th Guest, Myst, and Jurrasic Park (popular games on PC, Mac, Nintendo, and Sega platforms), all allow the player to travel in a first-person POV manner. Information organizers, such as

Packard Bell's Navigator and Apple's eWorld interface to online services, all use a first-person POV metaphor to organize information and to give users a sense of place and structure.

The VRML effort in particular has stimulated a number of efforts to link virtual environments to the World Wide Web (WWW). A number of interesting language proposals and demonstration systems can be found at various VRML Web sites.

Coupling of virtual environments with Mosaic and Netscape in the WWW is the next logical extension to these spatial types of interfaces. Mosaic and Netscape (the Web browsers) have provided a uniform interface to the Internet and WWW. Spatial interfaces can lead toward a more intuitive interface.

Integration of a virtual environment with the Web browsers can take two forms: inline graphics or external application. Both approaches have advantages and disadvantages, as discussed in the following sections.

This chapter describes several ways to use a computer-generated environment (virtual reality) with the Web browsers. Two approaches are taken. The first is to allow the user to interact with a virtual environment displayed as part of the Web browser's document, an inline image. The second is to create an independent process with which the user can have high-bandwidth interaction (real-time manipulations, which can drive the Web browsers remotely).

In the first case, an inline picture of a space is walked through in a virtual environment by allowing the user to select buttons that move the point of view of the user forward, backward, left, or right. Each user selection causes a network request to the Web browser site server, which renders a new scene or loads a new HTML page. This method has the advantage of being a pure Web browser application, and issues of portability are minimized; however, the cost is performance.

Using the second method—creating an independent process—a user is allowed to interact with a graphical process running on the user's workstation. At appropriate times in the interaction, the user selects an object. Objects can have a URL associated, which causes the Web browser process to go to that URL, using the remote control facility in the X version of the Web browsers. This method allows the user to have a great deal of interaction in real time with dynamic feedback. However, issues of portability become more important, as the real-time graphics process may be dependent on the particular platform. These techniques demonstrate that the use and interaction with spatially oriented information spaces are practical. Both techniques have advantages and disadvantages.

Inline Graphics Surrogate Travel

Using the inline graphics method of surrogate travel, as shown in Figure 7.1, the user is presented with a graphic that visualizes a first-person point of view (POV) in the middle of a Web browser page. In addition to the graphic, the page contains buttons that allow the user to control movement through the space in a virtual manner. When a button is selected, the user moves through the space, and the graphic is updated.

In the initial version of this experiment, each scene was hard coded into a separate HTML page (clearly a hack). Subsequently, a more extensive version (allowing more complete travel through the room) was developed and called the Virtual Corridor. In this version the user's movement commands interact with a cgi-bin command that computes the correct image to use and automatically provides the linking.

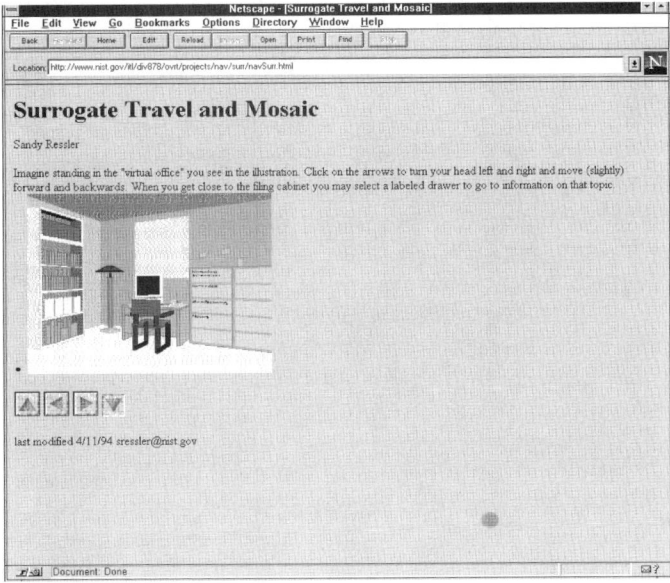

Figure 7.1 Inline Image Surrogate Travel: Netscape and Mosaic (actual demo)

External Graphics Surrogate Travel

Using this technique of surrogate travel, the user is presented with a completely separate application. This application drives the Web browsers via remote control. The principle advantage is that the user is able to manipulate a 3-D environment in real time, using all of the resources and performance of the graphics workstation and independently of the network bandwidth, as shown in Figure 7.2. The disadvantage is the loose coupling of the separate application with the Web browser and the need for a separate user interface.

The existing test application is a modification of SceneViewer, the Open Inventor application provided by Silicon Graphics, as shown in Figure 7.3. The SceneViewer program was modified to interpret object labels that are URLs. The URL is sent to a script, which generates the appropriate UNIX signal, causing the Web browsers to go to the URL in the label. Figure 7.3 shows a fragment of the Open Inventor file for the house containing a URL.

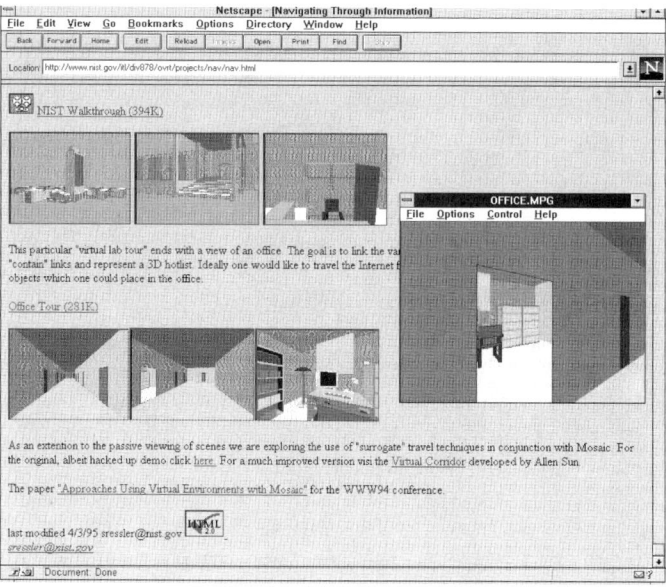

Figure 7.2 Workstation Screen With URL Viewer Driving Netscape and Mosaic

Chapter 7 Surrogate Travel on the Internet

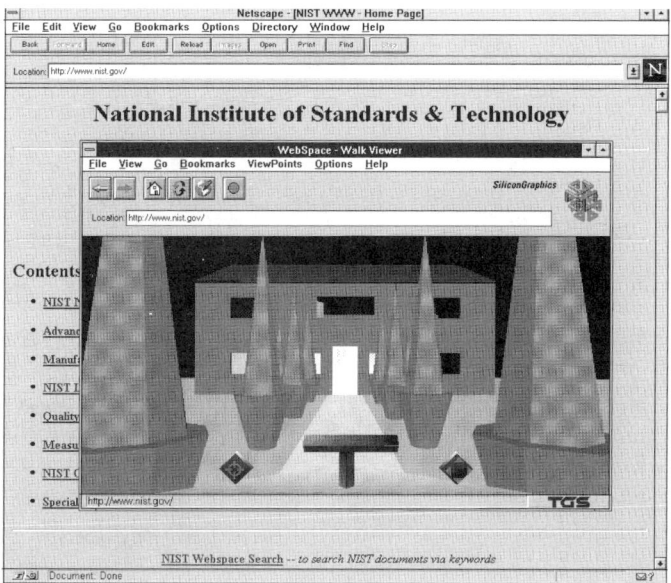

Figure 7.3 External Application (URLScene) Controlling Netscape and Mosaic

Future Directions

These experiments can take a number of directions. First, it would be useful to extend the inline graphics control to interact with a program that computes the views on the fly and returns a new inline image file. This approach should also be practical for wide Web browser distribution, as the 3-D computations and rendering take place on the Web site server, and image files could be sent back to less powerful CPUs (PCs).

In addition, extensions to the external application, URL viewer, to allow use of an immersive environment should prove useful. The addition of a 3-D position tracker and head-mounted display (HMD) would enable the user to become immersed in the environment and indirectly into the data. Current HMDs, however, are not of sufficient quality to allow for any significant amount of textual reading, so new representations of information would need to be developed.

Finally, there is also an opportunity for the generation of VR clipart that could be used in conjunction with these approaches. Although 3-D clipart has been around for a number of years, these clipart packages provide the end user with manipulable objects that are positioned and rotated to any orientation and then included into documents. For the WWW one would like to travel to a location (a dinosaur museum, for example), get a 3-D clipart object meaningful to the user, and place that object on one's virtual bookshelf. You then attach the URL to the object, and now you have a 3-D hotlist meaningful to the user.

From Here

Netscape and Mosaic have demonstrated the power of surrogate travel on the Internet that allows the user to interact in a virtual environment. Chapter 8 deals with *real* virtual reality on the Internet and addresses the fact that low-cost home virtual reality is closer to becoming a reality than most people realize.

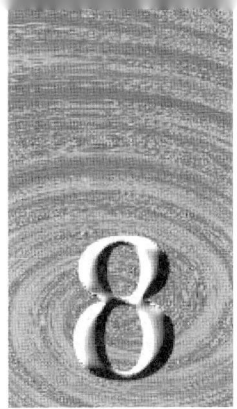

Real Virtual Reality on the Internet

Organizations such as the National Center for Supercomputing Applications (NCSA) at the University of Illinois, Urbana-Champaign, are moving at warp speed to develop new technologies for real VR development on the Internet. Over the past three years The Virtual Reality Lab at NCSA has been investigating the use of immersive technologies as a means for scientific visualization. Several custom applications have been developed to look at very specific data sets. Also, some tools and papers of potential interest to a wide community have been created.

The Papers subdirectory contains a paper on integrating virtual reality hardware with data flow packages. Prototype modules were developed on an alpha version of the Silicon Graphics' IRIS Explorer package. Modules will be made widely available as they are ported to the official release of of IRIS Explorer V2.0.

The Virtual-Devices subdirectory contains two utilities that allow some VR application development to be done offline at a programmer's desktop workstation. These utilities allow more time at a VR facility for application researchers to explore. The idea for these utilities came about during work on the Explorer VR modules. It was apparent that most of the time spent developing code didn't require the use of the equipment. Also, a small percentage of the time spent moving virtual reality devices was to make small movements in them to see whether they registered properly with the application display.

The two utilities contained in the subdirectory are for the virtual Binocular Omni-Orientation Monitor (BOOM) and a generic 6-D tracker device. There are plans for several more tools following the same idea. Glove interfaces and an interface for the CAVE are examples of what is in store.

Immersive Technologies

NCSA tries to provide a variety of VR technology to give users the opportunity to experiment with various immersive modalities. NCSA is collaborating with the Electronic Visualization Lab (EVL) at the University of Illinois at Chicago to create a CAVE at NCSA to develop both an emulation interface and an Explorer module interface for the CAVE (see Chapter 6).

To obtain more information about VR at NCSA or copies of tools and papers created there check the NCSA World Wide Web information site server (perhaps using NCSA's XMosaic information browser). To access the NCSA VR information, use the following URL:

```
http://www.ncsa.uiuc.edu/Viz/VR/vr_homepage.html
```

This ftp site will be updated as more items of interest are created. You can send e-mail to the coordinator of NCSA's VR lab at wsherman@ncsa.uiuc.edu.

Emerging Technologies

Since VR Internet technology is very scarce and lab time is at a premium, NCSA hopes that by allowing much of the development to be taken off-line, the VR labs will have a higher rate of being used for experiencing and experimenting with virtual environments on the Internet. Of course, occasionally development must take place in the lab. Testing the stereo algorithms of a program, for instance, is best done by wearing the equipment instead of passing off an interactive game screen as real virtual reality. Additionally, this will be useful in situations when a group of people are writing and testing code during the same time frame, as in a classroom or training environment.

To this end, NCSA is developing a collection of Internet tools that can move much development effort out of the VR labs and onto the programmer's desktop workstation. The first of these utilities is a pair of programs that emulate 6-D tracking systems used to give head or body location information to an application. These programs are called *virtual devices*. The first device developed was the virtual Binocular Omni-Orientation Monitor (BOOM), as shown in Figure 8.1. This device emulates the tracking hardware of a Fake Space Labs BOOM. The second utility is designed to emulate the hardware of generic 6-D tracking devices (the current version emulates only the Polhemus Isotrak system), as shown in Figure 8.2.

In order to use these two utilities, one piece of hardware is required—a cable to connect two RS-232 ports together with a null modem integration (basically, three wires). The cable is connected between two serial ports on the same machine or can connect two machines, allowing one to act as the tracking device and the other to run the applications. The virtual devices were written such that the application program reading from the serial port cannot distinguish between the actual device and the emulation program. The generic tracker program is not yet that robust, but a newer version is expected to be available soon.

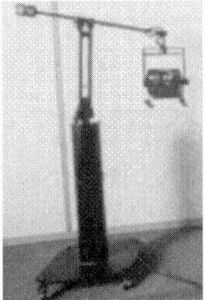

Figure 8.1 Virtual Binoccular Omni-Orientation Monitor (BOOM)

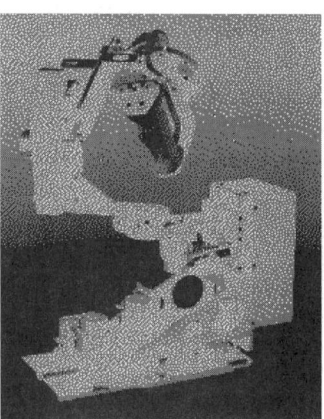

Figure 8.2 Generic 6D Tracking Devices

The BOOM position is controlled by six sliders at the top of the window, with the graphics section a representation of how the BOOM is oriented. Some direct control is done with the right and middle mouse buttons. There are also controls to reset the position of the BOOM and, of course, to exit the program.

The generic tracking program allows both for slider controls and trackball/translation control via the mouse. There is also a chooser for selecting the type of hardware to emulate (although this selection is currently limited to the Isotrak).

Current versions of these and new utilities are available via anonymous ftp at ftp.ncsa.uiuc.edu and probably some other VR archive sites throughout the Internet. Several new programs and enhancements for the current programs are in the works. In particular, emulators for the CAVE will be available soon, as well as glove and wand devices. Also, the use of sockets for transmitting the data will be enhanced and documented.

A goal of the NCSA VR facility is to provide a means to use immersive technology as an aid for visualization experimentation. Although better interactive results are achieved with customized application code, this will help broaden user access. Perhaps these modules will excite a researcher to develop a custom application to further examine his or her data. On the flip side of the coin, perhaps a scientist will decide that immersion has nothing to offer. Let's look at another VR research provider that promises the next generation of real virtual reality on the Internet.

The Diaspar Virtual Reality Network—the Next Generation

Founded in 1991 by David Mitchell (Coordinator, Laguna Beach, CA), the purpose of the Diaspar virtual reality network is to provide quality VR EduTainment (or educational entertainment) on the Internet, as shown in Figure 8.3. Education should be fun, and the best way to learn is by sharing information, products, and services with others on the Internet.

Diaspar is an experimental system focused on learning by doing. This means that it is not focused on projects with specific completion

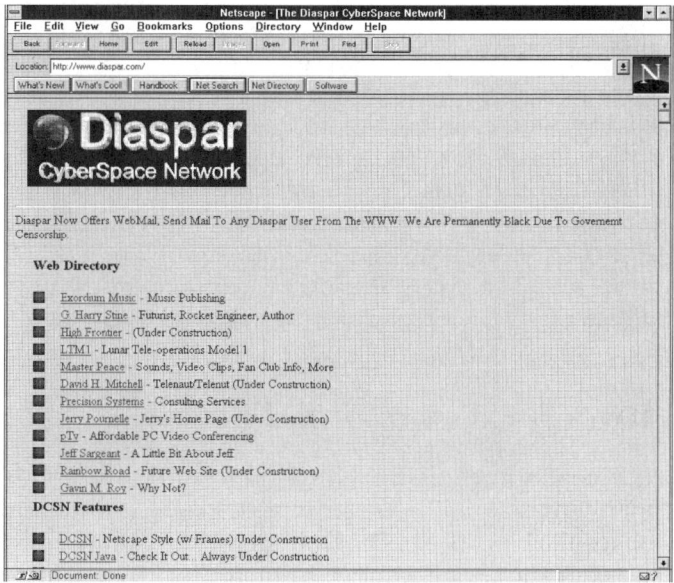

Figure 8.3 DIASPAR

dates or finite goals but rather on evolving exploration and growth. Today, right now, the network has the following:

- V-Nets—systems run by independent operators offering special services, products, and information;
- video and graphics—online video images and graphics using Dmodem;
- teleoperations—the ability to remotely control model vehicles;
- talk lines for live chat, conversation, and communication.

For the Future

Online seminars are where people meet to teach and learn. With virtual reality we have online shared worlds. Diaspar already has a two-user shared virtual world called POLY that you, the user, may try.

To accomplish these long-term goals, Diaspar has set out on a six-year plan to develop the tools necessary. Diaspar is five years into the plan, and it has changed a lot. It does still look possible to have low-cost home online virtual reality in 1997 for many people. Diaspar is an experimental system under construction, so the best way to learn more is to become involved.

But you don't have to wait until 1997 to start exploring the possibilities! POLY is a two-user shared virtual world that runs on most 386 and 486 PCs. You download the software, coordinate with someone else to meet online in the Polygon Playground (POLY) world, and then experience it. You can move objects, change your point of view, and see what the other world user is doing. POLY has been exhibited at the Exploratorium in San Francisco.

Toward Low Cost Home Virtual Reality

Low-cost home virtual reality is closer to becoming a reality than most people realize. All over the world, groups large and small are working on its development. Diaspar provides a conference for people interested in the area to share information. The company is also working on nonproprietary standards to handle basic virtual reality functions over normal communications circuits.

Researchers are welcome and encouraged to join Diaspar. The conference called Virtual Reality contains information, and you are invited to contact people here who share your interests.

As it develops low-cost home teleoperations capabilities, Diaspar looks forward to offering new ways to learn and explore; a lunar moon base model is under construction. Some test teleoperations sessions—allowing people to remotely drive a miniature lunar rover model—have been done. Diaspar is an experimental online system under construction.

The Lunar Teleoperations Model 1 {LTM1}

Diaspar is the sponsor of the Lunar Teleoperations Model 1, which is an EduTainment experiment, as shown in Figure 8.4. LTM1 is a miniature moon base colony model under construction!

This is a volunteer effort by a group of moonlighters who have the goal of building the model and enlightening people about the potential

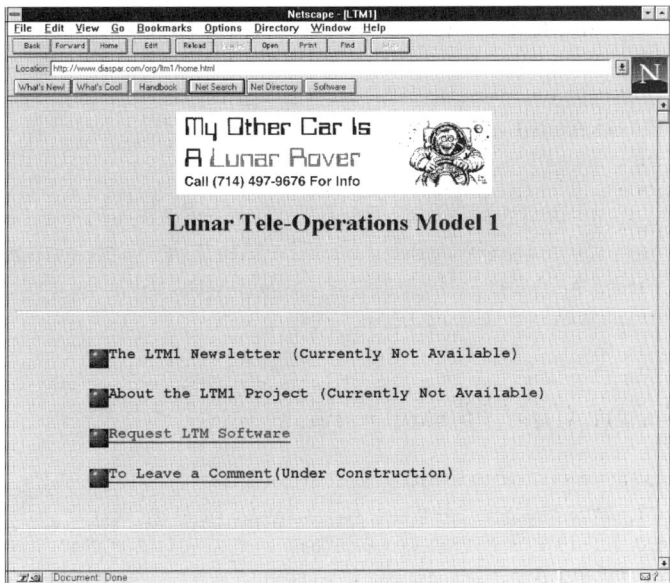

Figure 8.4 LTM1

for lunar exploration and development. Online meetings are usually held on Saturday evenings.

Take a drive on the moon! LTM1 has an operational model rover vehicle that you can control from your 386 or 486 PC. By downloading Diaspar's free software called Dmodem, you can receive live video images from a camera mounted on the LTM1 rover and control the vehicle. LTM1 is an experiment in low-cost home teleoperations, remote learning, and lunar base design.

Information about Virtual Networks

Virtual networks (V-Nets) are being added on Diaspar to meet the interests of members in various areas. Each V-Net has a system operator (sysop) that rents the V-Net from Diaspar for the purpose of conducting business in the V-Net. V-Nets are much like bulletin boards (bbs), except the sysop does not have to deal with owning hardware, software, and modems to run the bbs. So a V-Net is a way for someone who wants to provide information and products to Diaspar members to have an online office or store.

Diaspar currently has six V-Nets open to all members, and additional V-Nets are added periodically. The current list of V-Nets is as follows:

- Diaspar Lobby—system information and conference areas on virtual reality and events; file areas with Dmodem and POLY;
- LTM1—the Lunar Teleoperations Model 1;
- Planetary Society—the Online Planetary Society;
- Sense8—Sense8 virtual reality product support;
- Verdi—Verdi interactive product support;
- Precision Systems—online events and software products.

Getting Started

Cyberjunkies will be offered five hours of access on Diaspar at no charge on a one-time trial basis. This will give you "junkies" time to explore the system. After that, the basic cost to access the system is $1.00 per hour; there are no monthly membership fees to access many of the V-Nets. It is up to each V-Net sysop to charge a monthly membership fee if it wishes to. You will be advised in advance of any such charges, if applicable.

After subscribing, you will be given immediate access to the system to look around, on a read-only basis. You will also be able to download free software. It is suggested that you download Dmodem and use it with Diaspar (386 or 486 PC required). Then you can receive online graphics, sound, and video images—in live chat, by e-mail, and in posted conference messages. Without Dmodem, Diaspar appears as a typical text-based online system. With Dmodem, you can see graphics and video images—even take a drive on the moon by teleoperating a miniature lunar rover model vehicle.

When your account application has been processed, usually in less than a week, you will receive normal membership privileges. You may use the system immediately on a read-only basis, so do explore the system and download free software such as Dmodem—making online graphics and video available to you.

The next step in the process is the membership subscription procedure. It takes about five to ten minutes to read the information and fill out the online application. And first-time membership subscriptions get five hours of access at no charge—kind of a virtual test drive.

From Here

Now let's look at a prelude to the future development of VRML: multiuser domains (MUD) object-oriented (MOO) system. Chapter 9 discusses the architecture of the MOO-based HTML collaborative hypermedia system and its support for the emerging VRML standard.

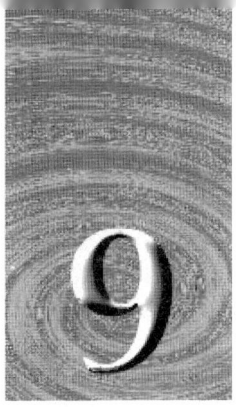

9

MOO-Based Collaborative Hypermedia System for WWW

This chapter describes the development of a networked collaborative hypermedia system intended to support groups of writers and scholars in writing and publishing hypertext fiction and criticism in a virtual reality environment. The current system supports the importation of individually developed Storyspace hypertext documents into a MUD-based (multiuser domains) collaborative workspace for integration and expansion and allows for the immediate publication of these dynamically generated multimedia documents with 3-D Web browsers. In addition, a forms-based writing and linking interface to the text is provided, so that writers use either the MUD-based or the forms-based authoring tools.

Since the HTML is generated dynamically from an underlying database, capabilities have been added to allow for user negotiation of content and bandwidth (only small virtual reality versions of the pictures, with the audio and text in German, with movies) and to provide the bandwidth-intensive media from distributed mirror sites. This system is being used by dozens of students, writers, and theorists around the world to support such projects as hypertext writing and theory classes at Brown and Vassar; a hypermedia version of a virtual reality feature-length film; WAX, or the discovery of television among the bees; a collaborative women's hypertext fiction-writing group; and the creation of an electronic journal to discuss the impact of technology on writing practice.

The World Wide Web has very quickly become one of the fundamental structures of the Internet. Although it provides a great deal of support for publishing information and navigating through it, it does not provide as much support for computer-supported collaborative work (CSCW)—where users can collectively write, annotate, and explore hypermedia documents.

A prototype system has been developed to support a collaborative virtual reality hypermedia writing space where users may write documents, annotate others' documents, engage in critical discussion, and have online classes or seminars. Although it was originally developed to support an undergraduate creative-writing class, it is now being used for film-based works and collaborative writing groups and as a reviewing system for refereed journals.

Hypermedia Models

The Dexter hypertext reference model (shown in Figure 9.1) describes a common set of abstractions found in hypertext systems— in order to both compare these systems and to develop interchange standards for them. Since this chapter describes the interactions among three complementary hypertext systems, the Dexter model will be used to highlight differences in the approaches taken by the various systems and the techniques used to convert among them.

However, since the Dexter model does not provide for the content-aware presentation of multimedia information, the Amsterdam hypertext model (AHM), shown in Figure 9.2, will also be used. This model represents multiple types of media information through the use of various channels and also is able to specify synchronization relationships among the various parts. Although the primary multimedia mechanism (typically Netscape or Mosaic) is not able to support synchronized multimedia information, and even though WWW does not even allow for the specification of temporal relationships, the information here will be described in terms of an ideal virtual reality

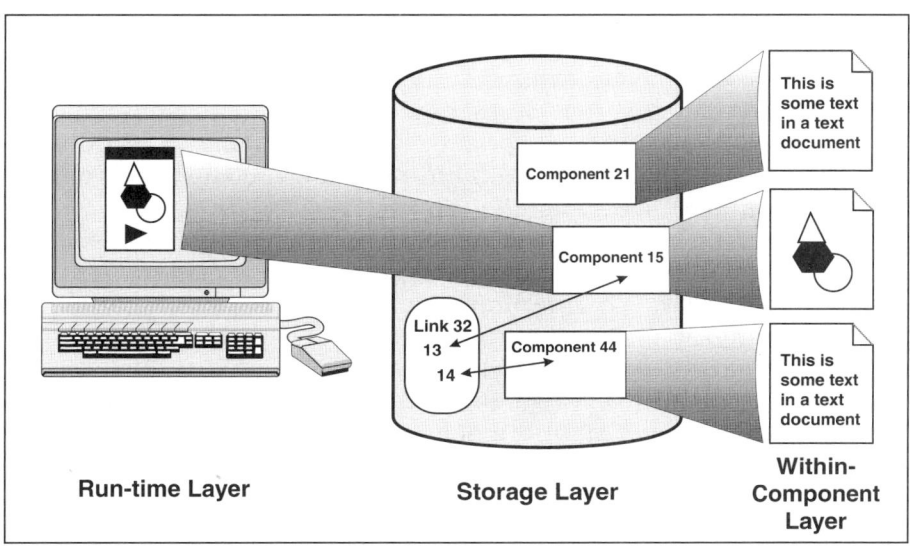

Figure 9.1 Dexter Hypertext Reference Model

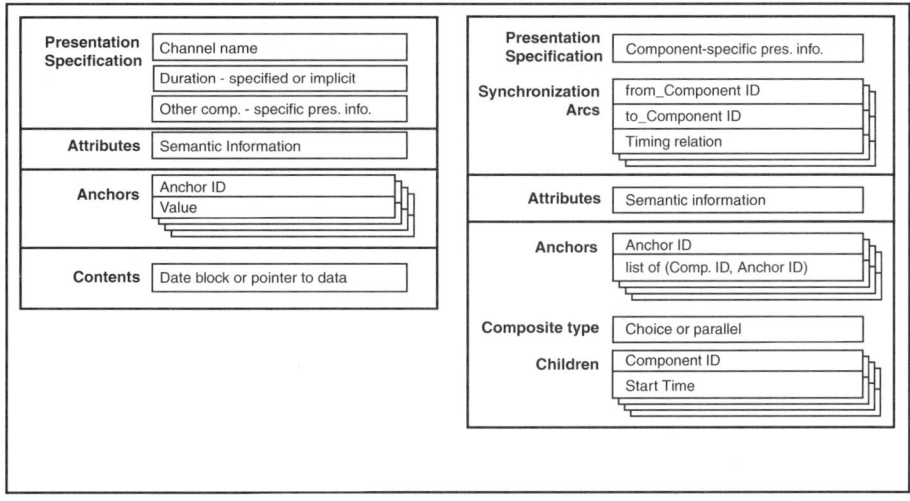

Figure 9.2 Amsterdam Hypertext Model

hypermedia implementation, not based on the limitations of any single environment.

The model used in the system consists of a central database that contains the text of each node, as well as additional information specifying the type, project info, and language of other multimedia information. This high-bandwidth multimedia information is typically stored at a number of distributed Web site servers on a per project basis. The centralized database contains low-bandwidth information (text and content coding) that is unlikely to change. On the other hand, the distributed multimedia servers contain high-bandwidth data (audio and video information) that will be modified much less frequently. At run time the central database server creates a specification of the text (based on current language and media preferences), with pointers to the multimedia information on the closest distributed server for that project. The model is a superset of the Dexter model but does not provide for the synchronization and timing relationships expressed by the AHM.

Storyspace

The Storyspace hypertext system was developed by writers who sought to build a tool that would encourage the process of writing and that would provide techniques useful in the creation of hypertext fiction. Storyspace uses guard fields, which provide for Boolean preconditions for following links. Many of the authors using Storyspace have used guard fields extensively in their writing, to provide for alternative narrative possibilities, based on what sections have previously been explored.

Storyspace has several interfaces for space (node) and link editing. These interfaces are based on the writer's preferred authoring style.

Publishing a read-only version of the text without any additional tools is easy. Several types of readers are available; they allow the user various levels of control and engagement with the text. However, they're not too overwhelming, with too complex an interface for the user.

Because of these features and because a number of early influential hypertext fictions were written in Storyspace (Michael Joyce's *Afternoon*), this system is now used by the majority of those writing hypertext fiction in academic environments. Eastgate Systems, the publisher of Storyspace, is also the primary publisher of texts written in the system and has a catalog of a few dozen titles, distributed primarily on floppy disk.

Storyspace is a classic hypertext system, providing for one-to-many and span-to-span unidirectional links. The primary part of the Storyspace system not covered under traditional hypertext models is the guard fields, which require a significant amount of user state.

Unfortunately Storyspace was originally intended to be a single-user and single-reader system. It provides only limited workgroup and versioning support and does not support simultaneous users on networked machines. The primary motivation in this work was to create a networked writing space with the narrative features of Storyspace, in order to encourage the creation of collaborative fiction.

MOO

MUDs, or multiuser domains, evolved out of multiplayer Adventure-style games in the early 1980s. These began as hack-and-slash-style games, but some of the MUDs began to evolve into more social areas, somewhat reminiscent of chat lines. Although many of the earlier systems relied on hard-coded behaviors, MUD systems began to incorporate internal scripting and virtual reality modeling languages. One particularly flexible Web site server, MOO (MUD object-oriented), is now being widely used by the research community to support collaborative work, due to the ease of modifying the virtual reality environment to support scholarship and sharing of information, as shown in Figure 9.3.

The MOO Web site server is distributed by Xerox PARC (Palo Alto Research Center) through its study of collaborative computer systems. Although a large number of MOOs are still devoted solely to socializing, MOO systems have been established at the MIT Media Lab (collaborative environment for media researchers), the University of Virginia (postmodern theorists), CalTech (astronomers) and the Weizmann Institute of Science in Israel (biologists).

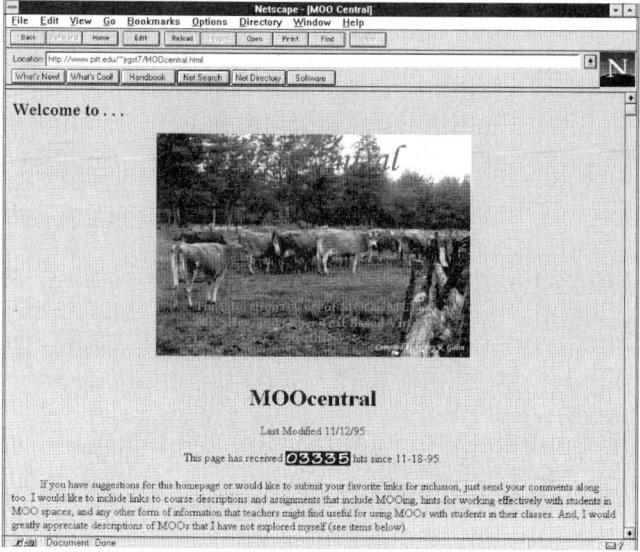

Figure 9.3 MOO

Hypertext in the MOO

It was apparent that the MOO system, could be easily modified to create a hypertext fictional VR environment, since the MOO architecture of rooms connected by various passages could correspond to the hypertext architecture of nodes connected by links. It seemed that it would be especially interesting to transform Storyspace documents into a MOO. This would keep the structural and narrative elements of the documents yet provide for the possibility of additional richness by the social environment. Writers could meet their readers in their text and engage in immediate dialogues with them, or writers could arrange to meet and work on collaborative works.

Creation of the Hypertext MOO

The creation of hypertext authoring tools in the MOO was straightforward, consisting of adding functionality to the generic rooms, exits, and players that already existed in the VR system. Because the MOO environment uses an interpreted object-oriented scripting language, the development of this part of the system was quite rapid.

Additionally, the import of the Storyspace documents into the MOO generally consisted of a one-to-one mapping between documents and rooms and between links and exits. A number of preexisting Storyspace documents were able to be imported into the system. Thus an immediate rich VR environment for authors to begin to work with was created.

Note that the interface to a MOO is quite primitive, since the software was designed to work through line-mode telnet. This means that the only interface is a command-line interface (even the editors are line editors). Since many of the standard MOO commands for building VR rooms and linking them are fairly arcane (@dig north,n to Room 211), the MOO interfaces are a bit difficult for a novice to learn, for example, since few computer users are accustomed to VR interfaces. In order to simplify the process of authoring hypertexts, all of the commonly used tools are written to consist of a one-word command. This in turn prompts the writer for as much additional information as necessary, by using simple menus.

Creating a WWW Site Server from the MOO

Within the past year, people at several MOOs have developed software that allows a MOO to serve as a WWW site server, responding to http requests and dynamically formatting the requested information. This is made especially easy due to the interpreted nature of the MOO language. The first MOO-based WWW server was developed at JaysHouseMOO. This MOO was devoted to exploring networking issues (a MOO-based gopher interface was also developed). Originally a modified version of the software was run. It ran an independent process that logs in as a character on the MOO and listens on another socket for http requests. Recently an integrated and modified version of the code has been developed at ChibaMOO. This code integrates the 3-D WWW site server very tightly into the MOO, without the necessity of an additional process to redirect the http requests. The VR graphical and multimedia capabilities of such WWW browsers as Netscape and Mosaic provide for a much more readable publishing medium than the early 1970s look that line mode telnet affords. However, there are many reasons to encourage the use of both interfaces. The MOO VR interface gives the user a great deal of programming control over the behavior of each node and also allows for real-time collaboration. Until a single viewer is developed with the best qualities of the two interfaces, the MOO version and the 3-D WWW version of the database will continue to be supported.

Dynamic Delivery of HTML Texts

All of the texts are stored internally to the MOO database, which consists of objects with methods and properties defined on them. The hypertexts are stored as texts marked up with an extended version of HTML. It's described here in more detail to provide for dynamic formatting of the data. This extended version of HTML is then parsed, all dynamic links are resolved, and it is then output as pure HTML.

Extensions to HTML

Three important extensions to HTML are provided. First is the specification of a generic media type, which allows for pictures at multiple possible resolutions. This occurs with client-based specification of the preferred data bandwidth—none of which standard http supports. It also allows for the user to specify that he or she would like to receive medium-sized pictures with video but without audio. Additionally, since the multimedia elements of the text are generally of a much higher bandwidth than the text, the specification of a number of large VR projects (WAXweb is an example of one such project) is allowed. Each of these projects has a set of mirror Web site servers defined for it. The server determines where the incoming request is coming from, and then points all the media references to the nearest server. Unfortunately, due to the present Internet name space, it is easy to determine the closest server only on a national level. Requests coming in from an address ending in .jp would be pointed to a mirror server in Japan, but it is difficult to distinguish between a .edu site in California and one in Maine.

Dynamic in-database virtual links are specified by using a dyn-link tag. This tag allows for the creation of floating links, and dynamic in-database links are specified using a dyn-link tag. This tag allows for the creation of floating virtual links and also provides for the maintenance of in-db state information passed through the URL. The state information is described later in the chapter.

Multiple-language support is provided through the <Q lang=> tag, which is defined as part of HTML+. The proposed definition of this tag, however, is primarily to guarantee that the language-specific layout conventions (hyphenation, text direction) are followed.

Adding State to WWW

There's a need to pass around a great deal of state to represent the current state of the reader. However, http is specified as a stateless mechanism for transferring hypertext. One common solution to this problem is to include the state as part of the URL associated with each link. This is not an incredibly clean solution to the problem of maintaining state. Since the state of a session could become arbitrarily complex with the inclusion of guard-field information, it is currently used quite heavily in the following situations:

- Authentication keys containing the current user and an encrypted password. Once a user is authenticated, he or she is able to access the authoring tools that require special privileges, and the database is able to keep track of more internal state describing a given user's preferred authoring modes or the user's bookmarks. Additionally, this allows tracking of the ownership of virtual links and nodes.
- The desired bandwidth level. This is where the information is stored about whether to display pictures, audio, or video to the user in a VR environment.
- The current language. The preferred language the user would like to use for text and audio is passed around.
- The current state of the user interface. A number of different interfaces may be opened or closed at any given time. The state between nodes should be maintained. These interfaces are described in greater detail later in the chapter.
- The support for guard fields. Although guard fields are not presently used, the information describing them on the individual nodes from Storyspace has been imported. This may be a feature that will be added to the state information that's stored, as documents are imported that make more extensive use of guards.

Forms-Based Authoring Tools

Most current implementations of 3-D Web viewers allow for the use of forms, which let an encapsulated user interface be included as part of the hypermedia content. Although the client deals with simple interaction, such as pop-up option menus, the 3-D WWW site server is responsible for handling updates from the forms. A number of expandable forms-based tools have been added VR authoring interface to the MOO. These include:

- modifying the current media defaults, including the level of VR picture detail, the types of media, and the current language for the text and audio;
- displaying authorship info, including the original creator of the text and a list of those who have added to it;
- showing comments and adding one's own to the text;
- adding and deleting bookmarks, and going to a specified bookmark;
- adding links to the text, and creating new nodes; and
- editing the text of nodes one owns.

The first three interfaces are available to any reader of the text. Only registered users are able to add bookmarks and VR links to the text. At the moment, a user can only edit text that he or she owns, although any registered user can add VR links between texts.

Security Issues

Although mechanisms for secure user authentication in the WWW are being developed, they currently allow for authentication for only a single document, due to the stateless nature of the protocol. Since one would rather not have the need for the reader to continually type in his or her password to be able to edit a set of pages, an authentication key has been added to the state passed around in the URL. At the moment, this consists of the user's account name (unique for the database) and an encrypted version of the password.

Consideration was given to making this encrypted password act as a token. However, it would be valid for only a short length of time—possibly a day. That way, users wouldn't be able to impersonate other users for more than a short period of time. However, this would make it difficult to take advantage of the current hotlist features of Mosaic or Netscape. Since this has also been confusing to users—it hasn't been done.

Currently the possibility of using a public-key cryptosystem to provide for a more secure interface is being explored. Of course, the consequences of a user impersonating another user of the system are fairly minor, limited to the ability to edit that user's texts. However, as this system is used for more important applications, security will become a critical issue.

Applications

The Hypertext Virtual Hotel was begun by the Hypertext Fiction Workshop at Brown University in 1991, using Intermedia, and ported to Storyspace in 1993. This historic collaborative document has been imported into the VR system. There it has continued to be extended and written on by writing students. The Storyspace version has also been added to. In addition, other people have written in the text and incorporated it with the other, newer areas of the VR system.

WAXweb is a hypermedia version of the VR film, WAX, or the discovery of television among the bees. This VR film was the first independent feature film edited using a nonlinear editing system. It was also the first film to be broadcast over the mbone (multimedia backbone) of the Internet. Originally the text of the film was to be put onto the Hypertest MOO to support a collaborative VR project in which 25 writers, filmmakers and theorists from around the world would add to the text of the movie and create a large body of associated hypertexts based on the film. The current project, which was premiered as part of The Edge at SIGGRAPH 94, consists of the script of the film, about 600 pages of supplementary text material; 2000 stills (one for each shot in the film); 600 MPEG-compressed video segments; and the entire audio of the film in English, French, German, and Japanese. This work has become the driving application for adding hypermedia functionality to the system.

Hi-Pitched Voices (a women's collaborative hypertext fiction working group) has been the most prolific part of the Hypertext MOO. This group was started to explore models of women's writing on the Net.

Another group, RhetNet, has also recently begun to use the Hypertext MOO to prepare a refereed electronic journal of technology and rhetoric. This group also held an online panel in the system, as part of the electronic version of the Computers and Writing conference.

WAXweb

Since WAXweb was the motivating application for the development of the 3-D WWW-based viewing and authoring tools, this section explores its structuring and artistic goals in greater detail. The media composition of the film WAX depends on a paradigm that might be described as anything, in any order, at any time. The film has no dialogue but instead a narrator who delivers much of the story through voiceover. This fact, combined with the film's natural resemblance to hypertext and the need for audience assembly, made it a natural retrofit into a constructive hypertext.

WAXweb began as an experiment in hypermedia authoring, trying to remove the time base from the film and increasing the number of pointers. The construction of the work began by developing a base layer of 600 nodes, roughly corresponding to each spoken line in the film's monologue. In each node, accompanying the text of the monologue, is the MPEG video and the audio of that scene. Additionally, each node contains stills (about 2000 total) representing each shot used in the video for that node. Each still has a commentary by the filmmaker. The entire text is also provided in video via English, French, German, and Japanese.

The base layer has several large-scale indexing structures:

- the linear path, which connects each node with the one immediately following it in the film;
- a tree structure, which establishes each node in its proper position in the act/scene hierarchy;
- shot overview maps such that clicking on an active still takes you to an index of similar pictures in the film (all the other pictures of hands);
- textual thematic paths; the text of the film has embedded links between words corresponding to the overall themes of the film (the path through all the instances of the word darkness);

- A random index, which consists of a page filled with Xs, each connected to a random starting point in the film.

Through a combination of these navigational techniques, it is expected that the reader will be able to understand the ideas expressed in WAX. So far, readers who have seen WAX as a film have reacted quite positively to experiencing it as a hypertext.

Future Work

A documented version of the Web site server for public use in the near future is planned for release with well-defined standard node types and more powerful workgroup functionality. Additional hypermedia projects are being planned and supported. Artists and critics are being sought who would like to explore their own ideas of hypermedia structures within a collaborative VR networked system.

Support for the emerging VRML standard is being planned in order to support a 3-D version of WAXweb. In the initial implementation 3-D models developed during the creation of WAXweb are also planned for use.

An integrated interface will be provided to the combined system, possibly by combining a Netscape- or Mosaic-like interface with a live stream of telnet data. Other groups are currently developing such tools. Additional issues that should be explored with a new system are as follows:

- Distributed hypermedia databases. At the moment, the architecture of the MOO system does not allow for multiple dynamic mirror sites of the same database.
- Scalability. Any global collaborative hypermedia system should be capable of supporting thousands or millions of simultaneous users. Distributing the database would help considerable with this problem.
- Guaranteed media delivery rates. This would allow for separate storage of synchronized video and audio in many languages and ensure a rapid and consistent delivery to the user.
- The additional collaborative 3-D media tools. Many of the current mbone tools would prove useful to this system, and work in this area is in progress in the Jupiter system.

Summary

The prototype CSCW system described in this chapter provides an interesting direction for further work in networked hypermedia systems. In particular, work still needs to be done on ensuring rapid interaction and time-critical display of 3-D multimedia information in a VR environment.

From Here

Chapter 10 consists of a brief discussion on cyberspace. The chapter outlines the requirements for VR architectures that can fully visualize 3-D Web environments. It also proposes solutions to the issues raised by these requirements.

Cyberspace

At least once a day, somebody in the Silicon Graphics Open Inventor group has a great idea. The following story is told by Rikk Carey[1] from inside the pits of Silicon Graphics Open Inventor Engineering. It's a short story about stumbling into cyberspace with an idea that didn't get away—VRML!

Sushi Lunch

"It all started last summer during one of our Thursday Open Inventor lunches. A bunch of the Silicon Graphics Inventor engineers were taking their shoes off at Yakko's Japanese Restaurant, when Gavin Bell[2] asked, 'Rikk,[3] ever heard of VRML?' I snapped back, 'Read this.' We ordered our food and sat in silence, drinking green tea, secretly waiting for the other to give in.

---

[1] Rikk Carey, Silicon Graphics, Inc., Visual Magic Division, nikk@sgi.com, 1995.
[2] Gavin Bell, Silicon Graphics, Inc., Visual Magic Division, gavin@sgi.com, 1994.
[3] Rikk Carey, op. cit.

"Eventually, I broke down and offered, 'Okay, smarty pants, what's VRML?' With a satisfied grin and a mouthful of unagi, Gavin described a movement on the WWW to define a language for connecting 3-D worlds onto the World Wide Web. He said that two guys, Mark Pesce (The Community Company)[4] and Brian Behlendorf (WIRED Magazine[5]), were spearheading the idea by posting messages and asking for help in defining a common language for describing 3-D objects and worlds for the WWW. They had a bunch of ideas and vision on where 3-D and the WWW should be heading but were looking for help on the technical details of the 3-D language.

"Ok, back to the sushi. Gavin then said that he had been thinking about 3-D on the Web for some time and wanted to get involved. I patiently explained to Gavin how this would never work. 'Nobody really cares about getting 3-D on the Web', I laughed with confidence. 'Second, we don't have time for this! Third . . .'

"But Gavin persisted. By the time we were done with lunch, I was a believer. Things took off quickly from there. Later that day, I saw my boss, Way Ting, in the hallway and asked, 'Way, ever heard of VRML?' Way shook his head. I quickly took advantage of the opportunity and informed him, 'Gosh, Way, you really need to be reading news more often.' With an engineer's smile, I told him that he would be hearing about it soon."

The Wheels Start Rolling

"Gavin immediately drafted a proposal for VRML V1.0. He based it on a subset of the Open Inventor 3-D Metafile format. Within a couple of weeks or so, his proposal was published on the Web. Reviews, raves, and flames came in immediately. The debate had begun!

"In the following weeks, we finally met in person with the primary troublemakers, Mark and Brian. Once again, it was an Open Inventor Thursday lunch that got us all together. We met at Thai City Restaurant in Palo Alto (excellent Panang Chicken) and started with a round of Thai iced tea. We quickly discovered that Mark has an assortment of amazing ideas and applications of VRML and is quite serious about making cyberspace a reality. Brian complements Mark with his pragmatic,

---

[4] Mark Pesce, The Community Company, mpesce@netcom.com, 1994.
[5] Brian Behlendorf, WIRED Magazine, brian@wired.com, 1994.

down-to-earth, get-it-done style. Both Mark and Brian are dedicated to the idea of building a VRML that is open and available. We discovered, over Pad Thai noodles, that we shared many of the same visions and goals and that we needed to work together. Mark and Brian made it clear that this was an open, public debate and that it was up to the www-vrml mail group to develop a consensus (and no amount of coconut ice cream would make a difference).

"Mark and Brian faithfully moderated the proposals and debates on the www-vrml e-mailing list. The variety of proposals on the table turned into a fierce debate, but Gavin's Open Inventor–based proposal had the strongest support. Gavin then began working with Tony Paris[6] on the final version, VRML V1.0 Specification. Mark, Tony, and Gavin announced VRML on October 1994 at the WWWF 94."

The Hard Part

"OK, so now that people were agreeing on the VRML language, we needed to get to work. The first thing we needed to do was find a volunteer to write the public domain VRML parser. Paul Strauss,[7] who is known for his eagerness to jump in at short notice and as the original architect of Open Inventor (among other things), volunteered for the job (well, sort of). Paul quickly cranked out a public domain reader for VRML, OvLib: Source Code for a VRML Parser. He named it 'QVLib' (a name so awful, Paul was sure somebody would rename it but nobody did). Mark Pesce took this and made it available to the public. It was then ported to Sun OS, LINUX, and Windows NT (coming soon to Macintosh and Solaris). This was ready in January 1995 and has enabled others to write their own VRML viewers.

"After that, we realized that maybe we should be writing a VRML viewer (brilliant!). At this point, Robert Weideman[8] of Template Graphics Software suggested that Silicon Graphics and Template Graphics work together on providing a publicly available VRML viewer that runs on a variety of platforms. (BTW: This is when I realized that we were on a runaway train. At this point, the phone started ringing, my voicemail filled up, and my mailbox was bursting with messages—all with

---

[6] Toni Parisi, The Community Company, dagobert.netcom.com, 1994.

[7] Paul Strauss, Silicon Graphics, Inc., Visual Magic Division, pss@sgi.com, 1994.

[8] Robert Weideman, Template Graphics Software, 1994.

questions on VRML.) All of this led to David Mott[9] (with lots of help from other Inventors) furiously writing WebSpace: A VRML Viewer *and the creation of a variety of VRML worlds."*

Future

"I will read news more frequently. I will listen carefully to everyone's lunch-time ideas. I will increase my voicemail limit (yippee!). And we'll continue to participate in the evolution of VRML, as well as to build really cool products that connect us to Cyberspace . . . ."

This story, as told by Rikk Carey, describes a visualization tool for the WWW: Labyrinth—which uses the WWW and a newly defined protocol, Cyberspace Protocol (CP)—to visualize and maintain a uniform definition of objects, scene arrangement, and spatiolocation that is consistent across all of the Internet. Several technologies have been invented to handle the scaling problems associated with widely shared spaces, including a distributed Web site server methodology for resolving spatial requests. Virtual Reality Modeling Language (VRML) was introduced as a beginning proposal for WWW visualization.

The emergence, in 1991, of the World Wide Web added a new dimension of accessibility and functionality to the Internet. For the first time, Internet users and programmers both could access all of the various types of services (FTP, Gopher, Telnet, etc.) through a consistent and abstract mechanism. In addition, the WWW added two new services: a rapid file-transfer mechanism and a universal locator mechanism for a data set resident anywhere within the Internet's domain.

The first major consequence of the presence of the WWW on the Internet has manifested itself in an explosion in the usability of datasets within it. This is directly correlatable to the navigability of these datasets. In other words, the Internet is useful (and will be used) to the degree that it is capable of conforming to requests made of it. The WWW has made the Internet navigable—where it was not before, except in the most occult and hermetic manner. It added a universal organization to the data within it. Through the WWW, all eight million

---

[9] David Mott, Silicon Graphics, Inc., Visual Magic Division, mott@sgi.com, 1994.

Internet hosts are treated as a single, unified data source. All of the data is treated as a single, albeit complexly structured, document.

It would appear that the WWW, as a phenomenon, has induced two other processes to begin. The first is an upswing in the amount of traffic on the Internet (1993 WWW traffic was 3000 times greater than in 1992!). The second is a process of organization—where the data available on Internet is being restructured—tailored to fit within the WWW. This is a clear example of the medium is the message as the presence of a new medium, the WWW, forces a reconfiguration of all preexisting media into it. This organization is occurring at right angles to the previous form of organization. That is to say, previously the Internet appeared as a linear source—a unidimensional stream. Now the Internet is an arbitrary linkage of documents in at least two dimensions (generally defined as pages). Fitting the organizational skills most common to Western civilization, this structure is often hierarchical, with occasional exceptions. Most rare are anti-hierarchical documents that are not intrinsically confusing.

Navigability in a purely symbolic domain has limits. The amount of depth present in a subject before it exceeds human capacity for comprehension (and hence navigation) is finite and relatively limited. Humans, however, are superb visualizers, holding within their craniums the most powerful visualization tool known. Human beings navigate in three dimensions; we are born to it. With the exception of cases due to severe organic damage, humans have a comprehensive ability to spatially locate and organize spatially.

It seems reasonable to propose that the WWW should be extended, bringing its conceptual model from two dimensions (out at a right angle) into three. To do this, two things are required: extensions to HTML to describe both geometry and space, and a unified representation of space across the Internet. This chapter proposes solutions to both of these issues and describes a WWW client built on them, called Labyrinth, which visualizes WWW as a space.

Visualization and VRML

As of this writing, HTML is capable of expressing both textual and pictorial data and can provide some limited formatting features for each of them. Beyond this, it provides a linkage mechanism to express the connection between datasets. HTML's roots are in text; its parent,

SGML, specifies a format for printed media, an expression that is intrinsically two-dimensional. For this reason, users have stepped outside of HTML in their language specifications for geometry and place, defining a simple, easily parsed scripting language for the generation of objects and spaces.

The basic functionality for any three-dimensional language interface to WWW is broken into three parts: *object definitions*, which include the definitions of the geometric representations for these objects; *scene definitions*, which define placement of these objects inside of a larger context; and a mechanism that binds a URL to an object within a scene. The current revision of Labyrinth's Virtual Reality Modeling Language (VRML), although unsophisticated, does fulfill all of these requirements. It also provides all of the basic functionality required in a fully visualized WWW client.

As currently defined, Labyrinth's VRML files are a unique data type, such as MPEG or AIFF. They must be integrated with MIME in order to launch a companion viewer. This is not an optimal solution, but it should be possible to extend HTML to encapsulate spatial data types. These data types could then be visualized or ignored, given the capabilities of the WWW client. The OpenGL, Open Inventor, or HOOPS specifications could form a basis. Insofar as object definitions are concerned for HTML extensions, it should be examined as a possible (and well-supported) solution to this issue. The scripting language should serve as a starting example rather than a proposal for an all-inclusive solution.

Any conceptualization of space contains within it, implicitly, the quality of number (how much or how far is contained within the simple expression of existence). Space, in its electronic representation, is numbered. If it is to be shared by billions of simultaneous participants, it must be consistent, unique, and very large/dense. Despite this, it is rarely necessary for a WWW client to deal with the totality of space. Operations occur local to the position of the WWW viewer, and this local description of space is nearly always a great deal more constrained than the entire spatial representation.

It is necessary for VRML to define a numbering system for visualization that conforms to the three principles outlined. Another section of this chapter describes such a system.

Cyberspace

For the purposes of continuity in navigation, it is necessary to create a unified conceptualization of space spanning the entire Internet—a spatial equivalent of WWW. This has been called cyberspace—in the sense that it has at least three dimensions. But it exists only as a consensual hallucination on the part of the hosts and users participating within it. There is only one cyberspace, just as there is only one WWW. To imply multiplicity is to defeat the objective of unity.

At its fundamental level, cyberspace is a map that is maintained between a regular spatial topology and an irregular network topology. The continuity of cyberspace implies nothing about the Internet work on which it exists. Cyberspace is complete abstraction, divorced at every point from concrete representation. All of the examples used in the following explanation of the algorithmic nature of cyberspace are derived from the implementation of a system—developed for TCP/IP and the Internet—that conforms to this basic principle.

Metrics in Cyberspace

The Internet defines an address space for its hosts, specifying these addresses as 32-bit numbers, expressed in dotted octet notation, where the general form is {s.t.u.v}. Into this unidimensional address space, cyberspace places a map of N dimensions (N-3 in the canonical, Gibsonian cyberspace under discussion here), so that any place is uniquely identified by the tuple {x.y.z}.

In order to ensure sufficient volume and density within cyberspace, it is necessary to use a numbering system that has a truly vast dynamic range. A system of address elements has been developed where each element contains a specific portion of the entire expressible dynamic range in the form {p.x.y.z}, where p is the place value, and x, y, and z are the metrics for each dimension. The address element is currently implemented as a 32-bit construct, so the range of p is ±127, and x, y, and z, are unsigned octets. Address elements may be concatenated to any level of resolution desired, because most operations in cyberspace occur within a constrained context of 32 bits. At most, 64 bits are sufficient to express the vast majority of interactions. This gives the numbering system the twin benefits of wide dynamic range and compactness. Compactness is an essential quality in a networked environment. This is only one possible numbering scheme. Other numbering schemes may be developed that conform to the principles as given, perhaps more effectively.

Cyberspace has now been given a universal, unique, dense numbering system. It is now possible to quantify it. The first quantification is that of existence (metrics). The second quantification is that of content. Content is not provided by cyberspace itself but rather by the participants within it. The only service cyberspace needs to provide is a binding between a spatial descriptor and a host address. This is described by the function: $\{f(s)= >a\}$, where s is a spatial identifier, and a is an internetwork address. This is the essential mathematical construction of cyberspace.

Implementation of Cyberspace Protocol

If cyberspace is reducible to a simple function, it is expressed through a transaction-based protocol, whereby every request yields a reply, even if that reply is AE. In the implementation under examination, Cyberspace Protocol (CP) is implemented through a straightforward client-server mechanism, in which there are very few basic operations: registration, investigation, and deletion.

In the registration process, a cyberspace client announces to a Web site server that it has populated a volume of space. In this sense, cyberspace does not exist until it is populated: This is a corollary to Benedict's Principle of Indifference, which states that absence from cyberspace will have a cost.

The investigation process will be discussed in detail later in this chapter. The basic transaction is simple: Given a circumscribed volume of space, return a set of all hosts that contribute to it. The reply to such a transaction could be NULL or practically infinite. Consider the case in which the request specifies a volume that describes the entirety of cyberspace. This implies that level of detail must be implemented within the transaction (and hence within registration) in order to optimize the process of investigation. Often it is enough to know that cyberspace is populated—nothing more. Many other times it is enough to know only the gross features of the landscape, not the particularities of it. In this sense level of detail is a quality intrinsic to cyberspace.

Registration contains within it the investigation process. Before a volume is registered successfully, permission must be received from cyberspace itself. This must include an active collaboration and authentication process with whatever other hosts help to define the volume. It is also an enforcement of the rule that forbids interpenetration of objects within the physical world. It need not be enforced, but unless it is observed in most situations, cyberspace will tend toward being intrinsically disorienting.

Finally, the deletion process—the logical inverse of the registration process—is when a volume defined by a client is removed from cyberspace. These three basic transactions form the core of CP, as implemented between the client and the Web site server.

Cyberspace Web Site Servers

Cyberspace is a unified whole. From a transaction-oriented point of view, every Web site server must behave exactly like any other server (specifically with respect to investigation requests). The same requests should evoke the same responses. This would appear to imply that every server must comprehend the totality of cyberspace, a requirement that is functionally beyond any computer yet. Otherwise, it places a severe restriction on the total content of cyberspace. Both of these constraints are unacceptable. A methodology to surmount these constraints must be incorporated into the cyberspace Web site server implementation.

The cyberspace Web site server is implemented as a three-dimensional database with at least three implemented operations: insertion, deletion, and search. These correspond to the registration, deletion, and investigation transactions. Each element within the database is composed of at least three items of data: the volumetric identifier of the space, the IP address of the host that manifests within that space and the IP address of the cyberspace server through which it is registered.

The investigation transaction is the core of the Web site server implementation. Cyberspace servers use a repeated, refined query mechanism. The mechanism interactively narrows the possible range of servers capable of affirmatively answering an investigation request until the set exactly conforms to the volumetric parameters of the request. This set of servers contains the entire possible list of hosts that collaborate in creating some volume of cyberspace. It will return a nonnull reply to an investigation request for a given volume of space.

An assumption implicit in the investigation algorithm is that investigative searches have depth—in other words, that investigation is not performed to its exhaustive limit but to some limit determined by both client and Web site server, based on the importance of the request. Registrations, on the other hand, must be performed exhaustively but can (and should) occur asynchronously. The primary side effect of this methodology is that cyberspace is not instantaneous, but is bounded by bandwidth, processor capacity, and level of detail. This is in the form $\{c = bp / \int dor.p(r,l)\}$, where c is a constant (the speed limit of cyberspace (as c is the speed of light in physical space); l is the level of detail, b is bandwidth of the internetwork, p is processor capacity, d is the number of dimensions of the cyberspace, and r is the position within the space. The function rho (o) defines the density of a volume of cyberspace under examination. This expression is intended to describe the primary relationships among the elements that create cyberspace. It is not mathematically rigorous.

Finally, because cyberspace Web site servers do not attempt to contain the entirety of cyberspace but rather search through it (based on client transaction requests), the content of a cyberspace server is determined entirely by the requests made to it by its clients. One way to visualize the operation of cyberspace Web site servers is with the metaphor of Indra's Net from Vedanta Hinduism—finely woven of glittering jewels, each jewel reflecting every other.

Cyberspace and the World Wide Web

Having defined, specified, and implemented an architecture that provides a binding between spatiolocation and dataset location, this architecture needs to be integrated with the existing WWW libraries so that their functionality is similarly extended. As location is being augmented by the addition of CP to WWW, it is the universal resource locator that must be extended to incorporate these new capabilities.

The URL, in its present definition, has three parts: an access identifier (type of service), a host name (specified as either an IP address or a DNS-resolvable name), and a file name, which is really more of a message passed along to the host at the point of service. CP fits well into this model, with two exceptions: multiple hosts that collaborate on a space, and the identification of a filename associated with a registered volume of space. A new URL of the following form is proposed, where {pn...} is a set of CP address elements:

cs://{pa.x.y.z} {pb.x.y.z}.../filename

Resolution of this URL into a dataset is a two-stage process: First, the client CP mechanism must be used to translate the given spatiolocation into a host address; then the request must be sent to the host address. Two issues arise here: multiple host addresses, as mentioned previously; and a default access mechanism for CP. If a set of host addresses is returned by CP, a request must be sent to each specified host; otherwise, the description of the space will be incomplete. Ideally, all visualized WWW clients will implement a threaded execution mechanism (with reentrant WWW libraries) so that these requests can occur simultaneously and asynchronously.

A default access mechanism for CP within WWW must be selected. HTTP has been selected for two reasons: It is efficient, and it is available at all WWW site servers. Nonetheless this is not a closed issue. It may make sense to allow for some variety of access mechanisms or perhaps a fallback mechanism. If one service is not present at a host, another attempt, on another service, could be made.

Labyrinth

It is now possible, from the previous discussion, to describe the architecture and operation of a fully visualized WWW client. It is composed of several pieces: WWW libraries with an integrated CP client interface; an interpreter for a VRML-derived language that describes object geometry, placement, and linkage; and a user interface that presents a navigable window on the Web.

The operation of the client is very straightforward, as is the case of the other WWW clients. After launching, the client queries the space at home and then loads the world as the axis mundi of the client's view of the Web. As a user moves through cyberspace, the client makes requests, through CP, to determine the content of all spaces passed through or looked on. A great deal of design effort needs to be put into the development of look-ahead caching algorithms for cyberspace viewers. Without the algorithms, the user will experience a discontinuous, jerky trip through cyberspace.

At this time, visualized objects in WWW have only two possible behaviors: no behavior at all or linkage through an attached URL to another dataset. This linkage could be to another world (actually another place in cyberspace), which is called a portal; or it could link to another data type, in which case the client must launch the appropriate viewer. Labyrinth is designed to augment the functionality of existing WWW viewers, such as NCSA Mosaic and Netscape. Labyrinth does not need a well-integrated facility for viewing other types of HTML documents.

Data Abstraction Protocols

As a specific implementation of a general theory that has implications well beyond WWW, CP is the solution in three dimensions of an N-dimensional practice for dataset location abstraction. Data abstraction places a referent between the name of a dataset locator and the physical location. It allows physical dataset location to become mutable.

If an implementation were to be developed for the case where $N=1$, it would be an effective replacement of the Internet's domain name service (DNS), which maintains a static mapping of names to IP addresses. Any network that used a dynamic abstraction mechanism could mirror or reassign hosts on a continuous basis (assuming that all write-through mirroring could be maintained by the hosts themselves). The reassignment of the hosts takes place so that the selection of a host for a transaction could be made based on criteria that would tend to optimize the performance of the network from the perspective of the transaction. It would also be easy to create a dataset that could follow its user(s), thus adjusting its location dynamically in response to changes in the physical location or connectivity of the user. In an age of wireless, worldwide networking, this could be a very powerful methodology.

Summary

This chapter attempts to outline the requirements for architectures that can fully visualize WWW and proposes solutions to the issues raised by these requirements. Although much further study needs to be done, this chapter is meant to serve as a starting point for an understanding of the subtleties of wide-area, distributed, visualized datasets.

Labyrinth and Cyberspace Protocol are logical extensions to the World Wide Web and the Internet. Indeed, without the existence of WWW, neither would be very useful immediately. They would operate but would lack content. Individuals would hardly be compelled to either use them or adapt their existing data sets to realize their new potentials. Used together, they work to make both the WWW and the Internet inherently more navigable. This is because they help to make the Internet more human-centered, adapting datasets to human capabilities rather than vice versa. It's also the single largest contribution that virtual reality research has offered to the field of computing: a human-centered design approach that lowers or erases the barriers to usage by creating user-interface paradigms that serve humans to the full of their potential.

Finally, network visualization marks the end of the first age of networking, in which protocols, services, and infrastructure dominated the discourse within the field. In the second age of networking, questions like data architecture and the inherent navigability of a well-designed dataset become infinitely more important than first-age questions. Where or how do I find what I'm looking for becomes more relevant than where did it come from.

From Here

Chapter 10 has laid the foundation for implementing real 3-D environments on the Internet. The next chapter provides an overview of the implementation of these environments as users create their own VRML Web sites. Part II of the book, which includes Chapters 11 to 14, will continue the theme of Chapter 11 by throughly explaining how users can create and implement virtual realitry applications on the Internet via the VRML standard.

Part II

Implementing the Future

VRML Architecture Group (VAG)

The VRML Architecture Group (VAG), as described in Chapter 2, is the official organization tasked with extending the VRML specification into what we all want—a scalable, fully interactive cyberspace. The VAG researchers will be participating directly in VRML futures meetings. Let's look at some of the research work that has been developed by VAG for implementation in future VRML standard releases.

Beyond VRML

This part of the chapter outlines a direction for VRML, based on trends and directions found in the rapidly forming 3-D graphics and networking markets. This discussion is intended as a guide in the development of interactive 3-D technology, not a hard or concrete platform on which to stand. Given that many such proposals exist, the final VRML solution will undoubtedly be a mixture of many technologies. The focus here is to outline priorities, reveal problems with VRML and provide some solutions, propose additions to the specification in the short term; and, finally, make some comments about the future.

Priorities

This is one of the most important aspects of the standard development process. Many companies and industries are already investing large amounts of time and resources to VRML technology. A standards group must be able to clearly state its intentions. An ordering of priorities is paramount when trying to develop a technology baseline, and it should be one of the first orders of business when defining the new VRML specification.

Additional work needs to be done in many areas. Because there are so many complicated issues, the areas listed here represent only what is thought to be of importance to VRML's future. By no means is this list complete.

- *Object references*—Attention needs to be given to how to name nodes.
- *Behaviors*—Many proposals already exist in this area.
- *Sound*—Again, proposals exist here as well.
- *Physics*—Another area is realistic object behavior. A physical object contains data that represents its physical properties. State changes in the object result from force and movement vectors applied from a previous event, as well as any new forces. At the end of simulation frame, the physics system will resolve the forces into object velocities and then into positions and orientations. Attachments points are needed. Would springs also be good to have? Also, the whole issue of collision detection must be determined. Without a fast and accurate algorithm, this can be a very difficult problem.
- *Networking*—Simple object position and orientation with very basic first, order approximation, broadcasting, multicast and point-to-point, global time, timestamped messages, and channels for multiple simultaneous simulations are needed.
- *Standard texture file formats such as* (raw, jpg, mpg, avi are needed).[1]

---

[1] Brian Blau, VRML 1.X and Beyond-Proposal Mania; Cyberspace Development, Autodesk, Inc., August 20, 1995.

There seems to be a clear distinction between trying to fix the current problems and specify what will happen in the future. It is obvious that the problems that exist today can be fixed, and that should be a clear focus of future VRML-a-Thon. Once that is in place, the industry will come forth with additional changes and recommendations. Capturing those ideas will become VRML V1.1. Finally, serious work needs to be done if VRML's basic architecture is going to be changed. That cannot possibly happen in a short amount of time if VRML stands a chance of becoming a standard picked up by the ISO or IEEE.

Changes to VRML Document

Reviewing the VRML document revealed several problems. Language problems are numerous. Only the most obvious will be listed. Many of the nodes have incomplete descriptions of properties. The many references to familiar notations and concepts need to be solidified and made concrete.

The VRML document should stand alone, with no other source of reference needed. As it exists now, one must purchase the series of Open Inventor books, published by Addison-Wesley, to fully understand the VRML technical specification. Even then SGI's WebSpace must be tested manually to fully understand the meaning of some properties. This will simply not work for the long run.

The specification should not contain any examples because an example shows only one case when there are typically many. If there are any questions about a field or value, the limits and scope should be explicitly stated.

A list of specific changes needed follows:

- The term "sensualized" from the Mission Statement section is misleading and needs to be revised.
- In the Language Basics section the node name is defined as a string that contains different kinds of symbols. It does not mention the # character (formally called an octothorp), and it really should.
- SFBitMask contains an obscure sentence. These names vary in this field for the node classes.

- In SFColor the term "scientific notation" is used without any reference. Which of the many scientific-notation standards does this reference?
- The SFImage basic scheme is three 8-bit numbers. This needs to be spelled out explicitly. SFMatrix needs to be fully explained.
- In the LOD section the statement "world-space eyepoint" is mentioned. This should be reworded to simply the camera or viewpoint.
- The cameras (orthographic and perspective) are lacking a complete description. How are the position and orientation fields used? What is the focal distance used (for the look-at point)? There needs to be a hither and-yon-value for the perspective camera. This node needs a complete description of how cameras should work. See the proposed camera nodes following.
- The scope of the Translate, Rotate, Scale, and Transform nodes must be spelled out explicitly. There is no way to determine the transformation order from the document.
- The Instancing section lists three spheres in one place and refers to two spheres in another, all using the same example.
- The Cube's default orientation must be specified. Which direction (or axis alignment) are the width, height, and depth? Possibly rename the fields; width becomes *x*dim, height becomes *y*dim, and depth becomes *z*dim.
- Explicitly state the meaning of the fields in the Material node (see proposed material node following). The emissiveColor field is misleading.
- Explicitly state the meaning of the properties in the SpotLight node. The dropOffRate and cutOffAngle are not specified.
- Lights are specified so that any one light may not illuminate some faces. This is difficult if not impossible for many renderers. Either remove this restriction or add a Boolean property to each light node that says whether it is to follow this rule.
- Under Browser Consideration/File Extensions, spell VRML correctly.[2]

---

[2] *Ibid.*

Nodes

Now let's look at proposals for new nodes and modifications to other nodes. We'll start with a brief discussion on animation.

Animation

Animations are important when specifying object actions. Although animations are repeatable segments of moving geometry, the combination of multiple animation tracks using the same object gives the illusion of continuous nonlinear behavior. When a modeling package that supports keyframed-based animation is used, no programming is necessary. Completely choreographed sequences of object movements are then possible.

The Animation key specifies a complete action for objects that are contained in the current group. Each entry in the keyframe tracks is a combination of a frame number and a data value. For location, rotation, roll, color, hide, and morph, the count of KeyNumbers must be equal to the count of Tracks. The number of keys in each track may differ from the others.

The location track specifies the position of object. The rotation track specifies the orientation. The roll track will cause the object to spin about its Y axis. The color track contains red, green, and blue values.

The hide track specifies when the object is visible and when it is not. By default all objects are visible. An entry in the hide track will cause the object to change its visibility at the given frame.

The morph track is a list of target objects (this assumes that VRML will have some kind of object reference mechanism). Every object in this list must have exactly the same number of vertices, and the face lists must equal in count and structure.

The Animation enums specify what type of interpolation is to be used. Most animation will look fine with simple linear, or spline-based interpolation. Using an enum leaves room for adding industry-specific interpolation methods. The last two properties are reserved for application-specific data. The size field defines the count of words in the interpolation track field.

Animation Interpolation Enums:

```
LINEAR—straight path between keys
BSPLINE—curved path between keys
3DSTUDIO—popular 3-D modeling animation software interpolation
  data format:
          easeFrom          # SFFloat
          eastTo            # SFFloat
          tension           # SFFloat
          continuity        # SFFloat
          bias              # SFFloat
```

File Format/Defaults:

```
AnimationKey {
    pivotPoint            0 0 0         # SFLong
    locationKeyNumber     0             # MFLong
    locationTrack         0 0 0         # MFVec3f
    rotationKeyNumber     0             # MFLong
    rotationTrack         0 0 1 0       # MFRotation
    rollKeyNumber         0             # MFLong
    rollTrack             0             # MFFloat
    colorKeyNumber        0             # MFLong
    colorTrack            0 0 0         # MFColor
    hideKeyNumber         0             # MFLong
    hideTrack             FALSE         # MFBool
    morphKeyNumber        0             # MFLong
    morphTargetTrack      " "           # MFString
    interpolation         LINEAR        # SFEnum
    appDataSize           0             # SFLong
    interpolationTrack    0             # MFLong (or MFChar)
}[3]
```

Materials

This Material node encompasses a full range of surface properties. Most renderers are capable of using many of these values.

The ambient factor regulates the intensity of the ambient light. The amount of ambient light reflected from the object's surface is determined by that ambient color. The same is true for diffuse and specular color.

---

[3] *Ibid.*

The specular exponent (really shininess) defines the surface highlight. If transparency is, the surface is opaque; if the value is 1, the surface is totally transparent.

File/Format Defaults:

```
Material {
    ambientFactor         0              # MFFloat    (New)
    ambientColor          0.2 0.2 0.2    # MFColor
    diffuseFactor         0              # MFFloat    (New)
    diffuseColor          0.8 0.8 0.8    # MFColor
    specularFactor        0              # MFFloat    (New)
    specularColor         0 0 0          # MFColor
    specular Component    0              # MFFloat    (New)
    transparency          0              # MFFloat
}4
```

Perspective and Orthographic Cameras

The specification of the camera's position and orientation needs to be simple and straightforward. Using the notion from, to, and up is unambiguous. It does require two additional floats.

HeightAngle specifies the field of view in the *Y* direction. AspectRatio specifies the ratio of the field of view in the direction divided by heightAngle. Hither is the near clipping plane, and yon is the far clipping plane.

The orthographic camera properties describe the parallelepiped anchored at the origin of the viewing coordinate system and pointing in the *Z* direction. Hither is the near clipping plane, and yon is the far clipping plane. The values *xmin, xmax, ymin, ymax, hither,* and *yon* define the size, and heightAngle and aspect field of the view define the volume in the *Y* and *X* directions.

File/Format Defaults:

```
PerspectiveCamera
    from          0 0 0        # SFVec3f    (New)
    to            0 0 1        # SFVec3f    (New)
    up            0 1 0        # SFVec3f    (New)
    heightAngle   0.785398     # SFFloat
    aspect        0            # SFFloat    (New)
```

---

[4] *Ibid.*

```
        hither           0.01          # SFFloat        (New)
        yon              5             # SFFloat        (New)
}
```

File/Format Defaults:

```
OrthographicCamera {
    from             0 0 1         # SFVec3f        (New)
    to               0 0 0 0       # SFVec3f        (New)
    up               0 1 0         # SFVec3f        (New)
    xmin             0             # SFFloat        (New)
    xmax             0             # SFFloat        (New)
    ymin             0             # SFFloat        (New)
    ymax             0             # SFFloat        (New)
    hither           0 0 1         # SFFloat        (New)
    yon              5             # SFFloat        (New)
}
```
[5]

Rendering

This node describes the current rendering method. All subsequent objects are to be rendered with this type until it is changed. Finding a suitable standard definition of wire, flat, gouraud, and textures should be possible. It will be more difficult for other rendering types, such as radiosity.

Rendering Enums:

```
    DEFAULT                  Browser decides
    INVISIBLE                No rendering done
    WIRE                         Wireframe rendering
    FLAT                         Flat shading, no textures
    FLATTEXTURED             Flat shading with textures applied
    GOURAUD                  Gouraud shading, no textures
    GOURAUDTEXTURED          Gouraud shading with textured applied
```

File/Format Default:

```
RenderingHints {
    value                    DEFAULT      # SFEnum
}
```

---

[5] *Ibid.*

Navigation

There is an integral connection between the model being viewed and the way in which you navigate. Some worlds need a fast plane; others need a car, a person, a molecule. The following hints and suggestions will give the user an experience that is appropriate with the world.

Constraints restrict the axis of translation and rotation. If the value is FALSE, movement along the axis or rotation about the axis is restricted.

Translation speeds (travel distance of the viewpoint from one frame to the next with respect to time) should be dependent on the size of the world. These three gauges set only the maximum translation and rotation speed. SLOW should be defined as 1 percent of the world's maximum dimension, MEDIUM as 5 percent of the world's maximum dimension, and FAST 10 percent of the world's maximum dimension.

Rotational speeds are constants: SLOW is 0.01 degree of rotation per second, MEDIUM is 0.5 degrees of rotation per second, and FAST is 2.0 degree of rotation per second.

Navigation Enums:

```
DEFAULT     Browser decides
FLY         Movement in all possible directions
ORBIT       Viewpoint always looking at the center of the world
```

Speed Enums:

```
DEFAULT     Browser decides, variable speed
SLOW        (see)
MEDIUM      (see)
FAST        (see)
```

File Format/Defaults:

```
Navigation {
constraintsTranslation   FALSE FALSE FALSE    # SFEnum3
constraintsRotation      FALSE FALSE FALSE    # SFEnum3
speedTranslation         MEDIUM               # SFEnum
speedRotation            MEDIUM               # SFEnum
defaultUp                0 1 0                # SFVec3f
navigationMode           FLY                  # SFEnum
}
```

Lights

A standard definition of lights should be designed to take advantage of as many rendering engines as possible. The current definition lacks some basic properties that many renderers are now supporting.

Attenuation is needed so that parallel surfaces of identical material that overlap in the image can be distinguished. The proposed additions are a common definition of attenuation.

```
total = 1.0 / (constant + (linear * D) + (squared + D * D))
```

The attenuation factors approximate lights that are close or far away. Total attenuation is clamped at 1. ConstantAttenuation is used to prevent the denominator from becoming too small; linearAttenuation and squaredAttenuation are used to approximate lights at a distance.

File Format/Default:

```
PointLight {
    on                      TRUE        # SFBool
    intensity               1           # SFFloat
    color                   1 1 1       # SFColor
    location                0 0 1       # SFVec3f
    constantAttenuation     1           # SFFloat    (New)
    linearAttenuation       0           # SFFloat    (New)
    squaredAttenuation      0           # SFFloat    (New)
```

Spotlights need not only attenuation but also a better definition of lights' distribution inside the cone of influence. Here is an attempt to define the current properties, as well as a new property.

CutOffAngle is the angle from the light's central axis to the outer edge of the illumination. No illumination is cast outside this angle. The default is 45 degrees (0.785398 radians). Its domain is 0 to 90 degrees inclusive (0.0 to 1.5707 radians).

File Format/Default:

```
SpotLight {
    on              TRUE        # SFBool
    intensity       1           # SFFloat
    color           1 1 1       # SFColor
    location        0 0 1       # SFVec3f
    direction       0 0 -1      # SFFVec3f
```

Chapter 11 VRML Architecture Group (VAG)

```
    dropOffRate              0             # SFFloat
    cutOffAngle              0.785398      # SFFloat
    constantAttenuation      1             # SFFloat    (New)
    linearAttenuation        0             # SFFloat    (New)
    squaredAttenuation       0             # SFFloat    (New)
```

Ambient light is a diffuse, nondirectional source of light. It is the product of many surfaces present in the world.

File/Format Defaults:

```
AmbientLight {
    color                    0.4 0.4 0.4   # SFColor
}
```

Geometry

Many possible geometrical shapes could be included in VRML. Currently cone, cube, cylinder, and sphere are the only choices. These features of VRML are extremely convenient, essentially opening the door for anyone who wants to build both simple and complex 3-D worlds. Additionally, the use of these primitives reduces the size of the file as compared to files that have the same geometry using point and face primitives.

The following new geometry primitives round out a somewhat standard set of shapes. Also, some of the exiting shapes need additional properties to make them even more useful, all without adding too many additional properties.

Cylinder

The new Cylinder node (if accepted as part of the standard) will eliminate the need for the Cone node. Both of these geometry structures are very similar and can be specified with a few simple properties.

The topRadius is a new property that specifies the radius of the top portion of the cylinder. If either the top or bottom radius is 0, the resulting geometry will be a cone. It is invalid to specify the radius for both top and bottom as 0.

The tessellation property of the cone determines the number of sides comprising the conical part. If the tessellation is not specified, the application will determine the number of sides.

The top and bottom positions of the cylinder specify displacements from the defaults. Changing these values creates a skewed cone or cylinder.

Parts Enum:

```
SIDES
BOTTOM
ALL
```

File Format/Defaults:

```
Cylinder {
    parts           ALL     # SFBitMask
    topRadius       1       # SFFloat      (New)
    bottomRadius    1       # SFFloat
    height          2       # SFFloat
    tessellation    8       # SFLong       (New)
    topPosition     000     # Sfvec3f      (New)
    bottomPosition  000     # SFVec3f      (New)
```

Sphere

The Sphere node should also have the tessellation property added. Here we have two properties for tessellation: latitude and longitude. If tessellation is not specified, the application must decide the default shape. The dome property specifies whether the sphere is to be cut in half. If TRUE, the sphere's bottom half (the negative Y portion) should be removed.

File Format/Defaults:

```
Sphere {
    radius              1       # SFFloat
    latitudeTessilation  8      # SFLong
    longitudeTessilation 8      # SFLong
    dome                FALSE   # SFBool
```

The torus is a donut-shaped object. The major property defines the larger radius; the minor property defines the smaller radius. Tessellation specify the face detail of the object. If tessellation are not specified, the application must determine how to represent the torus. The is centered at the origin and oriented along the Z axis.

File Format/Defaults

```
Torus
    major                   2       # SFFloat
    minor                   1       # SFFloat
    lattitudeTessilation    8       # SFLong
    longitudeTessilation    8       # SFLong
```

The Tower of VRML

VRML was the hottest topic at SIGGRAPH '95. VRML is a standard, the ideal starting point; it lets people create static scenes. Although easy to get done, it is far from a *Real* Virtual Reality Modeling Language. Already there is splintering: WebFX has collision detection, VRML+ has chat and interaction, IVRML is similar, and SGI is using features from Open Inventor. Further, there is the 3-D online gaming explosion.

This is not bad; this is good. However, it clearly points out that if VAG is to continue its success, it must spec out the next generation as soon as humanly possible.

Goal

The ultimate goal of VRML is to model the Black Sun in Neal Stephenson's *Snow Crash*. This allows a more or less realistic environment with physics-based modeling, autonomous agents, multi-user (or shared spaces), and no-excuses interaction. Hiro Protagonist can have a real swordfight. Emotions are apparent in facial features.

What is the short-term goal for VRML V2.0? Add multiuser spaces, interaction, and behaviors. What does this mean? Multiuser, or shared, spaces means that we can interact with others' avatars in some sort of meaningful way. Interaction means that we can control our avatar to our own satisfaction and use it to participate in the shared space. Behaviors means that we can imbue objects with the ability to react to the environment.

However, it appears that VAG only can do one more major revision of VRML. That should be the Grand Scheme, with VRML as a subset.

VAG is attempting to do the impossible. It is a near impossibility to do behavior, shared spaces, and interaction to everyone's satisfaction, and it is clear that these do not all belong in the geometry language of VRML. VAG is specifying more than VRML V2.0. It will be an architecture that will allow different vendors to plug in different behavior and physics models, different MUD/MOO engines, and, different interaction paradigms.

It will be useful to expand the number of buzzwords that are being used:

- VRML—Virtual Reality Modeling Language (geometry and simple behavior),
- COCO—Collision and constraint manager (complex behavior and physics),
- BSST—Black Sun Shared Tearoom (aka beast—the MUD/MOO manager).
- ACE—avatar control environment (interaction).
- VRAL—Virtual Reality Audio Lang (Owen Rowley, who calls COCO VRBL).[6]

Physics

The problem can be approached in three ways:

- Write a system that can solve ODEs and PDEs (ordinary and partial differential equations). Perhaps VAG just needs to approximate them.
- Build in material properties, density, bulk, shear, and poission Functions (or curves), because they vary depending on the conditions.
- Implement a good general-purpose computer engine (Java, for example).

If VRML could do what MATLAB does, it could do everything. The MATLAB language is a fourth generation language that allows compilation and has some sort of canonical interface (www.mathworks.com).

---

[5] Jan C. Hardenbergh, *The VRML of Babel*, jch@oki.com, August 18, 1995.

Behavior

There are at least two types of behavior: linear time-based behavior and behavior that does not fit into the definition of linear time-based.

In order to maintain frame rates of 15+ fps, we must download simple behaviors to the browser/rendering engine. An alternative would be to create a Java shell embedded in the browser and to keep all behavior out of the geometry. That would be a mistake. Geometry has behavior. (Certainly the BEF (www.besoft.com) is enmeshed in geometry.)

More complicated behaviors based on AI, behavior nets, or other high-level inventions are way beyond the scope of the most grandiose schemes for VRML. We need to define protocols that go between a high-level behavior engine and the browser/geometry or perhaps a Java front end.

Distributed Objects

The Grand Scheme must have some sort of distributed object infrastructure. It doesn't matter whether it is CORBA, OpenDoc, DOLE'3 (a.k.a. Cairo or COM?), OO Java, or whatever. The whole environment will not run on a PC; the multiuser aspect of it will need to be distributed. Ideally the system would be able to pass executing objects between servers, as the Emerald System could more than 10 years ago.

What would be *really* cool is to be able to specify interfaces to geometry, behavior, physics, shared spaces, interactions, etc., with a common IDL (Interface Definition Language). The OMG/CORBA IDL would be fine. Sun put out source code for the IDL parser in 1995.

MOO/MUD/Shared Space

Multiuser or shared space? Shared space is easier to say. VRML+ talks servers and passing avatars from server to server, doesn't it? We should look at the cellular phone technology(CD14A (code division multiplex?). The problems of load balancing, being able to register without a round-trip or perhaps only one round-trip; and keeping track of your neighbors in a dynamic environment seem to be the key issues.

Java Shell

We could use Java to create the medium-level behaviors and interfaces to the other engines driving the Grand Scheme. Of course, Java is not the only possibility. Python and SafeTCL come to mind, as well as more exotic solutions, such as Telescript. However, Java handles security (the issue of running code that may have viruses or be malignant is a huge concern. SafeTCL does this, too). The real deciding factor is that Java has joined VRML on the *WIRED* hype list.

ACE (Avatar Control Environment)

Perhaps a tight loop between the user and some server controlling the avatar and then the avatar could be devised. The avatar would coordinate with the other servers and engines in the Grand Scheme.

Protocol Conservation

Three or four protocols are mentioned here. Each would direct the VRML viewer/renderer from various points of view: behavior, physics, shared space, and interaction. This is possible, since the X server can handle many connections and several protocols gracefully. Granted, it was written by wizards, but many wizards are working on VRML.

Assume that it is possible. Is it desirable? Perhaps it would be better to combine these servers into one big server.

Network Issues

Minimizing round-trips and synchronous transactions will be key. A roll-forward and roll-back strategy is fine. It's better to have a fast world that makes mistakes than a slow world.

VRML V2.0 will either be a predictive standard, in which caseVAG must work on it with high energy for six to eight months or it should set the ground rules and foster many prototypes, picking one to be the winner. Either way, VAG must treat it like a crisis; otherwise it will have many competing incomparable standards to deal with, with close to a guarantee that the technically elegant will never win.

A major reason that standards are successful is that sample code reference is too much to hope for. It is made available at little or no cost. This was one reason that VRML V1.0 was a success, and it is a must for VRML V2.0

The Role of Sound in VRML

What is the role of sound in VRML? You might as well ask, What is the role of computer graphics in VRML? Although most important networking problems are not addressed in the VRML spec, VRML is a essentially a networking technology and is integral to communications via the Web, rather than being a 3-D description language for computer graphics. Now that VRML is completed and developers are scrambling to release VRML-compliant browsers, it is time to work toward defining standards that allow VRML worlds to become more than the austere and silent facades appearing at most sites today. The intention for the near term is to have VRML worlds become as fully sensualized as possible. Hearing is arguably the most important sense to stimulate when attempting to place the user within a virtual world, especially when the world is viewed via a 14-inch screen on a desktop.

The audio extensions that provide for this near-term solution will include only a means for specifying the 3-D spatial location of sound objects. Consistent with the minimally interactive nature of VRML, the VRML X.X audio extensions will merely establish a language for identifying and attaching sound objects to other items within the Web. Fully interactive sound services will be built on the method for supporting interactive behaviors that is slated for inclusion in VRML V2.0 (and is as yet only a gleam in the eyes of VRML V1.0 devotees). It should be clear it is most prudent to wait for the general solution to problems of interactivity within VRML worlds. Indeed, most of the difficult questions concerning interactive audio services in VRML are not audio-specific (such as streaming, caching and scaling); rather, they are problems that have been identified and discussed at length and are to be resolved for VRML X.X.

The audio services most important to a given VRML world will vary, but issues of streaming, caching, and scaling of audio data are important for nearly every world. For example, in a chatlike environment, some sonic events, such as the door-open and door-close events, are best cached. However, real-time teleconferencing, like features will require buffered streaming of audio data. Region-of-effect specifications for a given audio stream (read localized sound source) can go a long way toward reducing bandwidth requirements and also imply a simple audio rendering scheme that diminishes amplitude with distance to the threshold of audibility. Most VRML users would be satisfied simply to hear other users talking within the space they inhabit. To foreshadow the discussion of audio rendering to come, however, consider how frustratingly unintelligible most speakerphone-based teleconferencing is. Audio from more than two talkers in a space delivered over a single loudspeaker means drastically reduced speech intelligibility. Stereo panning of the sources toward a left or right loudspeaker will help a great deal, but head-related stereophony improves intelligibility even more. Compare your ability to listen selectively to a given conversation at a cocktail party to your ability to follow a conversation in a conventional stereo recording.

The importance of spatialized sound in sensualizing a VRML world will be obvious to the initiated, but one further observation should be stressed here before moving to the next topic of this chapter. The observation is that a primary role of spatial sound perception in the human is to direct focal vision to items of interest that may not be included in the current field of view. As an aid in navigating VRML worlds, spatially located sound can play a fundamental role in self-orientation and situational awareness.

History

There is very little history to recount regarding an audio spec for VRML. Some discussion of inlined sound can be found in the VRML Hypermail Archive. Very little of this was focused *on* audio spatialization per se. For those who took issue with the exclusion of audio from the VRML V 1.0 spec, all that can be said is that VRML V1.0 had to exclude many important concerns. This meant including the means for supporting interactive behaviors over the Net (considered to be quite critical to the building of cyberspace). The instigators of the VRML spec took the position that anything that they could not agree on quickly would be postponed for consideration in VRML V2.0. Several suggestions were made that would allow for rudimentary sound source description (both ambient and localized) to be included in V1.0, but it was concluded that more careful consideration was called for. With regard to the audio extensions currently under consideration for VRML X.X, a small advisory board has been formed by individuals already active in setting audio standards.

The same principles that guided VRML architects to adopt the Open Inventor ASCII file format from SGI for graphic object description may well guide VRML sound architects. However, no one API is truly comprehensive. Thus it has been proposed that VAG build an independent sound spec from the union of the features of the dominant audio spatialization APIs currently in use by developers. The APIs being compared include those from Creative Labs, Crystal River Engineering, Microsoft (DirectSound), and Roland. An informal survey suggests that most other audio-spatialization APIs describe only a subset of these more comprehensive and forward-looking designs. It remains to be seen whether any API provider will put a VRML-linkable C++ class library into the public domain.

Starting Point for the VRML X.X Audio Extentions

As a starting point in the discussion, it should be pointed out that the same language used in VRML to describe objects that are to be visually rendered via computer graphics may be used to describe sound objects. There is no need to supply redundant object information within the VRML file. If a sound object is to be attached to a graphic object, it moves past the observer as the observer navigates past the graphic object (thus the spec for the spatial location of sound objects is practically written already).

What will require further integration is support for further audio-rendering features, such as the simulation of reflected sound and reverberation. In addition, it is important to provide a means for obstacles to reduce or otherwise interfere with the propagation of sound through the VRML world when they are positioned between the sound source and the observer's position. Before going any further with this discussion, however, some further background material will be presented.

An analogy between the technologies of 3-D graphic rendering and 3-D audio rendering is drawn in order to teach distinctions in spatial sound processing to those more familiar with 3-D graphics. In each of four comparisons, a spatial sound-processing feature is added to those previously presented so that the complexity of 3-D audio rendering can be appreciated relative to the graphic rendering of a simple object, such as the sphere. The following respective graphic and audio features are discussed in turn: goraud shading versus directional filtering, shadows versus discrete reflections, ray tracing versus reverberation, and motion blur versus Doppler shift.

In order to teach some of the distinctions important in understanding levels of sophistication in three-dimensional (3-D) audio signal processing, VAG has prepared the following analogy in terms of 3-D graphic rendering technology. The analogy will be between the graphic rendering of a sphere on a visual display, such as a CRT screen, and the audio rendering of a sound source, such as the round tone of a low F on the trombone, via a pair of loudspeakers. In each case the minimal presentation simply gets the stimuli to their respective displays (the sphere on the screen appears as a solid white circle (no shading), and an identical monaural sound source emanates from both of the speakers (no signal processing). At each increase in the level of sophistication of audio rendering, new spatial sound-processing features are added that can be compared to increasingly complex graphic rendering of the sphere.

The first level of sophistication in audio rendering that might be called 3-D would be the simulation of the acoustical response of the ears for sound arriving from the direction of the trombone. If the sound is to appear to arrive somewhat from the right, the signal sent to the right speaker will have more high frequency energy than the signal sent to the left. This simulates the head shadow known to exist at high frequencies at the ear on the side of the head opposite the sound source. This acoustical phenomenon is analogous to the way in which the shading of the sphere changes as it moves across a space with a simulated light source at a fixed position. Just as the sphere looks more like an object in 3-D space and less like a circle of light on the screen, so the trombone tone sounds less like it is emanating from the speakers and more like it is arriving from a distinct position in space.

The second level of sophistication in 3-D audio rendering creates realistic impressions of distance for the trombone. Consider first what an observer might experience if the projection of a sphere on the screen gradually grows smaller and larger. Is the shaded sphere moving forward and back, or is its size shrinking and growing while it maintains a fixed position in space? The same ambiguity occurs when the loudness level of a sound source is modulated over time. Did the sound itself get softer and louder, or did it move forward and back while maintaining a constant volume? For both visual and sonic objects, simulating the interaction of the object with a wall provides a frame of reference that can help the observer decide between the two possibilities. If the sphere casts a shadow on the wall, the observer can infer from the behavior of the shadow whether the sphere is moving. The same is true of the sound that reflects off the surface of a wall. If a sound source gets softer and louder, so does a simulated reflection that arrives from a different direction and at a slight delay relative to the arrival of the direct sound. If a sound source moves away from the observer, both the direction and the time delay are modulated in a manner that is characteristic of a moving sound source. The more simulated walls producing sound reflections, the better the effect. The same is true of including more shadows for disambiguating the movement of the sphere.

The third level of sophistication in 3-D audio rendering is the simulation of the reverberation of a sound source throughout a 3-D space. This simulation is akin to ray tracing in graphic rendering in that it requires the calculation of how sound leaving the source in all directions eventually arrives at the observer's ears. If the surface of the sphere were made of shiny metal, graphic ray tracing would allow the textured walls of a room to be reflected to the observer's eyes according to the position and shape of the sphere. Including reverberation in 3-D audio rendering completes a spatial simulation in a most realistic fashion. When the sound source moves away from the observer, the overall level of the reverberation is hardly modulated at all while the level of the sound arriving directly from the source decreases. As with the single simulated reflection described previously, but much more powerfully, ambiguities of changing loudness versus sound source motion are easily resolved.

An additional 3-D graphic and audio-rendering feature that may or may not be included in the preceding levels of sophistication is motion-dependent modification of the graphic or sound object itself. When a graphic object moves quickly enough, it provides a good deal of realism if motion blur is added to the simulation. The image of the object will appear to be blurred along its direction of motion. Similarly when a sound source moves quickly enough away from the observer, its pitch will be decreased by an amount proportional to the sound source velocity. This feature provides a very salient cue to changes in sound source distance. In addition, if a sound source takes a circular path around the observer's head, the source is closer to one ear and then the other as it completes each revolution. As the source simultaneously moves toward one ear and away from the other, the pitch of the signal sent to one speaker is increased while the pitch to the other is decreased. This phenomenon adds a great deal to the sense of spatial motion not only when the sound source moves but also when the observer moves by a stationary sound source.

Areas for Further Development

VRML X.X will not include a spec for audiophile reproduction. But it will include a 0 dB SPL reference level, just as the THX specification does for film sound. Users can set their volume where they like, but if they want to listen at sound levels similar to those intended by the VRML file author, they can calibrate to a known standard. Although not many homes are equipped for spectral analysis, VRML X.X will also include a magnitude response curve that should be matched for keeping spectral balance as transparent as possible.

VRML X.X will not include a specification of audio signal processing for sound spatialization, just an Open Inventor does not specify the algorithms for rendering 3-D graphic objects). But it will include a set of parameters for controlling level of detail (LOD) in audio rendering on each sound object and, additionally, within 3-D bounding boxes that enclose sound objects. The parameters that describe LOD are scaled terms of computational load for each spatialization feature provided by the local audio-rendering engine. This flexible allocation of sound-processing resources does not make assumptions about what features will be most expensive when employing future technologies.

VRML X.X will make the following distinctions as well:

- Spatial positioning: Ambient versus object-attached sound 3-D located versus simply directionalized (2-D or 1-D).
- Real-time audio on the Web: Half-duplex versus full-duplex. Suggested sample-rates: 8 kHz, 11 kHz, 22.05 kHz, 44.1 kHz LOD-specified spatialization versus simple playback.
- MIDI sequencing: General MIDI (GM) versus RAM preloaded wavetable synthesis buffered real time versus background music and SFX.

- Other spatial enhancements: Any device that can be used actively or passively to process sound produced by the computer can be specified and controlled, preferably via MIDI SYSEX (system exclusive) commands.
- Emotion channels: The local interpretation of MIDI sequences can be influenced by data received via continuously modulated emotional-state descriptors in reserved emotion channels. These descriptors can also be used to modulate related rendering parameters, such as lighting.[7]

VRML's Associated Behavior

VRML, based on the Open Inventor ASCII file format, has rapidly become a standard 3-D modeling language for the Internet. However, it has two major limitations:

- The user may manipulate the camera and follow links, but no other types of interaction are supported.
- Only a very simple extension mechanism exists, and it does not allow one to specify the behavior of a new node type.[8]

VAG would like to provide for objects that can change over time and in response to external stimuli. In David Zeltzer's taxonomy of graphical simulation *systems (Autonomy, Interaction, and Presence)*, this corresponds to adding autonomy (animation, physics) and interaction (user manipulation) to the system. At the moment, presence is beyond the scope of VRML, since it refers to such things as the type and quality of the hardware used to interact with the virtual world.

Any proposed extension to VRML faces a unique set of challenges. It must be flexible enough to provide for the needs of an extremely diverse group of users, be on platforms ranging from PCs to supercomputers, and be able work over an untrusted wide area network. Additionally, it should fit the spirit of both VRML and the WWW, be defined through a process of group decision making, and should use public-domain tools where possible.

---

[7] William Martens, *Audio in VRML*, Headspace, wlm@netcom.com, August 19, 1995.

[8] Tom Meyer and D. Brookshire Conner, *Adding Behavior To VRML*, Brown Computer Graphics Group, NSF/ARPA Science and Technology Center for Computer Graphics and Scientific Visualization, twm@cs.brown.edu, 1995.

Existing Systems

A robust virtual-environment description language should be able to support time-varying models, user interaction, and multiuser sessions. In addition, it should be flexible, allowing for extensions in all aspects of functionality. A number of research and commercial systems which support some or all of these:

- *Open Inventor*, from SGI, is a 3-D graphics system written in C++ and is the one of the most commonly used interactive 3-D systems. It provides for nodes in a scene graph and for adding additional node types, using dynamically loaded C++ code. Internally Open Inventor makes use of multimethods, also used in Cecil and CLOS to provide for a scene graph that can perform several kinds of behaviors in an extensible way. For example, Open Inventor lets the programmer define both new nodes and new actions that nodes can perform (alternative rendering techniques).
- *TBAG*, developed at Sun Microsystems, is a functional, stateless 3-D system. Function objects in TBAG can be related to one another by multiway constraints and then evaluated with different parameters to create time-varying oruser-controlled geometries. TBAG also makes use of multimethods internally, even more pervasively than Open Inventor does
- The *UGA system*, which was developed at Brown University, uses an interpreted language called Flesh. This is a prototype-delegation object-oriented language that was developed specifically to rapidly prototype complex interactive 3-D scenes. It supports a variety of animation techniques, including keyframing, inverse kinematics, physically based modeling, and the evaluation of arbitrary functions.
- *Alice*, from the University of Virginia, is designed specifically to support rapid prototyping of 3-D immersive environments. It uses Python as an interpreted extension language.
- *ANIM3D* was developed at Digital to visualize algorithms and uses a custom prototype-delegation language. Obliq provides for concurrent behaviors.
- *Worlds*, a commercial product developed by Worlds, Inc., allows for multiple participants to take part in a dynamic environment with animations, spatialized audio, and texture-mapped video.

VRML+, which has been proposed by Worlds, includes a behavior extension protocol that should be language independent and also defines an API for modifying the scene graph. Also proposed is a networking protocol for connecting VRML servers and clients.

- The *BE system*, developed by the BE Software Company, provides an excellent system of Open Inventor–based node type for describing behaviors. A Pascal-based syntax is designed for embedding new behaviors inside nodes, and some nodes for physically based modeling are demonstrated.

Language Extension Mechanisms

Many extension mechanisms are available in contemporary programming languages, but they generally involve some combination of macro, function, or class definition. C++, for example, combines all three types of extension mechanisms and adds some very complex subclassing rules.

The graphics systems described previously, however, tend to use different mechanisms that are more powerful in many ways than the mechanisms provided by C++. Multimethods in a graphics system allow for the extension of both the set of primitives and the set of renderers. Most graphics systems use some form of dynamic object model, such as the prototype/delegation model used in the Self language. This model is especially prevalent in MOOs.

Finally, most of the systems described make some use of concurrency. Although not usually thought of as an extension mechanism, the use of concurrency permits the flexible extension of the system while it is running. Adding new behavior is simply a matter of adding a new thread (note that timer callbacks and similar mechanisms are essentially highly constrained forms of simulated concurrency).

Some have implied that all one needs to express behaviors in VRML is a good API (application programming interface). In practice, yes, an API is sufficient. However, if VRML lacks simple techniques for compositing node behaviors together and for defining nodes based on other nodes (inheritance), it will always be necessary to use an external programming language, even for fairly simple behaviors added to VRML.

VAG thinks that, given a suitable library of existing behaviors, most new behaviors should be simple to implement, based on compositions of other existing behaviors. Only if entirely new functionality is being added (for example, a node that opens up a socket and listens to it) should it be necessary to use an external programming environment. Additionally, a simple scripting language (Java Script) designed specifically for the requirements of VRML (flexible inheritance concurrency, VRML-embedded syntax) should be easier for nonprogrammers to learn.

Prototyping New Nodes

One of the more annoying parts of VRML right now is the impossibility of specifying a node separately from using it. VAG suggests a new type of separator (Prototypes) that doesn't render any of its children and that also provides a unified location for definitions.

This scheme has several benefits. It allows information about the contents of a scene (what kinds of nodes it contains) to be factored out into a separate world consisting of prototypes. Prototypes also provide the ability to define something without actually using it, a capability the current semantics of DEF don't support.

Consider a VRML file, that provides some sample geometries that can be used in a plug-and-play fashion, included via a WWWInline and used without duplicating models.

```
Prototype {
   DEF Refrigerator {
       fields [tempSetting SFFloat]
       tempSetting 40
       # Children for geometry here
       }
}[9]
```

VAG's Proposed Extension Mechanism

VRML provides a limited mechanism for adding new node types, using the *fields* and *isA* fields. In the VRML specification the Cube node could be specified as follows:

---

[9] *Ibid.*

```
Cube {
   fields [ SFFloat width, SFFloat height,
      SFFloat depth ]
}[10]
```

However, this extension mechanism is not powerful enough to describe the behavior of these new node types. VAG proposes an extension mechanism that permits new node types, browser extensions, the interaction of new node types, and new browser extensions. VAG's intention is to provide a mechanism that is simple and easy to understand and implement. VAG wishes to build as much as possible on VRML for backward compatibility, while adding just enough new syntax to get the job done.

The model VAG proposes allows for the prototype-delegation model, which has been found useful in a variety of interactive graphics systems. VAG suggests the minor extension that the isA field be an MFString rather than an SFString, allowing multiple inheritance while maintaining backward compatibility with old syntax.

In VRML the isA field is defined only to provide an alternative implementation of a new node if the VRML browser is not able to resolve the node. VAG would like to modify the semantics of isA to make it more like inheritance in a traditional programming language.

The first change is that any node that references another node using isA inherits all its field definitions. Also, since VAG may want to inherit from a specific instance of that node, the following syntax can be used:

```
DEF RedCube cube {
   color 1 0 0
}
AnotherRedCube {
   isa USE RedCube
}[11]
```

In this case AnotherRedCube inherits not only the fields of Cube but also the color value of RedCube. By default, this value is forwarded to/from the parent. This means that changing the color of AnotherRedCube actually changes the color of RedCube.

---

[10] *Ibid.*

[11] *Ibid.*

However, a new node may use the new reserved word COPY before the name of a prototype, thereby creating a copy of all of the fields of the prototype. Any field values copied using COPY can be changed in the copy independent of the original prototype's value. Thus a copy is considered dead, in that the new copy does not have any further ties to the object it was copied from. A copy, then, may be located on a different machine from its prototype, with contact occurring only during the initial copying.

For example, it could be specified that AnotherRedCube is a real copy of RedCube:

```
AnotherCube {
    isa COPY USE RedCube
}
```

Alternatively, a new node may use COPYALL, indicating that this should be a deep copy and that all the referenced nodes should be copied as well (VAG wants to ship an object and its references over the network to a remote machine).

If COPY is not used, values are shared, even remotely. Thus a simple way to provide networked shadows of remote objects is by using isA:

```
# Remote source
DEF Remote {
    fields { someValue SFBool }
    someValue TRUE
}
# Local source
DEF ShadowOfRemote {
    isA Remote
}
```
[12]

Combined with the use of the Prototypes nodes, this scheme provides some support for distribution of functionality, as the prototypes need not be in the same world as the nodes that inherit from them or copy them. Of course, using this mechanism too frequently could result in exceedingly slow worlds. VAG recommends that this be used only for cases in which two objects need to be seen in exactly the same way (a locked door is important, but fish in a bowl may not be).

---

[12] *Ibid.*

Since isA allows multiple strings, the possibility must be considered that a node inherits or copies several fields with the same name. The convention is that the first occurrence of the field is copied as is, with subsequent copies renamed to include the type name at the end of the new field name.

VAG suggests one additional optional field, designed to allow a node to be an executable thread of control. This field is code of type MFString. The strings in this field may be either a URI (pointing to a possible implementation of the object) or a list of *messages* described in the Sidebar.

Messages

A message is given in a very simple syntax. A message is one of the following:

- The name of a field of the current node. This indicates that, if the field refers to a node, that node's code should begin executing. As a special case the keyword SELF refers to the current node. If a field refers to a node, it may be followed by a period and the syntax for a message.
- The name of a field, an equal sign, and then a value (such as another field name, a USE of a DEF, or a literal) to indicate assignment.
- The new reserved word WAIT, followed by a field name. This indicates that execution of this code (and hence any following messages) should wait until the node refereed to by the field finishes its current execution.
- A USE, followed by the name of a node previously named using DEF, followed by a period, then followed by any of the previous syntaxes.

The following is a fragment of a YACC grammar describing a message. Note that the semicolons are part of the YACC syntax, not part of the message syntax. Messages in a series are separated by commas.

Sidebar

```
AnyMessage  :  Message
            |  UseMessage;
Message     :  Execute
            |  SetValue
            |  Wait;
Execute     :  fieldname
            |  SELF
            |  fieldname              .    Message;
SetValue    :  fieldname              =    Value;
Wait        :  WAIT fieldname;
UseMessage  :  USE nodename           .    Message;
Value       :  literal  |  fieldname  |    UseClause;
```

This syntax is quite simple, can easily be added to a parser, and supports a simple form of concurrency. As observed before, concurrency allows extension of behavior while the system is running. In addition, this form of concurrency is asynchronous, allowing for the possibility that the objects receiving messages may be widely distributed.

Setting and getting values are atomic operations (nothing else can change that value while it is being used), but in general all operations should be considered to happen in parallel. It is extremely important that these operations be atomic even when used with shared distributed objects. Several commercially available distributed databases might be useful to use as a general lock server in such environments.

Although conceptually every node on a single machine may be a thread, it need not be implemented in that way. A simple scheme would involve a round-robin of every node currently executing code, evaluating one message for each node in turn. A WAIT can be treated specially, taking the node waiting out of the round-robin. This provides conceptual concurrency without the use of operating system threads.

A Convention for Multimethods

Many object-oriented languages, such as C++, use single dispatching to determine which function to execute on an object when a method is called. In single dispatching, method lookup proceeds by searching for an appropriate method on the single object and proceeds to search up the inheritance tree for an appropriate method on any of its parents. Multimethods are the extension of this technique to multiple dispatching, whereby several objects together define the appropriate method to invoke. Consider the common case in which one is implementing a device-independent graphics library. Graphics hardware is not at all standardized, let alone consistent: Some graphics boards support fast sphere rendering, others support triangle strips, some provide for fast texture mapping, etc. In such cases the code is liberally sprinkled with switch statements and #ifdefs. With multimethods, general render method can be defined for the generic object/hardware combination. Then the inheritance can be used to simplify the amount of code specifying which method to invoke in which case. Multimethods have been widely used in such systems as CLOS and Cecil.

Time-Critical Behaviors

The types of time-critical behaviors that VAG would like to support are often classified under soft real-time systems: The system does not *guarantee* responsiveness but merely tries to meet deadlines (an MPEG decoder occasionally misses a frame). The LOD node in VRML, under some interpretations, already provides for such time-critical behavior when the system switches to a simpler model in order to increase scene update rates.

As a behavioral example of such a system, consider a physically based model of a pendulum. One could use several algorithms to simulate the motion of a pendulum, ranging from extremely inaccurate but fast (linear extrapolation of velocity), to accurate but slow (fourth-order Runge-Kutta with a small stepsize).

In previous work VAG has developed scheduling algorithms that attempt to balance computational demands versus rendering demands across multiple-processor systems in order to attain a constant frame rate in computationally demanding scientific-visualization environments. Such a complex system is not necessary in VRML, however, since such schedulers have high overhead, and simple reactive scheduling can be used to good effect, as is obvious in SGIs Webspace browser.

Since a Specific is just another node type, several versions of the same algorithm can be embedded inside a LOD node, as follows:

```
ComputePendulum {
    isA [ COPY SimpleBehavior, COPY Generic ]
    LOD {
        range [1 8]
        DEF ComputePendulumRK4 Prototype {
            isA [ COPY SimpleBehavior, COPY Specific
            generic USE ComputePendulum
            code "http://www.physics.com/rk4.java"
        }
        DEF ComputePendulumEuler Prototype {
            isA [ COPY SimpleBehavior, COPY Specific }
            generic USE ComputePendulum
            code "http://www.physics.com/euler.java"
        }
    }
}
```

Note that this assumes a slightly different interpretation of LOD than that traditionally used, but it is one that VAG would like to encourage. This interpretation is: LOD does not imply a set of representations of an object, to be interchanged based on distance from an object. Instead it defines a set of relative benefit values for alternative representations of an object or algorithm. The browser is responsible for choosing among the set of alternative representations, based on the actual cost of each representation relative to the benefit of that representation and the current load on the system. This interpretation allows for VRML scenes that can contain fast geometry and behaviors, independent of the speed of the host machine, but possibly sacrificing some accuracy.

Primitives

So far in this chapter high-level mechanisms have been described. The ability to give primitives an external scripting language will be useful, thus allowing programmers to code more complex behaviors, such as socket communication and protocols.

API Considerations

Some have assumed that the definition of a scripting language implies that one is opposed to the development of an API for VRML. This is not the case; it just postpones consideration of the proper API. Mitra from Worlds proposes a possible API that provides for the manipulation of the scene graph and individual fields and the insertion of new VRML code into a scene. Although this approach does not provide for data hiding and abstraction, it does provide a useful base to begin from.

Any proposed API should be able to be described in terms of both local invocations (direct function calls) and remote invocations (RPC, OLE, HTTP, etc.). VAG researchers would prefer a specification that respected the object-oriented nature of the scene graph, as well as provided for some ability to specify different levels of security (interface hiding—both on the local machine and remotely.

It is also necessary to provide an additional intermediate, device-independent API for managing such devices as the renderer, audio tools, video cameras, networking, etc. This is in itself a very difficult problem.

Extension Languages

Why do we need a language at all? After all, a large number of standards exist for executing (possibly external) code, such as CORBA, OLE, OpenDOC, and even HTTP. If all code could be efficiently executed remotely or if we could trust the remote server to give us safe code, such protocols would be perfect. However, we would like to be able to download code to execute locally, for efficiency. Because every possible language cannot be supported, it makes sense to require a standard extension language.

There are several important criteria for a 3-D behavior–specification language. They must have the following:

- support on the majority of Internet-based machines,
- ability to download safe code to execute on a local machine,
- protocols for invoking remote procedures,
- time-critical behaviors, and
- support for object-orientation, with flexible inheritance semantics.

Unfortunately no existing language satisfies all of these criteria. Python, Self, Tcl, and Java, among others, individually satisfy many of the requirements but fall short in others.

Java would seem to be a good enough choice for a common language for the World Wide Web, since it is advertised as a safe language. It is also considered to be a good choice because it is well defined and documented—released with source code for Sun Solaris. Netscape has recently licensed it for integration into its browser. Although the following examples are presented here in terms of Java, the API and protocols could be reworked in any other object-oriented language.

Worlds describes a process by which an interpreter for a new extension language could be downloaded dynamically. If this interpreter is able to generate code in the platform's native extension language, it is no longer necessary to choose a single language. Note that this may cause confusion and make it difficult to create new nodes based on existing code, but it may be a viable solution for the polyglot Web.

Due to time limitations, VAG has not yet attempted to describe how one would implement a new VRML node type in Java. This should happen relatively infrequently, since the language described so far is quite powerful. However, adding new functionality, such as the ability to open sockets, will require developing new libraries, probably in Java.

Example Primitives

Using Java, we can define primitive nodes that represent not geometry but time-varying behavior. Suggestions are made here for useful kinds of nodes, but keep in mind that different Web sites can define their own.

These nodes use fields to describe interesting values. These values would be more useful if VRML supported the ability to refer to only a particular field in a node, as can be done in Open Inventor. It is suggested that a simple syntax (the node, followed by a period, followed by the field name) should be adapted. VAG is already making use of this syntax in message sends.

- ***Browser***—The Browser node represents the capabilities of a generic VRML browser. Some agreement would have to be reached concerning the minimum functionality this object would support. But it seems that the object could be expected to support a few fields: Location, an *FVec2f*, representing the screen-space location of a mouse, button, and an SFBool, with TRUE if the mouse button were down and FALSE otherwise; and, *cameraPosition, cameraAt,* and *cameraUp*—a series of SFvec3 f representing the orientation of the camera.

Other prototypes could then represent special capabilities of other browsers. For example, this provides an alternative mechanism to WebSpace's use of DEF with Info nodes to set special parameters. Thus a prototype of WebSpace might support such fields as backgroundColor and viewer.

- **Location2**—This kind of node has one field, position of sFvec2 f, corresponding to the location of a pointer, such as a mouse. Other kinds of nodes can have a similar structure to correspond to other input devices. For example, a Location6 could correspond to a six degree-of-freedom input device with two fields: position of SFVec3 f and rotation of SFRotation.
- **VirtualSphere**—This kind of node has one field rotation, which contains the rotation. It results from a virtual sphere interaction with the user.
- **Toggle**—A Toggle node could have one value field containing either ON or OFF. An additional field could describe what device the field should get its value from, such as MOUSE_BTN_1 or a key on the keyboard.
- **CurrentSelection**—A node implementing the current selection can have two fields one for the geometry determining the pick (such as a ray or 3-D box) and one for the geometry that was picked.
- **Time**—This node has a single field (value) tied to the current wallclock time. This can be used to produce models that are intrinsically animated.

Sample Behavior Extensions

Earlier in the chapter, a description of how to implement a number of common browser functions with proposed additions to VRML was presented. Examples of more complex interactive behavior are provided here, with descriptions of how one might be able to approach implementing them in this system.

Magic Lenses

Magic lens filters consist of simulated filters that one can superimpose over a scene to hide or show various types of information. For example, a magic lens to show dependencies between objects could be composited with a magic lens that renders all objects semitransparently, to make it easier to see the lines illustrating the dependencies. These types of information-hiding and displaying tools could become very useful in complex, information-laden virtual environments.

Since some of these filters could be purely geometric, with others based on the semantics of the scene, generating useful composite behaviors is difficult for all scenes. However, multimethods can be used to determine how to render particular nodes for particular kinds of lenses.

Avatars

Avatars, or 3-D objects representing live participants in a shared virtual world, are a common feature of various real or imagined collaborative 3-D environments. In simple scenes these avatars could be implemented through VRML nodes representing a 3-D body with the possible input modalities. In the MERLE system, some participants are fully mobile in the 3-D scenes. Others, for whom only the head and arms are tracked, are represented as seated around a table.

Based on a combination of the possible input devices and the desired 3-D representation of the person, a live connection (possibly using mechanisms as simple as Java's existing networking code) would be kept between the local browser and the remote participant. This way users could experience real-time shared behavior.

Worlds has developed a set of documents on how one might develop shared, multiuser VRML worlds. VAG researchers are also currently writing a separate white paper on some of the important issues for multiuser worlds and how one might address them.

Collision Detection

Collision detection is another computationally demanding problem that is best dealt with on a scene-by-scene basis. This is absolutely necessary for many DOOM-like games and for collaborative systems, such as Worlds Chat. However, most CAD and drawing systems do not incorporate collision detection, and it is not clear that it would be useful when creating complex objects.

This is an ideal situation for multimethods. This is where browsers capable of computing collision detection could decide to subclass scene-navigation methods and detect collisions with standard objects. Or, a world creator could create a new class of collidable objects, all of which would register themselves with a collision-detection manager.

URNs and VRML

URNs are not the same thing as generic objects; rather, they are location-independent pointers to the same file or different representations of the same content. Generic objects are designed to handle the case of when you don't have the exact telephone but want any telephone. This VAG research proposal doesn't address generic objects except that they may be made easier by this.

URNs are a concept that's been around almost as long as URLs. Currently there is a consensus that they should look something like this:

```
urn:foo.com:abc123-Def
```

where:
The um says this is a URN and not a HTTP or other kind of URL; foo.com says that the issuing authority is foo.com. There is plenty of controversy about who and how these should be assigned; however, DNS names look like the best contenders; The opaque string ABC123-DEF is assigned by foo.com and can be any printable ASCII. And it may or may not be case dependent. For now it is recommended that all URNs be required to be lowercase.[13]

The IETF (Internet Engineering Task Force) could talk about this forever; a proposal merging three or four competing ideas and meeting the formal requirements document was presented in October 1995. But the IETF doesn't set timeliness, so other proposals keep appearing faster than they can be debunked.

For this proposal to succeed, VAG needs to address three timelines:

1. In the short term, VAG cannot assume any server infrastructure; everything must be happening at the client.

2. In the medium term, VAG can assume a server infrastructure created specifically for handling some URNs in relationship to VRML.

---

[13] Mitra, VRML and URN, mitra@earth.path.net, September 18, 1995.

3. In the long term, VAG can assume a global URN infrastructure; however, how long this will take is anyone's guess.[14]

In the short term VAG is relying on the client only; to do this, in brief, the client receives a URN as part of a WWWAnchor and then looks up in a hierarchy of tables to determine if/where it has a copy of the file. This requires four steps:

1. Make WWWInline a MFString rather than an SFString. This allows a client to see a list of potential locations for an object and to use the first one available. This is generally useful for clients that don't implement URNs, since it allows multiple alternative locations for the same file; thereby increasing reliability. It's also useful for the generic objects scenario, whereby a client can display a URL it does have cached while waiting for the correct one to be downloaded:

```
WWWInline {
  name [ "urn:foo.com:abc126,                       # A URN for the fancy
                                                      phone
         "http://www.foo.com/fancyphone.wrl",       # Where we know there
                                                      is a copy
         "http://vrml.org/generic/phone.wrl ]       # A generic version
                                                      to use now
}
```

2. Define a file format for resolving URNs. This format should allow easy future extension to support a networked URN resolution. A typical top-level URN file might look like this:

```
# We have the object library from foo.com here
urn:foo.com:* @file:c:/objectlib/foo/index.urn
# Maybe we have the URN cached from earlier
* @file:e:/objectcache/index.urn
#Try looking in d: (the CDROM) maybe its there
    @file:d:/index.urn
```
[15]

Note the use of @ to denote to look in that file rather than to return the file. Lower-level URN files would look something like this:

```
urn:foo.com:abc123 file:c:/objectlib/foo/table.wrl
urn:foo.com:abc124 file:c:/objectlib/foo/chair.wrl
```

---

[14] *Ibid.*

[15] *Ibid.*

Of course, a clever browser might implement its own, more efficient binary format, but there needs to be a common shared format.

3. Enable browsers to know where to go to find the top-level file (by looking in the .ini file).
4. Give CD-ROM makers a standard location to put a URN index of objects on their disks. The index.urn is suggested in the top directory.

In the medium term it is assumed that some server support exists for this. Then the client would want to be able to go across the network to resolve a URN. Retrieving a URN should be no different from retrieving a URL.

This is implemented by the following procedure:

1. A network format must be added to the URN file:

    urn:bar.com:*   @http://bar.com
    urn:*   @http://vrml.org

2. The client sends queries to the http server specified.
3. The server can return the document specified (typically this will be where it holds the document or is a caching server).
4. Alternatively, the server sends back an HTTP Redirect message (typically where the server is just providing resolution services).
5. The client interprets the redirect message to retrieve the file from the real server. We can add a form-based registration processes, so that sites like vrml.org can know where certain collections of objects are available.[16]

The following process gives a number of migration directions but only if and when URNs become widely deployed and supported.

1. Implement URN resolution or retrieval in common caching http servers.
2. Have caching servers and resolution servers that implement the official URN resolution method (whatever it is).
3. Use the real URN standard resolution method directly from the clients.

---

[16] *Ibid.*

VRML VAG Proposal

This final part of the chapter is a VAG proposal for VRML X.X, the next version of the VRML standard. It is intended to provide a framework for thinking about the important work to be done on VRML in the near future and to suggest an approach for getting there. It is a broad-brush discussion.

VRML X.X is a modest revision to the V1.0 and V1.1 specification. Its main goal is to repair problems in the current specification and to help clarify interpretation. This is important because the VRML community is in an unstable state now; none of the tools interoperate. This needs to be remedied, or VAG won't achieve a critical mass of content. VRML could die an early death. VAG researchers have instituted a process by which commercial ISVs can cooperate via Internet mail to stabilize this situation in the short term. Such a process will surely help, but it has to be supported by a formal specification effort.

A secondary goal of VRML X.X is to advance the scene description to the next level of interactivity and realism without compromising the long-term goal of creating a foundation for networked interactive simulation. The VAG proposal suggests a scope and ambition level for such changes.

The tasks before VAG for VRML X.X are to:

- fix trouble spots and correct minor oversights,
- review currently proposed extensions,
- add useful Open Inventor constructs,
- add support for simple reality,
- add API and behavior hooks,
- add location-independent name support, and[17]

Fix Trouble Spots and Correct Minor Oversights

The general idea is to find and fix the things VAG did wrong, forgot to put in, or are just proving troublesome. Some features present problems because they are too closely tied to the Open Inventor scene graph model and are troublesome for non–Open Inventor–based browsers. Others require too much bandwidth or rendering time to be practical. Some are features that just can't be done economically by low-end rendering engines.

---

[17] Tony Parisi, *VRML 1.1 Proposal*, Intervista Software, Inc., dagobent@netcom.com, August 19, 1995.

An example of an Open Inventor construct that may give VAG problems is the Group node. Because properties leak across them, they present certain difficulties. VAG researchers have suggested making Groups behave like Separators. Rather than break compatibility, a better idea is to suggest that everybody use Separators and to move people away from using Groups.

An example of a feature that eats rendering time is the defaults in the ShapeHints node. Because it defaults to UNKNOWN_ORDERING and UNKNOWN_SHAPE_TYPE, it puts the onus on the viewer to render back and front sides of a face. By defaulting to COUNTERCLOCKWISE vertexOrdering and SOLID shapeType, rendering time can be saved. Then the burden will rest with the content-creation tools to explicitly specify double faces.

An example of a feature that is not economical on a low-end renderer is the way lights are clipped within Separators. Most low-end renderers can handle only global lights. VAG should change this behavior to be more in line with low-end renderers.

Review Currently Proposed Extensions

Some browsers and authoring tools are using the extension capabilities of VRML to add features that are not in the specification. Many of these features are useful and should be incorporated into VRML X.X, as follows:

- SwitchButton—a Switch node that lets you cycle through children by clicking or some other control mechanism,
- Cameras—a list of viewpoints used by WebSpace and other browsers,
- CollisionHints—an Info node used by WebFX for simple collision detection,
- BackgroundColor and BackgroundTexture, and
- Title—the scene's title.[18]

Add Useful Open Inventor Constructs

When subsetting Open Inventor for VRML, good things were left out. Let's identify Inventor features that make VRML better and bring them in:

---

[18] *Ibid.*

- Environment, LightModel, TextureCoordinateBinding;
- nearDistance, farDistance fields in Camera nodes.[19]

Support for Simple Reality

It's going to be a while before VAG can build fully networked, multiuser interactive simulations. But there's an immediate need to make VRML worlds more compelling and to allay people's fears about VRML being able to specify only dead worlds. We should add:

- motion paths,
- simple animation,
- basic physics, and
- sound.[20]

These should be added in such a way that they can be hooked into to support arbitrary external control of the scene.

Add API and Behavior Hooks

VAG has to make sure that a VRML X.X scene can be controlled by an external API. Is it enough that a node has a name that can be turned into an API handle, or is something else needed?

Add Location-Independent Name Support

A relatively simple feature that buys big wins in bandwidth is the ability to refer to an object by name instead of URL. This allows objects to be stored locally on a hard disk or CD-ROM. One solid proposal in this area is the URN scheme. Ideally, VAG will take a serious look at this.

From Here

Open Inventor, as discussed in this chapter, might end up being used as a basis for the VRML standard. The next chapter presents a brief overview of Open Inventor as an object 3-D toolkit offering a comprehensive solution to interactive graphics programming problems.

---

[19] *Ibid.*

[20] *Ibid.*

Open Inventor

Open Inventor is an object-oriented 3-D toolkit offering a comprehensive solution to interactive graphics programming problems. It presents a programming model based on a 3-D scene database that dramatically simplifies graphics programming. It includes a rich set of objects, such as cubes, polygons, text, materials, cameras, lights, trackballs, handle boxes, 3-D viewers, and editors, that speed up your programming time and extend your 3-D programming capabilities. Open Inventor has the following characteristics:

- is built on top of OpenGL,
- defines a standard file format for 3-D data interchange,
- introduces a simple event model for 3-D interaction,
- provides animation objects called engines,
- provides high-performance object picking,
- is window system and platform independent.
- is a cross-platform 3-D graphics development system,
- supports PostScript printing, and
- encourages programmers to create new customized objects.
- Also, it is fun to use.[1]

---

[1] Gavin Bell, *Silicon Graphics, Inc.*, 1994, 1995, gavin @sgi.com.

IRIS Inventor Overview

IRIS Inventor was the first release of Inventor and is also known as Inventor V1.0 (Open Inventor is Inventor V2.0). IRIS Inventor is built on top of IRIS GL rather than OpenGL and has fewer features.

Inventor defines a powerful, extensible format for 3-D objects and scenes. The Inventor format is the standard for 3-D objects on Silicon Graphics machines and may become the standard for all machines.

However, Inventor is more than a 3-D object file format. It is a complete toolkit for writing interactive 3-D applications.

Inventor is for programmers writing 3-D applications and does not directly provide any way for users to create 3-D objects. Several Inventor applications have been written that create 3-D objects. Showcase V3.0, which is bundled with IRIX, is a fairly simple example. A much more sophisticated modeler called *Ez3d*, built on top of Inventor, is available from Radiance Software International.

Open Inventor contains mostly 3-D objects. There is little in the way of conventional user interface objects, such as buttons, dialogues, and menus. However, Open Inventor includes a full-fledged event model, a framework designed for 3-D user interaction, and some manipulator objects for 3-D user interface building. Note that the Open Inventor Xt Component and Utility Library includes some traditional 2-D user interface widgets.

Few GL programs achieve peak graphics performance, because most applications have natural application overhead, and many programmers lack a thorough understanding of the details and eccentricities of GL. If you are writing a simple display-only, immediate-mode GL program, it will run a bit faster using straight GL. However, if your program has scene traversal, interactivity, picking, bounding-box calculations, and other object space tasks, Open Inventor will perform better for you, because Open Inventor is specially tuned to make optimal use of GL on each SGI machine. Furthermore, Open Inventor supports render caching, which results in peak GL performance in most cases.

The VRML Architecture Group has found that in many cases, Open Inventor programs run faster than the original GL program. Thus the programmer productivity increases easily outweigh the overhead of the toolkit.

You can use the C API and never see or use C++. However, subclassing to extend the toolkit does require C++.

Open Inventor requires SGI's C++ compiler. The GNU C++ compiler and SGI's C++ compiler produce incompatible code, and Silicon Graphics does not ship an Open Inventor library compatible with GNU C++.

An Open Inventor Sampler: Hello Cone

This part of the chapter introduces Inventor programming and some key Inventor concepts. Most of the chapter provides variations on the Hello Cone program, a simple program that displays a cone on the screen.

Hello Cone is a 20-line program that opens an XtRenderArea in a window; creates a 3-D scene consisting of a camera, a light, and a red material; adds the scene to the XtRenderArea; and then enters the Xt main event loop, which takes care of rendering the cone in response to window system events. {Bonus information you won't find in the book: Several people in the Open Inventor group at SGI believe that these examples should have been expressed in the ASCII file format instead of being presented as programming exercises. However since Open Inventor is a programming library first and a file format second, the argument was lost. Nonetheless, the file format for the examples is being presented here. If you have an SGI machine, you can use the program '/usr/sbin/ivview' to view them.}

Here is HelloCone:

```
# Inventor V2.0 ascii
Separator {
   PerspectiveCamera
        position 0 0 4.18154
        nearDistance 2.44949
        farDistance 5.91359
        focalDistance 4.18154
   }
   DirectionalLight {}
   Material {
        diffuseColor [ 1 0 0 ]
   }
   Cone {}
}
```
[2]

---

[2] *Ibid.*

Variation 1: Using Engines to Make the Cone Spin

The first variation presented adds an engine to make the cone spin. A rotation transformation (RotationXYZ) is added to the scene, and an ElapsedTime engine is connected to the rotation's angle so that the angle of rotation in radians equals the time in seconds since the program started (the axis of rotation is set to the X-axis).

In the ASCII file format, this scene looks like:

```
#Inventor V2.0 ascii
Separator {
    PerspectiveCamera {
        position 0 0 4.18154
        nearDistance 2.44949
        farDistance  5.91359
        focalDistance 4.18154
    }
    DirectionalLight {}
    RotationXYZ {
        AXIS x
        angle = ElapsedTime{ }. timeOut
    }
    Material {
        diffuseColor [ 1 0 0 ]
    }
    Cone {}
}
```

Variation 2: Adding a Trackball Manipulator

Next, a trackball manipulator is used to allow the user to interactively manipulate the rotation of the cone. This is done by replacing the RotationXYZ node of the previous example.

This is done with a TrackballManip:

```
#Inventor V2.0 ascii
Separator {
    PerspectiveCamera {
        position 0 0 4.18154
        nearDistance 2.44949
```

```
        farDistance    5.91359
        focalDistance  4.18154
    }
    DirectionalLight { }
    TrackballManip { }
    Material {
        diffuseColor [ 1 0 0 ]
    }
Cone { }
}
```

Variation 3: Adding the Examiner Viewer

Finally, an XtExaminerViewer is used instead of a simple XtRenderArea. The XtExaminerViewer adds user interface controls to allow the user to manipulate his or her view of the scene. For example, this is like a zoom slider that controls the field of view (like a zoom lens on a camera) and thumbwheel widgets that control rotation about the screen X and Y axes, etc. The particular viewing paradigm used (ExaminerViewer, WalkViewer, FlyViewer, etc.) is not considered part of the scene and is not saved in the file format. So there is no corresponding file format example for this variant on Hello Cone.

Naming Scenes

Most Open Inventor C++ classes are prefixed with So, which stands for Scene Object (at least, that's the official explanation—insiders know that it really stands for Scenario, the internal name of the project before it had a name). All enumerated values are all uppercase, etc. The Open Inventor library also contains some useful low-level classes that are prefixed with Sb: SbLine, SbColor, and SbRotation.

Coordinate Systems

The convention for the coordinate system used by Open Inventor is a right-handed coordinate system with +z coming out of the screen. Angles are specified in radians, and objects may be defined in their own local coordinate system. The world coordinate space is the default coordinate space. An object can be transformed into world coordinates by applying all of the transformation affecting it.

Building a Scene Graph

This part of the chapter explains the concept of a scene graph and shows how to build scenes out of groups, properties, and shapes. It also describes the concepts of actions, traversal, and traversal state.

The phrase "*Open Inventor supports*" is used to indicate the features that are built in to Open Inventor. Programmers can extend the toolkit to support almost anything.

Open Inventor programs store their scenes in structures called *scene graphs*. A scene graph is made up of *nodes*, which represent 3-D objects that are drawn (shapes); *properties* of the 3-D objects (properties); groups, nodes that contain other nodes and are used for hierarchical grouping and others (cameras, lights, etc.).

Open Inventor defines a standard set of actions that can be applied to a scene, such as rendering, getting the world-space bounding box of the scene, or picking (finding out what objects are underneath the mouse pointer). Each node implements its own action behavior.

Nodes and Groups

Each node contains one or more pieces of information stored in fields. For example, the Sphere node contains only its radius, stored in its radius field. Each field class defines methods to get and set its values. Well behaved nodes (all standard Open Inventor nodes are well-behaved) use only the contents of their fields and their position in the scene to determine how they behave when traversed during an action.

Open Inventor supports the following shape nodes:

- Cone
- Cube
- Cylinder
- Sphere
- Text2

- Text3
- IndexedFaceSet
- IndexedLineSet
- IndexedTriangleStripSet
- FaceSet
- LineSet
- PointSet
- QuadMesh
- TriangleStripSet
- IndexedNurbsCurve
- IndexedNurbsSurface
- NurbsCurve
- NurbsSurface[3]

The way shapes are drawn is affected by property nodes in the scene. Open Inventor supports the following property nodes:

- BaseColor
- ColorIndex
- Complexity
- Coordinate3
- Coordinate4
- DrawStyle
- Environment
- Font
- LightModel
- Material
- MaterialBinding
- MaterialIndex
- Normal
- NormalBinding
- PackedColor
- PickStyle

---

[3] *Ibid.*

- LinearProfile
- NurbsProfile
- ProfileCoordinate2
- ProfileCoordinate3
- ShapeHints
- Texture2
- Texture2Transform
- TextureCoordinate2
- TextureCoordinateBinding
- TextureCoordinateDefault
- TextureCoordinateEnvironment
- TextureCoordinatePlane
- AntiSquish
- MatrixTransform
- ResetTansform
- Rotation
- Pendulum
- Rotor
- RotationXYZ
- Scale
- SuffoundScale
- Transform Translation
- Shuttle
- Units[4]

The order in which the shapes are drawn is determined by group nodes, which contain other nodes known as the group's "children." Open Inventor supports the following kinds of group nodes:

Open Inventor supports the following group nodes:

- Group
- Array
- LevelOfDetail

---

[4] *Ibid.*

- MultipleCopy
- PathSwitch
- Separator
- Annotation
- Selection
- Switch
- Blinker
- TransformSeparator

Open Inventor draws the scene graph in a recursive fashion, starting by drawing the first (root) node and then drawing its children (if it is a group). A property must be drawn before a shape node to affect it. The simplest kind of group node is Group, which just draws its children in order.

Separator nodes are used to isolate parts of scene from the rest of the scene. A property node inside a Separator will not affect any nodes outside the Separator.

For example, a robot's head and body might be specified in the file format like this:

```
#Inventor V2.0 ascii
Separator {
   Separator { # Body
      Transform { translation 0 3 0 }
      Material { A bronze color:
         ambientColor .33 .22 .27
         diffuseColor .78 .57 .11
         specularColor .99 .94 .81
         shininess .28
      }
      Cylinder { radius 2.5 height 6 }
   }
   Separator { # Head
      Transform { translation 0 7.5 0 }
      Material { # A silver color:
         ambientColor .2 .2 .2
         diffuseColor .6 .6 .6
         specularColor .5 .5 .5
         shininess .5
      }
```

```
        Sphere { }
    }
}
```

The use of Separator nodes keeps the translation of the body from affecting the translation of the head.

The *Switch* group has a field that specifies which children should be drawn. It can be set to draw only one child, to draw no children, or to draw all of the children (in which case it acts like a Group node).

LevelOfDetail is a kind of group that draws only one of its children, based on how big the object appears on the screen. It can be used to draw a simpler version of the object, with fewer polygons when the object is far away.

Adding the same node to more than one group creates a *shared instance*. Instancing is useful for geometry that is shared. Only one copy of the geometry needs to be read in and stored in memory.

For example, we can modify the robot scene graph to add legs, like this:

```
# Inventor V2.0 ascii
Separator {
    Separator{ # Body
        Transform { translation 0 3 0 }
        Material { # A bronze color:
            ambientColor .33 .22 .27
            diffuseColor .78 .57 .11
            specularColor .99 .94 .81
            shininess .28
        }
        Cylinder { radius 2.5 height 6 }
        Separator { # Left leg
            Transform { translation 1 -4.25 0 }
            DEF +0 Group { # Shared leg geometry
                Cube { width 1.2 height 2.2 depth 1.1 }
                Transform { translation 0 -2.25 0 }
                Cube { width 1 height 2.2 depth 1 }
                Transform { translation 0 -2 .5 }
                Cube { width .8 height .8 depth 2 }
            }
        }
```

```
        Separator { # Right leg
                Transform { translation -1 - 4.25 0 }
                USE +0 # Use the leg geometry again
            }
        }
        Separator { # Head
            Transform { translation 0 7.5 0 }
            Material { # A silver color:
                ambientColor .2 .2 .2
                diffuseColor .6 .6 .6
                specularColor .5 .5 .5
                shininess .5
            }
            Sphere { }
        }
    }
```

The DEF/USE +0 syntax is used to refer to the same node more than once. If several nodes were multiply instanced, Open Inventor would write out each with a unique number after the plus sign {+}.

Paths

The concept of a path is important when programming Open Inventor. A *path* is a chain of nodes, from parent to child, through the scene graph. Paths are returned from picking and searching. For example, if the user clicks the mouse on the left foot of the robot, a path from the root of the scene, through the body separator, the left-leg separator, through the leg group, and finally down to the last cube in the leg group would be returned. Paths are necessary because nodes may be multiple instances. The cube representing the foot cannot be returned when the user picks on the left foot, because the same cube is used for both the left and right feet.

Fields

Each type of field has its own set of methods for getting and setting its value(s). For example, MFFloat, which is a type of field that contains zero or more floating-point values, has methods for setting one value, for deleting a range of values, and for returning the number of values currently being stored, etc.

Fields have an ignored flag that can be set and queried. Fields in nodes that are marked ignored will have no effect. The ignore flag is written to file as a "-" character after (or in place of) the field's value.

Nodes have an override flag that can be used to force temporary changes to the scene. For example, to draw everything as lines, the following program might put a line near the beginning of the scene and set its ignored flag.

```
DrawStyle { style LINES }
```

Any subsequent DrawStyle nodes in the scene will be ignored. The override flag is not written to (or read from) file.

Node Mechanisms

Nodes are managed while in memory with a reference-counting mechanism that allows a node to be created, added to a scene, and then forgotten. The node gets properly deleted when the scene is deleted, even if it is multiply instanced.

Open Inventor provides programmers with a run-time type mechanism for its node, engine, action, detail, and event classes. It allows programmers to find out whether an object is of a given type, what class an object is derived from, etc.

Nodes can be given names. Once given a name, a node can be quickly looked up by name. Names follow the rules for C++ identifiers ([a-zA-Z_] [a-zA-Z0-9_]*.

The Open Inventor group will probably relax this to be any sequence of characters not containing the characters +,',",\,{}. Open Inventor V2.0 does not check to see whether names are valid and some Open Inventor customers already have programs that give their nodes names like Object1:foo[1,14]). Names are read and written to files by using the keyword 'DEF'.

For example, a cube named Joe would be written as:

```
DEF Joe Cube { }
```

Note: If multiply instanced, it might be written as Joe+1 8, but its name is still just Joe.

Cameras

Cameras and Lights, the Open Inventor node classes that allow you to see the objects that you create in your graph, are relatively intuitive. Lights provide the lighting for your scene Cameras provide the viewports to see them from.

The Camera class allows you to define a view of the scene. The two kinds of Camera nodes are *Orthographic* and *Perspective.* The Orthographic Camera class allows you to define cameras that do not preserve perspective, which can be useful for designing objects. Perspective cameras provide a more natural way of viewing scenes.

All Cameras have fields allowing you to set:

- the position of the camera in the scene;
- the orientation that the camera faces;
- the aspect ratio of the camera;
- the near and far clipping planes (so that you don't try to view things a millimeter away, or off in the extreme distance);
- a focal distance, when relevant; and
- a mapping flag, for use when the camera's proportions do not match those of the actual window that the user is looking at.[5]

When it encounters a camera is during traversal of a scene graph, Open Inventor figures out the volume of space that the camera covers (based on the angles it includes and the clipping planes) and doesn't draw any objects that aren't in that space. This space is called the *view volume*. You can orient a camera toward a specific object, using the pointAt() method, or examine an entire scene, using the viewAll() method.

Perspective Cameras provide one additional field: the vertical angle that the camera covers. By contrast, Orthographic Cameras instead have a field for the height of the volume that the camera should cover. Thus Perspective Cameras have (more or less) conical view volumes, and Orthographic ones have rectangular prisms for their view volumes.

You can have multiple cameras in a scene and switch between them dynamically. However, only one camera may be active at a time, and it must come before the objects it is to view.

---

[5] Mark Waks, *Silicon Graphics, Inc.*, 1995, justin@dsd.camb.inmet.com.

Lights

Like Cameras, lights should come before objects in the scene graph, and each light illuminates only the objects that come after it. There is a base class of Lights and several subclasses: Point Lights, Directional Lights, and Spotlights. All lights have several fields, indicating:

- whether the light is on,
- its intensity, and
- its color.[6]

Point Lights are balls of light at a particular point. They have one additional field, a location, and shine equally in all directions.

Directional Lights are like sunlight: They are infinitely far off and shine in one specific direction. They have one additional field, the direction of the light.

Spotlights are like real-world spotlights. They have a location in the scene and a direction of focus, as well as a falloff rate (indicating how much they are focused on one spot) and a cutoff angle beyond which no light goes. You can have an arbitrary number of lights in a scene.

Shapes, Properties, and Binding

This part of the chapter describes the basics of how you create shapes and how to apply properties to those shapes.

Shapes

All shapes are subclasses of the SoShape class. Shapes can be either simple or complex. Simple shapes include cubes, cones, spheres, and cylinders. Complex shapes allow you to describe more complex surfaces in a variety of ways—face sets, line sets, triangle strips, point sets, quad meshes, and NURBS.

Face Sets allow you to define a solid shape in terms of the polygons that make up its faces. You create an array of coordinates containing all of the vertices of all of the faces, in order. Note that this may involve duplication of vertices.

---

[6] *Ibid.*

An Indexed Face Set is like a Face Set, except that the vertices are indexed. This allows you to refer to vertices in any order and to reuse them, thus often saving some space.

A Triangle Strip Set allows you to create a surface out of a collection of triangles. It works much like a Face Set but is somewhat faster to render. However, it may be more inconvenient for some shapes. A Quad Mesh is similar to a Triangle Strip Set but uses an array of quadrilaterals to define the shape instead of triangles.

Properties

You can apply a number of kinds of *properties*, each with a different node class. Whereas shape nodes tell the rendering engine to draw the shape in question, property nodes affect the *state* of the rendering, changing the way that subsequent shapes will be drawn. Thus a property must always come before the shapes it is to affect.

The following properties are available:

- Materials—affects the color and reflectivity of objects;
- Draw Style—tells the renderer how to draw shapes;
- Light Model—affects how light is treated in the scene environment, specifying ambient properties such as fog and light attenuation;
- Shape Hints—permits certain rendering optimizations;
- Complexity—allows you to specify the level of detail to be drawn; and
- Units—allows you to define your units of measurement.

A SoMaterial node affects subsequent objects in the scene. This node allows you to specify the following for each object:

- ambient color—response to ambient light,
- diffuse color—base color of the object,
- specular color—reflected color,
- emissive color—color of radiated light,
- shininess, and
- transparency.[7]

---

[7] *Ibid.*

A SoDrawStyle lets you define whether shapes should be drawn as filled-in regions (the default), as outlines, as arrays of points, or left invisible. If you choose points, you can specify the size of those points. If you choose lines, you can specify the width and pattern of the lines.

A SoLightModel node allows you to specify whether to use Phong lighting (that is, use the light sources in the scene) or to just display each object in its base color. Phong lighting is the default and usually looks much more natural.

A SoEnvironment allows you to specify the *atmosphere* of the scene. Specifically you can describe:

- the intensity and color of the ambient light in the scene,
- how rapidly light attenuates away from its sources (which can be set to constant, linear, or squared attenuation),
- the kind of fog in the scene (there are several grades of fog: haze is light, fog is moderate, and smoke is quite dense),
- the color of the fog, and
- the distance at which the fog completely obscures the scene.[8]

A SoShapeHints node allows you to specify several characteristics of the subsequent shapes; doing so can speed up rendering of the scene. These hints include:

- the order of vertices in the faces of the shape,
- whether the shape is solid,
- whether all of the faces of the shape are convex, and
- the crease angle, which can help in automatically generating normals.[9]

A SoComplexity node allows you to specify how much you want the renderer to subdivide subsequent objects into polygons. If you specify less subdivision, rendering is generally faster.

You can tell it the following:

- to use fewer polygons for objects that are small on the screen,
- draw just bounding boxes,
- a hint about how much to subdivide (this is simply an abstract number between 0 and 1), and
- a hint about how carefully to texture the objects.

---

[8] *Ibid.*

[8] *Ibid.*

A SoUnits node allows you to specify the units of measurement for all subsequent shapes in the graph. Almost everything you are likely to want is available: from kilometers down to angstroms, including normal English units (feet, miles), and one or two esoteric ones (nautical miles). Meters are the default unit.

Bindings

A single Material is often insufficient for an object, particularly a complex object. Various parts or faces of the object may call for different colors or reflectivity. Thus, a SoMaterial node can actually hold an unlimited number of materials, each field in the node can have multiple values. The way that these values are applied to objects is determined by a SoMaterialBinding node.

You can specify a number of ways to bind a list of materials onto an object:

- the default, which tries to use the best binding (usually an overall binding), uses no materials;
- an overall binding, using the first material for the entire shape;
- the use of one material for each part of the shape, where part is appropriate to the kind of object in question;
- the use of one material per part, with indexing;
- the use of one material per face, optionally with indexing; and
- the use of one material per vertex, optionally with indexing.

If you use indexing, the object in question should use a *materialIndex* field to specify which materials are bound to which parts of the shape. If you bind materials to vertices, this field interpolates between those vertices. Several color plates are provided to illustrate the way Open Inventor handles materials, lights, and bindings.

Normals

Normals can be specified explicitly or generated automatically. You can specify them explicitly in much the same way that materials are specified and bound to objects. Most complex objects can compute their normals automatically, but this process is quite compute intensive and can slow things down.

Transformations

Transformations are similar to properties in that they affect the state of the rendering engine. However, they are cumulative; a transformation adds to previous transformations, unlike properties, which replace previous properties in the state. You can specify all of the usual sorts of transformations in a SoTransform node. Specifically, you can describe:

- translation in space,
- rotation,
- scaling factor,
- scaling rotation (a rotation to apply before scaling), and
- the center point of the object for rotation and scaling.

There are also separate node classes for rotation, translation, and scaling, which are convenient if you are performing only one transformation.

Text

Both two dimensional (2-D) and three dimensional (3-D) text can be added to a scene. Two-dimensional text is always displayed facing the screen. Three dimensional text appears as an object in the scene and can be viewed from any direction. The font type and size can be changed for both types of text, and the profile of the 3-D text can be modified.

A *SoText2* node is available for creating screen-aligned text. The origin of the text is (0,0,0), and the origin is transformed by the current transformation matrix. However, the text itself always faces the screen. The text can be justified with respect to the origin, and the line spacing can be modified. The 2-D text is not affected by perspective changes. In other words, the height and width of two-dimensional text does not change as the distance from the viewer changes. Two-dimensional text is useful for labeling graphs or points in a scene.

The primary difference between *SoText3* and *SoText2* is that 3-D text has a thickness and can be displayed as solid letters. *SoText3* is not constrained to face the screen. For instance, if the camera moves above the letters, the tops of the 3-D letters are displayed on the monitor.

The shape of the text displayed with a *SoText3* node can be changed by applying a custom extrusion profile. The profile can be defined by using either a *SoLinearProfile* node or a *SoNurbsProfile* node.[10] The profile can make the text appear beveled or curved instead of blocky.

Textures

Textures can greatly increase the quality of a rendered image. Textures are used to add visual detail to a model without increasing the number of polygons in the model.

To display a textured object, you need a list of polygons comprising the object on which the texture is to be displayed and a two-dimensional bitmap or image, which is called a texture map. The mapping between the texture and the polygons is controlled by assigning texture coordinates to individual vertices.

Two dimensional images used as texture maps can be read from file or stored in memory. Currently only SGI's RGB image format is supported on the SGIs, but there are many ways to convert image files to the SGI RGB format.

A texture map is described as being a 1 × 1 square. However, a texture map does not have to have the same dimension in height and in width. When a square or a rectangular bitmap is read into memory, it is assigned coordinates between 0.0 and 1.0 in both directions. These coordinates are mapped to the texture coordinates on the vertices of the polygon.

This example uses a SoTexture2 node to apply the bitmap contained in texture.rgb to a cube:

```
#Inventor V2.0 ascii
Separator {
   Texture2 {
       filename "texture.rgb-"
   }
   Cube {
   }
}
```
[11]

---

[10] John Barrus, Silicon Graphics, Inc., 1995, barrus@merl.com.

[11] *Ibid.*

The following list identifies and describes the nodes used for texture mapping:

SoTexture2	Used to specify bitmap for texturing.
SoTextureCoordinate2	Lists texture coordinates to be indexed by subsequent vertices.
SoTextureCoordinateBinding	Describes texture coordinate binding for following shape nodes.
SoTextureCoordinatePlane	To be determined.
SoTextureCoordinateEnvironment	Nodes that allow the use of spatial functions for creating texture coordinates.
SoTextureCoordinateDefault	Turns off previous texture coordinate functions.
SoTexture2Transform	Transforms a 2-D texture map.[12]

Texture maps can be used to modulate the color and the transparency of an object. Normally, when you draw shaded images, a polygon's color (or shaded color) is calculated, based on the current SoMaterial node. When a texture is used to *modulate* the color, the shaded color is combined with the texture color. When it is used as a *decal*, the texture color replaces the shaded color. With *blend* mode turned on and a one- or two-component texture map, the final color is blended between the shaded color and a constant blend color.

To map the texture onto the object, you can use the default texture mapping for the shape node, as in the previous example. However, you will often want more control over how the texture is mapped to the polygons of the object.

A SoTextureCoordinate2 node can be used to align specific texture coordinates to polygon vertices. Also, two texture coordinate functions can be applied to shapes: SoTextureCoordinatePlane and SoTextureCoordinateEnvironment.

---

[12] *Ibid.*

Nodekits

Nodekits are a collection of nodes with a specified arrangement, thereby simplifying the creation of consistent, structured databases. Nodekits also support nesting hierarchies, so many levels of relative motion can occur.

The template associated with the nodekit decides which nodes can be added and where they should be placed. Therefore you don't have to create and arrange each node individually.

When a nodekit is created, particular nodes are thereby default (separator nodes and internal nodes, for example); you must explicitly request other nodes to be created. The nodes can be created in any order, because the kit will put them in the right place as specified by the nodekit catalog. You don't have direct access to "hidden children", which are the nodes you create and remove in the nodekit. The nodekit takes care of the details for you.

An example can illustrate the ease of using nodekits for application-specific objects. With a cat simulation package, there are a several objects representing cats. Each cat has the same general structure in the scene graph for example, legs and head, as well as cat-specific actions (for example, ScratchingHead()). Each cat can be dealt with in a similar way. Knowing the details of the subgraph representing ScratchingHead() isn't necessary, because the general ScratchingHead() method exists. To create these new specific objects and methods, you need to extend Open Inventor by subclassing, which is described in Inventor Toolmaker.[13]

To select parts and to set values, you use something called "set()." You can also specify part names in the nodes of the nodekits. The other two basic methods are GetPart(), which returns the requested node, and setPart(), which inserts the node given as a new part in the nodekit. There are macros for these and two methods, called SO_GET_PART() and SO_CHECK_PART(), which perform casting and, additionally, type checking.

A path can be returned from a pick or a search action. The default is SoPath, which ends the path at the nodekit. You can also choose to cast SoFullPath, which includes hidden and public children of the nodekit; or SoNodEkitPath, which contains only the nodekits (not the intermediate nodes). It is also possible to create paths to a particular nodekit part.

---

[13] Ferguson, *Silicon Graphics, Inc.*, 1995, snpf@ugcs.caltech.edu.

Virtual Reality Modeling Language (VRML)

The Virtual Reality Modeling Language (VRML) is a language for describing multiparticipant interactive simulations—virtual worlds networked via the global Internet and hyperlinked with the World Wide Web. VRML can be used to specify all aspects of virtual world display, interaction, and Internetworking. It is the intention of its designers that VRML become the standard language for interactive simulation within the World Wide Web.

The first version of VRML allows for the creation of virtual worlds with limited interactive behavior. These worlds can contain objects that have hyperlinks to other worlds, HTML documents, or other valid MIME types. When a user selects an object with a hyperlink, the appropriate MIME viewer is launched. When the user selects a link to a VRML document from within a correctly configured browser, a VRML viewer is launched. Thus VRML viewers are the perfect companion applications to standard WWW browsers for navigating and visualizing the Web. Future versions of VRML will allow for richer behaviors, including animations, motion physics, and real-time multiuser interaction.

VRML Overview

The history of the development of the Internet has had three distinct phases. First was the development of the TCP/IP infrastructure, which allowed documents and data to be stored in a proximally independent way. That is, the Internet provided a layer of abstraction between datasets and the hosts that manipulated them. This abstraction was useful, but also confusing. Without any clear sense of what went where, access to the Internet was restricted to the class of sysops/net surfers who could maintain internal cognitive maps of the data space.

Next, Tim Berners-Lee's work at CERN, where he developed the hypermedia system known as World Wide Web, added another layer of abstraction to the existing structure. This abstraction provided an addressing scheme, a unique identifier (the Universal Resource Locator), which could tell anyone where to go and how to get there for any piece of data within the Web. Although useful, it lacked dimensionality. There's no *there* within the Web, and the only type of navigation permissible (other than surfing) is by direct reference. In other words, users can be directed on how to get to the VRML Forum home page only by saying http:Hwww.wired.com/, which is not human-centered data. So, although the World Wide Web provides a retrieval mechanism to complement the existing storage mechanism, it leaves a lot to be desired, particularly for human beings.

Finally, we move to perceptualized Internetworks, where the data has been sensualized or rendered sensually. If something is represented sensually, it is possible to make sense of it. VRML is an attempt (how successful, only time and effort will tell) to place humans at the center of the Internet, ordering its universe to out whims. In order to do that, the most important single element is a standard that defines the particularities of perception. Virtual Reality Modeling Language is that standard, designed to be a *universal description language for multiparticipant simulations.*

These three phases—storage, retrieval, and perceptualization—are analogous to the human process of consciousness, as expressed in terms of semantics and cognitive science. Events occur and are recorded (memory). Inferences are drawn from memory (associations), and maps of the universe are created (cognitive perception) from sets of related events. What is important to remember is that the map is not the territory, and we should avoid becoming trapped in any single representation or worldview. Although we need to *design to avoid disorientation*, we should always push the envelope in the kinds of experiences we can bring into manifestation!

This part of the chapter discusses the success of a process that was committed to being open and flexible and responsive to the needs of a growing Web community. Rather than reinvent the wheel, the VRML Architecture Group has adapted an existing specification (Open Inventor) as the basis from which its own work can grow, saving years of design work and perhaps many mistakes. Now the real work can begin: rendering its norspheric space.

History

VRML was conceived in the spring of 1994 at the first annual World Wide Web Conference in Geneva, Switzerland. Tim Berners-Lee and Dave Raggett organized a Birds-of-a-Feather (BOF) session to discuss virtual reality interfaces to the World Wide Web. Several BOF attendees described projects already under way to build three-dimensional graphical visualization tools that interoperate with the Web. Attendees agreed on the need for these tools to have a common language for specifying 3-D scene description and hyperlinks—an analog of HTML for virtual reality. The term Virtual Reality Markup Language (VRML) was coined, and the group resolved to begin specification work after the conference. The word Markup was later changed to Modeling to reflect the graphical nature of VRML.

Shortly after the Geneva BOF session, the www-vrml mailing list was created to discuss the development of a specification for the first version of VRML. The response to the list invitation was overwhelming: Within a week, there were more than a thousand members. After an initial settling-in period, list moderator Mark Pesce of Labyrinth Group announced his intention to have a draft version of the specification ready by the fall 1994 conference, a mere five months away. List members generally agreed that, although this schedule was aggressive, it was achievable, provided that the requirements for the first version were not too ambitious and that VRML could be adapted from an existing solution. The list members quickly agreed on a set of requirements for the first version and began a search for technologies that could be adapted to fit the needs of VRML.

The search for existing technologies turned up a several worthwhile candidates. After much deliberation, the list members came to a consensus: the Open Inventor ASCII File Format from Silicon Graphics, Inc. The Open Inventor File Format supports complete descriptions of 3-D scenes with polygonally rendered objects, lighting, materials, ambient properties, and realism effects. A subset of the Open Inventor File Format, with extensions to support networking, forms the basis of VRML. Gavin Bell of Silicon Graphics has adapted the Open Inventor File Format for VRML, with design input to the mailing list. SGI has publicly stated that the file format is available for use in the open market and has contributed a file format parser into the public domain to bootstrap VRML viewer development.

Requirements

VRML is designed to meet the following requirements:

- platform independence,
- extensibility, and
- ability to work well over low-bandwidth connections.[1]

As with HTML, these are absolute requirements for a network language standard. They should need little explanation here.

Early on, the designers decided that VRML would not be an extension to HTML, which is designed for text, not graphics. Also, VRML requires even more finely tuned network optimizations than HTML. It is expected that a typical VRML scene will be composed of many more inline objects and served up by many more servers than a typical HTML document. Moreover, HTML is an accepted standard, with existing implementations. To impede the HTML design process with VRML issues and to constrain the VRML design process with HTML compatibility concerns would do both languages a disservice. As a network language, VRML will succeed or fail independent of HTML.

VAG also decided that, except for the hyperlinking feature, the first version of VRML would not support interactive behaviors. This was a practical decision intended to streamline design and implementation.

---

[1] Gavin Bell, *Silicon Graphics, Inc.*, December 16, 1995.

Design of a language for describing interactive behaviors is a big job, especially when the language needs to express behaviors of objects communicating on a network. Such languages do exist. If VAG had chosen one of them, it would have risked getting into a language war. People don't get excited about the syntax of a language for describing polygonal objects; people get *very* excited about the syntax of real languages for writing programs. Religious wars can extend the design process by months or years. In addition, networked interobject operation requires brokering services such as those provided by CORBA or OLE—services that don't exist yet within WWW; VAG would have had to invent them. Finally, by keeping behaviors out of a version, VAG has made it a much smaller task to implement a viewer. VAG acknowledged that support for arbitrary interactive behaviors is critical to the long-term success of VRML. They will be included in Version X.X.

VRML Language Specification

The language specification deals with the following topics:

- language basics,
- coordinate system,
- fields,
- nodes,
- instantiation, and
- extensibility.[2]

Language Basics

At the highest level of abstraction, VRML is just a way for objects to read and write themselves. Theoretically the objects can contain anything—3-D geometry, MIDI data, JPEG images. VRML defines a set of objects useful for doing 3-D graphics. These objects are called *nodes*.

---

[2] *Ibid.*

Nodes are arranged in hierarchical structures called *scene graphs.* Scene graphs are more than just a collection of nodes. The scene graph defines an ordering for the nodes. The scene graph has a notion of *state.* Nodes earlier in the scene can affect nodes that appear later in the scene. For example, a Rotation or a Material node will affect the node after it in the scene. A mechanism is defined to limit the effects of properties (Separator nodes), allowing parts of the scene graph to be functionally isolated from other parts.

Applications that interpret VRML files need not maintain the scene graph structure internally. The scene graph is merely a convenient way of describing objects.

Node Characteristics

A node has the following characteristics:

Definition of what kind of object it is. A node might be a cube, a sphere, a texture map, a transformation, etc.

Parameters that distinguish this node from other nodes of the same type. For example, each Sphere node might have a different radius. And differTent texture maps nodes will certainly contain different images to use as the texture maps. These parameters are called fields. A node can have zero or more fields.

A name to identify this node. Being able to name nodes and to refer to them elsewhere is very powerful. It allows a scene's author to give hints to applications using the scene about what is in the scene and creates possibilities for very powerful scripting extensions. Nodes do not have to be named, but if they are named, they can have only one name. However, names do not have to be unique; several different nodes may be given the same name.

Child nodes. Object hierarchy is implemented by allowing some types of nodes to contain other nodes. Parent nodes traverse their children in order during rendering. Nodes that may have children are referred to as *group nodes.* Group nodes can have zero or more children.[3]

---

[3] Toni Parisi, *Intervista Software,* December 16, 1995.

The syntax chosen to represent these pieces of information is straightforward:

```
DEF objectname objecttype ( fields children )
```

Only the object type and braces are required. Nodes may or may not have a name, fields, and children. Node names must not begin with a digit and must not contain spaces or control characters, single or double quote characters, backslashes, braces, the plus character, or the period character.

General Syntax

For easy identification of VRML files, every VRML V1.1or VRML VX.X file must begin with the characters #VRML V1.1 utf8 or #VRML VX.X utf8.

The identifier utf8 allows for international characters to be displayed in VRML, using the UTF-8 encoding of the ISO 10646 standard. Unicode is an alternative encoding of ISO 10646. UTF-8 is explained later in the chapter.

Any characters after these on the same line are ignored. The line is terminated by either the ASCII newline or carriage-return characters.

The # character begins a comment. All characters until the next newline or carriage return are ignored. The only exception to this is within double-quoted SFString and MFString fields, where the # character will be part of the string.

Comments and whitespace may not be preserved. In particular, a VRML document server may strip comment and extraneous whitespace from a VRML file before transmitting it. Info nodes should be used for persistent information, such as copyrights or author information. Info nodes could also be used for object descriptions. New uses of named Iinfo nodes for conveying syntactically meaningful information are deprecated. Use the extension nodes mechanism instead.

Blanks, tabs, newlines, and carriage returns are whitespace characters wherever they appear outside of string fields. One or more whitespace characters separate the syntactical entities in VRML files, where necessary.

After the required header, a VRML file contains exactly one VRML node. That node may, of course, be a group node containing any number of other nodes.

Field names start with lowercase letters. Node types start with uppercase. The remainder of the characters may be any printable ASCII (2 1 H-7EH) except braces {{}}, brackets {[]}, single or double quotes {' "}, sharp {#}, backslash {\}, plus {+}, period {.}, or ampersand {&}.

Node names must not begin with a digit. But they may begin and contain any UTF-8 character except those below 2 1H (control characters and whitespace) and the characters {}, [], ",', #, \, +, ., and &.

VRML is case-sensitive. Thus "Sphere" is different from "sphere".

Coordinate System

VRML uses a Cartesian, right-handed, three-dimensional coordinate system. By default, objects are projected onto a two-dimensional device by projecting them in the direction of the positive Z-axis, with the positive X-axis to the right and the positive Y-axis up. A camera or modeling transformation may be used to alter this default projection.

The standard unit for lengths and distances specified is meters. The standard unit for angles is radians.

VRML scenes may contain an arbitrary number of local (or object-space) coordinate systems, defined by modeling transformations, using Translate, Rotate, Scale, Transform, and MatrixTransform nodes.

Suppose that one has a vertex V and a series of transformations, such as:

```
Translation { translation T }
Rotation { rotation R }
Scale { scaleFactor S }
Coordinate3 { point V } PointSet { numPoints 1 }
```

The vertex is transformed into world-space to get V' by applying the transformations in the following order:

V' = T-R-S-
V (if you think of vertices as column vectors) *or*
V' =
V-S-R-T (if you think of vertices as row vectors)[4]

---

[4] *Ibid.*

Conceptually VRML also has a world coordinate system, as well as a viewing, or camera-coordinate system. The various local coordinate transformations map objects into the world coordinate system. This is where the scene is assembled. The scene is then viewed through a camera, introducing another conceptual coordinate system. Nothing in VRML is specified using these coordinates. They are rarely found in optimized implementations where all of the steps are concatenated. However, having a clear model of the object, world, and camera spaces will help authors.

Fields

There are two general classes of fields: those that contain a single value (where a value may be a single number, a vector, or even an image), and those that contain multiple values. Single-valued fields all have names that begin with SF. Multiple-valued fields have names that begin with MF. Each field type defines the format for the values it writes.

Multiple-valued fields are written as a series of values separated by commas, all enclosed in brackets. If the field has zero values, only the brackets ([]) are written. The last may optionally be followed by a comma. If the field has exactly one value, the brackets may be omitted and just the value written. For example, all of the following are valid for a multiple-valued field containing the single integer value 1:

```
1
[1,]
[ 1 ]
```

SFBitMask is a single-value field that contains a mask of bit flags. Nodes that use this field class define mnemonic names for the bit flags. SFBitMasks are written to file as one or more mnemonic-enumerated type names, in this format:

```
( flag1 | flag2 |...)
```

If only one flag is used in a mask, the parentheses are optional. These names differ among uses of this field in various node classes.

SFBool is a field containing a single Boolean (true or false) value. SFBools may be written as 0 (representing FALSE), 1, TRUE, or FALSE.

SFColor/MFColor are fields containing one (SFColor) or zero or more (MFColor) RGB colors. Each color is written to file as an RGB triple of floating-point numbers in ANSI C floating-point format, in the range 0.0 to 1.0.

For example, this is an MFColor field containing the three colors red, green, and blue:

[1.0 0. 0.0, 0 1 0, 0 0 1][5]

SFEnum is a single-value field that contains an enumerated type value. Nodes that use this field class define mnemonic names for the values. SFEnums are written to file as a mnemonic enumerated type name. The name differs among uses of this field in various node classes.

SFFloat/MFFloat are fields that contain one (SFFloat) or zero or more (MFFloat) single-precision floating-point number. SFFloats are written to file in ANSI C floating-point format.

For example, this is an MFFoat field containing three values:

[3.1415926, 12.5e-3, .0001][6]

The *SFImage* field contains an uncompressed two-dimensional color or greyscale image. SFImages are written to file as three integers representing the width, height, and number of components in the image, followed by width*height hexadecimal values representing the pixels in the image, separated by whitespace. A one-component image will have one-byte hexadecimal values representing the intensity of the image. For example, 0xFF is full intensity and 0x00 is no intensity. A two-component image puts the intensity in the first (high) byte and the transparency in the second (low) byte. Pixels in a three-component image have the red component in the first (high) byte, followed by the green and blue components (so 0xFF0000 is red). Four-component images put the transparency byte after red/green/blue (so 0x0000FF80 is semitransparent blue). A value of 1.0 is completely transparent and 0.0 is completely opaque. Note that each pixel is read as a single unsigned number, so a three-component pixel with value 0x0000FF can also be written as 0xFF or 255 (decimal). Pixels are specified from left to right, bottom to top. The first hexadecimal value is the lower-left pixel of the image, and the last value is the upper-right pixel.

---

[5] *Ibid.*

[6] Gavin Bell, *Silicon Graphics, Inc.*, December 16, 1995.

For example, here is a greyscale image one pixel wide by two pixels high, with the bottom pixel white and the top pixel black:

```
1 2 1 0xFF 0x00
```

Here is an RGB image two pixels wide by four pixels high, with the bottom left pixel red, the bottom right pixel green, the two middle rows of pixels black, the top left pixel white, and the top right pixel yellow:

```
2 4 3 0xFF0000 0xFF00 0 0 0 0 0xFFFFFF 0xFFFF00[7]
```

The *SFLong/MFLong* fields contain one (SFLong) or zero or more (MFLong) 32-bit integers. SFLongs are written to file as an integer in decimal, hexadecimal (beginning with '0x'), or octal (beginning with '0') format.

For example, here is an MFLong field containing three values:

```
[ 17, -0xE20, -518820 ]
```

The *SFMatrix* field contains a transformation matrix. SFMatrices are written to file in row-major order as 16 floating-point numbers separated by whitespace.

For example, a matrix expressing a translation of 7.3 units along the X-axis is written as:

```
1 0 0 0   0 1 0 0   0 0 1 0   7.3 0 0 1
```

SFRotation is a field containing an arbitrary rotation. SFRotations are written to file as four floating-point values separated by whitespace. The four values represent an axis of rotation followed by the amount of right-handed rotation about that axis, in radians.

For example, a 180-degree rotation about the Y-axis is:

```
0 1 0   3.14159265
```

SFString/MFString are fields containing one (SFString) or zero or more (MFString) UTF-8 string (sequence of characters). Strings are written to file as a sequence of UTF-8 octets in double quotes (optional if the string doesn't contain any whitespace). Any characters (including newlines and #) may appear within the quotes. To include a double-quote character within the string, precede it with a backslash.

For example, all of these are valid strings:

---

[7] *Ibid.*

```
Testing
"One, Two, Three"
"He said, \"Immel did it!\""
```
[8]

SFVec2f/MFVec2f is a field containing a two-dimensional vector. SFVec2fs are written to file as a pair of floating-point values separated by whitespace.

SFVec3f/MFVec3f is a field containing a three-dimensional vector. SFVec3fs are written to file as three floating-point values separated by whitespace.

SFTime is a field containing a single time value. Each time value is written to file as a double-precision floating-point number in ANSI C floating-point format. Absolute SFTime is the number of seconds since Jan. 1, 1970 GMT.

Nodes

VRML defines several different classes of nodes. Most of the nodes can be classified into one of three categories: shape property, or group. Shape nodes define the geometry in the scene. Conceptually they are the only nodes that draw anything. Property nodes affect the way shapes are drawn. And grouping nodes gather other nodes together, allowing collections of nodes to be treated as a single object. Some group nodes also control whether their children are drawn.

Nodes may contain zero or more fields. Each node type defines the type, name, and default value for each of its fields. The default value for the field is used if a value for the field is not specified in the VRML file. The order in which the fields of a node are read is not important. For example, Cube { width 2 height 4 depth 6 } is equivalent to Cube { height 4 depth 6 width 2 }.

Cone is a node that represents a simple cone whose central axis is aligned with the *y*-axis. By default, the cone is centered at (0,0,0) and has a size of −1 to +1 in all three directions. The cone has a radius of 1 at the bottom and a height of 2, with its apex at 1 and its bottom at −1. The cone has two parts: the sides and the bottom.

The cone is transformed by the current cumulative transformation and is drawn with the current texture and material. If the current material binding is PER_PART or PER_PART_INDEXED, the first

---

[8] Toni Parisi, Intervista Software, December 16, 1995.

current material is used for the sides of the cone, and the second is used for the bottom. Otherwise, the first material is used for the entire cone.

When a texture is applied to a cone, it is applied differently to the sides and the bottom. On the sides the texture wraps counterclockwise (from above), starting at the back of the cone. The texture has a vertical seam at the back, intersecting the yz-plane. For the bottom a circle is cut out of the texture square and is applied to the cone's base circle. The texture appears right side up when the top of the cone is rotated toward the Z-axis.

The Coordinate3 node defines a set of 3-D coordinates to be used by a subsequent IndexedFaceSet, IndexedLineSet, or PointSet node. This node does not produce a visible result during rendering. It simply replaces the current coordinates in the rendering state for subsequent nodes to use.

The Cube node represents a cuboid aligned with the coordinate axes. By default, the cube is centered at (0,0,0) and measures two units in each dimension, from −1 to +1. The cube is transformed by the current cumulative transformation and is drawn with the current material and texture. A cube's width is its extent along its object-space X-axis, its height is its extent along the object-space Y-axis, and its depth is its extent along its object-space −Z-axis.

If the current material binding is PER_PART, PER_PART_IN-DEXED, PER_FACE, or PER_FACE_INDEXED, materials will be bound to the faces of the cube in this order: front (+Z), back (−Z), left (−X), right (+X), top (+Y), bottom (−Y). Textures are applied individually to each face of the cube. The entire texture goes on each face. On the front, back, right, and left sides of the cube, the texture is applied right side up. On the top the texture appears right side up when the top of the cube is tilted toward the camera. On the bottom the texture appears right side up when the top of the cube is tilted toward the −Z-axis.

Cylinder is a node that represents a simple capped cylinder centered around the y-axis. By default, the cylinder is centered at (0,0,0) and has a default size of −1 to +1 in all three dimensions. The cylinder has three parts: the sides, the top (y +1) and the bottom ($y = -1$). You can use the radius and height fields to create a cylinder with a different size.

The cylinder is transformed by the current cumulative transformation and is drawn with the current material and texture. If the current material binding is PER_PART or PER_PART_INDEXED, the first current material is used for the sides of the cylinder, the second is used for the top, and the third is used for the bottom. Otherwise, the first material is used for the entire cylinder.

When a texture is applied to a cylinder, it is applied differently to the sides, top, and bottom. On the sides the texture wraps counter-clockwise (from above), starting at the back of the cylinder. The texture has a vertical seam at the back, intersecting the yz-plane. For the top and bottom, a circle is cut out of the texture square and applied to the top or bottom circle. The top texture appears right side up when the top of the cylinder is tilted toward the +Z axis, and the bottom texture appears right side up when the top of the cylinder is tilted toward the −Z axis.

DirectionalLight is a node that defines a directional light source that illuminates along rays parallel to a given three-dimensional vector. A light node defines an illumination source that may affect subsequent shapes in the scene graph, depending on the current lighting style. Light sources are affected by the current transformation. A light node under a Separator does not affect any objects outside that Separator.

The *FontStyle* node defines the current font style used for all subsequent ASCII Text. Only font attributes are defined. It is up to the browser to assign specific fonts to the various attribute combinations. The size field specifies the height (in object-space units) of glyphs rendered and determines the vertical spacing of adjacent lines of text.

The *IndexedFaceSet* node represents a 3-D shape formed by constructing faces (polygons) from vertices located at the current coordinates. IndexedFaceSet uses the indices in its coordIndex field to specify the polygonal faces. An index of −1 indicates that the current face has ended and the next one begins. The vertices of the faces are transformed by the current transformation matrix.

Treatment of the current material and normal binding is as follows: The PER_PART and PER_FACE bindings specify a material or normal for each face. PER_VERTEX specifies a material or normal for each vertex. The corresponding _INDEXED bindings are the same but use the materialIndex or normalIndex indices. The DEFAULT material binding is equal to OVERALL. The DEFAULT normal binding is equal to PER_VERTEX_INDEXED. If insufficient normals exist in the state, vertex normals will be generated automatically.

Explicit texture coordinates (as defined by TextureCoordinate2) may be bound to vertices of an indexed shape by using the indices in the textureCoordIndex field. As with all vertex-based shapes, if a current texture is specified but no texture coordinates, a default texture coordinate mapping is calculated using the bounding box of the shape. The longest dimension of the bounding box defines the S coordinates, and the next longest defines the T coordinates. The value of the S coordinate ranges from 0 to 1, from one end of the bounding box to the other. The T coordinate ranges between 0 and the ratio of the second greatest dimension of the bounding box to the greatest dimension. Be sure that the indices contained in the coordIndex, materialIndex, normalIndex, and textureCoordIndex fields are valid with respect to the current state, or errors will occur.

The *IndexedLineSet* node represents a 3-D shape formed by constructing polylines from vertices located at the current coordinates. IndexedLineSet uses the indices in its coordIndex field to specify the polylines. An index of –1 indicates that the current polyline has ended and the next one begins. The coordinates of the line set are transformed by the current cumulative transformation.

Treatment of the current material and normal binding is as follows: The PER_PART binding specifies a material or normal for each segment of the line. The PER_FACE binding specifies a material or normal for each polyline. PER_VERTEX specifies a material or normal for each vertex. The corresponding _INDEXED bindings are the same but use the materialIndex or normalIndex indices. The DEFAULT material binding is equal to OVERALL. The DEFAULT normal binding is equal to PER_VERTEX_iNDEXED. If insufficient normals exist in the state, the lines will be drawn unlit. The same rules for texture coordinate generation as IndexedFaceSet are used.

The *Info* class defines an information node in the scene graph. This node has no effect during traversal. It is used to store information in the scene graph, typically for browser-specific purposes, copyright messages, or other strings.

The *LOD* node is used to allow browsers to switch between various representations of objects automatically. The children of this node typically represent the same object or objects at varying levels of detail, from highest detail to lowest. LOD acts as a Separator node, not allowing properties underneath it to affect nodes that come after it in the scene.

The distance from the viewpoint (transformed into the local coordinate space of the LOD node) to the specified center point of the LOD is calculated. If the distance is less than the first value in the ranges array, the first child of the LOD is drawn. If the distance between the first and second values in the ranges array, the second child is drawn, etc. If there are *N* values in the ranges array, the LOD group should have *N* + 1 children. Specifying too few children will result in the last child's being used repeatedly for the lowest levels of detail. If too many children are specified, the extra children will be ignored. Each value in the ranges array should be less than the previous value; otherwise, results are undefined. Not specifying any values in the ranges array (the default) is a special case that indicates that the browser may decide which child to draw to optimize rendering performance.

Authors should set LOD ranges so that the transitions from one level of detail to the next are barely noticeable. Browsers may adjust which level of detail is displayed to maintain interactive frame rates: to display an already fetched level of detail while a higher level of detail (contained in a line node) is fetched, or might disregard the author-specified ranges for any other implementation-dependent reason. Authors should not use LOD nodes to emulate simple behaviors, because the results will be undefined. For example, using an LOD node to make a door appear to open when the user approaches probably will not work in all browsers.

For best results, specify ranges only where necessary, and nest LOD nodes with and without ranges. For example:

```
LOD {
    range [100, 1000]
    LOD {
        Separator { ... detailed version... }
        DEF LoRes Separator { ... less detailed version ... }
    }
    USE LoRes
    Info { } # Display nothing
}[9]
```

In this example nothing will be displayed if the viewer is farther than 1000 meters away from the object. A low-resolution version of the object will be displayed if the viewer is between 100 and 1000 meters away. Also, a low-resolution or a high-resolution version of the object will be displayed when the viewer is closer than 100 meters from the object.

---

[9] *Ibid.*

Material is a node that defines the current surface material properties for all subsequent shapes. Material sets several components of the current material during traversal. Different shapes interpret materials with multiple values differently. To bind materials to shapes, use a MaterialBinding node.

The lighting parameters defined by the Material node are the same parameters defined by the OpenGL lighting model. Note that VRML provides no mechanism for controlling the amount of ambient light in the scene, so use of the ambientColor field is browser dependent. Several other parameters (such as light-attenuation factors) are also left as implementation details in VRML. Also note that OpenGL specifies the specular exponent as a nonnormalized 0–128 value, which is specified as a normalized 0–1 value in VRML (simply multiplying the VRML value by 128 to translate to the OpenGL parameter).

For rendering systems that do not support the full OpenGL lighting model, the following simpler lighting model is recommended. A transparency value of 0 is completely opaque, a value of 1 is completely transparent. Browsers need not support partial transparency but should support at least fully transparent and fully opaque surfaces, treating transparency values >= 0.5 as fully transparent.

Specifying only emissiveColors and zero diffuse, specular, emissive, and ambient colors is the way to specify precomputed lighting. It is expected that browsers will be able to recognize this as a special case and to optimize their computations.

For example:

```
Material {
ambientColor [] diffuseColor [] specularColor []
emissiveColor [0.1 0.1 0.2, 0.5 0.8 0.8 ]
}
```

Issues for Low-End Rendering Systems

Many low-end PC rendering systems are not able to support the full range of the VRML material specification. For example, many systems do not render individual red, green, and blue reflected values as specified in the specularColor field. Table 13.1 describes which Material fields are typically supported in popular low-end systems and suggests actions for browser implementors to take when a field is not supported. It is also expected that simpler rendering systems will be unable to support both lit and unlit objects in the same scene.

Table 13.1 Material Field Support

Field	Supported?	Suggested Action
ambientColor	No	Ignore
diffuseColor	Yes	Use
specularColor	No	Ignore
emissiveColor	No	Use in place of diffuseColor if != 0 0 0
shininess	Yes	Use
transparency	No	Ignore

Since Material nodes may contain more than one material, the *MaterialBinding* node specifies how the current materials are bound to shapes that follow in the scene graph. Each shape node may interpret bindings differently. For example, a Sphere node is always drawn using the first material in the Material node, no matter what the current MaterialBinding, whereas a Cube node may use six different Materials to draw each of its six faces, depending on the MaterialBinding.

The bindings for faces and vertices are meaningful only for shapes that are made from faces and vertices. Similarly, the indexed bindings are used only by the shapes that allow indexing.

Some renderers do not support per-vertex materials. The result is that MaterialBinding values PER_VERTEX and PER_VERTEX_INDEXED produce unpredictable results in different browsers.

The *MatrixTransform* node defines a geometric 3-D transformation with a 4-by-4 matrix. Only matrices that are the result of rotations, translations, and nonzero (but possibly nonuniform) scales must be supported. Noninvertable matrices should be avoided.

Matrices are specified in row-major order; thus, for example, a MatrixTransform representing a translation of 6.2 units along the local Z-axis would be specified as:[10]

---

[10] *Ibid.*

```
MatrixTransform { matrix
    1 0 0 0
    0 1 0 0
    0 0 1 0
    0 0 6.2 1
}
File Format/Defaults:
  MatrixTransform {
      matrix   1 0 0 0    SFMatrix
               0 1 0 0
               0 0 1 0
               0 0 0 1
```

The *Normal* node defines a set of 3-D surface normal vectors to be used by vertex-based shape nodes (IndexedFaceSet, IndexedLineSet, PointSet) that follow it in the scene graph. This node does not produce a visible result during rendering. It simply replaces the current normals in the rendering state for subsequent nodes to use. This node contains one multiple-valued field that contains the normal vectors.

To save network bandwidth, it is expected that implementations will be able to automatically generate appropriate normals if none are given. However, the results will vary from implementation to implementation.

NormalBinding specifies how the current normals are bound to shapes that follow in the scene graph. Each shape node may interpret bindings differently.

The bindings for faces and vertices are meaningful only for shapes that are made from faces and vertices. Similarly the indexed bindings are used only by the shapes that allow indexing. For bindings that require multiple normals, be sure to have at least as many normals defined as are necessary; otherwise, errors will occur.

OrthographicCamera defines a parallel projection from a viewpoint. This camera does not diminish objects with distance, as Perspective-Camera does. The viewing volume for an orthographic camera is a rectangular parallelepiped (a box).

By default, the camera is located at (0,0,1) and looks along the negative z-axis. The position and orientation fields can be used to change these values. The height field defines the total height of the viewing volume.

A camera can be placed in a VRML world to specify the initial location of the viewer when that world is entered. VRML browsers will typically modify the camera to allow a user to move through the virtual world.

The results of traversing multiple cameras are undefined. To ensure consistent results, place multiple cameras underneath one or more Switch nodes, and set the Switch's whichChild fields so that only one is traversed. By convention, these nontraversed cameras may be used to define alternative entry points into the scene. These entry points may be named by simply giving the cameras a name (using DEF). See the specification of Anchor for the conventional way of specifying an entry point in a URL.

Cameras are affected by the current transformation, so you can position a camera by placing a transformation node before it in the scene graph . The default position and orientation of a camera is at (0,0,1) looking along the negative z-axis, with the positive y-axis up.

The position and orientation fields of a camera are sufficient to place a camera anywhere in space with any orientation. The orientation field can be used to rotate the default view direction (looking down –z, with +y up) so that it is looking in any direction, with any direction "up."

The focalDistance field defines the point the viewer is looking at, and may be used by a browser as a navigational hint to determine how fast the viewer should travel, which objects in the scene are most important, etc. The nearDistance and farDistance are distances from the viewpoint (in the camera's coordinate system). Objects closer to the viewpoint than nearDistance or farther from the viewpoint than farDistance should not be seen. Browsers may treat these values as hints and may decide to adjust them as the viewer moves around the scene.

Most low-end rendering systems do not support the concept of focalDistance. Also, cameras are global to the scene. Placing a camera beneath a particular Separator is equivalent to placing it at outermost scope. For broadest compatibility, cameras should be placed only at outermost scope.

PerspectiveCamera defines a perspective projection from a viewpoint. The viewing volume for a perspective camera is a truncated right pyramid.

By default, the camera is located at (0,0, 1) and looks along the negative z-axis. The position and orientation fields can be used to change these values. The heightAngle field defines the total vertical angle of the viewing volume.

The *PointLight* node defines a point light source at a fixed 3-D location. A point source illuminates equally in all directions; that is, it is omnidirectional.

A light node defines an illumination source that may affect subsequent shapes in the scene graph, depending on the current lighting style. Light sources are affected by the current transformation. A light node under a Separator should not affect any objects outside that Separator (although some rendering systems do not currently support this).

PointSet represents a set of points located at the current coordinates. This node uses the current coordinates in order, starting at the index specified by the startIndex field. The number of points in the set is specified by the numPoints field. A value of -1 for this field indicates that all remaining values in the current coordinates are to be used as points.

The coordinates of the point set are transformed by the current cumulative transformation. The points are drawn with the current material and texture.

Treatment of the current material and normal binding is as follows: PER_PART, PER_FACE, and PER_VERTEX bindings bind one material or normal to each point. The DEFAULT material binding is equal to OVERALL. The DEFAULT normal binding is equal to PER_VERTEX. The startIndex is also used for materials or normals when the binding indicates that they should be used per vertex.

Many low-end renderers do not support the concept of per object lighting. This means that placing a light beneath a Separator, which implies lighting only the objects beneath the Separator with that light, is not supported in all systems. For the broadest compatibility, lights should be placed only at outermost scope.

The *Rotation* node defines a 3-D rotation about an arbitrary axis through the origin. The rotation is accumulated into the current transformation, which is applied to subsequent shapes.

Scale defines a 3-D scaling about the origin. If the components of the scaling vector are not all the same, a nonuniform scale is produced.

Separator is a group node that performs a push (save) of the traversal state before traversing its children and a pop (restore) after traversing them. This isolates the Separator's children from the rest of the scene graph. A Separator can include light, cameras, coordinates, normals, bindings, and all other properties. *Note*: A proposal to replace Separators with Frames and Leafs is at http://earth.path.net/mitra/papers/vrml-frames.html.

Separators can also perform render culling. Render culling skips over traversal of the Separator's children if they are not going to be rendered, based on the comparison of the Separator's bounding box with the current view volume. Culling is controlled by the renderCulling field. These are set to AUTO by default, allowing the implementation to decide whether to cull.

The *ShapeHints* node indicates that IndexedFaceSets are solid, contain ordered vertices, or contain convex faces. These hints allow VRML implementations to optimize certain rendering features. Optimizations that may be performed include enabling back-face culling and disabling two-sided lighting. For example, if an object is solid and has ordered vertices, an implementation may turn on back-face culling and turn off two-sided lighting. If the object is not solid but has ordered vertices, it may turn off back-face culling and turn on two-sided lighting.

The ShapeHints node also affects how default normals are generated. When an IndexedFaceSet has to generate default normals, it uses the creaseAngle field to determine which edges should be smoothly shaded and which ones should have a sharp crease. The crease angle is the angle between surface normals on adjacent polygons. For example, a crease angle of 0.5 radians (the default value) means that an edge between two adjacent polygonal faces will be smooth-shaded if the normals to the two faces form an angle that is less than 0.5 radians (about 30 degrees). Otherwise, it will be faceted.

The shapeType and vertexOrdering fields are used to determine whether to generate back faces for each polygon in a mesh. Most low-end rendering systems do not support built-in back-face generation. Browsers built on these systems need to create back faces explicitly.

The *Sphere* node represents a sphere. By default, the sphere is centered at the origin and has a radius of 1. The sphere is transformed by the current cumulative transformation and is drawn with the current material and texture.

A sphere does not have faces or parts. Therefore it ignores material and normal bindings, using the first material for the entire sphere and using its own normals. When a texture is applied to a sphere, the texture covers the entire surface, wrapping counterclockwise from the back of the sphere. The texture has a seam at the back on the yz-plane.

The *SpotLight* node defines a spotlight light source. A spotlight is placed at a fixed location in three-space and illuminates in a cone along a particular direction. The intensity of the illumination drops off exponentially as a ray of light diverges from this direction toward the edges of the cone. The rate of dropoff and the angle of the cone are controlled by the dropOffRate and cutOffAngle fields.

A light node defines an illumination source that may affect subsequent shapes in the scene graph, depending on the current lighting style. Light sources are affected by the current transformation. A light node under a Separator should not affect any objects outside that Separator (although some rendering systems do not currently support this).

Many low-end renderers do not support the concept of per object lighting. This means that placing a light beneath a Separator, which implies lighting only the objects beneath the Separator with that light, is not supported in all systems. For the broadest compatibility, lights should be placed only at outermost scope.

The *Switch* group node traverses one or none of its children. One can use this node to switch the effects of some properties on and off or to switch between properties.

The whichChild field specifies the index of the child to traverse, where the first child has index 0. This field is an input and thus can be modified by another node.

Open Issue

It is expected that in a future version of VRML, the Switch node will be defined to behave as a Separator node, not allowing its children to affect anything after it in the scene graph. To ensure future compatibility, it is recommended that all children of all Switch nodes be Separator nodes.

The Text node represents one or more text strings specified using the UTF-8 encoding of the ISO10646 character set. This is described later. An important note is that ASCII is a subset of UTF-8, so any ASCII strings are also UTF-8.

The text strings can be rendered in one of four directions: right to left (RL), left to right (LR), top to bottom (TB), or bottom to top (BT). The direction field governs this.

The justification field determines where the text will be positioned in relation to the origin (0,0,0) of the object coordinate system. The values for the justification field are BEGIN, END, CENTER. For a left-to-right (LR) direction, these would correspond to LEFT, RIGHT, CENTER.

For the directions RL and LR, the first line of text will be positioned with its baseline (bottom of capital letters) at $y = 0$. The text is positioned on the positive side of the x origin for the direction LR and justification BEGIN; the same for RL END. The text is on the negative side of X for LR END and RL BEGIN. For CENTER justification and horizontal text (RL, LR), each string will be centered at $x = 0$.

For the directions TB and BT, the first line of text will be positioned with the left side of the glyphs along the $y = 0$ axis. For TB BEGIN and BT END, the text will be positioned with the top left corner at the origin. For TB END and BT BEGIN, the bottom left will be at the origin. For TB and BT CENTER, the text will be centered vertically at $x = 0$.

The spacing field determines the spacing between multiple text strings. All subsequent strings advance in either x or y by −(size * spacing). A value of 0 for the spacing will cause the string to be in the same position. A value of −1 will cause subsequent strings to advance in the opposite direction.

The extent field will limit and scale the text string if the natural length of the string is longer than the extent. If the text string is shorter than the extent, it will not be scaled. The extent is measured horizontally for RL and LR directions, vertically for TB and BT.

The two-byte (UCS-2) encoding of ISO 10646 is identical to the unicode standard. In order to avoid introducing binary data into VRML, VAG has chosen to support the UTF-8 encoding of ISO 10646. This encoding allows ASCII text (0x0..0x7F) to appear without any changes and encodes all characters from 0x80.. 0x7FFFFFFF into a series of six or fewer bytes.

If the most-significant bit of the first character is 0, the remaining seven bits are interpreted as an ASCII character. Otherwise, the number of leading bits will indicate the number of bytes following. A 0 bit is always between the count bits and any data.

For example, the symbol for a register trademark is circled R, or 174 in both ISO/Latin-1 (8859/1) and ISO 10646. In hexadecimal it is 0xAE; in HTML. In UTF-8 it has the two-byte encoding 0xC2, 0XAE.

The text is transformed by the current cumulative transformation and is drawn with the current material and texture. Textures are applied to 3-D text as follows. The texture origin is at the origin of the first string, as determined by the justification. The texture is scaled equally in both S and T dimensions, with the font height representing one unit. S increases to the right, and T increases up.

In many languages the proper rendering of the text requires more than just a sequence of glyphs. The *TextLanguage* node allows the author to specify which, if any, language-specific rendering techniques to use. For simple languages, such as English, this node may be safely ignored.

The tag used to specify languages will follow RFC1766— Tags for the Identification of Languages {ftp://ftp.isi.edu/in-notes/rfc1766.txt}. This RFC specifies that a language tag may simply be a two-letter ISO 639 tag, such as en for English, ja for Japanese, and sv for Swedish. This may be optionally followed by a two letter country code from ISO 3166. So, Americans would be absolutely safe with en-US. ISO does not have documents online, yet. They can be ordered.

The *Texture2* property node defines a texture map and parameters for that map. This map is used to apply texture to subsequent shapes as they are rendered.

The texture can be read from the URL specified by the filename field. To turn off texturing, set the filename field to an empty string (....). Implementations should support at least the JPEG image file format. Also, supporting GIF and PNG formats is recommended.

If multiple URLs are presented, this expresses a descending order of preference. A browser may display a lower preference URL while the higher-order file is not available.

Textures can also be specified inline by setting the image field to contain the texture data. Supplying both image and filename fields will result in undefined behavior.

Texture images may be one component (greyscale), two component (greyscale plus transparency), three component (full RGB color), or four-component (full RGB color plus transparency). An ideal VRML implementation will use the texture image to modify the diffuse color and transparency of an object's material (specified in a Material node). It'll then perform any lighting calculations, using the rest of the object's material properties with the modified diffuse color to produce the final image.

The texture image modifies the diffuse color and transparency, depending on how many components are in the image, as follows:

- Diffuse color is multiplied by the greyscale values in the texture image.
- Diffuse color is multiplied by the greyscale values in the texture image; material transparency is multiplied by transparency values in texture image.
- RGB colors in the texture image replace the material's diffuse color.
- RGB colors in the texture image replace the material's diffuse color; transparency values in the texture image replace the material's transparency.

Browsers may approximate this ideal behavior to increase performance. One common optimization is to calculate lighting only at each vertex and to combine the texture image with the color computed from lighting (performing the texturing after lighting). Another common optimization is to perform no lighting calculations at all when texturing is enabled, displaying only the colors of the texture image.

Texture2Transform defines a 2-D transformation applied to texture coordinates. This affects the way textures are applied to the surfaces of subsequent shapes. The transformation consists of (in order) a nonuniform scale about an arbitrary center point, a rotation about that same point, and a translation. This allows a user to change the size and position of the textures on shapes.

TextureCoordinate2 defines a set of 2-D coordinates to be used to map textures to the vertices of subsequent PointSet, IndexedLineSet, or IndexedFaceSet objects. It replaces the current texture coordinates in the rendering state for the shapes to use.

Texture coordinates range from 0 to 1 across the texture. The horizontal coordinate, called S, is specified first, followed by the vertical coordinate, T.

The *WWWAnchor* group node loads a new scene into a VRML browser when one of its children is chosen. Exactly how a user chooses a child of the WWWAnchor is up to the VRML browser; typically, clicking on one of its children with the mouse will result in the new scene's replacing the current scene. A WWWAnchor with an empty ("")

name does nothing when its children are chosen. The name is an arbitrary URL.

If multiple URLs are presented, this expresses a descending order of preference, a browser may display a lower-preference URL if the higher order file is not available.

WWWAnchor behaves like a Separator, pushing the traversal state before traversing its children and popping it afterward. The description field in the WWWAnchor allows for a friendly prompt to be displayed as an alternative to the URL in the name field. Ideally browsers will allow the user to choose the description, the URL, or both to be displayed for a candidate WWWAnchor.

The WWWAnchor's map field is an enumerated value that can be either NONE (the default) or POINT. If it is POINT the object-space coordinates of the point on the object the user chose will be added to the URL in the name field, with the syntax "?x,y,z".

A WWW Anchor may also be used to take the viewer to a particular *viewpoint* in a virtual world by specifying a URL ending with #cameraName. Here cameraName is the name of a camera defined in the world.

The *WWWInline* node reads its children from anywhere in the World Wide Web. Exactly when its children are read is not defined. Reading the children may be delayed until the inline is displayed. A WWWInline with an empty name does nothing. The name is an arbitrary URL.

The effect of referring to a non-VRML URL in a WWWInline node is undefined. If multiple URLs are specified, this expresses a descending order of preference. A browser may display a URL for a lower-preference file while it is obtaining or if it is unable to obtain the higher-preference file.

If the WWWInline's bboxSize field specifies a nonempty bounding box (a bounding box is nonempty if at least one of its dimensions is greater than zero), the Inline's object-space bounding box is specified by its bboxSize and bboxCenter fields. This allows an implementation to quickly determine whether the contents of the WWWInline might be visible. This is an optimization hint only. If the true bounding box of the contents of the Inline is different from the specified bounding box, results will be undefined.

Pros and Issues

Adding such a node offers several advantages:

- It resolves the issue that most current scenes hover in black space.
- Implementation should make ground plane less expensive than general case.
- Geometry will provide good depth queue as closer objects move relative to the user.
- Geometry assumes nothing of what environment the author wants to portray.
- Geometry being part of scenegraph supports behaviors.
- Global coordinate space optimizes rendering of scenery.

However, issues remain:

- Global coordinates speed up implementation. If arbitrary ground plane is absolutely needed, consider a rotation and elevation to orient the ground plane in world space.
- There has been discussion of supporting different mapping for the background texture—a cylindrical, spherical hemisphere. However, current renderers do not support this functionality, and simulating it would be an unacceptable performance hit.

New Nodes for VRML

By providing a shaded ground plane, sky, and scenic textures, this node can be used to add substance to the void surrounding the scene. Only the first background node encountered is used, and it must be specified in the main file.

If ground colors are specified, a ground plane is added to the scenegraph at $Y = 0$ in global coordinate space. If more than one color is specified, the ground color is interpolated between colors from 0 degrees downward to 90 degrees at the horizon. Similarly, sky colors interpolate from the 90 degree mark to 180 degrees overhead.

A scene may describe a more precise atmosphere and include background scenery in the scenery field. This field is used to add a texture to the scene that is conceptually distant enough that it does not translate with respect to the eyepoint. The texture should be mapped wrapped around a cylinder so that it runs all the way around from $Y = 0$ in global coordinate space.

If multiple URLs are specified, this expresses a descending order of preference. A browser may display a URL for a lower-preference file while it is obtaining or if it is unable to obtain the higher-preference file.

CollideStyle specifies to a browser what objects in the scene should not be navigated through. It is useful to keep viewers from walking through walls in a building, for instance. Collision response is browser defined. For example, when the camera comes sufficiently close to an object to register as a collision, the browser may have the camera bounce off the object or simply come to a stop.

Since collision with arbitrarily complex geometry is computationally expensive, one method of increasing efficiency is to be able to define an alternative geometry that could serve as a proxy for colliding against. This collision proxy could be as crude as a simple bounding box or bounding sphere or could be more sophisticated (for example, the convex hull of a polyhedron). This proxy volume is used only to calculate the collision with the viewer and is not used for trivial rejection during the computation process. Efficient trivial rejection can be done by using hierarchical bounding boxes or some other technique, and its implementation is not specified in the language.

VRML represents collision proxy volumes for objects through the CollideStyle property node. A CollideStyle node sets the collision proxy volume for all the geometry in the scene graph that follows it up to the next CollideStyle node. Like all other properties, the current collision style would be saved and restored by Separators. Like all other shapes, the geometry is defined in object space and is transformed by the current modeling transformation.

CollideStyle contains two fields: collide (a Boolean) and proxy (a node). If the value of the collide field is FALSE, no collision is performed with the affected geometry. If the value of the collide field is TRUE, the proxy field defines the geometry against which collision testing is done. If the proxy value is undefined or NULL, the actual geometry is collided against. If the proxy value is not NULL, it contains the geometry that is used in collision computations.

Open Issues

An open issue exists here because there is no consensus by VAG on what collides with object. The viewer must have some geometry to collide against objects in the scene. In the future this would be an avatar geometry. For VRML X.X, the collisionRadius field Is of the NavigationInfo node is used

DirectedSound node defines a sound source that is located at a specific 3-D location and that emits primarily along a given direction. It adds directionality to the PointSound node. Besides the direction vector, minAngle and maxAngle fields specify how the intensity of the sound changes with direction. Within the cone whose apex is the sound location, whose axis is the direction vector, and whose angle is specified by minAngle, the DirectedSound behaves exactly like a PointSound. Moving along a constant radius (from the source location) from the surface of this cone to the surface of the similar cone whose angle is maxAngle, the intensity falls off to zero.

The *ElevationGrid* node creates a rectangular grid with varying heights, especially useful in modeling terrain and other space-creating surfaces. The model is specified primarily by a scalar array of height values that describe the height of the surface above each point of the grid.

The verticesPerRow and verticesPerColumn fields define the number of grid points in the Z and X directions, respectively, defining a surface that contains (verticesPerRow– 1) x (verticesPerColumn– 1) rectangles. The vertex locations for the rectangles are defined by the height field and the gridstep field. The vertex corresponding to the ith row and jth column is placed at (gridStep[0] * j, heights[i*verticesPerColumn+j], gridStep[1] * i) in object space, where 0<=i<=verticesPerRow, 0<=j<=verticesPerColumn.

The height field is an array of scalar values representing the height above the grid for each vertex. The height values are stored so that row 0 is first, followed by rows 1, 2, . . . verticesPerRow. Within each row the height values are stored so that column 0 is first, followed by columns 1, 2, . . . verticesPerColumn. The rows have fixed Z values, with row 0 having the smallest Z value. The columns have fixed X values, with column 0 having the smallest X value.

The default texture coordinates will range from [0,0] at the first vertex to [1,1] at the far side of the diagonal. The *S* texture coordinate will be aligned with *X* and the *T* texture coordinate with *Z*.

Treatment of the current material and normal binding is as follows: The PER_PART binding specifies a material or normal for each row of the mesh. The PER_FACE binding specifies a material or normal for each quadrilateral. The _INDEXED bindings are equivalent to their nonindexed counterparts. The default material binding is OVERALL. The default normal binding is PER_VERTEX.

If any normals (or materials) are specified, it is assumed that you provide the correct number of them, as indicated by the binding. You will see unexpected results if you specify fewer normals (or materials) than the shape requires. If no normals are specified, they will be generated automatically.

By default, the rectangles are defined with a counterclockwise ordering, so the *Y* component of the normal is positive. Setting the vertexOrdering field of the current ShapeHints node to CLOCKWISE reverses the normal direction. Back-face culling can be turned on as for all shapes, by defining a ShapeHints node prior to the ElevationGrid node, with the vertexOrdering field set to CLOCKWISE or COUNTER-CLOCKWISE and the shapeType field set to SOLID.

Pros

- This is an extremely compact way to represent geometry (key for transmission times).
- A lot of data available can be easily converted into this form (USGS Digital Elevation Models come to mind).
- Browsers can easily do automatic LOD degradation to keep performance up.

The *Environment* node describes global environmental attributes, such as ambient lighting, light attenuation, and fog. Ambient lighting is the amount of extra light impinging on each surface point. It is specified as an ambientColor and ambientIntensity. Light attenuation affects all subsequent lights in a scene. It is a quadratic function of distance from a light source to a surface point. The three coefficients are specified in the attenuation field. Attenuation works only for light sources with a fixed location, such as point and spot lights. The ambient lighting and attenuation calculations are defined in the OpenGL lighting model.

Fog has one of four types, each of which blends each surface point with the specified fog color. Each type interprets the visibility field to be the distance at which fog totally obscures objects. A visibility value of 0 (the default) causes the Environment node to set up fog so that the visibility is the distance to the far clipping plane of the current camera.

GeneralCylinder is a node for parametrically describing numerous families of shapes: extrusions (along an axis or an arbitrary path), surfaces of revolution, and bend/twist/taper objects. GeneralCylinders are defined by four piecewise linear curves: crossSection, profile, spine, and twist. Shapes are constructed as follows. The crossSection is a 2-D curve that is scaled, extruded through space, and twisted by the other curves. First, the crossSection is extruded and scaled along the path of the profile curve. Second, the shape is bent and stretched so that its central axis aligns with the spine curve. Finally, the shape is twisted about the spine by angles (in radians) given by the twist curve. The twist curve is a function of angle at given parametric distances along the spine.

With regard to surfaces of revolution, if the crossSection is a circle and the spine is straight, the GeneralCylinder will be equivalent to a surface of revolution, where the GeneralCylinder profile curve maps directly to that of the surface of revolution. Also, with regard to cookie-cutter extrusions, if both the profile and the spine are straight, then the crossSection acts like a cookie-cutter, with the thickness of the cookie equal to the length of the spine.

Shapes like Bend/Twist/Taper objects are the result of utilizing all four curves. The spine curve bends the shape, the twist curve twists it, and the profile curve tapers it.

Planar TOP and BOTTOM surfaces will be generated when the crossSection is closed (when the first and last points of the crossSection are equal). However, if the profile is also closed, the TOP and BOTTOM are not generated, because a closed crossSection extruded along a closed profile creates a shape that is closed without the addition of TOP and BOTTOM parts.

The parts field determines which parts are rendered. The notion of BOTTOM versus TOP is determined by the profile curve. The end of the profile curve with a lesser y value is the BOTTOM end.

The cone is transformed by the current cumulative transformation and is drawn with the current texture and material. The first material in the state is used for the entire GeneralCylinder, regardless of the current material binding.

GeneralCylinder automatically generates its own normals. NormalBinding in the state is ignored. Orientation of the normals is determined by the vertex ordering of the triangles generated by GeneralCylinder. The vertex ordering is in turn determined by the crossSection curve. If the crossSection is drawn counterclockwise, the polygons will have counterclockwise ordering when viewed from the "outside" of the shape (and vice versa for clockwise-ordered corrections). The GeneralCylinder responds to the fields of the ShapeHints node the same way as IndexedFaceSet.

Texture coordinates are automatically generated by GeneralCylinders. These will map textures like the label on a soup can. The coordinates will range in the u direction from 0 to 1 along the crossSection curve and in the v direction from 0 to 1 along the spine. If the TOP and BOTTOM exist, textures map onto them in a planar fashion.

When a texture is applied to a GeneralCylinder, it is applied differently to the sides, top, and bottom. On the sides, the texture wraps [0, 1] of the u direction of the texture along the crossSection from first point to last. It wraps [0, 1] of the v direction of the texture along the direction of the spine, from first point to last. When the crossSection is closed, the texture has a seam that follows the line traced by the correction's start/end point as it travels along the spine. For the top and bottom the crossSection is cut out of the texture square and applied to the top or bottom circle. The top and bottom texture's u and v directions correspond to the x and z directions in which the crossSection coordinate are defined.

Pros

- This is an extremely compact way to represent geometry (key for transmission times).
- Browsers can easily do automatic LOD degradation to keep performance up.

The *NavigationInfo* node contains information for the viewer through several fields: type, speed, collisionRadius, and headlight. The type field specifies a navigation paradigm to use. The types that all

VRML viewers should support are walk, examiner, fly, and none. A *walk* viewer would constrain the user to a plane (*x-z*), suitable for architectural walkthroughs. An *examiner* viewer would let the user tumble the entire scene, suitable for examining single objects. A *fly* viewer would provide six degree of freedom movement. The *none* choice removes all viewer controls, forcing the user to navigate using only WWWAnchors linked to viewpoints. The *type* field is multivalued, so that authors can specify fallbacks in case a browser does not understand a given type.

The speed is the rate at which the viewer travels through a scene in meters per second. Since viewers may provide mechanisms to travel faster or slower, this should be the default or average speed of the

Notes/Issues

- The following fields may be dynamic: speed, height, collisionRadius, worldUp.
- How is the kneecap height specified? That is, at what height does the browser climb something (like stairs), as opposed to collide with it (like a table)? This is currently browser defined (probably as some percentage of the collisionRadius).
- What happens when the user navigates the viewer off a cliff: Does the browser hover, drop to terrain instantaneously, or fall at some rate? Forces and masses could come into play here, but then browsers would be doing simulations, which is beyond the scope of VRML X.X.
- Currently most browsers automatically turn a headlight on. WebSpace turns a headlight on only if there are no lights in the scene. This means that scenes are rendered with different color saturations in different browsers. Adding a headlight field forces browsers to add headlights consistently.

viewer. In an examiner viewer this makes sense only for panning and dollying; it should have no effect on the rotation speed.

The collisionRadius field specifies the smallest allowable distance between the camera position and any collision object (as specified by CollideStyle) before a collision is detected.

The headlight field specifies whether a browser should turn a headlight on. A headlight is a directional light that always points in the direction the camera is looking. This effect can be had by adding a DirectionalLight in front of a camera in the scene. Instead, setting this field to TRUE allows the browser to provide a headlight, possibly with user interface controls to turn it on and off. Scenes that enlist precomputed lighting (radiosity solutions) can specify the headlight off here. The headlight should have intensity 1, color 1 1 1, and direction 0 0 − 1. The effects of specifying headlight on in a NavigationInfo node are equivalent to an author's adding a default DirectionalLight in front of a camera in the scene, except that using the NavigationInfo field allows a browser to provide user interface controlling the light.

This node defines a sound source located at a specific 3-D location. The name field specifies a URL from which the sound is read. Implementations should support at least the streaming-sound file formats. Streaming-sound files may be supported by browsers. Otherwise, sounds should be loaded when the sound node is loaded. Browsers may limit the maximum number of sounds that can be played simultaneously.

If multiple URLs are specified, this expresses a descending order of preference. A browser may use a URL for a lower-preference file while it is obtaining or if it is unable to obtain the higher-preference file.

The description field is a textual description of the sound, which may be displayed in addition to or in place of playing the sound. Also, the intensity field adjusts the volume of each sound source. An intensity of 0 is silence; an intensity of 1 is whatever intensity is contained in the sound file.

The sound source has a radius specified by the minRadius field. When the viewpoint is within this radius, the sounds' intensity (volume) is constant, as indicated by the intensity field. Outside the minRadius, the intensity drops off to zero at a distance of maxRadius from the source location. If the two radii are equal, the dropoff is sharp and sudden. Otherwise, the dropoff should be proportional to the square of the distance of the viewpoint from the minRadius.

Browsers may also support spatial localizations of sound. However, within minRadius, localization should not occur, so intensity is constant in all channels. Between minRadius and maxRadius, the sound location should be the point on the minRadius sphere that is closest to the current viewpoint. This ensures a smooth change in location when the viewpoint leaves the minRadius sphere. Note also that an ambient sound can therefore be created by using a large minRadius value.

The loop field specifies whether the sound is continually repeated. By default, the sound is played only once.

The start input specifies the time at which the sound should start playing. The pause input may be used to make a sound stop playing some time after it has started. If the pause time is less than the start time, it is ignored. Changing the start input while the sound is playing will result in undefined behavior. However, changing the start input after the sound is paused is well defined and useful. If the sound is not looped, the length of time the sound plays is determined by the sound file read and is not specified in the VRML file.

A sound's location in the scene graph determines its spatial location (the sound's location is transformed by the current transformation) and whether it can be heard. A sound can be heard only while it is part of the traversed scene. Sound nodes underneath LOD nodes or Switch nodes will not be audible unless they are traversed. If it is later part of the traversal again, the sound picks up where it would have been had it been playing continuously.

The *WorldInfo* node contains information about the world. The title of the world is stored in its own field, allowing browsers to display it, for instance, in their window border. Any other information about the world can be stored in the info field—for instance, the scene author, copyright information, and public domain information.

Prototyping

Prototyping is a mechanism that allows the set of node types to be extended from within a VRML file. It allows the encapsulation and parameterization of geometry, behaviors, or both.

A prototype is defined by using the PROTO keyword. A prototype is *not* a node. It merely defines a prototype (named *typename*) that can be used later in the same file as if it were a built-in node. The

Sidebar

Issues

- What sound-file formats does VAG want to support?
- Supporting real-time effects, such as frequency modulation, reverb, etc., requires too much CPU performance and is beyond the scope of this spec. Advanced browsers can always define more complicated sound sources and can use the IsA mechanism to maintain compatibility with less capable browsers.
- The scene graph semantics chosen allow sounds to be easily attached to objects. Putting an object underneath a Switch node is the way to make it (temporarily) disappear from the world. If the sound is part of the object, the sound should also disappear when this happens.

implementation of the prototype is contained in the scene graph rooted by *node*. That node may be followed by Logic or ROUTE declarations, as necessary to implement the prototype.

The eventIn and eventOut declarations export events inside the scene graph given by *node*. Specifying the type of each event in the prototype is intended to prevent errors when the implementation of prototypes is changed and to provide consistency with external prototypes. Specifying a name for each event allows several events with the same name to be exported with unique names.

Fields hold the persistent state of VRML objects. Allowing a prototype to export fields allows the initial state of a prototyped object to be specified by prototype instances.

The node names specified in the event and field declarations must be defined inside the prototype implementation. The first node defined in lexical (not traversal) order will be exported. It is an error (and results are undefined) if there is no node with the given name or if the first node found does not contain a field of the appropriate type with the given field name.

Prototype declarations have file scope, and prototype names must be unique in any given file. Only nodes defined inside the prototype may be used inside the prototype, and nodes defined inside the prototype are not visible (may not be used) outside the prototype.

A prototype is instantiated as if *typename* were a built-in node. A prototype instance may be defined or used.

VAG is making distinctions between fields, which can be given an initial value but cannot be changed except by the node that they're contained in, and events, which (at least for the built-in nodes) are requests to change fields. So if we want our TwoColorChair to have colors that can be changed, we'd need to expose the leg.setDiffuseColor 'eventIn' and seat.diffuseColor 'eventIn' events—all of which may make for confusing and wordy prototype declarations. Are there ever cases when you might want to allow only initial values to be set and *not* allow them to be changed later?

PROTO sort of gives people their noninstantiating DEF.- PROTOfoo [] Cube { } is roughly equal to DEF foo Cube { }, except that foo is now a type name instead of an instance name (and you say foo { } to get another cube instead of USEfoo). Smart implementations will automatically share the unchanging stuff in prototype implementations, so the end result will be the same.

What if we wanted a prototype that could be instantiated with arbitrary geometry? For example, we might want to define a prototype chair that allowed the geometry for the legs to be defined, with the default (perhaps) being a simple cylinder.

VRML X.X will include the SFNode field type—a field that contains a pointer to a node. We need some way of taking an SFNode field and inserting it into the scene.

Functionally; NodeReference is a do-nothing node—it just behaves exactly like whatever 'nodeToUse' points to (unless nodeToUse is NULL, of course, in which case NodeReference does nothing. NodeReference is interesting only if its nodeToUse field is exposed in a prototype (or it receives a nodeToUse event.

Note that SFNode fields follow the regular DEF/USE rules and that SFNode fields contain a pointer to a node. Using DEF/USE, an SFNode field may contain a pointer to a node that is also a child of some node in the scene graph and is pointed to by some other SFNode field, etc.

The NodeReference node has nice, clean semantics and allows a lot of flexibility and power for defining prototype. It also has some nice implementation side effects.

Browsers that want to maintain a different internal representation for the scene graph can implement NodeReference so that nodeToUse is read and the different internal representation is generated. Optimizations might also be performed at the same time.

Browsers that optimize scene graphs can implement NodeReference such that whenever nodeToUse changes, an optimized scene is created. When rendering, the optimized scene will be used instead of the unoptimized scene. A really smart browser will figure out that nobody is using the unoptimized scene and may free it from memory.

A second form of the prototype syntax allows prototypes to be defined in external files. In this case the implementation of the prototype is found in the given URL. The file pointed to by that URL must contain *only* a single prototype implementation (using PROTO). That prototype is then given the name typename in this file's scope (allowing possible naming clashes to be avoided). It is an error if the eventIn/eventOut declaration in the EXTERNPROTO is not a subset of the eventIn/eventOut declaration specified in URL.

The rules about allowing exporting only from files that contain a single PROTO declaration are consistent with the WWWInline rules. Until VAG has VRML-aware protocols that can send just one object or prototype declaration across the wire, VAG probably won't encourage people to put multiple objects or prototype declarations in a single file.

We need to think about scalability when using nested EXTERNPROTOS. EXTERNPROTOs don't have bounding boxes specified like WWWInlines, and they might need them. VAG is beginning to think about the need to add bboxCenter/Size fields to Separator instead of having them only on WWWInline. With animations possible, prespecifying maximum-possible bounding boxes could save a lot of work recalculating bounding boxes as things move.

Extensibility

Extensions to VRML are supported by supporting self-describing nodes. Nodes that are not part of standard VRML must write out a description of their fields first, so that all VRML implementations are able to parse and ignore the extensions. This description is written just after the opening brace for the node and consists of the keyword "fields", followed by a list of the types and names of fields used by that node, all enclosed in brackets and separated by commas.

Specifying the fields for nodes that *are* part of standard VRML is not an error. VRML parsers must silently ignore the field[] specification. However, incorrectly specifying the fields of a built-in node is an error.

The fields specification must be written out with every nonstandard node, whether or not that node type was previously encountered during parsing. For each instance of a nonstandard node, only the fields written as part of that instance need to be described in the fields[] specification. That is, fields that aren't written because they contain their default value may be omitted from the fields[] specification. It is expected that future versions of VRML will relax this requirement, requiring only that the first nonstandard node of a given type be given the fields[] specification.

Just like standard nodes, instances of nonstandard nodes do not automatically share anything besides the default values of their fields, which are not specified in the VRML file but are considered part of the implementation of the nonstandard nodes.

Using isA Relationships

A new node type may also be a superset of an existing node that is part of the standard. In this case if an implementation for the new node type cannot be found, the new node type can be safely treated as the existing node *it* is based on (with some loss of functionality, of course). To support this, new node types can define an MFString field, called isA, containing the names of the types of which it is a superset.

Multiple isA relationships may be specified in order of preference. Implementations are expected to use the first for which there is an implementation.

Note that isA and PROTO are different ways to define new nodes; they should not be used together. Nodes instantiated with isA should not copy default values or children from the first instantiation.

Using Alternative Representations

To allow extension nodes to be handled gracefully by browsers that don't recognize them, an alternateRep field is supported. This is an SFNode field that specifies what to use if the extension node is not recognized. Typically it will be a WWWInline for a more complex representation or a CGI script, which can generate the node dynamically.

Naming Conventions

Check the General Syntax section of this standard for the rules on valid characters in names.

To avoid name space collisions with nodes defined by other people, any of the following conventions should be followed.

- Anyone can pick names that include a suffix of an underscore followed by a domain name that you own, with the periods changed into underscores. For example, a company owning foo.com could create an extension node Cube_foo_com.
- If you are building a product—for example, an authoring tool or a browser—or defining a lot of new nodes, you can apply for a short prefix. Send e-mail to type_registry@vrml.org to register for the prefix. This will normally be accepted if it is the most significant part of a com, org or net address; in the example foo.com could register the extension _foo and create nodes of the form Cube_foo.
- Extensions supported by several companies should be registered and use the _X extension.

This process may change as more experience is gained.

URNs

VRML X.X browsers are not required to support URNs although if they don't then they should ignore URNs when they appear in MFString fields with URLs. URN support is specified in a separate document at http://earth.path.net/mitra/papers//vrml-urn.html, which may undergo minor revisions to keep it in line with parallel work happening at the IETF.

Browser Considerations

This final part of the chapter describes the file naming and MIME conventions to be used in building VRML browsers and configuring WWW browsers to work with them. The file extension for VMRL files is .wrl (for world). In addition, the MIME type for VRML files is defined as follows:

```
x-world/x-vrml
```

The MIME major type for 3-D world descriptions is x-world. The MIME minor type for VRML documents is x-vrml. Other 3-D world descriptions, such as oogl for The Geometry Center's Object-Oriented Geometry Language or iv for SGI's Open Inventor ASCII format, can be supported by using different MIME minor types.

It is anticipated that the official type will change to model/vrml; at this time servers should present files as being of type x-world/x-vrml. Browsers should recognize both x-world/x-vrml and model/vrml.

From Here

Now that VRML has been covered thoroughly, there also needs to be a very thorough discussion about the OpenGL Graphics System. After all, both OpenGL and Open Inventor are the bases, or foundations, on which VRML was created.

Chapter 14 describes the OpenGL graphics system: what it is, how it acts, and what is required to implement it. Programmers and experts in the computer graphics arena might also want to take a look at Appendixes C, D, and E for an in-depth look at the OpenGL environment.

The OpenGL Graphics System

This chapter describes the OpenGL graphics system: what it is, how it acts, and what is required to implement it. You must have at least a rudimentary understanding of computer graphics. This means that you must be familiar with the essentials of computer graphics algorithms, as well as with basic graphics hardware and associated terms.

Three Views of OpenGL

OpenGL (for Open Graphics Library) is a software interface to graphics hardware. The interface consists of a set of several hundred procedures and functions that allow a programmer to specify the objects and operations involved in producing high-quality graphical images—specifically color images of three-dimensional objects.

Most of OpenGL requires that the graphics hardware contain a frame buffer. Many OpenGL calls pertain to drawing objects, such as points, lines, polygons, and bitmaps, but the way that some of this drawing occurs (such as when antialiasing or texturing is enabled) relies on the existence of a frame buffer. Further, some of OpenGL is specifically concerned with frame buffer manipulation.

To the *programmer* OpenGL is a set of commands for the specification of geometric objects in two or three dimensions, together with commands that control how these objects are rendered into the frame buffer. For the most part OpenGL provides an immediate-mode interface, meaning that specifying an object causes it to be drawn.

A typical program that uses OpenGL begins with calls to open a window into the frame buffer into which the program will draw. Then calls are made to allocate a GL context and to associate it with the window. Once a GL context is allocated, the programmer is free to issue OpenGL commands. Some calls are used to draw simple geometric objects (points, line segments, and polygons). Others affect the rendering of these primitives, including how they are lit or colored and how they are mapped from the user's two- or three-dimensional model space to the two-dimensional screen. There are also calls to effect direct control of the frame buffer, such as reading and writing pixels.

To the *implementor* OpenGL is a set of commands for the operation of graphics hardware. If the hardware consists only of an addressable frame buffer, OpenGL must be implemented almost entirely on the host CPU. More typically the graphics hardware may comprise varying degrees of graphics acceleration—from a raster subsystem capable of rendering two-dimensional lines and polygons to sophisticated floating-point processors capable of transforming and computing on geometric data. The OpenGL implementor's task is to provide the CPU software interface while dividing the work for each OpenGL command between the CPU and the graphics hardware. This division must be tailored to the available graphics hardware to obtain optimum performance in carrying out OpenGL calls.

OpenGL maintains a considerable amount of state information. This state controls how objects are drawn into the frame buffer. Some of this state is directly available to the user: He or she can make calls to obtain its value. Some of it, however, is visible only by the effect it has on what is drawn. One of the main goals of this specification is to make OpenGL state information explicit, to elucidate how it changes, and to indicate what its effects are.

To me OpenGL is a state machine that controls a set of specific drawing operations. This model should engender a specification that satisfies the needs of both programmers and implementors. It does not, however, necessarily provide a model for implementation. An implementation must produce results conforming to those produced by the specified methods, but, there may be ways to carry out a particular computation that is more efficient than the one specified.

OpenGL Operation

OpenGL (henceforth the GL) is concerned only with rendering into a frame buffer (and reading values stored in that frame buffer). There is no support for other peripherals sometimes associated with graphics hardware, such as mice and keyboards. Programmers must rely on other mechanisms to obtain user input.

The GL draws primitives subject to a number of selectable modes. Each primitive is a point, line segment, polygon, or pixel rectangle. Each mode may be changed independently. The setting of one does not affect the settings of others (although many modes may interact to determine what eventually ends up in the frame buffer). Modes are set, primitives specified, and other GL operations described by sending commands in the form of function or procedure calls.

Primitives are defined by a group of one or more vertices. A vertex defines a point, an endpoint of an edge, or a corner of a polygon where two edges meet. Data (consisting of positional coordinates, colors, normals, and texture coordinates) are associated with a vertex. Each vertex is processed independently, in order, and in the same way. The only exception to this rule is if the group of vertices is clipped so that the indicated primitive fits within a specified region. In this case vertex data may be modified and new vertices created. The type of clipping depends on which primitive the group of vertices represents.

Commands are always processed in the order in which they are received, although there may be an indeterminate delay before the effects of a command are realized. This means, for example, that one primitive must be drawn completely before any subsequent one can affect the frame buffer. It also means that queries and pixel read operations return state consistent with complete execution of all previously invoked GL commands. In general, the effects of a GL command on either GL modes or the frame buffer must be complete before any subsequent command can have any such effects.

In the GL data binding occurs on call. This means that data passed to a command is interpreted when that command is received. Even if the command requires a pointer to data, the data is interpreted when the call is made, and any subsequent changes to the data have no effect on the GL (unless the same pointer is used in a subsequent command).

The GL provides direct control over the fundamental operations of 3-D and 2-D graphics. This includes specification of such parameters as transformation matrices, lighting equation coefficients, antialiasing methods, and pixel update operators. It does not provide a means for describing or modeling complex geometric objects. Another way to describe this situation is to say that the GL provides mechanisms to describe how complex geometric objects are to be rendered rather than mechanisms to describe the complex objects themselves.

The model for interpretation of GL commands is client-server. That is, a program (the client) issues commands, which are interpreted and processed by the GL (the server). The server may or may not operate on the same computer as the client. In this sense the GL is network transparent. A server may maintain a number of GL contexts, each of which is an encapsulation of current GL state. A client may choose to connect to any one of these contexts. Issuing GL commands when the program is not connected to a context results in undefined behavior.

The effects of GL commands on the frame buffer are ultimately controlled by the window system that allocates frame buffer resources. It is the window system that determines which portions of the frame buffer the GL may access at any given time and that communicates to the GL how those portions are structured. Therefore there are no GL commands to configure the frame buffer or to initialize the GL. Similarly display of frame buffer contents on a CRT monitor (including the transformation of individual frame buffer values by such techniques as gamma correction) is not addressed by the GL. Frame buffer configuration occurs outside of the GL in conjunction with the window system. The initialization of a GL context occurs when the window system allocates a window for GL rendering.

The GL is designed to be run on a range of graphics platforms with varying graphics capabilities and performance. To accommodate this variety, ideal behavior is specified here instead of actual behavior for certain GL operations. In cases where deviation from the ideal is allowed, the rules are also specified that an implementation must obey if it is to approximate the ideal behavior usefully. This allowed variation in GL behavior implies that two distinct GL implementations may not agree pixel for pixel when presented with the same input, even when run on identical frame-buffer configurations.

Finally, command names, constants, and types are prefixed in the GL (by gl, GL, and GL, respectively in C) to reduce name clashes with other packages. The prefixes are omitted in this chapter for clarity.

Floating-Point Computation

The GL must perform a number of floating-point operations during its operation. No specification is made here as to how floating-point numbers are to be represented or how operations on them are to be performed. Nevertheless it is required that numbers' floating-point parts contain enough bits and that their exponent fields are large enough so that individual results of floating-point operations are accurate to about 1 part in 10^5. The maximum representable magnitude of a floating-point number used to represent positional or normal coordinates must be at least 2^{32}. The maximum representable magnitude for colors or texture coordinates must be at least 2^{10}. The maximum representable magnitude for all other floating-point values must be at least 2^{32}. Most single-precision floating-point formats meet these requirements.

Any representable floating-point value is legal as input to a GL command that requires floating-point data. The result of providing a value that is not a floating-point number to such a command is unspecified, but must not lead to GL interruption or termination. In IEEE arithmetic, for example, providing a negative zero or a denormalized number to a GL command yields predictable results, whereas providing a NaN or an infinity yields unspecified results.

Some calculations require division. In such cases (including implied divisions required by vector normalizations) a division by zero produces an unspecified result but must not lead to GL interruption or termination.

GL State

The GL maintains considerable state. This chapter enumerates each state variable and describes how each variable can be changed. For purposes of discussion, state variables are categorized somewhat arbitrarily by their function. Although a description is provided of the operations that the GL performs on the frame buffer, the frame buffer is not a part of GL state.

There are two types of state distinguishers here. The first type of state, called GL server state, resides in the GL server. The majority of GL state falls into this category. The second type of state, called GL client state, resides in the GL client. Unless otherwise specified, all state referred to in this chapter is GL server state. GL client state is specifically identified. Each instance of a GL context implies one complete set of GL server state. Each connection from a client to a server implies a set of both GL client state and GL server state.

Although an implementation of the GL may be hardware dependent, this discussion is independent of the specific hardware on which a GL is implemented. There is a concern, therefore, with the state of graphics hardware only when it corresponds precisely to GL state.

GL Command Syntax

GL commands are functions or procedures. Various groups of commands perform the same operation but differ in how arguments are supplied to them. To conveniently accommodate this variation, a notation has been adopted for describing commands and their arguments.

GL commands are formed from a name followed, depending on the particular command, by up to four characters. The first character indicates the number of values of the indicated type that must be presented to the command. The second character or character pair indicates the specific type of the arguments: 8-bit integer, 16-bit integer, 32-bit integer, single-precision floating point, or double-precision floating point. The final character, if present, is **v**, indicating that the command takes a pointer to an array (a vector) of values rather than to a series of individual arguments.

Two specific examples come from the **Vertex** command:

```
void Vertex3f ( float x, float y, float z ) ;
```

and

```
void Vertex2sv ( short v[2] ) ;
```
[1]

Table 14.1 shows the correspondence of command suffix letters to GL argument types. Refer to Table 14.2 for definitions of the GL types.

---

[1] Mark Segal and Kurt Akeley, OpenGL Specification, *Utility Library Specification and GLX Protocol*, Silicon Graphics, Inc., January 16, 1995.

Table 14.1 GL Suffix Letters and Corresponding Argument Type

Letter	Corresponding GL Type
b	byte
s	short
i	int
f	f lost
d	double
ub	ubyte
us	ushort
ui	uint

The following examples show the ANSI C declarations for these commands. In general, a command declaration has the form

rtype Name { ∈ 1234} { ∈ b s i f d ub us ui} { ∈ v}
([*args* ,] T *arg1*, ... , T *argN* [, *args*]) ;

Note that the declarations shown in this chapter apply to ANSI C. Languages that allow passing of argument type information, such as C++ and Ada, admit simpler declarations and fewer entry points.

Rtype is the return type of the function. The braces ({}) enclose a series of characters (or character pairs) of which one is selected; ∈ indicates no character. The arguments enclosed in brackets ([*args* ,] and [, *args*]) may or may not be present. The *N* arguments *arg1* through *argN* have type *T*, which corresponds to one of the type letters or letter pairs as indicated in Table 14.1 (if there are no letters, the arguments' type is given explicitly). If the final character is not **v**, *N* is given by the digit **1**, **2**, **3**, or **4** (if there is no digit, the number of arguments is fixed). If the final character is **v**, only *arg1* is present, and it is an array of *N* values of the indicated type. Finally, an unsigned type is indicated by the shorthand of prepending u to the beginning of the type name (so that, for instance, unsigned char is abbreviated uchar).

For example,

void Normal3{fd}(T arg) ;

indicates the two declarations

void **Normal3f**(float *arg1*, float *arg2*, float *arg3*) ;
void **Normal3-D**(double *arg1*, double *arg2*, double *arg3*) ;

However,

void **Normal3**{**fd**}v(T *arg*) ;

means the two declarations

void **Normal3fv**(float *arg[3]*) ;
void **Normal3-Dv**(double *arg[S]*) ;

Arguments whose type is fixed (not indicated by a suffix on the command) are of one of 14 types (or pointers to one of these). These types are summarized in Table 14.2.

GL types are not C types. Thus, for example, GL type int is referred to as GLint outside this chapter and is not necessarily equivalent to the C type int. An implementation may use more bits than the number indicated in the table to represent a GL type. Correct interpretation of integer values outside the minimum range is not required, however.

Table 14.2 GL Data Types

GL Type	Minimum Number of Bits	Description
boolean	1 bit	Boolean
byte	8 bits	Signed two's complement binary integer
ubyte	8 bits	Unsigned binary integer
short	16 bits	Signed two's complement binary integer
ushort	16 bits	Unsigned binary integer
int	32 bits	Signed two's complement binary integer
uint	32 bits	Unsigned binary integer
sizei	32 bits	Nonnegative binary integer size
enum	32 bits	Enumerated binary integer value
bitfield	32 bits	Bit field
float	32 bits	Floating-point value
clampf	32 bits	Floating-point value clamped to [0,11]
double	64 bits	Floating-point value
clampd	64 bits	Floating-point value clamped to [0, 1]

Basic GL Operation

Figure 14.1 shows a schematic of the GL. Commands enter the GL on the left. Some commands specify geometric objects to be drawn, whereas others control how the objects are handled by the various stages. Most commands may be accumulated in a display list for processing by the GL at a later time. Otherwise, commands are effectively sent through a processing pipeline.

The first stage provides an efficient means for approximating curve and surface geometry by evaluating polynomial functions of input values. The next stage operates on geometric primitives described by vertices: points, line segments, and polygons. In this stage vertices are transformed and lit, and primitives are clipped to a viewing volume in preparation for the next stage-rasterization. The rasterizer produces a series of frame buffer addresses and values, using a two-dimensional description of a point, line segment, or polygon. Each fragment so produced is fed to the next stage which performs operations on individual fragments before they finally alter the frame buffer. These operations include conditioned updates into the frame buffer, based on incoming and previously stored depth values (to effect depth buffering); blending of incoming fragment colors with stored colors; as well as masking and other logical operations on fragment values.

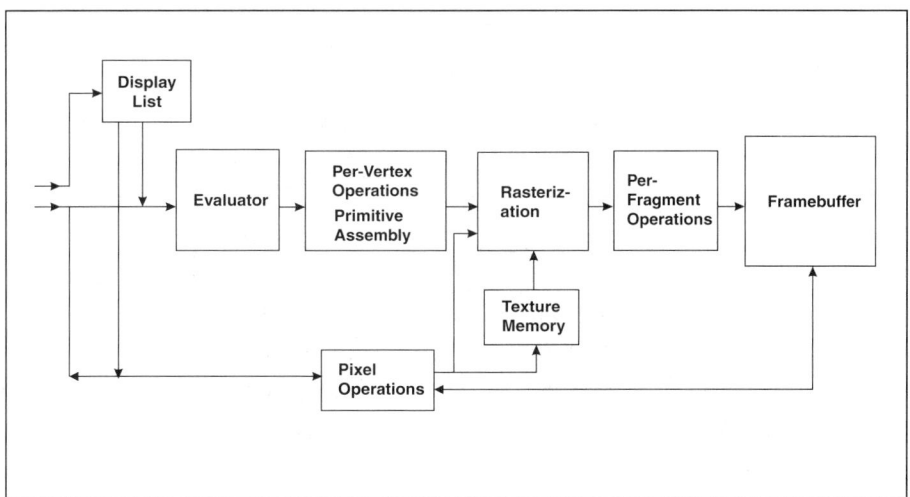

Figure 14. 1 Block Diagram of the GL

Finally, there is a way to bypass the vertex-processing portion of the pipeline to send a block of fragments directly to the individual fragment operations, eventually causing a block of pixels to be written to the frame buffer. Values may also be read back from the frame buffer or copied from one portion of the frame buffer to another. These transfers may include some type of decoding or encoding.

This ordering is meant only as a tool for describing the GL, not as a strict rule of how the GL is implemented. It is presented here only as a means to organize the various operations of the GL. Objects such as curved surfaces, for instance, may be transformed before they are converted to polygons.

GL Errors

The GL detects only a subset of those conditions that could be considered errors. This is because in many cases error checking would adversely impact the performance of an error-free program.

The following command is used to obtain error information:

```
enum GetError( void ) ;
```

is used to obtain error information.

Each detectable error is assigned a numeric code. When an error is detected, a flag is set and the code is recorded. Further errors, if they occur, do not affect this recorded code. When **GetError** is called, the code is returned and the flag is cleared, so that a further error will again record its code. If a call to **GetError** returns **NO_ERROR**, no detectable error has occurred since the last call to **GetError** (or since the GL was initialized).

To allow for distributed implementations, there may be several flag-code pairs. In this case after a call to **GetError** returns a value other than **NO_ERROR,** each subsequent call returns the nonzero code of a distinct flag-code pair (in unspecified order), until all non–**NO_ERROR** codes have been returned. When there are no more non–**NO_ERROR** error codes, all flags are reset. This scheme requires some positive number of pairs of a flag bit and an integer. The initial state of all flags is cleared, and the initial value of all codes is **NO_ERROR**.

Table 14.3 summarizes GL errors. Currently when an error flag is set, results of GL operation are undefined only if **OUT_OF_MEMORY** has occurred. In other cases, the command generating the error is

Table 14.3 Summary of GL Errors

Error	Description	Offending Command Ignored?
INVALID_ENUM	Enum argument out of range	Yes
INVALID_VALUE	Numeric argument out of range	Yes
INVALID_OPERATION	Operation illegal in current state	Yes
STACK_OVERFLOW	Command would cause a stack overflow	Yes
STACK_UNDERFLOW	Command would cause a stack underflow	Yes
OUT-OF-MEMORY	Not enough memory left to execute command	Unknown

ignored so that it has no effect on GL state or frame buffer contents. If the generating command returns a value, it returns 0. If the generating command modifies values through a pointer argument, no change is made to these values. These error semantics apply only to GL errors, not to system errors, such as memory access errors. This behavior is the current behavior. The action of the GL in the presence of errors is subject to change.

Two error-generation conditions are implicit in the description of every GL command. First, if a command that requires an enumerated value is passed, an enumerant that is not one of those specified as allowable for that command, the error **INVALID_EMUN** results. This is the case even if the argument is a pointer to an enumerated value if that value is not allowable for the given command. Second, if a negative number is provided where an argument of type **sizei** is specified, the error **INVALID_VALUE** results.

Begin/End Paradigm

In the GL most geometric objects are drawn by enclosing a series of coordinate sets that specify vertices and, optionally, normals, texture coordinates, and colors between Begin/End pairs. Ten geometric objects that are drawn this way: points, line segments, line segment loops, separated fine segments, polygons, triangle strips, triangle fans, separated triangles, quadrilateral strips, and separated quadrilaterals.

Each vertex is specified with two, three, or four coordinates. In addition, a *current normal*, *current texture coordinates*, and *current color* may be used in processing each vertex. Normals are used by the GL in lighting calculations. The current normal is a three-dimensional vector that may be set by sending three coordinates that specify it. Texture coordinates determine how a texture image is mapped onto a primitive.

A color is associated with each vertex as it is specified. This *associated* color is either the current color or a color produced by lighting, depending on whether lighting is enabled. Texture coordinates are similarly associated with each vertex. Figure 14.2 summarizes the association of auxiliary data with a transformed vertex to produce a *processed vertex*.

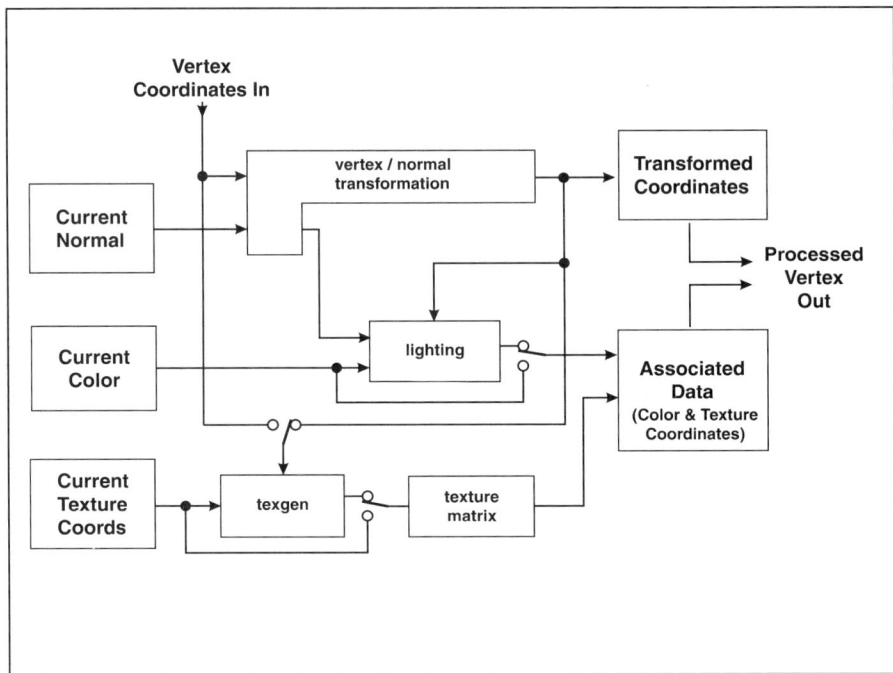

Figure 14.2 Association of Current Values with a Vertex. The heavy lined boxes represent GL state.

The current values are part of GL state. Vertices and normals are transformed. Colors may be affected or replaced by lighting. Texture coordinates are transformed and possibly affected by a texture coordinate-generation function. The processing indicated for each current value is applied for each vertex that is sent to the GL. The methods by which vertices, normals, texture coordinates, and colors are sent to the GL—as well as how normals are transformed and vertices are mapped to the two-dimensional screen—are discussed later.

Before a color has been assigned to a vertex, the state required by a vertex is the vertex's coordinates, the current normal, and the current texture coordinates. Once color has been assigned, however, the current normal is no longer needed. Because color assignment is done vertex by vertex, a processed vertex comprises the vertex's coordinates, its assigned color, and its texture coordinates.

Figure 14.3 shows the sequence of operations that builds a primitive (point, line segment, or polygon) from a sequence of vertices. After a primitive is formed, it is clipped to a viewing volume. This may alter the primitive by altering vertex coordinates, texture coordinates, and color. In the case of a polygon primitive, clipping may insert new vertices into the primitive. The vertices defining a primitive to be rasterized have texture coordinates and color associated with them.

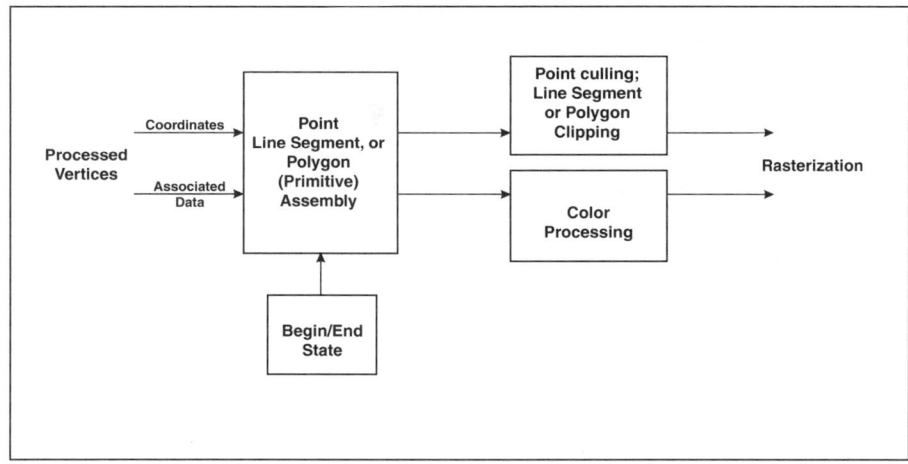

Figure 14.3 Primitive Assembly and Processing.

Begin and End Objects

Begin and **End** require one state variable with 11 values: one value for each of the 10 possible **Begin/End** objects and one other value indicating that no **Begin/End** object is being processed. The two relevant commands are:

```
void Begin( enum mode ) ;
void End( void ) ;
```

There is no limit on the number of vertices that may be specified between a Begin and an End.[2]

A series of individual *points* may be specified by calling Begin with an argument value of POINTS. No special state need be kept between Begin and End in this case, since each point is independent of previous and following points.

A series of one or more connected line segments, or *line strips*, is specified by enclosing a series of two or more end points within a Begin/End pair when Begin is called with LINE-STRIP. In this case the first vertex specifies the first segment's start point; the second vertex specifies the first segment's end point and the second segment's start point. In general, the ith vertex (for $i > 1$) specifies the beginning of the ith segment and the end of the i - 1st. The last vertex specifies the end of the last segment. If only one vertex is specified between the Begin/End pair, no primitive is generated.

The required state consists of the processed vertex produced from the last vertex that was sent (so that a line segment can be generated from it to the current vertex) and a Boolean flag indicating whether the current vertex is the first vertex.

Line loops, specified with the LINE-LOOP argument value to Begin, are the same as line strips, except that a final segment is added from the final specified vertex to the first vertex. The additional state consists of the processed first vertex.

Individual line segments, or separate lines, each specified by a pair of vertices, are generated by surrounding vertex pairs with Begin and End, when the value of the argument to Begin is LINES. In this case the first two vertices between a Begin and End pair define the first segment, with subsequent pairs of vertices each defining one more segment. If the number of specified vertices is odd, the last one is

---

[2] *Ibid.*, pp. 15–16.

ignored. The state required is the same as for lines but it is used differently: a vertex holding the first vertex of the current segment and a Boolean flag indicating whether the current vertex is odd or even (a segment start or end).

A *polygon* is described by specifying its boundary as a series of line segments. When Begin is called with POLYGON, the bounding line segments are specified in the same way as line loops. Depending on the current state of the GL, a polygon may be rendered in one of several ways, such as outlining its border or filling its interior. A polygon described with fewer than three vertices does not generate a primitive.

Only convex polygons are guaranteed to be drawn correctly by the GL. If a specified polygon is nonconvex (in particular, if its bounding edges, when projected onto the window, intersect anywhere other than at common end points), the rendered polygon need lie only within the convex hull of the vertices defining its boundary.

The state required to support polygons consists of at least two processed vertices (more than two are never required, although an implementation may use more). This is because a convex polygon can be rasterized as its vertices arrive, before all of them have been specified. The order of the vertices is significant in lighting, and polygon rasterization is discussed later in this chapter.

A *triangle strip* is a series of triangles connected along shared edges. A triangle strip is specified by giving a series of defining vertices between a Begin/End pair when Begin is called with TRIANGLE-STRIP. In this case the first three vertices define the first triangle (and their order is significant, just as for polygons). Each subsequent vertex defines a new triangle, using that point along with two vertices from the previous triangle. A Begin/End pair enclosing fewer than three vertices, when TRIANGLE-STRIP has been supplied to Begin, produces no primitive. See Figure 14.4.

The state required to support triangle strips consists of a flag indicating whether the first triangle has been completed, two stored processed vertices, (called vertex A and vertex B), and a one-bit pointer indicating which stored vertex will be replaced with the next vertex. After a **Begin(TRIANGLE-STRIP)**, the pointer is initialized to point to vertex A. Each vertex sent between a **Begin/End** pair toggles the pointer. Therefore the first vertex is stored as vertex A, the second stored as vertex B, the third stored as vertex A, and so on. Any vertex after the second one sent forms a triangle from vertex A, vertex B, and the current vertex (in that order).

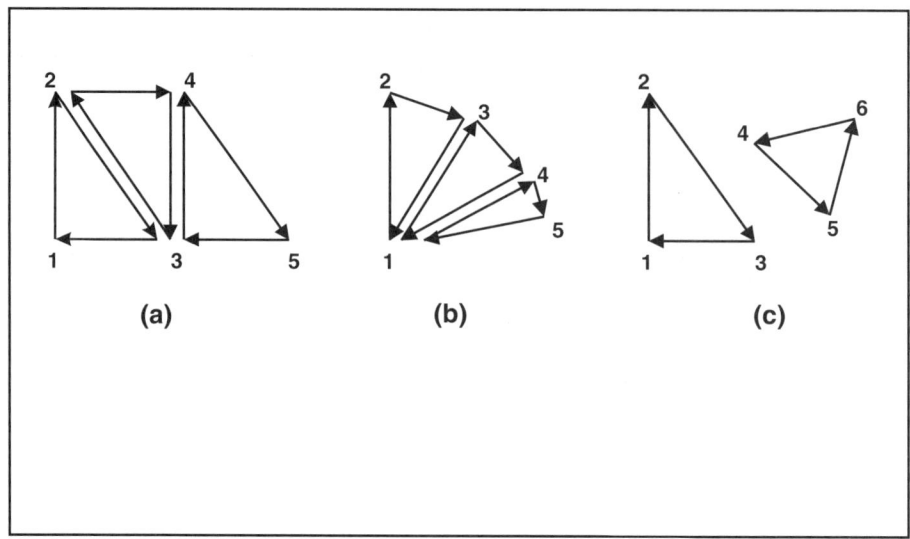

Figure 14.4 (a) Triangle Strip; (b) Triangle Fan; (c) Independent Triangles. The numbers give the sequencing of the vertices between Begin and End. Note that in (a) and (b) triangle edge ordering is determined by the first triangle, whereas in (c) the order of each triangle's edges is independent of the other triangles.

A *triangle fan* is the same as a triangle strip with one exception: Each vertex after the first always replaces vertex B of the two stored vertices. The vertices of a triangle fan are enclosed between Begin and End when the value of the argument to **Begin** is **TRIANGLE_FAN**.

Separate triangles are specified by placing vertices between **Begin** and **End** when the value of the argument to **Begin** is **TRIANGLES**. Otherwise, separate triangles are the same as a triangle strip. The rules given for polygons also apply to each triangle generated from a triangle strip, triangle fan, or separate triangles.

Quadrilateral {quad} strips generate a series of edge sharing quadrilaterals from vertices appearing between **Begin** and **End** when **Begin** is called with **QUAD_STRIP**. The state required is thus three processed vertices to store the last two vertices of the previous quad along with the third vertex (the first new vertex) of the current quad, a flag to indicate when the first quad has been completed, and a one-bit counter to count members of a vertex pair, as shown in Figure 14.5. The rules given for polygons also apply to each quad generated in a quad strip or from separate quads.

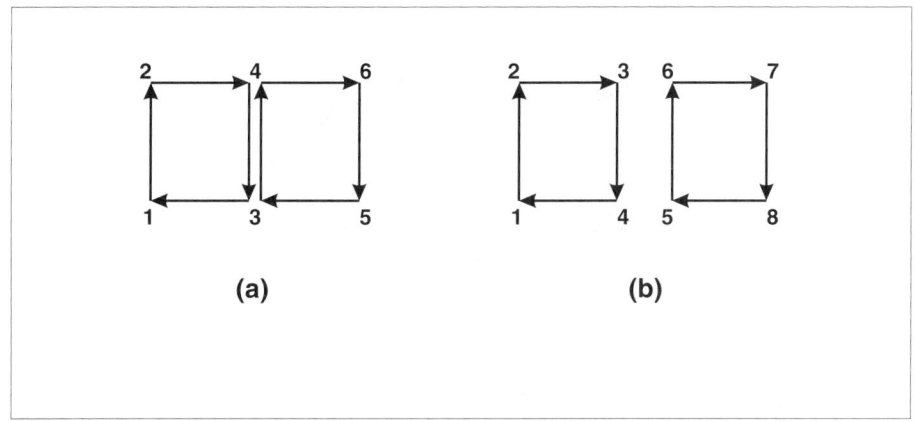

Figure 14.5 (a) Quad Strip;(b) Independent Quads. The numbers give the sequencing of the vertices between Begin and End.

A quad strip with fewer than four vertices generates no primitive. If the number of vertices specified for a quadrilateral strip between **Begin** and **End** is odd, the final vertex is ignored.

Polygon Edges

Each edge of each primitive generated from a polygon, triangle strip, triangle fan, separate triangle set, quadrilateral strip, or separate quadrilateral set is flagged as either boundary or nonboundary. These classifications are used during polygon rasterization. Some modes affect the interpretation of polygon boundary edges, as discussed later in the chapter. By default, all edges are boundary edges.

But the default flagging of polygons, separate triangles, or separate quadrilaterals may be altered by calling either of the following to change the value of a flag bit:

```
void EdgeFlag( boolean flag ) ;
void EdgeFlagv( boolean *flag
```

If flag is 0 the flag bit is set to FALSE. If flag is nonzero, the flag bit is set to TRUE.

When Begin is supplied with one of the argument values **POLYGON, TRIANGLES,** or **QUADS,** each vertex specified within a **Begin** and **End** pair begins an edge. If the edge flag bit is **TRUE,** each specified vertex begins an edge that is flagged as boundary. If the bit is **FALSE,** induced edges are flagged as nonboundary.

The state required for edge flagging consists of one current flag bit. Initially the bit is TRUE. In addition, each processed vertex of an assembled polygonal primitive must be augmented with a bit indicating whether the edge beginning on that vertex is boundary or nonboundary.

GL Commands within Begin/End

The only GL commands that are allowed within any **Begin/End** pairs are the commands for specifying vertex coordinates, vertex color, normal coordinates, and texture coordinates (**Vertex, Color, Index, Normal, TexCoord), EvalCoord,** and **EvalPoint** commands. Commands for specifying lighting material parameters (**Material** commands) are discussed later in the chapter, as well as display list invocation commands (**CallList** and **CallLists**) and the **EdgeFlag** command. Executing **Begin** after **Begin** has already been executed but before an **End** is issued generates the **INVALID_OPERATION** error, as does executing **End** without a previous corresponding **Begin**. Executing any other GL command within **Begin/End** results in the error **INVALID-OPERATION.**

Vertex Specification

Vertices are specified by giving their coordinates in two, three, or four dimensions. This is done by using one of several versions of the Vertex command:

```
void Vertex{1234}{sifd}( T coords ) ;
void Vertex{1234}{sifd}v( T coords ) ;
```

A call to any **Vertex** command specifies four coordinates: x, y, z, and w. The x coordinate is the first coordinate, y is second, z is third, and w is fourth. A call to *Vertex2* sets the x and y coordinates. The z coordinate is implicitly set to 0 and the w coordinate to 1. **Vertex3** sets x, y, and z to the provided values and w to 1. **Vertex4** sets all four coordinates, allowing the specification of an arbitrary point in projective three-space. Invoking a **Vertex** command outside of a **Begin/End** pair results in undefined behavior.

Current values used in associating auxiliary data with a vertex are discussed later in the chapter. A current value may be changed at any time by issuing an appropriate command.

The following commands specify the current homogeneous texture coordinates: named s, t, r, and q:

```
void TexCoord{1234}{sifd}( T coords ) ;
void TexCoord{1234}{sifd}v( T coords)
```

The **TexCoord1** family of commands set the s coordinate to the provided single argument while setting t and r to 0 and q to 1. Similarly **TexCoord2** sets s and t to the specified values, r to 0, and q to 1. **TexCoord3** sets s, t, and r, with q set to 1; **TexCoord4** sets all four texture coordinates.

The current normal is set using the following:

```
void Normal3{bsifd}( T coords ) ;
void Normal3{bsifd)v( T coords ) ;
```

The current normal is set to the given coordinates whenever one of these commands is issued. Byte, short, or integer values passed to Normal are converted to floating-point values as indicated for the corresponding (signed) type in Table 14.4.

Finally, there are several ways to set the current color. The GL stores both a current single-valued *color index* and a current four-valued RGBA color. One or the other of these is significant, depending on whether the GL is in *color index mode* or *RGBA mode*. The mode selection is made when the GL is initialized.

The command to set RGBA colors is:

```
void Color{34}{bsifd ubusui}( T components ) ;
void Color{34}{bsifd ubusui}v( T components ) ;
```

The **Color** command has two major variants: **Color3** and **Color4**. The four-value versions set all four values. The three-value versions set **R**, **G**, and **B** to the provided values. A is set to 1.0. The conversion of integer color components (R, G, B, and A) to floating-point values is discussed later in this chapter.

Versions of the **Color** command that take floating-point values accept values nominally between 0.0 and 1.0; 0.0 corresponds to the minimum, and 1.0 corresponds to the maximum (machine-dependent) value that a component may take on in the frame buffer. Values outside [0, 1] are not clamped.

The command

>   void **Index**{**sifd**}(T *index*) ;
>   void **Index**{**sifd**}**v**(T *index*) ;

Index updates the current (single-valued) color index. It takes one argument, the value to which the current color index should be set. Values outside the (machine-dependent) representable range of color indices are not clamped.

The state required to support vertex specification consists of four floating-point numbers to store the current texture coordinates s, t, r, and q; three floating-point numbers to store the three coordinates of the current normal; four floating-point values to store the current RGBA color; and one floating-point value to store the current color index. There is no notion of a current vertex, so no state is devoted to vertex coordinates. The initial values of s, t, and r of the current texture coordinates are 0. The initial value of q is 1. The initial current normal has coordinates (0, 0, 1). The initial RGBA color is (R, G, B, A) = (1, 1, 1, 1). The initial color index is 1.

A set of GL commands supports efficient specification of rectangles as two corner vertices:

>   void **Rect**{**sifd**}(T *x1,* T *y1,* T *x2,* **T** *y2*) ;
>   void **Rect**{**sifd**}**v**(T *v1[2],* T *v2[2]*) ;

Each command takes either four arguments organized as two consecutive pairs of (x, y) coordinates or two pointers to arrays, each of which contains an x value followed by a y value.

The effect of the **Rect** command—**Rect** (x_1, y_1, x_2, y_2) ;—has exactly the same effect as the following sequence of commands:

```
Begin(POLYGON) ;
     Vertex2 (x₁, y₁);
     Vertex2 (x₂, y₁);
     Vertex2 (x₂, y₂);
     Vertex2 (x₁, y₂);
End();
```

The appropriate **Vertex2** command would be invoked, depending on which of the **Rect** commands is issued.

Coordinate Transformations

Vertices, normals, and texture coordinates are transformed before their coordinates are used to produce an image in the frame buffer. Lets begin with a description of how vertex coordinates are transformed and how this transformation is controlled.

Figure 14.6 diagrams the sequence of transformations applied to vertices. The vertex coordinates that are presented to the GL are termed *object coordinates*. The *model-view* matrix is applied to these coordinates to yield *eye* coordinates. Then another matrix, called the *projection* matrix, is applied to eye coordinates to yield *clip* coordinates. A perspective division is carried out on clip coordinates to yield *normalized device* coordinates. A final *viewport* transformation is applied to convert these coordinates into *window coordinates*.

Object coordinates, eye coordinates, and clip coordinates are four-dimensional, consisting of x, y, z, and w coordinates (in that order). The model-view and perspective matrices are thus 4 x 4.

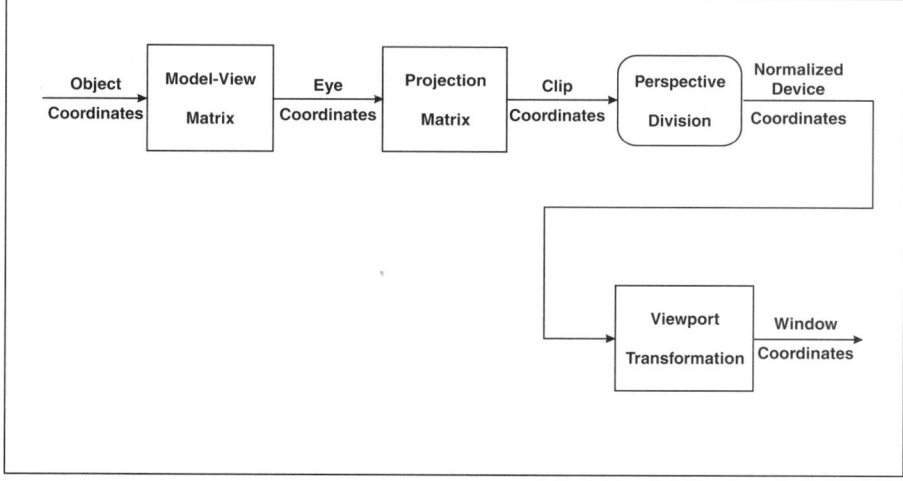

Figure 14.6 Vertex Transformation Sequence

Current Raster Position

The *current raster position* is used by commands that directly affect pixels in the frame buffer. These commands, which bypass vertex transformation and primitive assembly, are described later in the chapter. The current raster position, however, shares some of the characteristics of a vertex.

The current raster position consists of three window coordinates $\{x_w, y_w, \text{and } z_w\}$, a clip coordinate $\{w_c\}$ value, an eye coordinate distance, a valid bit, and associated data consisting of a color and texture coordinates. The current raster position is set by using one of the *RasterPos* commands:

```
void RasterPos{234}{sifd}( T coords ) ;
void RasterPos{234}{sifd}v( T coords ) ;
```

RasterPos4 takes four values indicating x, y, z, and w. **RasterPos3** (or **RasterPos2**) is analogous but sets only x, y, and z, with w implicitly set to 1 (or only x and y, with z implicitly set to 0 and w implicitly set to 1).

The coordinates are treated as if they were specified in a **Vertex** command. The x, y, z, and w coordinates are transformed by the current model-view and perspective matrices. These coordinates, along with current values, are used to generate a color and texture coordinates, just as is done for a vertex. The color and texture coordinates so produced replace the color and texture coordinates stored in the current raster position's associated data. The distance from the origin of the eye coordinate system to the vertex—as transformed by only the current model-view matrix—replaces the current raster distance. This distance can be approximated.

The transformed coordinates are passed to clipping as if they represented a point. If the point is not culled, the projection to window coordinates is computed and saved as the current raster position, and the valid bit is set. If the point is culled, the current raster position and its associated data become indeterminate, and the valid bit is cleared. Figure 14.7 summarizes the behavior of the current raster position.

The current raster position requires five single-precision floating-point values for its x_w, y_w, and z_w window coordinates; its w_c clip coordinate; its eye coordinate distance; a single valid bit; a color (RGBA and color index); and texture coordinates for associated data. In the

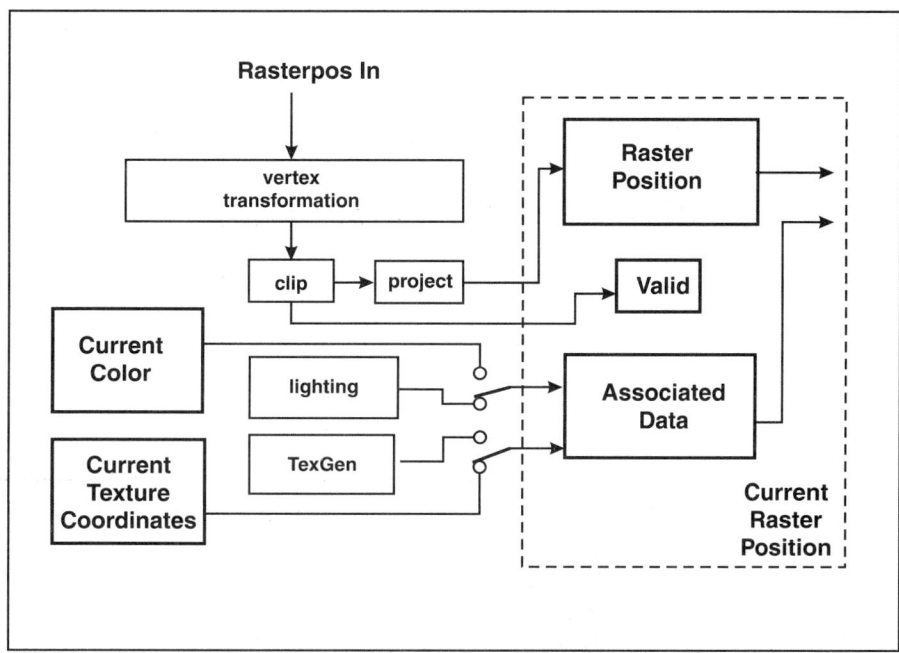

Figure 14.7 The Current Raster Position and How It Is Set

initial state the coordinates and texture coordinates are both (0, 0, 0, 1), the eye coordinate distance is 0, the valid bit is set, the associated RGBA color is (1, 1, 1, 1), and the associated color index color is 1. In RGBA mode the associated color index always has its initial value. In color index mode the RGBA color always maintains its initial value.

Colors and Coloring

Figure 14.8 diagrams the processing of colors before rasterization. Incoming colors arrive in one of several formats. Table 14.4 summarizes the conversions that take place on R, G, B, and A components, depending on which version of the **Color** command was invoked to specify the components. As a result of limited precision, some converted values will not be represented exactly. In color index mode a single-valued color index is not mapped.

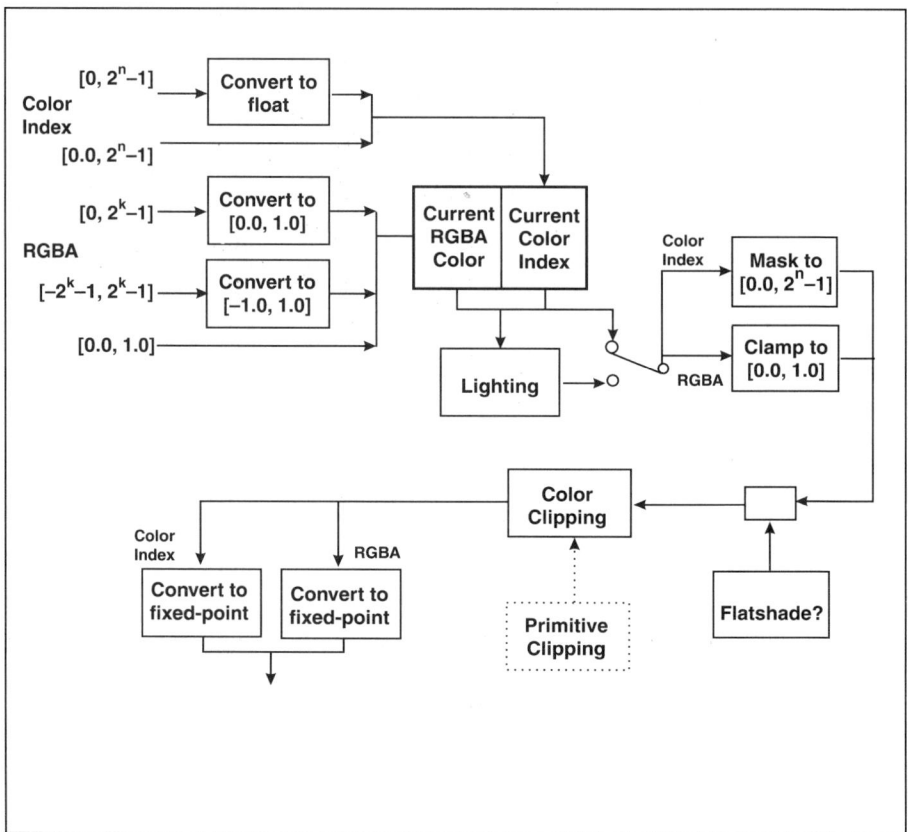

Figure 14.8. Processing of Colors: n is the number of bits in a color index; m is the number of bits in an R, G, B, or A component. See Table 14.4 for the interpretation of k.

Next, lighting, if enabled, produces a color. If lighting is disabled, the current color is used in further processing. After lighting, RGBA colors are clamped to the range [0, 1]. A color index is converted to fixed-point, and then its integer portion is masked. After being clamped or masked, a primitive may be flatshaded, indicating that all vertices of the primitive are to have the same color. Finally, if a primitive is clipped, colors (and texture coordinates) must be computed at the vertices introduced or modified by clipping.

Table 14.4 Component Conversions

GL Type	Conversion
ubyte	$c/(2^8 - 1)$
byte	$(2c + 1)/(2^8 - 1)$
ushort	$c/(2^{16} - 1)$
short	$(2c + 1)/(2^{16} - 1)$
uint	$c/(2^{32} - 1)$
int	$(2c + 1)/(2^{32} - 1)$
float	c
double	c

Color, normal, and depth components (c) are converted to an internal floating-point representation (f), using the equations in this table. All arithmetic is done in the internal floating-point format. These conversions apply to components specified as parameters to GL commands and to components in pixel data. The equations remain the same even if the implemented ranges of the GL data types are greater than the minimum required ranges. (Refer to Table 14.2.)

Lighting

GL lighting computes a color for each vertex sent to the GL. This is accomplished by applying an equation defined by a client-specified lighting model to a collection of parameters that can include the vertex coordinates, the coordinates of one or more light sources, the current normal, and parameters defining the characteristics of the light sources and a current material. The following discussion assumes that the GL is in RGBA mode. Color index lighting is described later in the chapter.

Lighting may be in one of two states: on or off. If lighting is off the color assigned to a vertex is the current color. If lighting is on, a vertex's color is found by computing a value given the current lighting parameters. Lighting is turned either on or off by using the generic **Enable** or **Disable** commands with the symbolic value **LIGHTING**.[3]

---

[3] *Ibid.*, pp. 38–39.

A lighting parameter is of one of five types: color, position, direction, real, or Boolean. A color parameter consists of four floating-point elements, one for each of R, G, B, and A, in that order. There are no restrictions on the allowable values for these parameters. A position parameter consists of four floating-point coordinates (x, y, z, and w) that specify a position in object coordinates (w may, in some cases, be 0, indicating a point at infinity in the direction given by x, y, and z). A direction parameter consists of three floating-point coordinates (x, y, and z) that specify a direction in object coordinates. A real parameter is one floating-point value. The various values and their types are summarized in Table 14.5. The result of a lighting computation is undefined if a value specified for a parameter is outside the range given for that parameter in the table.

Table 14.5 Summary of Lighting Parameters.

The range of individual color components is $(-\infty, +\infty)$.

Parameter	Type	Default Value	Description
Material Parameters			
a_{cm}	Color	(0.2, 0.2, 0.2, 1.0)	Ambient color of material
d_{cm}	Color	(0.8, 0.8, 0.8, 1.0)	Diffuse color of material
s_{cm}	Color	(0.0, 0.0, 0.0, 1.0)	Specular color of material
e_{cm}	Color	(0.0, 0.0, 0.0, 1.0)	Emissive color of material
s_{rm}	Real	0.0	Specular exponent (range: [0.0, 128.0])
a_m	Real	0.0	Ambient color index
d_m	Real	1.0	Diffuse color index
s_m	Real	1.0	Specular color index
Light Source Parameters			
a_{cli}	Color	(0.0, 0.0, 0.0, 1.0)	Ambient intensity of light i
$d_{cli}(i = 0)$	Color	(1.0, 1.0, 1.0, 1.0)	Diffuse intensity of light 0
$d_{cli}(i > 0)$	Color	(0.0, 0.0, 0.0, 1.0)	Diffuse intensity of light i

Table 14.5 *(continued)*

Parameter	Type	Default Value	Description
Light Source Parameters			
s$cli(i=0)$	Color	(1.0, 1.0, 1.0, 1.0)	Specular intensity of light
s$cli(i=0)$	Color	(0.0, 0.0, 0.0, 1.0)	Specular intensity of light i
Ppli	Position	(0.0, 0.0, 1.0, 0.0)	Position of light i
sdli	Direction	(0.0, 0.0, −1.0)	Direction of spotlight for light
$srli$	Real	0.0	Spotlight exponent for light i (range: [0.0, 128.0])
$crli$	Real	180.0	Spotlight cutoff angle for light i (range: [0.0,90.0],180.0)
koi	Real	1.0	Constant attenuation factor for light i (range: [0.0,∞))
$k1i$	Real	0.0	Linear attenuation factor for light i (range: [0.0,mbol∞))
$k2i$	Real	0.0	Quadratic attenuation factor for light i (range: [0.0,∞))
Lighting Model Parameters			
acs	Color	(0.2, 0.2, 0.2, 1.0)	Ambient color of scene
vbs	Boolean	**FALSE**	Viewer assumed to be at (0,0,0) in eye coordinates (**TRUE**) or (0, 0,∞) (**FALSE**)
tbs	Boolean	**FALSE**	Use two-sided lighting mode

Lighting Parameter Specification

Lighting parameters are divided into three categories: material parameters, light source parameters, and lighting model parameters (see Table 14.5). Sets of lighting parameters are specified with the following:

```
void Material{if}( enum face, enum pname, T param ) ;
void Material{if}v( enum face, enum pname, T params ) ;
void Light{if}( enum light, enum pname, T param ) ;
void Light{if}v( enum light, anum pname, T params ) ;
void LightModel{if}( enum pname, T param ) ;
void LightModel{if}v( enum pname, T params ) ;
```

Pname is a symbolic constant indicating which parameter is to be set (see Table 14.6). In the vector versions of the commands, *params* is a pointer to a group of values to which to set the indicated parameter. The number of values pointed to depends on the parameter being set. In the nonvector versions *param* is a value to which to set a single-valued parameter. If *param* corresponds to a multivalued parameter, the error **INVALID_ENUM** results. For the **Material** command, *face* must be one of **FRONT**, **BACK**, or **FRONT_AND_BACK_**, indicating that the property *name* of the front or back material, or both, respectively, should be set. In the case of **Light**, *light* is a symbolic constant of the form **LIGHT**i, indicating that light i is to have the specified parameter set. The constants obey **LIGHT**i = **LIGHT0** + i.

Table 14.6 gives, for each of the three parameter groups, the correspondence between the predefined constant names and their names in the lighting equations, along with the number of values that must be specified with each. Color parameters specified with Material and Light are converted to floating-point values (if specified as integers), as indicated in Table 14.4, for signed integers. The error I-NVALID-VALUE occurs if a specified lighting parameter lies outside the allowable range given in Table 14.5. The symbol Ĩ indicates the maximum representable magnitude for the indicated type.

ColorMaterial

One or more material properties can be attached to the current color, so that they continuously track its component values. This behavior is enabled and disabled by calling **Enable** or **Disable** with the symbolic value **COLOR_MATERIAL**. {See Figure 14.9.}

The command that controls which of these modes is selected is

```
void ColorMaterial( enum face, enum mode ) ;
```

Face is one of **FRONT**, **BACK**, or **FRONT_AND_BACK**, indicating whether the front material, back material, or both are affected by the current color. *Mode* is one of **EMISSION**, **AMBIENT**, **DIFFUSE**,

Table 14.6 Correspondence of Lighting Parameter Symbols to Names

Parameter	Name	Number of values
Material Parameters (Material)		
acm	AMBIENT	4
dcm	DIFFUSE	4
acm dcm	AMBIENT_AND_DIFFUSE	4
scm	SPECULAR	4
ecm	EMISSION	4
srm	SHININESS	1
a_m d_m, s_m	COLOR_INDEXES	3
Light Source Parameters (Light)		
acli	AMBIENT	4
dcli	DIFFUSE	4
scli	SPECULAR	4
Ppli	POSITION	4
sdli	SPOT_DIRECTION	3
srli	SPOT_EXPONENT	1
crli	SPOT_CUTOFF	1
$k0i$	CONSTANT_ATTENUATION	1
$k1i$	LINEAR_ATTENUATION	1
$k2i$	QUADRATIC_ATTENUATION	1
Lighting Model Parameters		
acs	LIGHT_MODEL_AMBIENT	4
vbs	LIGHT_MODEL_LOCAL_VIEWER	1
tbs	LIGHT_MODFEL_TWO_SIDE	1

AMBIENT_AND_DIFFUSE is used to set acm and Dcm to the same value.

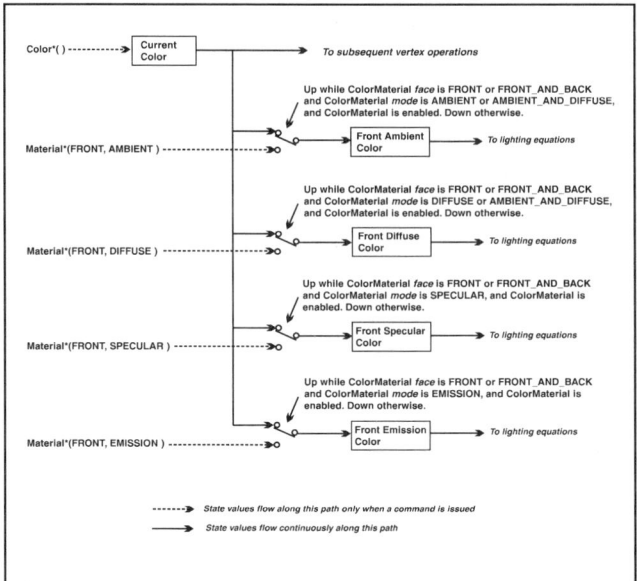

Figure 14.9 ColorMaterial Operation. Material properties are continuously updated from the current color while ColorMaterial is enabled and has the appropriate mode. Only the front material properties are included in this figure. The back material properties are treated identically.

SPECULAR, or **AMBIENT_AND_DIFFUSE** and specifies which material property or properties track the current color. If *mode* is **EMISSION**, **AMBIENT**, **DIFFUSE**, or **SPECULAR**, the value of e_{cm}, a_{cm}, d_{cm}, or s_{cm}, respectively, will track the current color. If *mode* is **AMBIENT_AND_DIFFUSE**, both a_{cm} and d_{cm}, track the current color.

The replacements made to material properties are permanent. The replaced values remain until changed by either sending a new color or by setting a new material value when **ColorMaterial** is not currently enabled to override that particular value. When **COLOR_MATERIAL** is enabled, the indicated parameter or parameters always track the current color. For instance, calling the following while **COLOR_MATERIAL** is enabled sets the front material, a_{cm}, to the value of the current color:

```
ColorMaterial(FRONT, AMBIENT)
```

Lighting State

The state required for lighting consists of all of the lighting parameters (front and back material parameters lighting model parameters at least eight sets of light parameters), a bit indicating whether a back color distinct from the front color should be computed, at least eight bits to indicate which lights are enabled, a five-valued variable indicating the current **ColorMaterial** mode, a bit indicating whether **COLOR_MATERIAL** is enabled, and a single bit to indicate whether lighting is enabled or disabled. In the initial state all lighting parameters have their default values. Back-color evaluation does not take place. **ColorMaterial** is **FRONT_AND_BACK** and **AMBIENT_AND_DIFFUSE**; both lighting and **COLOR_MATERIAL** are disabled.

Clamping or Masking

After lighting, RGBA colors are clamped to the range [0, 1]. For a color index the index is first converted to fixed point, with an unspecified number of bits to the right of the binary point. The nearest fixed-point value is selected. Then the bits to the right of the binary point are left alone while the integer portion is masked (bitwise ANDed) with $2n - 1$, where n is the number of bits in a color in the color index buffer. Buffers are discussed later in this chapter.

Flatshading

A primitive may be *flatshaded*, meaning that all vertices of the primitive are assigned the same color. This color is the color of the vertex that spawned the primitive. For a point this is the color associated with the point. For a line segment it is the color of the second (final) vertex of the segment. For a polygon the selected color depends on how the polygon was generated. Flatshading is controlled by:

    void ShadeModel(enum mode) ;

Mode value must be either of two symbolic constants. If node is **SMOOTH** (the initial state), vertex colors are treated individually. If mode is **FLAT**, flatshading is turned on. **ShadeModel** thus requires one bit of state.

Final Color Processing

For an RGBA color, each color component (which lies in [0,1]) is converted by rounding to the nearest fixed-point value with m bits; m must be at least as large as the number of bits in the corresponding component of the frame buffer. If the frame buffer does not contain an A component, m must be at least 2 for A. A color index is converted by rounding to the nearest fixed-point value with at least as many bits as there are in the color index portion of the frame buffer.

Suppose that lighting is disabled, the color associated with a vertex has not been clipped, and one of Colorub, Colorus, or Colorui was used to specify that color. When these conditions are satisfied, an RGBA component must convert to a value that matches the component as specified in the Color command. If m is less than the number of bits {b} with which the component was specified, the converted value must equal the most significant m bits of the specified value. Otherwise, the most significant b bits of the converted value must equal the specified value.

Rasterization

Rasterization is the process by which a primitive is converted to a two-dimensional image. Each point of this image contains such information as color and depth. Thus rasterizing a primitive consists of two parts. The first is to determine which squares of an integer grid in window coordinates are occupied by the primitive. The second is to assign a color and depth value to each square. The results of this process are passed on to the next stage of the GL (per fragment operations), which uses the information to update the appropriate locations in the frame buffer. Figure 14.10 diagrams the rasterization process.

A grid square along with its parameters of assigned color, z (depth), and texture coordinates is called a *fragment*. The parameters are collectively dubbed the fragment's *associated data*. A fragment is located by its lower-left corner, which lies on integer grid coordinates. Rasterization operations also refer to a fragment's *center*, which is offset by (1/2, 1/2) from its lower-left corner (and so lies on half-integer coordinates).

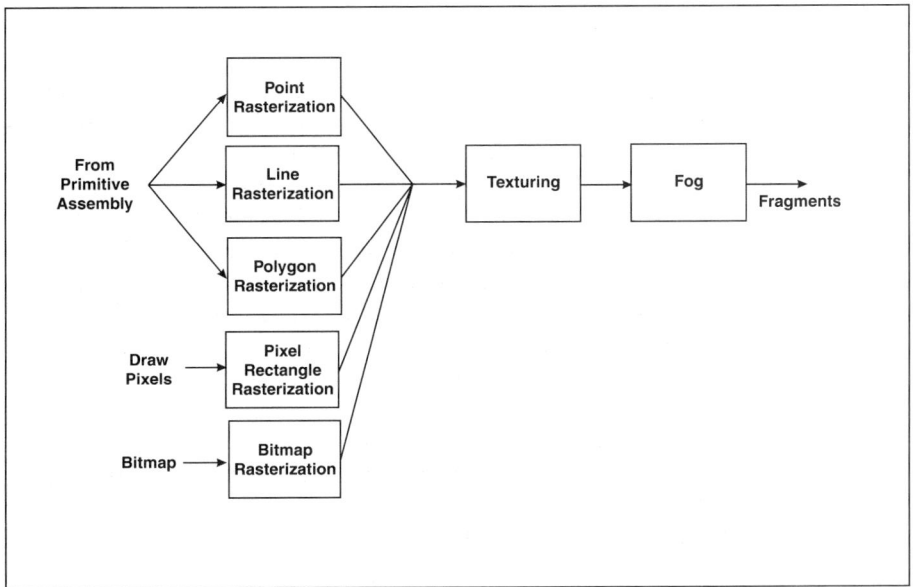

Figure 14.10 Rasterization

Grid squares need not actually be square in the GL. Rasterization rules are not affected by the actual aspect ratio of the grid squares. Display of nonsquare grids, however, will cause rasterized points and fine segments to appear fatter in one direction than in the other. Assume that fragments are square, since it simplifies antialiasing and texturing.

Several factors affect rasterization. Lines and polygons may be stippled. Points may be given differing diameters and line segments differing widths. A point, line segment, or polygon may be antialiased.

Invariance

Consider a primitive p' obtained by translating a primitive p through an offset (x,y) in window coordinates, where x and y are integers. As long as neither p' nor p is clipped, it must be the case that each fragment f' produced from p' is identical to a corresponding fragment f' from p' except that the center of f' is offset by (x, y) from the center of f.

Antialiasing of a point, line, or polygon is effected in one of two ways, depending on whether the GL is in RGBA or color index mode. In RGBA mode the R, G, and B values of the rasterized fragment are left unaffected, but the A value is multiplied by a floating-point value in the range [0, 1] that describes a fragment's screen pixel coverage. The per fragment stage of the GL can be set up to use the A value to blend the incoming fragment with the corresponding pixel already present in the frame buffer.

In color index mode the least-significant b bits (to the left of the binary point) of the color index are used for antialiasing, where $b = \min\{4,m\}$, and m is the number of bits in the color index portion of the frame buffer. The antialiasing process sets these b bits based on the fragment's coverage value: the bits are set to 0 for no coverage and to all 1s for complete coverage.

The details of how antialiased fragment coverage values are computed are difficult to specify in general. The reason is that high-quality antialiasing may take into account not only perceptual issues but also as characteristics of the monitor on which the contents of the frame buffer are displayed. Such details cannot be addressed within the scope of this chapter. Further, the coverage value computed for a fragment of some primitive may depend not just on the fragment's grid square but also on the primitive's relationship to a number of grid squares neighboring the one corresponding to the fragment. Another consideration is that accurate calculation of coverage values may be computationally expensive. Consequently a given GL implementation is allowed to approximate true coverage values by using a fast but not entirely accurate coverage computation.

A GL implementation may use other methods to perform antialiasing, subject to the following conditions:

- If f_1 and f_2 are two fragments and the portion of f_1 covered by some primitive is a subset of the corresponding portion of f_2 covered by the primitive, the coverage computed for f_1 must be less than or equal to that computed for f_2.
- The coverage computation for a fragment f must be local. It may depend only on f's relationship to the boundary of the primitive being rasterized. It may not depend on f's x and y coordinates.
- Desirable but not required is the sum of the coverage values for all fragments produced by rasterizing a particular primitive must be constant, independent of any rigid motions in window

coordinates, as long as none of those fragments lies along window edges.[4]

In some implementations varying degrees of antiabasing quality may be obtained by providing GL hints, thus allowing a user to make an image quality versus speed tradeoff.

Points

Point antialiasing is enabled or disabled by calling **Enable** or **Disable** with the symbolic constant **POINT_SMOOTH**. The default state is for point antialiasing to be disabled.

The rasterization of points is controlled with

```
void PointSize( float size ) ;
```

where *size* specifies the width or diameter of a point. The default value is 1.0. A value less than or equal to 0 results in the error **INVALID_VALUE**.

In the default state a point is rasterized by truncating its x_w and y_w coordinates (recall that the subscripts indicate that these are x and y window coordinates) to integers. This (x, y) address, along with the data associated with the vertex corresponding to the point, is sent as a single fragment to the per fragment stage of the GL.

All fragments produced in rasterizing a nonantialiased point are assigned the same associated data, which are those of the vertex corresponding to the point, as shown in Figure 14.11. If antialiasing is enabled, point rasterization produces a fragment for each fragment square that intersects the region lying within the circle having the diameter equal to the current point width and centered at the point's (x_w, y_w), as shown in Figure 14.12. The coverage value for each fragment is the window coordinate area of the intersection of the circular region with the corresponding fragment square. This value is saved and used in the final step of rasterization. The data associated with each fragment is otherwise the data associated with the point being rasterized.

Not all widths need be supported when point antialiasing is on, but the width 1.0 must be provided. If an unsupported width is requested, the nearest supported width is used instead. The range of supported widths and the width of evenly spaced gradations within

---

[4] *Ibid.*, p. 53.

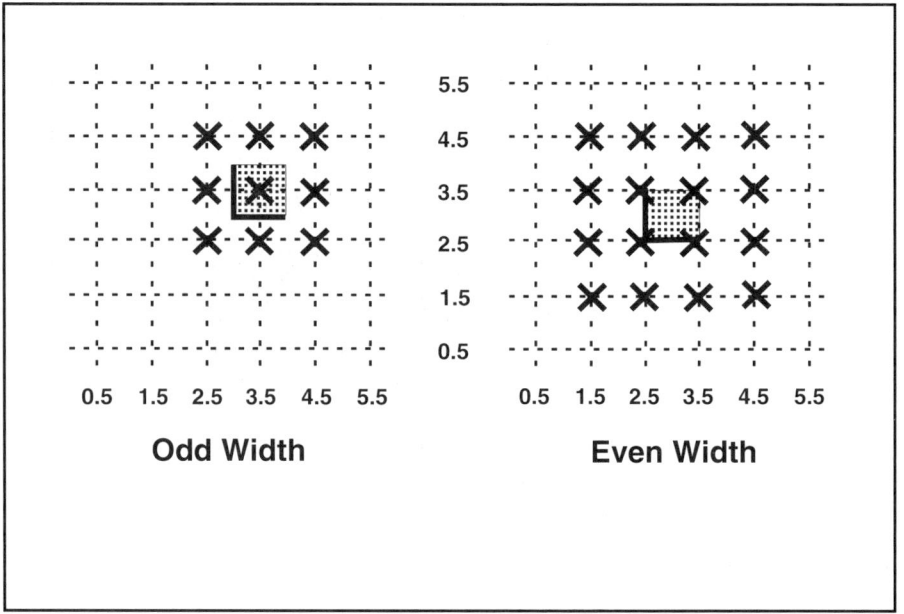

Figure 14.11 Rasterization of Nonantialiased Wide Points. The crosses show fragment centers produced by rasterization for any point that lies within the shaded region. The dotted grid lines lie on half-integer coordinates.

that range are implementation dependent. If, for instance, the width range is from 0.1 to 2.0 and the gradation width is 0.1, the widths 0.1, 0.2, ..., 1.9, 2.0 are supported.

The state required to control point rasterization consists in part of the floating-point point width. It also consists of a bit indicating whether antialiasing is enabled.

Line Segments

A line segment results from a line strip Begin/End object, a line loop, or a series of separate line segments. Line-segment rasterization is controlled by several variables.

Line width may be set by calling

```
void LineWidth( float width ) ;
```

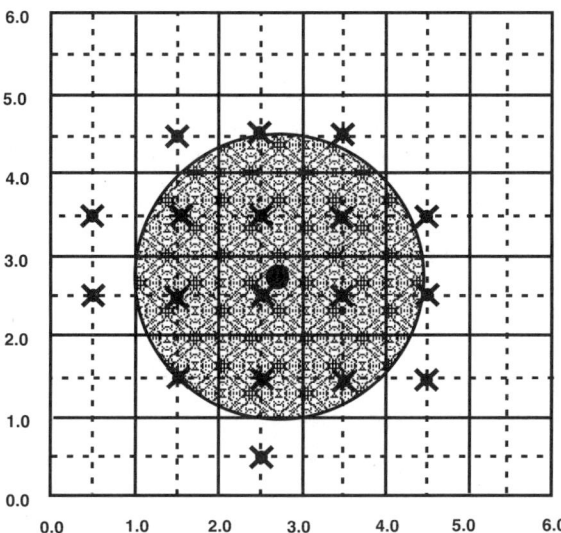

Figure 14.12 Rasterization of Antialiased Wide Points. The black dot indicates the point to be rasterized. The shaded region has the specified width. The X marks indicate those fragment centers produced by rasterization. A fragment's computed coverage value is based on the portion of the shaded region that covers the corresponding fragment square. Solid lines lie on integer coordinates.

with an appropriate positive floating-point width. Line width controls the width of rasterized line segments.

The default width is 1.0. Values less than or equal to 0.0 generate the error **INVALID_VALUE**. Antialiasing is controlled with **Enable** and **Disable,** using the symbolic constant **LINE_SMOOTH**. Finally, line segments may be stippled. Stippling is controlled by a **GL** command that sets a *stipple* pattern.

Antialiasing

Rasterized antialiased line segments produce fragments whose fragment squares intersect a rectangle centered on the line segment. Two of the edges are parallel to the specified line segment. Each is at a distance of one-half the current width from that segment: one above the segment and one below it. The other two edges pass through the line endpoints and are perpendicular to the direction of the specified line segment. Coverage values are computed for each fragment by computing the area of the intersection of the rectangle with the fragment square, as shown in Figure 14.13.

For purposes of antialiasing, a stippled line is considered to be a sequence of contiguous rectangles centered on the line segment. Each rectangle has width equal to the current line width and length equal to one pixel (except the last, which may be shorter). These rectangles are numbered from 0 to n, starting with the rectangle incident on the starting end point of the segment. Each of these rectangles is either eliminated or produced according to the procedure given under **Line Stipple**, above, where fragment is replaced with rectangle. Each rectangle so produced is rasterized as if it were an antiabased polygon, described later (but culling, nondefault settings of **PolygonMode** and polygon stippling are not applied).

Line Rasterization State

The state required for line rasterization consists of the floating-point line width, a 16-bit line stipple, the line stipple repeat count, a bit

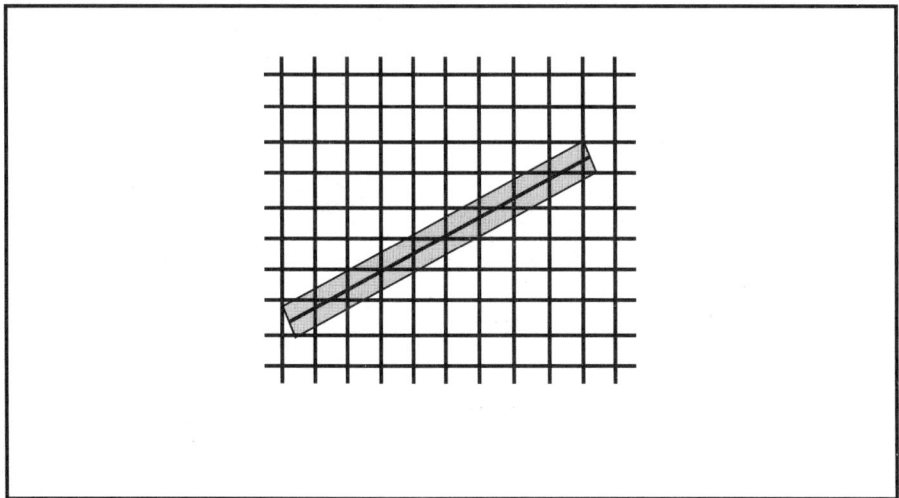

Figure 14.13. Region Used in Rasterizing and Finding Corresponding Coverage Values for an Antialiased Line Segment. (An x-major line segment is shown.)

indicating whether stippling is enabled or disabled, and a bit indicating whether line antialiasing is on or off. In addition, during rasterization an integer stipple counter must be maintained to implement line stippling. The initial value of the line width is 1.0. The initial value of the line stipple is *OxFFFF* (a stipple of all 1s). The initial value of the fine stipple repeat count is 1. The initial state of line stippling is disabled. The initial state of line segment antialiasing is disabled.

Polygons

A polygon results from a polygon **Begin/End** object. A triangle results from a triangle strip, a triangle fan, or a series of separate triangles or a quadrilateral arising from a quadrilateral strip, series of separate quadrilaterals, or a **Rect** command. Like points and line segments, polygon rasterization is controlled by several variables. Polygon antialiasing is controlled with **Enable** and **Disable** with the symbolic constant **POLYGON_SMOOTH**. The analog to line segment stippling for polygons is polygon stippling.

Stippling

Polygon stippling works much the same way as line stippling, masking out certain fragments produced by rasterization so that they are not sent to the next stage of the GL. This is the case regardless of the state of polygon antialiasing.

Stippling is controlled with

```
void PolygonStipple( ubyte pattern [] ) ;
```

The *pattern* is a pointer to memory into which a 32 x 32 pattern is packed. The pattern is unpacked from memory according to the procedure given later in the chapter for **DrawPixels**. It is as if the *height* and *width* passed to that command were both equal to 32, the *type* were **BITMAP**, and the *format* were **COLOR_INDEX**. The unpacked values (before any conversion or arithmetic would have been performed) are bitwise ANDed with 1 to obtain a stipple pattern of 0s and 1s.

Polygon stippling may be enabled or disabled with **Enable** or **Disable,** using the constant **POLYGON_STIPPLE**. When disabled, it is as if the stipple pattern were all 1s.

Antialiasing

Polygon antialiasing rasterizes a polygon by producing a fragment wherever the interior of the polygon intersects that fragment's square. A coverage value is computed at each such fragment, and this value is saved to be applied later. Associated data is assigned to a fragment by integrating the data's value over the region of the intersection of the fragment square with the polygon's interior and dividing this integrated value by the area of the intersection. For a fragment square lying entirely within the polygon, the value of the data at the fragment's center may be used instead of integrating the value across the fragment.

Options Controlling Polygon Rasterization

Face is one of **FRONT**, **BACK**, or **FRONT_AND_BACK**, indicating that the rasterizing method described by *mode* replaces the rasterizing method for front-facing polygons, back-facing polygons, or both front- and back-facing polygons, respectively. *Mode* is one of the symbolic constants **POINT**, **LINE**, or **FILL**. Calling **PolygonMode** with **POINT** causes certain vertices of a polygon to be treated, for rasterization purposes, just as if they were enclosed within a **Begin(POINT)** and **End** pair. The vertices selected for this treatment are those that have been tagged as having a polygon boundary edge beginning on them. **LINE** causes edges that are tagged as boundary to be rasterized as line segments. The line stipple counter is reset at the beginning of the first rasterized edge of the polygon but not for subsequent edges. **FILL** is the default mode of polygon rasterization. Note that these modes affect only the final rasterization of polygons. In particular a polygon's vertices are lit, and the polygon is clipped and possibly culled before these modes are applied.

The interpretation of polygons for rasterization is controlled by using

```
void PolygonMode( enum face, enum mode ) ;
```

Polygon antialiasing applies only to the **FILL** state of **PolygonMode**. For **POINT** or **LINE**, point antialiasing or line segment antialiasing, respectively, apply.

Polygon Rasterization State

The state required for polygon rasterization consists of a polygon stipple pattern, whether stippling is enabled or disabled, the current state of polygon antialiasing (enabled or disabled), and the current values of the **PolygonMode** setting for each of front- and back-facing polygons. The initial stipple pattern is all 1s. Initially stippling is disabled. The initial setting of polygon antialiasing is disabled. The initial state for **PolygonMode** is **FILL** for both front- and back-facing polygons.

Pixel Rectangles

Rectangles of color, depth, and certain other values may be converted to fragments by using the **DrawPixels** command. Some of the parameters and operations governing the operation of **DrawPixels** are shared by **ReadPixels** (used to obtain pixel values from the framebuffer) and **CopyPixels** (used to copy pixels from one frame buffer location to another). The discussion of **ReadPixels** and **CopyPixels**, however, is deferred until later in the chapter after the frame buffer has been discussed in detail. Nevertheless, it is noted here when parameters and state pertaining to **DrawPixels** also pertain to **ReadPixels** or **CopyPixels**.

A number of parameters control the encoding of pixels in client memory (for reading and writing) and how pixels are processed before being placed in or after being read from the frame buffer (for reading, writing, and copying). These parameters are set with three commands: **PixelStore**, **PixelTransfer**, and **PixelMap**.

Pixel Storage Modes

Pixel storage modes affect the operation of DrawPixels and ReadPixels (as well as other commands) when one of these commands is issued. This may differ from the time that the command is executed if the command is placed in a display list.

Pixel storage modes are set with

  void **PixelStore**{if}(enum *pname*, T *param*) ;

The *pname* is a symbolic constant indicating a parameter to be set, and *param* is the value to set it to. Table 14.7 summarizes the pixel

Table 14.7 *PixelStore* **Parameters Pertaining to** *DrawPixels*

Parameter Name	Type	Initial Value	Valid Range
UNPACK_SWAP_BYTES	Boolean	**FALSE**	TRUE/FALSE
UNPACK_LSB_FIRST	Boolean	**FALSE**	TRUE/FALSE
UNPACK_ROW_LENGTH	Integer	0	$[0, \infty)$
UNPACK_SKIP_ROWS	Integer	0	$[0, \infty)$
UNPACK_SKIP_PIXELS	Integer	0	$[0, \infty)$
UNPACK_ALIGNMENT	Integer	4	1,2,4,8

storage parameters, their types, their initial values, and their allowable ranges. Setting a parameter to a value outside the given range results in the error **INVALID_VALUE**.

The version of **PixelStore** that takes a floating-point value may be used to set any type of parameter. If the parameter is Boolean, it is set to **FALSE** if the passed value is 0.0 and **TRUE** otherwise. If the parameter is an integer, the passed value is rounded to the nearest integer. The integer version of the command may also be used to set any type of parameter. If the parameter is Boolean, it is set to **FALSE** if the passed value is 0 and **TRUE** otherwise; if the parameter is a floating-point value, the passed value is converted to floating point.

Pixel Transfer Modes

Pixel transfer modes affect the operation of **DrawPixels**, **ReadPixels**, and **CopyPixels** at the time when one of these commands is executed (which may differ from the time the command is issued).

Some pixel transfer modes are set with

```
void PixelTransfer{if}( enum param, T value ) ;
```

The *param* is a symbolic constant indicating a parameter to be set; *value* is the value to set it to. Table 14.8 summarizes the pixel transfer parameters that are set with **PixelTransfer**, their types, their initial values, and their allowable ranges. Setting a parameter to a value outside the given range results in the error **INVALID_VALUE**. The same

Table 14.8 Pixel Transfer Parameters

Parameter Name	Type	Initial Value	Valid Range
MAP_COLOR	Boolean	**FALSE**	TRUE/FALSE
MAP_STENCIL	Boolean	**FALSE**	TRUE/FALSE
INDEX_SHIFT	Integer	0.0	$(-\infty,\infty)$
INDEX_OFFSET	Integer	0.0	$(-\infty,\infty)$
RED_SCALE	Float	1.0	$(-\infty,\infty)$
GREEN_SCALE	Float	1.0	$(-\infty,\infty)$
BLUE_SCALE	Float	1.0	$(-\infty,\infty)$
ALPHA_SCALE	Float	1.0	$(-\infty,\infty)$
DEPTH_SCALE	Float	1.0	$(-\infty,\infty)$
RED_BIAS	Float	0.0	$(-\infty,\infty)$
GREEN_BIAS	Float	0.0	$(-\infty,\infty)$
BLUE_BIAS	Float	0.0	$(-\infty,\infty)$
ALPHA_BIAS	Float	0.0	$(-\infty,\infty)$
DEPTH_BIAS	Float	0.0	$(-\infty,\infty)$

versions of the command exist as for **PixelStore**, and the same rules apply to accepting and converting passed values to set parameters.

The other pixel-transfer modes are the various look-up tables used by **DrawPixels**, **ReadPixels**, and **CopyPixels**. These are set with

void **PixelMap**{**ui us f**}**v**(enum *map*, sizei *size*, T *values[]*) ;

The *map* is a symbolic map name, indicating the map to set *size* indicates the size of the map, and *values* is a pointer to an array of *size* map values.

The entries of a table may be specified by using one of three types: single-precision floating-point, unsigned short integer, or unsigned integer. This all depends on which of the three versions of **PixelMap** is called. A table entry is converted to the appropriate type when it is specified. An entry giving a color-component value is converted according to Table 14.4. An entry giving a color index value is converted from an unsigned short integer or unsigned integer to floating point. An entry giving a stencil index is converted from single-precision floating point to an integer by rounding to nearest. The various tables and their initial sizes and entries are summarized in Table 14.9. A table that takes an index as an address must have *size* = $2n$ or the error **INVALID_VALUE** results. The maximum allowable size of each table is implementation dependent but must be at least 32 (a single maximum applies to all tables). The error **INVALID_VALUE** is generated if a size larger than the implemented maximum, or less than zero, is given to PixelMap.

Rasterization of Pixel Rectangles

The process of drawing pixels encoded in host memory is diagramed in Figure 14.14. The stages of this process are described in the order in which they occur.

Pixels are drawn by using

```
void DrawPixels( sizei width, sizei height, enum format, enum type,
void *data ) ;
```

Table 14.9 *PixelMap* **Parameters.**

Map Name	Address	Value	Init. Size	Init. Value
PIXEL_MAP_I_TO_I	color idx	color idx	1	0.0
PIXEL_MAP_S_TO_S	stencil idx	stencil idx	1	0.0
PIXEL_MAP_I_TO_R	color idx	R	1	0.0
PIXEL_MAP_I_TO_G	color idx	G	1	0.0
PIXEL_KAP_I_TO_B	color idx	B	1	0.0
PIXEL_MAP_I_TO_A	color idx	A	1	0.0
PIXEL_MAP_R_TO_R	R	R	1	0.0
PIXEL_HAP_G_TO_G	G	G	1	0.0
PIXEL_MAP_B_TO_B	B	B	1	0.0
PIXEL_MAP_A_TO_A	A	A	1	0.0

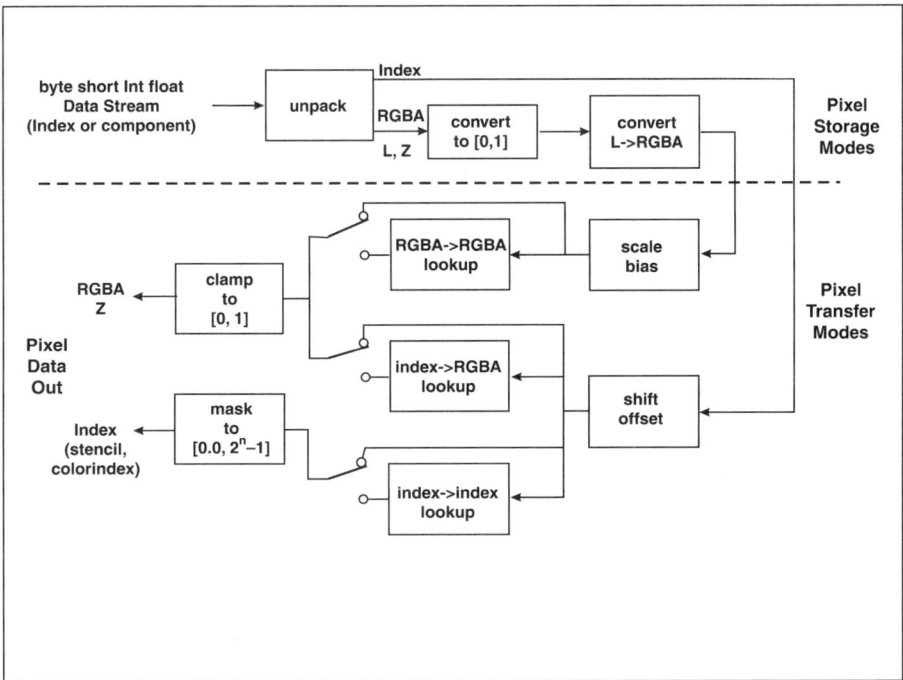

Figure 14.14 Operation of **DrawPixels**. The parameters controlling the stages above the dotted line are set with **PixelStore**; those controlling the stages below the line are set with **PixelTransfer** or **PixelMap**.

The *format* is a symbolic constant indicating what the values in memory represent; *width* and *height* are the width and height, respectively, of the pixel rectangle to be drawn; *data* is a pointer to the data to be drawn. The data is represented with one of seven GL data types, specified by *type*. The correspondence between the eight *type* token values and the GL data types they indicate is given in Table 14.10. If the GL is in color index mode and *format* is not one of **COLOR_INDEX**, **STENCIL_INDEX**, or **DEPTH_COMPONENT**, the error **INVALID_OPERATION** occurs.

Unpacking: Data is taken from host memory as a sequence of signed or unsigned bytes (GL data types byte and ubyte), signed or unsigned short integers (GL data types short and ushort), signed or

Table 14.10 *DrawPixels* and *ReadPixels* **Type Parameter Values and the Corresponding GL Data Types.**

Type Parameter Token Name	Corresponding GL Data Type
UNSIGNED_BYTE	ubyte
BITMAP	ubyte
BYTE	byte
UNSIGNED_SHORT	ushort
SHORT	short
UNSIGNED_INT	uint
INT	32-bit integer
FLOAT	float

Refer to Table 14.2 for definitions of GL data types.

unsigned integers (GL data types int and uint), or floating-point values (GL data type float). These elements are grouped into sets of one, two, three, or four values, depending on the *format*, to form a group. Table 14.11 summarizes the format of groups obtained from memory and also indicates those formats that yield indices and those that yield components.

By default, the values of each GL data type are interpreted as they would be specified in the language of the client's GL binding. If UNPACK_SWAP_BYTES is set to **TRUE**, however, the values are interpreted with the bit orderings modified as per Table 14.12. The modified bit orderings are defined only if the GL data type ubyte has eight bits and then for each specific GL data type only if that type is represented with 8, 16, or 32 bits.

The groups in memory are treated as being arranged in a rectangle. This rectangle consists of a series of rows, with the first element of the first group of the first row pointed to by the pointer passed to **DrawPixels**. If the value of **UNPACK_ROW_LENGTH** is not positive, the number of groups in a row is width. Otherwise, the number of groups is UNPACK_ROW_LENGTH.

Table 14.11 *DrawPixels* and *ReadPixels* **Formats.**

Format Name	Element Meaning and Order	Target Buffer
COLOR_INDEX	Color index	Color
STENCIL_INDEX	Stencil index	Stencil
DEPTH_COMPONENT	Depth component	Depth
RED	R component	Color
GREEN	G component	Color
BLUE	B component	Color
ALPHA	A component	Color
RGB	R, G, B components	Color
RGBA	R, G, B, A components	Color
LUMINANCE	Luminance component	Color
LUMINANCE_ALPHA	Luminance, A components	Color

The second column gives a description of and the number and order of elements in a group.

Conversion to floating-point: This step applies only to groups of components. It is not performed on indices. Each element in a group is converted to a floating-point value according to the appropriate formula in Table 14.4.

Table 14.12 Bit Ordering Modification of Elements when UNPACK_SWAP_BYTES is TRUE.

Element Size	Default Bit Ordering	Modified Bit Ordering
8 bit	[7..0]	[7..0]
16 bit	[15..0]	[7..0][15..8]
32 bit	(31..0)	[7..0][15..8][23..16][31..24]

These reorderings are defined only when GL data type ubyte has 8 bits and then only for GL data types with 8, 16, or 32 bits.

Conversion to RGB: This step is applied only if the *format* is **LUMINANCE** or **LUMINANCE_ALPHA**. If the *format* is **LUMINANCE**, each group of one element is converted to a group of R, G, and B (three) elements by copying the original single element into each of the three new elements. If the *format* is LUMINANCE_ALPHA, each group of two elements is converted to a group of R, G, B, and A (four) elements. This is done by copying the first original element into each of the first three new elements and copying the second original element to the A (fourth) new element.

Final expansion to RGBA: This step is performed only for nondepth component groups. Each group is converted to a group of four elements as follows: If a group does not contain an A element, A is added and set to 1.0. If any of R, G, or B is missing from the group, each missing element is added and assigned a value of 0.0.

Arithmetic on Components: This step applies only to component groups. Each component is multiplied by an appropriate signed scale factor: **RED_SCALE** for an **R** component, **GREEN_SCALE** for a **G** component, **BLUE_SCALE** for a **B** component, **ALPHA_SCALE** for an **A** component, or **DEPTH_SCALE** for a depth component. Then the result is added to the the appropriate signed bias: **RED_BIAS**, **GREEN_BIAS**, **BLUE_BIAS**, **ALPHA_BIAS**, or **DEPTH_BIAS**.

Arithmetic on Indices: This step applies only to indices. If the index is a floating-point value, it is converted to fixed point, with an unspecified number of bits to the right of the binary point. Indices that are already integers remain so; any fraction bits in the resulting fixed-point value are 0.

The fixed-point index is then shifted by | INDEX_SHIFT | bits, left if **INDEX_SHIFT** > 0 and right otherwise. In either case the shift is zero-filled. Then the signed integer offset INDEX_OFFSET is added to the index.

RGBA-to-RGBA lookup: This step applies only to RGBA component groups and is skipped if MAP-COLOR is FALSE. First, each component is clamped to the range [0, 1]. A table is associated with each of the R, G, B, and A component elements: PIXEL-KAP-R-TO-R for R, PIXEL-MAP-G-TO-G for G, PIXEL-MAP-B-TO-B for B, and PIXEL-MAPA-TOA for A. Each element is multiplied by an integer one less than the size of the corresponding table, and for each element, an address is found by rounding this value to the nearest integer. For each element the addressed value in the corresponding table replaces the element.

Index lookup: This step applies only to indices. If the GL is in RGBA mode, the integer part of the index is used to reference four tables of color components: **PIXEL_MAP_I_TO_R**, **PIXEL_MAP_I_TO_G**, **PIXEL_MAP_I_TO_B**, and **PIXEL_MAP_I_TO_A**. Each of these tables must have $2n$ entries for some integer value of n (n may be different for each table). For each table the index is first rounded to the nearest integer; the result is ANDed with $2n - 1$, and the resulting value used as an address into the table. The indexed value becomes an R, G, B, or A value, as appropriate. The group of four elements so obtained replaces the index, changing the group's type to component.

If the GL is in color index mode and if **MAP_COLOR** is **TRUE**, the index is looked up in the **PIXEL_MAP_I_TO_I** table (otherwise, the index is not looked up). Again, the table must have $2n$ entries for some integer n, and the integer part of the index is ANDed with $2n - 1$, producing a value. This value addresses the table, and the value in the table replaces the index. The floating-point table value is first rounded to a fixed-point value with unspecified precision. Finally, if *format* is **STENCIL_INDEX** and if **MAP_STENCIL** is **TRUE**, the index is looked up as described in the preceding paragraph but using the **PIXEL_MAP_S_TO_S** table.

Texturing

Texturing maps a portion of a specified image onto each primitive for which texturing is enabled. This mapping is accomplished by using the color of an image at the location indicated by a fragment's (s, t) coordinates to modify the fragment's RGBA color (r is currently ignored). Texturing is specified only for RGBA mode. Its use in color index mode is undefined.

The GL provides a means to specify the details of how texturing of a primitive is effected. These details include specification of the image to be texture mapped, the means by which the image is filtered when applied to the primitive, and the function that determines what RGBA value is produced given a fragment color and an image value.

The command used to specify a texture image is:

```
void TexImage2-D( enum target, int level, int components,
sizei width, sizei height, int border, enum format, enum
type, void *data ) ;[5]
```

---

[5] *Ibid.*, p. 81.

Currently *target* must be **TEXTURE_2-D**. The arguments *width*, *height*, *format*, *type*, and *data* correspond precisely to the corresponding arguments to **DrawPixels**. They specify the image's *width* and *height*, a *format* of the image data, the *type* of the data, and a pointer to the image data in memory. The image is taken from memory exactly as if these arguments were passed to **DrawPixels**, but the process stops just before final conversion. Each R, G, B, and A value so extracted is clamped to [0, 1]. The *formats* **STENCIL_INDEX** and **DEPTH_COMPONENT** are not allowed. Components are selected from the R, G, B, and A values to obtain a texture with *components* (the significance of the number of components is described later.) Table 14.13 summarizes the mapping of R, G, B, and A values to texture components. Specifying a number of components other than 1, 2, 3, or 4 generates the error **INVALID_VALUE**.

The image itself (pointed to by *data*) is a sequence of groups of values. The first group is the lower-left corner of the texture image. Subsequent groups fill out rows of *width* from left to right. *Height* rows are stacked from bottom to top.

The *level* argument to **TexImage2-D** is an integer *level-of-detail* number. Levels of detail are discussed later. The main texture image has the number 0 for level of detail.

The *border* argument to **TexImage2-D** is a border width. The significance of borders is described later. If *width* and *height* do not satisfy these relationships, the error **INVALID_VALUE** is generated. Currently if *b* is not either 0 or 1, the error **INVALID_VALUE** is generated. The maximum allowable width or height of an image is implementation dependent but must be at least 64. An excessive width or height or a width or height less than 0 generates the **INVALID_VALUE** error.

Table 14.13 Correspondence of Texture Components to Extracted R, G, B, and A Value

Components	RGBA Values	Texture Components
1	R	L
2	R, A	L, A
3	R, G, B	C
4	R, G, B, A	C, A

Another command is used to specify one-dimensional texture images:

void TexImage1D(enum *target*, int *level*, int *components*, sizei *width*, int *border*, enum *format*, enum *type*, void **data*) ;

Currently *target* must be the texture target **TEXTURE_1D**. For the purposes of decoding the texture image, **TexImage1D** is equivalent to calling **TexImage2-D** with corresponding arguments and a *height* argument of 1, except that the height of the image is always 1, regardless of the value of *border*.

An image with zero height or width (or zero width, for **TexImage1D**) indicates the null texture. If the null texture is specified for level-of-detail zero, it is as if texturing were disabled.

The image indicated to the GL by the image pointer is decoded and copied into the GL's internal memory. This copying places the decoded image inside a border of the maximum allowable width (currently 1), whether or not a border has been specified (see Figure 14.15). If no border or a border smaller than the maximum allowable width has been specified, the image is still stored as if it were surrounded by a border of the maximum possible width. Any excess border (which surrounds the specified image, including any border) is assigned unspecified values. A one-dimensional texture has a border only at its left and right ends.

An element (i, j) of the texture array is called a *texel* (for a one-dimensional texture, j is irrelevant). The *texture value* used in texturing a fragment is determined by that fragment's associated (s, t) coordinates but may not correspond to any actual texel. See Figure 14.15.

Various parameters control how the texture array is treated when applied to a fragment. Each parameter is set by calling

void TexParameter{if}(enum *target*, enum *pname*, T *param*) ;
void TexParameter{if}v(enum *target*, enum *pname*, T *params*);

The target is *Target*. Either **TEXTURE_1D** or **TEXTURE_2-D**, *pname* is a symbolic constant indicating the parameter to be set. The possible constants and corresponding parameters are summarized in Table 14.14. In the first form of the command, *param* is a value to which to set a single-valued parameter; in the second form of the command, *params* is an array of parameters whose type depends on the parameter being set. If the values for **TEXTURE_BORDER_COLOR**

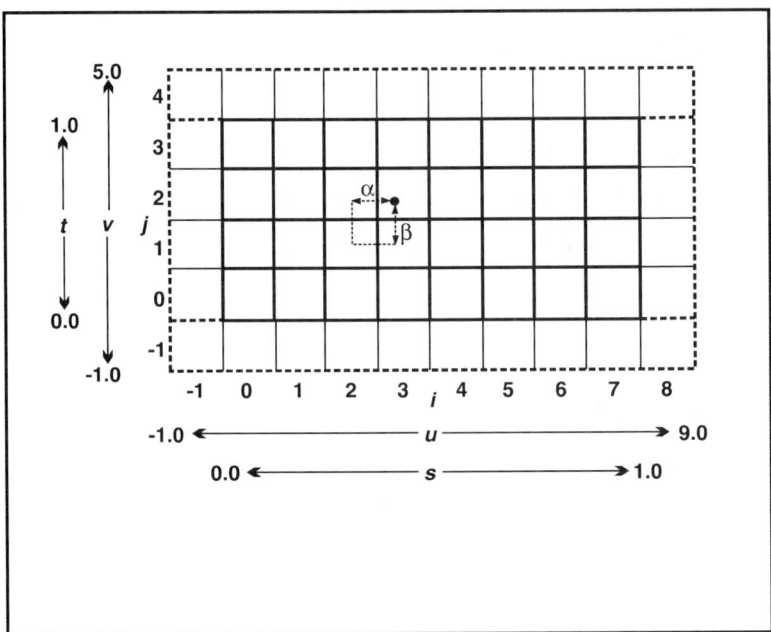

Figure 14.15 A Texture Image and the Coordinates Used to Access It. This is a two-dimensional texture with $n = 3$ and $m = 2$. A one-dimensional texture would consist of a single horizontal strip. The α and β values used in blending adjacent texels to obtain a texture value are also shown.

are specified as integers, the conversion for signed integers from Table 14.4 is applied to convert the values to floating point. Each of the four values set by **TEXTURE_BORDER_COLOR** is clamped to lie in [0, 1].

Texture Wrap Modes

If **TEXTURE_WRAP_S** or **TEXTURE_WRAP_T** is set to **REPEAT**, the GL ignores the integer part of s or t coordinates, respectively, using only the fractional part. For a number r, the fractional part is $r - \lfloor r \rfloor$, regardless of the sign of r; recall that the *floor* function truncates toward $-\infty$. **CLAMP** causes s or t coordinates to be clamped to the range [0, 1]. The initial state is for both s and t behavior to be that given by **REPEAT**.

Table 14.14 Texture Parameters and Their Values.

Name	Type	Legal Values
TEXTURE_WRAP_S	Integer	**CLAMP, REPEAT**
TEXTURE_WRAP_T	Integer	**CLAMP, REPEAT**
TEXTURE_MIN_FILTER	Integer	**NEAREST, LINEAR, NEAREST_MIPMAP_NEAREST, NEAREST_MIPMAP_LINEAR, LINEAR_MIPMAP_NEAREST, LINEAR_MIPMAP_LINEAR**
TEXTURE_MAG_FILTER	Integer	**NEAREST, LINEAR**
TEXTURE_BORDER_COLOR	Four Floats	any four values in [0, 1]

Texture Magnification

When λ indicates magnification, the value assigned to **TEXTURE_MAG_FILTER** determines how the texture value is obtained. There are two possible values for **TFXTURE_MAG_FILTER_NEAREST** and **LINEAR**. **NEAREST** behaves exactly as **NEAREST** for **TEXTURE_MIN_FILTER**. **LINEAR** behaves exactly as **LINEAR** for **TEXTURE_MIN_FILTER**. The level-of-detail 0 texture array is always used for magnification.

Finally, there is the choice of c, the minification versus magnification switchover point. If the magnification filter is given by **LINEAR** and the minification filter is given by **NEAREST_MIPMAP_NEAREST** or **LINEAR_MIPMAP_NEAREST**, $c = 0.5$. This is done to ensure that a minified texture does not appear sharper than a magnified texture. Otherwise, $c = 0$.

The state necessary for texture can be divided into two categories. First are the two sets of mipmap arrays (one-dimensional and two-dimensional) and their number. Each array has associated with it a width and height (two-dimensional only), a border width, and a four-valued integer describing the number of components in the image. Each initial texture array is null (zero width and height, zero border width, one component). Next are the two sets of texture properties. Each consists of the selected minification and magnification filters, the wrap modes for *s* and *t*, and the **TEXTURE_BORDER_COLOR**. In the initial state the value assigned to **TEXTURE_MIN_FILTER** is NEAREST_MIPMAP_LINEAR, and the value for **TEXTURE_MAG_FILTER** is **LINEAR**. Both *s* and *t* wrap modes are set to **REPEAT**. **TEXTURE_BORDER_COLOR** is (0,0,0,0).

Texture Environments and Texture Functions

Currently *target* must be the symbolic constant **TEXTURE_ENV**; *pname* is a symbolic constant indicating the parameter to be set. In the first form of the command, *param* is a value to which to set a single-valued parameter. In the second form, *params* is a pointer to an array of parameters: either a single symbolic constant or a value or group of values to which the parameter should be set. The possible environment parameters are **TEXTURE-ENV-MODE** and **TEXTURE_ENV_COLOR**. **TEXTURE_ENV_MODE** may be set to one of **MODULATE**, **DECAL**, or **BLEND**; **TEXTURE_ENV_COLOR** is set to an RGBA color by providing four single-precision floating-point values in the range [0, 1] (values outside this range are clamped to it). If integers are provided for **TEXTURE_ENV_COLOR**, they are converted to floating-point, as specified in Table 14.4 for signed integers.

The following command sets parameters of the *texture environment* that specifies how texture values are interpreted when texturing a fragment:

```
void TexEnv{if}( enum target, enum pname, T param ) ;
void TexEnv{if}v( enum target, enum pname, T params ) ;
```

Texture Application

Texturing is enabled or disabled by using the generic **Enable** and **Disable** commands, respectively, with the symbolic constant **TEXTURE-1D** or **TEXTURE_2-D** to enable the one-dimensional or two-dimensional texture. If both one- and two-dimensional textures are enabled, the two-dimensional texture is used. If all texturing is disabled, a rasterized fragment is passed on unaltered to the next stage of the GL (although its texture coordinates may be discarded). Otherwise, a texture value is found according to the parameter values of the currently bound texture image of the appropriate dimensionality. This texture value is used along with the incoming fragment in computing the texture function indicated by the currently bound texture environment. The result of this function replaces the incoming fragment's R, G, B, and A values. These are the color values passed to subsequent operations. Other data associated with the incoming fragment remains unchanged, except that the texture coordinates may be discarded.

The required state is two bits indicating whether each of one- or two-dimensional texturing is enabled or disabled. In the initial state all texturing is disabled.

Finally, if antialasing is enabled for the primitive from which a rasterized fragment was produced, the computed coverage value is applied to the fragment. In RGBA mode the value is multiplied by the fragment's alpha (A) value to yield a final alpha value. In color index mode the value is used to set the low-order bits of the color index value.

Per Fragment Operations and the Frame Buffer

The frame buffer consists of a set of pixels arranged as a two-dimensional array. The height and width of this array may vary from one GL implementation to another. For purposes of this discussion, each pixel in the frame buffer is simply a set of some number of bits. The number of bits per pixel may also vary, depending on the particular GL implementation or context.

Corresponding bits from each pixel in the frame buffer are grouped together into a bit plane, each containing a single bit from each pixel. These bit planes are grouped into several logical buffers: the color, depth, stencil, and accumulation buffers. The color buffer consists of a number of buffers: the front left buffer, the front right buffer, the back left buffer, the back right buffer, and some number of auxiliary buffers. Typically the contents of the front buffers are displayed on a color monitor, and the contents of the back buffers are invisible. Monoscopic contexts display only the front left buffer. Stereoscopic contexts display both the front left and the front right buffers. The contents of the auxiliary buffers are never visible. AU color buffers must have the same number of bit planes, although an implementation or context may choose not to provide right buffers, back buffers, or auxiliary buffers at all. Further, an implementation or context may not provide depth, stencil, or accumulation buffers.

Color buffers consist of either unsigned integer color indices or R, G, B, and, optionally, A unsigned integer values. The number of bit planes in each of the color buffers, the depth buffer, the stencil buffer, and the accumulation buffer is fixed and window dependent. If an accumulation buffer is provided, it must have at least as many bit planes per R, G, and B color component as do the color buffers.

The initial state of all provided bit planes is undefined.

Per Fragment Operations

A fragment produced by rasterization with window coordinates of (x_w, y_w) modifies the pixel in the frame buffer at that location, based on a number of parameters and conditions. These modifications and tests are described and diagramed in Figure 14.16, in the order in which they are performed.

Pixel Ownership Test

The first test is to determine whether the pixel at location (x^w, y^w) in the frame buffer is currently owned by the GL (more precisely, by this GL context). If it is not, the window system decides the fate of the incoming fragment. Possible results are that the fragment is discarded or that some subset of the subsequent per fragment operations is applied to the fragment. This test allows the window system to control the GL's behavior—for instance, when a GL window is obscured.

Scissor Test

If $left \leq x^w < left + width$ and $bottom \leq y_w < bottom + height$, the scissor test passes. Otherwise, the test fails and the fragment is discarded. The test is enabled or disabled by using **Enable** or **Disable,** using the constant **SCISSOR_TEST**. When disabled, it is as if the scissor test always passes. If either *width* or *height* is less than 0, the error **INVALID_VALUE** is generated. The state required consists of four integer values and a bit indicating whether the test is enabled or disabled. In the initial state *left* = *bottom* = 0. Both *width* and *height* are determined by the size of the GL window. Initially the scissor test is disabled.

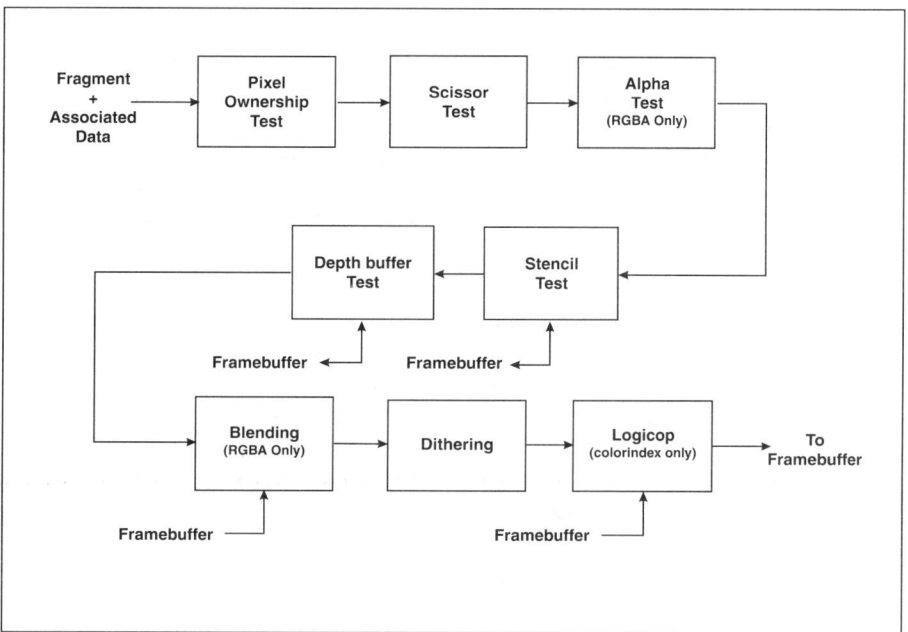

Figure 14.16 Per Fragment Operations

The scissor test determines whether (x^w, y^w) lies within the scissor rectangle defined by four values. These values are set with

void **Scissor**(int *left*, int *bottom*, sizei *width*, sizei *height*) ;

Alpha Test

This step applies only in RGBA mode. In color index mode proceed to the next step. The alpha test discards a fragment conditional on the outcome of a comparison between the incoming fragment's alpha value and a constant value. The comparison is enabled or disabled with the generic **Enable** and **Disable** commands, using the symbolic constant **ALPHA_TEST**. When disabled, it is as if the comparison always passes. The test is controlled with

void **AlphaFunc**(enum *func*, clampf *ref*) ;

The *func* is a symbolic constant indicating the alpha test function; *ref* is a reference value is clamped to lie in [0, 1], and then converted to a fixed-point value according to the rules given earlier in the chapter for an A component. For purposes of the alpha test, the fragment's alpha value is also rounded to the nearest integer. The possible constants specifying the test function are **NEVER, ALWAYS, LESS, LEQUAL, EQUAL, GEQUAL, GREATER,** or **NOTEQUAL,** or pass the fragment never, always, if the fragment's alpha value is less than, less than or equal to, equal to, greater than or equal to, greater than, or not equal to the reference value, respectively.

The required state consists of the floating-point reference value, an eight-valued integer indicating the comparison function, and a bit indicating whether the comparison is enabled or disabled. The initial state is for the reference value to be 0 and the function to be **ALWAYS.** Initially the alpha test is disabled.

Stencil Test

The test is enabled or disabled with the **Enable** and **Disable** commands, using the symbolic constant **STENCIL_TEST.** When disabled, the stencil test and associated modifications are not made, and the fragment is always passed.

The stencil test conditionally discards a fragment, based on the outcome of a comparison between the value in the stencil buffer at location (x^w, y^w) and a reference value. The test is controlled with

```
void StencilFunc( enum func, int ref, uint mask ) ;
void StencilOp( enum sfail, enum dpfail, enum dppass ) ;
```
[6]

The *ref* is an integer reference value that is used in the unsigned stencil comparison. It is clamped to the range [0, $2s - 1$], where *s* is the number of bits in the stencil buffer. The *func* is a symbolic constant that determines the stencil comparison function. The eight symbolic constants are **NEVER, ALWAYS, LESS, LEQUAL, EQUAL, GEQUAL, GREATER,** or **NOTEQUAL.** Accordingly the stencil test passes never, always, if the reference value is less than, less than or equal to, equal to, greater than or equal to, greater than, or not equal to the masked stored value in the stencil buffer. The *s* least-significant bits of *mask* are bitwise ANDed with both the reference and the stored stencil value. The ANDed values are those that participate in the comparison.

---

[6] *Ibid.*, p. 98.

StencilOp takes three arguments that indicate what happens to the stored stencil value if this or certain subsequent tests fail or pass; *sfail* indicates what action is taken if the stencil test fails. The symbolic constants are **KEEP, ZERO, REPLACE, INCR, DECR,** and **INVERT.** These correspond to keeping the current value, setting it to 0, replacing it with the reference value, incrementing it, decrementing it, or bitwise inverting it. For purposes of increment and decrement, the stencil bits are considered as an unsigned integer. Values clamp at 0 and the maximum representable value. The same symbolic values are given to indicate the stencil action if the depth buffer test fails *(dpfail)* or if it passes *(dppass)*. If the stencil test fails, the incoming fragment is discarded. The state required consists of the most recent values passed to **StencilFunc** and **StencilOp** and a bit indicating whether stencil testing is enabled or disabled. In the initial state stenciling is disabled the stencil reference value is 0, the stencil comparison function is **ALWAYS,** and the stencil *mask* is all 1s. Initially all three stencil operations are **KEEP.** If there is no stencil buffer, no stencil modification can occur, and it is as if the stencil tests always pass, regardless of any calls to **StencilOp.**

Depth Buffer Test

The depth buffer test discards the incoming fragment if a depth comparison fails. The comparison is enabled or disabled with the generic **Enable** and **Disable** commands, using the symbolic constant **DEPTH_TEST.** When disabled, the depth comparison and subsequent possible updates to the depth buffer value are bypassed, and the fragment is passed to the next operation. The stencil value, however, is modified, as if the depth buffer test passed. If enabled, the comparison takes place, and the depth buffer and stencil value may subsequently be modified. The comparison is specified with

```
void DepthFunc( enum func ) ;
```

This command takes a single symbolic constant: one of **NEVER, ALWAYS, LESS, LEQUAL, EQUAL, GREATER, GEQUAL, NOTEQUAL.** Accordingly, the depth buffer test passes never, always, if the incoming fragment's z_w value is less than, less than or equal to, equal to, greater than, greater than or equal to, or not equal to the depth value stored at the location given by the incoming fragment's (x_w, y_w) coordinates.

If the depth buffer test fails, the incoming fragment is discarded. The stencil value at the fragment's (x_w, y_w) coordinates is updated according to the function currently in effect for depth buffer test failure. Otherwise, the fragment continues to the next operation, and the value of the depth buffer at the fragment's (x_w, y_w) location is set to the fragment's z_w value. In this case the stencil value is updated according to the function currently in effect for depth buffer test success.

The necessary state is an eight-valued integer and a single bit indicating whether depth buffering is enabled or disabled. In the initial state the function is **LESS** and the test is disabled. If there is no depth buffer, it is as if the depth buffer test always passes.

Blending

Blending combines the incoming fragment's R, G, B, and A values with the R, G, B, and A values stored in the frame buffer at the incoming fragment's (x_w, y_w) location. This blending is dependent on the incoming fragment's alpha value and that of the corresponding currently stored pixel. Blending applies only in RGBA mode. In color index mode it is bypassed. Blending is enabled or disabled, using **Enable** or **Disable** with the symbolic constant **BLEND.** If it is disabled, proceed to the next stage.

The command that controls blending is

```
void BlendFunc( enum src, enum dst );
```

The *src* indicates how to compute a source blending factor, and *dst* indicates how to compute a destination factor. The possible arguments and their corresponding computed source and destination factors are summarized in Tables 14.15 and 14.16. In these tables A is a single alpha value, and C is a quadruplet of R, G, B, and A values. A subscript of s indicates a value from an incoming fragment; one of d indicates the corresponding current frame buffer value. Division of a quadruplet by a scalar means dividing each element by that value. Addition or subtraction of quadruplets or triplets means adding or subtracting them componentwise.

The computations in Tables 14.15 and 14.16 are carried out in floating point and yield floating-point blending factors. Destination (frame buffer) components referred to in the tables are taken to be fixed-point values represented according to the scheme given earlier in the chapter, as are source (fragment) components. Any implied conversion to floating-point must leave 0 and 1 invariant.

The state required is two integers indicating the source and destination blending functions and a bit indicating whether blending is enabled or disabled. The initial state of the blending functions is **ONE** for the source function and **ZERO** for the destination function. Initially blending is disabled.

Blending occurs once for each color buffer currently enabled for writing using each buffer's color for C_d. If a color buffer has no A value, then it is as if the destination A value is 1.

Dithering

Dithering selects between two color values or indices. In RGBA mode consider the value of any of the color components as a fixed-point value with m bits to the left of the binary point, where m is the number of bits allocated to that component in the frame buffer. Call each such value c. In color index mode the same rule applies, with c being a single color index. The c value must not be larger than the maximum value representable in the frame buffer for either the component or the index, as appropriate.

Table 14.15 Values controlling the source blending function and the source blending values they compute $f = \min(A_s, 1 - A_d)$.

Value	Blend Factors
ZERO	(0, 0, 0, 0)
ONE	(1, 1, 1, 1)
DST_COLOR	R_d, G_d, B_d, A_d
ONE_MINUS_DST_COLOR	$(1, 1, 1, 1) - (R_d, G_d, B_d, A_d)$
SRC_ALPHA	(A_s, A_s, A_s, A_s)
ONE_MINUS_SRC_ALPHA	$(1, 1, 1, 1) - (A_s, A_s, A_s, A_s)$
DST_ALPHA	(A_d, A_d, A_d, A_d)
ONE_MINUS_DST_ALPHA	$(1, 1, 1, 1) - (A_d, A_d, A_d, A_d)$
SR_ALPHA_SATURATE	$(f, f, f, 1)$

Table 14.16 Values controlling the destination blending function and the destination blending values they compute.

Value	Blend factors
ZERO	(0,0,0,0)
ONE	(1,1,1,1)
SRC_CCLOR	R_d, G_d, B_d, A_d
ONE_MINUS_SRC_COLOR	$(1, 1, 1, 1) - (R_d, G_d, B_d, A_d)$
SRC_ALPHA	(A_s, A_s, A_s, A_s)
ONE_MINUS_SRC_ALPHA	$(1, 1, 1, 1) - (A_s, A_s, A_s, A_s)$
DST_ALPHA	(A_d, A_d, A_d, A_d)
ONE_MINUS_DST_ALPHA	$(1, 1, 1, 1) - (A_d, A_d, A_d, A_d)$

Many dithering algorithms are possible, but a dithered value produced by any algorithm must depend only on the incoming value and the fragment's *x* and *y* window coordinates. If dithering is disabled, each color component is truncated to a fixed-point value with as many bits as there are in the corresponding component in the frame buffer. A color index is rounded to the nearest integer representable in the color index portion of the frame buffer.

Dithering is enabled with **Enable** and is disabled with **Disable,** using the symbolic constant **DITHER.** The state required is thus a single bit. Initially dithering is enabled. In RGBA mode this is the last operation, and the result goes into the frame buffer. In color index mode continue on to the last operation.

Logical Operation

Finally, a logical operation is applied between the incoming fragment and the value stored at the corresponding location in the frame buffer. The result replaces the current frame buffer value. The logical operation is enabled or disabled with **Enable** or **Disable**, using the symbolic constant **LOGIC-OP**. The logical operation is selected by

```
void LogicOp( enum op ) ;
```

The *op* is a symbolic constant. The possible constants and the corresponding logical operations are enumerated in Table 14.17. In this table s is the value of the incoming fragment, and d is the value stored in the frame buffer.

Note that the **SET** operation sets all bits of the result to 1. The result replaces the value in the frame buffer at the fragment's (x, y) coordinates. The numeric values assigned to the symbolic constants are the same as those assigned to the corresponding symbolic values in the X window system.

LogicOp applies only in color index mode. In RGBA mode it does not occur, and the previous operation is the last one applied to incoming fragments. **LogicOp** occurs once for each color buffer selected for writing. The required state is an integer indicating the logical

Table 14.17 Arguments to *LogicOp* and their corresponding operations.

Argument Value	Operation
CLEAR	0
AND	$s \wedge d$
AND_REVERSE	$s \wedge \varnothing\, d$
COPY	s
AND_INVERTED	$\neg s \wedge d$
NOOP	d
XOR	s xor d
OR	$s \vee d$
NOR	$\neg (s \vee d)$
EQUIV	$\neg (s$ xor $d)$
INVERT	$\neg d$
OR_REVERSE	$s \vee \neg d$
COPY_INVERTED	$\neg s$
OR_INVERTED	$\neg s \vee d$
NAND	$\neg (s \wedge d)$
SET	1

operation and a bit to indicate whether the logical operation is enabled or disabled. The initial state is for the logic operation to be given by **COPY**, and it is disabled.

Whole Frame Buffer Operations

Earlier this chapter described the operations that occur as individual fragments are sent to the frame buffer. We now turn to operations that control or affect the whole frame buffer.

Selecting a Buffer for Writing

The symbolic constant *buf* specifies zero, one, two, or four buffers for writing. The constants are **NONE, FRONT_LEFT, FRONT_RIGHT, BACK_LEFT, BACK_RIGHT, FRONT, BACK, LEFT, RIGHT, FRONT_AND_BACK,** and **AUX0** through **AUX**n, where $n+1$ is the number of available auxiliary buffers.

The first such operation is controlling the buffer into which color values are written. This is accomplished with

```
void DrawBuffer( enum buf ) ;
```

The constants refer to the four potentially visible buffers *front_left, front_right, back_left,* and *back_right* and to the *auxiliary* buffers. Arguments other than **AUX**i that omit reference to **LEFT** or **RIGHT** refer to both left and right buffers. Arguments other than **AUX**i that omit reference to **FRONT** or **BACK** refer to both front and back buffers. **AUX**i enables drawing only to auxiliary buffer i. Each **AUX**i adheres to **AUX**i = **AUX**$0 + i$. The constants and the buffers they indicate are summarized in Table 14.18. If **DrawBuffer** is supplied with a constant (other than **NONE**) that does not indicate any of the color buffers allocated to the GL context, the error **INVALID_OPERATION** results.

Indicating a buffer or buffers using **DrawBuffer** causes subsequent pixel color value writes to affect the indicated buffers. If more than one color buffer is selected for drawing, blending and logical operations are computed and applied independently for each buffer. Calling **DrawBuffer** with a value of **NONE** inhibits the writing of color values to any buffer.

Monoscopic contexts include only left buffers, whereas stereoscopic contexts include both left and right buffers. Likewise, single-buffered contexts include only front buffers, whereas double-buffered

Table 14.18 Arguments to DrawBuffer and the buffers they indicate.

Symbolic Constant	Front Left	Front Right	Back Left	Back Right	Aux i
NONE					
FRONT_LEFT	•				
FRONT_RIGHT		•			
BACK_LEFT			•		
BACK_RIGHT				•	
FRONT	•	•			
BACK			•	•	
LEFT	•		•		
RIGHT		•		•	
FRONT_AND_BACK	•	•	•	•	
AUXi					•

contexts include both front and back buffers. The type of context is selected at GL initialization.

The state required to handle buffer selection is a set of up to $4 + n$ bits. Four bits indicate whether the front left buffer, the front right buffer, the back left buffer, or the back right buffer are enabled for color writing. The other n bits indicate which of the auxiliary buffers is enabled for color writing. In the initial state the front buffer or buffers are enabled if there are no back buffers. Otherwise, only the back buffer or buffers are enabled.

Fine Control of Buffer Updates

Four commands are used to mask the writing of bits to each of the logical frame buffers after all per fragment operations have been performed.

The commands control the color buffer or buffers (depending on which buffers are currently indicated for writing):

```
void IndexMask( uint mask)
void ColorMask( boolean r, boolean g, boolean b, boolean a );
```

The least-significant n bits of mask, where n is the number of bits in a color index buffer, specify a mask. Where a 1 appears in this mask, the corresponding bit in the color index buffer (or buffers) is written. Where a 0 appears, the bit is not written. This mask applies only in color index mode. In RGBA mode **ColorMask** is used to mask the writing of R, G, B, and A values to the color buffer or buffers; r, g, b, and a indicate whether R, G, B, or A values, respectively, are written (a value of **TRUE** means that the corresponding value is written). In the initial state all bits (in color index mode) and all color values (in RGBA mode) are enabled for writing.

The depth buffer can be enabled or disabled for writing z. values, using

```
void DepthMask( boolean mask );
```

If *mask* is nonzero, the depth buffer is enabled for writing; otherwise, it is disabled. In the initial state the depth buffer is enabled for writing.

The command controls the writing of particular bits into the stencil planes:

```
void StencilMask( uint mask );
```

The least-significant s bits of *mask* comprise an integer mask (s is the number of bits in the stencil buffer), just as for **IndexMask**. The initial state is for the stencil plane mask to be all 1s.

The state required for the various masking operations is two integers and a bit: an integer for color indices, an integer for stencil values, and a bit for depth values. A set of four bits is also required, indicating which color components of an RGBA value should be written. In the initial state the integer masks are all 1s as are the bits controlling depth value and RGBA component writing.

Clearing the Buffers

The GL provides a means for setting portions of every pixel in a particular buffer to the same value.

The following command takes as an argument the bitwise OR of a number of values indicating which buffers are to be cleared:

void **Clear**(bitfield buf);

The values are **COLOR_BUFFER_BIT, DEPTH_BUFFER_BIT, STENCIL_BUFFER_SIT,** and **ACCUM_BUFFER_BIT,** indicating the buffers currently enabled for color writing, the depth buffer, the stencil buffer, and the accumulation buffer respectively. The value to which each buffer is cleared depends on the setting of the clear value for that buffer.

If the mask is not a bitwise OR of the specified values, the error **INVALID_VALUE** is generated. The following command sets the clear value for the color buffers in RGBA mode:

void **ClearColor**(clampf r, clampf g, clampf b, clampf a)

Each of the specified components is clamped to [0, 1] and converted to fixed-point according to the rules discussed earlier in the chapter. The following command sets the clear color index:

void **ClearIndex**(float $index$) ;

The $index$ is converted to a fixed-point value with unspecified precision to the left of the binary point. The following command takes a floating-point value that is clamped to the range [0, 1] and converted to fixed-point according to the rules for a window z value:

void **ClearDepth**(clampd d) ;

Similarly, the following command takes a single integer argument that is the value to which to clear the stencil buffer. s is masked to the number of bitplanes in the stencil buffer:

void **ClearStencil**(int s) ;

The following command takes four floating-point arguments that are the values, in order, to which to set the R, G, B, and A values of the accumulation buffer:

void **ClearAccum**(float r, float g, float b, float a) ;

These values are clamped to the range [−1,1] when they are specified.[7]

When **Clear** is called, the only per fragment operations that are applied (if enabled) are the pixel ownership test, the scissor test, and

---

[7] *Ibid.*, pp. 106–107.

dithering. The masking operations described earlier are also effective. If a buffer is not present, a **Clear** directed at that buffer has no effect.

The state required for clearing is a clear value for each of the color buffer, the depth buffer, the stencil buffer, and the accumulation buffer. Initially the RGBA color clear value is (0,0,0,0), the clear color index is 0, and the stencil buffer and accumulation buffer clear values are all 0. The depth buffer clear value is initially 1.0.

The Accumulation Buffer

The symbolic constant *op* indicates an accumulation buffer operation, and *value* is a floating-point value to be used in that operation. The possible operations are **ACCUM, LOAD, RETURN, MULT,** and **ADD.**

Each portion of a pixel in the accumulation buffer consists of four values: one for each of R, G, B, and A. The accumulation buffer is controlled exclusively through the use of

```
void Accum( enun op, float value ) ;
```

(except for clearing it).

The accumulation buffer operations apply identically to every pixel, so the effect is described of each operation on an individual pixel. Accumulation buffer values are taken to be signed values in the range [–1, 1]. Using **ACCUM** obtains R, G, B, and A components from the buffer currently selected for reading. Each component, considered as a fixed-point value in [0, 1], is converted to floating-point. Each result is then multiplied by *value*. The results of this multiplication are then added to the corresponding color component currently in the accumulation buffer. The resulting color value replaces the current accumulation buffer color value. The **LOAD** operation has the same effect as **ACCUM,** but the computed values replace the corresponding accumulation buffer components rather than being added to them.

The **RETURN** operation takes each color value from the accumulation buffer and multiplies each of the R, G, B, and A components by *value*. The resulting color value is placed in the buffers currently enabled for color writing, as if it were a fragment produced from rasterization. The exception is that the only perfragment operations applied are the pixel ownership test. If enabled, dithering is also applied. Color masking is applied as well.

The **MULT** operation multiplies each R, G, B, and A in the accumulation buffer by *value* and then returns the scaled color components to their corresponding accumulation buffer locations. **ADD** is the same as **MOLT**, except that *value* is added to each of the color components.

The color components operated on by **Accum** must be clamped only if the operation is **RETURN**. In this case a value sent to the enabled color buffers is first clamped to [0, 1]. Otherwise, results are undefined if the result of an operation on a color component is too large (in magnitude) to be represented by the number of available bits. When the scissor test is enabled, only those pixels within the current scissor box are updated by any **Accum** operation; otherwise, all pixels in the window are updated. If there is no accumulation buffer or if the GL is in color index mode, **Accum** generates the error **INVALID_OPERATION**. No state (beyond the accumulation buffer itself) is required for accumulation buffering.

Drawing, Reading, and Copying Pixels

Pixels may be written to and read from the frame buffer by using the **DrawPixels** and **ReadPixels** commands. **CopyPixels** can be used to **copy** a block of pixels from one portion of the frame buffer to another.

Writing to the Stencil Buffer

The operation of **DrawPixels** was described earlier. One exception would be if the format argument was **STENCIL_INDEX**. In this case all operations described for **DrawPixels** take place. But window (x, y) coordinates, each with the corresponding stencil index, are produced in lieu of fragments. Each coordinate stencil index pair is sent directly to the per fragment operations, bypassing the texture, fog, and antialiasing application stages of rasterization. Each pair is then treated as a fragment for purposes of the pixel ownership and scissor tests. All other per fragment operations are bypassed. Finally, each stencil index is written to its indicated location in the frame buffer, subject to the current setting of **StencilMask**. The error **INVALID_OPERATION** results if there is no stencil buffer.

Reading Pixels

The method for reading pixels from the frame buffer and placing them in client memory is diagramed in Figure 14.17. The stages of the pixel-reading process are discussed in the order in which they occur.

Pixels are read by using

```
void ReadPixels( int x, int y, sizei width, sizei height, enum format,
    enulm type, void *data ) ;
```

The arguments after x and y to **ReadPixels** correspond to those of **DrawPixels.** The pixel storage modes that apply to **ReadPixels** are summarized in Table 14.19.

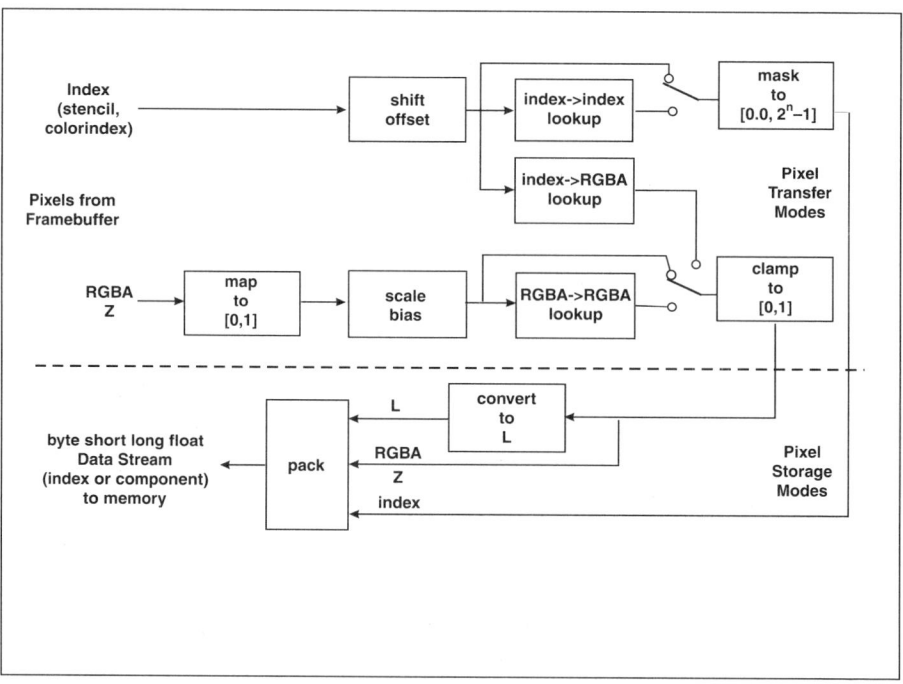

Figure 14.17 Operation of **PeadPixels.** The parameters controlling the stages above the dotted line are set with **PixelTransfer** or **PixelMap;** those controlling the stages below the line are set with **PixelStore.**

Table 14.19 PixelStore Parameters Pertaining to ReadPixels

Parameter Name	Type	Initial Value	Valid Range
PACK_SWAP_BYTES	Boolean	**FALSE**	**TRUE/FALSE**
PACK_LSB_FIRST	Boolean	**FALSE**	**TRUE/FALSE**
PACK_ROW_LENGTH	Integer	0	[0,∞)
PACK_SKIP_ROWS	Integer	0	[0,∞)
PACK_SKIP_PIXELS	Integer	0	[0,∞)
PACK_ALIGNMENT	Integer	4	1,2,4,8

1. *Obtaining pixels from the frame buffer*

If the format is **DEPTH_COMPONENT,** values are obtained from the depth buffer. If there is no depth buffer, the error **INVALID_OPERATION** occurs. If the format is **STENCIL_INDEX,** values are taken from the stencil buffer; again, if there is no stencil buffer, the error **INVALID_OPERATION** occurs. For all other formats, the buffer from which values are obtained is one of the color buffers. The selection of color buffer is controlled with **ReadBuffer.**

The following command

```
void ReadBuffer( enum src ) ;
takes a symbolic constant as argument:
```

The possible values are **FRONT_LEFT, FRONT_RIGHT, BACK_LEFT, BACK_RIGHT, FRONT, BACK, LEFT, RIGHT,** and **AUX0** through **AUXN. FRONT** and **LEFT** refer to the front left buffer, **BACK** refers to the back left buffer, and **RIGHT** refers to the front right buffer. The other constants correspond directly to the buffers they name. If the requested buffer is missing, the error **INVALID_OPERATION** is generated. The initial setting for **ReadBuffer** is **FRONT** if there is no back buffer and **BACK** otherwise.

The number of values obtained from the selected buffer depends on the *format*. If the *format* is **LUMINANCE,** R, G, and B values are obtained. If it is **LUMINANCE_ALPHA,** R, G, B, and A values are obtained. If the frame buffer does not support alpha values then the A that is obtained is 1.0. If the *format* is one of **RED, GREEN, BLUE, ALPHA, RGB, RGBA, LUMINANCE,** or **LUMINANCE_ALPHA** and if the GL is in color index mode, the color index is obtained. Otherwise, the type and number of values that are obtained from the selected buffer for each pixel are as shown in Table 14.11.

2. *Conversion of RGBA values*

This step applies only if the GL is in RGBA mode and then only if *format* is neither **STENCIL_INDEX** nor **DEPTH_COMPONENT**. The error **INVALID_OPERATION** results (in RGBA mode) if *format* is **COLOR_INDEX**. The R, G, and B (and possibly A) values form a group of elements. Each element is taken to be a fixed-point value in [0, 1] with m bits, where m is the number of bits in the corresponding color component of the selected buffer.

3. *Conversion to L*

This step applies only to RGBA component groups and only if the *format* is either **LUMINANCE** or **LUMINANCE_ALPHA**. A value L is computed as

$$L = R + G + B$$

where R, G, and B are the values of the R, G, and B components. The single computed L component replaces the R, G, and B components in the group.[8]

4. *Final conversion*

For an index, if the *type* is not **FLOAT**, final conversion consists of masking the index with the value given in Table 14.20. If the *type* is **FLOAT**, the integer index is converted to a GL float data value. For a component, each component is first clamped to [0, 1]. Then the appropriate conversion formula from Table 14.21 is applied to the component.

Groups of elements are placed in memory in the same way that they are taken from memory for **DrawPixels**. That is, the *i*th group of the *j*th row (corresponding to the *i*th pixel in the *j*th row) is placed in memory just where the *i*th group of the *j*th row would be taken from for **DrawPixels**. The only difference is that the storage mode parameters whose names begin with **PACK_** are used instead of those whose names begin with **UNPACK_**.

---

[8] *Ibid.*, p. 113.

Table 14.20 Index Masks Used by ReadPixels. Floating point is data are masked.

Type Parameter	Index Mask
UNSIGNED_BYTE	$2^8 - 1$
BITMAP	1
BYTE	$2^7 - 1$
UNSIGNED_SHORT	$2^{16} - 1$
SHORT	$2^{15} - 1$
UNSIGNED_INT	$2^{32} - 1$
INT	$2^{31} - 1$

Table 14.21 Reversed Component Conversions used when component data.

Type Parameter	GL Data Type	Component Conversion Formula
UNSIGNED_BYTE	ubyte	$c = (2^8 - 1)f$
BYTE	byte	$c = [(2^8 - 1)f - 1]/2$
UNSIGNED_SHORT	u hort	$c = (2^{16} - 1)f$
SHORT	short	$c = [(2^{16} - 1)f - 1]/2$
UNSIGNED_INT	uint	$c = (2^{32} - 1)f$
INT	int	$c = [(2^{32} - 1)f - 1]/2$
FLOAT	float	$c = f$

These are/is being returned to client memory. Color, normal, and depth components are converted from the internal floating-point representation (f) to a datum of the specified GL data type (c), using the equations in this table. All arithmetic is done in the internal floating-point format. These conversions apply to component data returned by GL query commands and to components of pixel data returned to client memory. The equations remain the same, even if the implemented ranges of the GL data types are greater than the minimum required ranges. (Refer to Table 14.2.)

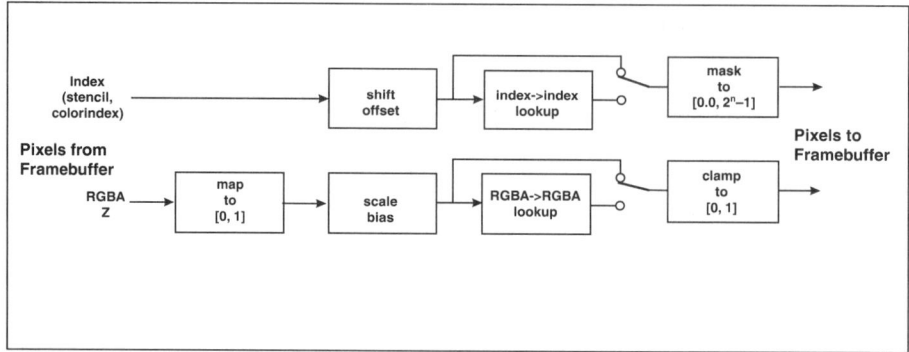

Figure 14.18 Operation of **CopyPixels**. All parameters affecting pixel copying are set with **PixelTransfer** or **PixelMap**.

Copying Pixels

CopyPixels transfers a rectangle of pixel values from one region of the frame buffer to another. Pixel copying is diagrammed in Figure 14.18.

This command has the form

    void **CopyPixels**(int x, int y, sizei width, sizei height, enum type);

The *type* is a symbolic constant that must be one of **COLOR, STENCIL,** or **DEPTH,** indicating that the values to be transferred are colors, stencil values, or depth values, respectively. The first four arguments have the same interpretation as the corresponding arguments to **ReadPixels.** Values are obtained from the frame buffer, converted (if appropriate), subjected to arithmetic operations, and looked up in tables, just as if **ReadPixels** were called with the corresponding arguments. If the *type* is **STENCIL** or **DEPTH,** it is as if the *format* for **ReadPixels** were **STENCIL_INDEX** or **DEPTH_COMPONENT,** respectively. If the type is **COLOR,** the GL is in RGBA mode. If the *format* were **RGBA** while the GL is in color index mode, it is as if the *format* were **COLOR INDEX.** The groups of elements so obtained are then written to the frame buffer just as if **DrawPixels** had been given width and height, beginning with final conversion of elements. The effective format is the same as that already described.

Pixel Draw/Read State

The state required for pixel operations consists of the parameters that are set with **PixelStore, PixelTransfer,** and **PixelMap.** This state has been summarized in Tables 14.7, 14.8, and 14.9. The current setting of **ReadBuffer,** a 12-valued integer, is also required, along with the current raster position. State set with **PixelStore** is GL client state.

Special Functions

Some GL functionality does not fit easily into any of the preceding chapters. This functionality consists of evaluators (used to model curves and surfaces), selection (used to locate rendered primitives on the screen), feedback (which returns GL results before rasterization), display lists (used to designate a group of GL commands for later execution by the GL), flushing and finishing (used to synchronize the GL command stream), and hints.

Evaluators

Evaluators provide a means to use a polynomial or rational polynomial mapping to produce vertex, normal, and texture coordinates and colors. The values so produced are sent on to further stages of the GL as if they had been provided directly by the client. Transformations, lighting, primitive assembly, rasterization, and perpixel operations are not affected by the use of evaluators.

```
void Map1{fd}( enum type, T u_1, T u_2, int stride, int order, T points );
```

The *type* is a symbolic constant indicating the range of the defined polynomial. Its possible values, along with the evaluations that each indicates, are given in Table 14.22. The *order* is equal to $n + 1$. The error **INVALID_VALUE** results if *order* is less than 1 or greater than **MAX_EVAL_ORDER.** The value *points* is a pointer to a set of $n + 1$ blocks of storage. Each block begins with k single-precision floating-point or double-precision floating-point values, respectively. The rest of the block may be filled with arbitrary data. Table 14.22 indicates how k depends on *type* and what the k values represent in each case.

Table 14.22 Values Specified by the target to Map1.

target	k	Values
MAP1_VERTEX_3	3	x, y, z vertex coordinates
MAP1_VERTEXA	4	x, y, z, w vertex coordinates
MAP1_NDEX	1	Color index
NAPI_COLORA	4	R, G, B, A
MAP1_NORMAL	3	x, y, z normal coordinates
MAP1_TEXTUFLE_COORD_1	1	s texture coordinate
MAP1_TEXTURE_COORD_2	2	s, t texture coordinates
MAP1_TEXTURE_COORD_3	3	s, t, r texture coordinates
MAP1_TEXTURE_COORD_4	4	s, t, r, q texture coordinates

Values are given in the order in which they are taken.

The number of single- or double-precision values (as appropriate) in each block of storage is stride. The error **INVALID_VALUE** results if *stride* is less than *k*. The order of the polynomial, *order*, is also the number of blocks of storage containing control points.

Figure 14.19 describes map evaluation schematically. An evaluation of enabled maps is effected in one of two ways. The first way is to use:

```
void EvalCoord{12}{fd}( T arg ) ;
void EvalCoord{12}{fd}v( T arg ) ;
```

EvalCoord1 causes evaluation of the enabled one-dimensional maps. The argument is the value (or a pointer to the value) that is the domain coordinate, u'. **EvalCoord2** causes evaluation of the enabled two-dimensional maps. The two values specify the two domain coordinates, u' and v', in that order.

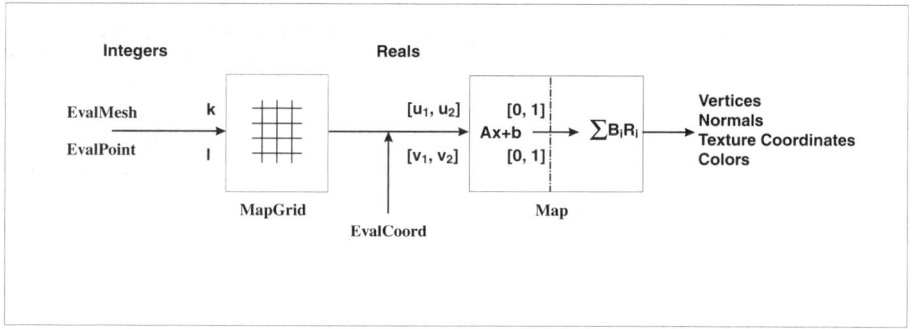

Figure 14.19 Map Evaluation

When one of the **EvalCoord** commands is issued, all currently enabled maps of the indicated dimension are evaluated. Then, for each enabled map, it is as if a corresponding GL command were issued with the resulting coordinates, with one important difference. The difference is that when an evaluation is performed, the GL uses evaluated values instead of current values for those evaluations that are enabled (otherwise, the current values are used). The order of the effective commands is immaterial, except that **Vertex** (for vertex coordinate evaluation) must be issued last. Use of evaluators has no effect on the current color, normal, or texture coordinates.

No command is effectively issued if the corresponding map (of the indicated dimension) is not enabled. If more than one evaluation is enabled for a particular dimension (**MAP1_TEXTURE_COORD_1** and **MAP1_TEXTURE_COORD_2**), only the result of the evaluation of the map with the highest number of coordinates is used.

Finally, if either **MAP2_VERTEX_3** or **MAP2_VERTEX_4** is enabled, the normal to the surface is computed analytically. If automatic normal generation is enabled, this computed normal is used as the normal associated with a generated vertex. Automatic normal generation is controlled with **Enable** and **Disable** and the symbolic constant **AUTO_NORMAL**. If automatic normal generation is disabled, a corresponding normal map, if enabled, is used to produce a normal. If neither automatic normal generation nor a normal map is enabled, no normal is sent with a vertex resulting from an evaluation (the effect is that the current normal is used).

The state required for evaluators potentially consists of nine one-dimensional map specifications and nine two-dimensional map specifications, as well as corresponding flags for each specification indicating which are enabled. Each map specification consists of one or two orders, an appropriately sized array of control points, and a set of two values (for a one-dimensional map) or four values (for a two-dimensional map) to describe the domain. The maximum possible order, for either u or v, is implementation dependent (one maximum applies to both u and v) but must be at least eight. Each control point consists of between one and four floating-point values (depending on the type of the map). Initially all maps have order 1 (making them constant maps). AD vertex coordinate maps produce the coordinates (0, 0, 0, 1) (or the appropriate subset). All normal coordinate maps produce (0, 0, 1). RGBA maps produce (1,1,1,1). Color index maps produce 1.0. In the initial state all maps are disabled. A flag indicates whether automatic normal generation is enabled for two-dimensional maps. In the initial state automatic normal generation is disabled. Also required are two floating-point values, an integer number of grid divisions for the one-dimensional grid specification, four floating-point values, and two integer grid divisions for the two-dimensional grid specification. In the initial state the bounds of the domain interval for 1-D is 0 and 1.0, respectively. For 2-D, they are (0, 0) and (1.0, 1.0), respectively. The number of grid divisions is one for 1-D and one in both directions for 2-D. If any evaluation command is issued when no vertex map is enabled, nothing happens.

Selection

A programmer uses selection to determine which primitives are drawn into some region of a window. The region is defined by the current model-view and perspective matrices.

Selection works by returning an array of integer-valued *names*. This array represents the current contents of the *name stack*. This stack is controlled with the commands

```
void InitNames( void ) ;
void PopName( void ) ;
void PushName( uint name ) ;
void LoadName( uint name ) ;
```

InitNames empties (clears) the name stack. **PopName** pops one name off the top of the name stack. **PushName** causes *name* to be pushed onto the name stack. **LoadName** replaces the value on the top of the stack with *name*. Loading a name onto an empty stack generates the error **INVALID_OPERATION**. Popping a name off of an empty stack generates **STACK_UNDERFLOW**. Pushing a name onto a full stack generates **STACK_OVERFLOW**. The maximum allowable depth of the name stack is implementation dependent but must be at least 64.

In selection mode no fragments are rendered into the frame buffer. The GL is placed in selection mode with

```
int RenderMode( enum mode ) ;
```

The *mode* is a symbolic constant: one of **RENDER, SELECT,** or **FEEDBACK**. **RENDER** is the default, corresponding to rendering as described until now. **SELECT** specifies selection mode, and **FEEDBACK** specifies feedback mode. Use of any of the name stack manipulation commands while the GL is not in selection mode has no effect.

Selection is controlled by using

```
void SelectBuffer( sizei n, uint *buffer ) ;
```

The *buffer* is a pointer to an array of unsigned integers (called the selection array) to be potentially filled with names and *n* is an integer indicating the maximum number of values that can be stored in that array. Placing the GL in selection mode before **SelectBuffer** has been called results in an error of **INVALID_OPERATION**, as does calling **SelectBuffer** while in selection mode.

In selection mode if a point, line, polygon, or the valid coordinates produced by a **RasterPos** command intersect the clip volume, then this primitive (or **RasterPos** command) causes a selection *hit*. In the case of polygons, no hit occurs if the polygon would have been culled. But selection is based on the polygon itself, regardless of the setting of **Polygonmode**. In selection mode whenever a name stack manipulation command is executed or **RenderMode** is called and there has been a hit since the last time the stack was manipulated or **RenderMode** was called a *hit record* is written into the selection array.

A hit record consists of the following items in order: a nonnegative integer giving the number of elements on the name stack at the time of the hit, a minimum depth value, a maximum depth value, and the name stack with the bottommost element first. The minimum and maximum depth values are the minimum and maximum taken over all the window coordinate z values of each (postclipping) vertex of each primitive that intersects the clipping volume since the last hit record was written. The minimum and maximum (each of which lies in the range [0, 1]) are each multiplied by $2^{32} - 1$ and rounded to the nearest unsigned integer to obtain the values that are placed in the hit record.

Hit records are placed in the selection array by maintaining a pointer into that array. When selection mode is entered, the pointer is initialized to the beginning of the array. Each time a hit record is copied, the pointer is updated to point at the array element after the one into which the topmost element of the name stack was stored. If copying the hit record into the selection array would cause the total number of values to exceed n, as much of the record as fits in the array is written, and an overflow flag is set.

Selection mode is exited by calling **RenderMode** with an argument value other than **SELECT**. Whenever **RenderMode** is called in selection mode, it returns the number of hit records copied into the selection array and resets the **SelectBuffer** pointer to its last specified value. Values are not guaranteed to be written into the selection array until **RenderMode** is called. If the selection array overflow flag was set, **RenderMode** returns –1 and clears the overflow flag. The name stack is cleared and the stack pointer reset whenever **RenderMode** is called.

The state required for selection consists of the address of the selection array and its maximum size, the name stack and its associated pointer, a minimum and maximum depth value, and several flags. One flag indicates the current **RenderMode** value. In the initial state the GL is in the **RENDER** mode. Another flag is used to indicate whether a hit has occurred since the last name stack manipulation. This flag is reset entering selection mode and whenever a name stack manipulation takes place. One final flag is required to indicate whether the maximum number of copied names would have been exceeded. This flag is reset entering selection mode. This flag, the address of the selection array, and its maximum size are GL client state.

Feedback

Feedback, like selection, is a GL mode. The mode is selected by calling **RenderMode** with **FEEDBACK**. When the GL is in feedback mode, no fragments are written to the frame buffer. Instead, information about primitives that would have been rasterized is fed back to the application, using the GL.

Feedback is controlled by using

   void **FeedbackBuffer**(sizei *n*, enum *type*, float **buffer*) ;

The *buffer* is a pointer to an array of floating-point values into which feedback information will be placed; *n* is a number indicating the maximum number of values that can be written to that array; and *type* is a symbolic constant describing the information to be fed back for each vertex. The error **INVALID_OPERATION** results if the GL is placed in feedback mode before a call to **FeedbackBuffer** has been made or if a call to **FeedbackBuffer** is made while in feedback mode.

While in feedback mode, each primitive that would be rasterized (or bitmap or call to **DrawPixels** or **CopyPixels,** if the raster position is valid) generates a block of values that get copied into the feedback array. If doing so would cause the number of entries to exceed the maximum, the block is partially written so as to fill the array (if any room is left at all). The first block of values generated after the GL enters feedback mode is placed at the beginning of the feedback array, with subsequent blocks following. Each block begins with a code indicating the primitive type, followed by values that describe the primitive's vertices and associated data. Entries are also written for bitmaps and pixel rectangles. Feedback occurs after polygon culling and **PolygonMode** interpretation of polygons have taken place. It may also occur after polygons with more than three edges are broken up into triangles (if the GL implementation renders polygons by performing this decomposition). The *x*, *y*, and *z* coordinates returned by feedback are window coordinates. If *w* is returned, it is in clip coordinates. In the case of bitmaps and pixel rectangles, the coordinates returned are those of the current raster position. The texture coordinates and colors returned are those resulting from the clipping operations.

The ordering rules for GL command interpretation also apply in feedback mode. Each command must be fully interpreted and its effects on both GL state and the values to be written to the feedback buffer completed before a subsequent command may be executed.

The GL is taken out of feedback mode by calling **RenderMode** with an argument value other than **FEEDBACK**. When called while in feedback mode, **RenderMode** returns the number of values placed in the feedback array and resets the feedback array pointer to be *buffer*.

The return value never exceeds the maximum number of values passed to **FeedbackBuffer.** If writing a value to the feedback buffer would cause more values to be written than the specified maximum number of values, then the value is not written and an overflow flag is set. In this case **RenderMode** returns –1 when it is called, after which the overflow flag is reset. While in feedback mode, values are not guaranteed to be written into the feedback buffer before **RenderMode** is called.

Table 14.23 gives the correspondence between feedback buffer and the number of values returned for each vertex.

The following command may be used as a marker in feedback mode:

```
void PassThrough( float token ) ;
```

The value of *token* is returned as if it were a primitive. It is indicated with its own unique identifying value. The ordering of any **PassThrough** commands with respect to primitive specification is maintained by feedback. **PassThrough** may not occur between **Begin** and **End**. It has no effect when the GL is not in feedback mode.

The state required for feedback is the pointer to the feedback array, the maximum number of values that may be placed there, and the feedback type. An overflow flag is required to indicate whether the maximum allowable number of feedback values has been written. Initially this flag is cleared. These state variables are GL client state.

Table 14.23 Correspondence of Feedback Type to Number of Values per Vertex.

Type	Coordinates	Color	Texture	Total Values
2-D	x, y	—	—	2
3-D	x, y, z	—	—	3
3-D_COLOR	x, y, z	k	—	3 + k
3-D_COLOR_TEXTURE	x, y, z	k	4	7 + k
4D_COLOR_TEXTURE	x, y, z, w	k	4	8 + k

Note that k is 1 in color index mode and 4 in RGBA mode.

Feedback also relies on the same mode flag as selection to indicate whether the GL is in feedback, selection, or normal rendering mode.

Display Lists

A display list is simply a group of GL commands and arguments stored for subsequent execution. The GL may be instructed to process a particular display list (possibly repeatedly) by providing a number that uniquely specifies it. Doing so causes the commands within the list to be executed just as if they were given normally. The only exception pertains to commands that rely on client state. When such a command is accumulated into the display list (that is, when issued, not when executed), the client state in effect at that time applies to the command. Only server state is affected when the command is executed. As always, pointers passed as arguments to commands are dereferenced when the command is issued.

A display list is begun by calling

```
void NewList( uint n, enum mode ) ;
```

n is a positive integer to which the display list that follows is assigned, and *mode* is a symbolic constant that controls the behavior of the GL during display list creation.[9]

If *mode* is **COMPILE,** commands are not executed as they are placed in the display list. If *mode* is **COMPILE_AND_EXECUTE,** commands are executed as they are encountered, then placed in the display list. If $n = 0$, the error **INVALID_VALUE** is generated. If the size of the display list exceeds the available memory, an **OUT_OF_MEMORY** error is generated.

After calling **NewList,** all subsequent GL commands are placed in the display list (in the order the commands are issued) until a call to

```
void EndList( void ) ;
```

After that occurs the GL returns to its normal command execution state.

It is only when **EndList** occurs that the specified display list is associated with the index indicated with NewList. The error **INVALID_OPERATION** is generated if EndList is called without a previous

---

[9] *Ibid.*, p. 128.

matching NewList or if **NewList** is called a second time before calling **EndList.** Once defined, a display list is executed by calling

```
void CallList( uint n ) ;
```

n gives the index of the display list to be called.

This causes the commands saved in the display list to be executed, in order, just as if they were issued without using a display list. If n = 0, the error **IRVALID-VALUE** is generated.

The command provides an efficient means for executing a number of display lists:

```
void CallLists( sizei n, enum type, void *lists ) ;
```

n is an integer indicating the number of display lists to be called, and *lists* is a pointer to an array of offsets.

Each offset is constructed as determined by *lists*, as follows. First, *type* may be one of the constants **BYTE, UNSIGNED_BYTE, SHORT, UNSIGNED_SHORT, INT, UNSIGNED_INT,** or **FLOAT.** This indicates that the array pointed to by *lists* is an array of bytes, unsigned bytes, shorts, unsigned shorts, integers, unsigned integers, or floats, respectively. In this case each offset is found by simply converting each array element to an integer (floating-point values are truncated).

Indicating a display list index that does not correspond to any display list has no effect. **CallList** or **CallLists** may appear inside a display list. If the *mode* supplied to **NewList COMPILE_AND_EXECUTE**, the appropriate lists are executed. But the **CallList** or **CallLists**, rather than those lists' constituent commands, is placed in the list under construction. To avoid the possibility of infinite recursion resulting from display lists calling one another, an implementation, dependent limit is placed on the nesting level of display lists during display list execution. This limit must be at least 64.

Two commands are provided to manage display list indices. One is

```
uint GenLists( sizei s ) ;
```

This command returns an integer n such that the indices $n, \ldots, n + s - 1$ are previously unused (that is, there are s previously unused display list indices starting at n).

GenLists also has the effect of creating an empty display list for each of the indices $n, \ldots, n + s - 1$, so that these indices all become used. **GenLists** returns 0 if there is no group of s contiguous previously unused display list indices or if $s = 0$.

The second command is top here

```
boolean IsList( uint list );
```

This command returns **TRUE** if *list* is the index of a display list. A contiguous group of display lists may be deleted by calling

```
void DeleteLists( uint list, sizei range );
```

Here *list* is the index of the first display list to be deleted, and *range* is the number of display lists to be deleted.

All information about the display lists is lost, and the indices become unused. Indices to which no display list corresponds are simply ignored. If range = 0, nothing happens.

Certain commands, when made within a display list, are not compiled into the display list but are executed immediately. These are **IsList, GenLists, DeleteLists, FeedbackBuffer, SelectBuffer, RenderMode, ReadPixels, PixelStore, Flush, Finish, IsEnabled,** and all of the **Get** commands.

Display lists require one bit of state to indicate whether a GL command should be executed immediately or placed in a display list. In the initial state commands are executed immediately. If the bit indicates display list creation, an index is required to indicate the current display list being defined. Another bit indicates, during display list creation, whether commands should be executed as they are compiled into the display list. One integer is required for the current **ListBase** setting. Its initial value is 0. Finally, state must be maintained to indicate which integers are currently in use as display list indices. In the initial state no indices are in use.

Flush and Finish

The following command

```
void Flush( void );
```

indicates that all commands that have previously been sent to the GL must complete in finite time:

The following command forces all previous GL commands to complete:

```
void Finish( void );
```

Finish does not return until all effects from previously issued commands on GL client and server state and the frame buffer are fully realized.

Hints

The symbolic constant *target* indicates the behavior to be controlled, and *hint* is a symbolic constant indicating what type of behavior is desired. The *target* may be one of **PERSPECTIVE_CORRECTION_HINT.** This indicates the desired quality of parameter interpolation. **POINT_SMOOTH_HINT** indicates the desired sampling quality of points. **LINE_SMOOTH_HINT** indicates the desired sampling quality of lines. **POLYGON_SMOOTH_HINT** indicates the desired sampling quality of polygons. **FOG_HINT** indicates whether fog calculations are done per pixel or per vertex. *Hint* must be one of **FASTEST** {indicating that the most efficient option should be chosen}, **NICEST** {indicating that the highest quality option should be chosen}, or, **DONT_CARE** {indicating no preference in the matter}.

Certain aspects of GL behavior, when there is room for variation, may be controlled with hints. A hint is specified by using

```
void Hint( enum target, enum hint ) ;
```

The interpretation of hints is implementation dependent. An implementation may ignore them entirely.

State and State Requests

The commands obtain Boolean, integer, floating-point, or double-precision state variables. The symbolic constant *value* indicates the state variable to return, and *data* is a pointer to an array of the indicated type in which to place the returned data.

In addition, the following can be used to determine whether value is currently enabled (as with **Enable**) or disabled:

```
boolean IsEnabled( enum value ) ;
```

The values of most GL state variables can be obtained by using a set of **Get** commands. There are four commands for obtaining simple state variables:

```
void GetBooleanv( enum value, boolean *data );
void GetIntegerv( enum value, int *data );
void GetFloatv( enum value, float *data );
void GetDoublev( enum value, double *data );
```

If a **Get** command is issued that returns value types different from the type of the value being obtained, a type conversion is performed. If **GetBooleanv** is called, a floating-point or integer value converts to **FALSE** if and only if it is 0 (otherwise it converts to **TRUE)**. If **GetIntegerv** (or any of the **Get** commands following) is called, a Boolean value is interpreted as either 1 or 0, and a floating-point value is rounded to the nearest integer, unless the value is an RGBA color component, a **DepthRange** value, a depth buffer clear value, or a normal coordinate. In these cases, the **Get** command converts the floating-point value to an integer according the **INT** entry of Table 14.21. A value not in [−1, 1] converts to an undefined value.

If **GetFloatv** is called, a Boolean value is interpreted as either 1.0 or 0.0; an integer is coerced to floating point, and a double-precision floating-point value is converted to single precision. Analogous conversions are carried out in the case of **GetDoublev.** If a value is so large in magnitude that it cannot be represented with the requested type, the nearest value representable using the requested type is returned.

Other commands exist to obtain state variables that are indexed by a target:

```
void GetClipPlane( enum plane, double eqn[4] );
void GetLight{if}v( enum light, enum value, T data );
void GetMaterial{if}v( enum face, enum value, T data );
void GetTexEnv{if}v( enum env, enum value, T data );
void GetTexGen{if}v( enum coord, enum value, T data );
void GetTexParameter{if}v( enum target, enum value, T data );
void GetTexLevelParameter{if}v(enum target, int lod, enum value, T data );
void GetPixelMap{ui us f}v( enum map, T data );
void GetMap{ifd}v( enum map, enum value, T data );
```

GetClipPlane always returns four double-precision values in *eqn*. These are the coefficients of the plane equation of *plane* in eye coordinates (these coordinates were computed when the plane was specified).

GetLight places information about *value* (a symbolic constant) for *light* (also a symbolic constant) in *data*. **POSITION** or **SPOT_DIRECTION** returns values in eye coordinates (again, these coordinates were computed when the position or direction was specified).

GetMaterial, GetTexGen, GetTexEnv, and **GetTexParameter** are similar to **GetLight,** placing information about *value* for the target indicated by their first argument into *data*. The *face* argument to **GetMaterial** must be either **FRONT** or **BACK,** indicating the front or back material, respectively. The *env* axgument to **GetTexEnv** must currently be **TEXTURE_ENV.** The *coord* argument to **GetTexGen** must be one of **S, T, R,** or **Q**. For Get**TexGen, EYE_LINEAR** coefficients are returned in the eye coordinates computed when the plane was specified. **OBJECT_LINEAR** coefficients are returned in object coordinates.

For **GetTexParameter** and **GetTexLevelParameter,** *target* must currently be either **TEXTURE_1D** or **TEXTURE_2-D,** indicating the target from which information is to be obtained. *Value* is a symbolic value indicating which texture parameter is to be obtained. The *lod* argument to **GetTexLevelParameter** determines which level-of-detail's state is returned. If the *lod* argument is less than 0 or if it is larger than the maximum allowable level of detail, the error **INVALID_VALUE** occurs.

For **GetPixelMap,** the map must be a map name from Table 14.9. For **GetMap,** *map* must be one of the map types described earlier, and *value* must be one of **ORDER, COEFF,** or **DOMAIN.GetTexImage** is used to obtain texture images.

```
void GetTexImage( enum tex, int lod, enum format, enum type,
   void *img ) ;
```

It is somewhat different from the other get commands; *tex* is a symbolic value indicating which texture is to be obtained. **TEXTURE_1D** indicates a one-dimensional texture, whereas **TEXTURE_2-D** indicates a two-dimensional texture. *Lod* is a level-of-detail number; *format* is a pixel format from Table 14.11; *type* is a pixel type from Table 14.10; and *img* is a pointer to a block of memory. **GetTexImage** obtains component groups from a texture image with the indicated level of detail, starting with the first group in the first row, and continuing by obtaining groups in order from each row and proceeding from the first row to the last. The number of components in a group is the number of components of the texture. The components are assigned among R, G, B, and A according to Table 14.13. These groups are then packed and placed in client memory as described earlier in the chapter. The row length and number of rows are determined by the size of the texture image (including any borders). Calling **GetTexImage** with *lod* less than 0 or larger than the maximum allowable causes the error **INVALID_VALUE**. Calling **GetTexImage** with format of **COLOR_INDEX, STENCIL_INDEX,** or **DEPTH_COMPONENT** causes the error **INVALID_ENUM**. The following command obtains the polygon stipple:

```
void GetPolygonStipple( void *pattern ) ;
```

The pattern is packed into memory according to the procedure given earlier for **ReadPixels.** It is as if the *height* and *width* passed to that command were both equal to 32, the *type* were **BITMAP,** and the format were **COLOR_INDEX.** Finally, a pointer to a static string describing some aspect of the current GL connection is returned by:

```
ubyte *GetString( enum name ) ;
```

The possible values for name are **VENDOR, RENDERER, VERSION,** and **EXTENSIONS.** The format of the **RENDERER** and **VERSION** strings is implementation dependent. The **EXTENSIONS** string contains a space-separated list of extension names The extension names themselves do not contain any spaces. The **VERSION** string is laid out as follows:

```
<version number><space><vendor-specific information>
```

The version number is either of the form *major-number.minor-number* or *major-number.minor-number.release-number*, where the numbers all have one or more digits. The vendor-specific information is optional. However, if it is present, it pertains to the server, and the format and contents are implementation dependent.

GetString returns the version number (returned in the **VERSION** string) and the extension names (returned in the **EXTENSIONS** string) that can be supported on the connection. Thus if the client and server support different versions or extensions, a compatible version and Est of extensions is returned.

Tables 14.24 and 14.25 indicate which state variables are obtained with what commands. State variables that can be obtained using any of **GetBooleanv, GetIntegerv, GetFloatv,** or **GetDoublev** are listed with just one of these commands—the one that is most appropriate given the type of the data to be returned. These state variables cannot

Table 14.24 Attribute Groups

Attribute	Constant
accum-buffer	**ACCUM_BUFFER_BIT**
color-buffer	**COLOR_BUFFER_BIT**
current	**CURRENT_BIT**
depth-buffer	**DEPTH_BUFFER_BIT**
enable	**ENABLE_BIT**
eval	**EVAL_BIT**
fog	**FOG_BIT**
hint	**HINT_BIT**
lighting	**LIGHTING_BIT**
line	**LINE_BIT**
list	**LIST_BIT**
pixel	**PIXEL_MODE_BIT**
point	**POINT_BIT**
polygon	**POLYGON_BIT**
polygon-stipple	**POLYGON_STIPPLE_BIT**
scissor	**SCISSOR_BIT**
stencil-buffer	**STENCIL_BUFFER_BIT**
texture	**TEXTURE_BIT**
transform	**TRANSFORM_BIT**
viewport	**VIEWPORT_BIT**
	ALL_ATTRIB_BITS
client	**can't be pushed** or **pop'd**

be obtained using **IsEnabled**. However, state variables for which **IsEnabled** is listed as the query command can also be obtained by using **GetBooleanv**, **GetIntegerv**, **GetFloatv**, and **GetDoublev**. State variables for which any other command is listed as the query command can be obtained only by using that command.

Table 14.25 State Variable Types

Type code	Explanation
B	Boolean
C_-	Color (floating-point R, G, B, and A values)
CI	Color index (floating-point index value)
T	Texture coordinates (floating-point s, t, r, q values)
N	Normal coordinates (floating-point x, y, z values)
V	Vertex, including associated data
Z	Integer
Z+	Non-negative integer
$Z_k, \_Z_{k*}$	k-valued integer ($k*$ indicates that k is minimum)
R	Floating-point number
R+	Nonnegative floating-point number
Rk	k-tuple of floating-point numbers
P	Position (x, y, z, w floating-point coordinates)
D	Direction (x, y, z floating-point coordinates)
M4	$4 * 4$ *floating-point matrix*
I	Image
A	Attribute stack entry, including mask
$n \times type$	n copies of type *type* ($n*$ indicates that n is minimum)

Unless otherwise indicated, multivalued state variables return their multiple values in the same order as they are given as arguments to the commands that set them. For instance, the two **DepthRange** parameters are returned in the order n followed by f. Similarly, points for evaluator maps are returned in the order that they appeared when passed to **Map1**. **Map2** returns **R**ij in the [($uorder$)$i + j$]th block of values.

Besides providing a means to obtain the values of state variables, the GL also provides a means to save and restore groups of state variables. The **PushAttrib** and **PopAttrib** commands are used for this purpose.

The following command takes a bitwise OR of symbolic constants indicating which groups of state variables to push onto an attribute stack:

> void **PushAttrib**(bitfield *mask*) ;

Each constant refers to a group of state variables. The classification of each variable into a group is indicated in the following tables of state variables.

The following command resets the values of those state variables that were saved with the last **PushAttrib:**

> void **PopAttrib**(void) ;

Those not saved remain unchanged. It is an error to pop an empty stack or to push onto a full one. Table 14.24 shows the attribute groups with their corresponding symbolic constant names.

The depth of the attribute stack is implementation dependent but must be at least 16. The state required is potentially 16 copies of each state variable, 16 masks indicating which groups of variables are stored in each stack entry and an attribute stack pointer. In the initial state the attribute stack is empty.

In Tables 14.24, and 14.25 a type is indicated for each variable. Table 14.25 explains these types. The type identifies all state associated with the indicated description. In certain cases only a portion of this state is returned. This is the case with all matrices, where only the top entry on the stack is returned; with clip planes, where only the selected chp plane is returned; with parameters describing lights, where only the value pertaining to the selected light is returned; with textures, where only the selected texture or texture parameter is returned; and with evaluator maps, where only the selected map is returned. Finally, a "-" in the attribute column indicates that the indicated value is not included in any attribute group (and thus cannot be pushed or popped with **PushAttrib** or **PopAttrib).**

Invariance

The OpenGL specification is not pixel exact. It therefore does not guarantee an exact match between images produced by different GL implementations. However, the specification does specify exact matches, in some cases, for images produced by the same implementation.

This part of the chapter identifies and provides justification for those cases that require exact matches.

Repeatability

The obvious and most fundamental case is repeated issuance of a series of GL commands. For any given GL and frame buffer state vector, and for any GL command, the resulting GL and frame buffer state must be identical whenever the command is executed on that initial GL and frame buffer state.

One purpose of repeatability is avoidance of visual artifacts when a double-buffered scene is redrawn. If rendering is not repeatable, swapping between two buffers rendered with the same command sequence may result in visible changes in the image. Such false motion is distracting to the viewer. Another reason for repeatability is testability.

Repeatability, although important, is a weak requirement. Given only repeatability as a requirement, two scenes rendered with one (small) polygon changed in position might differ at every pixel. Such a difference may be within the law of repeatability but is certainly not within its spirit. Additional invariance rules are desirable to ensure useful operation.

Multipass Algorithms

Invariance is necessary for a whole set of useful multipass algorithms. Such algorithms render multiple times, each time with a different GL mode vector, to eventually produce a result in the frame buffer. Examples of these algorithms include:

- erasing a primitive from the frame buffer by redrawing it, either in a different color or using the XOR logical operation; and
- using stencil operations to compute capping planes.[10]

On the other hand, invariance rules can greatly increase the complexity of high-performance implementations of the GL. Even the weak repeatability requirement significantly constrains a parallel implementation of the GL. Because GL implementations are required to implement *all* GL capabilities, not just a convenient subset, those that

---

[10] *Ibid.*, p. 158.

use hardware acceleration are expected to alternate between hardware and software modules based on the current GL mode vector. A strong invariance requirement forces the behavior of the hardware and software modules to be identical. This is something that may be very difficult to achieve if, for example, the hardware does floating-point operations with different precision than the software. What is desired is a compromise that results in many compliant, high-performance implementations and in many software vendors' choosing to port to OpenGL.

Invariance Rules

For a given instantiation of an OpenGL rendering context, three rules apply.

Rule 1 *For any given GL and frame buffer state vector and for **any** given GL command, the resulting GL and frame buffer state must be identical each time the command is executed on that initial GL and frame buffer state.*

Rule 2 *Changes to the following state values have no side effects (the use of **any** other state value is not affected by the change):*

The following are required:

- frame buffer contents (all bit planes);
- the color buffers enabled for writing;
- the values of matrices other than the top-of-stack matrices;
- scissor parameters (other than enable);
- writemasks (color, index, depth, stencil);
- clear values (color, index, depth, stencil, accumulation);
- *current values (color, index, normal, texture coords, edgeflag);*
- *current raster color, index and texture coordinates;*
- *material properties (ambient, diffuse, specular, emission, shininess).*

Strongly suggested:

- *matrix mode;*
- *matrix stack depths;*

- *alpha test parameters (other than enable);*
- *stencil parameters (other than enable);*
- *depth test parameters (other than enable);*
- *blend parameters (other than enable);*
- *logical operation parameters (other than enable);*
- *pixel storage and transfer state; and*
- *evaluator state (except as it affects the vertex data generated by the evaluators).*

Corollary 1 *Fragment generation is invariant with respect to the state values marked with* **bullets** *in Rule 2.*

Corollary 2 *The window coordinates (x, y, and z) of generated fragments are also invariant with respect to the following requirements:*

- *current values (color, color index, normal, texture coordinates, edge flag);*
- *current raster color, color index, and texture coordinates; and*
- *material properties (ambient, diffuse, specular, emission, shininess).*

Rule 3 *The arithmetic of each per-fragment operation is invariant except with respect to parameters that directly control it (the parameters that control the alpha test, for instance, are the alpha test enable, the alpha test function, and the alpha test reference value).*

Corollary 3 *Images rendered into different color buffers, either simultaneously or separately using the same command sequence, are pixel identical. (Note that this does not hold between X * pirmaps and color buffers, however.)*Hardware-accelerated GL implementations are expected to default to software operation when some GL state vectors are encountered. Even the weak repeatability requirement means, for example, that OpenGL implementations cannot apply hysteresis to this swap. It must instead guarantee that a given mode vector implies that a subsequent command is *always* executed in either the hardware or the software machine.

The stronger invariance rules constrain when the switch from hardware to software rendering can occur, given that the software and hardware renderers are not pixel identical. For example, the switch can be made when blending is enabled or disabled, but it should not be made when a change is made to the blending parameters.

Because floating-point values may be represented using different formats in different renderers (hardware and software), many OpenGL state values may change subtly when renderers are swapped. This is the type of state value change that Rule 1 seeks to avoid.

From Here

The intense interest expressed within the WWW community during 1995 (especially the last six months) for a visualized interface to bring virtual reality to the Internet and the Web has exploded beyond all expectations. Part III and following chapters will present those visions as to what the Web community wants to be able to do with VRML.

Chapter 15 will begin this visionary journey by taking a brief tour of proposed VRML research projects and systems. Other chapters will follow with a discussion of VRML applications and other futuristic related research projects and proposals.

PART III

Results and Future Directions

Proposed VRML Systems

This chapter begins the visionary quest of briefly visiting the numerous proposed VRML research projects and systems. The chapter guides you through the development of ongoing realistic VRML research projects and proposals from the newly developed Active VRML to VRML behaviors. Keep in mind, though, that the VRML technology is not yet stable. Therefore some of these research projects and proposals could drastically change in design and functionality at any time.

Adding Behavior to VRML

The German National Research Center for Information Technology (GMD) agrees with most other writers of proposals that interaction and behavior are essential for the future of VRML, since without them, real VRML applications will not be possible. However, the GMD thinks that most existing approaches are not flexible enough. Most of them provide mechanisms that are either specialized or not powerful enough to support complex behavior.

On first sight, the GMD approach seems to be much more complex than the existing ones. Nevertheless, it is just the formal specification that is more complicated. If you look at the examples, you will realize that the behavior specifications are actually very short and simple.

GMD's Goals

Simplicity

The designer of a VRML world should be able to add behavior to virtual world objects without any knowledge of programming. It should be possible to define even complex behaviors with simple mechanisms.

Reusability

One major goal of GMD's approach is to support reusability. Behaviors (especially complex ones) once realized should be easily applied to new artifacts (virtual world objects).

Dynamics

The behavior mechanism should be flexible enough to apply a single behavior to several artifacts at the same time. It should even be possible to apply existing behaviors to new entities joining the virtual world dynamically.

Authoring

GMD's approach supports the interactive modeling of interactions and behavior. Even complex interactions or interaction hierarchies can easily be applied to virtual worlds or parts of them. In the future this could even be done by using an interactive tool.

Scripting

GMD thinks that scripting languages are necessary to realize VRML applications, but they are not needed for most (more than 90 percent) of the object behaviors. However, the GMD model also provides the possibility of including arbitrary scripting languages.

Sharing

In a distributed multiuser virtual world, special mechanisms to support shared interactions and behavior are required. The GMD approach can easily be extended to support multiuser interactions, as well as synchronized shared behavior. Sharing behavior is performed by using a generalized *dead reckoning* mechanism.

This approach is based on an interaction model GMD developed for collaborative distributed virtual environments, not in particular for VRML. The model was presented at the ACM SIVE95 (Iowa City) and was adapted for VRML, which is used as an evaluation platform.

Artifacts

GMD proposes to add a new node type, which is guaranteed to be kept by the internal representation of the browser. Thus it can be addressed during the lifetime of the world. An Artifact node will traverse its children similarly to the new-style Separator node.

An Artifact node (like a Separator node) may have arbitrary children. However, all transformations are combined into a single child. Only the last property node of each type is traversed. Transformations and properties apply before shape nodes and subgroups. Subgroups are traversed after all other nodes. Thus property changes within subgroups do not influence the nodes of the Artifact node or any node above it. We could also think of a more restrictive Artifact node, where children will be forced to meet the required order, and only one child of each property node will be allowed

Subclassing

Subclassing provides the possibility of creating new classes within a VRML file and using them later as if they were built-in nodes. GMD's main purpose here was to provide a possibility of realizing new behavior classes and inheriting new classes from existing ones. There are some differences to the prototyping mechanism proposed by SGI, but GMD can also think of extending its approach in this direction.

Events

GMD's behavior approach is based entirely on an object-oriented event model. It achieved a high flexibility by providing the user with built-in event objects and the additional possibility of adding arbitrary user-defined events within a VRML file. GMD is aware of the fact that many people do not like the idea of having an additional type of objects that have to be specified within VRML. But it gives GMD the possibility of specifying behavior in a much more flexible and artifact-independent way.

Behavior

GMD's behavior model is based on the subclassing mechanism. It allows the user to define arbitrary new behavior nodes (classes) by combining behavior components. Behavior nodes— whether used to compute user interactions or independent artifact behavior—can always be assembled from a basic set of components. These basic components can be subdivided into the classes triggers, actions, engines, semantic, activate, deactivate, scripts, and sensors.

By providing specialized or preconfigured realizations of certain components, most common behaviors can be realized with minimal effort. However, more complex behavior can still be realized by assembling those components but will usually be based on more powerful, configurable ones.

Distributed Behavior

These are some very rough ideas to extend the behavior model to support multiuser interactions (several users interact with the same artifact concurrently), as well as synchronized distributed behavior. Support for shared distributed multiuser worlds can easily be integrated within GMD's approach by adding two modified components types: shared trigger and synchronized engines.[1]

MultiUser Representation of Virtual Worlds to Support VRML

In a cooperative, virtual organization teams of users can be formed at will to share and interact with abstract artifacts and to communicate with one another through these artifacts. In such a world users can be aware of one another's activities, interact with shared objects and have their own 3-D representation (or embodiment). This part of the chapter shows how multiple users can be supported by using VRML/HTTP. The GMD describes how VRML can be extended and

---

[1] Wolfgang Broll, *Adding More Behaviors To VRML*, GMD-German National Research Center for Information Technology, wolfgang.broll@gmd.de, December 6, 1995.

supported with extended clients and servers to provide mechanisms for awareness, embodiment, and access control.

The key distinction between CSCW (Computer Support for Cooperative Work) systems and applications aimed at individual computer users is that CSCW systems allow users to coordinate their activities around a group of tasks. The form of coordination is very loose. Users might use social protocols or a model, as in work-flow systems. Social protocols are currently the most popular way of supporting user coordination, as they allow users to develop methods of cooperation and coordination that can be tailored to their specific tasks. The goal of the work at GMD is to show how virtual reality and VRML can be used to enhance CSCW applications. GMD research shows how VRML/HTTP can be used as a basis for this aim by supporting multiple users. GMD wants to establish the cooperative context in which a multiple-user VRML/HTTP architecture would be used.

What are the artifacts that GMD might wish to model in VRML to support cooperating users? Many CSCW systems attempt to provide analogs of the features of real-world organizations. However, to adequately support social and organizational protocols, GMD needs to provide some underlying mechanisms with which users can establish their own cooperation environment. GMD needs to provide mechanisms that support important concepts, such as:

- awareness,
- access control,
- group membership, and
- version control.[2]

Most existing work on multiuser virtual reality has concentrated on visualizing the first two items. In virtual reality awareness is more graphic: Users are present as visual objects, or embodiments. We can actually see who is around, what they are doing, and which artifacts they are working on (see Figure 15.1). The spatial model takes this further and allows users to control what they see and how they are seen. Users can set a focus on vision and sound, and they can also set an aura, which defines when they become visible (or audible) to

---

[2] Wolfgang Broll and David England, *Bringing Worlds Together: Adding Multiuser Support to VRML*, GMD-German National Research Center for Information Technology Institute for Applied Information Technology, (wolfgang.broll@gmd.de; david.england@gmd.de), D-53754 Sankt Augustin, Germany, 1995.

Figure 15.1 Multiuser Virtual World

others. In conventional systems access control is usually displayed by showing that objects or commands are either available or not. Commonly unavailable commands are grayed out. The idea of boundaries in VR takes the idea of graying out further by representing the access state of objects by different graphical properties. So, for example, a completely inaccessible object may be hidden behind a wall. An object that is visible but not accessible may be shown behind a window. When GMD wants a user to be aware of the existence of an object but not its details, it may hide the object behind frosted glass. The boundaries idea mixes access control and awareness. This demonstrates one of the benefits of VR for CSCW. GMD can combine (with careful design) many properties and mechanisms in the visualization of one object and thus give more information to users.

VRML provides an additional medium for visualizing awareness and access control. Visualizations can, of course, be provided in two dimensions, but they produce greater clutter of limited display space. The third dimension and the dimension of time provide the means for viewing more attributes simultaneously. For example, suppose we have a virtual library in which the users are embodied and the query from shared bibliographic searches is visualized. In such a scenario

GMD can spread the results of the query into, for example, a pyramid. Users can be seen moving about this pyramid and and watch them as they choose individual artifacts returned by the query. Different users librarian and readers—may have different styles of embodiment. Readers may find that some artifacts are not accessible to them; their visualization represents the state of their accessibility (by boundary objects). Another user might make a further refining query that changes the population of the data landscape. Other users may come in and out of the system and become visible to their co workers.

However before GMD can provide VRML models that visualize awareness and access features, it first needs to examine the existing model of distribution. In the current vision of the World Wide Web information is shared only in that multiple users are able to simultaneously view pages put up by many providers. The users are just browsers of the information provided, and interaction is limited to following links or completing forms. The control of information remains largely with the information provider. The traditional client-server model of distribution supports this type of information exchange well. However, for truly cooperative work, such as that researched at GMD, researchers need to support awareness and access control as described earlier. Some Web products, such as Virtual Places for Windows, from Ubique, provide a crude notion of awareness, but this is not adequate. In addition, there are requirements for the consistency of views on a virtual world that cannot be met by the current WWW architecture.

GMD is examining how VRML could be extended to support cooperative, multiuser worlds on the Internet. GMD stresses cooperative in addition to multiuser worlds, as shown in Figure 15.1.[3] Many systems are multiuser but not cooperative; that is, users cannot coordinate their activities through the system. GMD is also examining how cooperation can be supported without radically altering VRML. Radical changes are unacceptable for an emerging standard. Ideally, GMD feels, it should be able to provide a smooth transition from the existing, isolated-client model to a communicating-clients model.

What are the functional requirements for a VRML/HTTP basis for GMD's virtual library world? First, it needs to be able to create a VRML scene graph of the preceeding query result. This can be done with

---

[3] Wolfgang Broll, *Adding More Behaviors To VRML*, GMD-German National Research Center for Information Technology, wolfgang.broll@gmd.de, December 6, 1995.

current technology. Individual users could then view the scene graph. However, as VRML objects (currently) have no behavior they could not interact with the objects (unless they were links). The addition of behaviors to VRML would support interaction with the artifacts and the representation of access to artifacts, which could be given different behaviors when chosen by different users. As users joined the system, GMD could create a VRML scene graph of their embodiment and add that to the query scene graph. However, this updated scene graph would be visible only to the user currently joining and to later users. For existing users to be made aware of the new user would require the server (or other clients in a peer-to-peer approach) to notify the connected clients. This is not part of the WWW architecture. However, work at GMD by the BSCW project (Basic Support for Cooperative Work) shows how this might be done by modifying servers and clients so that server-to-client notification is possible. Now as users move about the virtual world, other users would need to be made aware of their changes in position. Again, GMD would need some form of server-to-client notification of these changes.

The problem of the distribution of artifacts in virtual worlds can be tackled at two levels. First, there are problems of multiuser access to documents and how changes to shared documents might be managed. Second, there is the question of how the visualization of objects in a shared space might be kept consistent. Some existing work has looked at the problems of distributed virtual environments. For example the DIS protocol has been used to support distributed applications with more than 300 participants. However, this requires the use of a dedicated network. In further enhancements to NPSNET (based on DIS), it is shown how multicasting can be used to reduce network and computing requirements. In this part of the chapter we will discuss GMD's use of multicasting to support multiuser VRML. NPSNET is limited to military simulations, and this limitation is most evident in its restriction to the use of dead reckoning for propagate changes. For the wider spectrum of VR applications, GMD needs to move toward distributing behaviors.

In the rest of this chapter we will look in more detail at GMD's approaches to distributing changes to user representations and how interactions on artifacts may be distributed. The focus here is on the topology and protocol of communications between server and clients. Finally, we will look at some proposals for further extension to VRML in terms of object naming and multiuser interactions.

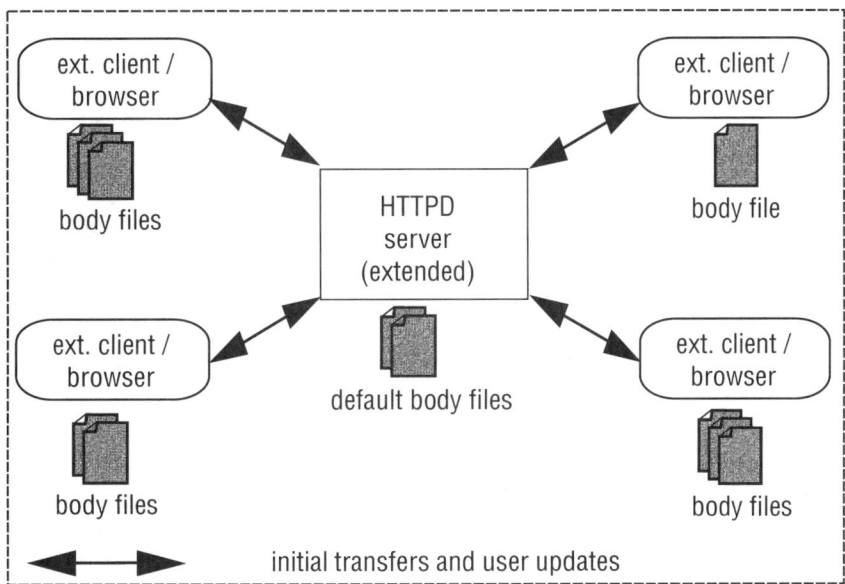

Figure 15.2 Multiuser Support Using Direct Client/Server Connections

Multiuser Representation

Let's look at GMD's two approaches to supporting several users using VRML, based on slight extensions to the existing HTTP protocol and servers. The two approaches are very different.

Minimal-Changes Approach

GMD's first approach requires only minimal changes to VRML clients/browsers, such as WebSpace or WorldView, and slight extension to the HTTPD server. Most of the server extensions might even be realized by CGI scripts. All clients communicate directly with the server.

Each user can define his or her own representation within a local VRML file (myBody.wrl). The browser will use this file or even several files for different user representations (see Figure 15.2).[4] A user might be presented by a human model within an office environment but a space ship representation when in a solar system world. However,

---

[4] *Ibid.*

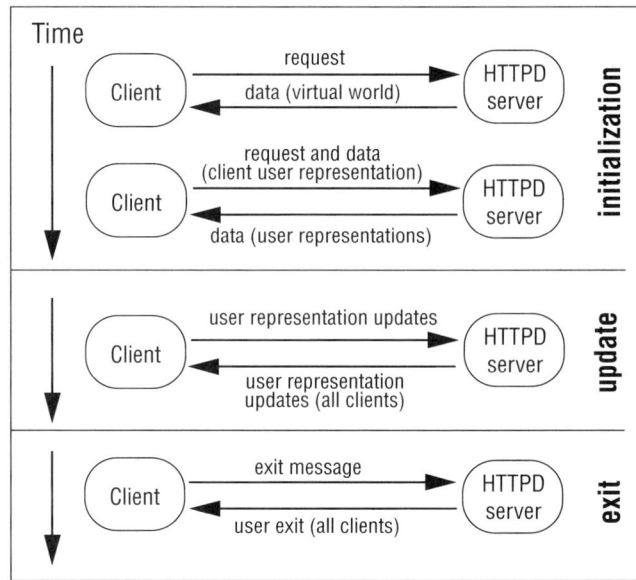

Figure 15.3 Extended Protocol for Multiuser Support

multiuser-capable browsers should also provide at least one default user representation.

The protocol extensions used to distribute user representations and to update their locations (or even other attributes) will be described later (see Figure 15.3).[5]

The browser first sends a request for the world description to the server. The server returns the VRML file. This is the standard mechanism used to transmit VRML files by HTTP. If the browser supports user representations, it sends a request for the representations of the other users along with the location (position/direction) and, if available, local representation of the user. The multiuser-capable server will return the current locations of other users in the same world, followed by their individual representations. User representations for a specific world might be provided by the author of the world. The server will send the data received from the browser to all other participants of the world. The local browser then adds the incoming user representations to the local scene graph. It sends any updates on the location of the local user to the server (using some kind of threshold

---

[5] *Ibid.*

or a dead-reckoning mechanism to reduce network load) and listens for updates on other user locations from the server. As soon as the local browser moves to another virtual world location (VRML file), it sends a quit message to the server. The server eliminates the user from the world and distributes this information among the participants. The server should also realize a time-out mechanism to eliminate users who have not updated their positions for a certain time. Additionally, the server may limit the total number of displayed user embodiments or the number of users participating in the world.

Caching might be used to reduce the amount of transmitted data. Servers (or even browsers) may keep user representations for a certain time to reduce retransmission when the user returns to a previous page. Servers might also use the transmitted user representation if the browser switches to another document on the same server.

The approach allows arbitrary user representations of a theoretically unlimited number of users for each world. However, servers of popular sites will very quickly become a bottleneck, since they have to handle the communication of all participants of all provided multiuser worlds.

It would be preferable if the server could also add user representations to pages requested by clients not capable of multiuser support. Currently the user description cannot be included within the virtual world description, since the naming mechanism used in VRML is not general enough to identify different users and different types of user representations. Thus VRML could be extended to allow the identification of a subtree of the scene graph as a user or the server distinguishes between the different clients; it would include the user embodiments as parts of the scene graph by default (this can be realized within a simple CGI script). Or VRML could send those embodiments separately on request to multiuser-capable clients.

Multicast Approach

GMD's second approach, very different from the first one, moves many tasks from the server to decentralized components. As shown earlier, central servers can very quickly become a bottleneck of a distributed system, especially when adding further enhancements, such as interaction within shared worlds. The central-server approach is no longer suitable, since it is not scalable. The second approach uses the multicast mechanism, which has already proved to be suitable for large-scale interactive multiuser virtual environments, such as NPSNET and DIVE.

The initial setup of the connections is the same as in the first approach: The browser contacts the server to receive the VRML page. Afterward the client will introduce itself as a user to the server, and the server will respond by sending the user embodiment files of the current users. Along with this, the client receives a multicast address and port number. The multicast address will usually refer to the server; the port number to the individual world. However, in large virtual worlds or when separating groups of users by replicated worlds, different relations might be used. The browser now sends its current user description, including the location, to the mutlicast address. All participants, as well as the server, get the new user information from the multicast address. The browser now listens to the multicast address for updates of other user representations, for new users, and for quit messages of existing users. A time-out mechanism can be provided by the server as in the first approach. In this case the server sends the quit message to the multicast address instead of to the client.

This approach reduces server communication dramatically, since the update messages are sent by clients. Thus they are reduced to necessary updates only. Additionally, sending the messages directly via the multicast address increases the average update time significantly, since the messages need not be redistributed by the server (see Figure 15.4).[6]

Compared to the average network load based on browsing through VRML pages, or even HTML pages, the number of messages in a multiuser virtual world will be significantly higher. Instead of loading a new page every few minutes, updates will be necessary at least every few seconds.

Using the using traditional client/server connections, a small number of participants in a multiuser virtual world would make it impossible for the server to realize realistic (almost real-time) updates of user representations. Multicast has been proved to be suitable for this task. In contrast to symmetrical (non-server based, systems without any central components) distributed multiuser VR systems, GMD's second approach still includes a central server. But this server is used to provide a uniform address to "dial in" the world (to get the multicast address) and to provide all participants with the same set of

---

[6] *Ibid.*

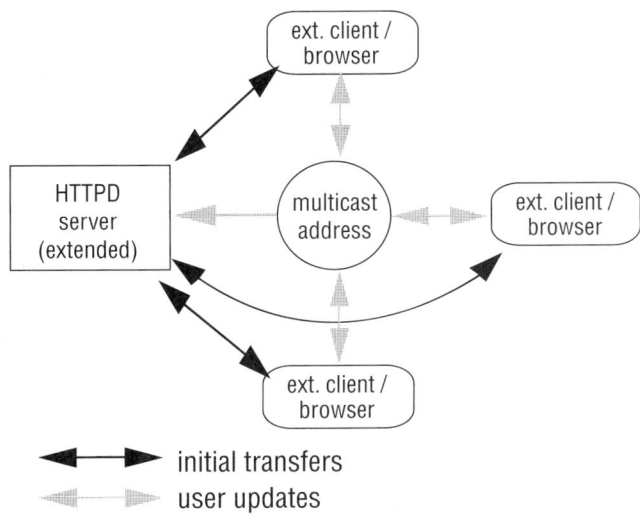

Figure 15.4 Multiuser Support Using Multicast Groups

virtual world contents. These services cannot be provided for frequently changing (connecting, disconnecting) hosts. Within specialized systems, such as NPSNET, such problems do not occur, since they are limited to a certain kind of application. Within its limited world (military simulation), all entities are well defined, so each participating site can use a fixed database to set up the world. But this approach is not to be suitable for general-purpose virtual environments, especially when sites participate at worlds for a rather short period.

Sharing and Distributed Interactions

Real distributed, multiuser, virtual environments require sharing of not only a static world and dynamic user representations but also interactions. So users should be able to change the virtual world or parts of it and have these modifications distributed among all current and future participants of the specific world. Other users should realize who is participating in the shared world and what the participants are doing—was referred to earlier as *awareness*.

One problem, well known from distributed databases and from existing distributed VR systems, is that of providing consistency among the different sites. Another problem, specific to VRML, is the implementation of user movement between different worlds. Users should be able to move easily between different worlds. Portals seem to be a more adequate metaphor for that purpose than simple links. This issue was very controversial during the specification of VRML but was not resolved. Moving objects or entities (currently parts of the scene graph) from one world to another is an important issue, which has to be addressed within this topic.

Let's look at GMD's approach to handling the sharing of objects and interactions and allowing users to exchange objects as well as their own representations between several worlds. The approach is an extension of the multicast approach.

Realizing Consistency of Virtual Worlds

Before we look at possible solutions to managing access in distributed VRML-based systems and to keeping distributed virtual worlds consistent, let's look at GMD's answer to the question Why do we need access control at all? There are several examples of multiuser applications in the VR context and in the CSCW context. These examples show that access management can be solved on social rather than on technical mechanisms. Imagine a group of users standing in front of a virtual whiteboard: Only one user writes at the whiteboard at any time, so no access control is necessary. If you extend this to a large virtual world (or even a MUD), this world will be completely anarchistic but might still work.

However, another example that shows some problems which might occur when consistency among worlds or views of worlds is not supported. Imagine a user who wants to move an object (a picture in his or her virtual office). Thus he or she will grab the object, move it, and release it. The object should now be placed at the new location. If we allow several people to change and modify parts of the world, without any consistency control, a second user might also grab the object within his or her local copy of the world at the same time. When one of the users releases the object and the object's final position is distributed among all sites, the other user's view will certainly be distorted. The object will appear at a new location, while he or she is supposed to have grabbed it. Thus it is sometimes very important to define and realize a certain level of access control. GMD has some possible solutions. Let's review their advantages and disadvantages.

1. *No Access Management*

If no access management is provided, each client is allowed to change the scene graph independently. All modifications are posted to the multicast address and distributed among the other clients and the server. This method is very fast, since no additional information other than the modifications of the scene graph has to be distributed. For that reason it might be used for the modification of worlds, where reliability of modifications and consistency among the worlds is not a major requirement. Consistency cannot be guaranteed, since concurrent access is not detected. Additionally, modifications of the virtual world may arrive at the individual client sites in different orders.

2. *Active Locking without Acknowledge*

Active locking without acknowledging requires at least three times as many messages as without any access management (see Figure 15.5).[7] Object modifications or a block of them have to be preceded by a locking message on the specific objects. After the distribution of the modifications, a release message has to be distributed. Locks are not acknowledged by the individual clients or by the server. But the server will manage multiple locks on the same object. Different kinds of locks might be used to support various kinds of reliability requirements. Locks should not be understood to guarantee absolute access to an object. This kind of lock has failed in most cooperative environments. GMD sees locks, rather, as a guarantee of achievable consistency, based on a prediction of the client's future activities. This mechanism provides a kind of soft locks, which may be broken for the price of a certain loss of consistency.

However, this scheme may lead to rejections of locking requests. Thus an appropriate message can be sent to the client to reset its lock. Additionally, the client might send a request to the server to restore the object. The server will also distribute the current lock status to all new clients joining the world. Again the server will be responsible for releasing a lock after a certain timeout and to achieve consistency.

---

[7] *Ibid.*

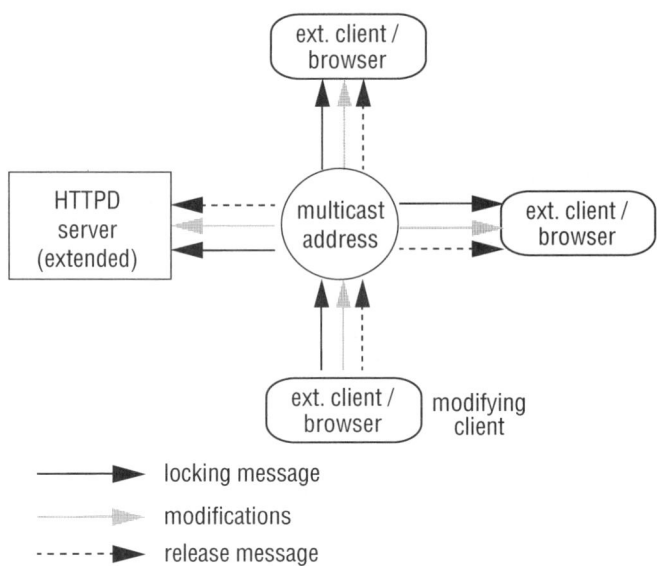

Figure 15.5 Active Locking without Acknowledging

3. *Active Locking with Acknowledge*

Active locking with acknowledgment requires only small extensions to the previous method. The main difference is that the server always sends an acknowledge message of the lock to the client (see Figure 15.6).[8] This is an improvement over sending an acknowledge message to every client. The latter would either cause an unnecessary heavy load on the multicast address or require that each client be able to communicate with all other clients directly (peer to peer).

This would then require the distribution of all client addresses and heavily increase the load on the locking client. Additionally, the locking phase would be extended to an unacceptable length, and clients not capable of locking or with slow network connections would slow down the whole process.

4. *Decentralized Access Management*

The mechanisms discussed are based on a central access management provided by the server. In a large-scale virtual environment

---

[8] *Ibid.*

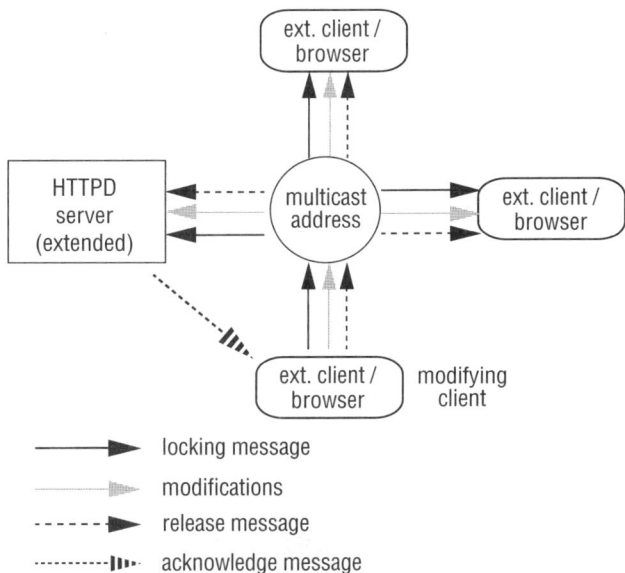

Figure 15.6 Active Locking with Acknowledge

including a large number of participants, the server will again become a bottleneck. System performance will decrease, even when using the multicast distribution mechanism, since access control is performed entirely on the server.

Decentralized mechanisms to manage access control include migration and master entities. Migration does not seem to be very useful in the VRML context, since the graphical representation of all virtual world contents has to be locally available. Also, VRML does not provide any additional object representation. Nevertheless, migration has proved suitable even for distributed VR (in the AVIARY system). It might be a solution, as soon as object identification and naming are solved within VRML in an appropriate way, and objects may hold more information than just a graphical representation.

Master entities provide a mechanism for flexible access in a distributed system. Access control for each part of the virtual world (objects, artifacts, or just subtrees of the scene graph) is located at potentially different sites. The object copy at the managing site (also called the owner of the object) is called master entity. When changes to certain objects are closely related to their owners, this method provides a very fast mechanism, even in distributed systems. If access has to be provided for different sites (clients), but it's concentrated at each time to one of them, master entities (object ownerships) can be migrated.

In a central server system, pure master-entity mechanisms are not appropriate. As there might not be any clients at all, the server has to be the owner of all master entities, at least at startup time. Clients can request ownerships from the server. The server keeps track of the current owner and gets the master entity back by migration, disconnection of the client, or after a timeout. So far, there is almost no difference to the locking schemes described before. But master entities might also be transferred directly from one client to another. This can be done by using the multicast connection, since all clients and the server always have to know the current owner of the object.

When supporting multiple locks for each object, migration cannot be used as a general mechanism to provide access for sites other than the current owner. For that reason, the owner has to provide server functionality for access management. This can be achieved either by direct (peer-to-peer) connections between the two sites or via the multicast address. Both solutions raise some problems. Direct connections require the distribution of all participants' addressees and may cause a heavy load on some participating sites (especially when they own several master entities). Using the multicast address will increase the load of all participants, even those for which the access for this particular object is not of any interest. The main problem with this kind of decentralized access management is to find an appropriate algorithm to decide under which conditions master entities (rights) are relocated to achieve a good performance.

Beyond the access mechanisms shown here, there exist several more. These could be applied to support multiuser virtual worlds. But they do not seem to be suitable for smooth VRML/HTTP extensions.

GMD will now try to review the different approaches to get an idea of the final approach, which may be used for future VRML releases. On the one hand, many virtual worlds will not need any kind of access control, since consistency is not a major problem if users use social protocols. This allows the server to stay almost passive after the initialization phase and for that reason reduces server and network load. On the other hand, at least for some objects of the world (including avatars) or for certain kinds of interactions (grabbing, moving), consistency is important. Thus it should be possible to specify consistency either on an object (subgraph) level or on an interaction level. This will require extensions to the VRML specification or will have to be included in the interaction and behavior specification, respectively.

As long as GMD distinguishes between servers and clients (a more or less centralized system), decentralized access mechanisms do not seem to be advantageous especially since all virtual world contents are originally located at the server. However, this may change if all users have a basic common library of objects on their local system. Thus a participating site (server/client) would have to supply only some special objects.

For the central server architecture, a rather simple approach should be used. GMD thinks that access should not be restricted by default, but it should be possible to manage access on a soft lock mechanism, if required.

Moving Objects and Users Through Multiple Worlds

Another important issue to the realization of multiple users and interactions is the question, How can users and object move among several worlds? Currently VRML uses hyperlinks realized by Anchor nodes to switch to other virtual worlds. With some late extensions of the specification, it is possible to specify the destination location in the new world, if it is another VRML page. The term *portal* is used to specify a special kind of link, potentially bidirectional, and also capable of connecting points within the same world. However, a portal can always be realized by a pair of hyperlinks specifying the world and the position in the appropriate counterpart. It has to be part of the client realization to provide mechanisms to avoid unnecessary reloading of pages.

Since portals and links connect different worlds or parts of them, they are closely related to the movement of user representations and objects among such worlds. In GMD's approach user representation is provided by the client and sent to the server for each page separately. However, as mentioned earlier, user movements among several worlds on the same server should be cached to reduce network transfers.

Moving objects can be realized by the same mechanism. The object, or even several objects, become parts of the user representation. They are distributed along with it but have to be identified as independent objects. The user needs to be able to drop objects in a world so that they can be manipulated or modified by other users. However, picking, grabbing and dropping objects will require further extensions to VRML to realize interaction and behavior. This is not part of this chapter. Additionally, some extensions are necessary to specify whether objects can be removed or just copied and whether it is possible to add objects to a world. Authors of virtual worlds might also want to specify objects or parts of their worlds so that they can be neither removed nor copied. But since all transferred VRML data is accessible, restrictions could be applied only to the unexpected copying or removing of objects. This would not allow an author to restrict access to his or her virtual world data (although this might be useful for some commercial use of VRML in the future).

Further Extensions

This part of the chapter presents some GMD extensions to the VRML specification as well as its approach for multiuser support. The VRML extensions can simplify the management of users and artifacts and enforce the possibilities of distributing multiuser world descriptions to standard (not multiuser-capable) browsers.

User and Artifact Naming and Identification

As already mentioned, users or user representations and objects or artifacts should be identified within a scene graph to support the described functionality. Currently there are two methods of doing this within the VRML specification: info nodes and the DEF keyword.

Although Info nodes are already widely used by browsers (such as WebSpace) to set up browser parameters, they should not be used to identify structures of the scene graph (otherwise, GMD could represent almost every node as an Info node). They should be used to include safe comments on nodes into the scene graph.

The DEF keyword, currently used to name nodes, could be used to identify a single user: DEF User Separator {...}. But with multiple users (as in the server), the naming convention has to be extended (Userl, User2, etc.). When several user representations are provided for the same user, names can become unreadable (User1 Car, User2b, etc.), especially since there is no way of identifying a user or to set a user type that can be used by the server to select the appropriate user representation for the current scene. In a cooperative world users will need to get more information on the individual user or its organization.

Since GMD supports individual user representations, Anchor nodes might be used as parts of the user embodiment to point to the user's personal home page or his or her organization.

The key requirements for working together in shared virtual worlds are awareness and access control. Without these, coworkers have great difficulties coordinating their activities. They need to be aware of the presence and actions of others. They need to be aware of the state of shared artifacts and interactions on those artifacts. Authors who are also coworkers need to be able to restrict access according to the demands of the shared tasks. GMD can use VR models within the VRML/HTTP framework to support these requirements.

Distributed Interactive Virtual Environment {DIVE}

DIVE is an Internet-based multiuser VR system in which participants navigate in 3-D space and see, meet, and interact with other users and applications. The DIVE software is a research prototype covered by licenses. Binaries for noncommercial use, however, are freely available for a number of platforms. The first DIVE version appeared in 1991.

The SICS DIVE is an experimental platform for the development of virtual environments, user interfaces, and applications, based on shared 3-D synthetic environments. DIVE is especially tuned to multiuser applications, in which several networked participants interact over the Internet.

DIVE is based on a peer-to-peer approach with no centralized server, where peers communicate by reliable and nonreliable multicast, based on IP multicast. Conceptually the shared state can be seen as a memory shared over a network, where a set of processes interact by making concurrent accesses to the memory.

Consistency and concurrency control of common data (objects) are achieved by active replication and reliable multicast protocols. That is, objects are replicated at several nodes, where the replica is kept consistent by being continuously updated. Update messages are sent by multicast so that all nodes perform the same sequence of updates.

The peer-to-peer approach without a centralized server means that as long as any peer is active within a world, the world, along with its objects, remains alive. Since objects are fully replicated (not approximated) at other nodes, they are independent of any one process and can exist independently of the creator.

The dynamic behavior of objects may be described by interpretative scripts in DIVE/Tcl that can be evaluated on any node where the object is replicated. A script is typically triggered by events in the system, such as user interaction signals, timers, and collisions.

Users navigate in 3-D space and see, meet, and collaborate with other users and applications in the environment. A participant in a DIVE world is called an *actor* and is either a human user or an automated application process. An actor is represented by a body-icon (or avatar) to facilitate the recognition and awareness of ongoing activities. The body-icon may be used as a template on which the actor's input devices are graphically modeled in 3-D space.

A user "sees" a world through a rendering application called a *visualizer* (the default is currently called Vishnu). The visualizer renders a scene from the viewpoint of the actor's eye. Changing the position of the eye or changing the eye to an another object will change the viewpoint. A visualizer can be set up to accommodate a wide range of I/O devices, such as an HMD, wands, datagloves, etc. Further, it reads the user's input devices and maps the physical actions taken by the user to logical actions in the DIVE system. This includes navigation in 3-D space, clicking on objects, and grabbing objects.

In a typical DIVE world a number of actors leave and enter worlds dynamically. Additionally, any number of application processes (applications) exist within a world. Such applications typically build their user interfaces by creating and introducing necessary graphical objects. Thereafter they listen to events in the world, so that when an event occurs, the application reacts according to some control logic.

The software is a research prototype and is therefore provided on an as-is basis, with no provisions for support or future enhancements.

Behavior Representation

VRML is a recently defined standard for representing 3-D scenes on the World Wide Web. The phrase VRML refers to a currently active effort to extend VRML to the realm of behavior. The format described here is based on technology developed at BE Software Company (BE), which is making this preliminary specification public in order to contribute to the VRML V2.0 debate and also as a first step toward making the format and its browsing technology widely available.

This part of the chapter outlines a proposed extension of VRML that covers behavior. This format, called BEF (for behavior format), can be viewed as a frontal attack on the problem originally posed by the concept of VRML V2.0 in that it embeds behavioral descriptions directly into the format as a new kind of data.

In practice, VRML V2.0 may well end up being defined as a standardized API for modifying the rendered world, together with hooks that allow a variety of mechanisms for defining behavior to transmit what they need over the Web and to access the API. The virtue of the latter approach is that it will not lock in a scheme for behavior representation at a stage when most technology of this kind is quite immature, compared to rendering technology. If the API approach is taken and yields good results, what BE has to propose here will fit in well as one possible scheme for representation of behavior. The generality of the proposal and the fact that it based on technology that is relatively well tested and has been in commercial use for a number of years should make it a candidate for the next stage of standardization—VRML V3.0 or VRML V2.0 in the case that the API step is skipped.

Principal Features of BEF

Here are the principal features of BEF:

- *Legibility and (comparative) simplicity.* Like HTML and VRML, a BEF file is comprehensible, with a little study, to any computer-literate newcomer. The caveat is that real expertise may be required to understand particular behaviors whose definition exploits specialized knowledge.
- *Full expressiveness.* BEF has the same level of expressive power as the current generation of object-oriented languages.
- *Full efficiency.* Due to the strong typing available in BEF, its algorithmic content can be implemented via fast pseudocode interpretation without overhead beyond that imposed by any interpreter.
- *Clean integration of behavioral objects with other objects.* Behavioral information can be embedded in any object, and any object can be embedded within a behavioral description.

- *Simple and uniform mechanisms for hierarchical assembly, disassembly, and abstraction of systems.* Any system built using the BEF formalism can always be used as a component in a larger system.
- *A VRML extension, not modification.* A VRML file is a legal BEF file that happens not to include behaviors.
- *Inclusion of HTML documents.* Since they can appear within BEF, this allows behaviors to be embedded into HTML in the same manner as they are embedded into the geometric world. Thus the links and forms of the HTML portion of a BEF document can trigger behaviors relating to the geometric world, and vice-versa.

BEF supports the definition of behavior for many purposes, including:

- simulation of physical systems;
- interactions with the user;
- computation of geometry from parametric descriptions;
- definition of rules for rendering, such as computed (rather than predefined). levels of detail; and
- communication of behavioral descriptions between browsers for distributed applications.[9]

The technology underlying BEF has been developed during more than a decade of work in the domain of simulation at BE Software and previously at SILMA Incorporated (now a division of Adept Technologies). The expressiveness of BEF can be judged from the fact that the products from BE Software are written largely in the programming formalism of BEF itself. SILMA's extensive range of simulation products was written almost entirely in a language called SIL (which is BEF's predecessor) and which BEF extends. Current products from BE Software implement a binary format for behavior with similar content and structure to BEF as proposed here but with a basis in Open Inventor rather than VRML.

---

[9] *Format For Representing Behavior,* The BE Software Company, 1995.

VRML Extension Process

The process by which VRML is extended to BEF can be divided into the following major steps:

1. introduction of a way of naming a child in the context of its parent (rather than in the context of the entire file, as in DEF/USE);
2. introduction of new nodes for the following types: primitive types (real, string, integer), the type ntype of all types (so that definitions of types and classes can appear within the node graph), a root class for behavior, behavior subclasses defined by algorithmic programming (control structures, functions, the HTML type, collection types, and references;
3. extension of the format to cover dynamic objects whose class membership may change over time;
4. definition of a collection of primitive operations on the node graph, and on the available data types;
5. definition of the BEF model of time and concurrency;
6. definition of node types supporting user interaction; and
7. introduction of classes for kinematic links and for motion in kinematic and Cartesian space.[10]

The classes and their operations listed in step 7 are expressed within BEF by ordinary BEF files, so they can be regarded as content *in the format* rather than part *of the format*. Nonetheless, motion and kinematics are central to many potential applications, so it is worthwhile proposing a standard treatment.

It would be possible to use syntax in the VRML style for all of the types listed in step two. For example, the semantics of HTML could be preserved while replacing tag/end-tags by VRML node syntax. However, there is no benefit beyond a superficial uniformity to be gained by such a transformation. So HTML nodes within BEF use ordinary HTML syntax, except for the addition of a new tag for embedding behavior (the tag <behavior>). The same consideration applies to algorithmic objects, for which BE chose a conventional syntax based on Pascal.

---

[10] *Ibid.*

References are the mechanism by which objects are symbolically named from within other objects. A reference is a kind of path name in the name space generated by the child-naming facility just alluded to. Within algorithmic objects, constants, variables, classes, and functions are most often designated by using references rather than simple names. Use of references has the effect that all symbolic naming is hierarchical and is localized in an explicit way within the node graph. This in turn means that assembling and disassembling node graphs that include behavior can be done in a uniform fashion.

Separable Aspects of this Proposal

BEF is defined in several parts. Modifications or replacements of some parts are possible without affecting the benefits yielded by others.

Naming and Assembly

The core idea behind BEF is to provide a unified name space for objects of all kinds, including behaviors and types, with an architecture that supports assembly of systems from components. These notions are defined via extensions to the VRML syntax. Needless to say, the details of how these extensions are accomplished can be modified without affecting the content they convey.

The Object Model

At the next level is an object model that defines the structure of objects denoted by BEF files. The proposed model is fairly simple but incorporates significant flexibility not found in standard object models, such as that underlying C++ and SmallTalk, or in newer variants, such as the Java model.

The Language

BEF uses the syntax and control structures of Pascal for the textual programming part of its definition of behavior. Alternative choices of syntax and control structures, based on C syntax, for example, would be possible. However, this possibility does not extend to other, less superficial, aspects of the language.

BEF integrates the language very tightly with the naming scheme underlying the format as a whole and with the object model. The scheme used in the language to name functions, classes, and variables is exactly the same hierarchical scheme employed for naming throughout the format. The possibility of doing assembly of behavioral systems from components depends on this uniformity. So although syntax and control structures could be changed without major effects, it is just not the case with C, C++, Tcl, or Java. They all have their own naming schemes and object (or data) models and could be substituted easily. An API allowing manipulation of BEF structures from external code could be defined, with useful consequences. But this would not by itself unify the external language's classes, variables, and functions with the corresponding entities within BEF.

Predefined Operations

BEF defines a base set of types for primitive entities, such as numbers and strings, for geometry and for elements of the node graph. It also defines the operations available for modifying the node graph. These are independent aspects of the proposal. In particular, if VRML V2.0 specifies an API different from what BE has anticipated, adjustment of BEF to fit this specification should not have major effects on other aspects of the proposal.

User Interaction

VRML V1.0 is a derivative of the file format for Open Inventor from SGI. Open Inventor defines node types, called SoSelection and SoDragger for user interaction. SoSelection supports graphical selection by the user of objects on the screen, and the various subclasses of SoDragger support graphical manipulations of objects, such as moving and scaling.

BEF includes nodes for interaction that follow the Open Inventor model, with the difference that the behaviors resulting from dragging or selection are defined within BEF rather than (as in the case of Open Inventor) as C++ callbacks. So, for example, the behavior resulting from selection of an object is simply a field of the Selection node.

Details on this aspect of the BEF specification are still under consideration. The prototype implementation directly imports Open Inventor primitives, and a design that reduces Open Inventor dependencies is still in progress.

Kinematics and Motion

The aspects of BEF defined so far constitute an adequate foundation on which to build behavioral descriptions. Additional capabilities can be built within BEF as libraries of standard objects, classes, and behaviors—libraries that can be distributed on the WWW. Nonetheless, several basic mechanisms and behaviors are relevant to such a large fraction of potential applications that it is worthwhile standardizing them at the outset. Kinematic linkages and motion in Cartesian space are mechanisms of this kind.

High-Performance Rendering Capabilities of High-End VR Systems

This part of the chapter presents i3-D from the Center for Advanced Studies, Research and Development in Sardinia (CASRDS). This system combines the 3-D input and high-performance rendering capabilities of high-end virtual reality systems with the data-fetching abilities of network browsers. Using a *spaceball*, the user can intuitively navigate inside the three-dimensional data while selecting 3-D objects. All of this is done with the mouse trigger's requests for access to remote media documents that can be text, still images, animations, or even other 3-D models. Time-critical rendering techniques allow the system to display complex 3-D scenes at high and constant frame rates, making it possible to use it in the context of large-scale projects. The system is currently being used at *CERN* as a visualization and data management tool for the design of the new Large Hadron Collider and at *CRS4* for the *Virtual Sardinia* project. The i3-D is available through anonymous ftp from various sites on the Internet.

The World Wide Web has rapidly become one of the fundamental structures of the Internet. It adds a universal organization to the data made available on the Internet. It allows a view of all hosts as a unique data source, as well as treating all of this data as parts of a single structured document. The HyperText Markup Language used to describe WWW documents has its roots in SGML, a format for printed media, and is therefore intrinsically suited for the composition of bidimensional documents composed of textual and pictorial data.

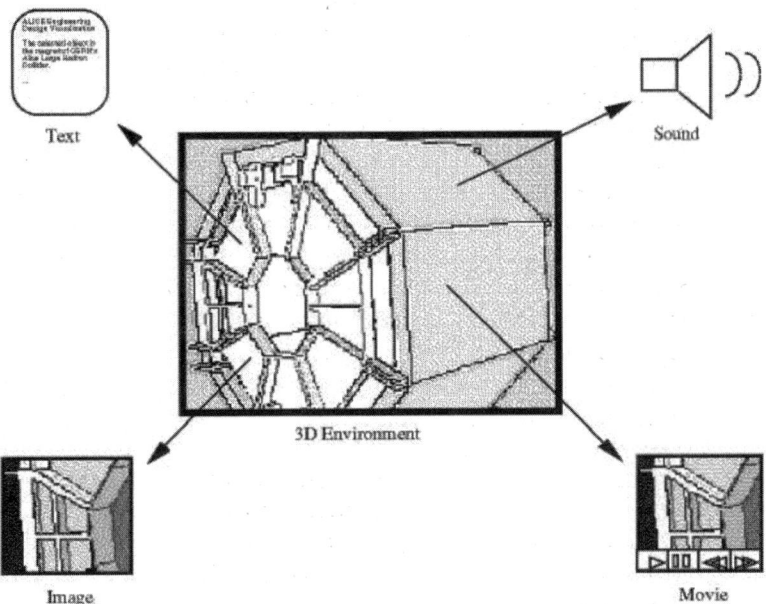

Figure 15.7 Annotated 3-D Model

Other types of media, such as digital video and sound, are accessible through the invocation of external specialized viewer applications.

The availability, at relatively low costs, of 3-D graphics workstations that are able to display scenes composed of thousands of polygons at interactive speeds has made it possible to bring 3-D data to the World Wide Web through specialized viewers for this new kind of media. However, it has been rapidly identified that the effectiveness of interactive 3-D viewers in communicating information about 3-D environments can be dramatically enhanced by attaching digital media annotations to the environment's models. By allowing users to interactively recall and view the attached information by selecting objects of interest during navigation, the interactive 3-D viewer becomes a natural front end for querying information about 3-D models. Annotations can refer to text, still images, animations, or even other 3-D models, thus exploiting all of the digital media capabilities of current workstations, as shown in Figure 15.7.[11]

---

[11] Jean-Francis Balaguer and Enrico Gobbetti, *A High-Speed 3-D Web Browser*, Center for Advanced Studies, Research and Development In Sardinia, Via Sauro, 10, I-09123 Cagliari, (balaguer@cern.ch and gobbetti@cs.umbc.edu), 1995.

As an example, in architectural CAD applications the virtual building representation could be augmented by linking to its various components the original drawings showing engineering details of the structure, photographs of the real site, and so on. The interactive 3-D model can therefore be used for data management purposes during the design phase. Information about the building can be presented to the client with maximum efficiency.

When exploring three-dimensional environments, navigation using interactive control of virtual camera motions is often the most important form of three-dimensional interaction. Multiple degree-of-freedom input devices, such as the s*paceball* and the 3-D mice, allows interactive 3-D viewing with continuous viewpoint control. Hence providing visual cues are of invaluable help in understanding the structure of the three-dimensional data. It requires that images be rendered smoothly and quickly enough so that an illusion of real-time exploration of a virtual environment can be achieved as the simulated observer navigates through the model.

Characteristics of a 3-D Environment

To best perform its function, an interactive system for exploring annotated 3-D environments should combine the following characteristics:

- *Interactive 3-D viewing capabilities.* Effective exploration of a 3-D environment requires the ability to directly specify 3-D motions and the generation of enough depth cues to understand the structure of the 3-D world.
- *Time-critical rendering.* High feedback bandwidth and low response times are crucial for an interactive 3-D graphics system, where motion parallax is obtained only by means of high frame rates and continuous motion specification. In order to guarantee low response times when handling large datasets, the system must be able to adoptively trade rendering and computation quality with speed.
- *Distribution and* sharing. With the World Wide Web, two standard mechanisms for defining distributed documents and sharing information over a network have been introduced: the *uniform resource locator (URL)* mechanism, for locating information

residing anywhere within the Internet domain, and the *Hypertext Transfer Protocol (HTTP)*, for rapid file transfer. By using URLs to represent annotations on 3-D models and H= to fetch the documents on request, annotated 3-D environments can be distributed and shared over the Internet.

- *Multiple kinds of annotations.* Users should be given the possibility of attaching to 3-D models the kinds of digital media that are best suited to convey their ideas. The 3-D system should thus be able to recognize multiple kinds of annotation and to communicate with other viewers capable of handling the various digital media (images, hypertexts, movies). The hypertext transfer protocol HTTP uses the multipurpose Internet mail extensions {MIME}, which describe a set of mechanisms for specifying and describing the format of Internet message bodies for request and response message formats. This allows servers to use a standard notation for describing document contents. When a client receives a MIME message, the content is used to invoke the appropriate viewer by analyzing the mailcap configuration file that describes the bindings between document types and viewer applications. That way, it is easy to add local support for a new format without changes to the Web browser.[12]

A number of systems currently have some of these capabilities, but none possesses them all. Visual simulation and virtual reality systems, such as *dVISE* and *Performer*, strive at providing support for high-performance rendering and multidimensional input but do not permit the annotation of 3-D models with other digital media. *Iris Annotator* is a 3-D view-and-markup utility that allows users to attach digital media annotations to 3-D objects. However, *Iris Annotator*'s documents are monolithic and cannot be shared over the network. WWW browsers, such as *NCSA Mosaic* or *Netscape,* are good at fetching many kinds of data over the Internet but are currently not able to deal with annotated 3-D objects. To overcome this limitation, 3-D geometry viewers such as *Geomview,* have been connected to WWW browsers to permit the inclusion of 3-D models as elements of a hypertext document. The new language, VRML, has been defined to serve as a standard for defining 3-D scenes hyperlinked with the World Wide Web. VRML browsers, such as WebView from the San Diego Supercomputing Center and

---

[12] *Ibid.*

WebSpace from Silicon Graphics, are both based on Open Inventor and have been developed recently. The integration of a standard network browser with a 3-D geometry viewer offers an ideal basis for a system geared towards the exploration of annotated 3-D environments. However, the geometry viewers that have been integrated with the WWW to date, as well as available 3-D browsers, are limited to mouse-based interaction. They are also not able to ensure constant high frame rates when dealing with large datasets, thus limiting their appropriateness for large-scale projects.

The i3-D System

The i3-D system for the interactive exploration of annotated 3-D models described using VRML or a proprietary file format incorporates the 3-D input and high-performance rendering capabilities of a high-end VR system with the data-fetching abilities of network browsers. The system is currently being used at CERN as a visualization and data management tool for the design of the new Large Hadron Collider and at CRS4 for the Virtual Sardinia project. Beginning in June 1995, unsupported binaries of i3-D were also made publicly available by *CRS4* through anonymous ftp at the address *ftp//sgvenus.cern.ch/pub/I3-D*. Mirror sites are listed in *http://sgvenus.cern.ch/i3-D/i3-D-install.html*.

Future work will concentrate on improving the interaction with the system by providing additional navigation metaphors and by adding the capability to annotate the 3-D scene interactively. CASRDS finds it also necessary to widen the range of supported file format for data importation. Improved visual cues for media annotations are planned so that the user can quickly identify the type of the annotation and determine whether it has already been accessed.

The i3-D tool allows the exploration of three-dimensional scenes annotated with any kind of media documents that can be accessed on the World Wide Web. It is implemented on top of *XI* I and *OpenGL*. It runs on Silicon Graphics workstations. Using a 3-D device, the user can explore its three-dimensional data and request access to other documents. When retrieving and displaying media documents, i3-D handles directly the three-dimensional data and collaborates with NCSA Mosaic or Netscape for other types of media.

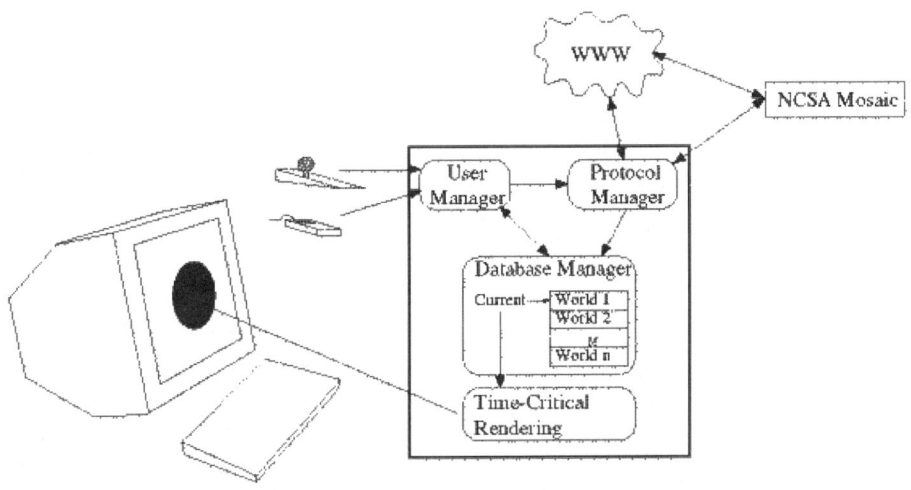

Figure 15.8 Application Overview

Application Overview

As shown in Figure 15.8, i3-D is composed of the following units:

- The *user manager* is responsible for sensing and analyzing the user's movements and actions in order to recompute the new viewpoint position and orientation; to trigger retrieval of media documents by the protocol manager; and, to navigate among the stack of worlds that is maintained by the database manager;
- The *protocol manager* is responsible for the retrieval of media documents from the World Wide Web. Three-dimensional scenes as well as inlined worlds and textures are loaded locally and transmitted to the database manager. This is all happening while requests for other types of media documents are delegated to a WWW browser *(NCSA Mosaic or Netscape)* for retrieval and display by the most adequate viewer application;
- The *database manager* maintains the state of the 3-D scenes in order to provide the necessary geometrical information and visual attributes for the user and rendering managers to perform their tasks. It also maintains a stack of the scenes that

Figure 15.9 Device Configuration i3-D

have been visited to reach the current world and provides fast world switching on user manager's requests;

- The *rendering manager* is responsible for the generation of the visual representation *of the current* scene at a high and constant frame rate.[13]

User Interaction

The i3-D's device configuration uses a spaceball and a mouse as input devices for the continuous specification of the camera's position and orientation to select objects and access media documents, respectfully. Both of a user's hands can therefore be employed simultaneously to input information (Figure 15.9).[14] Additionally, abstractions of the 2-D mouse motions into 3-D transformations are also provided so that navigation is possible when no *spaceball* is available. A pop-up menu and keyboard commands are used to control various visibility

---

[13] *Ibid.*

[14] *Ibid.*

flags and rendering modes. The ability to continuously specify complex camera motions in an intuitive way, together with high visual feedback rates, provides an accurate simulation of motion parallax. This is one of the most important depth cues when dealing with large environments.

To explore three-dimensional worlds, the user can either free-fly, using an eye-in-hand metaphor, or can inspect the scene or the currently selected object, using a slide-on-ball thus allowing the camera to rotate around its interest point, by placing it at the center of the object's (or scene's) bounding box. While navigating inside a three-dimensional scene, the user can request additional information by accessing media documents associated with geometrical data. Since annotated geometries are drawn with a blue silhouette, they can be easily identified. Selecting an annotated geometry by clicking on its visual representation with the mouse triggers the document retrieval and display. For three-dimensional scenes, i3-D maintains a stack of active worlds. Through keyboard commands, the previous or next world in the stack can be made current, thus providing a means to quickly navigate among active worlds.

Application Examples

Defining annotated three-dimensional scenes using the i3-D file format is made easy by the simple three-dimensional scene shown in Figure 15.10.[15] The scene is composed of three textured cubes. The material and the triangle list defining the cube's geometry are shared among the 3-D objects. Each cube is associated with a different texture image that is accessed through HTTP. Media annotations link the cubes to three documents: the cube on the left references an HTML document; the center cube references an MPEG movie; and the cube on the right references an alternative 3-D scene.

1. *The CERN VENUS Project*

The European Laboratory for Particle Physics (CERN) is currently involved in designing its next-generation particle accelerator, namely, the Large Hadron Collider (LHC). In any project of this scale, the

---

[15] *Ibid.*

Figure 15.10 A Simple Annotated 3-D Scene

design phase is probably the most delicate one, as this is when some critical choices are to be taken that might dramatically affect the final results, timing, and costs. The ability to visualize the model in depth is essential to a good understanding of the interrelationships among the parts. An iterative design-optimization process can improve remarkably issues of space management and ergonomics. However, with the visual capability of the present CAD tools, it takes a fair amount of time and imagination to isolate eventual design faults. A pilot project, named VENUS (Virtual Environment Navigation in the Underground Sites) was started at CERN in January 1994. Its mandate was to produce a detailed virtual prototype of the LHC premises and to allow navigation and access to engineering data in the form of fly-through by natural interaction. The i3-D system is being actively used for the exploration of the virtual prototype. Figure 15.11 shows a snapshot of a typical i3-D session.[16]

The VENUS virtual prototype is entirely extracted from the original EUCLID CAD database. As soon as engineers add new drawings, these are extracted and converted to the i3-D format in two steps: First,

---

[16] *Ibid.*

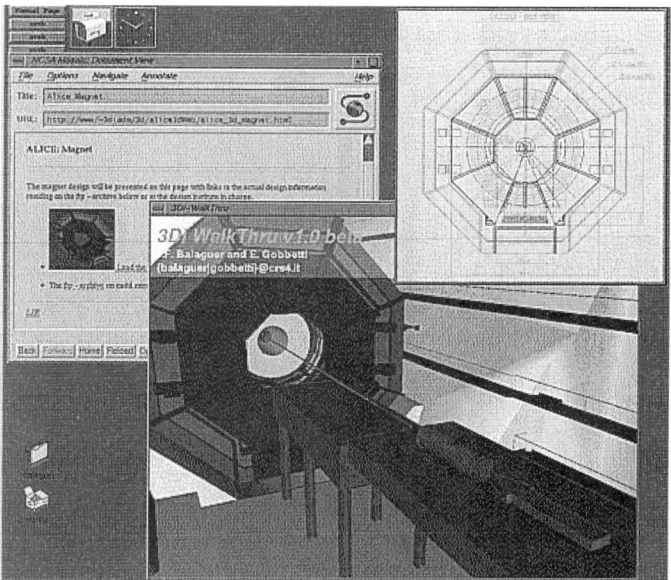

Figure 15.11 Exploring CERN Alice

EUCLID data is converted to Wavefront OBJ format; second, the resulting Wavefront objects are converted to i3-D and assembled into a scene. Some minor manual treatment is necessary at the moment to compensate for lack of some features (color and textures) in the EUCLID-to-Wavefront converter utility supplied by Matra-Datavision. Annotations that refer to various sources of information are then added by associating URLs to relevant 3-D objects. A further step is necessary to optimize the geometry for interactive navigation. All the process is fairly automatic and does not require major efforts, since the data conversion and optimization are handled by software utilities. The entire conversion process should be completely automated in the near future, triggered from the EUCLID side on any significant changes to the geometry. This way the virtual prototype will always reflect the latest state of the design.

The i3-D is made available to all CERN users. This allows any CERN user with a Silicon Graphics workstation to connect to the CERN server, to fly through the latest models of the detectors, and to inspect all the information attached to the three-dimensional model (latest CAD drawings, technical papers).

Figure 15.12 Exploring Sardinia

Objects in the scene are specified at one or two levels of detail. Perhaps the user specified an expected frame rate of 20 frames/second and a desired graphical load of 80 percent. This means that the user desired a constant frame duration of 50 ms, with 40 ms allocated to rendering and 10 ms for all other tasks. By combining hierarchical culling and level-of-detail selection, the system is able to adhere to the timing requirements.

2. *The Virtual Sardinia Project*

This project, under realization at CRS4, aims at providing on the Internet easily accessible information on the island of Sardinia, as shown in Figure 15.12.[17] Using i3-D, users can explore a 3-D model of the island, built from digital terrain model data textured with satellite images. Various 3-D markers are positioned on the surface of the terrain to indicate sites of interest. The interactive selection of one of these markers during navigation triggers the request for accessing a descriptive document. This occurs while the selection of

---

[17] *Ibid.*

a location on the terrain triggers the request to view a high-resolution version of the area surrounding the selected point.

The possibilities of i3-D are exploited to allow the exploration of detailed terrain models on a range of machines. To produce the i3-D description of the terrain, the original terrain data (a regular grid) is subdivided into subregions that can be drawn and culled independently. Each subregion is described at various levels of detail by transforming the original regular grid into simpler irregular triangular meshes through a decimation process that iteratively groups nearly coplanar polygons and simplifies them. Different tolerances for planarity checks are used to produce the various levels of detail. To avoid cracking problems, small tolerances are used at the borders of the subregions. In addition to the optimization of the geometric model, images that are to be used as textures are clipped and rescaled so as to have them fit into texture memory. All these optimizations are done automatically by a tool that takes as input the original digital terrain model, the satellite images, and, a list of descriptions of geographical location that have to be marked and associated to a hyperlink. Thanks to hierarchical culling and on-the-fly level-of-detail selection, the resulting model can be explored at interactive speed (more than 10 frames per second) on a Silicon Graphics Onyx RE2.

MPh 1a—{Metaphysical Modeling Language}

MPh is a proposal for a language to describe the metaphysics of various models of reality. The basis of MPh is the concept of an interaction between objects as an object type itself. An interaction consists of a list of actors, the effects of the action on each of the actors, and whether each of the actors has a choice. A field called mutability determines whether subclasses of the actor classes will be able to alter the implementation of the interaction. Using this model, a wide range of phenomena and belief systems can be simulated.

The intent of this theoretical language description is to stimulate discussion in the field of reality modeling. This gets down to those essential nitty-gritty questions of what is reality and what is the basis of our models of reality.

Physics is the study of interactions between objects. Physics and biology can be modeled by using MPh.

Interacting with Intelligent Objects with Simple Behaviors

Silicon Graphics has a goal to design a set of extensions to VRML that give the user a much richer experience than is now possible in VRML. SGI believes that the ability to interact with intelligent objects with simple behaviors, the ability to create animated 3-D objects, and the addition of sound into 3-D worlds will provide the rich, interactive experience that will enable a completely new set of applications of VRML.

SGI's design was guided by the following constraints (in rough order of priority):

- *Performance:* SGI believes that speed is a key to a good interactive experience, and that it is important to design the system so that VRML browsers will be able to optimize the VRML world.
- *Scalability:* SGI's goal is to allow the creation of very large virtual worlds. Any feature that limits scalability is unacceptable.
- *Composability* SGI wants to be able to compose VRML worlds or objects to create larger worlds. SGI assumes that it will be able to compose worlds that are created by different people simply by creating a metaworld that refers to the other worlds.
- *Authoring:* SGI assumes that sophisticated VRML authoring tools will be created and wishes to make it possible to perform most of the tasks necessary to create an interesting, interactive VRML world using a graphical user interface. SGI believes that VRML will not be successful until artists and creative people not interested in programming are able to create compelling, interactive VRML content.
- *Power:* SGI feels it must allow programmers to seamlessly extend VRML's functionality by allowing them to create arbitrary scripts/applets/code that can then be easily reused by the nonprogrammer.
- *Multiuser potential:* SGI expects VRML to evolve into a multiuser shared experience in the near future, allowing complete collaboration and communication in interactive 3-D worlds. SGI has attempted to anticipate the needs of multiuser VRML, considering the possibility that VRML browsers might eventually need to support synchronization of changes to the world

by locking persistent distributed worlds, event rollback, and dead reckoning in the future.[18]

The essence of simple behaviors is changes to the world over time. With a single spectator interacting with the world, SGI identifies three sources of change: user events from some device, translated into affects on the 3-D world; time; and real-world sources of input, accessed through some scripting/logic language, perhaps by a process running synchronously to the VRML browser.[19]

SGI is proposing a model for describing how changes are communicated between objects in the VRML scene. Objects are defined to send or receive events or messages. The names and types of events that can be sent or received is defined by each object. A generic object (the Script node) is defined to allow user-defined processing and generation of events. This change-communication model is combined with a new prototyping capability that allows the encapsulation and reuse of objects, behaviors, or both.

For some applications of VRML (such as database visualization, scientific visualization, and possibly shared, multiuser, distributed worlds), it is desirable to allow the creation and modification of VRML scene graphs. SGI addresses this need by allowing arbitrary changes to the well-defined parts of the world.

VR Data Structures

In some of the previous HTML documents that the surfer may have browsed, there was mention of transport of graphical objects over the Web. Think about it. If you can transport a lamp over the Web, you can transport a room over the Net. If you can transport a room over the Net, you can transport a virtual environment over the Net—not just the picture or a set of pictures that can be pieced together to form a virtual reality scene, but the real unreal thing.

---

[18] Mitra, Yasuaki Honda, Kovichi Matsuda, Gavin Bell, Chee Yu, Chris Marrin, *Moving Worlds: Behaviors for VRML,* World Maker, Sony Computer Science Laboratory, and Silicon Graphics, December 11, 1995.

[19] *Ibid.*

Many systems bring you VR data structures. Most CAD and architectural systems are examples. Brigham Young University has the RLE format.

So, what do we need that they don't have? Consider this. Animation is just a moving picture of a dynamic situation. So we need dynamic information. One easy way to think of the problem is to classify it as a simulation problem. So we need simulation information, such as position, motion, state information; connectivity information; lists of static architectural/terrain constraints; and models for motion, feeding, interaction and their data elements. One of the goals of the BOLTS group is to generate such a data structure.[20]

Virtual Society Project

The Virtual Society Project (VSP) is an umbrella for a set of research projects within Sony CSL. The overall goal of the project is to investigate how the future online community will evolve.

It is CSL's belief that future online systems will be characterized by a high degree of interaction, support for multimedia, and, most important, the ability to support shared 3-D spaces. Users will not simply access textual-based chat forums but will enter into 3-D worlds where they will be able to interact with the world and with other users in that world.

CSL is looking at several issues. These issues include the basic networking structure, distributed consistency, continuous media support, and support for many hundreds of users.

CSL's original work was based on the DIVE system from SICS. CSL is currently collaborating with SICS to investigate how to support a DIVE-like system in a wide area Internet-based environment. CSL is also experimenting with Apertos running on ATM networks to investigate resource-related issues. CSL will eventually port itsshared 3-D platform to machines running Apertos.

CSL believes that the growth of the WWW and its open architecture is a perfect opportunity to further study a large scale shared 3-D space. To achieve this CSL is investigating how to merge its shared 3-D

---

[20] *Virtual Reality Standard Data Structure*, VR Data Structure, richards@marlin.nosc.mil, 1995.

infrastructure and the WWW. An initial draft proposal discusses an open architecture combining the WWW and the Virtual Society system.

Currently CSL interfaces to its shared 3-D world by using traditional 2-D screens. NaviCam is an investigation into hand-held access device that will free users from traditional desktop terminals.

CyberLab is a longer-term project that aims to pull together some of the other projects to investigate the use of shared 3-D spaces as support for CSCW. The main aim of CyberLab is to build a shared 3-D space that seamlessly integrates a virtual world and the real world.

There is considerable interest at CSL in agent-based computing. CSL is currently investigating how to apply A-Life techniques to create and evolve intelligent agents who inhabit the shared 3-D worlds.

Other Proposed VRML Systems

- *ActiveVRML*—Microsoft's Active Virtual Reality Modeling Language (ActiveVRML). It is a *descriptive* (also known as a *declarative* or *modeling*) framework for constructing interactive animations. Using ActiveVRML, one can create simple or sophisticated animations without programming in the usual sense of the word.

- *Database visualization and VRML*—an SGI proposal on how VRML can be used together with database technology to achieve on-the-fly world building and more intuitive representations of data sets.

- *Distributed virtual reality*—one of the hottest topics in virtual reality research. A lot of ideas have been tossed around in various newsgroups and mailing lists. This proposal is an attempt by the University of Waterloo to bring together some of the more interesting concepts and to organize them in a way that's easy to follow.

- *Division Ltd. products*—including dVS, the virtual reality operating environment; dVISE, a ready-to-use VR application providing a virtual design environment for traditional CAD users; the fully integrated ProVision range of affordable virtual reality platforms; and Pixel-Planes, the massively parallel rendering engine that offers new levels of visual realism and supercomputer performance to virtual worlds.

Recently there has been a great deal of discussion on the mailing lists about making VRML more object oriented. There has also been a lot of work done on adding behavior to VRML. However, there are still a number of unresolved issues that may prove to be sources of conflict. The University of Waterloo has a proposal to address some of these unresolved issues and to propose a way of making VRML more object oriented. This proposal is an attempt to gather and organize some ideas related to the idea of behavior in VR systems, particularly distributed (networked) VR systems. Many of these ideas have come from discussions on the Net.

Sony has a proposal consisting of a list of nodes that constitute its extensions to the current VRML V1.0 standard. The new proposed nodes describe scripting, object attributes, and sound features.

The Virtual Environment Systems Protocol from the DEC Computer Lab, Utah State University, for a protocol to handle multiple streams and sockets via TCP/IP, is intended for use with integrating VRML into these systems. Also being proposeed is virtual HTML, a modification of HTML in order to have it work in a stream rather than a document.

From Here

This chapter has presented proposals for many VRML systems that will be developed or are currently being implemented. The next chapter examines VRML concepts that would allow VR environments to be incorporated into the WWW, thereby allowing users to walk around and push through doors to follow hyperlinks to other parts of the Web. VRML is examined as a logical modeling format for nonproprietary platform-independent VR. The format describes VR environments as compositions of logical elements. Additional details are specified, using a universal resource naming scheme supporting retrieval of shared resources over the Network. The chapter closes with ideas on how to extend this to support virtual presence teleconferencing.

VRML Concepts

This chapter describes preliminary ideas for extending the World Wide Web to incorporate virtual reality (VR), the primary focus of this book. By the end of this decade, the continuing advances in price/performance will allow affordable desktop systems to run highly realistic virtual reality models. VR will become an increasingly important medium, and the time is now ripe to develop the mechanisms for people to share VR models on a global basis.

VR systems at the low end of the price range show a 3-D view into the VR environment together with a means of moving around and interacting with that environment. At the minimum you could use the cursor keys for moving forward and backward and turning left and right. Other keys would allow you to pick things up and put them down. A mouse improves the ease of control, but the realism is determined primarily by the latency of the feedback loop from control to changes in the display. Joysticks and spaceballs improve control but cannot compete with the total immersion offered by head-mounted displays (HMDs). High end systems use magnetic tracking of the user's head and limbs, together with such devices as 3-D mice and datagloves, to yet further improve the illusion.

Sound can be just as important to the illusion as the visual simulation: The sound of a clock gets stronger as you approach it. An airplane roars overhead crossing from one horizon to the next. High-end systems allow for tracking of multiple moving sources of sound. Distancing is the technique whereby you get to see and hear more detail as you approach an object. The VR environment can include objects with complex behavior, just like their physical analogs in the real world (drawers in an office desk, telephones, calculators, and cars). The simulation of behavior is frequently more demanding computationally than updating the visual and aural displays.

The virtual environment may impose the same restrictions as in the real world (gravity and restricting motion to walking, climbing up/down stairs, and picking up or putting down objects). Alternatively, users can adopt superpowers and fly through the air or even through walls with ease! When using a simple interface (a mouse), it may be easier to learn whether the range of actions at any time is limited to a small set of possibilities (moving forward toward a staircase causes you to climb the stairs). A separate action is unnecessary, as the VR environment builds in assumptions about how people move around. Avatars are used to represent the user in the VR environment. Typically these are simple disembodied hands, which allow you to grab objects. This avoids the problems in working out the positions of the user's limbs and cuts down on the computational load.

Platform Independent VR

Is it possible to define an interchange format for VR environments that can be visualized on a broad range of platforms from PCs to high-end workstations? At first sight there is little relationship between the capabilities of systems at either extreme. In practice many VR elements are composed from common elements (rooms have floors, walls, ceilings, doors, windows, tables, and chairs). Outdoors there are buildings, roads, cars, lawns, and trees, etc. Perhaps VAG can draw on experience with document conversion and the Standard Generalized Markup Language (SGML) and specify VR environments at a logical level, leaving browsers to fill in the details according to the capabilities of each platform.

The basic idea is to compose VR environments from a limited set of logical elements (chair, door, and floor). The dimensions of some of these elements can be taken by default. Others, such as the dimensions of a room, require lists of points (to specify the polygon defining the floor plan). Additional parameters give the color and texture of surfaces. A picture frame hanging on a wall can be specified in terms of a bitmapped image.

These elements can be described at a richer level of detail by reference to external models. The basic chair element would have a subclassification (office chair), which references a detailed 3-D model, perhaps in the DXF format.

Keeping such details in separate files has several advantages:

- High-level VR markup format can be simplified. This makes it easier to create and revise VR environments than with a flat representation.

- Models can be cached for reuse in other VR environments. Keeping the definition separate from the environment makes it easy to create models in terms of existing elements and saves resources.

- Models can be shared over the Net. Directory services can be used to locate and retrieve the model. In this way a vast collection of models can be shared across the Net.

- Alternative models can be provided according to each browser's capabilities.[1]

Authors can model objects at different levels of detail according to the capabilities of low-, mid-, and high-end machines. The appropriate choice can be made when querying the directory service (by including machine capabilities in the request). This kind of negotiation is already in place as part of the World Wide Web's HTTP protocol.

Limiting VR environments to compositions of known elements would be overly restrictive. To avoid this, it is necessary to provide a means of specifying novel objects, including their appearance and behavior. The high-level VR markup format should therefore be dynamically extendable. The built-in definitions are merely a shortcut to avoid the need to repeat definitions for common objects.

---

[1] David Raggett, *Extending WWW To Support Platform Independent Virtual Reality*, Hewlett Packard Laboratories (dsr@hplb.hpl.hp.com), 1995.

Universal Resource Locators (URLS)

The World Wide Web uses a common naming scheme to represent hypermedia links and links to shared resources. It is possible to represent nearly any file or service with a URL.

The first part of the URL always identifies the method of access (or protocol). The next part generally names an Internet host and is followed by path information for the resource in question. The syntax varies according to the access method given at the start. Here are some examples:

- http://info.cern.ch/hypertext/WWW/TheProject.html
  This is the CERN home page for the World Wide Web project. The prefix http implies that this resource should be obtained by using the hypertext transfer protocol (HTTP).
- http://cui_www.unige.ch/w3catalog
  This is the searchable catalog of WWW resources at CUI, in Geneva; it is updated daily.
- news:comp.infosystems.www
  This is the Usenet newsgroup comp.infosystems.www. This is accessed via the NNTP protocol.
- ftp://ftp.ifi.uio.no/pub/SGML
  This names an anonymous FTP server: ftp.ifi.uio.no, which includes information relating to the Standard Generalized Markup Language (SGML).[2]

The URL notation can be used in a VR markup language for referencing wire frame models, image tiles, and other resources—for example, a 3-D model of a vehicle or an office chair. Resources may be defined intentionally and generated by the server in response to the user's request.

Major museums could provide educational VR models on particular topics. Hypermedia links (to other parts of the Web) would allow students to easily move from one museum to another by walking through links between the different sites.

One drawback of URLs is that they generally depend on particular servers. VAG is working to provide widespread support for lifetime identifiers that are location independent. This will make it possible to

---

[2] *Ibid.*

provide automated directory services akin to X.500 for locating the nearest copy of a resource.

Multipurpose Internet Mail Extensions {MIME}

MIME describes a set of mechanisms for specifying and describing the format of Internet message bodies. It is designed to allow multiple objects to be sent in a single message, to support the use of multiple fonts plus nontextual material, such as images and audio fragments. Although it was conceived for use with e-mail messages, MIME has a much wider applicability. The hypertext transfer protocol HTTP uses MIME for request and response message formats. This allows servers to use a standard notation for describing document contents (image/gif for GIF images and text/html for hypertext documents in the HTML format). When a client receives a MIME message, the content type is used to invoke the appropriate viewer. The bindings are specified in the mailcaps configuration file. This makes it easy to add local support for a new format without changes to your mailer or Web browser. You simply install the viewer for the new format and then add the binding into your mailcaps file.

VAG anticipates the development of a public domain viewer for a new MIME content type: video/vrml. A platform-independent VR markup language would allow people to freely exchange VR models either as e-mail messages or as linked nodes in the World Wide Web.

VRML Issues

A major distinction appears to be indoor and outdoor scenes. Indoors, the scene is constructed from a set of interconnected rooms. Outdoors, you have a landscape of plains, hills, and valleys on which you can place buildings, roads, fields, lakes, and forests, etc. The following sketch is in no way comprehensive but should give a flavor of how VRML would model VR environments. Much work remains for VAG to turn this vision into a practical reality.

Indoor Scenes

The starting point is to specify the outlines of the rooms. Architects' drawings describe each building as a set of floors, each of which is described as a set of interconnected rooms. The plan shows the position of windows, doors and staircases. Annotations define whether a door opens inward or outward and whether a staircase goes up or down. VRML directly reflects this hierarchical decomposition with separate modeling elements for buildings, floors, rooms, doors, and staircases, etc. Each element can be given a unique identifier. The modeling for adjoining rooms uses this identifier to name interconnecting doors. Rooms are made up from floors, walls and ceilings. Additional attributes define the appearance (the color of the walls and ceiling). This would be the kind of plaster covering used to join walls to the ceiling, as well as the style of windows. The range of elements and their permitted attributes are defined by a formal specification analogous to the SGML document type definition.

Rooms have fittings: carpets, paintings, bookcases, kitchen units, tables, and chairs, etc. A painting is described by reference to an image stored separately (like inlined images in HTML). The browser retrieves this image and then applies a parallax transformation to position the painting at the designated location on the wall. Wallpaper can be modeled as a tiling, where each point on the wall maps to a point in an image tile for the wallpaper. This kind of texture mapping is computationally expensive, and low-power systems may choose to employ a uniform shading instead. Views through windows to the outside can be approximated by mapping the line of sight to a point on an image acting as a back cloth and effectively at infinity. Kitchen units, tables, and chairs, etc., are described by reference to external models. A simple hierarchical naming scheme can be used to substitute a simpler model when the more detailed one would overload a low-power browser.

Hypermedia links can be represented in a variety of ways. The simple approach used in HTML documents for depicting links is almost certainly inadequate. A door metaphor makes good sense when transferring to another VR model or to a different location in the current model. If the link is to an HTML document, an obvious metaphor is opening a book (by tapping on it with your virtual hand?). Similarly a radio or audio system makes sense for listening to a audio link, a television for viewing an MPEG movie.

Outdoor Scenes

A simple way of modeling the ground into plains, hills, and valleys is to attach a rubber sheet to a set of vertical pins of varying lengths and placed at irregular locations: $zi = fi(x, y)$. The sheet is single-valued for any x and y, where x and y are orthogonal axes in the horizontal plane. Smooth terrain can be described by interpolating gradients specified at selected points. The process is applied only within polygons for which all vertices have explicit gradients. This makes it possible to restrict smoothing to selected regions as needed.

The next step is to add scenery onto the underlying ground surface by texture wrapping—mapping an aerial photograph onto the ground surface. This works well if the end user is flying across a landscape at a sufficient height that parallax effects can be neglected for surface detail such as trees and buildings. Realism can be further enhanced by including an atmospheric haze that obscures distant details, such as plants. These come in two categories: pointlike objects, such as individual trees, and arealike objects, such as forests, fields, weed patches, lawns, and flower beds.

A tree can be placed at a given (x, y) coordinate and scaled to a given height. A range of tree types can be used (deciduous and coniferous). The appearance of each type of tree is specified in a separate model, so VRML needs only the class name and a means of specifying the model's parameters (in many cases defaults will suffice). Extended objects, such as forests, can be rendered by repeating an image tile or generated as a fractal texture, using attributes to reference external definitions for the image tile or texture. Other examples of extended objects include:

- water—streams, rivers, and waterfalls; ponds, lakes, and the sea. The latter involves attributes for describing the nature of the beach: muddy estuary, sandy, rocky, and cliffs.
- borders—fences, hedges, walls, etc., which are fundamentally linelike objects.
- roads—number of lanes, types of junctions, details for signs, traffic lights, etc.[3]

---

[3] *Ibid.*

Each road can be described in terms of a sequence of points along its center and its width. Road lights and crash barriers can be generated by default according the attributes describing the kind of road. Road junctions could be specified in detail. But it seems possible to generate much of this locally on the basis of the nature of the junction and the end points of the roads it connects: freeway exit, clover-leaf junction, four-way stop, roundabout, etc. In general, VRML should avoid specifying detail where this can be inferred by the browsing tool. This reduces the load on the Network and allows browsers to show the scene in the detail appropriate to the power of each platform. Successive generations of kit can add more and more detail, leading to increasingly realistic scenes without changes to the original VRML documents.

Most buildings (houses, skyscrapers, factories, filling stations, barns, silos, etc.) can be specified by using constructive geometry (as a set of intersecting parts, each of which is defined by a rectangular base and some kind of roof). This approach describes buildings in a compact style and makes it feasible for VRML to deal with a rich variety of building types. The texture of walls and roofs, as well as the style of windows and doors, can be defined by reference to external models.

A scene could consist of a number of parked vehicles (and other moving objects) and a number of vehicles moving along the road. Predetermined trajectories are rather unexciting. A more interesting approach is to let the behavior of the set of vehicles emerge from simple rules governing the motion of each vehicle. This could also apply to pedestrians moving on a sidewalk. The rules would be defined in scripts associated with the model and not part of VRML itself. The opportunities for several users to meet up in a shared VR scene are discussed later.

Distant scenery (a mountain range on the horizon) is effectively at infinity and can be represented as a backcloth hung in a cylinder around the viewer. It could be implemented by using bitmap images (in GIF or JPEG formats). One issue is how to make the appearance change according to the weather/time of day.

Outdoor scenes wouldn't be complete without a range of weather types (and sky)! Objects should gradually lose their color and contrast as their distance increases. Haze is useful for washing out details, as the browser can then ignore objects beyond a certain distance. The opacity of the haze will vary according to the weather and time of day. Fractal techniques can be used to synthesize cloud formations. The color of the sky should vary as a function of the angle from the sun and the angle above the horizon. For VRML the weather would be characterized as a set of predetermined weather types.

The illusion will be more complete if you can see more detail the closer (distancing) you get. Unfortunately it is impractical to explicitly specify VR models in arbitrary detail. Another approach is to let individual models to reference more detailed models in a chain of increasingly fine detail. A model that defines a lawn as a green texture can reference a model that specifies how to draw individual blades of grass. The latter is needed only when the user zooms in on the lawn. The browser then runs the more detailed model to generate a forest of grass blade.

Actions and Scripts

Simple primitive actions, such as the ability of the user to change position/orientation and to pick up/put down or press objects, are part of the VRML model. Other behavior is the responsibility of the various objects and lies outside the scope of VRML. Thus a virtual calculator would allow users to press keys and carry out calculations just like the real thing. This rich behavior is specified as part of the model for the calculator object class, along with details of its appearance. A scripting language (Java Script) is needed for this. But it will be independent of VRML; indeed, there could be a variety of languages. The format negotiation mechanism in HTTP seems appropriate to this, as it would allow browsers to indicate which representations are supported when sending requests to servers.

Achieving Realism

Another issue is how to provide realism without excessive computational demands. To date the computer graphics community has focused on mathematical models for realism (ray tracing with detailed models for how objects scatter or transmit light). An alternative approach could draw on artistic metaphors for rendering scenes. Paintings are not like photographs, and artists don't try to capture all details; rather, they aim to distill the essentials with a much smaller number of brush strokes. This is akin to symbolic representations of scenes. VAG may be able to apply this to VR. As an example, consider the difficulty in modeling the folds of cloth on your shirt as you move your arm around. Modeling this computationally is going to be very expensive; perhaps a few rules can be used to draw in folds when you fold your arms.

Virtual Presence Teleconferencing

The price performance of computer systems currently doubles about every 15 months. This has happened for the last five years, and industry pundits see no end in sight. It therefore makes sense to consider approaches that today are impractical but will soon come within reach.

A world without people would be a dull place indeed! VRML allows us to define shared models of VR environments, so the next step is to work out how to allow people to meet in these environments. This comes down to two parts:

- the protocols needed to ensure that each user sees an up-to-date view of all the other people in the same virtual location, whether this is a room or somewhere outdoors; and
- a way of visualizing people in the virtual environment. This in turn begs the question of how to sense each user—the expressions, speech, and movements.[4]

For people to communicate effectively, the latency for synchronizing models must be on the order of 100 milliseconds or less. You can get by with longer delays, but it gets increasingly difficult. Adopting a formal system for turn taking helps, but you lose the ability for nonverbal communication. In meetings it is common to exchange glances with a colleague to see how he or she is reacting to what is being said. The rapid feedback involved in such exchanges calls for high-resolution views of people's faces, together with very low latency.

A powerful technique will be to use video cameras to build real-time 3-D models of people's faces. As the skull shape is fixed, the changes are limited to the orientation of the skull and the relative position of the jaw. The fine details in facial expressions can be captured by

---

[4] *Ibid.*

wrapping video images onto the 3-D model. This approach greatly reduces the bandwidth needed to project lifelike figures into the VR environment. The view of the back of the head and the ears, etc., is essentially unchanging and can be filled in from earlier shots or, if necessary, synthesized from scratch to match visible cues.

In theory the approach needs a smaller bandwidth than conventional video images, as head movements can be compressed into a simple change of coordinates. Further gains in bandwidth could be achieved at a cost in accuracy by characterizing facial gestures in terms of a composition of identikit stereotypes (shots of mouths that are open or closed, smiling or frowning). The face is then built up by blending the static model of the user's face and jaw with the stereotypes for the mouth, cheeks, eyes, and forehead.

Although head-mounted displays offer total immersion, they also make it difficult to sense the user's facial expressions. They are also uncomfortable to wear. Virtual presence teleconferencing is therefore more likely to use conventional displays-together with video cameras mounted around the user's workspace. Lightweight headsets are likely to be used in preference to stereo or quadraphonic loudspeaker systems, as they offer greater auditory realism and avoid trouble when sound spills over into neighboring work areas.

The cameras also offer the opportunity for hands-free control of the user's position in the VR environment. Tracking of hands and fingers could be used for gesture control without the need for 3-D mice or spaceballs, etc. Another idea is to take cues from head movements. Moving your head from side to side could be exaggerated in the VR environment to allow users to look from side to side without needing to look away from the display being used to visualize that environment.

Where Next?

For workstations running the XI I windowing system, the PEX library for 3-D graphics is now available on most platforms. This makes it practical to start developing proof of concept platform–independent VR. The proposed VRML interchange format could be used within the World Wide Web or for e-mail messages. All users would need to do is to download a public domain VRML browser and add it to their mailcaps file. I am interested in getting in touch with people willing to collaborate in turning this vision into a reality.

From Here

As interest in computer graphics has grown, so has the desire to be able to write VRML applications that run on a variety of platforms—the premise of this chapter. The next chapter describes how VRML applications and other considerations have governed the selections and presentation of graphical operators in OpenGL.

The OpenGL Graphics Interface Design

OpenGL is an emerging graphics standard that provides advanced rendering features while maintaining a simple programming model. Because OpenGL is only for rendering, it can be incorporated into any window system (and has been, into the X Window System and a soon to be released version of Windows) or can be used without a window system. An OpenGL implementation can efficiently accommodate almost any level of graphics hardware, from a basic frame buffer to the most sophisticated graphics subsystems. It is therefore a good choice for use in interactive 3-D, 2-D graphics, and VRML applications.

This chapter describes how these and other considerations have governed the selection and presentation of graphical operators in OpenGL. Complex operations have been eschewed in favor of simple, direct control over the fundamental operations of 3-D and 2-D graphics. Higher-level graphical functions (such as virtual reality) may, however, be built from OpenGL's low-level operators. The operators have been designed with such layering in mind.

Computer graphics (especially 3-D graphics, and interactive 3-D graphics in particular) is finding its way into an increasing number of VRML applications, from simple graphing programs for personal computers to sophisticated modeling and visualization software on workstations and supercomputers. As the interest in computer graphics has grown, so has the desire to be able to write VRML applications that run on a variety of platforms with a range of graphical capabilities. A graphics standard eases this task by eliminating the need to write a distinct graphics driver for each platform on which the VRML application is to run.

To be viable, a graphics standard intended for interactive 3-D applications must satisfy several criteria. It must be implementable on platforms with varying graphics capabilities without compromising the graphics performance of the underlying hardware and without sacrificing control over the hardware's operation. It must provide a natural interface that allows a programmer to describe rendering operations tersely. Finally, the interface must be flexible enough to accommodate extensions so that as new graphics operations become significant or available in new graphics subsystems, these operations can be provided without disrupting the original interface.

OpenGL meets these criteria by providing a simple, direct interface to the fundamental operations of 3-D graphics rendering. It supports basic graphics primitives, such as points, line segments, polygons, and images, as well as basic rendering operations, such as affine and projective transformations and lighting calculations. It also supports advanced rendering features such as texture mapping and antialiasing.

Several other systems provide an API (application program interface) for effecting graphical rendering. In the case of 2-D graphics, the PostScript page description language has become widely accepted, making it relatively easy to electronically exchange and, to a limited degree, manipulate static documents containing both text and 2-D graphics. Besides providing graphical rendering operators, PostScript is also a stack-based programming language.

The X window system has become standard for UNIX workstations. A programmer uses X to obtain a window on a graphics display into which either text or 2-D graphics may be drawn. X also provides a means for obtaining user input from such devices as keyboards and mice. The adoption of X by most workstation manufacturers means that a single program can produce 2-D graphics or obtain user input on a variety of workstations by simply recompiling the program. This integration even works across a network: The program may run on one workstation but display on and obtain user input from another, even if the workstations on either end of the network are made by different companies.

For 3-D graphics, several systems are in use. One relatively well-known system is PHIGS (Programmer's Hierarchical Interactive Graphics System). Based on GKS (Graphics Kernel System), PHIGS is an ANSI (American National Standards Institute) standard. PHIGS (and its descendant, PHIGS+) provides a means to manipulate and draw 3-D objects by encapsulating object descriptions and attributes into a *display list* that is then referenced when the object is displayed or manipulated. One advantage of the display list is that a complex object need be described only once even if it is to be displayed many times. This is especially important if the object to be displayed must be transmitted across a low-bandwidth channel (such as a network). One disadvantage of a display list is that it can require considerable effort to respecify the object if it is being continually modified as a result of user interaction. Another difficulty with PHIGS and PHIGS+ (and with GKS) is lack of support for advanced rendering features, such as texture mapping.

PEX extends X to include the ability to manipulate and draw 3-D objects. PEXlib is an API employing the PEX protocol. Originally based on PHIGS, PEX allows *immediate mode* rendering, meaning that objects can be displayed as they are described rather than having to first complete a display list. PEX currently lacks advanced rendering features (although a compatible version that provides such features is under design) and is available only to users of X. Broadly speaking, however, the methods by which graphical objects are described for rendering using PEX (or, rather, PEXlib) are similar to those provided by OpenGL.

Like both OpenGL and PEXlib, Renderman is an API that provides a means to render geometric objects. Unlike these interfaces, however, Renderman provides a programming language (called a shading language) for describing how these objects are to appear when drawn. This programmability allows for generating very realistic-looking images, but it is impractical to implement on most graphics accelerators, making Renderman a poor choice for interactive 3-D graphics.

Finally, some APIs provide access to 3-D rendering as a result of methods for describing higher-level graphical objects. Chief among these are HOOPS and IRIS Inventor. The objects provided by these interfaces are typically more complex than the simple geometry describable with PEXlib or OpenGL. They may comprise not only geometry but also information about how they are drawn and how they react to user input. HOOPS and Open Inventor free the programmer from tedious descriptions of individual drawing operations. But simple access to complex objects generally means losing fine control over rendering (or at least making such control difficult). In any case OpenGL can provide a good base on which to build such higher-level APIs.

Overview of OpenGL

OpenGL draws *primitives* into a frame buffer, subject to a number of selectable modes. Each primitive is a point, line segment, polygon, pixel rectangle, or bitmap. Each mode may be changed independently. The setting of one does not affect the settings of others, although many modes may interact to determine what eventually ends up in the frame buffer. Modes are set, primitives specified, and other OpenGL operations described by issuing *commands* in the form of function or procedure calls.

Figure 17.1 shows a schematic of OpenGL.[1] Commands enter OpenGL on the left. Most commands may be accumulated in a *display list* for processing at a later time. Otherwise, commands are effectively sent through a processing pipeline.

The first stage provides an efficient means for approximating curve and surface geometry by evaluating polynomial functions of input values. The next stage operates on geometric primitives described by vertices: points, line segments, and polygons. In this stage vertices are transformed and lit, and primitives are clipped to a viewing volume in preparation for the next stage, rasterization. The rasterizer produces a series of frame buffer addresses and values, using a two-dimensional description of a point, line segment, or polygon. Each *fragment* so produced is fed to the next stage which performs operations on individual fragments before they finally alter the frame buffer. These operations include conditional updates into the frame buffer, based

---

[1] Mark Segal and Kurt Akeley, *The Design Of The OpenGL Graphics Interface*, Silicon Graphics Computer Systems, 2011 N. Shoreline Blvd., Mountain View, CA., 94039, 1994, p. 2.

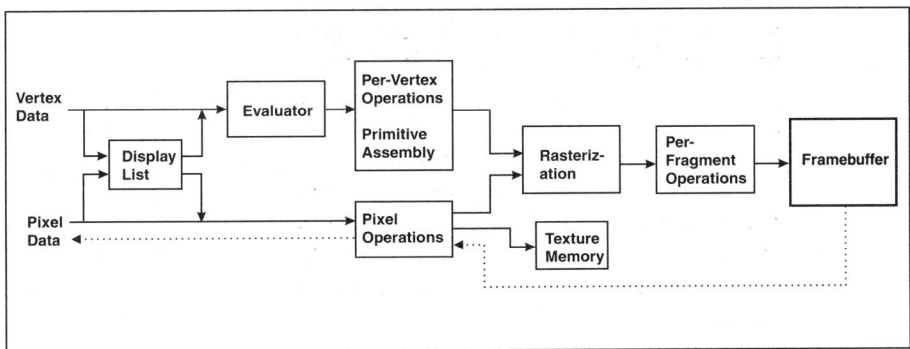

Figure 17.1 Block Diagram of OpenGL

on incoming and previously stored depth values (to effect depth buffering); blending of incoming fragment colors with stored colors; as well as masking and other logical operations on fragment values.

Finally, pixel rectangles and bitmaps bypass the vertex-processing portion of the pipeline to send a block of fragments directly through rasterization to the individual fragment operations, eventually causing a block of pixels to be written to the frame buffer. Values may also be read back from the frame buffer or copied from one portion of the frame buffer to another. These transfers may include some type of decoding or encoding.

Design Considerations

Designing any API requires tradeoffs among a number of general factors such as simplicity in accomplishing common operations versus generality or many commands with few arguments versus few commands with many arguments. This part of the chapter describes considerations peculiar to 3-D API design that have influenced the development of OpenGL.

Performance

A fundamental consideration in interactive 3-D graphics is performance. Numerous calculations are required to render a 3-D scene of even modest complexity, and a scene in an interactive application must generally be redrawn several times per second. An API for use in interactive 3-D applications must therefore provide efficient access to the capabilities of the graphics hardware of which it makes use. But different graphics subsystems provide different capabilities, so a common interface must be found.

The interface must also provide a means to switch various rendering features on and off. Some hardware may not provide support for some features and so cannot provide those features with acceptable performance; also, even with hardware support, enabling certain features or combinations of features may decrease performance significantly. Slow rendering may be acceptable, for instance, when producing a final image of a scene, but interactive rates are normally required when manipulating objects within the scene or adjusting the viewpoint. In such cases the performance-degrading features may be desirable for the final image but undesirable during scene manipulation.

Orthogonality

Since it is desirable to be able to turn features on and off, it should be the case that doing so has few or no side effects on other features. If, for instance, it is desired that each polygon be drawn with a single color rather than interpolating colors across its face, doing so should not affect how lighting or texturing is applied. Similarly, enabling or disabling any single feature should not engender an inconsistent state in which rendering results would be undefined. These kinds of feature independence are necessary to allow a programmer to easily manipulate features without having to generate tests for particular illegal or undesirable feature combinations that may require changing the state of apparently unrelated features. Another benefit of feature independence is that features may be combined in useful ways that may have been unforeseen when the interface was designed.

Completeness

A 3-D graphics API running on a system with a graphics subsystem should provide some means to access all the significant functionality of the subsystem. If some functionality is available but not provided, the programmer is forced to use a different API to get at the missing features. This may complicate the application because of interaction between the two APIs.

On the other hand, if an implementation of the API provides certain features on one hardware platform, those features should, generally speaking, be present on any platform on which the API is provided. If this rule is broken, it is difficult to use the API program that is certain to run on diverse hardware platforms without remembering exactly which features are supported on which machines. In platforms without appropriate acceleration, some features may be poor performers (because they may have to be implemented in software), but at least the intended image will eventually appear.

Interoperability

Many computing environments consist of a number of computers (often made by different companies) connected together by a network. In such an environment it is useful to be able to issue graphics commands on one machine and have them execute on another (this ability is one of the factors responsible for the success of X). Such an ability (called *interoperability*) requires that the model of execution of API commands be *client-server*. The client issues commands, and the server executes them. Interoperability also requires that the client and the server share the same notion of how API commands are encoded for transmission across the network. The client-server model is just a prerequisite. Of course, the client and the server may be the same machine.

Since API commands may be issued across a network, it is impractical to require a tight coupling between client and server. A client may have to wait for some time for an answer to a request presented to the server (a *round-trip*) because of network delays, whereas simple server requests not requiring acknowledgment can be buffered up into a large group for efficient transmission to and execution by the server.

Extensibility

As was discussed earlier, a 3-D graphics API should, at least in principle, be extendable to incorporate new graphics hardware features or algorithms that may become popular in the future. Although attainment of this goal may be difficult to gauge until long after the API is first in use, steps can be taken to help to achieve it. Orthogonality of the API is one element that helps achieve this goal. Another is to consider how the API would have been affected if features that seem consciously omitted were added to the API.

Acceptance

It might seem that design of a clean, consistent 3-D graphics API would be a sufficient goal in itself. But unless programmers decide to use the API in a variety of applications, designing the API will have served no purpose. It is therefore worthwhile to consider the effect of design decisions on programmer acceptance of the API.

Design Features

This part of the chapter highlights the general features of OpenGL's design. Illustrations and justifications of each, using specific examples, are also provided.

Based on IRIS GL

OpenGL is based on Silicon Graphics' IRIS GL. Although a completely new API could have been designed, experience with IRIS GL provided insight into what programmers want and don't want in a 3 D graphics API. Further, making OpenGL similar to IRIS GL where possible makes OpenGL much more likely to be accepted. There are many successful IRIS GL applications, and programmers of IRIS GL will have an easy time switching to OpenGL.

Low-Level API

An essential goal of OpenGL is to provide device independence while still allowing complete access to hardware functionality. The API therefore provides access to graphics operations at the lowest possible level that still provides device independence. As a result, OpenGL does not provide a means for describing or modeling complex geometric objects. Another way to describe this situation is to say that OpenGL provides mechanisms to describe how complex geometric objects are to be rendered rather than mechanisms to describe the complex object themselves.

One benefit of a low-level API is that there are no requirements **on** how an application must represent or describe higher-level objects (since there is no notion of such objects in the API). Adherence to this principle means that the basic OpenGL API does not support some geometric objects that are traditionally associated with graphics APIs. For instance, an OpenGL implementation need not render concave polygons. One reason for this omission is that concave polygon-rendering algorithms are of necessity more complex than those for rendering convex polygons, and different concave polygon algorithms may be appropriate in different domains. In particular, if a concave polygon is to be drawn more than once, it is more efficient to first decompose it into convex polygons (or triangles) once and to then draw the convex polygons. Another reason for the omission is that to render a general concave polygon, all of its vertices must first be known. Graphics subsystems do not generally provide the storage necessary for a concave polygon with a (nearly) arbitrary number of vertices. Convex polygons, on the other hand, can be reduced to triangles as they are specified, so no more than three vertices need be stored.

Another example of the distinction between low level and high level in OpenGL is the difference between OpenGL evaluators and NURBS. The evaluator interface provides a basis for building a general polynomial curve and surface package on top of OpenGL. One advantage of providing the evaluators in OpenGL instead of a more complex NURBS interface is that applications that represent curves and surfaces as other than NURBS or that make use of special surface properties still have access to efficient polynomial evaluators (that may be implemented in graphics hardware) without incurring the costs of converting to a NURBS representation.

Concave polygons and NURBS are, however, common and useful operators. They were familiar (at least in some form) to users of IRIS GL. Therefore a general concave polygon decomposer is provided as part of the OpenGL utility library, which is provided with every OpenGL implementation. The library also provides an interface, built on OpenGL's polynomial evaluators, to describe and display NURBS curves and surfaces (with domain space trimming), as well as a means of rendering spheres, cones, and cylinders. The utility library serves both as a means to render useful geometric objects and as a model for building other libraries that use OpenGL for rendering.

In the client-server environment a utility library raises an issue: Utility library commands are converted into OpenGL commands on the client. If the server computer is more powerful than the client, the client-side conversion might have been more effectively carried out on the server. This dilemma arises not just with OpenGL but with any library in which the client and server may be distinct computers. In OpenGL the base functionality reflects the functions efficiently performed by advanced graphics subsystems, because no matter what the power of the server computer relative to the client, the server's graphics subsystem is assumed to efficiently perform the functions it provides. If in the future, for instance, graphics subsystems commonly provide full trimmed NURBS support, such functionality should likely migrate from the utility library to OpenGL itself. Such a change would not cause any disruption to the rest of the OpenGL API. Another block would simply be added to the left side in Figure 17.1.

Fine-Grained Control

In order to minimize the requirements on how an application using the API must store and present its data, the API must provide a means to specify individual components of geometric objects and operations on them. This fine-grained control is required so that these components and operations may be specified in any order and so that control of rendering operations is flexible enough to accommodate the requirements of diverse applications.

In OpenGL most geometric objects are drawn by enclosing a series of coordinate sets that specify vertices and, optionally, normals, texture coordinates, and a colon between glBegin/glEnd command pairs.

For example, to specify a triangle with vertices at (0, 0, 0), (0, 1, 0), and (1, 0, 1), one could write:

```
glBegin(GL_POLYGON);
    glVertex3i(0,0,0);
    glVertex3i(0,1,0);
    glVertex3i(1,0,1);
glEnd();
```
[2]

Each vertex may be specified with two, three, or four coordinates (four coordinates indicate a homogeneous three-dimensional location). In addition, a *current normal, current texture coordinates,* and *current color* may be used in processing each vertex. OpenGL uses normals in lighting calculations. The current normal is a three-dimensional vector that may be set by sending three coordinates that specify it. Color may consist of red, green, blue, and alpha values (when OpenGL has been initialized to RGBA mode) or a single color index value (when initialization specified color index mode). One, two, three, or four texture coordinates determine how a texture image maps onto a primitive.

Each of the commands specifying vertex coordinates, normals, colors, or texture coordinates comes in several flavors to accommodate differing applications' data formats and numbers of coordinates. Data may also be passed to these commands either as an argument list or as a pointer to a block of storage containing the data. The variants are distinguished by mnemonic suffixes.

A procedure call is used to specify each individual group of data that together define a primitive; this means that an application may store data in any format and order that it chooses. Data need not be stored in a form convenient for presentation to the graphics API, because OpenGL accommodates almost any data type and format, using the appropriate combination of data-specification procedures. Another advantage of this scheme is that by simply combining calls in the appropriate order, different effects may be achieved. Figure 17.2 shows an example of a uniformly colored triangle obtained by specifying a single color that is inherited by all vertices of the triangle.[3] A smooth-shaded triangle is obtained by respecifying a color before each vertex. Not every possible data format is supported (byte values may not be given for vertex coordinates, for instance) because it was found

---

[2] *Ibid.*, p. 4.

[3] *Ibid.*, p. 3.

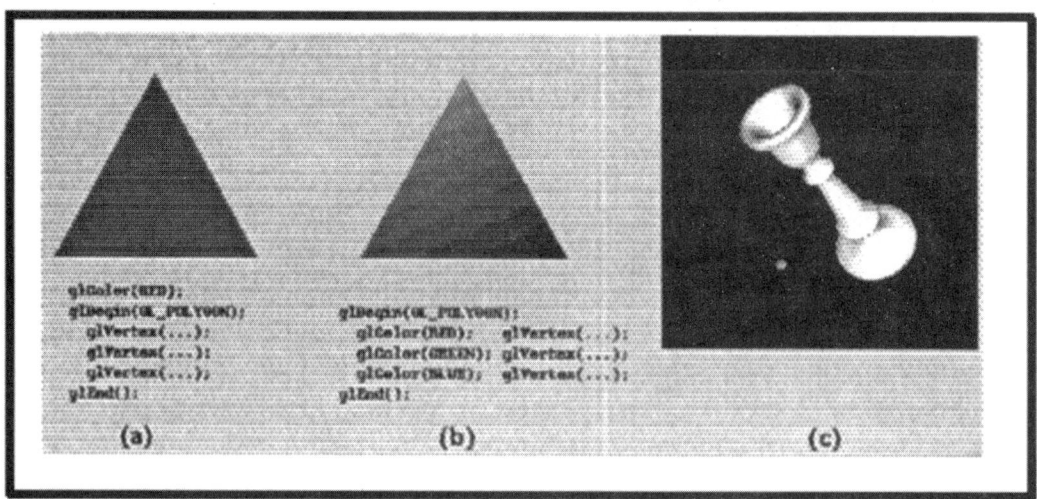

Figure 17.2 (a) A Uniformly Colored Triangle (b) Gouraud Shaded Triangle (c) Scene Consisting of Many Lit, Shaded Polygons

from experience with IRIS GL that not all formats are used. Adding the missing formats in the future, however, would be a trivial undertaking.

One disadvantage of using procedure calls on such a fine grain is that it may result in poor performance if procedure calls are costly. In such a situation an interface that specifies a format for a block of data that is sent all at once may have a performance advantage. The difficulty with specifying a block of data, however, is that it either constrains the application to store its data in one of the supported formats or requires the application to copy its data into a block structured in one of those formats, resulting in inefficiency. Allowing any format arising from an arbitrary combination of individual data types is impractical, because there are so many combinations.

In OpenGL the maximum flexibility provided by individual procedure calls was deemed more important than any inefficiency induced by using those calls. This decision is driven partly by the consideration that modem compilers and computer hardware have improved to the point where procedure calls are usually relatively inexpensive, especially when compared with the work necessary to process the geometric data contained in the call. This is one area in which OpenGL differs significantly from PEX, a primitive's vertices (and associated data) are generally presented all at once in a single army. If it turns out that fine-grained procedure calls are too expensive, it may be necessary to add a few popular block formats to the OpenGL API or to provide a mechanism for defining such formats.

Modal API

As a consequence of fine-grained control, OpenGL maintains considerable state, or modes, that determines how primitives are rendered. This state is present in lieu of having to present a large amount of information with each primitive that would describe the settings for all the operations to which the primitive would be subjected. Presenting so much information with each primitive is tedious and would result in excessive data being transmitted from client to server. Therefore essentially no information is presented with a primitive except what is required to define it. Instead a considerable proportion of OpenGL commands are devoted to controlling the settings of rendering operations.

One difficulty with a modal API arises in implementations in which separate processors (or processes) operate in parallel on distinct primitives. In such cases a mode change must be broadcast to all processors so that each receives the new parameters before it processes its next primitive. A mode change is thus processed serially, halting primitive processing until all processors have received the change, and reducing performance accordingly. One way to lessen the impact of mode changes in such a system is to insert a processor that distributes work among the parallel processors. This processor can buffer up a string of mode changes, transmitting the changes all at once only when another primitive finally arrives.

Another way to handle state changes relies on defining groups of named state settings, which can then be invoked simply by providing the appropriate name (this is the approach taken by X and PEX). With this approach a single command naming the state setting changes the server's settings. This approach was rejected for OpenGL for several reasons. Keeping track of a number of state vectors (each of which may contain considerable information) may be impractical on a graphics subsystem with limited memory. Named state settings also conflict with the emphasis on fine-grained control. In some cases changing the state of a single mode when transmitting the change directly is more convenient and efficient than first setting up and then naming the desired state vector. Finally, the named state–setting approach may still be used with OpenGL by encapsulating state-changing commands in display lists.

Matrix Stack

Three kinds of transformation matrices are used in OpenGL: the *model-view* matrix, which is applied to vertex coordinates; the *texture* matrix, which is applied to texture coordinates; and the *projection* matrix, which describes the viewing frustum and is applied to vertex coordinates after they are transformed by the model-view matrix. Each of these matrices is 4×4.

Any of one these matrices may be loaded with or multiplied by a general transformation. Commands are provided to specify the special cases of rotation, translations and scaling (since these cases take only a few parameters to specify rather than the 16 required for a general transformation). A separate command controls a mode indicating which matrix is currently affected by any of these manipulations. In addition, each matrix type consists of a stack of matrices that can be pushed or popped. The matrix on the top of the stack is the one that is applied to coordinates and that is affected by matrix-manipulation commands.

The retained state represented by these three matrix stacks simplifies specifying the transformations found in hierarchical graphical data structures. Other graphics APIs also employ matrix stacks but often only as a part of more general attribute structures. But OpenGL is unique in providing three kinds of matrices that can be manipulated with the same commands. The texture matrix, for instance, can be used to effectively rotate or scale a texture image applied to primitive and, when combined with perspective viewing transformations, can even be used to obtain projective texturing effects, such as spotlight simulation and shadow effects using shadow maps.

State Queries and Attribute Stacks

The value of nearly any OpenGL parameter can be obtained by an appropriate get command. There is also a stack of parameter values that can be pushed and popped. For stacking purposes, all parameters are divided into 21 functional groups. Any combination of these groups can be pushed onto the attribute stack in one operation (a pop operation automatically restores only those values that were last pushed). The get commands and parameter stacks are required so that various libraries may make use of OpenGL efficiently without interfering with one another.

Frame Buffer

Most of OpenGL requires that the graphics hardware contain a frame buffer. This is a reasonable requirement, since nearly all interactive graphics applications (as well as many noninteractive ones) ran on systems with frame buffer. Some operations in OpenGL are achieved only through exposing their implementation using a frame buffer (transparency using alpha blending and hidden-surface removal using depth buffering are two examples). Although OpenGL may be used to provide information for driving such devices as pen plotters and vector displays, such use is secondary.

Multipass Algorithms

One useful effect of making the frame buffer explicit is that it enables the use of multipass algorithms, in which the same primitives are rendered several times. One example of a multipass algorithm employs an *accumulation buffer*: A scene is rendered several times, each time with a slightly different view, and the results are averaged in the frame buffer. Depending on how the view is altered on each pass, this algorithm can be used to achieve full-window antialiasing, depth-of-field effects, motion blur, or combinations of these. Multipass algorithms are simple to implement in OpenGL, because only a small number of parameters must be manipulated between passes. Changing the values of these parameters is both efficient and without side effects on other parameters that must remain constant.

Invariance

Consideration of multipass algorithms brings up the issue of how what is drawn in the frame buffer is or is not affected by changing parameter values. If, for instance, changing the viewpoint affected the way in which colors were assigned to primitives, the accumulation buffer algorithm would not work. For a more plausible example, if some OpenGL feature is not available in hardware, an OpenGL implementation must switch from hardware to software when that feature is switched on. Such a switch may significantly affect what eventually reaches the frame buffer, because of slight differences in the hardware and software implementations.

The OpenGL specification is not pixel exact. It does not indicate the exact values to which certain pixels must be set given a certain input. The reason is that such specification, besides being difficult, would be too restrictive. Different implementations of OpenGL ran on different hardware with different floating-point formats, rasterization algorithms, and frame buffer configurations. It should be possible, nonetheless, to implement a variety of multipass algorithms and expect to get reasonable results.

For this reason the OpenGL specification gives certain invariance rates that dictate under what circumstances one may expect identical results from one particular implementation given certain inputs (implementations on different systems are never required to produce identical results given identical inputs). These rates typically indicate that changing parameters that control an operation cannot affect the results due to any other operation,but that such invariance is not required when an operation is turned on or off. This makes it possible for an implementation to switch from hardware to software when a mode is invoked without breaking invariance. On the other hand, a programmer may still want invariance even when toggling some mode. To accommodate this case, any operation covered by the invariance rates admits a setting of its controlling parameters that cause the operation to act as if it were turned off even when it is on. A comparison, for instance, may be turned on or off, but when on, the comparison that is performed can be set to always (or never) pass.

Not Programmable

OpenGL does not provide a programming language. Its function may be controlled by turning operations on or off or specifying parameters to operations, but the rendering algorithms are essentially fixed. One reason for this decision is that, for performance reasons, graphics hardware is usually designed to apply certain operations in a specific order. Replacing these operations with arbitrary algorithms is usually unfeasible. Programmability would conflict with keeping the API close to the hardware and thus with the goal of maximum performance.

The model of command execution in OpenGL is that of a *pipeline* with a fixed topology (although stages may be switched in or out). The pipeline is meant to mimic the organization of graphics subsystems. The final stages of the pipeline, for example, consist of a series of tests on and modifications to fragments before they are eventually placed in the frame buffer. To draw a complex scene in a short amount of time, many fragments must pass through these final stages on their way to the frame buffer, leaving little time to process each fragment. Such high *fill rates* demand special-purpose hardware that can perform only fixed operations with minimum access to external data.

- Even though fragment operations are limited, many interesting and useful effects may be obtained by combining the operations appropriately. Per-fragment operations provided by OpenGL include:
- Alpha blending: blend a fragment's color with that of the corresponding pixel in the frame buffer based on an alpha value.
- Depth test: compare a depth value associated with a fragment with the corresponding value already present in the frame buffer and discard or keep the fragment based on the outcome of the comparison.
- Stencil test: compare a reference value with a corresponding value stored in the frame buffer and update the value or discard the fragment based on the outcome of the comparison.[4]

Alpha blending is used to achieve transparency or to blend a fragment's color with that of the background when antialiasing. The depth test can effect depth buffering (and thus hidden-surface removal). The stencil test can be used for a number of effects, including highlighting interference regions and simple CSG (constructive solid geometry) operations. These (and other) operations may be combined to achieve, for instance, transparent interference regions with hidden surfaces removed or any number of other effects.

The OpenGL graphics pipeline also induces a kind of orthogonality among primitives. Each vertex, whether it belongs to a point, line segment, or polygon primitive, is treated in the same way. Its coordinates are transformed, and lighting (if enabled) assigns it a color. The

---

[4] *Ibid.*, p. 6.

primitive defined by these vertices is then rasterized and converted to fragments, as is a bitmap or image rectangle primitive. All fragments, no matter what their origin, are treated identically. This homogeneity among operations removes unneeded special cases (for each primitive type) from the pipeline. It also makes natural the combination of diverse primitives in the same scene without having to set special modes for each primitive type.

Geometry and Images

OpenGL provides support for handling both 3-D (and 2-D) geometry and 2-D images. An API for use with geometry should also provide support for writing, reading, and copying images, because geometry and images are often combined, as when a 3-D scene is laid over a background image. Many of the per fragment operations that are applied to fragments arising from geometric primitives apply equally well to fragments corresponding to pixels in an image, thus making it easy to mix images with geometry. For example, a triangle may be blended with an image, using alpha blending. OpenGL supports a number of image formats and operations on image components (such as lookup tables) to provide flexibility in image handling.

Texture mapping provides an important link between geometry and images by effectively applying an image to geometry. OpenGL makes this coupling explicit by providing the same formats for specifying texture images as for images destined for the frame buffer. Besides being useful for adding realism to a scene (Figure 17.3a), texture mapping can be used to achieve a number of other useful effects. Figures 17.3b and 17.3c show two examples in which the texture coordinates that index a texture image are generated from vertex coordinates.[5] OpenGL's orthogonality makes achieving such effects with texture mapping simply a matter of enabling the appropriate modes and loading the appropriate texture image, without affecting the underlying specification of the scene.

---

[5] *Ibid.*, p. 7.

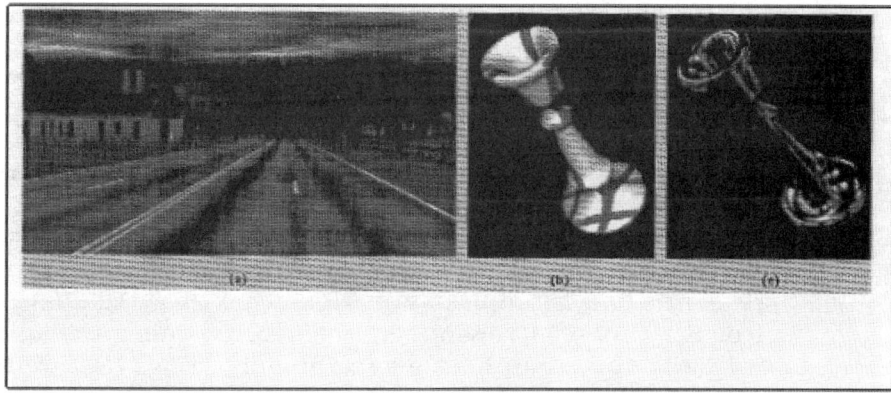

Figure 17.3 (a) A Scene with a Number of Textures Mapped onto Primitives; (b) Contouring Achieved with Texture Mapping and a Texture Coordinate Generation Function; (c) Reflectance Mapping with a Texture Coordinate Generation Function

Immediate Mode and Display Lists

The basic model for OpenGL command interpretation is *immediate mode*, in which a command is executed as soon as the server receives it. Vertex processing, for example, may begin even before specification of the primitive (of which it is a part) has been completed. Immediate-mode execution is well suited to interactive applications in which primitives and modes are continually altered. In OpenGL the fine-grained control provided by immediate mode is taken as far as possible: Even individual lighting parameters (the diffuse reflectance color of a material, for instance) and texture images are set with individual commands that have immediate effect. Although immediate mode provides flexibility, its use can be inefficient if unchanging parameters or objects must be respecified. To accommodate such situations, OpenGL provides *display lists*. A display list encapsulates a sequence of OpenGL commands (all but a handful of OpenGL commands may be placed in a display list) and is stored on the server. The display list is given a numeric name by the application when it is specified. The application need only name the display list to cause the server to effectively execute all the commands contained within the list. This mechanism provides a straightforward, effective means for an application to transmit a group of commands to the server just once even when those same commands must be executed many times.

Display List Optimization

Accumulating commands into a group for repeated execution presents possibilities for optimization. Consider, for example, specifying a texture image. Texture images are often large, requiring a large, and therefore possibly slow, data transfer from client to server (or from the server to its graphics subsystem) whenever the image is respecified. For this reason some graphics subsystems are equipped with sufficient storage to hold several texture images simultaneously. If the texture image definition is placed in a display list, the server may be able to load that image just once when it is specified. When the display list is invoked (or reinvoked), the server simply indicates to the graphics subsystem that it should use the texture image already present in its memory, thus avoiding the overhead of respecifying the entire image.

Examples like this one indicate that display list optimization is required to achieve the best performance. In the case of texture image loading, the server is expected to recognize that a display list contains texture image information and to use that information appropriately. This expectation places a burden on the OpenGL implementor to make sure that special display list cases are treated as efficiently as possible. It also places a burden on the application writer to know to use display lists in cases where doing so could improve performance. Another possibility would have been to introduce special commands for functions that can be poor performers in immediate mode. But such specialization would clutter the API and blur the clear distinction between immediate mode and display lists.

Display List Hierarchies

Display lists may be redefined in OpenGL but not edited. The lack of editing simplifies display list memory management on the server, eliminating the penalty that such management would incur. One display list may, however, invoke others. An effect similar to display list editing may thus be obtained by building a list that invokes a number of subordinate lists and redefining the subordinate lists. This redefinition is possible on a fine grain: A subordinate display list may contain anything (even nothing), including just a single vertex or color command.

There is no automatic saving or restoring of modes associated with display list execution. If desired, such saving and restoring may be performed explicitly by encapsulating the appropriate commands in the display list. This allows the highest possible performance in executing a display list, since there is almost no overhead associated with its execution. It also simplifies controlling the modal behavior of display list hierarchies: Only modes explicitly set are affected.

Lack of automatic modal behavior in display lists also has a disadvantage: it is difficult to execute display lists in parallel, since the modes set in one display list must be in effect before a following display list is executed. In OpenGL display lists are generally not used for defining whole scenes or complex portions of scenes but rather for encapsulating groups of frequently repeated mode-setting commands (describing a texture image, for instance) or commands describing simple geometry (the polygons approximating a toms, for instance).

Depth Buffer

The only hidden-surface removal method directly provided by OpenGL is the depth (or z) buffer. This assumption is in line with that of the graphics hardware containing a frame buffer. Other hidden-surface removal methods may be used with OpenGL (a BSP tree coupled with the painter's algorithm, for instance), but it is assumed that such methods are never supported in hardware and thus need not be supported explicitly by OpenGL.

Local Shading

The only shading methods provided by OpenGL are local. That is, methods for determining surface color, such as ray tracing or radiosity, that require obtaining information from other parts of the scene are not directly supported. The reason is that such methods require knowledge of the global scene database. But so far, specialized graphics hardware is structured as a pipeline of localized operations and does not provide facilities to store and traverse the large amount of data necessary to represent a complex scene. Global shading methods may be used with OpenGL only if the shading can be precomputed and the results associated with graphical objects before they are transmitted to OpenGL.

Rendering Only

OpenGL provides access to rendering operations only. There are no facilities for obtaining user input from such devices as keyboards and mice, since it is expected that any system (in particular, a window system) under which OpenGL runs must already provide such facilities. Further, the effects of OpenGL commands on the frame buffer are ultimately controlled by the window system (if there is one) that allocates frame buffer resources. The window system determines which portions of the frame buffer OpenGL may access and communicates to OpenGL how those portions are structured. These considerations make OpenGL window system independent.

Integration in X

X provides both a procedural interface and a network protocol for creating and manipulating frame buffer windows and drawing certain 2-D objects into those windows. OpenGL is integrated into X by making it a formal X extension called *GLX*. GLX consists of about a dozen calls (with corresponding network encodings) that provide a compact, general embedding of OpenGL in X. As with other X extensions (two examples are Display PostScript and PEX), there is a specific network protocol for OpenGL rendering commands encapsulated in the X byte stream.

OpenGL requires a region of a frame buffer into which primitives may be rendered. In X such a region is called a *drawable*. A *window*, one type of drawable, has associated with it a *visual* that describes the window's frame buffer configuration. In GLX the visual is extended to include information about OpenGL buffers that are not present in unadorned X (depth, stencil, accumulation, front, back, etc.).

X also provides a second type of drawable, the *pixmap*, which is an off-screen frame buffer. GLX provides a GI-Y pixmap that corresponds to an X pixmap but with additional buffers as indicated by some visual. The GLX pixmap provides a means for OpenGL applications to render off screen into a software buffer.

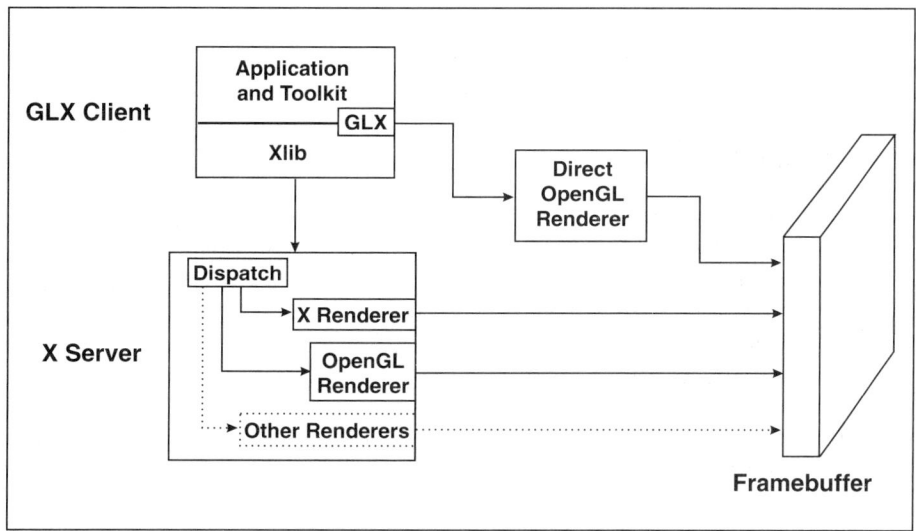

Figure 17.4 GLX Client, X Server, and OpenGL Renderers

To make use of an OpenGL-capable drawable, the programmer creates an OpenGL *context* targeted to that drawable. When the context is created, a copy of an OpenGL renderer is initialized with the visual information about the drawable. This OpenGL renderer is conceptually (if not actually) part of the X server, so that once created, an X client may *connect* to the OpenGL context and issue OpenGL commands (Figure 17.4).[6] Multiple OpenGL contexts may be created that are targeted to distinct or shared drawables. Any OpenGL-capable drawable may also be used for standard X drawing (those buffers of the drawable that are unused by X are ignored by X).

A GLX client that is running on a computer of which the graphics subsystem is a part may avoid passing OpenGL tokens through the X server. Such direct rendering may result in increased graphics performance, since the overhead of token encoding, decoding, and dispatching is eliminated. Direct rendering is supported but not required by GLX. Direct rendering is feasible, because sequentiality need not be maintained between X commands and OpenGL commands except where commands are explicitly synchronized.

---

[6] *Ibid.*, p. 8.

Because OpenGL comprises rendering operations only, it fits well into existing window systems (integration into Windows is similar to that described for X) without duplicating operations already present in the window system (such as window control or mouse event generation). It can also make use of window system features, such as off-screen rendering, which among other uses can send the results of OpenGL commands to a printer. Rendering operations provided by the window system may even be interspersed with those of OpenGL.

API Not Protocol

PEX is specified primarily as a network protocol; PEXlib is a presentation of that protocol through an API. OpenGL, on the other hand, is specified primarily as an API. The API is encoded in a specified network protocol when OpenGL is embedded in a system (like X) that requires a protocol. One reason for this preference is that an applications programmer works with the API and not with a protocol. Another is that different platforms may admit different protocols (X places certain constraints on the protocol employed by an X extension, whereas other window systems may impose different constraints). This means that the API is constant across platforms even when the protocol cannot be, thereby making it possible to use the same source code (at least for the OpenGL portion) without regard for any particular protocol. Further, when the client and server are the same computer, OpenGL commands may be transmitted directly to a graphics subsystem without conversion to a common encoding.

Interoperability between diverse systems is not compromised by preferring an API specification over one for a protocol. Tests in which an OpenGL client running under one manufacturer's implementation was connected to another manufacturer's OpenGL server have provided excellent results.

Example: Three Kinds of Text

To illustrate the flexibility of OpenGL in performing different types of rendering tasks, three methods for the particular task of displaying text are outlined. The three methods are using bitmaps, using line segments to generate outlined text, and using a texture to generate antialiased text.

The first method defines a font as a series of display lists, each of which contains a single bitmap:

```
for i = start + 'a' to start + 'z' {
    glBeginList(i);
        glBitmap( ... );
glEndList();
```

glBitmap specifies both a pointer to an encoding of the bitmap and offsets that indicate how the bitmap is positioned relative to previous and subsequent bitmaps.[7]

In GLX the effect of defining a number of display lists in this way may also be achieved by calling glXUseXFont, which generates a number of display lists. Each display list contains the bitmap (and associated offsets) of a single character from the specified X font.

In either case the string Bitmapped Text whose origin is the projection of a location in 3-D is produced by:

```
glRasterPos3i(x, y, z);
glListBase(start);
glCallLists("Bitmapped Text",14,GL_BYTE);
```
[8]

In Figure 17.5 (a) glListBase sets the display list base so that the subsequent glCallLists references the characters just defined.[9] GlCallLists invokes a series of display lists specified in an array. Each value in the array is added to the display list base to obtain the number of the display list to use. In this case the array is an array of bytes representing a string. The second argument to glCallLists indicates the length of the string. The third argument indicates that the string is an array of 8-bit bytes (16- and 32-bit integers may be used to access fonts with more than 256 characters).

The second method is similar to the first but uses line segments to outline each character. Each display list contains a series of line segments:

```
glTranslate(ox, oy, 0);
glBegin (GL_LINES);
    glVertex( ... );
    ...
```

---

[7] *Ibid.*, p. 9.

[8] *Ibid.*, p. 9.

[9] *Ibid.*, p. 9.

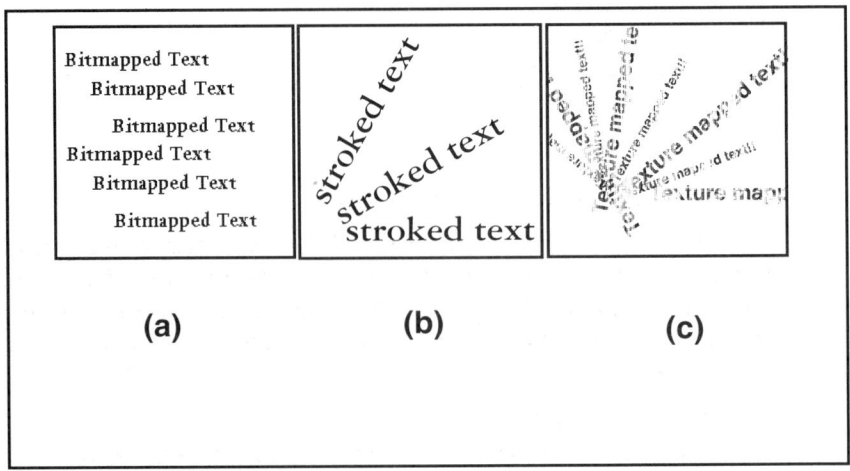

Figure 17.5 (a) Bitmap Example; (b) Stroke Font Example; (c) Texture-Mapped Font Example

```
glEnd ();
glTranslate(dx-ox, dy-oy, 0);
```

The initial glTranslate updates the transformation matrix to position the character with respect to a character origin. The final glTranslate updates that character origin in preparation for the following character. A string is displayed with this method just as in the previous example, but since line segments have 3-D position, the text may be oriented as well as positioned in 3-D (Figure 17.5b).[10] More generally the display lists could contain both polygons and line segments, and these could be antialiased.

Finally, a different approach may be taken by creating a texture image containing an array of characters. A certain range of texture coordinates thus corresponds to each character in the texture image.

Each character may be drawn in any size and in any 3-D orientation by drawing a rectangle with the appropriate texture coordinates at its vertices:

---

[10] *Ibid.*, p. 9.

```
glTranslate(ox, oy, 0);
glBegin(GL_QUADS)
    glTexCoord( ... );
    glVertex( ... );
        ...
glEnd ();
glTranslate(dx-ox, dy-oy, 0);
```

If each group of commands for each character is enclosed in a display list, and the commands for describing the texture image itself (along with the setting of the list base) are enclosed in another display list called TEX. Then, the string Texture mapped text!! may be displayed by:

```
glCallList(TEX);
glCallLists("Texture mapped text!!",21,GL_BYTE);
```

One advantage of this method is that, by simply using appropriate texture filtering, the resulting characters are antialiased (Figure 17.5c).

Summary

OpenGL is a 3-D graphics API intended for use in interactive applications. It has been designed to provide maximum access to hardware graphics capabilities, no matter at what level such capabilities are available. This efficiency stems from a flexible interface that provides direct control over fundamental operations. OpenGL does not enforce a particular method of describing 3-D objects and how they should appear but instead provides the basic means by which those objects, no matter how described, may be rendered. Because OpenGL imposes minimum structure on 3-D rendering, it provides an excellent base on which to build libraries for handling structured geometric objects, no matter what the particular structures may be.

The goals of high performance, feature orthogonality, interoperability, implementability on a variety of systems, and extensibility have driven the design of OpenGL's API. This chapter has shown the effects of these and other considerations on the presentation of rendering operations in OpenGL. The result has been a straightforward API with few special cases, which should be easy to use in a variety of applications.

Future work on OpenGL is likely to center on improving implementations through optimization and extending the API to handle new techniques and capabilities provided by graphics hardware. Likely candidates for inclusion are image-processing operators, new texture-mapping capabilities, and other basic geometric primitives, such as spheres and cylinders. If care is taken in the design of the OpenGL API, it will make these as well as other extensions simple and will result in OpenGL's remaining a useful 3-D graphics API for many years to come.

From Here

Now that we've discussed OpenGL graphics interface design considerations, let's look at behavior engine technology and its comparison to a behavior language protocol for VRML. These topics are discussed in the next chapter.

Virtual Behavior Engines

The technology underlying the behavior engine (BE) was developed during nearly ten years of work in the domain of manufacturing simulation. This technology allows simulations, as well as the documents through which the reader accesses them, to be built by linking and embedding components distributed on the WWW. Thus a repair manual for an automobile can be constructed by linking or embedding documents and simulations of its parts. Creation of the compound simulation includes specification of the behavioral interactions among the simulations of the parts.

The BE includes utilities supporting creation of a variety of behaviors, including motion of kinematic devices. At the same time, the authoring environment is fully open and allows description of arbitrarily complex behaviors in a programming formalism called *BEyond*. The power, efficiency, and completeness of this formalism are indicated by the fact that the behavior engine itself was implemented in BEyond.

Overview of BE

The basic technical idea underlying the behavior engine is the embedding of all of the varieties of information needed to describe objects and their behavior, including classes, algorithms, and specialized parametric behavioral forms, such as motion, into a unified structure with common methods for hierarchical assembly and hierarchical naming. This contrasts to conventional simulation and programming technology in which the realms of code and data are separated. Classes and behavior are on the code side, and code-side naming is of fixed depth (package/class/method).

As a result of the unified approach implemented by the behavior engine, behavior can be alloyed with other attributes of objects so that things, such as simulated mechanical devices, carry their behaviors within themselves. Assembly of systems and documents with associated behavior then goes very smoothly, because there is only one kind of glue needed to connect them—glue that works on behavioral and nonbehavioral elements alike.

BE products have three levels of technical content. The fundamental level supports creation of a kind of Web-distributed software component called a Being, which is the external form of a BE object and implements the uniformities just described. In addition to embedding classes and their behavior, BEings support parameterization of their content, temporal modeling, versioning and configuration management, and object evolution; so objects can change class membership, as well as other properties, over their lifetimes.

The second level applies this general infrastructure to documents and three-dimensional objects and their behaviors. A BEing that incorporates these elements can serve as a parameterized document that embeds interactive 3-D simulations.

The third level adds support that is specifically useful to mechanical product modeling and simulation. For example, kinematic modeling, with associated user interfaces, allows creation of documented simulations of mechanisms.

Objects and Classes

As in most object systems, a BE class specifies a collection of typed fields. However, BE classes dictate the structure of their members less strictly than do conventional systems, such as C++, Smalltalk, or Java. BE objects can change their class membership over time and can have their own attributes in addition to those dictated by their classes.

Naming

A BE name (called a reference) is a kind of path name that specifies a way to navigate to the named object through the object structure. References play all of the naming roles in the behavior engine—they serve as program variables, names of functions and classes, and path names of geometric objects in the hierarchically structured 3-D world model. References may appear as data embedded in any kind of object. They can be mentioned, as well as used, by programs.

BEings

A BEing is a BE object that is meaningful as a separate entity—an object that can be stored, sent as a message, or served on the WWW. A BEing, like any BE object, can serve as a programming context within which functions, classes, and global variables are defined. BEings can be assembled to form a hierarchically structured programming environment. All entities, including classes and functions, can appear at arbitrary depth in such a hierarchical structure and can be named by references. This contrasts to conventional programming formalisms (including C++, Smalltalk, CLOS, Java, etc.), in which classes and functions/methods must be organized in a structure of a fixed depth of 1, 2, or 3, and hierarchical assembly cannot be done directly but only via some kind of flattening. BEings are typically used to represent units of BE functionality, such as simulations of mechanical assemblies.

Assembly

The basic assembly operations are embedding or linking BEings into BEings at the next larger scale. These operations use one uniform mechanism—resolution of references—to connect BEings. This uniformity is possible because references cover all varieties of symbolic naming.

Each level of a hierarchy is represented by a BEing with its own models, functions, behaviors, and classes. New levels are built by embedding, linking, or sharing BEings from the existing levels. A typical BEing is a simulation of a component of a system at a particular scale. For example, a mechanical assembly is modeled by a hierarchy of BEings mirroring the part-subpart structure of the assembly. BEings at each level fully encode the behavior and classes relevant at that level.

Time and Concurrency

The BE programming formalism includes a full complement of constructs for modeling time and concurrent activity. When modeling a temporal process using computation, some computations determine the state of a simulation at a particular instant of time, and other computations step through a duration of simulated time determining the sequence of events which will take place. For example, the computation that determines the gravitational forces acting on astronomical objects at a given instant of time in a planetary simulation is of the former kind. Of course, the computation takes time on the computer executing the simulation but should not be allocated any duration in the simulated world.

The behavior engine model posits that the state of the simulated world at any given moment consists of the following components:

- a real-valued clock whose state reflects the current time in the simulated world;
- an ordered set of instantaneous computations, called influences, representing the conditions and constraints currently in force; and
- a current set of temporal behaviors—behaviors with nonzero duration in simulated time.[1]

The influences are computations that update the state of the world, based on the current clock value. An influence can be sampled at any time while it is in force. Temporal behaviors are discrete threads of activity, including instantaneous acts interleaved with waits for events or semaphores, and delays in simulated time. Many temporal behaviors are effectively described by objects rather than directly by code. For example, there is a class motion whose subclasses are used to describe many varieties of motion in 3-D space, including articulated

---

[1] Behavior Engine Technology, The BE Software Company, 1995.

motions of kinematic mechanisms. Programmers are free to add their own temporal behavior classes to the existing hierarchy.

Programming the Behavior Engine

The programming formalism used in the BE is called BEyond. BEyond's syntax and semantics make it particularly suitable for use by people with an engineering or scientific background, who may not necessarily fit the profile of professional software developers. A programmer can get started and do useful work by treating BEyond as an interactive implementation of Pascal and pick up the more advanced features as needed.

Comparison to Other Simulation Technology

Many simulation systems exist, covering a wide variety of behaviors. But in traditional implementations of simulation software, the bulk of what it takes to describe and render complex behavior is rigidly fixed in the code that makes up the implementation. This makes it difficult or impossible to create kinds of behavior not contemplated by the architects of available simulators or to assemble disparate kinds of behavioral objects into a single system or document, even if each constituent of the system is addressed by one or another existing simulation product. The aim of the behavior engine is to provide an infrastructure for creation of simulation-enriched documents that does not place *a priori* constraints on the kinds of behavior that can be included.

Java is an adaptation of C++ that supports transmission of platform-independent executable code on the Internet. Java has been integrated with the WWW browser technologies HotJava (from Sun Microsystems) and Netscape Navigator Version 2. Those familiar with Java may wonder about how Java and BE technologies compare. Before embarking on a detailed discussion of this issue, it should be pointed out that the behavior engine is integrated with Netscape Navigator 2.0, which includes Java applets, enabling use of the two technologies in concert.

Like the behavior engine, Java-based technology exists at more than one level: at the fundamental level independent of applications, at the level of generic browser applications, and at the level of uses in particular industries. But Java and the behavior engine have several differences at the fundamental level.

First, Java, like the behavior engine, supports WWW distribution of software components. But in the current implementation, Java provides support for distribution only of classes, not instances. Although descriptions of instances can be encoded in classes (by constants or by algorithms that generate the instances), the classes still arise from source code. No generic support is available for saving or distributing an object that has been created or modified in the course of a Java session. To put it succinctly, Java technology in its current form supports distribution of code but not data. BE, on the other hand, supports saving any kind of structure, including those that mix classes, behaviors, and ordinary objects.

Of course, Java programmers, like programmers in any language, are free to design application-specific formats for transmitting their data, but the likely consequence is that multiple formats will prevent assembly of content from diverse sources. Also, generic support for persistent and distributable objects may well be added to Java in the future. But there is as yet no indication of what this support will look like or when it will arrive. The remaining differences between Java and BE are architectural and will not disappear with the addition of features to Java.

Second, BE, unlike Java, provides direct and generic support for hierarchical assembly of behavioral systems. In the BE classes, behaviors, and all other kinds of objects are embedded in a common hierarchy with a common naming scheme. Java takes a more conventional approach: All behavior is held in the methods of classes, and classes are effectively organized as a flat, not a hierarchical, structure (despite superficial appearance). The practical effect is that BE provides much more effective support for hierarchical assembly of systems and widespread distribution of components that can be used together freely at a later time than does Java. Here are the details.

In Java behavior is defined by methods within classes, and any object gets all of its behavior from its class. Within Java code a class is referenced by a simple name or a fully qualified name (package + name). Either way, by the time the Java compiler generates byte codes, all such names have been resolved to fully qualified names. Although the programmer may have included dots or other symbols in the class and package names to represent a mental hierarchy, the name is treated as atomic by the time it is turned into byte code. Thus in Java, as in C++, objective C, and Smalltalk, classes are organized in a flat name space. Behaviors appear as methods of classes. This leads to fundamental difficulties in the construction of hierarchical systems from distributed components.

For example, in BE it is commonplace to make a copy B of a system A and subsequently modify B, including internal classes and behaviors. Later on, A and the modified B might end up as parts of the same assembly. This might take place after a long separation and many previous assembly steps. None of this is problematic in BE. But in Java, under the same assumptions, A and B would have to remain forever separate. They could never end up together in the same assembly, because they include different classes with the same name. These names propagate upward through arbitrarily many levels of assembly. In Java it is necessary to rename any class that is modified, especially if there is any chance of its bumping into its old self out on the Net. Java class names (and behavior names in the form of class.method), like IP addresses, must be unique on a planetary scale if all assembly dangers are to be avoided. But forcing uniqueness of names causes its own problems: Any code that mentioned an old version of a class by name and that is needed in a context where the new version is relevant must be not only recompiled but also rewritten.

Third, in the BE objects can evolve: They can acquire new behaviors, lose old behaviors, and change class membership over time. This possibility for evolution is built into the structure of all objects. In Java, as in C++, objects are much more rigid; their class memberships, and thus their signatures (how their attributes are named), are frozen at creation time. The evolutionary features of BE objects are important both for simulation and for effectively supporting components that may have long lives traveling the Internet.

Finally, Java's reflective capabilities are better than C++ but still weak compared to BE. In Java a class is an object, but the internal structure of classes is not available for manipulation; nor are the contents of an object accessible except by code, which has its class compiled in. In BE all metadata, including the structure of classes and of behavior, is fully available. The practical effect is that general-purpose code can be developed in BE that applies to objects whose classes and interfaces are not known in advance. For example, generic user interfaces for browsing objects and metalevel facilities, such as systems for managing class repositories, can be developed within BE for dealing with its own content.

Other differences between Java and BE exist at the fundamental level, but an exhaustive list is beyond the scope of this chapter. There are also significant differences in the way that the two technologies are applied in the context of documents with active content. In the Netscape Navigator 2.0 and HotJava WWW browsers, Java serves as the implementation language for applets. An applet is a small application that presents itself to the user within a window allocated for it in an HTML document. In this approach applets are elements of a document, not the other way around.

In contrast, BEings typically include documents as part of their content. Parameterized BEings may include document generators, which compute appropriate HTML from the values supplied for parameters. Three-dimensional content is treated the same way: as an element of a BEing that may be computed from parameters—often the same parameters as govern an associated document.

A BEing representing a complex set of data, such as assembly and maintenance methods for a mechanical system, should be viewed as a unified whole presented to the user by a collection of interactive documents. This approach allows both the content of the documents and the interpretation of user interactions with the document to be derived from a unified underlying model.

Example Applications

The behavior engine can be used to create owner's manuals for mechanical equipment that incorporates detailed simulations of the equipment's behavior. For example, Figure 18.1 shows an image of a radial arm saw as it would appear in the behavior engine's 3-D window.[2] Simulated operation of the saw is controlled by clicking on text or submitting forms from the associated document or, more directly, by manipulating the saw, using the mouse in the 3-D window. The details of how the saw works govern what can be done in the simulation.

---

[2] *Ibid.*

The simulated world can also be affected by links or forms in the Web document. For example, clicking on a link called New Board in the document causes a 2×4 to appear on the saw table. Thereafter, dragging the blade over the 2×4 results in the simulated board being cut in two.

The BE edition of the owner's manual thus includes a working model of the thing it describes. The manual also includes step-by-step instructions for saw operations, which are illustrated by simulation and exercises in which operation of the saw by the reader is monitored and corrected.

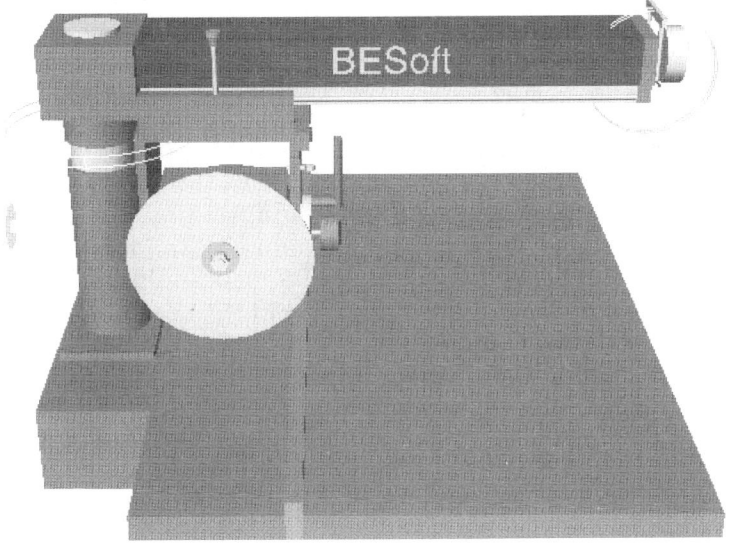

Figure 18.1 Image of a Radial Arm Saw as it Would Appear in BE's 3-D Window

Repositories of Parameterized Objects, Behaviors, and Documents

A central feature of BE technology is that it supports creation of repositories of software components, called BEings, that can be distributed on the World Wide Web and that serve as reusable building blocks for related applications. BEings include all of the varieties of data needed to represent an object, its behaviors, and the active documents via which the user interacts with the object. The next example illustrates the use of BEing repositories in creating online simulation-based documentation for a line of related products. The same general points apply to many classes of products, but for the sake of simplicity and familiarity, the example described here will be assembly-required furniture kits.

There are three kinds of users in this scenario: repository builders, who add new BEings to the repository; document authors, who develop new individual documents by drawing on the repository; and the final customer, who learns how to assemble the furniture kit by interacting with an assembly document for that kit—that includes detailed 3-D simulations of the assembly steps. The repository builders may need some knowledge of BE technology, but neither the document author nor the final customer need any special expertise. Creating new documents for new kits is very efficient, because most of the elements of documentation, modeling, and simulation will be present already in parametric form in the repository.

Although this example is quite simple, exactly the same approach applies to the creation and use of simulation-based documentation for complex mechanical products, where the end user of the documentation is an engineer or maintenance person rather than a consumer. The objective in any case is to efficiently codify and reuse parametric descriptions of documents, mechanical parts, and mechanical behavior in the sharing of engineering knowledge.

The individual BEings in the repository for the furniture kit example hold the following varieties of information:

- *Classes*, that is, generic part descriptions. Examples are parameterized models of fasteners, such as screws and dowels; parameterized models of furniture elements, such as boards; parameterized models of tools, such as wrenches, screw drivers, and so forth.

- *Behaviors*, including mating behaviors (bringing furniture parts into correct relative position for an assembly operation) and fastening behaviors, such as use of tools to perform a fastening operation. Behaviors are also parameterized and described by classes.
- *User interfaces* for assisting the designer in creating the particular parts, fasteners, and behaviors needed for a particular furniture assembly.
- *Parameterized documents* describing steps of assembly. A parameterized document in this case is a schematicized document and associated 3-D simulation describing an assembly step. Instances of such documents are used as parts of the final assembly instructions seen by the customer. So far, all the BEings have been of a parametric nature, and form a common base for designing and documenting many individual furniture kits.

From these parameterized BEings, the following concrete models and documents are created:

- particular part and behavior models,
- particular assembly sequences, and
- asembly instruction documents for particular kits.[3]

Behavior Engine Products

The BEyond programming environment provides the tools necessary for developers to access behavior engine classes and to create new behaviors and behavior classes. BEyond is suitable for creating BEyond dcuments that do not include 3-D content or for developing simulation applications in which 3-D model is not appropriate. BEyond supports assembly of complex systems of behavior from components and is fully integrated with World Wide Web technology.

---

[3] *Ibid.*

BE Designer

BE Designer extends the BEyond programming environment with behavior classes supporting three-dimensional simulations. It provides all of the facilities needed to create BEyond documents incorporating 3-D content, including utilities for creating simple kinematic mechanisms, and for basic temporal path planning and motion. The Open Inventor 3-D library supplies rendering and modeling functionality; 3-D models in any of the many formats convertible into Open Inventor format can be loaded into BE Designer as the starting point for creation of 3-D simulations. BEyond documents created with BE Designer can be served to the WWW by standard servers, such as Netscape Commerce Server or the NCSA HTTPD server.

BE Player

BE Player is the viewer or player for BEyond documents created with BE Designer. BE Player works with an HTML browser, such as Netscape Navigator or NCSA Mosaic. Like any browser, BE Player can access BEyond documents stored in the local file system or remotely on the WWW.

Virtual Reality Behavior System (VRBS)

VRBS (pronounced verbs) is a VRML behavior scripting system prototype developed by the San Diego Supercomputer Center (SDSC). This system is proposed as the basis of behavior support within VRML.

SDSC's VRML work is centered on the development of an experimental VRML browser, WebView. Source code for WebView is available for Version 1.0 beta, which does not include VRBS support. Version 1.1 beta, which will include VRBS support, is expected to be released in late 1996.

VRML provides constructs for controlling the shape, appearance, position, size, and orientation of 3-D objects. It does not include constructs to change these features in response to user interaction or automated actions. Such behaviors are clearly needed. To provide the flexibility and power needed for complex behaviors, a scripting language (Java Script) is necessary. Several possible languages have been proposed by the VRML community. A common denominator, however, is the need for an interprocess communications protocol that links an executing behavior script to a VRML browser.

A *behavior* is the description of a response to a user interaction or an automatic event (such as a timer alarm going off). Such a response may cause a scene shape to move, a color to change, or a light to turn on or off. In more complex applications behaviors alter multiple scene nodes or restructure entire chunks of the world.

The wide applicability of VRML makes efforts to standardize on a few built-in behaviors impractical. Instead, a general-purpose behavior description mechanism is needed. Several *behavior languages* have been proposed, including Perl, Tcl, and Java. In each case a behavior *script* is written in one of these languages and bound to a VRML file. When the VRML file is downloaded into the browser, the script is run. Thereafter, as users interact with the scene, the script responds and alters scene content. Later, when the user leaves the scene or quits the browser, the behaviors are flushed from the system.

To implement such a system requires that several key issues be addressed:

- How are behaviors bound to VRML files? When are they downloaded?
- When and how are behaviors started, stopped, and flushed from the system?
- How do behaviors and the browser communicate? How do behaviors respond to user interaction and automatic events?
- In what language are behaviors written?[4]

The first issue requires a script node extension to the VRML syntax; the second the definition of a behavior system structure and the semantics of behavior startup and shutdown; the third a communications protocol to be developed whereby the browser and running behaviors may communicate; and the fourth the development of a scripting language and an API for browser-behavior communications.

The first three issues are independent of the choice of a behavior language. It is these issues that are addressed here and by prototype *VRBS*.

---

[4] David R. Nodeau and John L. Moreland, The Virtual Reality Behavior System (VRBS): A Behavior Language Protocol for VRML, San Diego Supercomputer Center (SDSC), Association of Computing Machinery (ACM), December 15, 1995.

The VRBS System Structure

A *system structure* defines system components and how and when they interact. The VRML browser reads and presents VRML files retrieved from the Internet. Embedded within VRML files are URLs for associated behavior scripts. Behavior scripts are retrieved by the browser and passed to a *separate* behavior interpreter process. That process, implementing a specific behavior language, executes the script.

Issues include:

- Are the browser and language interpreter the same program or separate?
- If separate, which is started up first, how and when are the remaining components started, how and when are they shut down, and what happens if there's a problem?
- Which component does what task?
- Can individual components be replaced with alternative implementations without affecting the others?

Figure 18.2 shows the VRBS system structure. The principal components are:

- a VRML browser,
- a behavior interpreter,
- one or more VRML world files, and
- one or more behavior script files.[5]

A behavior language API provides functions to the script that allow it to query and change scene content by communicating with the browser. In response, the browser parses behavior requests and updates the scene. For user- or time-triggered actions, a behavior nominates callbacks, asking the browser to notify it for desired events. When an event occurs, the browser sends the event to the interpreter, which executes the behavior callback.

The VRBS protocol ties the browser and interpreter together. It defines messages to communicate scene changes and events, as well as messages to control the startup and shutdown of the interpreter and its behaviors.

---

[5] *Ibid.*

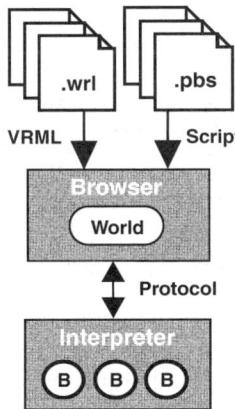

Figure 18.2 VRBS System Structure

The VRBS system structure is similar to that common to interactive applications. The use of separate processes allows the independent development of browsing and behavior language functionality:

- The browser is ignorant of behavior language syntax. Its roles are to display VRML scenes, get behavior scripts from the Internet and hand them to the interpreter, and respond to interpreter requests.
- The interpreter is ignorant of VRML syntax, Internet protocols, or windowing system details. Its roles were to execute scripts sent to it by the bTowstT, and provide an API so that scripts can send messages to and receive events from the browser.[6]

The following discussion walks through the prototype VRBS system structure. It starts with linking a behavior script to a VRML scene, through the VRBS protocol, and returning again to system structure to discuss system startup and handshaking.

The WWWScript Node

An assumption implicit in discussion of behaviors is that there is some way for a scene author to associate behaviors with a world. The

---

[6] *Ibid.*

most natural mechanism is through the introduction of a new VRML node type: WWWScript.

A WWWScript node, like existing WWWInline nodes, provides the URL of a remote file. Where a WWWInline loads a VRML scene file, a WWWScript loads a VRML behavior file.

As with all URLS the MIME type or file name extension of a file indicates the type of data being read. As the industry explores different behavior language options, different MIME types will be defined for different languages.

When a WWWScript node is processed by the browser, the script is retrieved from the Internet, its MIME type checked, and the user's mailcap file scanned for the name of an appropriate behavior language interpreter to invoke. In this way the same VRML node syntax can be used to generically reference a behavior of any behavior language.

WWWScript nodes are not restricted to one per scene. When multiple WWWScript nodes are encountered, each node's script is loaded into the same interpreter.

To reduce name space collisions, the behavior language interpreter is provided both the script text and the name of the VRML WWWScript node. That node name can be used to group script functions within their own name space. In a Perl implementation, for instance, the node name is used as a Perl package name. The script's code is loaded into that package.

When multiple behavior scripts are loaded simultaneously, each into a different package, scripts may make calls to one another, using the package name. This is stylistically similar to the use of a node's name for VRML USE node instancing.

Where an author has omitted a name for a WWWScript node, a unique package name is automatically generated. SDSC WebView, for instance, generates a name of the form b#, where # is a unique random number.

A WWWScript node may occur anywhere within a scene graph, including within a VRML file loaded by a WWWInline. The *root world* of a tree of WWWInline'd worlds is said to be the owner of the entire behavior set, including those loaded by it directly, those loaded by WWWInline'd files, and so on down the world tree. This serves to flatten the behavior script name space, allowing scripts of WWWInline'd worlds to easily access script functions loaded at other points in the scene graph.

Each root world has its own behavior set and its own behavior language interpreter. This establishes a natural border between worlds, preventing all the scripts of all the worlds ever loaded in to a browser from piling up indefinitely. Instead, a behavior set exists only as long as the root world exists. When the browser flushes the root world from its memory, the associated interpreter and its behaviors are flushed as well.

To load a retrieved script into an interpreter and later communicate with that script, the browser and interpreter must use a mutually agreed on communications protocol. The prototype VRBS protocol and its design motivation are discussed later in the chapter.

VRBS Behavior Protocol Goals and Style

The browser-behavior interprocess communications protocol must meet several key goals that in turn dictate a protocol design. Different VRML browser implementations will use different VRML implementation approaches. Where SGI/TGS WebSpace and SDSC WebView both use Open Inventor as the implementation base, other browsers may use other techniques. For broad applicability, the behavior protocol cannot make assumptions about the browser implementation.

A prime example of this issue is the *scene graph*. A scene graph is a *conceptual* data structure expressed by an input VRML file. It is not necessarily a convenient internal *implementation* data structure for all browsers. A generic behavior protocol cannot, therefore, depend on such a structure. An abstraction is needed to provide browser implementors with the flexibility to define their own efficient and appropriate data structures for their target graphics platform.

The VRBS protocol allows scripts to query and change only those scene nodes given *names* via the VRML DEF construct. This is stylistically compatible with the VRML USE construct, which allows scene nodes with names, and only those nodes, to be repeatedly instanced.

VRBS does not require that there be an internal scene graph representation, only that the named nodes of a VRML scene be accessible within the browser. The browser must, however, retain the semantics of VRML scene node relationships.

A behavior may access the named Material node sphereColor to, say, change it from red to blue. Regardless of the internal browser data structure used, the Sphere should turn blue, and the Cone should not.

Behavior Language Independent

The protocol should make minimal assumptions about the abilities of a behavior language. The language must be free to define it's own package, class, and function mechanisms, naming conventions, scoping, data types, and so forth. It is only with such minimal assumptions that the VRML Architecture Group (VAG) could allow for the development of new, and perhaps radically different, behavior languages in the future.

For example, the VRBS protocol does not require that the scripting language have a notion of *objects*. The application of an object-oriented programming style is entirely up to the scripting language. The protocol simply defines messages to notify the interpreter when events have occurred. It is up to the interpreter to decide how it delivers those events and to whom.

The VRBS protocol *does* assume that the language has some support for name space segregation, typically via package, module, or class structures. In the absence of such, it is expected that the language interpreter will process incoming scripts and adjust function and variable names to automatically avoid name space collisions.

Platform Independent

Different compute architectures have different word sizes, byte orders, and floating-point formats. Conversion between byte orders is tedious and, between floating-point formats, problematic. To reduce these problems, the protocol should allow for similar and convenient implementations regardless of architecture attributes.

The VRBS protocol is entirely *string-based*. No multibyte binary data is included, thereby avoiding byte order and floating-point issues.

Easily Parsed by Scripting Languages

Typical (but not necessarily all) behavior languages will be based on scripting languages, such as Perl, Java Script, TCL, and so forth.

Such languages frequently have a text-processing history and provide efficient support for dealing with text-based messages. They may not, however, support binary data operations with equal ease and efficiency.

Traditional protocol-building tools, such as XDR, build binary packets. Although efficient in C, they can be problematic for text-processing style scripting languages. Additionally, they require porting a support library and its integration into a language interpreter.

To achieve a script-friendly protocol, the VRBS protocol is, again, entirely string based. Messages are easily handled, using simple text operations already available in any language. No modifications or additional support libraries are needed to enable typical existing languages to use the VRBS protocol.

Extensible

Clearly a protocol cannot anticipate every possible desired feature. So the design must support the addition of new messages and define the actions to be taken on receipt of an unrecognized message.

In VRBS the protocol allows for the definition of new opcodes and arguments. An interpreter may query the protocol version number supported by a browser, as well as the set of extensions supported by that browser. Receipt of a message with an unknown opcode is treated as a nonfatal error, allowing the browser or interpreter to continue on.

Similarly, individual scripts may query the features supported by a browser and compute platform, then adapt accordingly. This allows a script run on, say, a PC to perform differently from one run on an SGI Onyx Reality Engine II.

Reasonably Secure

A behavior script is a program executed, behind the scenes, on the user's local host. The potential for viruslike abuse is huge. The design of the behavior protocol can help to control this problem.

The VRBS protocol distinguishes between two stages of behavior initialization: *load* and *startup*. When a browser encounters a WWWScript node, it retrieves the script and hands it off to an appropriate language interpreter. The interpreter is asked to *load* the script only but not to execute it. During the load phase, the interpreter should *sanitize* the script, watching for illegal or unsecure operations.

A Perl implementation, for instance, parses an incoming script and blocks all access to *eval, require, undef,* and so forth. Additionally, it traps calls to open files, allowing it to redirect file access to a user-defined temporary directory.

Once an interpreter has finished loading a new behavior, it notifies the browser. The browser responds by requesting the interpreter to *start up* the behavior. If any sanitization problems occurred, the browser will not start up the script.

The differentiation between *load* and *startup* also allows a browser to preload scripts or maintain them in a local loaded cache. If the language supports script precompilation, the *load* stage does this work, allowing the *startup* stage to get straight to executing the behavior.

VRBS Protocol Messages

The VRBS prototype implements a simple protocol based on the goals given and design decisions stated here. VRBS protocol *messages* are composed of three parts:

- the preheader,
- the header, and
- the body.

The *preheader* gives the size, in bytes, of the *header* that follows. The *header* names the operation to be performed and gives the size, in bytes, of the *body* that follows. Finally, the *body* provides arguments to the operation. The preheader, header, and body may not be interleaved with other data. They always occur together in that sequence.

All message header and body components are NULL-terminated ASCII strings. All numbers are expressed in decimal as strings and are constrained to be storable (when converted to binary) within a 32-bit variable.

Preheader

The preheader contains a single unsigned 1byte binary integer that gives the size, in bytes, of the message header that follows. The preheader tells a browser or interpreter how many bytes to read from the connection in order to retrieve the entire message header.

Note that, unlike the remainder of a message, the preheader is binary rather than a NULL-terminated string. This allows a message parser to read exactly 1 byte with a single read call instead of looping to read a variable-length NULL-terminated string. This helps to keep the number of read calls down and to increase the performance of message parsing. By keeping the preheader to a single byte, the protocol also avoids byte-order issues.

Header

The header is a list of NULL-terminated strings whose total byte count, including NULLS, sums to HeaderNBytes, the size given in the preheader. The opcodeClass is a signed integer that indicates the general category of operation to be performed. The opcode is a signed integer that indicates the specific operation to be performed.

The BodyNBytes is a positive signed integer that indicates the number of bytes that follow as part of the message body. The preheader's HeaderNBytes field always gives the actual size of the transferred header, which may be greater than that required for the components. This allows future versions of the protocol to add additional header fields (such as a time stamp) without breaking existing applications. Older applications that do not recognize the new fields will silently skip over the extra header fields by using the HeaderNBytes byte count.

Body

The message body provides arguments to the message's OpcodeClass and Opcode. Arguments are always provided as a list of NULL-terminated strings whose length, including the NULLs, sums to the BodyNBytes value in the header.

For example, the OpGetNodeField opcode requests the browser to change the value of a field of a named node. Each argument in a string nodeName gives the name of the node to change; fieldName gives the name of a field in that node (such as diffuseColor for a Material node). FieldValue is the new value for the field.

The WorldId field is discussed later in the chapter. It is provided on some, but not all, protocol messages.

The body is always BodyNBytes long, which may be larger than that required for the opcode's arguments. Again this allows for protocol changes in the future that may add additional optional arguments to individual opcodes. Older applications will use the BodyNBytes field to silently skip extra data in a message body.

Opcode Classes and Opcodes

Opcode classes group opcodes by category, whereas opcodes indicate the specific operation to perform within that category. The initial VRBS protocol defines the following opcode classes:[7]

```
ClBehaviorToWorld
ClBehaviorToBehavior
ClBehaviorToBrowser
ClBehaviorToInterpreter

ClBrowserToWorld
ClBrowserToBehavior
ClBrowserToBrowser
ClBrowserToInterpreter

ClInterpreterToWorld
ClInterpreterToBehavior
ClInterpreterToBrowser
ClInterpreterToInterpreter

ClWorldToWorld
ClWorldToBehavior
ClWorldToBrowser
ClWorldToInterpreter
```

The intent of opcodes within a given opcode class is clear from the name: ClBehaviorToWorld. OpCodes are messages from a behavior to a world; clWorldToBehavior opcodes are the reverse, and so on. This naming structure makes clear the 16 initial possibilities for messages to and from behaviors, browsers, interpreters, and worlds. Nothing in the protocol, however, prohibits additional classes. Possible future classes might include those for messages to and from behavior library servers, databases, the window system, and so forth.

---

[7] *Ibid.*

The prototype VRBS protocol defines opcodes for some, but not all, of these classes. The ClBrowserToBrowser class, for instance, is currently empty. Key protocol messages include those in the ClBehaviorToWorld Class, which describes operations to be performed on a node or queries about a node field's value.

The ClBehaviorToBrowser class includes opcodes to query the browser's abilities, including what VRML node types and node fields it supports and what viewer types it implements. Also, the ClWorldToBehavior class supports opcodes to start and stop a world's behavior set and to deliver user and timer events to the behavior.

Key administrative tasks are included as opcodes within the clWorldToInterpreter class. Typical operations include loading a behavior in to the interpreter and telling the interpreter to quit when a world is flushed from a browser's memory.

Following is a brief list of the VRBS opcode classes and opcodes.[8] The list is provided to illustrate the protocol's style. Opcode argument details are left to the protocol manual.

```
ClBehaviorToWorld
    OpGetWorldUrl
    OpGetNodeNames
    OpGetNodeBBox
    OpGetNodeType
    OpSetNodeField
    OpGetNodeField
    OpSetNodeFieldl
    OpGetNodeFieldl
    OpDeleteNode
    OpInsertNode
    OpReplaceNode

ClBehaviorToBrowser
    OpGetBrowserHost
    OpGetBrowserPort
    OpGetBrowserName
    OpGetBrowserVersion
    OpGetBrowserFeatures
    OpGetBrowserNodeTypes
    OpGetBrowserNodeFields
    OpGetBrowserViewerTypes
```

---

[8] *Ibid.*

```
ClInterpreterToWorld
    OpAddEventInterest
    OpRemoveEventInterest
    OpReady

ClInterpreterToBrowser
    OpHello
    OpInformation

ClWorldToBehavior
    OpBehaviorStart
    OpBehaviorStop
    OpBehaviorEvent

ClWorldToInterpreter
    OpLoadBehavior
    OpLo&dBehaviorFile
    OpQuitInterpreter
```

World Identifiers

Throughout the protocol, a WorldId is required as an argument to most messages. Recall that a *root world* maintains a behavior set that is loaded into a single instance of a language interpreter. Behaviors within that set, when executing, must be able to query and change nodes in their *root world* or any of the WWWInline'd worlds beneath it. A browser may, however, have multiple root *worlds* loaded at the same time, as when it maintains a cache of the last few worlds encountered while walking through an anchor chain. To indicate which world to change with an OpSetNodeField message, for instance, the browser needs a world identifier.

The VRBS protocol defines that a WorldId is a unique identifier for a *root world* within a browser. It does not define the nature of that identifier. It could be a name, a number, an address, or whatever. For example, SDSC WebView generates a unique random number for each V@ world and treats that as a WorldId. WorldIds of consecutively loaded worlds may not have any relationship to one another (and do not in SDSC WebView). WorldIds may or may not be reused during a browser session (they are not in SDSC WebView).

Events

Behaviors can affect changes to a scene, such as with the opsetNodeField message. They can also respond to user interactions. VRBS supports the traditional notion of an *event* that notifies a behavior when something of interest has occurred. Typical events include:

- mouse button presses and releases,
- atop a node,
- atop a region of the window,
- keyboard key presses and releases,
- pointer (cursor) motion,
- timer alarms,
- node and field changes, and
- World enter and leave.[9]

Like the X Window System, Open Inventor, HyperCard, and most other interactive systems, a behavior must first indicate its interest in a type of event. Later, each time that event occurs, the browser sends a message back to the interpreter.

The VRBS protocol supports the OpAddEventInterest message through which an interpreter requests notification of world events. OpRemoveEventInterest cancels such an interest.

Typical language implementations will cover these opcodes with an API that allows a script to nominate a function to be called each time a desired event arrives at the interpreter. SDSC's prototype Perl implementation, for instance, maintains a set of Perl functions to call on each event type. In any case, an interpreter's response to an incoming event is not defined by the VRBS protocol. Only the names and parameters of events are defined.

Handshaking

In many protocols a message sent from one party to another requires an *acknowledgment*, or *Ack*. VRBS defines a nonsymmetric client-server relationship between the browser (server) and interpreter (client). Each message from the interpreter to the browser is Acked,

---

[9] *Ibid.*

indicating whether the browser executed the request or rejected it because of an error. Typically the interpreter will pass error codes back to the behavior script, allowing it to detect when it's made an illegal operation.

Messages from the browser to the interpreter, such as events, are not Acked by the interpreter. This lack of symmetry prevents deadlock situations. For example, suppose that both the browser and the interpreter had to Ack the other on each message. Now let them both send a message to the other at exactly the same time and then enter a read waiting for an Ack back. The browser, expecting an Ack from its message to the interpreter, instead gets a new request. Similarly, the interpreter, expecting an Ack from its message to the browser, instead gets a new event. Both shelve the request or event and reenter a read in hopes of finding an Ack. Since both have put off processing the other's message, neither can send back an Ack, and they both hang, waiting for the other. To avoid this problem, the browser never waits for an Ack, and the interpreter never sends one.

Several alternative protocol designs are possible to avoid this kind of deadlock situation. For instance, browsers and interpreters could avoid blocking on reads and, using a message ID, track Acks and messages despite possible interleaved delivery. This kind of approach works but has several side effects.

Interleaved message handling breaks the *remote procedure call* style visible to a behavior script. Ideally a script simply calls a function in an API. The API function packages a message, sends it off to the browser, awaits a response, and then returns a status or query answer to the script just by the function call returning. The remote execution of the call is not visible to the script.

However, requiring interleaved message handling either forces the interpreter to allow message functions to return before getting answers or requires the interpreter to support multithreaded execution (so that one script can continue while another waits for a message answer). In the former case a script function call that sends a message would return nothing. Some indeterminate time later the answer would arrive back from the browser, be saved within the interpreter, and the script told of its arrival. The script is responsible for getting this late answer and trying to pick up where it left off earlier. This can create very inconvenient program structure, making it problematic to write even simple behaviors.

Supporting multithreaded script execution is also a problem. It is difficult to implement within a language interpreter and is not supported by most current scripting languages.

An alternative approach is to skip Acks altogether. Roughly this is the case with the X Window System protocol. Xlib queues packets destined for the server, flushing them periodically or when a client makes a server query. Xlib calls return immediately, without error codes indicating whether the server liked or disliked what it was sent. Sometime later faulty applications see a protocol error message show up on stderr if there was a problem. Again, this can make authorship of even simple scripts problematic.

The VRBS protocol's nonsymmetric handling of Acks eliminates most of these problems. Scripts make API function calls to send messages. The call blocks, waiting for the Ack back from the browser. When received, the call returns the status, error code, or query answer exactly like returning from a function call. Script writing is straight forward, with all message handling looking like function calls.

If the browser quits, messages destined for it from the interpreter have no place to go. The interpreter is expected to detect this and quit as well. Detection of browser or interpreter death is left up to the operating system's interprocess communications utilities. For example, on UNIX systems, SDSC WebView uses sockets. A read or write on a socket to a process that has died will return an error, letting the interpreter know that the browser has died unexpectedly. The protocol needn't support any explicit process death detection.

Interpreter and Behavior Startup Sequence

Previous parts of the chapter have covered each component of the VRBS system, including the WWWScript node, browser responsibilities, interpreter responsibilities, and the VRBS protocol for sending messages to and from each. Putting it all together, this part of the chapter discusses the interpreter and behavior startup sequence.

When a browser encounters a WWWScript node, it uses the script's URL to retrieve the script file to local disk. It also looks up the script's MIME type in the user's mailcap file. The appropriate entry's language interpreter is invoked, passing it:

- the browser's host name,
- the browser's port number, and
- a world's WorldId.[10]

The behavior script itself is not yet passed to the interpreter. Instead it is queued, awaiting transfer.

The combination of host name and port number uniquely addresses an open interprocess communications port on an Internet host. The interpreter, on startup, opens a connection back to the browser, on that host and at that port number. Its opening message to the browser, OpHello, queries the browser's VRBS protocol version and features. From this information the interpreter can adapt to variations in VRBS protocol revisions.

The interpreter then issues an OpReady Message back to the browser, passing it the initial WorldId. It indicates that it is ready to receive a behavior script for the world. The browser checks its transfer queue, pulls out the top pending behavior script, and, using an OpLoadBehavior message, sends it to the interpreter for loading and sanitization.

When the interpreter finishes with that script, it again sends OpReady, and so on until all behavior scripts pending in the browser have been loaded. At that point the browser issues an opBehaviorStart for each loaded behavior. This starts execution of the behavior within the interpreter.

Behaviors may be loaded into an interpreter at any time. They needn't be loaded all at once. For instance, suppose that a WWWScript node is a child of an LOD node. The browser could encounter the script and load it only when the LOD triggers the child by user proximity.

Browsers also may delay issuing an OpBehaviorstart as they see fit. A browser may, for instance, preload scripts, starting them up only as needed. In the LOD example an alternative implementation would load the WWWScript's script before the LOD triggers the child. Only the *startup* of the script would be delayed until the LOD trigger. The semantics of behavior execution remain the same, but the implementation varies to adapt to different browser styles.

In any case, when a behavior script is finally started, it typically immediately expresses interest in one or more events, nominating callback functions for each. The interpreter sends the browser an

---

[10] *Ibid.*

OpAddEventInterest message. Thereafter the browser sends events to the interpreter as they occur. The interpreter makes the callbacks, and the behavior script reacts to the events as it sees fit.

Changing Other Worlds

The use of a WorldId on all scene change messages allows a behavior to direct its operations at any world for which it has a valid WorldId. Behavior scripts may, at their discretion, communicate their WorldId to other scripts running in different interpreters on, perhaps, different hosts. It is through this mechanism that simple collaborative environments can be built.

Consider a VRML file with a behavior script. The script, at startup, gets its WorldId, opens a network connection to a remote collaboration server, and passes the WorldId, browser host name, and port number to the server. The collaboration server opens a connection back to the browser and starts issuing scene change messages, just as a behavior running within a local interpreter would.

World events may be delivered back to the collaboration server, allowing it to detect user actions. It responds by issuing messages to the user's browser, as well as messages to the browsers of all other network users viewing the same world. If one user, say, reaches out and starts a cube spinning in the scene, all users viewing the same world via the collaboration server see a cube start spinning. The simplicity of the VRBS protocol, and its independence from assumptions about the client, allows this kind of flexibility.

The Virtual Reality Behavior System (VRBS) is a prototype implementation of behavior scripting within VRML. It was designed to be straightforward to implement and as generic as practical. Its purpose was to begin exploring the issues involved in behavior scripting and to create a testbed for trying out alternative solutions.

Key VRBS features include:

- dynamic loading from one or more WWWScript nodes within a VRML file,
- independence from browser implementation style,
- independence from behavior language features,
- independence from compute architecture attributes,
- script-friendly protocol,

- extensibility and reasonability secure, and
- support a traditional event model.[11]

The VRBS protocol has been implemented at SDSC within SDSC WebView, a publicly available VRML browser. A prototype implementation of a behavior scripting language supporting the VRBS protocol has been implemented atop Perl, a publicly available scripting language.

SDSC is working to develop enhancements to the VRBS system to support:

- behaviors that travel from world to world, allowing, say, a paper airplane to be flown out the door of one world and into the next;
- higher-level tools and libraries to more easily support common behavior operations; and
- a binary variant of the VRBS protocol for use when a scripting language can easily deal with binary data.[12]

Perl: The Standard VRML Behavior Language

This part of the chapter presents a prototype implementation of a behavior system for VRML to demonstrate the requirements and the real-world problems involved in creating a behavior system. It also uncovers some of the more esoteric problems one finds in the finer implementation details of a VRML behavior language. Implementation details having to do with system and network security are specifically discussed.

The choice of Perl as a behavior language was made not necessarily because Perl should become the standard VRML behavior language but rather for convenience of implementation and demonstration purposes. The choice of Perl also permits the demonstration of several techniques to enable the repurposing of an existing scripting language as a VRML behavior language.

VRML is a developing standard for describing interactive three-dimensional scenes delivered across the Internet. The first version of the VRML specification, however, did not include semantics for describing

---

[11] *Ibid.*

[12] *Ibid.*

interactive behaviors in a scene. Instead, this task was left to be defined in future revisions of the standard.

The implementation of a prototype behavior system for VRML has helped to demonstrate many unique requirements and real-world problems involved in creating a future behavior system standard for VRML. Having implemented such a prototype, the VRML Architecture Group (VAG) has found that there is an inherent competition between providing required functionality and dealing with the pitfalls of network security, system security, performance issues, and portability.

Functional Requirements

To describe the advantages and disadvantages of a specific language implementation, it is useful to define the basic functional requirements necessary in general for a VRML behavior language. VAG may then set out to define the specific language features and to identify problems involved in providing those features in a nonprototype language implementation.

Architecture Independent

The language should not be tied to any specific hardware architecture. This includes such issues as assuming word size, byte ordering, memory layout, etc.

Operating System Independent

The language should not be tied to any specific operating system. This includes such issues as assuming a process management model, directory path notation, or file name formats.

Portable and Powerful

The interpreter should be available on or easily ported to a wide variety of computer systems. The intent is to provide a language that can be shared over a network among many different heterogeneous systems. A developer should also be provided with sufficiently powerful tools (language features/libraries) to be able to author arbitrarily sophisticated environments.

Usable

The language should be easy to author and learn and should provide a quick development cycle. Convoluted syntax and overly intricate semantics will discourage the majority of users.

Network and System Secure

The language should provide some well-defined networking capabilities, but limit the scope to prevent intentional or unintentional network security problems. In addition, the language should provide certain well-defined system access capabilities (such as file I/O, process creation, etc.) but limit the scope to prevent intentional or unintentional system security problems.

Perl Behavior System (PBS)

Several scripting languages fulfill these requirements. Perl, in particular, is powerful, portable, available for most systems, and very C-like. It is the network and system security requirements that tend to be troublesome for most languages, however.

There are, perhaps, many more language feature requirements that should be addressed in a standards specification. The items listed here are sufficient, however, to demonstrate specific language features that will be presented. They will help to identify most of the problems uncovered in SDSC's prototype implementation.

The Perl Behavior System (PBS) is a prototype implementation of a behavior language. PBS uses the VRBS to communicate with a VRML browser (SDSC WebView). PBS itself consists of a wrapper script (written in Perl) that provides a preprocessor for end user scripts and a small number of simple routines used to interact with VRML worlds, as shown in Figure 18.3.[13]

VRBS is a simple message-passing protocol used to communicate commands, requests, and data to the VRML browser. It also accepts events and messages back from the VRML browser and distributes those events to the correct behavior script. It is the separation of

---

[13] John L. Morland and David R. Nadeau, The Virtual Reality Behavior system (VRBS): Using Perl As A Behavior Language For VRML, San Diego Supercomputer Center (SDSC) Association of Computing Machinery (ACM), December 15, 1995.

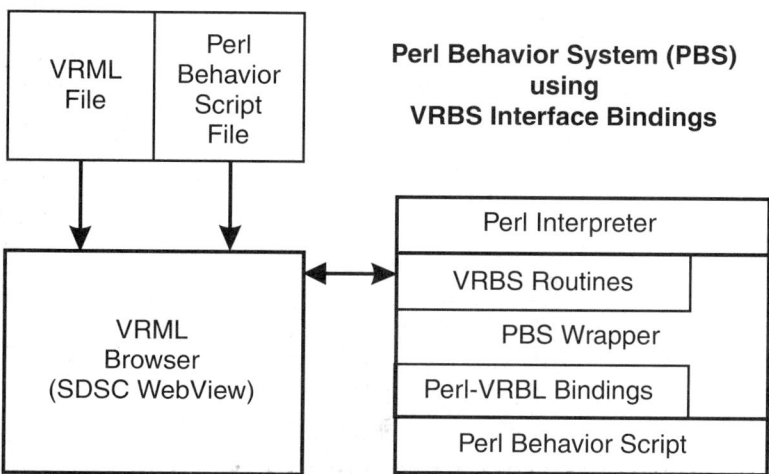

Figure 18.3 Perl Behavior System, Using VRBS Interface Bindings

behavior protocol from behavior language that makes it possible to use any scripting language or even any program as a behavior system. It is SDSC's intent, however, to focus on the script-based behaviors, since they are capable of being downloaded over a network connection and present the most challenges.

PBS/VRBS-Browser Interaction

In the SDSC WebView/PBS environment, behavior scripts are downloaded by the SDSC WebView browser. Each time a new world is encountered by the browser, a new Perl interpreter is started. The interpreter is killed when the browser flushes a world from its memory cache. So there may be more than one interpreter running at any given time. However, any number of behavior scripts that are part of the same world may be running simultaneously under one interpreter. This enables several scripts from one world to interact with the same scene.

When a new interpreter is started for a world, the following sequence of events takes place:

1. *Browser executes PBS/Perl.* The PBS wrapper script is handed parameters for the hostname, port, and worldId by the browser.
2. *PBS performs internal initialization.* PBS initializes static variables, tables, and other data structures in preparation to begin handling requests for a world.
3. *PBS connects to browser.* PBS opens a connection to the browser and sends a message telling the browser that the interpreter is ready to begin processing requests.
4. *Browser sends a behavior to PBS.* The browser sends PBS a command telling the interpreter to load a behavior script along with the name of the behavior, and either the filename or the actual text of the behavior script.
5. *PBS verifies the behavior script.* PBS runs the script through a filter to check for known dangers or illegal behaviors, then caches the script, based on the node name of the Script node.
6. *Browser asks to start a behavior.* The browser sends PBS a command telling the interpreter to begin execution of a named, cached behavior.
7. *PBS runs the behavior code.* PBS calls Perl's *eval* function on the cached behavior and continues waiting for message from the browser.

After step 7, the behavior script can then begin execution and may run Perl code, which includes calls to the Perl-VRBS User-level Binding routines.[14]

Perl-VRBS User Bindings

PBS contains a Perl implementation of the VRBS protocol routines. These are low-level routines that are intended to be called not by end user scripts but by a language-specific user-level binding layer.

In addition to the calls that a user makes to PBS, the PBS wrapper also makes calls to user routines through event callbacks. Event callbacks are user-defined routines that are added to an internal PBS list by calling the AddEvent routine. The user routines are later called as a result of some specific event sent from the browser.

---

[14] *Ibid.*

An event callback mechanism is used for the following reasons:

- A behavior script does not have to poll for user events.
- The user script does not block execution. It returns control back to the PBS wrapper.[15]

Of particular interest to this discussion is the method in which a user behavior uses these routines to interact with the PBS wrapper and with a specific VRML world.

PBS Internals

Each time the user's script calls the AddEvent routine, the PBS wrapper adds an entry to an event table, as shown in Table 18.1. This event table enables the PBS wrapper to call the correct user-nominated callback routine when the browser sends an event.[16] At this stage, however, the browser does not know that PBS is interested in seeing events of the given type. The AddEvent routine must also determine whether it has ever asked the browser to start sending the event type (that is, whether the given event type is ever generated by some user action or other behavior interaction).

After the PBS wrapper has cached the event in its event table it then determines whether it needs to register a new event type with the browser. It does this by looking in its own list of event types whose entries denote the number (count) of user callback routines that have previously been registered for the event type.

By using the event numbers as an index into the eventList cache, we can quickly determine whether we need to tell the browser to respond to specific event types. In this case the table indicates that there has been one EvTimer event registered and one NodeChange event registered.

Note that the finite number, type, and capabilities of the events that VRBS provides leaves the implementors in control of what kind of calls are made between the browser and behaviors. This in turn limits the scope of what an ill-mannered script could do to an unsuspecting user's environment. However, the calls that can be made by

---

[15]*Ibid.*

[16]*Ibid.*

Table 18.1 Event Table

id	world	event	func	data	params
0	2001	EvTimer	rotate	Fred	1000
1	42	NodeChan	doIt	toIt	milk

the behavior to the scripting language interpreter itself present more difficult access control issues.

Behavior Language Restraints

One of the unique aspects of developing a behavior model for VRML is the notion that scripts can be downloaded from a remote machine on a network. Once downloaded, the script is then executed on the local machine. The potential for intentional or unintentional inclusion of a software pathogen (computer virus) is quite real.

Even if a language were to fulfill the behavior language requirements, a language that does not meet the requirements could potentially be too dangerous to trust when used as a behavior system. The issue is access. That is, the ability to make use of system or network resources can potentially lead to exploitation of the capabilities of those resources.

To illustrate some of the potential problems in allowing a behavior language to make unrestrained calls, SDSC's researchers have classified some of Perl's built-in subroutines and examined the positive and negative aspects of their use in a behavior script. The two main types of potentially dangerous language features are internal language parsing constructs and external communications constructs. The external communications classification can be further broken down into three subcategories: file operations, system interaction, and network access.

Language-Specific Constructs

Most of the Perl functionality in this category involves the creation or execution of Perl code fragments. Let's look at some of these.

1. *Code creation and deletion*

   Perl uses the *sub* keyword to define a code fragment for a subroutine call. This capability is most certainly useful and often necessary for scripts of even moderate complexity. However, when the *sub* keyword is used more than once with the same subroutine name, the prior definition of the subroutine is lost. In this case it may be possible for a downloaded behavior script to override even PBS routines such that subsequent behaviors use redefined subroutines.

   Another Perl function that is quite useful for initialization but potentially hazardous is the *undef* routine. This enables a script to undefine any variable or subroutine such that it no longer has any definition whatsoever. The concern here is similar to that of the *sub* keyword. An ill-mannered behavior could completely remove the ability for other scripts to function.

2. *Code execution*

   The Perl *eval* function enables a script to ask the interpreter to parse and execute a code fragment contained in a variable. This routine is of particular interest because it is the very mechanism that the PBS wrapper script uses to interpret a behavior script. The key danger here lies in the fact that a behavior script could, through the use of the *eval* function, completely bypass the preprocessing stage of pbs. Any checks for valid or dangerous code, therefore, are also bypassed.

   Since a string to be executed in Perl can be computed at run time, we have a further problem in determining what in a user behavior looks dangerous. Any language that wishes to execute fragments of its own language may have a similar code-evaluation capability. Therefore there should be similar concern on behalf of other behavior languages.

3. *Code acquisition and execution*

   Perl provides two functions—*do* and *require*—that enable a script to have a file containing Perl code to be loaded, parsed, and executed. This is similar to a C preprocessor #include statement. Code fragments are read from an external file at the line in the calling file where the *do* or *require* statements occur.

This functionality is particularly insidious, since it is both accessing arbitrarily named external files and is executing code that a preprocessing stage can not catch.

A scripting language processor can grant as few or as many capabilities to a script as the language specification allows. A preprocessor can even detect and remove existing constructs before they ever get to the interpreter. SDSC's researchers can even modify the interpreter itself to remove any built-in language constructs that can cause the kind of grief that's been discussed. But modifying the interpreter means changing the language, which in this case defeats the purpose of using a standard scripting language. However, access to resources outside of the language interpreter itself is a far more difficult issue than internal interpreter issues.

External Communications

SDSC's researchers would like to provide as much capability to a behavior author as is possible without sacrificing their local system or network security. Specifically, there are functions that they would like to provide to the user even if they provide them with slightly limited capabilities. Three categories of external communications functions that deserve attention.

1. *File operations*

The need for a behavior script to have file access is clear. Opening a writable file for caching state information, outputting results of a simulation, or reading a configuration file are a few examples.

Perl provides the following functionality for accessing or manipulating local files: (glob), chdir, chmod, chown, dbmopen, link, lstat, mkdir, open, opendir, readlink, rename, rmdir, stat, symlink, truncate, unlink, and utime. The justification for allowing or disallowing use of each of these routines in turn can be easily proposed. However, it is more important to ask to what extent the functions should be allowed. Ideally SDSC's researchers can justify the validity of one solution to this problem.

2. *System interaction*

Interaction with operating system functionality, although not particularly portable, is often very useful. It is easy to demonstrate situations in which executing an external program is desirable, such as a VRML world that presents a directory tree where doors represent directories and images on the wall represent files. The execution of the UNIX ls command would be quite handy in this case.

Perl provides the following routines for interaction with operating system–level functionality: chroot, die, exec, exit, fork, getgrp, getlogin, getpid, getpriority, glob, kill, setgrp, setpriority, sleep, syscall, system, umask, wait, waitpid, and (accent graves).

In SDSC's researchers' virtual directory-structure room, they could imagine providing a more limited form of an ls-like command. But providing this sort of functionality directly in the language, could become unwieldy, not to mention nonportable (as is the case for the ls command).

3. Network access

One can easily imagine a behavior needing to open a network connection to a large database server. It could send queries and render scenes based on the returned data. One can also imagine an ill-mannered script that reads the local host's password database (such as the /etc/passwd file on a UNIX host) and then promptly opens a network connection to a remote host to hand off that data.

Perl provides the following functions to enable TCP/IP socket connections that could easily be abused: accept, bind, connect, and listen. Allowing a network connection to an unfamiliar host through an untrusted port using an arbitrary protocol has obvious problems. But as in the first example, it also has some notable benefits.

The key to all of these problems is, again, resource access. If a language and interpreter or even a network or operating system grant the ability to access specific resources, the game is over. The solution, therefore, is to not allow access to critical resources to begin with, or at least to limit the extent of access capabilities.

Sanitizing Perl

As SDSC's researchers have demonstrated, the danger in a behavior language lies in the unrestrained access a language has to both internal and external resources. One method that has proved useful in avoiding resource access problems is to preprocess the incoming behavior script before it is ever passed to the interpreter. In essence, a sanitizing pass is run on the behavior script to disable or replace any built-in access-granting routines or any user-level code fragments that have the potential of being antisocial.

A feature of Perl that allows implementation of a sanitizing pass is that a Perl script cannot compute and then call a built-in function name. This has to do with the function-call syntax of Perl itself. Calls to built-in Perl function names are not preceded by an ampersand (&) character. This is not the case for user-defined routines. The difference in implementation is that built-in function names are bound to interpreter code at compile time, whereas user-defined routines are bound to interpreter code at run time.

Several key points come to mind that can help solve some problems. One can choose routines to remove from a behavior script. For example, the system call could be removed, because one cannot predict which commands the script will try to run. The user could be warned about questionable code. The browser user could be told that a behavior that was about to start was potentially too dangerous to run. Or the script would just not run in this case. One could also select a subset of routines to modify. The open call could be changed to restrict opened files to one fixed directory. The script itself does not have to know this.

The last option means that SDSC researchers could simply wrap the routines they have deemed dangerous with their own code. In other words, code that has parameter-compatible arguments with the real routines provides reduced access to resources.

It is clear that there are resource-access problems involved in downloading a behavior script from a remote system and running a script on a local machine. The solutions are less clear. The restrictions one places on a language can clearly hamper the usefulness of the language. By the same token, it is also clear that unlimited resource access by a behavior is potentially dangerous. Determining what is enough access or too much access is an interesting and worthy area of future research.

From Here

Now that I've thoroughly explored the intricacies of behavior engine technology as it relates to VRML, let's look at the numerous VRML applications that have been derived from this technology. The next chapter looks at numerous VR applications that have been developed and delivered via the Internet. They range from architectural models, to commercial (virtual banking and retailing), to military, space related, medical, and last but not least, other miscellaneous applications. Now that I've thoroughly explored the intricacies of Behavior Engine Technology as it relates to VRML, the next chapter covers other ongoing VR research projects that will eventually be imported to the Internet.

Other VR Research

Chapter 15 presented numerous proposed VRML research projects and systems. This chapter will guide you through the development of ongoing realistic VR projects within the commercial, military, government, and medical communities for eventual importation to the Internet as possible VRML applications.

Commercial: VRML Making VISA More Competitive in the Financial Services Market

Visa and Worlds Inc. are working together to develop virtual banking and retailing applications delivered via the Internet. The partners will combine the power of multiuser virtual reality and secure transaction processing to create advanced online environments for consumers, merchants, and financial institutions.

A prototype, called The Electronic Courtyard, is being developed that includes an interactive bank branch in which consumers can check account balances, transfer funds, and apply for loans. The flat, two-dimensional "home pages" available on the Internet today will evolve into compelling three-dimensional Web sites where people bank, shop, and interact. This alliance represents a powerful combination. The advanced technologies—coupled with VISA's global transaction processing systems give VISA the ability to deliver compelling new electronic services to its members and their customers.

The Electronic Courtyard is an example of a three-dimensional, commercial online environment that can be deployed today over the Internet. It is a radical departure from traditional text- and icon-based applications. Rendered in rich three-dimensional graphics, environments like The Electronic Courtyard allow users to explore their surroundings from a first-person perspective, using a mouse or a keyboard. Within virtual rooms and spaces, individual users can interact with bank tellers, loan officers, financial advisors, and salespeople who can help the user conduct business online or purchase merchandise electronically. This technology has already proved itself in a VRML online chat environment. Combined with and enhanced by VISA's transaction-processing capabilities, users will be able to not only chat but also shop, bank, and access an array of financial services within a shared virtual world.

The Electronic Courtyard will use VISA's remote banking subsidiary, VISA Interactive, to provide connectivity between financial institutions and consumers. Leveraging the VISA infrastructure to provide the back-end processing will enable banks to reach their customers in new and innovative ways without creating costly new systems.

Visa's members know that investing in bricks and mortar is no longer the way to reach new customers. This new interface will give financial institutions the opportunity to use cyberbricks and mortar to build environments in which they can offer services to consumers—at a fraction of the investment of the traditional branch.

Like other services offered by VISA Interactive, the virtual branches will be bank-branded and designed to the specifications of the member financial institution. VISA members will be able to tailor the virtual environment to suite the needs of their market and their customers.

Visa, the world's largest consumer payment system, plays a pivotal role in developing and implementing new technologies that benefit member financial institutions, their cardholders, businesses, governments, and the global economy. San Francisco–based VISA and its 19,000 member financial institutions worldwide serve more than 12 million merchants and service more than 402 million cards. VISA also owns and operates VISA Interactive, which provides remote banking solutions to member and Visa/PLUS, the largest global automated teller machine (ATM) network. In 1994 VISA card (credit and debit) transactions totaled more than $630 billion worldwide. More information on VISA can be obtained through its home page on the Internet's World Wide Web at http://www.visa.com.

Military: DIVE Technology

Until recently no serious effort was under way to develop virtual environments to allow individual combatants access to the virtual battlefield. As new technologies allow the individual soldier to employ increasingly lethal smart weapons, the importance of the virtual soldier will be even greater on future battlefields.

Simulation and training systems currently under development, such as the Close Combat Tactical Trainer (CCTT), provide only a minimal ability to simulate the effects of dismounted infantry. Moreover, these systems do not provide any means to train infantry in even an approximately realistic setting.

Recent research conducted by the United States Army Simulation Training and Instrumentation Command (STRICOM) and Avatar Partners, Inc., Boulder Creek, CA, attempts to enable the realistic simulation of combined arms combat, including dismounted infantry. The proposed approach will allow individual soldiers to enter the virtual battlefield through specially designed gateways known as Dismounted Infantry Virtual Environment (DIVE) chambers—instrumented rooms—that allow the soldiers to immerse themselves in a virtual environment, as shown in Figure 19.1. Within this environment a soldier will be able to navigate through a variety of terrain, engage in combat, communicate with both real and synthetic forces, and train for a variety of combat scenarios. Moreover, the DIVE system will connect to the defense simulation Internet (DSI), allowing the dismounted soldier to participate in larger distributed interactive simulation (DIS) exercises (environments that permit mechanized units to fight on a simulated battlefield).

Avatar Partners, Inc., was recently awarded a $1 million research and development contract from STRICOM to develop the DIVE system.

This wireless unencumbered virtual reality system for infantry training applications represents a significant step forward in synthetic environment technology in terms of both immersion and realism. DIVE is the first step toward the creation of a holodecklike virtual reality system.

The DIVE system consists of a network of up to 20 individual DIVE chambers, each of which generates a window into a shared synthetic environment. Each chamber generates a window into a shared synthetic environment: an immersive three-dimensional visual, audio, and tactile environment that allows individual participants to enter a

Figure 19.1 DIVE Chamber

shared virtual battlefield. Applications of the DIVE system include hazardous-operations training and simulation for both military and civilian operations and location-based entertainment.

Technical Approach

Similar to the system seen in the popular movie *Disclosure*, the DIVE system combines unencumbered and immersive virtual reality technologies into a single full-body tracking system. This system allows the user's body to be tracked without encumbering cables or tethers. Within the virtual environment the user sees an animated character or virtual body that follows his or her body motions in real time. This virtual body enables natural navigation of the virtual environment when walking, climbing, and running or when manipulating virtual objects.

The DIVE technical approach focuses on minimum encumbrance, deep immersion (sensory and functional), and body centered interaction. These goals are accomplished by using a variety of innovative technologies: video-based body tracking system, shared memory heterogeneous multiprocessing, physics-based modeling, synthetic agents, and speaker-independent voice recognition.[1]

Minimum Encumbrance

One of the goals of the DIVE system is to eliminate the perceivable interface between the participant and the equipment comprising the virtual environment. Optimally the participant would wear no special equipment or devices to experience the synthetic environment.

Technology limits the degree to which the participant can be unencumbered. The current state of the art requires that the user carry various electronic devices, a portable computer, and other devices.

Deep Immersion

The degree of immersion is determined by the extent that the participant in a virtual environment feels that he or she is in the virtual space. Immersion is related to presence—the sensation of being located at a place—in this case a location within the virtual environment. Immersion and presence can (and should) be measured.

Deep immersion occurs when the virtual environment becomes more real to the participant than the physical environment. Deep immersion produces suspension of disbelief. Immersion can be decomposed into two components: sensory and functional. Sensory immersion refers to the replacement of the normal sensory stimulus with artificially generated or synthetic sources. The majority of work in virtual environments has focused on sensory immersion (head-mounted display technology). Functional immersion refers to the operation of the virtual environment, that is, the physical simulation that lies behind the sensory stimuli (the simulation of gravitational properties of objects, weapons, effects, etc.). If either the sensory or functional immersion breaks, the illusion is disturbed and total immersion suffers.

---

[1] John R. Vacca, *Dismounted Infantry Virtual Environment (DIVE) Technology*, Virtual Reality Special Report, Vol. 2, No. 5, November-December, 1995, pp. 49.

Body-Centered Interaction

Experimental results indicate that there is a connection between the presence of a virtual body within a synthetic environment and the reported degree of presence in the environment. Presence refers to a measure of the participant's sense of being at a location within the virtual space rather than the physical space. Body-centered interaction focuses on developing interaction techniques that match sensory data (primarily visual) with proprioceptive feedback (sensed body position).

Video-Based Body Tracking

The eventual goal of the Avatar approach is to create a completely "unencumbered" system in which the participant wears only the normal battlefield equipment. Avatar has developed a proprietary video-based tracking methodology that is implementable with commercially available image processing systems. Multiple video cameras are arranged around the DIVE chamber, and positions of key body locations are triangulated to determine positions within the chamber.

Heterogeneous Multiprocessing

Reducing system latency (also referred to as lag) is one of the primary challenges in designing any virtual reality system. In addition to judicious design of the system, employing parallel processing and multiprocessing can greatly reduce system latency.

Avatar has developed a heterogeneous multiprocessing architecture, based on industry standard and COTS components, that implements a large scale multiprocessing system. Each DIVE chamber includes approximately 12 processing systems that all act as a single shared-memory computer. The entire DIVE network (consisting of as many as 40 chambers) connects to the same fiber-optic LAN, effectively creating an enormous multiprocessing computer.

Physics-Based Modeling

The DIVE system architecture is concerned largely with the creation of an ultrarealistic physical environment. Multiple compute servers are dedicated to realistic modeling of gravitational effects, inertia, rigid and nonrigid body collision, weapons effect, fire simulation, etc. DIVE is a distributed real-time physics based modeling environment.

Synthetic Agents

DIVE supports synthetic agents both to generate enemy forces and to fill out friendly forces. Agents have realistic sensory and cognitive limitations (they can't see behind them and can't do 10 things at once). Synthetic agents use a separately compiled map of the virtual environment to simplify sensing and navigation.

Agents use preprogrammed sequences of actions or scripts to implement specific activities, such as room entry and clearing. They communicate with one another and with human participants, using voice and hand signals. Agent body motion is then computed in real time using inverse kinematics and prerecorded motion sequences.

Voice Recognition

The system includes a capability for human participants to communicate with synthetic agents via voice and hand/arm gestures. A speaker-independent voice-recognition system, coupled with an English-like command syntax, allows the human participants to command a force of synthetic agents.

Additionally, agents can be communicated with via hand/arm signals. The outputs of the body-tracking system are interpreted as gestures, such as "come here", "get down", "halt", etc. They also know how to respond to these commands.

Physiological and Psychological Requirements

In order to begin defining requirements for a dismounted-infantry training system, Avatar began by examining the ultimate system performance. The ultimate DIVE-type simulator would have the following properties:

- From the soldier's point of view, the virtual environment is indistinguishable from reality.
- From the trainer's point of view, the soldier's actions are indistinguishable from battlefield performance.
- Any mission can be simulated.[2]

---

[2] *Ibi\d.*, p. 50.

Detailed requirements of the ultimate DIVE simulator are defined by examining each of the sensory channels available to the immersed soldier. People are used to talking about the five senses, but in fact human sensory perception is much more complex. According to Avatar, the human sensory system includes the following categories:

- visual,
- auditory and vibratory,
- olfactory,
- tactile,
- temperature,
- pain, and
- propioceptive and kinesthetic.[3]

Most virtual reality research focuses on systems and technologies for supporting the visual channel. The ultimate performance of the visual channel is determined by examining the capabilities of the human eye. The instantaneous field of view of the eye is approximately 100 degrees in the horizontal and vertical axes. At the center of the field of view the visual acuity of the human eye is about one arc minute. This rolls off approximately by 20 percent at 10 degrees from center of the field of view. The eye can saccade rapidly +/- 45 degrees y shuts down for about 100 milliseconds. By combining the maximum motion about the center of the field of view and the instantaneous field of view, thel system, the ultimate DIVE simulator would also need to completely model the visual appearance of the world in such a way that the simulated world is indistinguishable from the real world. According to Avatar, this leads to the following set of requirements for the visual channel: resolution equivalent to performance of the human visual system, textures on everything, full color, complex lighting that includes shadows and reflections, and no perceivable lag.[4]

The second major sensory channel is the auditory channel. The frequency range of human hearing is typically quoted as ranging from 20–20,000 Hz, although lower-frequency vibrations can be experienced as tactile sensations. Avatar has been able to locate sounds fairly accurately within a range of 5–10 degrees. Localization is a complex function of time delays, frequency differences, and other cues.

---

[3] *Ibid.*, p. 50.

[4] *Ibid.*, p. 50.

Modeling the auditory environment is almost as complex as modeling the visual environment. The real world has a potentially infinite number of sound sources, which may be located arbitrarily and can be directional. Moving sources are subject to both atmospheric absorption and the Doppler effect. Reverberation and echoes can be very complex and are time varying.

The olfactory channel (smell) is perhaps the least explored of the human senses in current virtual environment research. The human olfactory system is very sensitive and capable of detecting minute amounts of chemical substances in the air. The human olfactory system is also capable of distinguishing individual odors in mixes, estimating the intensity of an odor, and to some extent determining the direction or point of origin of an odor.

The human skin is capable of sensing a variety of stimuli, including touch, pain, and temperature. According to Avatar, three mechanical stimuli can produce the sensation of touch: step functions—a displacement of the skin for an extended time; impulse functions—transitory displacements of the skin, lasting only a few milliseconds; and periodic functions—repeat regular or irregular displacements of the skin.[5]

The frequency range over which the skin is sensitive to touch ranges from 0 to about 300 Hz. Different frequency ranges activate different nerve fibers. Texture sensing occurs as a relative motion between the textured object and the skin receptors.

The skin can also sense temperature. The skin generally maintains a temperature of about 33 degrees Celsius; when in contact with a warmer or cooler medium, it changes temperature. These changes can be sensed and the location and extent determined.

Often overlooked, the sensation of pain is itself a separate and important sensory mechanism. In the case of the skin, pain generally occurs from damage to the skin from piercing, cutting, or burning. Pain sensations are localized but can become unlocalized in certain cases.

The propioceptive and kinesthetic sensory systems allow the body to sense its position and motion in the environment. The human being is extremely sensitive to differences in joint angles and forces exerted on the body. For example, specific joint angles can be easily duplicated accurately and remembered for extended periods. Joint-angle differences below one degree can be sensed, depending on the particular joint in question and the motion of the specific joint.

---

[5] *Ibid.*, p. 51.

All of the sensory information received by the human being is processed in real time to produce high-level sensations, such as presence or immersion. These terms are often used in the VR literature to describe the effectiveness of VR simulations but at best are poorly defined and understood.

Generally speaking, immersion refers to the feeling of being contained inside a space, whereas presence refers to the sensation of being at a place or part of an experience. Although there is little data available that would enable either of these terms to be quantified, some factors that impact immersion and presence have been identified and serve as pointers for further research.

Perceived presence in the virtual environment can contribute significantly to the training effectiveness of the system. For example, in the case of the proposed DIVE system, the participants' willingness to believe that they might be injured or killed by taking the wrong action, as well as the fear of being surprised, are important components of the simulation experience. If the participants do not seek to avoid injury, they may take actions that are unrealistic for a given situation. Additionally, fear and excitement cause the release of adrenaline into the participants, and that can alter the caloric consumption during the performance of a task.

Presence is defined as the degree to which, while immersed in the virtual environment, it becomes more "real" or "present" than everyday reality. Clearly, increasing the participants' perception of presence will also increase the likelihood that they will perform tasks as if they were actually performing them and will limit their willingness to take unrealistic risks.

As stated earlier, perceived presence can be decomposed into two components: sensory and functional. The sensory component refers to sensory immersion that is the focus of most virtual reality research. Functional presence refers to the behavioral and operational components of a virtual environment that contribute to presence. For example, if light switches do not operate, objects on a desk cannot be moved or picked up, and the participant will have a decreased sense of presence. Avatar refers to environments that exhibit both sensory and functional aspects of presence as deep, or immersive.

Body awareness, the ability to sense and see one's own body, contributes immensely to the sense of presence. Several controlled experiments have been conducted to determine the relationship among presence, the representation of a virtual body, and the method of navigation within the environment. Motion of the body in space is also related to the ability to remember directions and to navigate in an environment. The results of these studies indicate a very strong coupling between the degree of presence reported and the connection of a natural mode of navigation (walking) with a virtual body.

According to Avatar, participants in these experiments were asked to perform the degree of perceived presence under the following conditions: no virtual body, navigate by pointing; virtual body, navigate by pointing; and virtual body, navigate by walking.[6] According to Avatar, the results indicate that there was practically no difference in perceived presence between the first two conditions. However, the participants who navigated by walking reported a statistically significant increase in perceived presence.

High-resolution visual imagery over a wide field of view has been shown to contribute to the sensation of immersion, although a number of experiments have indicated that high-resolution imagery is necessary only over a small region of the field of view. The ability to look into any direction, and in particular to move the head while navigating, contributes to the feeling of immersion and aids the construction of an internal model of a space.

Appropriately placed and triggered audio cues can significantly enhance the overall realism of a virtual experience. Researchers have found that well-produced audio can cause users to report that graphics of video games are of a higher quality than the same graphics presented without audio. The effective use of audio within a virtual environment is similarly important.

Unencumbered Virtual Reality Technology

Virtual reality technology provides a means by which members of the infantry can be immersed in a virtual environment and to participate in a DIS exercise. However, achieving this goal requires the development of new approaches and innovative combinations of these technologies.

Historically the virtual reality community has been split between those who have favored total immersion and those favoring unencumbered approaches. By donning a head-mounted display with six

---

[6] *Ibid.*, p. 52.

degrees of freedom head tracking, the total immersion approach places the user inside of a three-dimensional synthetic environment.

The immersive approach requires the user to wear a variety of equipment, and this equipment (often weighing several pounds) is generally connected to one or more computers by a variety of cables. The combination of the equipment worn by the user and the cables connecting this equipment to computers encumber the user, thus restricting his movement substantially. Usually the user of an immersive system is required to stand in a specific spot or sit to avoid tripping over the myriad of cables.

Head-mounted immersive systems also suffer from the fact that the user's body disappears when entering the virtual environment (you can't see your hands or feet). According to Avatar, with systems such as VPL's DataGlove, a portion of the user's body enters the virtual environment, but this experience is somewhat dissatisfying and unnatural for many applications. The loss of body awareness is particularly troubling when the user attempts to navigate in the virtual environment by using full body motion.

According to Avatar, the unencumbered approach to virtual environments uses video-based pattern recognition and tracking techniques to allow the user to interact with virtual (computer-generated) objects without wearing any specialized equipment or tracking systems. The user sees a graphical representation or video image of himself or herself projected inside of a virtual environment (second-person VR). Historically these systems have been limited to two-dimensional video game worlds. The existing unencumbered approaches allow the user to retain body awareness, but do not produce a total immersion experience.

Proposed Solution

The proposed effort will result in the development of a hybrid virtual reality interface combining total immersion with unencumbered body tracking to allow dismounted infantry people to engage directly in simulated exercises. DIVE will provide an interactive simulation environment that, for the first time, will allow people to be completely immersed in simulation exercises. By combining technology developed by both total immersion and unencumbered approaches, a system will be developed that allows for a total immersion experience in a virtual environment in which the user retains body awareness and can see his or her hands and feet. This capability will provide a major advance in the realism of infantry and combined infantry/mechanized training.

The DIVE project is more than the development a single simulation system; it is also the development of an open system architecture that will be made available to other vendors to allow their equipment and software to interface with the DIVE network and eventually the Internet. An interface control document describing the DIVE system interfaces will be published by Avatar and be made available to interested parties in late 1996.

Government: NASA Virtual Reality Projects

Virtual environment (VE) technology is still in its infancy. However, there is a great potential for this technology for the National Aeronautics and Space Administration (NASA). Several NASA centers, following initial research and development at the Ames Research Center (ARC), Moffett Field, CA, in the Aerospace Human Factors Division, are now investigating and developing VE technology for specific NASA tasks and missions. (See Figure 19.2.)[7]

Research support for VE technology development has been a part of NASA's human factors research program since 1985. Under the auspices of the Office of Aeronautics and Space Technology (OAST), initial funding was provided to ARC, which resulted in the origination of this technology. Since 1985, other NASA centers have begun using and developing this technology. At each research and space flight center, NASA missions have been major drivers of the technology. Let's look at an overview of each VE project, the technology, and its applications in NASA centers the potential roles it can take in NASA and a roadmap of the next four years.

Ames Research Center (ARC)

The Ames Research Center is responsible for human performance research relevant to developing virtual environments for NASA

---

[7] John R. Vacca, *NASA VR Projects: Part 1*, *VR World*, Vol. 3, No. 2, March/April, 1995, p. 48.

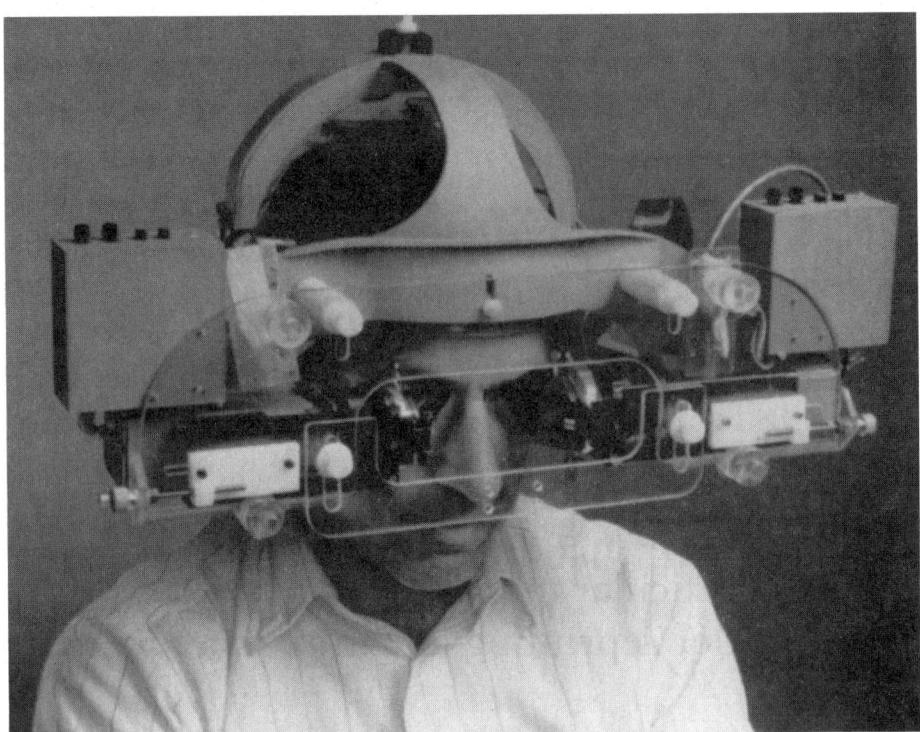

Figure 19.2 Early Head-Mounted Haploscope for Studying the Apparent Depth of Stereo Virtual Images

applications and for the development of human-centered technology for aeronautics. Figure 21.3 shows some of the current research and development in VE technology that's going on there: (See Figure 19.3).[8]

Dynamic Response of Spatial Sensors

The research objective of this project is to characterize the dynamic response of displacement transducers commonly used in VE applications. Currently a testbed and a method for measuring the dynamic response characteristics of position and orientation sensors have

---

[8] *Ibid.*

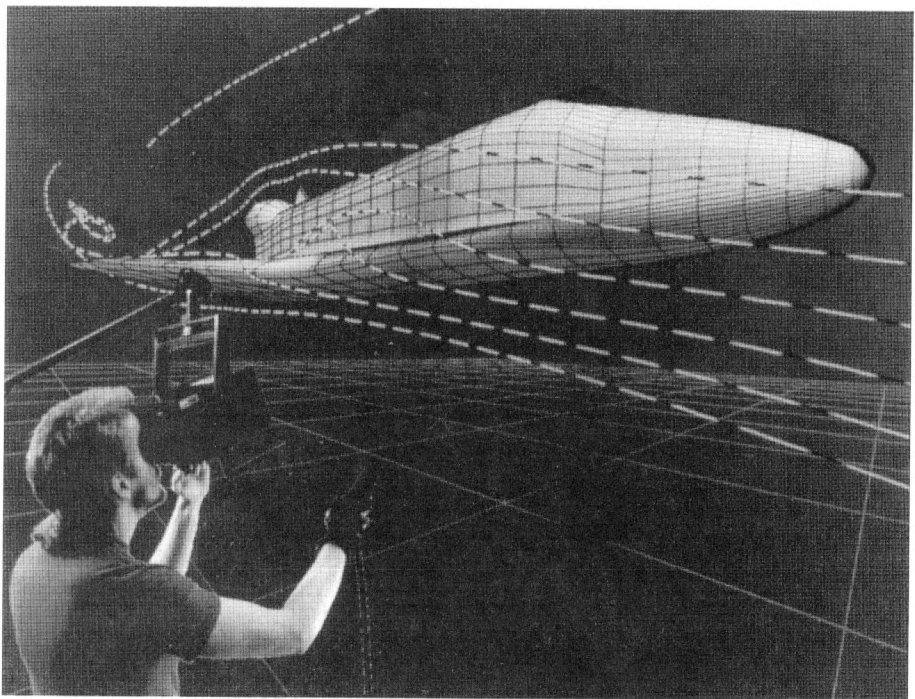

Figure 19.3 The NASA Ames Virtual Wind Tunnel

been developed. The testbed consists of a motorized swing arm that imparts known displacement inputs to the VE sensor. The experimental method involves a series of tests in which the sensor is displaced back and forth at a number of controlled frequencies that span the bandwidth of volitional human movement. During the tests, actual swing arm angle, as determined by an optical encoder at the motor shaft, and reported VE sensor displacements are collected and time stamped. Because of the time-stamping technique, the response time of the sensor can be measured directly, independent of latencies in data transmission from the sensor unit and any processing by the interface application running on the host computer. Analysis of these experimental results allows sensor time delay and gain characteristics to be determined as a function of input frequency. Results from tests on several commercially available VE spatial sensors have been obtained and documented.

In the future additional sensors will be tested. The test method and hardware will be extended to measure dynamic response of complete—sensor-to-display—VE systems.

Head-Slaved Roll Compensation in Virtual/Remote Target Acquisition Tasks

This project examines whether the addition of a head-slaved roll degree of freedom in a computer-synthesized scene or in a camera platform assists human subjects in judgment of the planar position and planar orientation of objects in virtual or remote environments.

It has been suggested that inclusion of the roll degree of freedom (DOF) in either computer-synthesized or remotely viewed scenes may improve situation awareness in such tasks as teleoperation.

Six subjects were required to match the position and orientation of a series of stationary target markers on a remote taskboard by manually placing similar response markers on an identical local taskboard. The subjects could view the remote taskboard only through a head-mounted display driven by the cameras on the platform. They could not see either the local board or their own limbs. The target locations spanned the full range of head azimuth for each subject and necessitated near maximal head elevation at maximum azimuth magnitudes.

The data shows that the addition of head-slaved roll compensation to the platform had no statistically discernible effect on the ability of the subjects to match the position (azimuth and elevation) of the remote targets. Nonetheless, systematic position errors were noted regardless of the roll condition. Absence of the roll DOF, however, did affect the subjects' judgment of target orientation when their heads were at peak attainable elevations for full magnitude azimuth rotations.

In the future further target acquisition experiments requiring head azimuth-elevation-roll will be conducted in a VE. The objective of the work will be the development of minimum kinematic degrees of freedom models of head motion.

Interface Control Parameters for Effective Haptic Display

The objective of this project is to understand the mechanical impedance and digital (discrete time) control requirements for effective presentation of haptic information through force reflecting interfaces. Currently a haptic, or kinesthetic, virtual environment incorporates two principal components—the computer model (algorithms or equations) describing the physical dynamics of the objects in the VE and the interface hardware that allows the human to interact with the VE. Because a haptic interface uses the same piece of hardware that serves as both control output and sensory input for the human operator, information transfer entails significant bidirectional mechanical power flow. Thus to optimize information transfer to the human, physical power flow must be modulated by selecting the appropriate impedance (mechanical characteristics) for the interface.

In this work psychophysical experiments were conducted to see how interface computer control parameters affect haptic perception. Parameters of interest are controller sample-and-hold update rates and phase lag—features akin to screen-refresh rates and persistence in CRT video displays.

Future plans for this project include examining how intrinsic mechanical properties of the interface, such as friction, inertia, and compliance, affect haptic perception of virtual objects.

3-D Auditory Displays in Aeronautical Applications

The purpose of this research is to implement and test auditory display concepts that will allow a pilot, crew member, or air traffic controller (ATC) controller to immediately, accurately, and inexpensively monitor three-dimensional information, such as traffic location, through the use of a virtual acoustic display.

Hardware has been designed and implemented for experiments in the following areas: spoken audio warning signals, TCAS (Traffic Collision Avoidance System) advisories, and cockpit radio communications. The TCAS traffic advisory consists of the spoken word "traffic." The position of the traffic is usually obtained visually, through instrument monitoring or out-the-window acquisition. In the ACFS flight simulator the out-the-window position of the traffic is linked to the virtual auditory position of the word "traffic" heard through headphones.

A pilot experiment was recently completed to determine whether the time interval for traffic acquisition is reduced when binaural sound delivery is used to suggest the direction for head-up visual search of the target, compared to monotic (single-ear piece), normal practice conditions. Results showed that there was a 2.2 second improvement in acquisition time.

An experiment currently under development pits a normal TCAS visual display against a 3-D auditory and visual head-up display. For communications, a 3-D sound hardware system can place various radio communication streams (ATIS, ATC, VOR) in separate virtual auditory positions around the pilot. The purpose of the system is to allow greater intelligibility against noise or when more than one frequency must be monitored, such as in the vicinity of an airport. Preliminary investigations have shown a 6–7 dB intelligibility improvement over monaural systems.

Basic research in the area of human headphone localization is also under way that supports these applied research efforts. A study was completed that compared inexperienced listeners' headphone localization of speech to previous studies using noise. Another study was completed that used artificial spatial reverberation to increase the veridicality of the 3-D sound display. Another study determined that there was no perceptual degradation when using a 20:1 data reduction of the filter parameters used in the 3-D sound display hardware.

Future plans include additional experiments involving target acquisition and speech intelligibility.

The Virtual Wind Tunnel

The objective of this project is to make possible the visualization and exploration of three-dimensional CFD solution datasets in a natural and efficient manner. In addition, the objective is to explore the applicability of VE technology to numerical flow visualization.

A VE for the exploration of three-dimensional numerically generated flow fields has been implemented. The analogy is to a wind tunnel, with the user able to move freely about the flow, injecting "virtual smoke" into the flow to make it visible, and yet not disturbing the flow in any way. The current environment allows the exploration of large single-grid three-dimensional steady flow fields or small single-grid three-dimensional unsteady flow fields. The environment supports several numerical flow visualization techniques, including streamlines, streaklines, particle-paths, and tufts. Collections of tools that generate these flow visualizations may be repositioned or reoriented in the flow in real time. Time can be frozen for detailed exploration of complex spatial structures. A new version of the software has been written that uses a convex minisupercomputer for memory-intensive and compute-intensive tasks but still uses the IRIS workstation for rendering and display.

The system is being extended to handle a larger class of engineering flows. This involves support for multiple zone grids and large disk-resident unsteady flows on the convex. The software is also being enhanced to support multiple users exploring the same flow together in real time. A new generation of hardware, namely, the Fake Space Labs BOOM IIC high-resolution two-color display and Silicon Graphics dual-pipe Skywriter, is being integrated into the virtual windtunnel.

Measurement and Calibration of Static Distortion of Position Data from 3-D Trackers

The purpose of this research is to characterize the accuracy of the position sensitivity of trackers commonly used in VE systems. Additionally, the various methods for correcting the deficiencies in their accuracy will be studied.

Three-dimensional trackers are becoming increasingly important as user inputs in interactive computer systems. These trackers give the position of a sensor in three dimensions. If the tracker were perfect, the position returned by the tracker would exactly correspond to the position of the sensor in appropriate coordinates. In reality trackers fail to be perfect. Distortions are introduced into the tracking data so that the position returned by the tracker corresponds only loosely to the position of the sensor and then only with a limited volume of space. This distortion is typically a function of the sensor's distance from some source and is dependent on the ambient environment. If this distortion is constant in time, it can be measured, and the position of the sensor can be inferred from the distorted data. This is called calibrating the tracker.

Detailed measurements have been made of the tracker output for a known set of tracker positions. These known tracker positions fill a volume of space with a resolution of 12 inches. These measurements can be used to determine the distortion of the tracker data. Calibration methods that partially correct for the distortion have been implemented. These measurements have been performed on a Polhemus Isotrack tracker, an electrogmagnetically based tracking system that provides three-dimensional position and orientation of a sensor. The measurements have been taken twice within the same location and at different locations to measure the dependence of the distortion on the ambient electromagnetic environment.

Study of the noise and repeatability imply limits on calibration success. When tracking greater than 50 inches from the source, the tracking signal is so noisy that no useful calibration can be expected. Inside this distance, repeatability implies a limit of about an inch in calibration accuracy. Both fourth order polynomial calibration and bump-lookup calibration perform close to these limits.

Further study in the calibration question can proceed in two obvious directions. The success of polynomial and lookup calibrations suggests that a three-dimensional spline calibration, a combination of global polynomials and lookup tables, should work quite well. Lookup calibration requires more study of the weighting and interpolation question. The bump-lookup calibration method fails for overly distorted data sets and can be refined.

This research addresses only static position calibration. These trackers also produce orientation data, and the study of distortion in the calibration should be performed.

Goddard Space Flight Center (GSFC)

This center is responsible for scientific studies and applications for unmanned space flight in the areas of space physics, astrophysics, earth sciences, and flight project support. Figures 19.4, and 19.5 show some of the current research and development in VE technology going on there.[9]

The research objective is to provide earth and space science researchers with a VE based on a familiar user interface so as to introduce and evaluate VEs as a research tool.

Research scientists working in the earth and space sciences require VE tools that they can immediately use as an extension of their existing tools and methods. In this way they can minimize both

---

[9] *Ibid.*, p. 51.

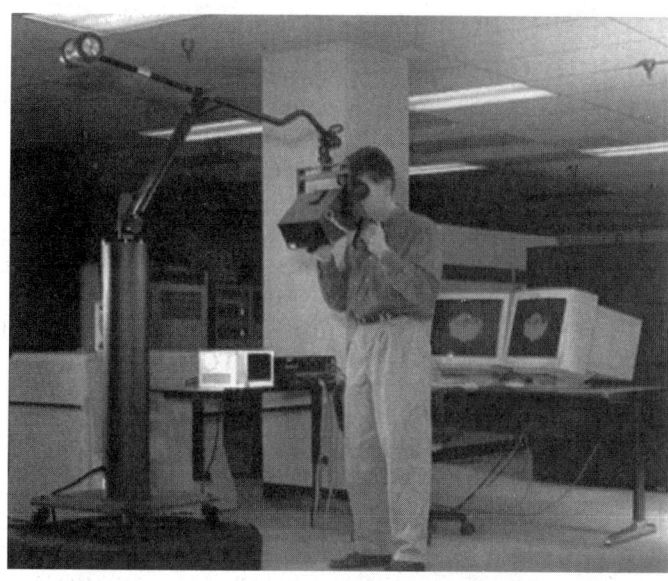

Figure 19.4 Goddard Scientific Virtual Environment.

learning and development time and can evaluate VEs directly as a research tool. The Flow Analysis Software Toolkit (FAST) is a popular NASA-developed visualization tool, specifically designed to visualize the physics of three-dimensional flows and optimized for high-end graphics hardware. By using a subset of FAST modules for data input, analysis, and visualization control, a VE version of FAST is being developed (VR-FAST), which will allow research scientists to work with a VE package they are already familiar with.

Initial development of the VR-FAST is in progress. The development hardware system has been purchased and delivered to Sterling Software, the developers of FAST. Helmet-tracking modifications have been integrated, and 75 percent of the glove software is done (innate gestures and learn gestures done, with applications integration in progress).

Figure 19.5 Globe Map in Goddard Space Flight Center's VR-FAST System.

The initial deliverable VR-FAST system has been completed. Immediate subsequent development will focus first on a multiple-user version, for collaborative research efforts, and then on versions that are distributed over multiple machines and graphics hardware and are paralleled for high performance.

Johnson Space Center (JSC)

JSC is responsible for manned space flight research, development, and applications; and, for astronaut training. Figures 19.6 and 19.7 show some of the current research and development in VE technology that's going on there.[10]

---

[10] *Ibid.*, pp. 54-55.

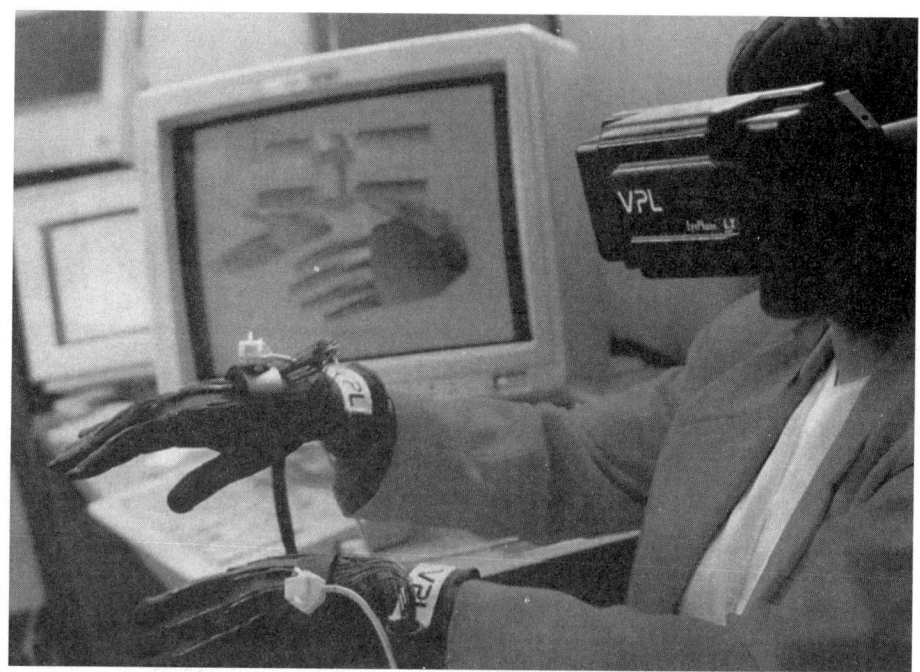

Figure 19.6 NASA CAVE (Applications and Virtual Environments) Developed in 1993 at JSC

Workload Assessment Using a Synthetic Work Environment

The objective of this project is to quantify the additional mental workload imposed by microgravity. This includes developing tools for assessing the mental workload imposed by spacecraft systems.

Currently a series of mental workload studies using a synthetic work environment has been completed. These studies sought to demonstrate the utility of response surface methodology (RSM) central-composite designs for predicting mental workload. The intent was to conduct the first in a series of studies that would ultimately establish systems operating conditions for proposed spacecraft systems that do not overload the capabilities of the operator. Eight subjects participated in a testing situation—a synthetic work environment consisting of four tasks: visual monitoring, Sternberg memory, arithmetic computations, and auditory monitoring.

Figure 19.7 NASA CAVE (Applications and Virtual Environments) Developed in 1993 at MSFC

Preliminary results suggest that RSM provides an effective tool for evaluating operating conditions in synthetic work environments in terms of the imposed mental workload. Plans call for augmentation of the first-order model to a second-order central composite design to more accurately characterize the response surface. Then, the predictively validity of the response surfaces will be established, further demonstrating the utility of RSM for evaluating the operating conditions in proposed spacecraft systems.

The results of these studies will advance current understanding of the relation between the simultaneous effects of various systems, operating conditions and how they impact the mental workload imposed by spacecraft systems proposed for extended-duration spaceflight. However, the synthetic work environment does not provide the fidelity necessary for comprehensive human workload analysis. Virtual reality technology can be expected to provide a new level of fidelity and an enhanced capability for in-depth evaluation of the workload imposed by microgravity and by proposed spacecraft systems.

Device for Orientation and Motion Environments (DOME)–Preflight Adaptation Trainer (PAT)

The purpose of this research is to develop training devices and procedures to preadapt astronauts to the sensory stimulus rearrangements of microgravity. The trainers are intended to demonstrate sensory phenomena likely to be experienced in flight and immediately postflight, allow astronauts to train preflight in an altered sensory environment, alter sensorimotor reflexes (appropriate for microgravity), and eliminate or reduce space motion sickness and orientation and motion disturbances.

The DOME-PAT system is currently being used to train astronauts in the recognition and quantitative description of perceptual experiences associated with head and body movements made on orbit, during entry, and immediately postflight. Postflight astronauts report which set(s) of conditions in the DOME are similar to their flight-related perceptual experiences and help evaluate potentially useful training tasks. The system is a 3.7-m diameter spherical dome with a 1.8-m diameter hole in the bottom.

The inner surface of the dome serves as a projection surface for two Triumiplex video projectors with custom wide angle optics mounted on a 1.8-m diameter rotating base that fills the hole in the bottom of the dome. The trainee restraint adjusts for positioning the trainee to sit upright, lie on either the left or right side, or lie supine. A 6 DOF isometric joystick or forceplate is used by the trainee or the instructor for virtual motion within the visual environment. The joystick can be used to control real whole-body rotation when the rotating base is enabled. Position signals derived from torque sensors in a trainee head-restraint assembly can also be used to drive the visual scene in a manner appropriate for either real or intended head movement. Real head movements are permitted only in a plane orthogonal to gravity to eliminate a gravity stimulus to the gravity receptors in the inner ear.

In the near-term future new training tasks/protocols will be developed and evaluated by astronauts as part of an ongoing detailed supplementary objective (DSO) activity, criteria for evaluating the efficacy of various training protocols will be determined, and a visual data base for simulating EVA will be developed. Ultimately the full complement of training procedures is expected to be implemented as part of the astronaut's operational training.

Training for EVA Satellite Grapple

The objective here is to develop a proof-of-concept training environment that provides astronauts with a simulation of satellite dynamics that match those observed during STS-49. A proof-of-concept VE for EVA satellite grapple is under development. Elements include models of the orbiter, the RMS, and Intellsat. The Intellsat model is dynamic and will respond to impulses imparted by a human hand or a hardware fixture. A polhemus device is used to track hand or fixture motion. The model detects collisions and infers the impulse imparted to the payload from a simple mass model of the hand or fixture and its velocity on collision with the payload. If the proof-of-concept system is judged to be valuable for training by training personnel and experienced astronauts, a more complete model will be developed and delivered as a training system for future payload retrieval missions.

Shared Virtual Environments

The research objective is to develop the capability for sharing VEs via long-distance networks. The capability of sharing the same VE between JSC and MSFC has been demonstrated. Such a shared environment permits personnel at both centers to simultaneously observe and interact with the same virtual objects. The use of existing networks imposes unpredictable latencies due to other network traffic.

The installation of a dedicated communication link between JSC and MSFC is planned. The nature of the shared environments will be increased in complexity, and more interactive tasks will be performed.

Marshall Space Flight Center (MSFC)

MSFC is responsible for spacecraft design, structure, development, and operations. Let's look at some of the current research and development in VE technology that's going on there.

Researchers wanted to develop, assess, and validate VR as a macroergonomics analysis tool for considering operational, viewing, and reach-envelope requirements in the topological design of work areas. To develop, assess, and validate scalable user anthropometry attributes, a study will compare Virtual Payload Operations Control Centers (VPOCC) with the existing Payload Operations Control Center (POCC).

Two VPOCCs have been developed that contain the basic objects of the POCC (tables, monitors, printers, communication panels, etc.) and their spatial layout. One operational VPOCC permits the relocation of objects that are generally moveable and moved in an operational environment (keyboards). Another nonoperational VPOCC permits the relocation of all objects that can be moved in the real world (tables).

Test scenarios will be performed in both the POCC and operational VPOCC and their results compared to ascertain what, if any, distortions arise in a virtual world (VW). The test scenarios will focus on what one can see from a variety of eye reference points, using a range of real and virtual anthropometric sizes. These scenarios will also include operationally driven components, such as translation paths among the various console, printer, fax, and file locations.

An algorithm has been developed to rescale use anthropometric attributes to any desired virtual anthropometry. Thus a 95th percentile male could view and reach as a virtual 5th percentile female and vice-versa.

The nonoperational VPOCC will be used to explore alternative POCC configurations (different topological arrangements of consoles, printers, faxes, files, etc. The various configurations will be compared, using much the same methodology developed for the operational VPOCC.

As confidence is gained in VR as a macroergonomic analytical tool, it will be applied in upcoming topological design efforts, such as the Space Station Payload Operations Integrated Center (POIC). Specific options to be addressed in the design of the POIC, in addition to "standard" topological design issues, include slanted walls (to cover utility runs) and tiering of the control room and viewing area floors. The validated scalable user anthropometry capability will be applied in future macro- and icroergonomic analysis.

These centers have worked together to develop the current state of VE technology, plan for future activities and organize their individual projects.

Since beginning research and technology development in 1985, NASA centers have learned important lessons about the technology itself and the value it can provide in accomplishing the gamut of NASA's missions in aeronautics, science, and space. Cost savings could be dramatic, since virtual environment can potentially allow change to be made in a small way that can have a large effect, can potentially analyze situations with VE with capabilities not heretofore available, can potentially analyze situations more quickly and more cheaply than with conventional methods, and analysis can potentially be done that allows unique insights for investigators/scientists. It's very probable that several of the technologies discussed will similarly be tailored and eventually priced into the commercial VR industry to be delivered via the Internet.

Medical: VR Technology and Project ARCANA

Immersive virtual reality (IVR) is a mature technology to assist cognitive psychologists and therapists in their clinical work with brain-damaged patients. The rationale, the software, and the hardware of the first IVR system application—Advanced Research for the Computer-Based Assessment of Neuropsychological Ailments (ARCANA 1)—being developed by the Medical Division of Cyberfunk Italy Srl, Signoressa, Italy (a subsidiary of Cyberfunk, Inc., of Tucson AZ), provides a concrete example of what the role of IVR as a clinical tool will be. Although prospects are exciting, extensive research is needed to validate this new approach and reveal both its limits and advantages.

The Project ARCANA. has been promoted to develop IVR models to assist clinical psychologists, neurophyschologists, and cognitive therapists in their work with cognitively impaired patients. The main project is articulated into subprojects dealing with various aspects of IVR modeling and simulation. Each of the latter will have a completely worked-out rationale, evaluation protocol, and a specific cognitive model to which it is referred.

ARCANA 1 Project Description

The first subproject, termed ARCANA 1, started in October 1993 from a collaboration of the Medical Division of Cyberfunk Italy. As a cognitive paradigm, ARCANA 1 has been developed from well-known examples of the neuropsychological testing tradition. The Wisconsin Card Sorting Test (WCST), in particular, has been taken as a reference. The choice to create a hybrid (a program with both the formal characteristics of a standardized test and those of a more open-ended situation) has been made for a number of reasons.

First, it will allow cognitive psychologists not to break with a consolidated approach of assessment. Second, it will serve as an entry-level program to IVR, to probe both patient and therapist attitudes toward this new technology. Third, although it will benefit from a solid theoretical and experimental background, it will also allow for more empirical and behaviorally oriented approaches.

Given its origins, ARCANA 1 is more suited for diagnostic purposes. Nonetheless, since it has been fully parameterized (can be configured in a number of ways and its cognitive demands can be graded), it may be suitable also for retraining purposes.

The artificial environment of ARCANA 1 is a virtual building (a series of rooms of variable shape with entrance and exit doors). The rooms are connected with corridors of variable length. Rooms and corridors may be empty or may contain a number of fixed or animated objects. In its basic version, however, the environment is very simple, as shown in Figures 19.8 and 19.9.[11]

The interaction is also kept as simple as possible. The user can freely navigate the environment by simply holding a pointing device (a jokerstick) in the direction of the intended movement. The doors open when touched on the knob with a virtual key.

The basic goal is to exit the castle in the shortest possible time. This implies the selection of an efficient strategy to move from one room to the next. A room can be left only by selecting the correct door. The cue for selecting the exit door is obtained by looking at the entrance door, which is marked by a yellow wall. Only one cue operates at any time and should be selected to identify the exit door, which shares with the entrance door the same cue. To be identified as a cue, a given characteristic must be categorized. For example, valid cues are the color or the shape of a door. Any combination of cues is treated as a wrong criterion. One cannot be certain that the selection is correct until the exit door is reached.

---

[11] Tullio Bortoletto, *ARCANA Project*, Cyberfunk Italy Srl, Medical Division, Via Livenza, 5, Signoressa, Italy, 1995.

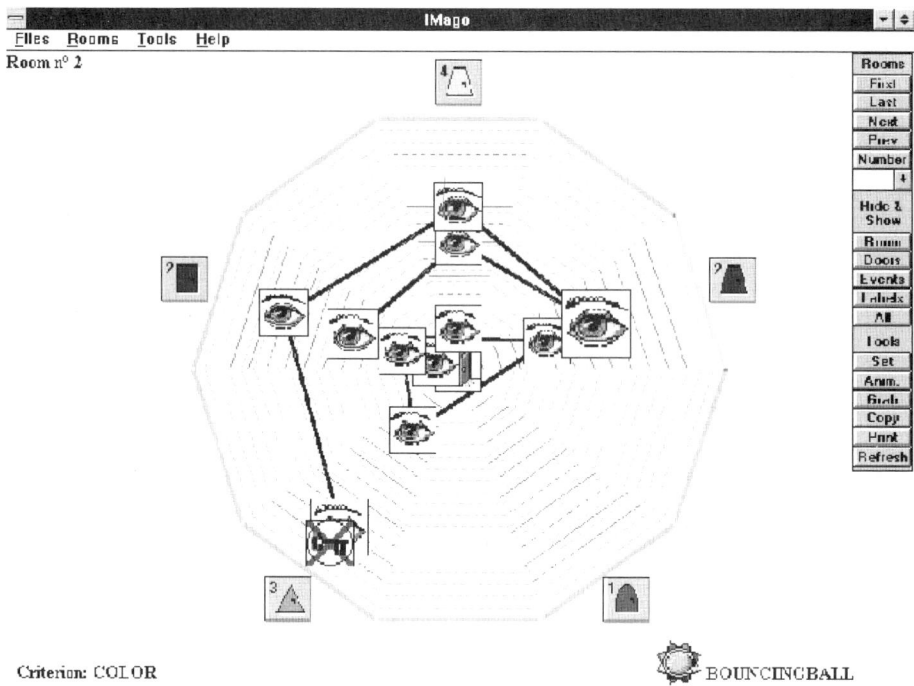

Figure 19.8 ARCANA 1 Virtual Building

The opening of the exit door is an implicit confirmation of correctness. If the door stays shut, the strategy should be reconsidered and corrected. In the basic configuration, a shift in the criterion occurs every seven consecutive right selections. That a shift has occurred is to be inferred by an unseen lack of confirmation of a previously correct solution. Once a new solution is found by trial and error, the criterion should be maintained until the next shift.

The Cognitive Demands and the Interpretive Model

As in the standard paper-and-pencil test, motivational processes are required to carry out the task, as are a number of other special-purpose cognitive processes of the type that standard neuropsychological tests measure. For example, sustained attention, visual scanning, recognition of objects and object characteristics, spatial memory,

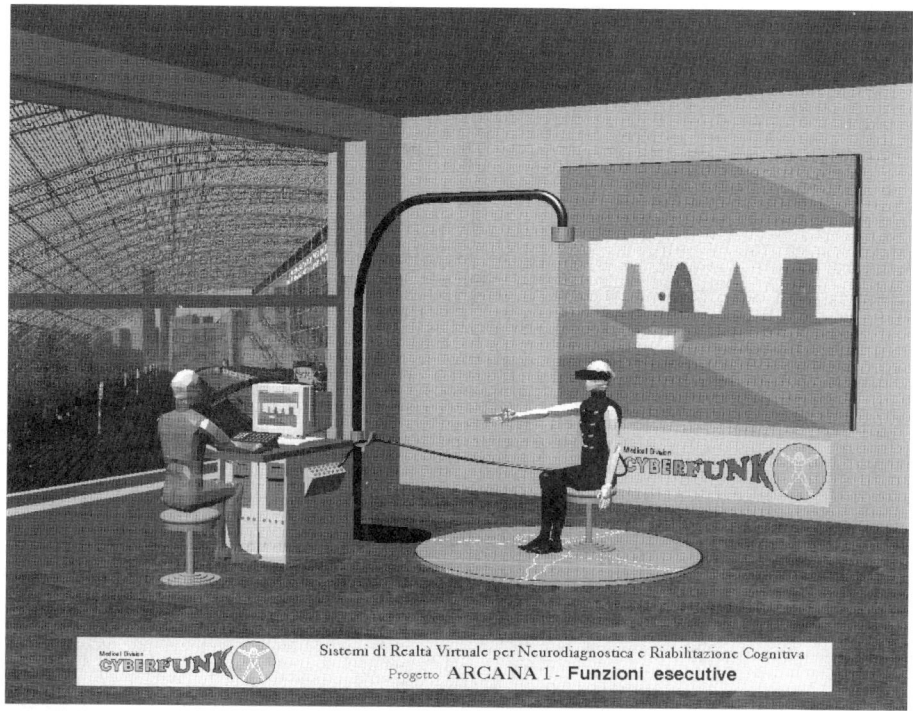

Figure 19.9 ARCANA 1 Environment

retrospective verbal memory, categorization, concept formation, abstract reasoning, inference, utilization of nonverbal feedbacks, criterion maintenance and shifting, inhibition of impulsive behavior, and adherence to rules are all component abilities that are called into action. In addition, since IVR configures a spatially more complex situation and the action is carried out on a broader time scale, there are a number of so-called bridge processes that enable the previously described basic cognitive abilities to be used efficiently to satisfy motivational requirements. These processes allow the creation and maintenance of goals and their realization at appropriate times.

As already mentioned, in real as well as in simulated situations, when routine actions will not achieve a goal satisfactorily, the problem-solving process required (the supervisory attentional system involves at least four stages, which can be called into action in a recursive way. An achievable goal must be specified, a plan must be formulated, a solution is attempted, and the result is assessed. Bridge processes link the schematic plan to the potential to realize it at some adequate future time.

A marker is a message relevant to a certain behavior that can be called at any point in time during a future event. Thus a task rule would be realized through a marker becoming activated when the instructions are understood that something has to be done when a marked event occurs. In summary, then, the proposed function of the system is to control: goal articulation, provisional plan formulation, marker allocation, and marker triggering by an appropriate event. An evaluation process can take place at any time; if the solution is not satisfactory, this would lead to a plan modification.

When applied to Cyberfunk's simulation and prior information is limited to a minimum, this schema would give the following results

- *Situation:* being inside a building;
- *Goal articulation:* to exit as soon as possible;
- *General plan formulation or evaluation:* to proceed by trial and error until an effective strategy is identified;
- *Local plan formulation or evaluation:* selecting a cue from the entrance door;
- *Marker creation:* upon entering a room looking back at the entrance door to get the cue;
- *(When entering a new room)* marker triggers the preselected behavior;
- *Provisional solution attempted;* and
- *Local (or general) plan* re-evaluation if solution is not adequate.[12]

Evaluation of the Cognitive Performance

Cognitive performance on an IVR test such as ARCANA 1 can then be analyzed in at least two complementary ways: first, according to a quantitative scoring system that counts errors and sorts them according to a taxonomy of specific mental processes involved, as is done in standard neuropsychological tests; according to the component processes model in a practical problem-solving situation as

---

[12] *Ibid.*

suggested. It is acknowledged, however, that in more open-ended situations, such as those that will be modeled in future system applications of the ARCANA series, a cognitive process model approach will be applied more effectively to the evaluation of performance. The latter will be also based on:

- a normative task analysis to yield a taxonomy of elementary behaviors for performing the task, their sequence, duration, frequency, relevance, and flexibility;
- an analysis of the perceptual steps involved (mostly basic visual routines, such as detection, orientation, localization, and recognition); and
- a learning curve.[13]

Automatic Scoring of Events

As in any computerized technology, IVR should also give the experimenter the opportunity to obtain objective measurements from a behaving subject. The tracking system is able to monitor a subject's head and arm movements and his body position in space. This information can be used to interpret a subject's intentions while he or she is interacting with the artificial environment.

Every move and every event in the virtual world is detected, and the time of occurrence can be stored in a report file. The latter is then analyzed to give summary reports and graphical displays of the most significant events that occurred and of their parameters in space and time. This data adds significant information for both statistical and assessment purposes. For example, the visual scanning strategy of a subject in the virtual environment of ARCANA 1 can be easily detected in this way and the data related to specific steps of the process model such as marker creation and triggering, as shown in Figure 19.10.[14]

An audiovisual monitoring device is also integrated in the IVR system of ARCANA 1. This device sample frames of the subjective vision display and synchronizes them with an outside view of the behaving subject taken by a VHS camera, as shown in Figure 19.8. A couple of

---

[13]*Ibid.*
[14]*Ibid.*

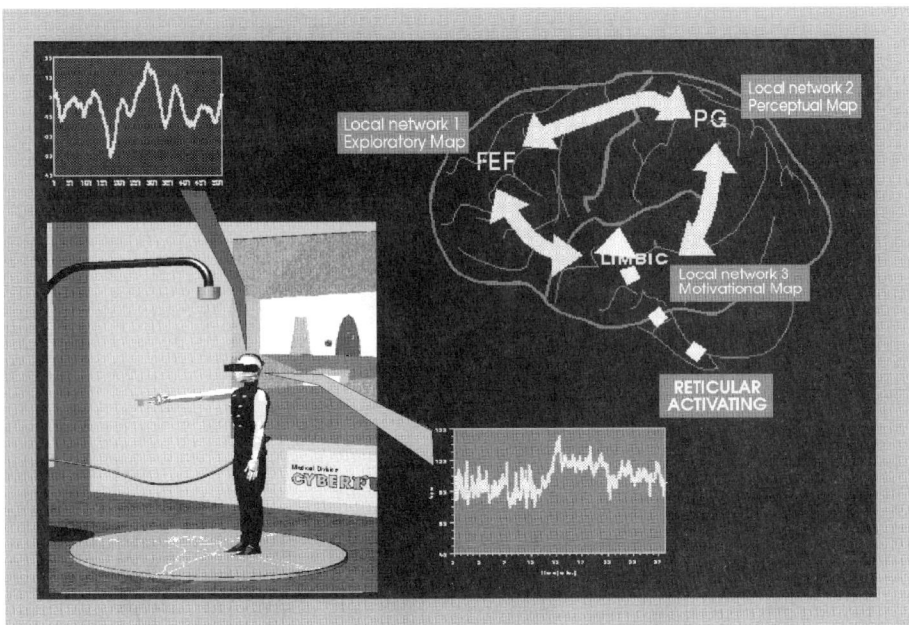

Figure 19.10   Marker Creation Triggering

combined images is then stored every 250 msec on a standard VHS tape ready to be replayed back for off-line analysis.

Biomedical Data Acquisition and Analysis

It is frequently stated that quantitative measurement of psychophysiological activity during purposeful tasks allows us to quantitatively characterize individual cognitive styles. The IVR system can be connected and synchronized with other external systems devoted to biomedical data acquisition and analysis. This is obtained by triggering the external devices with input signals generated at selected time points by the IVR system. For example, Cyberfunk is using this facility to recover auditory and visual event-related potentials from polygraph recordings of behaving subjects during their IVR experience. Signals from the body surface can be fed directly to an acquisition system (a commercial computerized EEG system) or, more conveniently, to a portable light-weight and battery-operated recording device that does not encumber the subject with additional wires that connect to an external device.

The aim of recording biological signals during the IVR immersion is complex. First, it can be useful to address research questions. One that is interesting to Cyberfunk is whether it can obtain a direct index of the mental resources a subject is devoting to the task. It has approached this problem, using auditory event-related potentials (ERPs). For each subject it can generate a function that describes the relationship between sound intensity and ERP parameters (amplitude) in baseline conditions.

By analogy, Cyberfunk can then use this function to measure with the same units the variations of ERP parameters that it observes during IVR when the subject is supposed to be actively engaged in the primary task and only a fraction of his or her processing abilities is devoted to an auditory input, as shown in Figure 19.11.[15] The recording of body signals can serve two other important functions in IVR applications monitoring psychophysiological reactions and implementing biocybernetic paradigms. As far as the first is concerned, Cyberfunk has already found it useful to record and analyze heart rate during performance in IVR systems to document the degree of cardiovascular stress imposed to the subject by the paradigm simulated and its setup.

In contrast to a VR driving simulation that Cyberfunk has used in the past, the ARCANA 1 paradigm does not seem to induce as large an increase in cardiac activity of volunteers. This is important to document when developing VR applications for the disabled, since stressful paradigms may inadvertently affect a subject's performance and learning. On the other hand, mild degrees of stress may facilitate performance in apathetic individuals. Further, meaningful correlations with performance measures can be drawn to assist the interpretation, as shown in Figure 19.12.[16]

The recording of eye movements during visualization of virtual environments can further improve the analysis of the scanning behavior of patients with associated impairments of oculomotor function. Cyberfunk has used it to show that the commonly held belief that using HMDs with a limited total FoV greatly reduces the frequency and

---

[15]*Ibid.*
[16]*Ibid.*

Figure 19.11 Auditory Input

amplitude of saccadic EM is basically incorrect, as shown in Figure 19.13.[17]

Hardware and Software

Stated, there is no doubt that an affordable IVR system can be assembled from over-the-shelf technology. However, this is true only if its overall performance on the field as a real-time simulator must not be pushed to a level of absolute realism and especially if it is conceived not as an enabling device but rather as a cognitive trainer.

---

[17] *Ibid.*

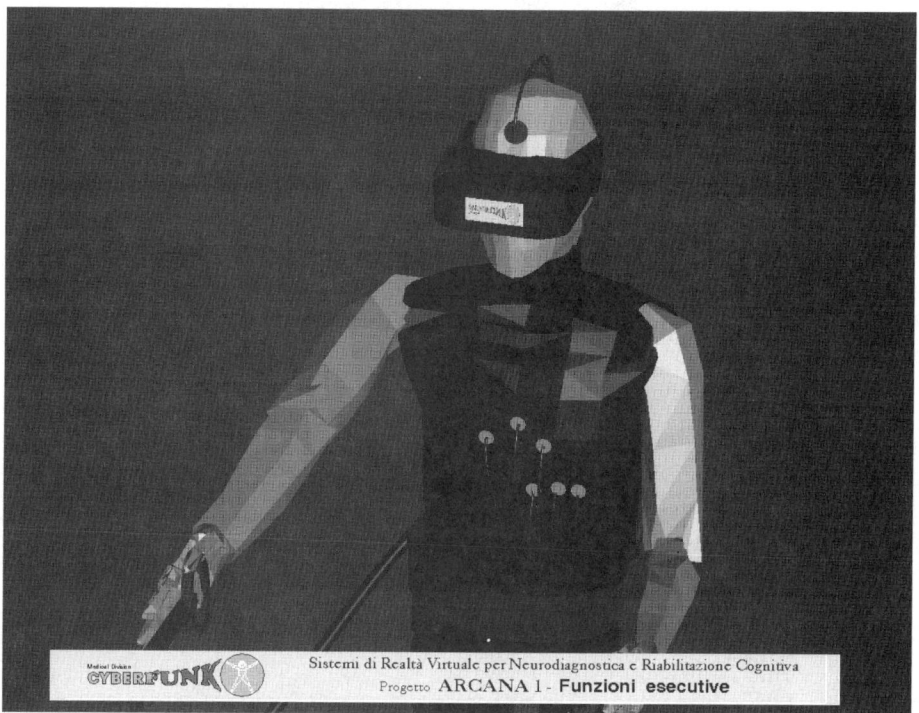

Figure 19.12 Performance Measures

This consideration is, in Cyberfunk's view, of paramount importance for the assessment of cost/effectiveness issues of many IVR systems proposed for training applications. As an example, it reports general specifications for such an IVR system devoted to the cognitive retraining of patients who may also happen to have a moderate limb sensory motor impairment, as shown in Figure 19.8.

In such a system no expensive engineering is requested to customize the interfaces for retraining of sensory motor skills, because the emphasis is put on the cognitive and perceptual domains. Drawing from the experience of Cyberfunk Italy's Medical Division, which has developed the hardware and software for ARCANA 1 to meet certain specifications, the major R&D efforts had to be directed to the development of software modules required by the system.

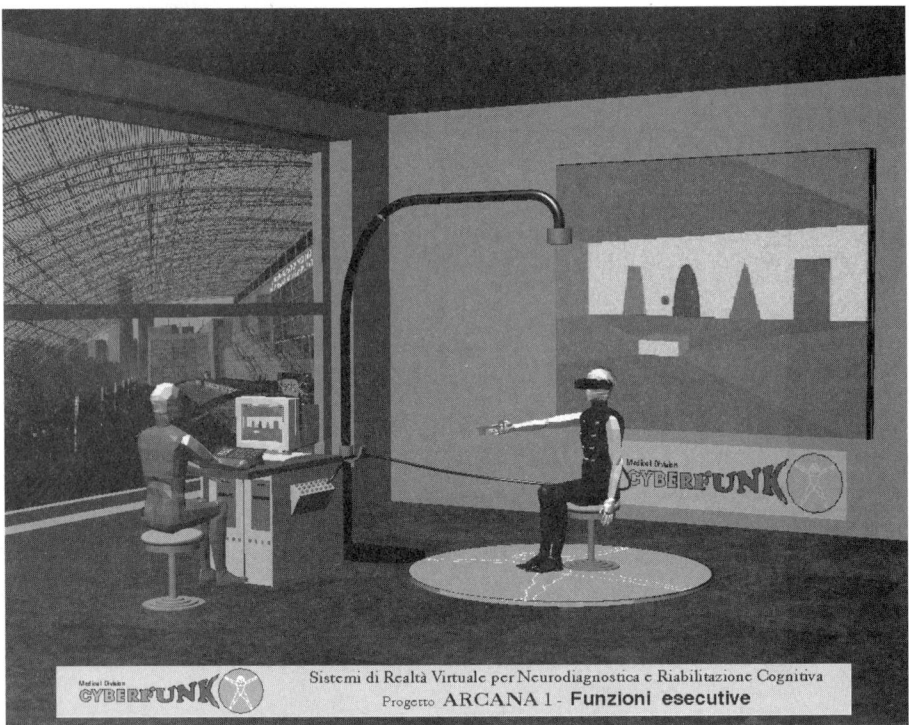

Figure 19.13 Saccadic EM

It must be noted that the system software is not directed just to generate a virtual environment but rather to generate a virtual paradigm in which several technical aspects must be integrated:

- parametric setting of the IVR in all its components: graphics and sound, dimensioning and shaping of the objects, lows of motion, strategies for the tasks, triggering and synchronization of the biomedical data;
- biomedical data acquisition to be correlated to salient moments to facilitate subsequent performance analysis with the concurring need to operate on data base easily accessible;
- design of operator-friendly interfaces to offer both the researcher and the therapist the possibility to have at their disposal an easy and useful instrument that would not encapsulate in a rigid context but rather offer the possibility to tailor

the virtual paradigm as well as the assessment and the therapeutical plans according to their experience and the patient steps of improvement in the retraining process.[18]

Cyberfunk feels that it is fundamental that there be close cooperation between the doctors and the hardware and software design engineers in order to have reciprocal exposure to the clinical needs, technological possibilities, and constraints. Only from a mutual understanding of sometimes conflicting needs can the opportunity come to develop concrete projects.

Limitations and Constraints of Present-Time VR Technology

Technological limits and constraints of IVR, however, do exist; many of them are still unavoidable and must be carefully understood and considered in relation to clinical applications. Limitations are broadly classifiable into the following categories: encumbering factors, factors introducing perceptual errors and time delays, and factors affecting novelty.

Encumbering factors limit a user's motility in various ways and are typical of HMDA (Head-mounted displays), data gloves, and any other device that is worn by the user and needs to be connected to the VR server. Needless to say, the encumbering should be avoided as much as possible. Patients should be informed adequately and made acquainted with the devices and their use before experiencing IVR.

Factors introducing perceptual errors and time delays typically originate from graphic computing and rendering and tracking devices. Delays of more than 100 msec are said to cause both discomfort and to affect the experience of a smooth, continuous visual environment and of motion (zooming effect).

In many IVR systems of low performance and cost-significant time delays can be introduced only when the subject stares at quite complex visual scenes. The rate at which frames can be generated then drops dramatically, say, to below 10/sec to revert to an acceptable value a few seconds later once the subject has moved his or her sight to another point in space.

---

[18] *Ibid.*

The discontinuity can be so prominent to generate surprise and an orienting reaction which interrupts the ongoing cognitive processing. Encumbering factors, time delays, and the absence of sensory feedbacks typical of natural motion are also involved in the generation of so-called cybersickness.

This topic has been repeatedly covered by recent papers and will not be examined in any detail here. The introduction of faster image processors and of lightweight high-resolution HMDA, however, has considerably limited the incidence of cybersickness, thus proving that sensorial conflict is only one possible factor.

Once a specific task is identified, the sense of realism (or of novelty) can be affected by the tradeoff among the amount of graphic complexity required, the level of interaction needed, and the speed of rendering. The debate between those in favor of an absolute realism and those who do not consider this requisite as a fundamental one for clinical VR applications is still unsettled.

A fundamental issue is the amount of prior knowledge of what can be used to build an internal representation of the specific environment. If this cognitive process is not greatly impaired, a sketchy version of the real world can be used without confusing the patient. Moreover, human factors that may also pose limits to applicability should be examined in greater detail.

In principle, patients with cognitive deficits are inherently at risk for showing maladaptive responses and behaviors and hence to have problems accepting an unusual experience, such as IVR, and to experience difficulties understanding the scope of its wired devices, such as HMD, data gloves, and the like.

Although psychological reactions to IVR have to be studied in greater detail, Cyberfunk's still growing experience with a variety of mentally disabled subjects exposed to IVR for relatively brief periods is completely in contrast with this expectation. Although some of them may not understand enough of the rationale and frequently take it merely as a game, most of them liked it and would experience it again. Hence VR technology per se does not appear to be a limiting factor.

Comment

It seems that a new class of clinical tools is about to emerge from the attempt to apply IVR technology to the cognitive rehabilitation of acquired cognitive impairments. Problems of transfer to real-life situations, generalization of results, prediction, and assessment of outcome for specific behavioral-cognitive treatments may be approached from a novel stance.

Cyberfunk has briefly discussed the rationale and the most relevant methodological aspects for the design of an IVR system devoted to this aim. The latter is part of an extended project, which will be completed in 1996.

Cyberfunk has also provided a few examples drawn from the ongoing preliminary clinical experience with this tool. A large number of approaches and models are amenable to be implemented by means of VR, those dealing with higher cognitive functions have attracted interest because they are the least represented in the variety of technological aids for cognitive assessment and rehabilitation.

More basic functions, such as attention, memory, and language, are already successfully retrained by means of more traditional computerized procedures. There are hints, however, that IVR could be superior to the latter, thanks to its greater ability to mobilize mental resources and to be closer to the ideal rehabilitative cognitive aid: one that can easily and realistically simulate any situation and any paradigm, giving a full sense of immersion to the patient and that of full control to the therapist.

In the never-ending process of research and discovery, IVR may be the technique to bring about a new revolution in the methodologies in assessing cognitive abilities and to compensate for their impairments. Prospects are exciting, but extensive research and development will have to be carried out in order to approximate this end.

Problems of transfer of diagnostic information to real-life situations via the Internet, generalization of trained skills, and prediction of outcome for specific behavioral-cognitive treatments may be approached from a novel stance. Within a large collaborative project for the development of a cognitive retraining system based on IVR technology called ARCANA, Cyberfunk has developed a first system in which IVR is used to assist in the assessment of those control components of cognitive activity (so-called executive functions) that enable more basic abilities to be used efficiently.

The system is described as an example of what Cyberfunk believes should be implemented to make IVR a useful clinical tool. Wearing a stereoscopic lightweight color HMD, the patient must find his way out of a building. Visual cues will help the patient select the correct exit doors that connect one room to the next.

A general plan will have to be drawn up, and several local strategies will have to be identified and possibly changed by the patient in order to complete the journey inside the building. Non-verbal (visual and auditory) feedback will be released by the system at every correct or incorrect move. Both the visual representation of the artificial environment and the modality of interaction are kept as simple as possible. However, the overall complexity can be increased, and every detail can be easily changed by simply typing in the modifications needed. The model can then be reconfigured according to, for example, an incremental training program or the necessity to disassemble the task into simpler subtasks.

The system stores behavioral data into exportable files and realtime images of both subjective and external views and sends synchronizing signals to other devices enabling the monitoring of biomedical data. Behavioral data analysis can be carried out according to standardized criteria, as in traditional neuropsychological tests, or to a model which classifies errors according to control cognitive processes. The recording of psychophysiological parameters enables meaningful correlations to be drawn with behavioral data. Ongoing research with this instrument is focused on its clinical validation and the assessment of all potential hazards, physical and psychological effects of IVR simulations for clinical purposes to be eventually imported to the Internet.

From Here

This chapter presented other VR research that is taking place for eventual deliverance to the Internet. The next chapter concludes by taking a peek at the next generation of VRML application development through the use of high-performance computing. How far will high-performance VRML go? In what direction will development take place? How quickly will it evolve?

20

Summary, Conclusions, and Recommendations

How far can high-performance VRML go? In what direction will it develop? How quickly will it evolve? These questions can be answered by examining the various pieces of the puzzle and looking at application trends and future possibilities.

We now have lots of little pieces of the future floating around, but how they intersect or bond to one another will depend largely on the marketability of their potential outcomes. We have certainly excelled on the hardware side of high-performance VRML machines. Virtual reality (VR) software has also rapidly evolved, especially in the cinematic and advertising realms. Virtual reality, still a fledgling science, is appealing to both the would-be reality escapee and the consumer product marketeer. Artificial intelligence, another fledgling science, still remains largely stuck in the halls of academia.

Meanwhile, the market for VR-based products is hot in three major areas: fantasy adventure games, training simulators, and sex-oriented media. These markets have experienced the type of growth that most entrepreneurs have only dreamed about during restless nights.

These market successes, as with many others, are prompting regulators and our unduly elected officials in Washington to produce some political hay. The moral concerns of the imaginary heartland and the First Amendment rights are once again clashing like titans. It is not that the governmental transients in Washington have much going for them in the way of morals, but they do like to get themselves on TV and hustle votes and campaign contributions. It is likely that political interest will attempt to choke certain aspects of the market, especially the sexually oriented graphics market. But while the politicians blow hot air, momentum in high-performance VRML development is growing.

We have been provided with a fantasy of what high-performance computer VR could do for us by our science fiction writers. They have woven a vision of reality in their millions of words of pulp-style prophecy about our future, our explorations, our quest, and indeed our destiny and how they would all be constructed with computers at our beck and call. These dreams come to life in the concept of the StarTrek holodeck, that place where anything can happen any time we want it to, without risk to life, limb, or physical being.

One of the futures for high-performance graphics, I contend, is the development of StarTrek holodecklike applications. These applications will serve as escape mechanisms, recreational alternatives, and training environments. It will be like Jurassic Park, with the dinosaurs replaced by anything that meets the fancy of the individuals who are willing to pay the bill. The religious could meet their god, the sex-starved could indulge in their own self-styled orgies, and those with killer instincts could slaughter and conquer. This may all be closer than we think.

Performance and Price

We have been taking large leaps in price/performance as increased power and capacity trickle down to smaller and less expensive machines, including raw speed, memory capacity, and storage capacity. Consumer-oriented desktop units are changing very rapidly, with a price/performance improvement rate of about 100 percent a per year.[1]

---

[1] Michael Erbschloe, consultant, educator, and writer who specializes in the strategic use of computer technology at Oklahoma State University, erbschloe@hpcwire.tge.com.

The more expensive systems, such as high-end UNIX based workstations, are experiencing about 100 percent price/performance improvements every 18 months. The largest systems are experiencing the same rate of price/performance improvement about every 24 months.

We also occasionally experience what I call megaleaps in commonly available price/performance improvements, which will start to come much more quickly than they have in the past. We are on the edge of our next megaleap as we migrate to 64-bit systems. This evolution will be followed with the emergence of 128-bit machines by the year 2000.

The first step, to 64-bit platforms, has been a little slow but should pick up speed during the next two years. Again, it is not the existence of the machines themselves but the commonplace availability that is key to developers' being able to exploit the technology for the consumer market.

The emergence and common utilization of object-oriented development techniques will ease the move from the 64-bit platforms to the 128-bit platforms. Likewise this opens the door for an even faster acceptance and market for 256-bit machines by the year 2005. Again, common acceptability, availability, and accessibility are the key elements to a successful market for software developers.

Software and Hardware

During the last two generations of business computers, we have seen software trailing the availability of machines by 18 to 36 months.[2] However, as de facto standards, or market domination, solidifies in the hands of the few, like Microsoft products for PCs, mainstream business software developers are shortening the time lag between hardware availability and software availability. This lag time could potentially be reduced to just a few months as long as the haggling between dominant players and smaller applications developers doesn't heighten their licensing conflicts and developers continue the steady evolution into object-oriented design methodologies for their products.

VR and multimedia software developers, now about to reach puberty, have experienced similar lags between common hardware availability and delivery of their products. This lag will decrease rapidly. In fact, I contend, as the VR market grows consumer-oriented

---

[2] *Ibid.*

hardware, packagers may have difficulty keeping up with VR software products.

The leaders in the use of VR, now mostly in the entertainment industry, will always continue to push the threshold of demand for more capable, less expensive development platforms. This in turn will provide funding for hardware companies and will result in the development of higher performance technology that can be more quickly trickled down to commonly available consumer machines.

We will also experience a more rapid trickling down, more like a waterfall, as hardware developers scurry to recoup their R&D investments so they can fund additional R&D. This dynamic will fuel the faster migration of VR software to 64-bit and 128-bit machines, which in turn will increase demand for these platforms and result in faster common availability.

Overall these dynamics, although they will result in pain for those companies that cannot keep up with the rapid pace of change, will be beneficial to high-performance VRML applications developers. The primary benefit is a more open and viable market.

The secondary benefit will be obtained by those developers willing to risk the funds necessary to initiate development of VR applications or entertainment packages for future platforms. The more rapid introduction of higher performance consumer computers or the waterfall of price/performance, the less the risk that developers will face when preparing products for platforms that will not be commonly available for two, three, or even four years.

Although this may seem to be a long time for venture capitalists to wait for a return on their investment, it is still a shorter time between megaleaps in price/performance than we experienced during the 1980s.[3] It also lessens the pain of investment in early versions of computing platforms, because the lag between early and more expensive versions of an architecture and the common availability of that architecture will decrease.

Artificial Intelligence and Virtual Reality

So far consumer-oriented graphic-based products such as Myst and a wide variety of sex games, have been built on a series of predetermined outcomes, or scripts, that are invoked by specific actions of

---

[3] *Ibid.*

Chapter 20 Summary, Conclusions, and Recommendations

their human players. Although these games make for great puzzles, they will rapidly fade into the dark ages as artificial intelligence (AI) and high-performance graphics merge into a new generation of AIgraphic applications.

Instead of predetermined outcomes or even simple randomly invoked outcomes available from a library, the fantasy game of the future will be more capable of emulating real life, or shall I say real adventure. This could occur in two ways. First, and probably sooner on the evolutionary path, players will be able to intentionally create their own libraries of scripts, making them as complex as they like. This is similar to some of the virtual reality applications now on the market.

Second, and further into the future, script creation will be based on a psychological analysis of individual players. The psych battery will be built into the game or training package and will automatically develop a profile of each individual as he or she uses the software. These psycho-based scripts could potentially evolve on their own, growing more complex as player skills improve.

VR applications also extend beyond entertainment. Our military has been a leader in computer-based simulation training. These applications, to date, have been built like many of the $79.00 fantasy games you can buy at a local store.[4] That is, scripts and outcomes are predetermined, based on training goals.

By adding an AI feature, scripts or outcomes in these training simulators could evolve in a more natural way, based on the ability and the experience of individual trainees. The knowledge base for each trainee would be stored and reinvoked by entering an identification number and pressing the start button.

The development of AIgraphic applications will require all around high-performance platforms with a minimum of 64-bit massive parallel architectures, terabytes of memory and storage, and fiber-optic light speed data channels, with dynamic and logical allocation of system resources. Development platforms will likely remain in the supercomputer class, but the VR applications could be accessed via high-performance workstation servers. Other requirements for product delivery are high-resolution floor-to-ceiling monitors to display the AIgraphic images, a high-quality sound system, and a voice-recognition interface for players to issue commands.

---

[4] *Ibid.*

Market Drivers

The U.S. military and the sex industry have been leading the way in the use of computer graphics, each in its own unique fashion. For more than a decade the military has been using graphics based simulators for technology and battle training. This experience, combined with the potential costs savings for using simulators and the financial ability to support development, gives the military a healthy lead in the field.

If the government loosens up and moves the military technology into the private sector through a defense conversion program, VR development for commercial purposes will likely accelerate. It would make good business sense to do this, so we can probably not count on its happening.

The sex industry, in its own way, has also been a leader in developing and marketing VR-based applications. These applications range from digitized images on the low end up to pseudointeractive games on the high end. The games are becoming more and more popular and will continue to be a thriving market.

The main obstacle to growth in the sex sector is the pending Communications Decency Act, which has been appended to the 1995[5] Telecommunications Act. The debate about this rages. Conservative voteseeking politicians in Washington and across the country want to regulate access to sexually oriented material via the Internet.

If the politicians win this one, it is likely that they will get onto a smut-irradication campaign that could stifle growth in the sex sector. This is bad news. Regardless of whether people agree with the intent and method of the Communications Decency Act, its passage may very well have a negative impact on the cash flow of the sex industry.

First Amendment and free-commerce issues held constant, a decrease in cash flow for developers of existing VR-based sex products will impact their ability to fund development of more sophisticated VR AIgraphic–type products in the future. This is not good for a free-market economy.

---

[5] *Ibid.*

Index

A

Acceptance, OpenGL, 424
Accumulation buffer, 330–331, 431
Ack, 469–471
Actions, 413
ActiveVRML, 403
AddEvent routine, 479
Address
　element, 147
　multicast, 372
Agora, 56–57
Alice, 180
Alpha blending, 322–323, 433
Alpha test, 319–320
AlternateRep field, 260
Ambient light, 167
Ames Research Center, VR research, 499–506
　haptic display, interface control parameters, 503
　head-slaved roll compensation, 502
　measurement and calibration of static distortion of position data, 505–506
　spatial sensor dynamic response, 500–502
　3D auditory displays, aeronautical applications, 503–504
　virtual wind tunnel, 504–505
Amsterdam hypertext model, 128–130
Animation
　CAVEview, 102–103
　interpolation enums, 162
　nodes, 161–162
ANIM3D, 180
Annotated 3-D model, 389
Antialiasing, 296–297
　line segments, 299–300
　point, OpenGL, 297–298
AntiSquish, 89
API, 189–191
　adding hooks to VRML, 198
　extension languages, 189–190
　graphical rendering, 418–420
　low-level, OpenGL, 425–426
　model, OpenGL, 429–430
ARCANA 1
　automatic scoring of events, 519–520

ARCANA 1 *(continued)*
  biomedical data acquisition and analysis, 520–522
  cognitive demands and interpretive model, 516–518
  cognitive performance evaluation, 518–519
  hardware and software, 522–525
  limitations and constraints of VR technology, 525–526
  project description, 514–516
Architecture, OpenGL, 61–62
Array node, 88
Art galleries, 42–44
Artifact node, 363
Artifacts
  distribution, in virtual worlds, 368
  naming and identification, 380–381
Assembly
  behavior engines, 447–448
  behavior format, 386
Attribute groups, OpenGL, 351–352
Attribute stack, OpenGL, 430–431
Audio, CAVEview, 105
Auditory environment, modeling, 494–495
Authoring package, 15–16
Authoring tools
  commercial availability, 39–40
  forms-based, 136
Avatar, 192
Avatar control environment, 172

B

BaseColor, 79–80
BASE_COLOR lighting model, 89
Basic Support for Cooperative Work project, 368

BE Designer, 456
Begin/End objects, 276–279
Begin/End pairs, 280
Begin/End pairs, OpenGL, 273–275
Behavior, 171
  adding hooks to VRML, 198
  adding to VRML, 361–364
  behavior engines, 455
  definition, 457
  distributed, 364
  key issues, 457
  simple, intelligent objects with, 400–401
  time-critical, 187–188
Behavior engines, 445–485, *see also* Virtual Reality Behavior System
  applications, 452–455
  assembly, 447–448
  BEings, 447, 452, 454–455
  comparison to other simulation technology, 449–452
  naming, 447
  objects and classes, 446
  overview, 445–446
  Perl, 474–484
  products, 455–456
  programming, 449
  reflective capabilities, 451–452
  repositories of parameterized objects, behaviors, and documents, 454–455
  time and concurrency, 448–449
Behavior extensions, sample, 191–192
Behavior format, 383–388
  features, 383–384
  kinematics and motion, 388
  language, 386–387
  naming and assembly, 386
  object model, 386
  predefined operations, 387

user interaction, 387
VRML extension process, 385–386
Behavior model, 364
Behavior representation, 382–388
Behavior script startup, VRBS, 472–473
BEings, 447, 452, 454–455
BE objects, evolution, 451
BE Player, 456
BE system, 181
Binary format, Open Inventor, 90
Binding nodes, 74–76
Bindings, Open Inventor, 215
Binocular Omni-Orientation Monitor, 119–120
Biomedical data, acquisition and analysis, 520–522
Birds-of-a-Feather session, 223
Bitmaps, OpenGL, 441–442
Blending, OpenGL, 322–323, 433
Blinker, 88
Body, 465–466
    awareness, 496–497
    tracking, video-based, 492
BOOM, 119–120
Browser node, 190
Browsers, *see also* Web browsers
    PBS/VRBS interaction, 477–478
    recommending, 28–29
    specialized, 23
    standards, 33–35
    VRML considerations, 262
BSCW project, 368
Business
    advantages of VRML, 45–47
    requirements for benefits of VRML, 47–49
Caligari trueSpace, 22
Cameras, *see also* Orthographic camera; Perspective camera
    Open Inventor, 82–84, 211
    traversing multiple, 240
CAVE, 100–101
CAVE simulator, 101–102
CAVEview, 99–109
    animation, 102–103
    audio, 105
    control panel, 104
    data file, 107
    3-D mouse, 105
    dynamic link, 107
    features, 103
    flying mouse, 105
    implementation and development, 106
    as presentation tool, 104
    scripts, 106
    tracking, 105
    viewing modes, 104
    VROOM, 108
CERN VENUS project, 395–398
Child nodes, 226
Clamping, 293
Classes, behavior engines, 446, 454
Client server applications development environments, VRML implications, 45
Client server environment, VRML implications, 44–45
Client-server model, 266, 367
ClipPlane, 88
CollideStyle node, 249–250
Collision detection, 192–193
CollisionRadius field, 255
Color
    associated with vertex, 274
    final processing, OpenGL, 294
    indexed per vertex, 70–72
    OpenGL, 281
    processing, OpenGL, 285–287

C

ColorMaterial, OpenGL, 290, 292
Comments, Open Inventor, 95
Commercial applications, 42–43
Communications, external, PBS, 482–483
Completeness, OpenGL, 423
Complexity node, 77
Computer Support for Cooperative Work systems, 365
Concurrent engineering, 44
Cone node, 232–233
Coordinate3 node, 73–74, 233
Coordinate4, 90
Coordinate space conventions, 96
Coordinate systems, Open Inventor, 203–204
Coordinate transformations, OpenGL, 283
COPY, 184
CopyPixels, 303–305
CSCW systems, 365
Cube node, 232–233
Curent raster position, OpenGL, 284–285
CurrentSelection node, 191
Cyberfunk, 519–521, 523, 525, 527
CyberLab, 403
Cybersickness, 526
Cyberspace, 141–153
  concept, 147
  data abstraction protocols, 152
  labyrinth, 151–152
  metrics, 147–148
  Web site servers, 149–150
  World Wide Web, 150–151
Cyberspace protocol, implementation, 148–149
Cylinder node, 167–168, 233–234

D

Data abstraction protocols, 152
Database manager, 393–394
Database visualization, 403
Data file, CAVEview, 107
Data structure
  implementation, 461
  VR, 401–402
Depth buffer, OpenGL, 321–322, 433, 437–438
Device for orientation and motion environments, 511–512
Dexter hypertext reference model, 128–129
Diaspar virtual reality network, access to, 125
DirectedSound node, 250
Directional Lights, 212, 234
Display list, OpenGL, 345–347, 435–437
  hierarchies, 436–437
  optimization, 436
DistanceSwitch, 79
Distancing, 406
Distributed interactive virtual environment, 381–382
Distributed objects, 171
Distributed virtual reality, 403
Dithering, OpenGL, 323–324
DIVE system, 489–499
  body-centered interaction, 492
  deep immersion, 491–492
  heterogeneous multiprocessing, 492
  hybrid VR interface, 498–499
  minimum encumbrance, 491
  physics-based modeling, 492
  physiological and psychological requirements, 493–497
  synthetic agents, 493
  technical approach, 490–493

unencumbered VR technology, 497–498
video-based body tracking, 492
voice recognition, 493
Division Ltd. products, 403
Document, parameterized, behavior engines, 455
Document authors, 454
DOME-PAT system, 511–512
Draggers, 87
Drawable, 438–439
DrawBuffer, 326–327
DrawPixels, 303–305, 307–309
DrawStyle, 88
dVISE, 391

E

Earth, simulation, 53–55
Edge flagging, 279–280
The Electronic Courtyard, 487–488
ElevationGrid node, 250
Emerging technologies, 118–121
EndList, 345–346
Engineering applications, 41
Environment node, 88, 251–252
Errors, OpenGL, 272–273
EvalCoord commands, 338–339
Eval function, 481
Evaluators, OpenGL, 337–340
EVA satellite grapple, training, 512
eventIn and eventOut declarations, 257, 259
Events, 363
   automatic scoring, ARCANA 1, 519–520
   VRBS, 469
Extensibility, 93–94, 259–261
   OpenGL, 424
Extension languages, 189–190

External graphics, surrogate travel, 114–115

F

Face Sets, 212
Feedback, OpenGL, 342–345
Fields, 69, 229–232
   classes, 91–92
   Open Inventor, 209–210
   syntax, 91–92
File
   contents, Open Inventor, 95
   extension, Open Inventor, 96
   operations, PBS, 482
   size, reducing, 28
   transfer, Web browsers, 107
Finish, 348
Flatshading, OpenGL, 293
Floating-point computation, OpenGL, 267
Flow Analysis Software Toolkit, 507–508
Flush, 347
Flying mouse, CAVEview, 105
focalDistance field, 240
Font node, 87
FontStyle node, 234
Frame buffer, 326–331, 431
   accumulation, 330–331
   clearing, 328–330
   fine control of updates, 327–328
   invariance, 431–432
   multipass algorithms, 431
   OpenGL, 317
      copying pixels, 336
      pixel draw/read state, 337
      reading pixels, 332–336
      writing to stencil buffer, 331
   selecting, 326–327

G

GeneralCylinder node, 252–253
GenLists, 346–347
Geometry, 167–169
    OpenGL, 434–435
German National Research Center for Information Technology
    behavior model, 364
    distributed behavior, 364
    enhanced CSCW applications, 365
    events, 363
    goals, 362–363
    subclassing, 363
    VRML extension to support cooperative, multitasking worlds, 367
Get, 349
GetClipPlane, 349–350
GetError, 272
GetFloatv, 349
GetLight, 350
GetMaterial, 350
GetPart(), 219
GetString, 351
GetTexImage, 350–351
GetTexParameter, 350
Goddard Space Flight Center, VR research, 506–508
GOPHER site, 53
Graphical rendering, API, 418–420
Group nodes, 77–78, 197, 226
    Open Inventor, 206–207
Groups, Open Inventor, 204–209

H

Handshaking, VRBS, 469–471
Haptic display, interface control parameters, 503

Hardware
    ARCANA 1, 522–525
    requirements, 51–52
Header, 465
    Open Inventor, 94–95
Headlight field, 255
Head-mounted display, 115
Hello Cone, 201–204
    adding trackball manipulator, 202–203
    coordinate systems, 203–204
    engines to spin cone, 202
    naming scenes, 203
    XtExaminer Viewer, 203
High-end VR systems, high-performance rendering capabilities, *see* i3-D
HTML, extensions, MOO hypermedia system, 134–135
HTML browsers, extensions, 39
HTML texts, dynamic delivery, 134
Hypermedia system, 127–140, *see also* MOO hypermedia system
    models, 128–130
    Storyspace, 130–131
Hypertext, MOO hypermedia system, 132–133
Hypertext virtual hotel, 137–138

I

i3-D, 388, 392–399
    application, 393–394
    CERN VENUS project, 395–398
    user interaction, 394–395
    virtual Sardinia project, 398–399
Images, OpenGL, 434–435
Immersion, 118
    DIVE system, 491–492
Index command, 282
IndexedFaceSet node, 70–72, 213, 234

IndexedLineSet node, 75–76, 235
Indoor scenes, 410
Info node, 84–85, 235
Information, visualization, 17–18
Inline graphics, surrogate travel, 113
Inline node, 8–9
Instancing, 92–93, 208
Integrated Data Systems, 26
Interactions, distributed, 373–374
Internet
    conceptualization of space spanning, 147
    history of development, 222
    real virtual reality on, 117–126
        Diaspar virtual reality network, 121–123
        emerging technologies, 118–121
        immersive technologies, 118
        low cost home, 123
        Lunar Teleoperations Model 1, 123–124
        POLY, 122–123
        virtual networks, 124–125
Interoperability, OpenGL, 423
Interpreter, VRBS, 471–473
Invariance, 431–432
    OpenGL, 295–297, 355–358
Iris Annotator, 391
IRIS GL, 59–60, 424
IRIS Inventor, 200–201
isA relationships, 260
ISO 10646, encoding, 244–245

J

Java, 449–452
    reflective capabilities, 451

Java shell, 172
Johnson Space Center, VR research, 508–512
Justification field, 244

K

Kinematics, behavior format, 388

L

Labyrinth, 144, 151–152
    VRML files, 146
Language extension mechanisms, 181–193
    API considerations, 189–191
    avatars, 192
    behavior extensions, 191–192
    collision detection, 192–193
    example primitives, 190–191
    extension languages, 189–190
    magic lenses, 192
    messages, 185–186
    multimethod convention, 186–187
    primitives, 188
    prototyping new nodes, 182
    time-critical behaviors, 187–188
    VAG's proposed extension mechanism, 182–185
Language specification
    coordinate system, 228–229
    extensibility, 259–261
    fields, 229–232
    general syntax, 227–228
    language basics, 225–226
    naming, conventions, 261
    node characteristics, 226–227
    prototyping, 256–259
    URNs, 261
Latency, synchronizing models, 414

LevelOfDetail, 78–79
   Open Inventor, 208
Lighting
   color from, 286
   OpenGL, 287–288
   Open Inventor, 84, 212
   parameter, 288–291
Lighting state, OpenGL, 293
LightModel, 89
Light node, 166–167, 241, 243
Line loops, 276
Line segments, OpenGL, 298–301
   antialiasing, 299–300
   rasterization state, 300–301
   outlining characters, 441–442
Line strips, 276
Liquid Reality with Hot Java, 5–6
Load, 463–464
Location2 node, 191
LOD node, 8–9, 235–236
Logical operation, OpenGL, 324–326
LogicOp, 324–325
Loop field, 256
Lunar Teleoperations Model 1, 123–124

M

Magic lens filters, 192
Magnification, texture, 315–316
Marketing, 42
Marketplace, 55
Marshall Space Flight Center, VR research, 512–514
Masking, 293
Master entity, 377–378
MaterialBinding node, 238
Material field, 237–238
Material node, 79–80, 162–163, 237

Matrix stack, OpenGL, 430
MatrixTransform node, 82, 238–239
maxRadius, 255–256
Medical research, 41–42
Messages, 185–186
Metaphysical modeling language, 399
Metrics, cyberspace, 147–148
MFColor, 229–230
MFFloat, 230
MFLong, 231
MFString, 231–232
MIME, 409
Minimal-changes approach, 369–371
minRadius, 255–256
Modeling, physics-based, 492
Model-view matrix, 283
MOO hypermedia system, 131–140
   adding state to WWW, 135
   applications, 137–139
   creating WWW site server from, 133–134
   forms-based authoring tools, 136
   future work, 139–140
   HTML, extensions, 134–135
   HTML texts, dynamic delivery, 134
   hypertext, 132–133
   security issues, 136–137
   WAXweb, 138–139
MOO/MUD/shared space, 171
MOO Web site server, 131
Mosaic, 99
   coupling of virtual environments with, 112
Motion, behavior format, 388
Mouse, three dimensional, 105
MPh, 399
MUD-based collaborative workspace, 127
Multicast approach, 368, 371–373
Multimethods, convention for, 186–187

Multipass algorithms, OpenGL, 355–356, 431
MultipleCopy node, 88
Multiprocessing, heterogeneous, 492
Multipurpose Internet Mail Extensions, 409
Multiuser representation, virtual worlds, *see* Virtual worlds
Museums, virtual, 42–44

N

Name stack, 340–341
Name support, location-independent, 199
Naming
  behavior engines, 447
  behavior format, 386
  conventions, 261
  Open Inventor, 92
NavigationInfo node, 254–255
Navigation nodes, 165
NCSA VR facility, goal, 120–121
NCSA World Wide Web information site server, 118
Netscape, 99
  coupling of virtual environments with, 112
Network issues, 172–173
NewList, 345–346
Nodekits, Open Inventor, 87, 219–220
NodeReference node, 258–259
Nodes, 67, 161–167, 232–237, *see also* specific nodes
  animation, 161–162
  characteristics, 226–227
  classes, 232
  contents, 69–70
  cylinder, 167–168
  lights, 166–167
  materials, 162–163
  mechanisms, Open Inventor, 210
  navigation, 165
  new
    prototyping, 182
    VRML, 248–250
    Open Inventor, 204–209
  perspective and orthographic cameras, 163–164
  rendering, 164
  sphere, 168–169
NO_ERROR, 272
Normal nodes, 73–74, 239
Normals, Open Inventor, 215
NURBS, 87, 425–426

O

Object
  Begin/End, 276–279
  behavior engines, 446
  coordinates, 283
  definitions, 146
  distributed, 171
  hierarchy, 70
  intelligent, with simple behaviors, 400–401
  moving through multiple worlds, 379–380
Object model, behavior format, 386
Olfactory channel, 495
Opcode classes and opcodes, 466–468
OpenGL, 59–65, 263–358, 417–444, *see also* Frame buffer; Rasterization
  acceptance, 424
  alpha test, 319–320
  API, not with a protocol, 440
  architecture, 61–62

OpenGL *(continued)*
   attribute groups, 351–352
   attribute stacks, 430–431
   based on IRIS GL, 424
   Begin and End objects, 276–279
   begin/end paradigm, 273–275
   bitmaps, 441–442
   blending, 322–323, 433
   block diagram, 271, 421
   clamping or masking, 293
   ColorMaterial, 290, 292
   colors and coloring, 285–287
   command execution model, 433
   commands within Begin/End, 280
   command syntax, 268–270
   completeness, 423
   coordinate transformations, 283
   curent raster position, 284–285
   current value association with vertex, 274
   data types, 270
   depth buffer test, 321–322, 433, 437–438
   design considerations, 421–424
   display lists, 345–347, 435–437
      hierarchies, 436–437
      optimization, 436
   dithering, 323–324
   errors, 272–273
   evaluators, 337–340
   extensibility, 62–64, 424
   features, 60
   feedback, 342–345
   final color processing, 294
   fine-grained control, 426–429
   flatshading, 293
   floating-point computation, 267
   flush and finish, 347–348
   frame buffer, 317
   geometry and images, 434–435
   governance, 64
   immediate mode, 435
   implementor's view, 264
   integration, 62–64
      in X, 438–440
   interoperability, 423
   invariance, 355–358
      rules, 356–358
   licensing program, 64
   lighting, 287–288
   lighting model, 237
   lighting state, 293
   line segments to outline each character, 441–442
   local shading, 437–438
   logical operation, 324–326
   low-level API, 425–426
   matrix stack, 430
   model API, 429–430
   multipass algorithms, 355–356
   not programmable, 432–434
   online information, 64
   operation, 265–267, 271–272
   orthogonality, 422
   overview, 420–421
   performance, 422
   per fragment operations, 318–326
   pixel ownership test, 318
   polygon edges, 279–280
   primitives, 265
      assembly and processing, 275
   procedure calls, 427–429
   programmer's view, 264
   rendering, 438–440
   repeatability, 355
   scissor test, 318–319
   selection, 340–342
   state and state requests, 267–268, 348–354, 430–431

state variable, 351–353
stencil test, 320–321, 433
texture image containing array
    of characters, 442–443
three views, 263–265
vertex specification, 280–282
Open Inventor, 67–98, 180,
        199–220
    adding contructs to VRML, 198
    AntiSquish, 89
    array node, 88
    binary format, 90
    binding nodes, 74–76
    bindings, 215
    Blinker, 88
    building a scene graph, 204–210
        fields, 209–210
        group nodes, 206–207
        node mechanisms, 210
        paths, 209
        property nodes, 205–206
        separator nodes, 207–208
        shape nodes, 204–205
        switch group, 208
    cameras, 82–84, 211
    characteristics, 199
    ClipPlane, 88
    comments, 95
    Coordinate3 and Normal nodes,
        73–74
    Coordinate4, 90
    coordinate space conventions, 96
    draggers, 87
    DrawStyle, 88
    Environment node, 88
    extensibility, 93–94
    features, 97
    field
        classes, 91–92
        syntax, 91–92
    file
        contents, 95
        extension, 96
    File Format, 224
    font, 87
    group nodes, 77–78
    header, 94–95
    Hello Cone, 201–204
    IndexedFaceSet, 70–72
    IndexedLineSet, 75–76
    info node, 84–85
    instancing, 92–93
    IRIS Inventor, 200–201
    LevelOfDetail, 78–79
    LightModel, 89
    lights, 84, 212
    material node, 79–80
    MultipleCopy node, 88
    naming, 92
    node content, 69–73
    nodekits, 87, 219–220
    normals, 215
    NURBS, 87
    object-oriented file format, 67
    Pendulum, 88
    PointSet, 76
    primitive shapes, 76–77
    ProfileCoordinate2, 90
    ProfileCoordinate3, 90
    properties, 213–215
    ResetTransform, 89
    RotationXYZ, 89
    Rotor, 88
    scene graphs, 68–69
    SceneViewer, 114
    separator node, 78
    ShapeHints, 72–73
    shapes, 212–213
    Shuttle, 88
    terminology, 97

Open Inventor *(continued)*
   text, 216–217
   Text2, 87
   Text3, 86–87
   TextureCoordinate2, 81
   TextureCoordinateEnvironment, 90
   TextureCoordinatePlane, 90
   textures, 80, 217–218
   transformations, 81–82, 216
   Units, 89
   VRML extensions, 85–86
   whitespace, 95
Orthogonality, OpenGL, 422
Orthographic camera, 163–164, 239–240
   Open Inventor, 82–83, 211
Outdoor scenes, 411–413

P

PackedColor, 79–80
Papers subdirectory, 117
Paths, Open Inventor, 209
Payload Operations Control Center, 513
Pendulum, 88
Performance, OpenGL, 422
Performer, 391
Per fragment operations, OpenGL, 318–326
Perl, 474–484
   architecture independent, 475
   network and system secure, 476
   operating system independent, 475
   portable and powerful, 475
   sanitizing, 483–484
   usability, 476
Perl Behavior System, 476–477
   behavior language restraints, 480–483
   browser interaction, 477–478
   external communications, 482–483
   internals, 479–480
   language-specific constructs, 480–482
   user bindings, 478–479
Perspective camera, 163–164, 240–241
   Open Inventor, 82–83, 211
PEX, 419
PHIGS, 419
PHONG lighting model, 89
Physics, 170
Pixel
   copying in frame buffer, 336
   reading from frame buffer, 332–336
   storage modes, 303–304
   transfer modes, 304–306
PixelMap, 305–306
Pixel ownership test, 318
Pixel rectangles, OpenGL, 303–311
   conversion to floating-point, 309
   pixel storage modes, 303–304
   pixel transfer modes, 304–306
   rasterization, 306–311
Pixmap, 438–439
Platform independent VR, 407–409
Pname, 290
Point, antialiasing, OpenGL, 297–298
PointLight node, 212, 241
Point of view model, first-person, 111
PointSet node, 76, 241
POLY, 122–123
Polygon, 277
   concave, 425–426
   edges, 279–280
   OpenGL, 301–303
PopAttrib, 354
Portable Graphics, 26
PostScript, 418
Preflight Adaptation Trainer, 511–512

Preheader, 464–465
Presence, virtual environment, 496–497
Presentation tool, CAVEview, 104
Primitives, 188
  assembly and processing, OpenGL, 275
  example, 190–191
  OpenGL, 265, 420
  shapes, 76–77
ProfileCoordinate2, 90
ProfileCoordinate3, 90
Property nodes, Open Inventor, 205–206, 213–215
Protocol
  conservation, 172
  extensions for multiuser support, 370
  VRBS
    extensibility, 463
    goals and style, 461–464
    messages, 464–466
Protocol manager, 393
Prototyping, 256–259
PushAttrib, 354

Q

Quadrilateral strips, 278–279
QuickDraw 3-D, 25, 36–37

R

Rasterization, OpenGL, 294–317
  invariance, 295–297
  line segments, 298–301
  pixel rectangles, 303–311
  points, 297–298
  polygons, 301–303
  texturing, 311–317

ReadPixels, 303–305, 308–309, 332–333
Realism, achieving, 413–414
Reality, simple, support for, 198
Rectangles, *see* Pixel rectangles
Rect command, 282
Rendering
  low-end systems, VRML issues, 237–243
  nodes, 164
  OpenGL, 438–440
Rendering manager, 394
Renderman, 419
RenderMode, 341–344
Repeatability, OpenGL, 355
Repository builders, 454
Research, 41–42
ResetTransform, 89
Response surface methodology, 509–510
RFC1786, 245
RGB, conversion to, pixel rectangles, 310
Roads, 412
Roll compensation, head-slaved, 502
Rotation node, 241
RotationXYZ node, 89, 202
Rotor, 88
Rtype, 269

S

Sardinia, virtual project, 398–399
Scale node, 242
Scene graphs, 68–69
Scenes
  definitions, 146
  indoor, 410
  outdoor, 411–413
SceneViewer, 114
Scissor test, 318–319
Scripting languages, VRBS parsed by, 462–463

Scripts, 413
   CAVEview, 106
Security issues, MOO hypermedia system, 136–137
Selection, OpenGL, 340–342
Senate, 56–57
Separator node, 78, 242, 244
   Open Inventor, 207–208
setPart(), 219
SFBitMask, 229
SFColor, 229–230
SFEnum, 230
SFFloat, 230
SFImage, 230–231
SFLong, 231
SFMatirx, 231
SFNode field, 258
SFRotation, 231
SFString, 231–232
SFTime, 232
Shading, local, OpenGL, 441–438
ShapeHints node, 72–73, 242
Shape notes, Open Inventor, 204–205
Shapes, Open Inventor, 212–213
Shuttle, 88
SIGGRAPH, 4–5
   VROOM, 108
Silicon Graphics Computer Systems, 59
   VRML extensions, 400–401
6D tracking devices, 119–120
SoComplexity node, 214
SoDrawStyle, 214
SoEnvironment, 214
Softimage, 21
Software
   ARCANA 1, 522–525
   requirements, 51–52

SoLightModel, 214
SoMaterial node, 213
Sony CSL, 402–403
SoShape class, 212
SoShapeHints node, 214
SoText2 node, 216
SoText3 node, 216–217
SoTexture2 node, 217–218
Sound, 406
   DirectedSound node, 250
   frequency range of human hearing, 494
   role in VRML, 173–179
      areas for further development, 178–179
      history, 174–175
      VRML X.X audio extension, 175–178
   spatial localizations, 256
SoUnits node, 215
Spacing field, 244
Spatial model, 365–366
Spatial sensors, dynamic response, 500–502
Sphere node, 69, 168–169, 243
Spotlights, 166, 212, 243
Standards
   browser, 33–35
   VRML, 32–33
Start input, 256
Startup, 463–464
State queries, OpenGL, 430–431
State variable, OpenGL, 351–353
Static distortion, measurement and calibration, position data from 3-D trackers, 505–506
Stencil buffer, writing to, 331
StencilOp, 321
Stencil test, 320–321, 433
Stippling, polygon, 301

Storyspace, 130–131
Strata Inc., 25
Strata studio, 22
Subclassing, 363
Sub keyword, 481
Surrogate travel, 111–116
    external graphics, 114–115
    future directions, 115–116
    inline graphics, 113
Switch group, Open Inventor, 208
Switch group node, 243–244
Synthetic agents, DIVE system, 493

T

TBAG, 180
Technology, advantages of VRML, 45–47
Teleconferencing, virtual presence, 414–415
TexImage2-D, 311–313
Text, Open Inventor, 216–217
Text2, 87
Text3, 86–87
TextLanguage node, 245
Text node, 244
Texture
    applied to
        cone, 233
        cylinder, 234
    OpenGL, 311–317
        application, 316–317
        environments and functions, 316
        magnification, 315–316
        wrap modes, 314
    Open Inventor, 80, 217–218
TextureCoordinate2, 81, 234–235, 246–247
TextureCoordinateBinding node, 74
TextureCoordinateEnvironment, 90
TextureCoordinatePlane, 90
Texture coordinates
    default, 251
    OpenGL, 281
Texture environments, 316
Texture images, 246
    containing character array, OpenGL, 442–443
Texture2 node, 245
Texture2Transform node, 81–82, 246
3-D audio signal processing, 176–177
3-D auditory displays, aeronautical applications, 503–504
3-D creation tools, 20–23
    evaluating features, 26–29
3-D environment
    builders, 10
    characteristics, 390–392
    ease of access, 14–16
    ease of building, 13–14
    future promise, 29–30
    limitation, 13–14
    on the Web, 5–7
    practical value, 16–18
3-D graphics rendering, 418
3-D studio, 21
Time node, 191
Toggle node, 191
Touch, sensation of, 495
TrackballManip, 202–203
Tracking, CAVEview, 105
Traffic Collision Avoidance System, 503–504
Transformations, Open Inventor, 81–82, 216
TransformSeparator, 78
Triangle fan, 278
Triangles, separate, 278
Triangle strip, 213, 277–278

2-D tools, compatibility with 3-D tools, 27
Typename, 257–258

U

UGA system, 180
U. S. Holocaust Museum, 52
U. S. Library of Congress, 53
Units, 89
Universal Resource Locator, 150–151
  multiple, 245, 247, 255
URLScene, 115
URNs, 193–196, 261
User bindings, Perl-VRBS, 482–479
User manager, 393
Users
  interfaces, behavior engines, 455
  moving through multiple worlds, 379–380
VERSION string, 351

V

Vertex
  specification, OpenGL, 280–282
  transformation sequence, OpenGL, 283
Vertical industries, VRML planned use, 40
verticesPerColumn field, 250–251
verticesPerRow field, 250–251
Viewers, commercial availability, 39
Viewing volume, 239
ViewportMapping, 83
View volume, 211
Virtual-Devices subdirectory, 117
Virtual environment
  coupling with Mosaic and Netscape, 112
  integration with Web browsers, 112
  shared, 512
Virtual museums and art galleries, 42–44
Virtual networks, information about, 124–125
Virtual Payload Operations Control Centers, 513
Virtual presence teleconferencing, 414–415
Virtual reality, toward low cost home, 123
Virtual Reality Behavior System, 456–474
  behavior language independent, 462
  behavior protocol goals and style, 461–464
  body, 465–466
  browser interaction, 477–478
  changing other worlds, 473–474
  enhancements, 474
  events, 469
  extensibility, 463
  features, 473–474
  handshaking, 469–471
  header, 465
  interpreter and behavior startup sequence, 471–473
  opcode classes and opcodes, 466–468
  parsed by scripting languages, 462–463
  platform independent, 462
  preheader, 464–465
  protocol messages, 464–466
  security, 463–464
  system structure, 458–459
  user bindings, 478–479
  world identifiers, 468
  WWWScript node, 459–461, 471

Virtual reality data structures,
    401–402
Virtual Reality Modeling Language,
    see VRML
Virtual reality research
    commercial, 487–488
    government, 499–514
    medical, 514–528
    military, 489–499
Virtual reality technology,
    limitations and constraints,
    525–526
Virtual Sardinia project, 398–399
Virtual Society Project, 402–403
VirtualSphere node, 191
Virtual wind tunnel, 504–505
Virtual worlds
    multiuser representation,
        364–381
        access control, 365–367
        active locking, 375–377
        artifact distribution, 368
        awareness, 365–367
        decentralized access
            management, 376–379
        functional requirements,
            367–368
        minimal-changes approach,
            369–371
        moving objects and users
            through multiple worlds,
            379–380
        multicast approach, 371–373
        no access management, 375
        sharing and distributed
            interactions, 373–374
        user and artifact naming and
            identification, 380–381
    realizing consistency, 374–379
VISA, 487–488

Visual channel, ultimate performance,
    494
Visualization, 367
    VRML, 145–146
Voice recognition, DIVE system, 493
VRealm Builder, 26
VRML, *see also* Language specification
    adding behavior, 361–364
    authoring package, 15–16
    authoring tools, commercial
        availability, 39–40
    browser
        considerations, 262
        standards, 33–35
        specialized, 23
    commercial acceptance, 47–48
    commercial availability, 38–40
    designed to meet requirements,
        224–225
    development stage, 35–38
    document, changes to, 159–160
    extensions
        BEF, 385–386
        Open Inventor, 85–86
    first version, 221
    future, 49
    GMD goals, 362–363
    goal, 169
    history, 223–224
    inline node, 8–9
    limitations, 179
    LOD node, 8–9
    new nodes, 248–250
    open issue, 244–248
    overview, 222–223
    planned applications, 40–44
    priorities, 158–159
    pros, 251–256
    standard, 32–33
    standardization, 48

VRML *(continued)*
  viewers, commercial availability, 39
  visualization, 145–146
  visualizing awareness and access control, 366–367
VRML+, 24–25
VRML V2.0, 38
VRML Architecture Group, 32–33, 36
  making distinctions between fields, 258
  proposal for VRML X.X, 196–199
  URNs, 193–196
  VRML revision, 170
VROOM, 108

W

WAXweb, 138–139
Weather maps, 53–54
Web browsers, 99–100
  file transfer, 107
  integration with virtual environment, 112
  3-D, 25
Web builders, 3-D, 25
Webfx, 33–34
Webspace, 5, 7, 33–34
WebSpace Navigator, 16–17
WebView, 456

whichChild field, 243
Whitespace, Open Inventor, 95
Whurlwind, 25
Workload, assessment using synthetic work environment, 509–511
World identifiers, 468
WorldInfo node, 256
Worlds, 180–181
Worldview, 5–6, 33, 35
World wide marketplace, 55
World Wide Web
  adding state to, 135
  consequences of presence on the Internet, 144–145
  cyberspace, 150–151
  site server
    creating from MOO, 133–134
    cyberspace, 149–150
  3-D environments on, 5–7
Wrap modes, texture, 314
WWWAnchor, 85–86, 194
  map field, 247
WWWAnchor group node, 247
WWWInline node, 85, 194, 247–248
WWWScript node, 459–461, 471

X

XtExaminerViewer, 203
X window system, 418–419

About the CD-ROM

The CD-ROM included with this book provides users the ability to view the latest and the best VRML and 3D browsers, viewers, modeling tools, and models available on the market. Users will be able to view these products from just about any platform environment. A word viewer for windows is also provided in the CD-ROM that allows users to view appendices which are in a MS Word 6.0 format. Additionally, a readme.txt file is included in the CD-ROM that provides instructions on how to install the software, product or tool.

The CD-ROM's file system has the following structure: platform, type of tool, company/vendor and the product file names. This CD-ROM was mastered to ISO9660 specifications which allows PCs, Macintoshes, and UNIX systems to access its file system.

Some of the tools featured include **Virtus'** *Virtus Voyager*, **IBM's** *Virtual World*, **Visible Decision's** *Discovery for Developers*, **Strata's** *StudioPro Blitz*, **Caligari's** *Fountain*, **Autodesk's** *Hot Java*, **Apple's** *Whurlwind*, and many more!

System Requirements

The CD-ROM will run on the following platforms:
Macintosh / Power Mac (System 7.5.1 and higher)
PC, Windows 3.1, 95 and NT 3.51
HP-UX
SUN (OS and Solaris)
SGI IRIX
DEC (Alpha and Ultrix)
Linux
IBM AIX
Note: See individual 'Read Me' files accompanying each software offering for any specific requirements (RAM, soundcards, etc.)